2001

Better Homes and Gardens®

ANNUAL
Recipes
2001

Better Homes and Gardens® Books
Des Moines, Iowa

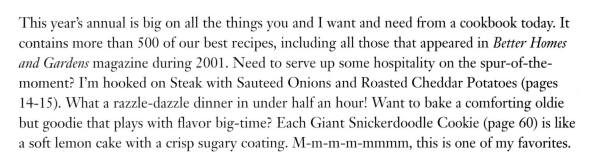

Welcome to the *Better Homes and Gardens® Annual Recipes 2001* cookbook.

Chances are as an owner of this book, you and I have a few things in common. I get as much pleasure from chopping, stirring, cooking, or baking as I do from serving a special meal to my family and friends. Collecting cookbooks and poring over the tempting food and flavor combinations is a favorite pastime. Ever get enough recipes? Not me.

This year's annual is big on all the things you and I want and need from a cookbook today. It contains more than 500 of our best recipes, including all those that appeared in *Better Homes and Gardens* magazine during 2001. Need to serve up some hospitality on the spur-of-the-moment? I'm hooked on Steak with Sauteed Onions and Roasted Cheddar Potatoes (pages 14-15). What a razzle-dazzle dinner in under half an hour! Want to bake a comforting oldie but goodie that plays with flavor big-time? Each Giant Snickerdoodle Cookie (page 60) is like a soft lemon cake with a crisp sugary coating. M-m-m-m-mmmm, this is one of my favorites.

As you page through the book, you'll find more help, more photos, more tips, more how-to techniques than ever. Also new to each chapter is a special feature of the month, starting with January's winter-warming Casserole Classics (pages 18-19) and ending with December's magical Classic Candies (pages 304-305).

The food ideas inside don't get any better than this. So let's get cooking!

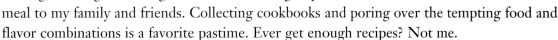

Nancy Byal
Executive Food Editor
Better Homes and Gardens® Magazine

Better Homes and Gardens® Books
An Imprint of Meredith® Books

Better Homes and Gardens® Annual Recipes 2001

Project Editor: Chuck Smothermon
Contributing Editors: Shelli McConnell,
  Margaret Smith
Associate Art Director: Lynda Haupert
Copy Chief: Terri Fredrickson
Editorial Operations Manager: Karen Schirm
Managers, Book Production: Pam Kvitne,
  Marjorie J. Schenkelberg
Electronic Production Coordinator: Paula Forest
Editorial and Design Assistants: Judy Bailey,
  Mary Lee Gavin
Test Kitchen Director: Lynn Blanchard
Test Kitchen Home Economists: Judy Comstock,
  Jennifer Kalinowski, Maryellyn Krantz, Jill Lust,
  Jill Moberly, Dianna Nolin, Kay Springer,
  Colleen Weeden, Lori Wilson,
  Charles Worthington

Meredith® Books

Editor in Chief: James D. Blume
Design Director: Matt Strelecki
Managing Editor: Gregory H. Kayko
Executive Food Editor: Jennifer Dorland Darling

Director, Sales, Special Markets: Rita McMullen
Director, Sales, Premiums: Michael A. Peterson
Director, Sales, Retail: Tom Wierzbicki
Director, Book Marketing: Brad Elmitt
Director, Operations: George A. Susral
Director, Production: Douglas M. Johnston

Better Homes and Gardens® Magazine

Editor in Chief: Karol DeWulf Nickell
Executive Food Editor: Nancy Byal
Senior Food Editor: Nancy Wall Hopkins
Nutrition Editor: Jeanne Ambrose
Associate Editors: Richard Swearinger, Stephen J. Exel
Editorial Assistants: Karen Pollock, Anna Anderson

Meredith Publishing Group

President, Publishing Group: Stephen M. Lacy

Meredith Corporation

Chairman and Chief Executive Officer:
  William T. Kerr

Chairman of the Executive Committee:
  E. T. Meredith III

Cover photograph: Walnut Molasses Pie *(page 232)*
Page 1: Christmas Eve Lamb Stew and Mashed Sweet
  Potatoes *(page 294)*
Page 2: Grape Mini Pies *(page 235)*
Page 4: Top left, Tortellini Emilia *(page 206)*;
Top right, Coconut Eggnog *(page 308)*;
Bottom, Feta Cheese Appetizers *(page 218)*

Our seal assures you that every recipe in *Better Homes and Gardens® Annual Recipes 2001* has been tested in the Better Homes and Gardens® Test Kitchen. This means that each recipe is practical and reliable, and meets our high standards of taste appeal. We guarantee your satisfaction with this book for as long as you own it.

All of us at Better Homes and Gardens® Books are dedicated to providing you with the information and ideas you need to create delicious foods. We welcome your comments and suggestions. Write to us at:
Better Homes and Gardens Books, Cookbook Editorial Department, 1716 Locust Street, LN 112, Des Moines, IA 50309-3023.

If you would like to order additional copies of this book, call 800-439-4119.

CONTENTS

---

30 MINUTE

When this symbol appears with a recipe, rest assured that you can prepare the dish—start to finish—in 30 minutes or less.

LOW FAT

Any recipe that bears this low-fat symbol meets our guideline of having no more than 10 grams of fat per serving (see page 8).

30 MINUTE, LOW FAT

This symbol is assigned to recipes that are both low in fat and can be prepared—start to finish—in 30 minutes or less.

PRIZE WINNER

The recipes that display this blue-ribbon symbol have earned top honors in our monthly Prize Tested Recipes contest.

Nutrition Information

With each recipe, we give you useful nutrition information you easily can apply to your own needs. First read "What You Need" (below) to determine your dietary requirements. Then refer to the Nutrition Facts listed with each recipe. You'll find the calorie count and the amount of fat, saturated fat, cholesterol, sodium, carbohydrates, fiber, and protein for each serving. In most cases, along with the Nutrition Facts per serving, you'll find the amount of vitamin A, vitamin C, calcium, and iron noted as a percentage of the Daily Values. The Daily Values are dietary standards set by the Food and Drug Administration. To stay in line with the nutrition breakdown of each recipe, follow the suggested number of servings.

How We Analyze

The Better Homes and Gardens® Test Kitchen computer analyzes each recipe for the nutritional value of a single serving.
● The analysis does not include optional ingredients.
● We use the first serving size listed when a range is given. For example: If we say a recipe "Makes 4 to 6 servings," the Nutrition Facts are based on 4 servings.
● When ingredient choices (such as margarine or butter) appear in a recipe, we use the first one mentioned for analysis. The ingredient order does not mean we prefer one ingredient over another.
● When milk is a recipe ingredient, the analysis is calculated using 2-percent (reduced-fat) milk.

What You Need

The dietary guidelines below suggest nutrient levels that moderately active adults should strive to eat each day. As your calorie levels change, adjust your fat intake, too. Try to keep the percentage of calories from fat to no more than 30 percent. There's no harm in occasionally going over or under these guidelines, but the key to good health is maintaining a balanced diet *most of the time.*

Calories: About 2,000
Total fat: Less than 65 grams
Saturated fat: Less than 20 grams
Cholesterol: Less than 300 milligrams
Carbohydrates: About 300 grams
Sodium: Less than 2,400 milligrams
Dietary fiber: 20 to 30 grams

Low-Fat Recipes

For recipes that meet our low-fat criteria, a main-dish serving must contain 10 or fewer grams of fat. For side dishes or desserts, the serving must contain 5 or fewer grams of fat. These recipes are flagged with a low-fat symbol.

january

IN THIS CHAPTER

30-minute recipes indicated in COLOR.
Low-fat and no-fat recipes indicated
with a ♥.
Photographs indicated in italics.
***Bonus recipe**

Feta-Fruit Appetizer

A melon baller or plain teaspoon will work to hollow out the cheese; work gingerly to keep the sides from crumbling.

Start to finish: 35 minutes

- 2   8-oz. blocks feta cheese
- 2   cups assorted chunks of peeled fresh tropical fruit, such as kiwi fruit, pineapple, papaya, guava, or mango
- 1   cup cubed honeydew melon
- 1   cup smoked almonds
- 2   Tbsp. snipped fennel tops or 1 tsp. fennel seed, crushed
      Pita bread wedges

1 Using a melon baller or butter curler, carefully remove cheese from the center of the blocks of feta to create "bowls" with sides about ½ inch thick. Hollow carefully to avoid cutting through the bottom. Transfer the scooped cheese to a small serving bowl.

2 Arrange tropical fruit, melon, and almonds in and around the hollowed cheese bowls. Stir fennel tops or fennel seed into reserved cheese and serve with cheese bowls of fruit and pita bread wedges. Makes 8 appetizer servings.

Nutrition Facts per serving: 350 cal., 22 g total fat (9 g sat. fat), 50 mg chol., 856 mg sodium, 25 g carbo., 4 g fiber, 14 g pro. **Daily Values:** 11% vit. A, 51% vit. C, 37% calcium, 11% iron.

Smoked Salmon Appetizer

No smoked salmon on hand? Substitute drained canned tuna. (See the photograph on page 38.)

Start to finish: 40 minutes

- 3   Tbsp. sliced green onions
- 1½ tsp. finely shredded lemon peel
- 4   tsp. lemon juice
- 4   tsp. olive oil
- 4   tsp. capers
- 1½ tsp. anchovy paste (optional)
- 2   cloves garlic, minced
- ¼   tsp. freshly ground pepper
- 1   4-oz. piece smoked salmon, cut ½ to 1 inch thick
       Pitted niçoise olives or olive medley, cut up (about 24 olives)
       Coarsely chopped roasted red sweet peppers
- 6   hard-cooked eggs, cut into ½-inch slices
       Crackers or toasted pita wedges

1 In a small serving bowl stir together green onions, lemon peel, lemon juice, olive oil, capers, anchovy paste, garlic, and ground pepper.

2 To assemble, place salmon on a serving plate. Surround with small bowls of olives, roasted red pepper, egg slices, and caper mixture. Serve with crackers or toasted pita wedges. Makes 12 appetizer servings.

Nutrition Facts per serving: 93 cal., 5 g total fat (1 g sat. fat), 108 mg chol., 233 mg sodium, 7 g carbo., 1 g fiber, 4 g pro. **Daily Values:** 7% vit. A, 13% vit. C, 3% calcium, 5% iron.

Stuffed Celery Bites

For easiest preparation, spread the cream cheese mixture in the celery first, then slice.

Start to finish: 30 minutes

-     Nonstick cooking spray
- 2   Tbsp. pine nuts
- 1   clove garlic, minced
- 8   stalks celery
- 1   8-oz. tub cream cheese with dried tomato or cream cheese
- ¼ cup shredded Italian cheese blend (1 oz.)
- 2   Tbsp. dry-roasted shelled sunflower seeds
      Celery leaves (optional)

1 Lightly coat a skillet with nonstick cooking spray. Add pine nuts and garlic. Cook over medium heat 3 to 5 minutes or until nuts are golden brown, stirring frequently. Set aside.

2 Remove tops and wide base from celery. Using a vegetable peeler, remove two thin strips from the rounded side of the celery, creating a flat surface.

3 In a small bowl combine the cream cheese and shredded Italian cheese. Spread or spoon cheese mixture into celery.

4 Cut each filled stalk of celery into 2-inch pieces. Sprinkle half the pieces with the pine nut mixture and half with the sunflower seeds. Top with celery leaves, if desired. Makes 8 appetizer servings.

To Make Ahead:
Stuff celery up to 4 hours before serving; cover and chill. Cut into 2-inch pieces and add nuts and seeds just before serving.

Nutrition Facts per serving: 132 cal., 13 g total fat (7 g sat. fat), 31 mg chol., 152 mg sodium, 3 g carbo., 1 g fiber, 4 g pro. **Daily Values:** 7% vit. A, 5% vit. C, 6% calcium, 3% iron.

PRIZE WINNER

Spinach and Bean Salad

Patricia A. Harmon
Baden, Pennsylvania
$200—Beans, Split Peas, and Lentils

Prep: 25 minutes **Chill:** 2 hours

 1   15-oz. can black beans, rinsed and drained
 ½   cup snipped dried apricots
 ½   cup chopped red and/or yellow sweet pepper
 1   green onion, thinly sliced
 1   Tbsp. snipped fresh cilantro
 1   clove garlic, minced
 ¼   cup apricot nectar
 2   Tbsp. salad oil
 2   Tbsp. rice vinegar
 1   tsp. soy sauce
 1   tsp. grated fresh ginger
 4   cups shredded fresh spinach

1 In a medium mixing bowl combine black beans, apricots, sweet pepper, green onion, cilantro, and garlic. In a screw-top jar combine apricot nectar, oil, vinegar, soy sauce, and ginger. Cover and shake well. Pour over bean mixture; toss gently to coat. Cover and refrigerate for 2 to 24 hours.

2 To serve, add spinach to black bean mixture, tossing to mix. Season to taste with salt. Makes 4 main-dish servings.

Nutrition Facts per serving: 192 cal., 7 g total fat (1 g sat. fat), 0 mg chol., 381 mg sodium, 29 g carbo., 10 g fiber, 9 g pro. **Daily Values:** 43% vit. A, 79% vit. C, 8% calcium, 24% iron.

Mixed Bean and Herb Salad

Prep: 25 minutes **Stand:** 30 minutes

 1   15-oz. can red kidney or black beans, rinsed and drained
 1   15-oz. can chickpeas (garbanzo beans), rinsed and drained
 1   15-oz. can cut green beans, drained
 ½   cup chopped onion
 ½   cup chopped red sweet pepper
 ¼   cup chopped green sweet pepper
 ¼   cup olive oil
 2   Tbsp. snipped fresh basil
 2   Tbsp. snipped fresh cilantro
 2   Tbsp. snipped fresh tarragon or oregano
 ¼   cup red wine vinegar
 1   Tbsp. Dijon-style mustard
 ¼   tsp. black pepper
 ⅛   tsp. salt

1 In a large mixing bowl combine beans; set aside. In a large skillet cook onion, red sweet pepper, and green sweet pepper in olive oil about 5 minutes or just until tender. Add to beans along with basil, cilantro, and tarragon or oregano. Toss to mix.

2 In a small mixing bowl whisk together wine vinegar, mustard, black pepper, and salt. Pour mixture over beans; toss gently to coat. Cover and let stand at room temperature about 30 minutes before serving. Makes 8 to 10 side-dish servings.

EDITOR'S TIP

Dieters Need to Bone Up on Calcium

You might think that dropping pounds is always good for your overall health and self-image, but it can be hard on your bones.

A study conducted of 236 women between the ages of 44 and 50 found that women who lost about 7 pounds within 18 months also lost twice as much bone density in their hips and spines as women who didn't lose any weight.

Although the rate of bone density loss connected with weight loss is moderate, it could put women at risk for osteoporosis at an earlier age, says Dr. Loran Salamone, assistant professor of epidemiology at the University of Pittsburgh.

"As you approach menopause, rate of bone loss is 1 to 2 percent a year," she says. "If you add bone loss due to dieting, you could be at a greater risk for fractures sooner in life."

To protect your bones, especially if you watch your waistline, Dr. Salamone suggests getting 1,200 milligrams of calcium each day. A daily vitamin D supplement containing 400 to 800 international units will help your body absorb the calcium it needs.

Dr. Salamone also recommends slipping on your walking shoes to help your bones. Three to four hours of moderate exercise a week, such as walking a 15-minute mile, can help keep bones strong. Women in the study who lost weight and increased their exercise did not decrease bone density.

To Make Ahead:
Cover and chill salad for up to 24 hours. Let stand at room temperature for 30 minutes just before serving.

Nutrition Facts per serving: 182 cal., 8 g total fat (1 g sat. fat), 0 mg chol., 370 mg sodium, 24 g carbo., 6 g fiber, 7 g pro. **Daily Values:** 44% vit. C, 5% calcium, 10% iron.

- Italian Lentil Soup (see below right)

- Salad of fresh romaine, marinated artichoke hearts, and thinly sliced onions, tossed with Caesar dressing and topped with Parmesan cheese shavings

- Crusty peasant-style bread with olive oil for dipping

- Coconut Sno-Cakes (see page 22)

30 MINUTE

Red Lentil Soup

Although they are called red lentils, their color is actually orange. Once the lentils are added to the soup, be sure to cook only five minutes or the lentils will be overcooked.

Start to finish: 30 minutes

- 1 cup chopped onion
- ¼ cup chopped carrot
- ¼ cup chopped celery
- 1 Tbsp. olive oil
- ½ tsp. fennel seed, crushed
- ¼ tsp. ground turmeric
- ¼ tsp. ground coriander
- ⅛ tsp. black pepper
- ⅛ tsp. ground red pepper
- 2½ cups dry red lentils, rinsed
- 4 cups chicken broth
- 2¼ cups water
- 1 7-oz. jar roasted red sweet peppers, drained
- 1 Tbsp. olive oil
- ⅓ cup plain low-fat yogurt
- 2 Tbsp. snipped fresh cilantro

1 In a large saucepan cook the onion, carrot, and celery in 1 tablespoon hot olive oil until onion is tender. Stir in fennel seed, turmeric, coriander, black pepper, and ground red pepper. Stir in lentils, chicken broth, and water. Bring to boiling; reduce heat. Cover and simmer about 5 minutes or until lentils are very tender.

2 Meanwhile, in a blender container or food processor bowl combine the red sweet peppers and the olive oil. Cover and blend or process until nearly smooth. Stir into the cooked lentil mixture; heat through.

3 To serve, ladle soup into bowls. Stir together yogurt and cilantro; dollop atop each serving. Makes 6 to 8 side-dish servings.

Nutrition Facts per serving: 346 cal., 6 g total fat (1 g sat. fat), 1 mg chol., 562 mg sodium, 51 g carbo., 13 g fiber, 23 g pro. **Daily Values:** 118% vit. C, 10% calcium, 26% iron.

PRIZE WINNER

Italian Lentil Soup

Dee Carona
Albany, New York
$400—Beans, Split Peas, and Lentils

Prep: 15 minutes **Cook:** 50 minutes

- 1 cup sliced carrots
- ½ cup sliced celery
- ⅓ cup chopped onion
- 1 Tbsp. olive oil
- 5 cups water
- ½ of a small head cabbage, cored and cut into 1-inch pieces (4 cups)
- 1 cup dry lentils, rinsed and drained
- 1 cup tomato puree
- 1½ tsp. sugar
- 1½ tsp. salt
- ½ tsp. dried oregano, crushed
- ¼ tsp. pepper

1 In a large saucepan cook carrots, celery, and onion in hot olive oil about 5 minutes or until crisp-tender. Stir in water, cabbage, lentils, tomato puree, sugar, salt, oregano, and pepper. Bring to boiling; reduce heat. Cover and simmer about 45 minutes or until lentils are very soft.

2 To serve, ladle soup into bowls. Makes 5 main-dish servings.

Nutrition Facts per serving: 210 cal., 3 g total fat (0 g sat. fat), 0 mg chol., 938 mg sodium, 35 g carbo., 15 g fiber, 13 g pro. **Daily Values:** 76% vit. A, 49% vit. C, 8% calcium, 26% iron.

30 MINUTE, LOW FAT

Eggplant and White Bean Soup

Select eggplants that are glossy, feel heavy for their size, and have no brown spots. Flesh should spring back when lightly pressed. The peak season for eggplants is from July to October.

Start to finish: 25 minutes

- 1 Tbsp. olive oil
- 2 cloves garlic, minced
- 1 small onion, cut into thin wedges (½ cup)
- 1 lb. eggplant, any type, peeled and cut into ¾-inch cubes (4 to 5 cups)
- 2 14½-oz. cans vegetable broth or reduced-sodium chicken broth

1 15-oz. can navy, cannellini, or
   Great Northern beans, rinsed
   and drained
3 Tbsp. tomato paste
2 tsp. snipped fresh marjoram or
   tsp. dried marjoram, crushed
⅛ tsp. ground black pepper
2 Tbsp. snipped fresh parsley
   Fresh marjoram sprigs (optional)

1 In a large saucepan cook and stir garlic in hot olive oil over medium-high heat for 30 seconds. Add onion; cook and stir 2 minutes. Add eggplant; cook and stir 3 minutes more.

2 Stir in vegetable or chicken broth, beans, tomato paste, marjoram, and pepper. Bring to boiling; reduce heat. Cover and simmer about 5 minutes or until eggplant is just tender. Do not overcook.

3 To serve, ladle soup into bowls. Sprinkle with parsley. Garnish with marjoram, if desired. Makes 4 main-dish servings.

Nutrition Facts per serving: 199 cal., 5 g total fat (1 g sat. fat), 0 mg chol., 1,342 mg sodium, 36 g carbo., 4 g fiber, 10 g pro. **Daily Values:** 6% vit. A, 18% vit. C, 5% calcium, 21% iron.

30 MINUTE, LOW FAT
Italian Bean Soup

Blend or puree half of the beans and tomatoes to thicken this homey soup.

Start to finish: 25 minutes

2 15-oz. cans red kidney beans,
   rinsed and drained
1 15-oz. can Great Northern beans,
   rinsed and drained

1 14½-oz. can diced tomatoes with
   basil, oregano, and garlic
5 cups water
½ of a 6-oz. can Italian-style
   tomato paste (⅓ cup)
1 Tbsp. instant chicken bouillon
   granules
1 tsp. dried basil, crushed
1 tsp. dried oregano, crushed
½ tsp. ground white pepper
1 cup wide egg noodles
1 Tbsp. snipped fresh parsley

1 In a blender container or food processor bowl combine one can of the red kidney beans, ⅔ cup of the Great Northern beans, ¾ cup of the undrained tomatoes, and 1 cup of the water. Cover and blend or process until nearly smooth. Transfer mixture to a 4-quart Dutch oven.

2 Stir in the remaining beans, remaining tomatoes, remaining water, tomato paste, bouillon granules, basil, oregano, and white pepper. Bring to boiling; stir in noodles. Return to boiling; reduce heat. Cover and simmer for 15 minutes.

3 Just before serving, stir parsley into soup. Ladle soup into bowls. Makes 8 main-dish servings.

Nutrition Facts per serving: 218 cal., 1 g total fat (0 g sat. fat), 7 mg chol., 1,025 mg sodium, 40 g carbo., 11 g fiber, 12 g pro. **Daily Values:** 18% vit. A, 8% calcium, 17% iron.

- Stuffed Celery Bites (see page 10)

- Steak with Sautéed Onions (see page 15)

- Garlic mashed potatoes (see page 55)

- Steamed green beans

- Red wine, such as Cabernet Sauvignon

30 MINUTE, LOW FAT

Split Pea Tortellini Soup

Using dried ingredients, this soup makes the perfect gift jar of food. If your grocery store doesn't carry dried chopped carrots, order them online at www.justtomatoes.com.

Prep: 15 minutes

    3   oz. dried cheese-filled tortellini
        (⅔ cup)
    ¼   cup snipped dried tomatoes
    ⅓   cup dried split green peas
    ½   cup dried chopped carrots
    1   Tbsp. instant chicken bouillon
        granules
    1   Tbsp. dried minced onion
    1½ tsp. dried basil, crushed
    1½ tsp. dried thyme, crushed
    ½   tsp. garlic powder
    ¼   tsp. pepper

1 Layer ingredients in a clean 1-pint glass canning jar in the following order (from bottom to top): tortellini, dried tomatoes, split peas, dried carrots, bouillon granules, dried onion, basil, thyme, garlic powder, and pepper. Cover the jar and attach a gift tag with directions for cooking.

Gift Tag Directions:
Empty jar ingredients into a 3-quart saucepan. Add 5 cups of water. Bring mixture to boiling; reduce heat. Cover and simmer about 50 minutes or until peas are tender. Add 1 cup chopped cooked ham or sausage, if desired. Heat through. Makes 4 main-dish servings.

Nutrition Facts per serving: 188 cal., 3 g total fat (0 g sat. fat), 0 mg chol., 964 mg sodium, 31 g carbo., 5 g fiber, 9 g pro. **Daily Values:** 13% vit. C, 12% calcium, 11% iron.

Roasted Cheddar Potatoes

To keep hot potatoes available, divide the wedges into two batches to heat one at a time. The second batch will be ready to eat just as guests finish the first round. (See the photograph on page 38.)

Prep: 10 minutes **Bake:** 25 minutes

    1   24-oz. pkg. frozen potato
        wedges (skins on)
    2   Tbsp. cooking oil
    4   cloves garlic, minced
    1   tsp. smoked paprika or paprika
    ¼   tsp. salt
        Nonstick cooking spray
    1   cup shredded white cheddar or
        other cheddar cheese (4 oz.)
    ⅔   cup crushed croutons (about
        1 cup croutons)
        Dairy sour cream (optional)

1 Preheat oven according to package directions for potatoes. Place frozen potatoes in a large self-sealing plastic bag. Combine cooking oil, garlic, paprika, and salt. Drizzle over potato wedges. Seal bag and shake to coat potatoes.

2 Lightly coat a 15×10×1-inch baking pan with nonstick cooking spray. Spread potatoes in a single layer on prepared pan. Bake potato wedges according to package directions, turning once.

3 In a small bowl combine the cheddar cheese and crushed croutons. Sprinkle over the potatoes the last 3 minutes of baking. Use a large spatula to transfer potato wedges to a platter or large plate (keep potatoes in a single layer). Serve with sour cream, if desired. Makes 8 side-dish servings.

Nutrition Facts per serving: 165 cal., 8 g total fat (4 g sat. fat), 15 mg chol., 217 mg sodium, 19 g carbo., 1 g fiber, 5 g pro. **Daily Values:** 6% vit. A, 5% vit. C, 11% calcium, 2% iron.

Oven Pancake with Sausage and Pears

Plan to seat guests at the table before you take this from the oven because the pancake deflates quickly. (See the photograph on page 40.)

Prep: 40 minutes **Bake:** 25 minutes

    ¼   cup margarine or butter, cut up
    4   eggs
    1   cup milk

1 cup all-purpose flour

⅛ tsp. salt

1 medium onion, cut into wedges

1 Tbsp. margarine or butter

8 oz. fully cooked bratwurst or
   other fully cooked smoked
   sausage links, bias-sliced

2 large green pears, cored and cut
   into 1-inch pieces (or 1 pear
   and 1 apple, cored and cut
   into 1-inch pieces)

⅓ cup dried tart red cherries
   Maple syrup

1 Preheat oven to 400°F. Place the ¼ cup margarine or butter in a 2½-quart oval or round baking dish. Place dish in oven for 5 minutes or until margarine or butter melts.

2 In a large bowl beat eggs with a rotary beater or an electric mixer until combined. Add milk, flour, and salt. Beat until smooth. (Or place eggs in a blender container or food processor bowl. Cover and blend or process for 30 seconds. Add milk, flour, and salt. Cover and blend for 30 seconds more or until smooth, scraping down sides as necessary.)

3 Immediately pour batter over melted margarine in the hot baking dish. Bake about 25 minutes or until puffed and well browned.

4 Meanwhile, in a large saucepan cook onion wedges in the 1 tablespoon hot margarine or butter over medium heat about 5 minutes or until tender. Add sausage slices; cook until lightly browned. Stir in pears or apples and dried cherries; add salt and pepper to taste. Cook about 5 minutes or until fruit is slightly softened.

5 To serve, spoon sausage mixture into center of puffed pancake. Cut into wedges. Drizzle each serving with maple syrup. Makes 6 servings.

Nutrition Facts per serving: 445 cal., 24 g total fat (7 g sat. fat), 167 mg chol., 434 mg sodium, 45 g carbo., 2 g fiber, 14 g pro. Daily Values: 22% vit. A, 6% vit. C.

30 MINUTE

Steak with Sautéed Onions

Based on a recipe from a beloved, now closed, Des Moines restaurant, this recipe is easily doubled. (See the photograph on page 39.)

Start to finish: 25 minutes

6 4-oz. beef tenderloin steaks
   (1 inch thick)

¼ tsp. salt

¼ tsp. pepper

2 Tbsp. margarine or butter

1 small red onion, cut into
   6 wedges

2 cloves garlic, minced

1 tsp. dried basil, crushed

½ tsp. dried oregano, crushed

2 Tbsp. whipping cream

6 Tbsp. onion marmalade or
   orange marmalade

1 Sprinkle meat with salt and pepper. In a large skillet melt margarine or butter over medium heat. Add onion wedges and garlic. Cook and stir for 6 to 8 minutes or until onion is tender but not brown. Remove onion from skillet.

2 Increase heat to medium-high. Add steaks to skillet; cook to desired doneness, turning once. (For rare, cook meat about 4 minutes on each side. Allow 2 to 3 minutes longer for medium.) After turning, sprinkle meat with basil and oregano.

3 Remove meat from skillet; keep warm. Return onion to skillet. Heat onion through. Remove skillet from heat. Stir in whipping cream.

4 To serve, place a steak on each of six dinner plates. Spoon cream over steaks. Top each steak with 1 tablespoon of the marmalade, and then divide cooked onions evenly among the steaks. Makes 6 servings.

Nutrition Facts per serving: 271 cal., 13 g total fat (4 g sat. fat), 63 mg chol., 110 mg sodium, 14 g carbo., 0 g fiber, 24 g pro. **Daily Values:** 6% vit. A, 3% vit. C, 3% calcium, 19% iron.

30 MINUTE, LOW FAT

Crunchy Parmesan Turkey

Walk into your kitchen after work and have this healthy meal prepared in 30 minutes. Prepare the fresh salad while the turkey and pasta cook.

Prep: 15 minutes **Bake:** 12 minutes

  12 **oz. turkey tenderloin**
   3 **Tbsp. Grape Nuts cereal**
   3 **Tbsp. grated Parmesan or Romano cheese**
  ¾ **tsp. dried Italian seasoning, crushed**
  ⅛ **to ¼ tsp. ground red pepper**
   1 **egg white**
   1 **Tbsp. water**
   1 **12-oz. pkg. dried spinach fettuccine**
   4 **medium zucchini or yellow summer squash, halved lengthwise and thinly sliced (about 3½ cups)**
   2 **cups low-fat chunky tomato pasta sauce**

1 Preheat oven to 400°F. Cut turkey tenderloin into six even pieces. In a shallow bowl combine Grape Nuts cereal, Parmesan or Romano cheese, Italian seasoning, and ground red pepper. In another shallow bowl slightly beat together egg white and water. Dip tenderloin pieces in the egg white mixture, then coat with cereal mixture.

2 Place turkey in a lightly greased baking pan. Bake for 12 to 15 minutes until turkey is no longer pink, turning once.

3 Meanwhile, prepare pasta according to package directions. During the last 2 minutes of cooking pasta, add zucchini or summer squash. Drain pasta mixture; set aside and keep warm. In a small saucepan heat pasta sauce.

4 To serve, arrange pasta mixture on each of six dinner plates. Top with turkey and pasta sauce. Makes 6 main-dish servings.

Nutrition Facts per serving: 340 cal., 4 g total fat (1 g sat. fat), 27 mg chol., 126 mg sodium, 55 g carbo., 3 g fiber, 23 g pro. **Daily Values:** 11% vit. A, 18% vit. C, 9% calcium, 19% iron.

Chicken and Mushrooms

Whether to slice mushrooms or not depends on their size. If they're larger than 1½ inches in diameter, slice them. Otherwise, leave them whole. (See the photograph on page 41.)

Prep: 15 minutes **Cook:** 40 minutes

  ¼ **cup all-purpose flour**
  ¼ **tsp. salt**
  ¼ **tsp. pepper**
  ¼ **tsp. paprika**
   4 **chicken thighs, skinned**
   4 **chicken drumsticks, skinned**
   2 **Tbsp. cooking oil**
   1 **medium onion, sliced**
   2 **cups whole or sliced fresh mushrooms**
   1 **medium red sweet pepper, cut into 1-inch strips**
   3 **cloves garlic, minced**
  ½ **cup dry red wine or beef broth**
   2 **Tbsp. balsamic vinegar**
   1 **14½-oz. can diced tomatoes**
   2 **tsp. dried Italian seasoning, crushed**
  ¼ **cup half-and-half or light cream**
   1 **Tbsp. all-purpose flour**
  ¼ **cup snipped fresh flat-leaf parsley**
      Hot cooked pasta (optional)

1 In a large self-sealing plastic bag combine the ¼ cup flour, salt, pepper, and paprika. Add 2 or 3 pieces of chicken to the bag at a time. Seal and shake to coat well.

2 In a very large skillet heat the 2 tablespoons oil over medium heat. Cook chicken in hot oil about 10 minutes or until well browned, turning to brown evenly. Remove chicken from skillet, reserving drippings in the skillet.

3 Add onion, mushrooms, sweet pepper, and garlic to skillet. Cook and stir for 2 minutes. Add red wine or beef broth and balsamic vinegar. Cook and stir 5 minutes more.

4 Add undrained tomatoes and Italian seasoning. Bring to boiling, scraping up browned bits from the bottom of the skillet. Return chicken to the skillet; reduce heat. Cover and simmer about 20 minutes or until chicken is tender and no longer pink. Remove chicken; keep warm.

5 Stir together half-and-half or light cream and the 1 tablespoon flour; add to skillet. Cook and stir until slightly thickened and bubbly. Cook and stir 1 minute more. Return chicken to skillet; heat through. Sprinkle with parsley. Serve over hot cooked pasta, if desired. Makes 4 to 6 servings.

Nutrition Facts per serving: 323 cal., 13 g total fat (3 g sat. fat), 89 mg chol., 400 mg sodium, 21 g carbo., 2 g fiber, 25 g pro. Daily Values: 26% vit. A, 132% vit. C, 10% calcium, 18% iron.

Celebration Shrimp-Stuffed Chicken

Perfect for a party—these festive chicken bundles are worth the effort.

Prep: 1 hour Bake: 25 minutes

- 6 oz. medium shrimp in shells
- 2 oz. fresh shiitake or button mushrooms
- ¼ cup chopped green onions
- ¼ cup chopped walnuts
- 1 clove garlic, minced
- 2 Tbsp. olive oil
- 3 Tbsp. fine dry bread crumbs
- 4 large skinless, boneless chicken breast halves
- ¾ cup dry white wine
- 1 ½-inch piece fresh ginger
- 1 medium tomato, peeled, seeded, and chopped
- 2 Tbsp. butter or margarine, softened
- ¼ cup snipped fresh cilantro
- 2 tsp. lemon juice

1 Remove shells from shrimp; reserve shells. Chop shrimp; set aside. Remove stems from mushrooms; set aside. Chop the mushroom caps. For filling, in a large skillet cook the shrimp, mushroom caps, green onions, walnuts, and garlic in 1 tablespoon of the olive oil over medium-high heat about 3 minutes or

until shrimp turn opaque. Stir in bread crumbs, ¼ teaspoon salt, and ⅛ teaspoon pepper; set aside.

2 Preheat oven to 350°F. Place each chicken piece, boned side up, between two pieces of plastic wrap. Pound lightly with a meat mallet to a rectangle ¼- to ⅛-inch thick. Remove plastic wrap. Sprinkle with salt and pepper. Place one-fourth of the filling on one end of each chicken piece. Fold in sides and roll up. Secure with wooden toothpicks.

3 In the large skillet cook chicken in the remaining 1 tablespoon olive oil over medium heat 2 to 3 minutes per side or until browned. Transfer to a 2-quart rectangular baking dish. Bake, uncovered, about 25 minutes or until chicken is tender and no longer pink and filling is 160°F.

4 Meanwhile, for sauce, place the reserved shrimp shells and mushrooms stems in a medium saucepan. Add white wine, ginger, ¼ teaspoon salt, and ⅛ teaspoon pepper. Bring to boiling; reduce heat. Cover; simmer for 10 minutes. Strain liquid through a fine mesh strainer; discard solids. Return liquid to saucepan. Stir in tomato. Bring to boiling; reduce heat. Boil gently, uncovered, 5 minutes or until most of the liquid has evaporated. Remove from heat. Whisk in butter. Stir in cilantro and lemon juice.

5 To serve, place one chicken roll on each of four dinner plates. Spoon sauce over chicken. Serves 4.

Nutrition Facts per serving: 416 cal., 21 g total fat (6 g sat. fat), 150 mg chol., 659 mg sodium, 7 g carbo., 1 g fiber, 42 g pro. Daily Values: 20% vit. C, 7% calcium, 15% iron.

LOW FAT

Chocolate-Covered Grapes

The grapes must be dry before dipping because one drop of water in the melted mixture will cause the chocolate to harden and become unusable (seizing). Wash the grapes and let them dry for several hours. (See the photograph on page 38.)

Prep: 30 minutes Chill: 30 minutes

- 1 bunch seedless grapes (1 lb.)
- 4 oz. milk chocolate pieces
- 4 oz. semisweet chocolate pieces
- 2 Tbsp. shortening

1 Wash grapes. Drain thoroughly on paper towels for several hours. Line a baking sheet with waxed paper; set aside.

2 In a small saucepan combine milk chocolate, semisweet chocolate, and shortening. Heat and stir over low heat until chocolate is melted. Holding grape bunch by stem, dip grapes partially into melted chocolate. If necessary, spoon chocolate over grapes to coat. Let excess chocolate drip off. Place grapes, stem side up, on prepared baking sheet.

3 Chill the grapes until the chocolate is firm, from 30 minutes to 6 hours. Makes about twenty 3- to 5-grape servings.

Nutrition Facts per serving: 86 cal., 5 g total fat (1 g sat. fat), 1 mg chol., 6 mg sodium, 11 g carbo., 1 g fiber, 1 g pro. Daily Values: 4% vit. C, 2% calcium, 2% iron.

CASSEROLE CLASSICS

When winter's chill is on, spooning into a bubbly hot one-dish meal warms the tummy and comforts the senses. You'll receive added comfort and smiles of delight when you unveil a casserole that has filled the kitchen with mouthwatering aroma. Here's a collection of favorites from years gone by.

Pork and Green Chiles Casserole

Diced green chile peppers and a little salsa add spunk to this hearty rice, bean, and pork dish. For those who love Mexican-style food, it rates at the top.

Prep: 25 minutes **Bake:** 25 minutes
Stand: 3 minutes

- 1¼ lb. lean boneless pork
- 1 Tbsp. cooking oil
- 1 15-oz. can black beans or pinto beans, rinsed and drained
- 1 14½-oz. can diced tomatoes
- 1 10¾-oz. can condensed cream of chicken soup
- 2 4½-oz. cans diced green chile peppers, drained
- 1 cup quick-cooking brown rice
- ¼ cup water
- 2 Tbsp. bottled salsa
- 1 tsp. ground cumin
- ½ cup shredded cheddar cheese (2 oz.)

1 Preheat oven to 375°F. Cut pork into thin bite-size strips. In a large skillet stir-fry pork, half at a time, in hot oil until no pink remains; drain. Return all meat to skillet. Stir in beans, undrained tomatoes, soup, chile peppers, brown rice, water, salsa, and cumin. Heat and stir just until bubbly; pour into a 2-quart casserole.

2 Bake, uncovered, for 25 minutes. Remove from oven. Sprinkle with cheese; let stand for 3 to 4 minutes to melt cheese. Serves 6.

Nutrition Facts per serving: 350 cal., 14 g total fat (5 g sat. fat), 69 mg chol., 1,242 mg sodium, 28 g carbo., 5 g fiber, 30 g pro. **Daily Values:** 9% vit. A, 58% vit. C, 15% calcium, 14% iron.

Spaghetti Pie

Better Homes and Gardens magazine featured this popular casserole on the cover in 1974.

Prep: 25 minutes **Bake:** 25 minutes

- 6 oz. packaged dried spaghetti
- 2 Tbsp. margarine or butter
- ⅓ cup grated Parmesan cheese
- 2 eggs, well beaten
- 1 lb. lean ground beef or bulk pork sausage
- ½ cup chopped onion
- ¼ cup chopped green sweet pepper
- 1 7½-oz. can tomatoes, cut up
- 1 6-oz. can tomato paste
- 1 tsp. sugar
- 1 tsp. dried oregano, crushed
- ½ tsp. garlic salt
- 1 cup cream-style cottage cheese
- ½ cup shredded mozzarella cheese (2 oz.)

1 Preheat oven to 350°F. Cook spaghetti according to package directions; drain (about 3¼ cups cooked spaghetti). Stir margarine into hot spaghetti. Stir in Parmesan cheese and eggs. Form spaghetti mixture into a "crust" in a buttered 10-inch pie plate.

2 In a large skillet cook the ground beef, onion, and sweet pepper until meat is brown. Drain well. Stir in the undrained tomatoes, tomato paste, sugar, oregano, and garlic salt. Heat through.

3 Spread cottage cheese over spaghetti mixture in pie plate. Top with meat mixture. Bake, uncovered, for 20 minutes. Sprinkle mozzarella cheese over top. Bake 5 minutes more or until cheese melts. Makes 6 servings.

Nutrition Facts per serving: 452 cal., 22 total fat (9 g sat. fat), 128 mg chol., 554 mg sodium, 32 g carbo., 2 g fiber, 31 g pro. **Daily Values:** 14% vit. A, 26% vit. C, 19% calcium, 20% iron.

Vegetarian Lasagna

This hearty lasagna is one of the many top-notch recipes we have created in response to the request for more meatless main dishes.

Prep: 25 minutes **Bake:** 30 minutes
Stand: 10 minutes

- 9 packaged dried lasagna noodles
- 2 cups sliced fresh mushrooms

- 1 cup coarsely shredded carrot
- ½ cup chopped onion
- 1 Tbsp. cooking oil
- 1 15-oz. can tomato sauce
- 1 6-oz. can tomato paste
- ½ cup chopped pitted ripe olives
- 1½ tsp. dried oregano, crushed
- 2 cups cream-style cottage cheese, drained
- 1 egg, slightly beaten
- 2 cups shredded Monterey Jack cheese (8 oz.)
- 1 10-oz. pkg. frozen chopped spinach, thawed and well drained

  Grated Parmesan cheese

1 Preheat oven to 375°F. Grease a 3-quart rectangular baking dish. Set aside. Cook lasagna noodles according to package directions; drain and set aside.

2 Meanwhile, in a medium saucepan cook mushrooms, carrot, and onion in hot oil until tender. Stir in tomato sauce, tomato paste, olives, and oregano. In a medium mixing bowl stir together cottage cheese and egg. Set aside ¼ cup of the Monterey Jack cheese.

3 In the prepared baking dish layer one-third of the lasagna noodles, one-third of the cottage cheese mixture, one-third of the spinach, one-third of the remaining Monterey Jack cheese, and one-third of the tomato mixture; repeat the layers twice. Sprinkle with the reserved Monterey Jack cheese.

4 Bake, uncovered, about 30 minutes or until heated through. Let stand 10 minutes before serving. Pass Parmesan cheese. Makes 8 to 10 servings.

Nutrition Facts per serving: 333 cal., 15 g total fat (7 g sat. fat), 59 mg chol., 834 mg sodium, 30 g carbo., 4 g fiber, 21 g pro. **Daily Values:** 191% vit. A, 25% vit. C, 30% calcium, 15% iron.

Deep-Dish Chicken Pie

To achieve the same delicious results and save time, substitute refrigerated unbaked piecrust for the Pastry Topper. Pour the chicken mixture into a 2-quart round casserole, top with piecrust, flute, brush, and bake.

Prep: 30 minutes **Bake:** 30 minutes
Cool: 20 minutes

- 1 recipe Pastry Topper (see right)
- 2 Tbsp. margarine or butter
- 3 medium leeks or 1 large onion, chopped
- 1 cup sliced fresh mushrooms
- ¾ cup sliced celery
- ½ cup chopped red sweet pepper
- ⅓ cup all-purpose flour
- 1 tsp. poultry seasoning
- 1½ cups chicken broth
- 1 cup half-and-half, light cream, or milk
- 2½ cups chopped, cooked chicken
- 1 cup loose-pack frozen peas
- 1 egg, beaten

1 On a lightly floured surface, roll Pastry Topper into a rectangle ⅛-inch thick. Trim to 1 inch larger than a 2-quart rectangular baking dish. Using a sharp knife or small cookie cutter, cut shapes from the center of the pastry. Set aside.

2 Preheat oven to 400°F. In a large saucepan melt margarine over medium heat. Add the leeks or onion, mushrooms, celery, and red sweet pepper; cook until tender, about 5 minutes. Stir in flour, poultry seasoning, and ¼ teaspoon each salt and pepper. Add broth and half-and-half; cook and stir until thickened and bubbly. Stir in chicken and peas. Pour into baking dish.

3 Place pastry over the hot chicken mixture. Turn under edges of pastry and flute to top edges of dish. Brush with egg. Place reserved pastry shapes on top of pastry. Brush again with egg.

4 Bake for 30 to 35 minutes until crust is golden brown. Cool 20 minutes before serving. Serves 6.

Pastry Topper

Stir together 1¼ cups flour and ¼ teaspoon salt. Cut in ⅓ cup shortening to make small pea sizes. Sprinkle 1 tablespoon cold water over part of the mixture; gently toss with a fork. Push moistened dough to side of bowl. Repeat with 3 to 4 tablespoons cold water, 1 tablespoon at a time, until dough is moistened. Form into a ball.

Nutrition Facts per serving: 489 cal., 26 g total fat (8 g sat. fat), 102 mg chol., 615 mg sodium, 39 g carbo., 3 g fiber, 26 g pro. **Daily Values:** 26% vit. A, 48% vit. C, 11% calcium, 22% iron.

TEST KITCHEN TIP

Can I Freeze Cookie Dough? How Should Cookies Be Stored?

Most cookie doughs can be refrigerated or frozen for baking later. The exceptions are meringue or macaroon mixtures and thin batters, such as bar cookie batters.

Store cookie dough in a tightly covered container in the refrigerator for up to three days, or freeze for up to six months. To freeze cookie dough, pack it into freezer containers or shape slice-and-bake dough into rolls and wrap in foil. For drop cookie dough, go a step further, using a small ice cream scoop to form balls. Freeze the balls on a baking sheet and transfer them to a plastic freezer bag after they freeze.

To bake, thaw frozen dough in containers in the refrigerator. If the thawed dough is too stiff to work with, let it stand at room temperature for a few minutes until it is easy to handle.

To store baked cookies, follow these guidelines:

● Cool the cookies completely on a wire rack. If they're warm, they'll likely stick together.

● Place cookies in plastic bags or containers that seal tightly.

● Store cookies unfrosted; frosting causes cookies to stick together. Royal Icing separates from cookies and colored icing may develop light spots when frozen. Frosted cookies lose crispness as they absorb moisture from frosting.

Store cookies at room temperature for up to three days. Pack crisp and soft cookies separately—stored together, they all become soft. Store bar cookies, cut or uncut, in tightly covered containers.

Store cookies with frosting or filling that contains cream cheese or yogurt in the refrigerator.

LOW FAT

Brownie Meringues

Letting egg whites stand at room temperature allows them to gain greater volume when beaten with sugar than if they were cold.

Prep: 15 minutes **Stand:** 30 minutes
Bake: 10 minutes per batch

  2 egg whites
  ½ tsp. vinegar
  ½ tsp. vanilla
     Dash salt
  ½ cup sugar
  1 cup semisweet chocolate pieces, melted and cooled
  ¾ cup chopped walnuts
  ½ cup semisweet chocolate pieces
  1 tsp. shortening

1 Preheat oven to 350°F. Grease baking sheets; set aside. For meringue, place egg whites in a large mixing bowl; let stand at room temperature for 30 minutes. Add the vinegar, vanilla, and salt. Beat with an electric mixer on medium speed until soft peaks form (tips curl). Add sugar, 1 tablespoon at a time, beating on high speed about 4 minutes or until stiff peaks form (tips stand straight) and the sugar is almost dissolved. Fold in the melted chocolate and nuts.

2 Drop mixture from teaspoons onto prepared baking sheets. Bake for 10 to 12 minutes or until edges are firm. Transfer cookies to wire racks; let cool. In a small saucepan heat the ½ cup semisweet chocolate pieces and the shortening until melted. Drizzle over cookies. Makes 24 cookies.

Nutrition Facts per cookie: 95 cal., 5 g total fat (2 g sat. fat), 0 mg chol., 11 mg sodium, 8 g carbo., 2 g fiber, 1 g pro. **Daily Values:** 1% iron.

LOW FAT

Lemonade Cookies

The tangy citrus flavor of these cakey cookies comes from frozen lemonade concentrate. They're marvelous with ice cream or as a snack.

Prep: 20 minutes
Bake: 6 minutes per batch

  1 cup butter
  1 cup granulated sugar
  1 tsp. baking soda
  2 eggs
  1 6-oz. can (¾ cup) frozen lemonade concentrate, thawed
  3 cups all-purpose flour
     Granulated sugar or coarse sugar

1 Preheat oven to 400°F. In a medium mixing bowl beat butter with an electric mixer on medium speed for 30 seconds. Add the 1 cup granulated sugar and the baking soda. Beat until combined. Beat in eggs and ½ cup of the lemonade concentrate. Beat in as much of the flour as you can. Stir in any remaining flour with a wooden spoon.

2 Drop dough by rounded teaspoons 2 inches apart on ungreased baking sheets. Bake for 6 to 7 minutes or until lightly brown around the edges. Cool on baking sheet for 1 minute. Transfer cookies to a wire rack. Brush hot cookies lightly with remaining lemonade concentrate; sprinkle with granulated or coarse sugar. Let cool. Makes about 48 cookies.

Nutrition Facts per cookie: 90 cal., 4 g total fat (3 g sat. fat), 20 mg chol., 70 mg sodium, 12 g carbo., 0 g fiber, 1 g pro. **Daily Values:** 4% vit. A, 1% vit. C, 2% iron.

Cookies and Cream

Choose your favorite cookie. Any type works as long as it's soft enough to be cut with a fork. (See the photograph on page 41.)

Start to finish: 15 minutes

- ½   **cup whipping cream**
- 2   **Tbsp. honey**
- ½   **cup dairy sour cream**
- 24 **purchased large soft cookies, such as ginger or oatmeal**
      Honey
      Candied violas or other edible flower petals (optional)

1 In a small chilled mixing bowl combine whipping cream and the 2 tablespoons honey. Beat with chilled beaters of an electric mixer on medium speed until soft peaks form. Fold in sour cream.

2 To serve, lay one cookie on each of eight dessert plates. Top with a spoonful of whipped cream mixture. Top with another cookie, and another spoon of whipped cream mixture. Top with a third cookie and more whipped cream mixture. Drizzle with additional honey and, if desired, sprinkle with flower petals. Makes 8 servings.

To Make Ahead:

Prepare whipped cream mixture; cover and chill up to 1 hour before serving. Assemble individual desserts just before serving.

Nutrition Facts per serving: 456 cal., 21 g total fat (10 g sat. fat), 43 mg chol., 310 mg sodium, 61 g carbo., 2 g fiber, 5 g pro. **Daily Values:** 12% vit. A, 1% vit. C, 6% calcium, 9% iron.

Ranger Cookies

For gift giving, the colorful fruit-flavored crisp rice cereal looks pretty in the jar. If you prefer, substitute the plain crisp rice cereal.

Prep: 20 minutes

- 1¼ **cups all-purpose flour**
- ½   **tsp. baking powder**
- ¼   **tsp. baking soda**
- ½   **cup shortening**
- 2   **cups fruit-flavored crisp rice cereal**
- ⅔   **cup packed brown sugar**
- ⅓   **cup shredded or flaked coconut**

1 In a medium mixing bowl stir together flour, baking powder, and baking soda. Use a pastry blender to cut in shortening until well blended. Layer ingredients in a clean 1-quart glass canning jar in the following order: half of the cereal, flour mixture, brown sugar, remaining cereal, and coconut. Cover jar and attach gift tag with directions for mixing and baking.

Gift Tag Directions:

Use within 1 month. Preheat oven to 375°F. Empty contents of jar into large mixing bowl. Stir in 1 beaten egg, 2 tablespoons milk, and 1 teaspoon vanilla until combined. Drop by rounded teaspoon 2 inches apart on an ungreased cookie sheet. Bake for 8 to 9 minutes or until edges are golden brown. Cool on cookie sheet 1 minute. Transfer to a wire rack; let cool. Makes 24 cookies.

Nutrition Facts per cookie: 106 cal., 5 g total fat (1 g sat. fat), 9 mg chol., 48 mg sodium, 14 g carbo., 0 g fiber, 1 g pro. **Daily Values:** 2% calcium, 4% iron.

Peanut Butter Pizzas

Use any form of pizza dough you like with this recipe. Refrigerated is the most convenient—frozen or homemade dough works equally well.

Prep: 20 minutes **Bake:** 10 minutes

- 1   **10-oz. pkg. refrigerated pizza dough**
- ⅔   **cup chunky peanut butter**
- 2   **cups assorted toppers, such as grape jelly or strawberry preserves, marshmallow creme, miniature marshmallows, chocolate-hazelnut spread, fresh sliced strawberries, peanuts, and/or sliced bananas**
      Cinnamon-sugar (optional)

1 Preheat oven to 375°F. To make individual pizzas, lightly grease two baking sheets. Divide dough into five or six pieces. Cover; let rest for 10 minutes. Roll each piece into a 6-inch circle. Place on baking sheet. Prick dough generously with a fork (do not allow to rise). Bake for 10 to 12 minutes or until lightly browned.

2 Remove from oven. While still warm, spread bread circles with peanut butter. Arrange on a serving board or platter. Serve warm with remaining toppings. Sprinkle with cinnamon-sugar, if desired. Makes 5 or 6 individual pizzas.

Nutrition Facts per pizza: 523 cal., 26 g total fat (4 g sat. fat), 0 mg chol., 490 mg sodium, 62 g carbo., 4 g fiber, 15 g pro. **Daily Values:** 8% vit. C, 2% calcium, 11% iron.

30 MINUTE, LOW FAT

Coconut Sno-Cakes

Start with cupcakes—made from scratch, from a mix, or purchased. Use extra-fine sugar to make the smoothest frosting.

Start to finish: 25 minutes

- 1½ cups extra-fine granulated sugar or granulated sugar
- ⅓ cup water
- 2 egg whites
- ¼ tsp. cream of tartar or 2 tsp. light-colored corn syrup
- 1 tsp. vanilla
- 36 unfrosted white cupcakes in paper liners
  Toasted coconut

1 In the top of a double boiler stir together sugar and water. Add egg whites and cream of tartar. Beat with an electric mixer on low speed for 30 seconds. Place over boiling water (upper pan should not touch water). Cook, beating constantly on high speed, about 7 minutes or until stiff peaks form. Remove from heat; add vanilla. Beat 2 to 3 minutes more or until easy to spread.

2 Spread on cupcakes. Top with coconut. Serve the same day. Makes 36 cupcakes.

Nutrition Facts per serving: 188 cal., 127 cal., 2 g total fat (0 g sat. fat), 0 mg chol., 154 mg sodium, 25 g carbo., 0 g fiber, 1 g pro. Daily Values: 4% calcium, 2% iron.

30 MINUTE

Iced Cocoa-Coffee

Start to finish: 10 minutes

- 2 cups strong black coffee, chilled
- ½ cup whipping cream
- ½ cup chocolate-flavored syrup
  Ice cubes

1 In a blender container combine chilled coffee, whipping cream, and chocolate-flavored syrup. Cover and blend until combined. Serve over ice. Makes 4 servings.

Nutrition Facts per serving: 188 cal., 11 g total fat (7 g sat. fat), 41 mg chol., 50 mg sodium, 23 g carbo., 1 g fiber, 1 g pro. Daily Values: 3% calcium, 5% iron.

30 MINUTE, LOW FAT

Mocha au Lait

Here's a homemade birthday gift for someone you want to remember when you're not sure what to buy.

Prep: 10 minutes

- 1½ cups nonfat dry milk powder
- ⅓ cup packed brown sugar
- ½ cup instant coffee crystals
- ⅔ cup miniature semisweet chocolate pieces

1 In a medium mixing bowl stir together milk powder, brown sugar, coffee crystals, and chocolate

pieces. Divide mixture into three 1-cup gift containers. Seal containers and attach gift tag directions.

Gift Tag Directions:

Pour ⅔ cup boiling water into a blender container. Add ¼ cup of the mocha mix. Cover and blend until well combined and frothy. (Or beat with wire whisk or electric mixer.) Pour into a mug and enjoy.

Nutrition Facts per serving: 133 cal., 4 g total fat (2 g sat. fat), 2 mg chol., 51 mg sodium, 21 g carbo., 0 g fiber, 4 g pro. Daily Values: 1% vit. C, 12% calcium, 3% iron.

PRIZE WINNER

Holiday Cider

Jeanne Berkley
Washington, Pennsylvania
$200—Holiday Nogs and Punches

Start to finish: 55 minutes

- 2 to 4 medium baking apples, cored
- 2 tsp. whole cloves
- ⅓ cup water
- 4 crab apples (optional)
- 4 medium oranges
- 4 medium lemons
- 8 cups apple cider
- ½ cup sugar
- 12 inches stick cinnamon
- 1 tsp. ground allspice
- ½ tsp. ground nutmeg

1 Preheat oven to 350°F. Insert about half the cloves into 2 baking apples. Place the apples in a 2-quart square baking dish. Add the water. Bake apples, uncovered, for 15 minutes. Add crab apples, if desired. Bake an additional 25 to

30 minutes or until apples and crab apples are tender; cool slightly. Halve or quarter baking apples. Set aside.

2 Meanwhile, squeeze juice from oranges and lemons (you should have 1⅓ cups orange juice and ¾ cup lemon juice). In a 4-quart Dutch oven combine orange and lemon juices, apple cider, sugar, cinnamon, remaining cloves, allspice, and nutmeg. Bring to boiling; reduce heat. Simmer, uncovered, for 20 minutes. Use a slotted spoon to remove whole cloves and stick cinnamon from the cider mixture.

3 To serve, place apples in a large heat-proof punch bowl; carefully pour cider mixture into bowl. Makes 12 to 16 servings.

Nutrition Facts per serving: 125 cal., 0 g total fat, 0 mg chol., 1 mg sodium, 17 g carbo., 1 g fiber, 0 g pro. Daily Values: 1% vit. A, 39% vit. C, 2% calcium, 4% iron.

NO FAT
Spirited Cranberry Slush

Store a batch of this frosty drink in the the freezer to serve when unexpected guests drop by.

Prep: 20 minutes **Freeze:** Overnight **Stand:** 10 minutes

- 4 cups cranberry juice
- 1 12-oz. bag cranberries
- 1 12-oz. can frozen pink lemonade concentrate, thawed
- 2 cups vodka
    Lemon-lime or grapefruit carbonated beverage, chilled
    Mint sprig, optional

1 In a blender container combine 2 cups of the cranberry juice and the cranberries. Cover and blend using on/off turns just until cranberries are finely chopped. Transfer mixture to a 3-quart freezer container. Stir in remaining cranberry juice, lemonade concentrate, and vodka. Cover and freeze overnight.

2 To serve, let mixture stand at room temperature for 10 minutes. Use a large spoon to scrape across frozen mixture and spoon about ½ cup into a chilled 8-ounce glass. Fill glass with carbonated beverage. Garnish with mint sprig, if desired. Makes 22 servings.

Nutrition Facts per serving: 164 cal., 0 g total fat, 0 mg chol., 15 mg sodium, 29 g carbo., 1 g fiber, 0 g pro. Daily Values: 35% vit. C, 1% calcium, 2% iron.

Non-Spirited Cranberry Slush
Prepare slush as directed at left, except omit the vodka and use 6 cups total of the cranberry juice. Let the frozen slush stand for 30 minutes before scraping.

LOW FAT
Melon Snowball Slush

Blend frozen cantaloupe for a refreshing beverage with slushy snow consistency. Tag this page so you'll be able to turn to it quickly in the heat of summer.

Prep: 20 minutes **Freeze:** 1 hour

- 1 large cantaloupe
- 1 cup apricot nectar, chilled

- ¼ cup frozen orange juice concentrate
- ¼ cup lime juice
- ¼ cup extra-fine granulated sugar

1 Peel and seed cantaloupe. Cut melon into ½-inch cubes. (You should have 6 to 7 cups melon.) Place melon cubes in a self-sealing plastic bag; seal and partially freeze, about 1 hour.

2 In a 2-cup glass measure combine apricot nectar, orange juice concentrate, lime juice, and sugar. Place half of the melon into a blender container. Pour half of the juice into the container. Cover and blend until slushy. Pour into chilled glasses. Repeat blending remaining melon and juice mixture. Makes 6 servings.

Nutrition Facts per serving: 132 cal., 1 g total fat (0 g sat. fat), 0 mg chol., 16 mg sodium, 33 g carbo., 2 g fiber, 2 g pro. Daily Values: 115% vit. C, 3% calcium, 3% iron.

Mango Mash

Skewers of pineapple, mango, and kiwi fruit decorate each glassful of mango- and tangerine-flavored punch.

Start to finish: 25 minutes

- 1 small pineapple, peeled, cored and cubed
- 1 ripe mango, seeded, peeled, and cubed
- 12 to 14 whole baby kiwi fruit, halved, or 6 kiwi fruit, peeled and quartered
- 12 to 14 6-inch wooden skewers
- 1 pint mango sorbet, softened
- 4 cups tangerine juice blend, chilled
- 1¼ tsp. ground ginger
- 1 2-liter bottle ginger-flavored carbonated beverage, chilled

1 Thread pineapple cubes, mango cubes, and kiwi fruit onto wooden skewers. Set aside.

2 In a large punch bowl stir together the softened sorbet, 2 cups of the tangerine juice blend, and the ground ginger until smooth. Stir in remaining juice blend and carbonated beverage.

3 To serve, ladle punch into chilled glasses. Garnish each serving with a fruit skewer. Makes 12 to 14 servings.

Nutrition Facts per serving: 190 cal., 1 g total fat (0 g sat. fat), 0 mg chol., 14 mg sodium, 47 g carbo., 2 g fiber, 1 g pro. Daily Values: 28% vit. C, 4% calcium, 4% iron.

Raspberry Melba Punch

Pretty in pink, this sherbety not-too-sweet drink is the light fruity choice for a children's party.

Start to finish: 10 minutes

- 1 12-oz. can frozen raspberry juice blend concentrate, thawed
- 1 12-oz. can frozen pink or regular lemonade concentrate, thawed
- 2 cups peach or apricot nectar, chilled
- 1 cup cold water
- 1 2-liter bottle carbonated water or lemon-lime carbonated beverage, chilled
- 1 quart raspberry sherbet

1 In a large punch bowl combine raspberry juice blend concentrate, lemonade concentrate, peach or apricot nectar, and water. Slowly add carbonated beverage, stirring gently. Add small scoops of sherbet. Serve at once. Makes 18 to 20 servings.

Nutrition Facts per serving: 140 cal., 1 g total fat (1 g sat. fat), 2 mg chol., 46 mg sodium, 34 g carbo., 0 g fiber, 1 g pro. Daily Values: 49% vit. C, 3% calcium, 1% iron.

Raspberry Shrub

Hunter Marlo
Charlottesville, Virginia
$400—Holiday Nogs and Punches

Prep: 25 minutes **Cool:** 2 hours

- 3 12-oz. pkg. frozen lightly sweetened red raspberries (about 9 cups)
- 1½ cups honey
- 1 cup sugar
- ⅓ cup water
- 2 lemons
- 12 inches stick cinnamon, broken
- 2 Tbsp. snipped fresh rosemary or 2 to 3 tsp. dried rosemary, crushed
- 9 or 10 whole cloves
- ⅓ to ½ cup light rum or ½ cup water
- 2 to 3 cups ice cubes
- 1 750 ml bottle Champagne or sparkling grape juice, chilled
  Fresh rosemary sprigs (optional)

1 In a 4-quart Dutch oven combine raspberries, honey, sugar, and water. Cook and stir over medium heat until sugar dissolves. Use a vegetable peeler to remove strips of peel from lemons. Juice the lemons (you should have ½ cup lemon juice). Add strips of lemon peel, lemon juice, cinnamon, rosemary, and cloves to Dutch oven. Bring mixture just to boiling; stir occasionally. Remove from heat. Cover; cool to room temperature. Press mixture through a sieve; discard solids. (You should have about 4 cups syrup.)

2 To serve, in a punch bowl combine syrup, rum or water, and ice cubes. Slowly add Champagne or sparkling juice. Stir gently. Serve over ice in small glasses or punch cups. Garnish with fresh rosemary sprigs, if desired. Makes about 16 servings.

To Make Ahead:

Prepare raspberry syrup mixture. Cover and store in the refrigerator for up to 3 days. Combine syrup, rum, and ice just before serving.

Nutrition Facts per serving: 217 cal., 0 g total fat, 0 mg chol., 2 mg sodium, 46 g carbo., 1 g fiber, 0 g pro. Daily Values: 8% vit. C, 2% iron.

february

IN THIS CHAPTER

**30-minute recipes indicated in COLOR.
Low-fat and no-fat recipes indicated
with a ♥.
Photographs indicated in italics.
*Bonus recipe**

Cheese Puffs

These flaky morsels appeared as a *Better Homes and Gardens* Prize Tested Recipe in 1974.

Prep: 30 minutes **Bake:** 12 minutes

 1 **3-oz. pkg. cream cheese, softened**
 1 **egg yolk**
 1 **tsp. lemon juice**
 1 **tsp. snipped fresh chives**
    Dash pepper
 ½ **cup shredded white cheddar cheese (2 oz.)**
 2 **slices bacon, crisp-cooked, drained, and crumbled**
 1 **17¼-oz. pkg. (2 sheets) frozen puff pastry, thawed**
    Milk

1 Preheat oven to 400°F. For filling, in a small mixing bowl combine cream cheese, egg yolk, lemon juice, chives, and pepper. Beat with an electric mixer on medium speed until nearly smooth. Stir in cheddar cheese and bacon.

2 On a lightly floured surface, roll one of the pastry sheets to a 12-inch square. Cut into sixteen 3-inch squares. Top each square with 1 teaspoon of filling. Brush edges with milk. Fold in half diagonally. Seal edges by pressing with tines of a fork or with fingers. Place on an ungreased baking sheet. Repeat with remaining pastry sheet and filling.

3 Bake for 12 to 15 minutes or until golden brown. Remove from baking sheet; serve warm. Makes 32 puffs.

Nutrition Facts per puff: 87 cal., 7 g total fat (1 g sat. fat), 12 mg chol., 83 mg sodium, 6 g carbo., 0 g fiber, 1 g pro. **Daily Values:** 2% vit. A, 2% calcium.

LOW FAT

Warm Hearts

Talk about a sweetheart of a deal. These buttery nibbles, just right for a snack or appetizer, take a little heat from the ground red pepper and the jalapeños in the cheese. These tidbits are a perfect match for a glass of wine, especially Shiraz or Zinfandel. (See the photograph on page 43.)

Prep: 30 minutes **Bake:** 8 minutes

 ½ **cup all-purpose flour**
 ¼ **tsp. ground cumin**
 ⅛ **tsp. salt**
 ⅛ **tsp. ground red pepper**
 2 **Tbsp. cold butter, cut up**
 ½ **cup shredded Monterey Jack cheese with jalapeño peppers (2 oz.)**
 1 **to 2 Tbsp. water**
    Grated Parmesan cheese (optional)
 ½ **tsp. paprika (optional)**

1 Preheat oven to 400°F. In a large mixing bowl* stir together flour, cumin, salt, and ground red pepper. Cut in butter until the size of coarse crumbs. Stir in the Monterey Jack cheese. Sprinkle water over the mixture, stirring until all the dough is moistened.

2 Turn dough onto a large piece of waxed paper or plastic wrap. Use your hands to gather dough into a ball and flatten into a disk. If necessary, wrap and refrigerate the dough at least 30 minutes or until easy to handle.

3 On a lightly floured surface roll dough to about ⅛-inch thickness. Use a floured 1-, 1½-, and/or 2-inch heart-shape or other cookie cutter(s) to cut dough, rerolling as necessary.

Place hearts about ½ inch apart on ungreased cookie sheets. Sprinkle Parmesan cheese on some of the hearts, if desired.

4 Bake about 8 minutes or until hearts are golden brown around the edges. Transfer to a wire rack to cool completely. Sprinkle paprika lightly over hearts without Parmesan cheese, if desired. Makes ninety-six 1-inch crackers, forty-eight 1½-inch crackers, or thirty 2-inch crackers.

To Store:

Place baked crackers in an airtight container. Store at room temperature for up to 2 days.

*Note: Or in a food processor bowl combine the flour, cumin, salt, and ground red pepper. Drop the pieces of butter through the feed tube with the motor running. Process until fine crumbs form. Add the Monterey Jack cheese. Process again until well blended. Add water; process just until all the dough is moistened.

Nutrition Facts per 2-inch cracker: 21 cal., 1 g total fat (1 g sat. fat), 4 mg chol., 28 mg sodium, 2 g carbo., 0 g fiber, 1 g pro. **Daily Values:** 1% vit. A, 1% calcium, 1% iron.

LOW FAT

"Reddy" and Waiting Onion Cups

Roasted onions make tasty edible bowls—especially when filled with a savory vegetable mixture.

Prep: 30 minutes **Roast:** 20 minutes

 ½ **cup dairy sour cream**
 1½ **tsp. prepared horseradish**

4 medium red onions, peeled
    (8 to 10 oz. each)
1 Tbsp. olive oil
¼ tsp. salt
¼ tsp. pepper
2 slices bacon
1¼ cups chopped red sweet pepper
1 clove garlic, minced
1 16-oz. can diced beets, drained
2 tsp. snipped fresh rosemary or
    1 tsp. dried rosemary, crushed
    Fresh rosemary sprigs (optional)

1 Preheat oven to 400°F. In a small bowl combine sour cream and horseradish. Cover and chill until serving time.

2 Cut onions in half lengthwise. Use your fingers to carefully remove all but the 2 outermost rings to make 8 onion cups; reserve remaining onion. Place the onion cups, cut side down, in a shallow roasting pan. Brush with the 1 tablespoon olive oil. Sprinkle lightly with ⅛ teaspoon each of the salt and pepper. Roast, uncovered, for 15 to 20 minutes or until the onions are nearly tender.

3 Meanwhile, chop enough of the remaining onion to make 1 cup; set aside. In a large skillet cook bacon over medium heat until crisp. Drain bacon on paper towels, reserving 1 tablespoon drippings in skillet. Crumble bacon; set aside.

4 In the same skillet cook chopped onion, sweet pepper, and garlic in drippings about 5 minutes or until tender. Stir in beets, rosemary, and remaining salt and pepper.

5 Carefully turn onion cups cut side up. Divide cooked vegetable mixture among cups, mounding if necessary. Roast, uncovered, 5 minutes more or until onion cups are tender.

6 To serve, top each onion with crumbled bacon. Serve with sour cream-horseradish mixture and, if desired, a rosemary sprig. Makes 8 side-dish servings.

Nutrition Facts per serving: 123 cal., 5 g total fat (2 g sat. fat), 7 mg chol., 282 mg sodium, 16 g carbo., 4 g fiber, 3 g pro. **Daily Values:** 15% vit. A, 77% vit. C, 5% calcium, 3% iron.

Glorious Greens

The inspiration for this stacked salad came from a creation that chef Todd English served at his Miramar restaurant in Westport, Connecticut. The salad is topped with a shower of Spain's famed mellow-rich manchego cheese—although freshly shredded Parmesan works wonders too. To finely shred cheese, use a handheld microplane grater.

Start to finish: 40 minutes

1 recipe Hazelnut Vinaigrette
    (see right)
2 heads butter lettuce, bibb
    lettuce, and/or Boston lettuce
1 cup chopped roma tomatoes
½ cup finely sliced red onion slivers
¼ cup coarsely chopped toasted
    hazelnuts (filberts)
1 oz. manchego cheese or
    Parmesan cheese,
    finely shredded

1 Prepare Hazelnut Vinaigrette. Set aside. (Vinaigrette can be made a day ahead. Whisk before using.)

WINTER DINNER

- Roast beef or beef steaks

- "Reddy" and Waiting Onion Cups (see page 26)

- Oven-roasted potato wedges

- Crusty peasant-style bread

2 Separate leaves from each head of lettuce. Each individual salad requires 5 leaves, ranging in size from about 4 inches in diameter to 1½ inches in diameter.

3 To compose salad, on each of four plates, layer the largest leaf (about 4 inches), a few chopped tomatoes, a few red onion slivers, a sprinkling of nuts, and a drizzle of Hazelnut Vinaigrette. Repeat layering, stacking carefully, until all of the lettuce leaves are used. Top each serving with finely shredded manchego or Parmesan cheese. Makes 4 side-dish salads.

Hazelnut Vinaigrette
In a small bowl whisk together 3 tablespoons Champagne vinegar or white wine vinegar, 1 tablespoon finely chopped shallots, ½ teaspoon salt, and ¼ teaspoon pepper. Slowly whisk in 3 tablespoons hazelnut oil.

Nutrition Facts per serving: 199 cal., 17 g total fat (2 g sat. fat), 6 mg chol., 374 mg sodium, 7 g carbo., 2 g fiber, 5 g pro. **Daily Values:** 9% vit. A, 23% vit. C, 9% calcium, 5% iron.

Me and My Bread Machine

The small appliance that electrified a nation of adult bread bakers and put warm, homemade bread back on the table has found an enthusiastic crop of young fans. That's right. Bread machines are catching on with kids. Besides, January is National Bread Machine Baking Month, as named by an industry group.

We should have seen it coming. Bread machines are kid friendly. They enable kids to work in the kitchen with relative independence. The machines eliminate tricky kneading with the sort of techno-wizardry that computer-savvy kids understand. "While adults view bread machines as appliances, kids embrace them as computers that bake yummy bread," says Ann Parrish, president of

Innovative Cooking Enterprises, a testing firm for bread machines.

Do techno-gadgets give you the high-tech jitters? Don't worry. Bread machines are child's play. The hard part isn't operating one; it's choosing between all the available models. Shop around and read the owner's manual before you begin. After that, all you do is measure and push a few buttons. Program the machine to knead, rise, and bake. Or remove risen dough to shape and bake in your oven. Don't worry if the finished loaf doesn't look picture-perfect. Kids don't mind. The pride in their handiwork far outweighs a few wrinkles, bumps, and dings. Especially when—like this delicious cheese bread—it tastes so good.

LOW FAT

Favorite Cheese Bread

Prep: 7 minutes **Bake:** 2½ hours

1½-lb. loaf ingredients
- 1 cup water
- 3 cups white bread flour
- 1 Tbsp. sugar
- 1 tsp. salt
- 1 Tbsp. powdered buttermilk
- ¼ cup dairy sour cream
- ½ cup shredded cheddar cheese
- 1 Tbsp. dried chives
- 1 Tbsp. dry ranch salad-dressing mix
- 1 tsp. active dry yeast or bread-machine yeast

2-lb. loaf ingredients
- 1¼ cups water
- 4 cups white bread flour
- 2 Tbsp. sugar
- 1½ tsp. salt
- 2 Tbsp. powdered buttermilk
- ½ cup dairy sour cream
- 1 cup shredded cheddar cheese
- 2 Tbsp. dried chives
- 2 Tbsp. dry ranch salad-dressing mix
- 1¼ tsp. active dry yeast or bread-machine yeast

1 Select loaf size.* Add ingredients to bread machine according to manufacturer's directions. Select basic white bread cycle. Makes 16 slices (1½-pound loaf).

*Note: For 1½-pound loaf, machine pan must have capacity of 10 cups or more; for 2-pound loaf, pan must have capacity of 12 cups or more.

Nutrition Facts per slice: 120 cal., 2 g total fat (1 g sat. fat), 5 mg chol., 208 mg sodium, 20 g carbo., 1 g fiber, 4 g pro. Daily Values: 4% calcium, 7% iron.

Pepper-and-Onion Bread Pudding

A savory twist on a typical dessert, this bread pudding is a tantalizing side dish. Serve the bread pudding with roasted chicken or pork—it's like having your own individual serving of stuffing.

Prep: 20 minutes **Bake:** 30 minutes
Stand: 10 minutes

- 8 oz. crusty Italian bread
- 2 Tbsp. butter or margarine, softened
- 3 eggs, slightly beaten
- 1½ cups milk
- 1 12-oz. jar roasted red sweet peppers, well-drained and coarsely chopped (about 1½ cups)
- ½ cup thinly sliced green onions
- 3 Tbsp. snipped fresh oregano or 2 tsp. dried oregano, crushed
- ½ to 1 tsp. bottled hot pepper sauce
- ¼ tsp. salt
- ¼ tsp. pepper
- 1 cup shredded fontina or provolone cheese (4 oz.)

1 Preheat oven to 350°F. Cut the bread into 1-inch slices. Spread the slices with butter or margarine, then tear the bread into bite-size pieces. Set aside. Grease eight 6-ounce custard cups or ramekins; set aside. (Or grease a 1½-quart soufflé dish; set aside.)

2 In a large mixing bowl beat together the eggs and milk. Stir in chopped sweet peppers, green onions, oregano, hot pepper sauce, salt, and pepper. Add bread pieces and fontina or provolone cheese, stirring well to coat bread.

3 Divide mixture among custard cups (or spoon into a prepared soufflé dish). Lightly press down the mixture with the back of a wooden spoon.

4 Bake custard cups, uncovered, about 30 minutes or until tops are puffed and golden brown and a knife inserted near the center comes out clean. Let stand for 10 minutes before serving. (Or bake a large soufflé, uncovered, for 40 minutes or until the top is puffed and golden brown and a knife inserted near the center comes out clean. Let stand for 15 to 20 minutes before serving.) Makes 8 side-dish servings.

Nutrition Facts per serving: 220 cal., 11 g total fat (6 g sat. fat), 108 mg chol., 432 mg sodium, 20 g carbo., 2 g fiber, 10 g pro. Daily Values: 27% vit. A, 130% vit. C, 18% calcium, 10% iron.

PRIZE WINNER

Two-Pepper Burgers

Emma Little
Austin, Texas
$200—Great Hamburger Ideas

Prep: 15 minutes Broil: 12½ minutes

- ½ cup mayonnaise or salad dressing
- ½ to 1 chipotle pepper in adobo sauce, finely chopped
- ⅓ cup finely chopped onion
- 3 to 5 fresh jalapeño peppers, seeded and finely chopped*
- 4 cloves garlic, minced
- 2 tsp. Cajun or Creole seasoning
- 1½ lb. lean ground beef
- 4 oz. Monterey Jack cheese, sliced
- 6 hamburger buns, split and toasted

1 In a small bowl stir together mayonnaise and chipotle pepper. Cover and chill until serving time.

2 In a large mixing bowl combine onion, jalapeño pepper, garlic, and Cajun seasoning. Add ground beef; mix well. Shape beef mixture into six ¾-inch-thick patties.

3 Place patties on the unheated rack of a broiler pan. Broil 4 to 5 inches from heat for 12 to 14 minutes or until done (160°F), turning once. Top with cheese slices; broil 30 seconds more until cheese slices are melted. Serve on buns with mayonnaise-pepper mixture. Makes 6 servings.

*Note: Hot peppers contain oils that can burn eyes, lips, and sensitive skin, so wear gloves while preparing them and be sure to wash your hands thoroughly afterward.

Nutrition Facts per serving: 557 cal., 38 g total fat (12 g sat. fat), 93 mg chol., 578 mg sodium, 24 g carbo., 2 g fiber, 29 g pro. Daily Values: 9% vit. A, 5% vit. C, 22% calcium, 19% iron.

Firecracker Turkey Burgers

Cool and creamy garlic sauce helps tame the fire from the spice and peppers in these smoky grilled patties. (See the photograph on page 42.)

Prep: 20 minutes Grill: 14 minutes

- ½ cup mayonnaise or salad dressing
- ¼ cup dairy sour cream
- 1 clove garlic, minced
- ½ tsp. cracked black pepper
- ¼ cup fine dry bread crumbs
- 2 Tbsp. water
- 2 cloves garlic, minced
- 1 Tbsp. chili powder
- 1 or 2 canned chipotle peppers in adobo sauce, drained and chopped (reserve 2 Tbsp. adobo sauce)
- ¼ tsp. salt
- 1 lb. ground raw turkey or ground raw chicken
- 4 poppy seed rolls or hamburger buns, split and toasted
- 4 lettuce leaves
- 4 tomato slices
- 8 to 12 avocado slices (optional)

1 For sauce, in a small bowl stir together the mayonnaise, sour cream, the 1 clove garlic, and the black pepper. Cover and chill until serving time.

2 For burgers, in a large mixing bowl combine bread crumbs, water, the 2 garlic cloves, the chili powder, chipotle peppers, and salt. Add ground raw turkey or chicken; mix well. Shape turkey mixture into four ¾-inch-thick patties.

3 Grill burgers on the rack of an uncovered grill directly over medium coals for 14 to 18 minutes or until done (165°F), turning once halfway through grilling.

4 To serve, spread bottoms of rolls with adobo sauce. Top each with a turkey patty. Spoon mayonnaise-sour cream mixture over top. Add lettuce leaves, tomato slices, and, if desired, avocado slices. Cover with the roll top. Makes 4 servings.

Nutrition Facts per serving: 517 cal., 32 g total fat (8 g sat. fat), 111 mg chol., 700 mg sodium, 31 g carbo., 3 g fiber, 25 g pro. Daily Values: 23% vit. A, 12% vit. C, 13% calcium, 21% iron.

Grilled Poblano Chile Burgers

Prep: 45 minutes **Grill:** 16 minutes

  2 fresh medium poblano peppers
  1 egg, beaten
  ¾ cup soft bread crumbs (1 slice)
  ½ cup shredded carrot
  2 Tbsp. water
  2 cloves garlic, minced
  1 tsp. dried oregano, crushed
  ½ tsp. salt
  ¼ tsp. pepper
  1 lb. lean ground beef
  ¼ cup purchased guacamole
  ½ of a medium tomato, sliced
  4 kaiser rolls, split and toasted

1 Preheat oven to 425°F. To roast peppers, halve peppers and remove stems, membranes, and seeds.* Place peppers, cut side down, on a foil-lined baking sheet. Roast in the oven for 20 to 25 minutes or until skin is bubbly and browned. Wrap the peppers in foil and let stand for 20 to 30 minutes or until cool enough to handle. Use a paring knife to gently and slowly pull the skin off peppers. Chop the peppers.

2 In a large mixing bowl combine chopped peppers, egg, bread crumbs, carrot, water, garlic, oregano, salt, and pepper. Add ground beef; mix well. Shape mixture into four ¾-inch-thick patties.

3 Grill burgers on the rack of an uncovered grill directly over medium coals for 14 to 18 minutes or until done (160°F), turning once. Top each with 1 tablespoon guacamole and a tomato slice and grill 2 minutes more. Serve on toasted rolls. Makes 4 servings.

*Note: Hot peppers contain oils that can burn eyes, lips, and sensitive skin, so wear gloves while preparing them and be sure to wash your hands thoroughly afterward.

Broiler Method:

Prepare and shape burgers as directed. Place burgers on the unheated rack of a broiler pan. Broil 4 inches from the heat for 12 to 14 minutes or until done (160°F), turning once. Top burger with 1 tablespoon guacamole and a tomato slice and broil for 2 minutes more. Serve as directed.

Nutrition Facts per serving: 482 cal., 21 g total fat (7 g sat. fat), 123 mg chol., 755 mg sodium, 43 g carbo., 3 g fiber, 30 g pro. **Daily Values:** 216% vit. C, 11% calcium, 33% iron.

PRIZE WINNER

Onion Burger Melt

Mari G. Chandler
Anniston, Alabama
$400—Great Hamburger Ideas

Prep: 20 minutes **Grill:** 14 minutes

  3 cups sliced onions
  4 tsp. olive oil
  ¼ tsp. salt
  ¼ tsp. coarsely ground pepper
  1 lb. lean ground beef
  2 Tbsp. Worcestershire sauce
  ½ tsp. coarsely ground pepper
  2 cloves garlic, minced
  ¾ cup shredded Swiss cheese
      (3 oz.)
  4 ¾-inch-thick diagonally cut
      French bread slices
  1 Tbsp. olive oil

1 In a large skillet cook the onions in the 4 teaspoons hot olive oil over medium heat about 10 minutes or until golden brown, stirring occasionally. Stir in salt and the ¼ teaspoon pepper. Cover and keep onions warm.

2 Meanwhile, in a large mixing bowl combine beef, Worcestershire sauce, the ½ teaspoon pepper, and the garlic. Divide into eight equal portions. Shape each portion into a 4-inch-diameter patty. Place one-fourth of the cheese on each of four of the patties. Top with remaining patties; press down lightly, sealing edges well.

3 Grill burgers on the rack of an uncovered grill directly over medium coals for 14 to 18 minutes or until done (160°F), turning once halfway through grilling.

4 Brush bread slices lightly with the 1 tablespoon olive oil. Add bread slices to grill rack the last 2 to 3 minutes of cooking time or until toasted, turning once. To serve, place burger on a toasted French bread slice; top with onion mixture. Makes 4 servings.

Broiler Method:

Prepare and shape burgers as directed. Place burgers on the unheated rack of a broiler pan. Broil 4 inches from the heat for 12 to 14 minutes or until done (160°F), turning once halfway through broiling. Prepare bread as directed, except broil instead of grill.

Nutrition Facts per serving: 455 cal., 25 g total fat (9 g sat. fat), 91 mg chol., 480 mg sodium, 26 g carbo., 3 g fiber, 30 g pro. **Daily Values:** 6% vit. A, 14% vit. C, 26% calcium, 20% iron.

Greek Burgers

Prep: 15 minutes **Broil:** 10 minutes

  1 egg, beaten
  2 Tbsp. milk or water
  ¾ cup soft bread crumbs (1 slice) or
      ¼ cup fine dry bread crumbs
  ½ tsp. garlic powder
  ½ tsp. lemon-pepper seasoning
  ¼ tsp. salt
  8 oz. ground lamb
  8 oz. ground beef
  ½ cup crumbled feta cheese
      (2 oz.)
  ½ cup dairy sour cream
  ¼ cup seeded and coarsely
      shredded cucumber
  2 Tbsp. finely chopped onion
  1 Tbsp. snipped fresh mint
  2 cups shredded romaine or
      spinach
  3 pita bread rounds,
      halved crosswise

1 In a large bowl combine the egg
    and milk or water. Stir in bread
crumbs, garlic powder, lemon pepper,
and salt. Add ground lamb and ground
beef; mix well. Gently stir in feta
cheese. Shape into six 5×2×½-inch
oval-shaped patties.

2 Place burgers on the unheated
    rack of a broiler pan. Broil
burgers 4 inches from the heat for
10 to 12 minutes or until done
(160°F), turning once halfway
through broiling.

3 Meanwhile, in a small bowl stir
    together the sour cream,
cucumber, onion, and mint; set aside.
Place some of the shredded romaine
in each of the pita bread round halves.
Place patties in halved bread rounds
and top each with some of the sour
cream mixture. Makes 6 servings.

Grill Method:

Prepare and shape burgers as directed.
Grill burgers on the rack of an
uncovered grill directly over medium
coals for 10 to 12 minutes or until
done (160°F), turning once midway
through grilling.

Nutrition Facts per serving: 329 cal.,
18 g total fat (8 g sat. fat), 101 mg chol.,
537 mg sodium, 22 g carbo., 1 g fiber,
20 g pro. Daily Values: 60% vit. C,
12% calcium, 15% iron.

Gingery Chutney Burgers

Expect the ground meat mixture to be
a little soft—when the burgers cook,
they'll be just right.

Prep: 35 minutes **Grill:** 16 minutes

  1 egg, beaten
  ¼ cup fine dry bread crumbs
  ¼ cup snipped fresh cilantro or
      parsley
  ¼ cup finely chopped onion
  ½ cup mango chutney (snip any
      large pieces)
  1 Tbsp. finely chopped fresh
      ginger
  ⅛ tsp. ground cumin
  ⅛ tsp. salt
  ⅛ tsp. pepper
  1 lb. lean ground beef
  4 slices Monterey Jack cheese with
      jalapeño peppers
  4 hamburger buns, split and
      toasted
      Onion slices, tomato slices, and
      lettuce leaves (optional)

1 In a medium mixing bowl combine
    egg, bread crumbs, cilantro, onion,
¼ cup of the chutney, 2 teaspoons of
the ginger, the cumin, salt, and

pepper. Add ground beef; mix well.
Shape meat mixture into four ¾-inch-
thick patties.

2 Grill burgers on the rack of an
    uncovered grill directly over
medium coals for 14 to 18 minutes
or until done (160°F), turning once
halfway through. Top with cheese
slices. Grill, uncovered, about
2 minutes more or until the cheese
begins to melt.

3 In a small bowl stir together the
    remaining chutney and remaining
ginger. Spread chutney mixture onto
buns. Serve patties on buns. Serve
with sliced onion, sliced tomato, and
lettuce leaves, if desired. Makes
4 servings.

Nutrition Facts per serving: 555 cal.,
23 g total fat (10 g sat. fat), 138 mg chol.,
582 mg sodium, 56 g carbo., 3 g fiber,
30 g pro. Daily Values: 31% vit. C,
200% calcium, 22% iron.

TEST KITCHEN TIP
Sizzlin' Solutions

**Making burgers is simple when
you follow these tips:**

● Be sure your ground meat is fresh.
It should be bright pink without any
unpleasant odors or dark spots.

● Grill burgers over medium heat to
keep them flavorful and juicy.

● Resist pressing down on the
burgers with the spatula while they
grill! This squeezes out the juices,
making them dry and tough.

● Never cook burgers to the point of
dryness; however, the meat should
show no signs of pinkness and the
juices should run clear.

Getting Your Vitamins

Experts recommend a boost in antioxidants. They also say it's not necessary to spend megabucks on megadoses of vitamins.

Put away the pills and keep eating those fruits and vegetables. You've heard this before from nutritionists who for years have said that a balanced diet ought to be enough to keep us healthy. After an exhaustive review of research, the nation's top scientists have come to the same conclusion.

If you eat a healthy diet, there is rarely a need for antioxidant supplements, according to a report by the Institute of Medicine, a part of the National Academies of Sciences. Researchers found no evidence that large doses of antioxidants—vitamins C and E, selenium, and beta-carotene—prevent chronic diseases.

Setting Limits

The group did, however, revise the Recommended Dietary Allowances (RDAs) for antioxidants and, for the first time, set an upper intake level—the largest amount that a person can take without risking health problems.

"I'm glad they set a limit. A lot of people assume a little is good, but more is better. That isn't always the case," says Chris Rosenbloom, Ph.D., spokesperson for the American Dietetic Association and acting chair of the nutrition department at Georgia State University.

The report seems to contradict earlier information about antioxidants. There is evidence that free radicals (compounds that cause damage to cells) are linked to a risk of cancer and heart disease, but there is no proof that antioxidants in humans attack free radicals or limit their damage. It's only been proven in laboratories. Therefore, no evidence exists that taking megadoses of antioxidants prevents cancer, heart disease, or Alzheimer's disease.

"The public is very confused because often when these studies get reported all the facts aren't in," says Sandra Schlicker, director of the study at the Institute of Medicine.

Five-a-Day Way

In revising the RDAs, the panel looked at published studies and focused on trials involving humans—not animals. The take-home message of this report is simple: Eat more fruits and vegetables every day. Although the panel did not say how many to eat, it did endorse the five-a-day eating plan, advising people to eat at least five servings of fruits and vegetables a day.

A typical serving is ½ cup of berries, cut-up fruit, or cooked vegetables. One 6-ounce glass of orange juice also is considered a serving. The report, "Dietary Reference Intakes for Vitamin C, Vitamin E, Selenium, and Carotenoids," is available online at http://books.nap.edu/catalog/9810.html.

Here are some of the new recommendations.

Vitamin E

Old RDA: Women, 8 milligrams (12 IU). Men, 10 milligrams (15 IU).
New RDA: 15 milligrams (22 IU) of natural vitamin E, also called d-alpha-tocopherol, for men and women.

Upper intake limit: 1,000 milligrams. Anything higher increases your risk of uncontrolled bleeding. Vitamin E has been associated with reducing heart disease because it blocks oxidation of LDL (bad) cholesterol, making the cholesterol less likely to cling to artery walls. However, only one out of four large-scale trials of megadoses of vitamin E showed a reduced risk of heart attacks.

"The literature is very conflicting," says Maret Traber, Ph.D., associate professor at the Linus Pauling Institute at Oregon State University and Institute of Medicine panelist. "There is a lot of experimental data on human tissue and in test tubes, but the studies done on humans are not conclusive enough to prove a beneficial effect."

Because vitamin E is found in fat, some people may need to meet the RDA by taking a supplement. "If you're eating 3,000 calories a day, it's easy to get your 15 milligrams, so don't worry about it," Traber says. "If you're eating only 1,500 calories a day, you may have trouble getting there. I'd rather see someone take a vitamin E supplement and eat a low-fat, low-calorie diet rich in fruits and vegetables than for the person to eat more fat just to get the vitamin E," Traber says.

When buying the supplement, look for natural vitamin E, also known as d-alpha-tocopherol. Researchers used to think synthetic vitamin E, known as dl-alpha-tocopherol, was just as effective, but it is not, Traber says. Many multivitamins contain synthetic vitamin E, Traber warns, so check labels carefully.

Best food sources: Vegetable oils, such as sunflower and safflower; nuts; and seeds. Smaller amounts of vitamin E are found in dairy foods, eggs, beef, whole grains, fruits, and vegetables.

Vitamin C

Old RDA: 60 milligrams.
New RDA: Women, 75 milligrams. Men, 90 milligrams. People who smoke should increase the RDA of vitamin C by 35 milligrams.

Upper intake limit: 2,000 milligrams for men and women. Taking more than the recommended upper limit may cause gastrointestinal distress. Studies found an association between vitamin C and a reduced risk for cancer and heart disease, but few established a true cause-and-effect relationship.

Robert A. Jacob, Ph.D., a member of the institute's panel and research chemist with the USDA Western Human Nutrition Research Center in Davis, California, says most of the studies on megadoses of vitamin C had mixed results or were neutral, including those that linked vitamin C to staving off the common cold or preventing heart disease and cancer.

"Studies didn't show harmful outcomes. But if they didn't show consistently positive results, you can't use that as a basis for an RDA," Jacob says.

Most of the research on vitamin C has never shown direct cause and effect. Studies have found only an "association" with health benefits. For example, research may show that people with high vitamin C intake have lower blood pressure. However, there is no scientific proof that the vitamin is responsible, because other components of a healthy diet may lower blood pressure. "There is an association, but it doesn't prove that vitamin C lowers blood pressure," Jacob says.

It's easy to get enough vitamin C in your diet. One 6-ounce glass of orange juice has enough vitamin C—about 78 milligrams—to meet the RDA for women. Vitamin C-rich fruits and vegetables typically average about 40 milligrams per serving, Jacob says.

Best food sources: Citrus fruits and juices, kiwi fruit, broccoli, strawberries, and red or green sweet peppers.

Selenium

Old RDA: Women, 55 micrograms. Men, 70 micrograms.
New RDA: 55 micrograms for men and women.

Upper intake limit: 400 micrograms. Higher amounts can cause brittleness in hair and nails. Studies suggesting a link between selenium intake and reduced risk of prostate, colon, and lung cancer aren't conclusive enough to warrant adding a supplement. In fact, if you live in the United States, chances are you're getting enough selenium in your diet. The reason: selenium is in the soil. Produce grown in selenium-rich soil will contain the mineral, says Dr. Raymond Burk, director of clinical nutrition research unit at Vanderbilt University.

Burk says the old RDA that distinguished between men and women was based on body weight, and new research shows that's not necessary. An upper limit of 400 micrograms was set because too much selenium causes hair to fall out; it also causes other problems with fingernails and toenails.

Best food sources: Brazil nuts, seafood, meat, chicken, and whole-grain foods.

Beta-Carotene and Other Carotenoids
(lutein, zeaxanthin, and lycopene)

Old RDA: None. There never was one.
New RDA: None.

Upper intake limit: Beta-carotene supplements are not advised other than as a source of vitamin A. There appears to be a link between carotenoids and a decreased risk of age-related macular degeneration, cataracts, and some cancers. However, no clinical trial has shown that carotenoids—compounds found in red and yellow plants—are responsible for lowering risk.

"There is encouraging research with certain carotenoids in the prevention of some diseases, but not enough to say what the requirement should be," says Susan Taylor Mayne, Ph.D., associate professor of epidemiology and public health at Yale University School of Medicine. There are some promising associations, such as with lutein and macular degeneration, but they are preliminary, she says.

So all the articles written about the effect of lycopene on prostate cancer don't mean much?

"It's all interesting data, but at this point, it is far from proven," Mayne says. "And most of the studies have been done on food, not pills." Mayne recommends getting your carotenoids by eating a variety of foods.

Best food sources: Sweet potatoes, carrots, tomatoes, peppers, spinach, kale, collard greens, squash, apricots, mangoes, cantaloupe, and papayas.

- **Meatballs in Pasta Nests (see below)**

- **Salad of torn romaine, tomato wedges, and Parmesan cheese shavings with Italian vinaigrette**

- **Chocolate cake with chocolate frosting**

Meatballs in Pasta Nests

These bitty meatballs, inspired by the Italian classic osso buco, are tucked into a bed of pasta. This Americanized version is topped with a chunky sauce of carrots, onion, and fennel. (See the photograph on page 43.)

Prep: 40 minutes **Cook:** 8 minutes

- 1   egg, slightly beaten
- ¼   cup fine dry bread crumbs
- 3   large cloves garlic, minced
- 1   tsp. dried sage, crushed
- ½   tsp. salt
- ¼   tsp. pepper
- 1   lb. ground veal or lean ground beef
- 2   Tbsp. olive oil
- 6   dried vermicelli nests (6 oz.)
- 2   Tbsp. snipped fennel tops
- 1   Tbsp. finely shredded lemon peel
- 1   recipe Lemony Vegetable Sauce (see right)
    Snipped fresh parsley and/or fennel tops (optional)
    Toasted baguette slices (optional)

1 For meatballs, in a large mixing bowl combine egg, bread crumbs, garlic, sage, the ½ teaspoon salt, and the ¼ teaspoon pepper. Add ground veal or beef. Mix well. Form the mixture into 36 meatballs, about 1 inch in size.

2 In a skillet heat oil. Add meatballs; cook for 8 to 10 minutes, turning once, or until browned on all sides and meat is done (160°F). Remove meatballs from skillet, reserving drippings for use in Lemony Vegetable Sauce (see recipe, right). Cover meatballs; keep warm.

3 In a large saucepan or Dutch oven cook vermicelli nests according to package directions, stirring the snipped fennel tops and lemon peel into the cooking water. Use a slotted spoon to carefully remove nests to a colander to drain. Cover and keep pasta warm.

4 Prepare Lemony Vegetable Sauce. Divide the pasta nests among six plates. Spoon meatballs into nests. Spoon the vegetable sauce over meatballs and pasta nests. Sprinkle with additional parsley and fennel sprigs and serve with baguette slices, if desired. Makes 6 main-dish servings.

Nutrition Facts per serving: 52 cal., 16 g total fat (4 g sat. fat), 97 mg chol., 411 mg sodium, 31 g carbo., 6 g fiber, 21 g pro. Daily Values: 55% vit. A, 21% vit. C, 6% calcium, 13% iron.

Lemony Vegetable Sauce

This zesty sauce is similar to Italian gremolata—a peppy seasoning made with parsley and lemon peel.

Start to finish: 15 minutes

- 2   Tbsp. olive oil
- 1   cup finely chopped onion
- 1   cup finely chopped fennel bulb
- 1   cup finely chopped carrots
- ¼   tsp. salt
- ¼   tsp. pepper
- ⅓   cup snipped fresh parsley
- 1   Tbsp. finely shredded lemon peel

1 For vegetable sauce, add oil to the reserved drippings in the skillet used for the meatballs. Cook and stir onion, chopped fennel bulb, carrots, salt, and pepper over medium heat for 2 minutes. Remove from heat. Stir in parsley and lemon peel.

Crispy Chicken with Mango-Berry Salsa

Your family will request this crunch-coated, oven-baked favorite time and time again.

Prep: 20 minutes **Bake:** 40 minutes

    Nonstick cooking spray
- ½   cup toasted wheat germ
- ¾   tsp. seasoned salt
- ½   tsp. onion powder
- ½   tsp. dried basil, crushed
- ⅓   cup milk
- 2   lb. meaty chicken pieces (breasts, thighs, and drumsticks)
- 1   mango, peeled and chopped (1 cup)
- ½   cup raspberries

2 Tbsp. frozen orange juice
   concentrate, thawed

1 Preheat oven to 400°F. Line a 13×9×2-inch baking pan with foil; lightly coat with nonstick cooking spray; set aside.

2 In a shallow dish combine wheat germ, seasoned salt, onion powder, and basil. Place milk in another shallow dish. Roll chicken first in milk and then in wheat germ mixture to coat.

3 Arrange chicken in the prepared pan. Bake, uncovered, for 40 to 45 minutes or until chicken is tender and no longer pink (180°F).

4 Meanwhile, for salsa, in a small mixing bowl stir together chopped mango, raspberries, and orange juice concentrate. Serve salsa with chicken. Makes 4 to 6 servings.

Nutrition Facts per serving: 571 cal., 35 g total fat (10 g sat. fat), 171 mg chol., 307 mg sodium, 18 g carbo., 3 g fiber, 45 g pro. **Daily Values:** 58% vit. C, 5% calcium, 16% iron.

Golden Gingered Drumsticks

The not-too-sweet, not-too-spicy marinade doubles as a sauce.

Prep: 15 minutes **Marinate:** 4 hours
Bake: 40 minutes

8 to 12 chicken drumsticks
   (about 2 lb.)
⅔ cup frozen pineapple-orange
   juice concentrate, thawed
2 Tbsp. soy sauce
1½ tsp. ground ginger
1 tsp. garlic salt

½ tsp. ground red pepper
3 Tbsp. brown sugar

1 Place chicken in a self-sealing plastic bag set in a shallow dish. For marinade, stir together the pineapple-orange juice concentrate, soy sauce, ginger, garlic salt, and ground red pepper. Reserve ⅓ cup for sauce. Pour remaining mixture over chicken; seal bag. Marinate in the refrigerator for 4 to 24 hours, turning the bag occasionally.

2 For the brush-on mixture, stir brown sugar into reserved soy sauce mixture. Cover and chill until ready to use.

3 Preheat oven 375°F. Drain chicken, discarding marinade. Place chicken in a shallow baking pan. Bake, uncovered, for 25 minutes. Brush both sides of chicken with sauce. Bake 15 to 20 minutes more or until chicken is tender and no longer pink (180°F), brushing once or twice with sauce. Makes 4 to 6 servings.

Nutrition Facts per serving: 371 cal., 17 g total fat (5 g sat. fat), 117 mg chol., 631 mg sodium, 26 g carbo., 0 g fiber, 27 g pro. **Daily Values:** 139% vit. C, 3% calcium, 8% iron.

Mediterranean-Style Chicken

Several *Better Homes and Gardens* readers rank this tomato- and cinnamon-spiced chicken as one of the all-time best recipes.

Start to finish: 1 hour

2 Tbsp. cooking oil
2½ to 3 lb. meaty chicken pieces
   (breasts, thighs, and
   drumsticks), skinned
1 14½-oz. can tomatoes,
   undrained and cut up
¼ cup dry white wine or chicken
   broth
3 Tbsp. regular onion soup mix
1 9-oz. pkg. frozen artichoke
   hearts
½ cup pitted ripe olives, halved
⅛ tsp. ground cinnamon
1 Tbsp. cold water
2 tsp. cornstarch
   Hot cooked couscous or hot
   cooked rice

1 In a 12-inch skillet heat oil over medium heat. Add chicken and cook, uncovered, for 10 minutes, turning to brown evenly. Drain well.

2 Stir together the undrained tomatoes, wine or broth, and soup mix. Add to chicken in skillet. Bring to boiling; reduce heat. Simmer, covered, for 30 minutes. Stir in artichoke hearts, olives, and cinnamon. Simmer, covered, for 8 to 10 minutes more or until chicken is tender and no longer pink and artichoke hearts are tender. Use a slotted spoon to transfer chicken and solids to a serving platter.

3 Skim fat from broth mixture. Combine the cold water and cornstarch. Add the cornstarch mixture to the broth mixture in the skillet. Cook and stir until thickened and bubbly; cook for 2 minutes more. Spoon over chicken. Serve with couscous or rice. Makes 6 servings.

Nutrition Facts per serving: 363 cal., 12 g total fat (2 g sat. fat), 78 mg chol., 513 mg sodium, 31 g carbo., 5 g fiber, 31 g pro. **Daily Values:** 11% vit. A, 26% vit. C, 8% calcium, 13% iron.

Roast Chicken with Olive-Raisin Sauce

When you're in a hurry to present a special main dish, this easy-to-prepare recipe satisfies elegantly. (See photograph on page 37.)

Prep: 12 minutes **Roast:** 25 minutes

    2   whole chicken breasts, halved
    8   to 12 fresh sage leaves or
        24 sprigs fresh marjoram
   ½   cup sliced celery (½-inch pieces)
   ½   cup chopped onion
    2   large cloves garlic, minced
    2   Tbsp. olive oil
   ½   cup chicken broth
   ½   cup dry red wine or additional
        ⅓ cup chicken broth plus
        2 Tbsp. balsamic vinegar
   ½   cup pitted and halved mixed
        olives or Kalamata olives
   ½   cup golden raisins
   ⅛   tsp. ground red pepper
        (optional)
    1   Tbsp. snipped fresh marjoram
        Cooked red Swiss chard
        (optional)

1 Preheat oven to 425°F. Loosen chicken skin and place 2 to 3 sage leaves or 6 sprigs of marjoram under skin of each piece of chicken. Sprinkle chicken with ¼ teaspoon salt and ¼ teaspoon pepper.

2 Place chicken, skin side up, in a roasting pan. Roast, uncovered, for 25 to 30 minutes or until chicken is golden brown and no longer pink (180°F).

3 Meanwhile, in a large skillet cook celery, onion, and garlic in hot oil until tender. Add the broth, wine, olives, raisins, and, if desired, ground red pepper. Bring mixture to boiling; reduce heat. Simmer, uncovered, for 7 minutes or until slightly thickened. Stir in the snipped marjoram and simmer 1 minute more.

4 To serve, spoon sauce over roasted chicken breast halves. Serve with cooked Swiss chard, if desired. Makes 4 servings.

Nutrition Facts per serving: 412 cal., 18 g total fat (3 g sat. fat), 95 mg chol., 555 mg sodium, 20 g carbo., 3 g fiber, 35 g pro. **Daily Values:** 4% vit. A, 8% vit. C, 5% calcium, 12% iron.

What-a-Catch Citrus Scallops

Israeli couscous, sometimes called pearl pasta, looks like tiny round pearls. Look for it in major markets and in specialty food stores. (See the photograph on page 37.)

Start to finish: 35 minutes

    1   lb. fresh or frozen jumbo sea
        scallops
    2   Tbsp. all-purpose flour
    1   cup Israeli couscous (about 5 oz.)
    2   Tbsp. cooking oil
    2   cups chicken broth
    8   oz. haricots verts (long, thin green
        beans) or thin green beans
    2   Tbsp. butter or margarine
   1½   cups orange-tangerine juice or
        orange juice
    1   Tbsp. snipped fresh tarragon or
        ¾ tsp. dried tarragon, crushed
    2   small blood oranges,
        clementines, or other oranges,
        peeled and sliced
        Fresh tarragon sprigs (optional)
        Orange wedges (optional)

1 Thaw scallops, if frozen. In a plastic bag combine flour and ⅛ teaspoon each of salt and pepper. Add scallops; toss to coat. Set aside.

2 In a medium saucepan cook and stir couscous in hot oil over medium heat for 3 to 4 minutes or until couscous is slightly golden brown. Carefully add broth. Bring mixture to boiling; reduce heat. Cover and simmer for 8 to 10 minutes or until couscous is tender.

3 Meanwhile, in a medium saucepan cook haricots verts or green beans, covered, in a small amount of boiling water for 10 to 15 minutes or until crisp-tender. Drain; keep warm.

4 In a large skillet heat butter or margarine. Add scallops; cook over medium-high heat 2 minutes per side or until golden brown. (Reduce heat slightly, if necessary, to prevent overbrowning.) Scallops should be opaque in center when done. Remove scallops from pan and transfer to a baking sheet, reserving drippings. Place scallops in a warm oven.

5 For sauce, add orange-tangerine juice and snipped tarragon to skillet. Bring to boiling, stirring browned bits from bottom of skillet. Reduce heat. Cook, uncovered, about 7 minutes or until sauce is reduced by half (¾ cup) and slightly thickened. Season with ⅛ teaspoon each salt and pepper. Cool slightly.

6 To serve, place sauce in four glasses or cups. Divide cooked couscous, haricots verts, and slices of blood oranges among four dinner plates. Place the scallops next to couscous mixture. Serve with sauce. If desired, garnish sauce with fresh tarragon and orange wedges. Serves 4.

Nutrition Facts per serving: 512 cal., 19 g total fat (5 g sat. fat), 52 mg chol., 1,204 mg sodium, 60 g carbo., 5 g fiber, 28 g pro. **Daily Values:** 20% vit. A, 137% vit. C, 10% calcium, 12% iron.

Left: Roast Chicken with Olive-Raisin Sauce (page 36)
Below: What-a-Catch Citrus Scallops (page 36)

Left: Roasted Cheddar Potatoes (page 14)

Below left: Chocolate-Covered Grapes (page 17)

Below right: Smoked Salmon Appetizer (page 10)

Page 39: Steak with Sautéed Onions (page 15)

Page 40: Oven Pancake with
Sausage and Pears (page 14)
Above: Chicken and
Mushrooms (page 16)
Left: Cookies and Cream
(page 21)

Top: Firecracker Turkey Burgers
(page 29)
Left: Chocolate Meringue Mountains
(page 46)
Page 43, top: Meatballs in Pasta Nests
(page 34)
Page 43, bottom left: Warm Hearts
(page 26)
Page 43, bottom right: Chocolate-
Topped Fruited Phyllo Tarts (page 46)

Left: S'More Sundaes (page 45)
Below: A Billow of Berries 'n' Brownies (page 45)

S'More Sundaes

Serve these sundaes with frothy mugs of cocoa for a quick and easy snack. Or put them on a plate and watch them disappear. You'll have no problem figuring out what to do with the extra graham shortbread cookies. (See the photograph on page 44.)

Start to finish: 25 minutes

- 6 Tbsp. butter
- ¼ cup packed light brown sugar
- 1 tsp. vanilla
- ¼ tsp. ground cinnamon
- ⅛ tsp. salt
- ⅔ cup all-purpose flour
- ¼ cup graham cracker crumbs
- ½ cup pink or white miniature marshmallows
- 1½ pints strawberry ice cream
  Purchased dark chocolate ice cream topping

1 Preheat oven to 375°F. For shortbread, in a medium saucepan melt butter. Remove pan from heat and stir in brown sugar, vanilla, cinnamon, and salt. Stir in the flour and graham cracker crumbs. Pat dough evenly onto the bottom of an ungreased 8×8×2-inch baking pan. Bake about 12 minutes or until edges are firm. Remove from oven.

2 Preheat broiler. Arrange marshmallows evenly across top of hot shortbread. Broil 4 inches from the heat about 45 to 60 seconds or until marshmallows are soft and golden brown. (Watch carefully to prevent burning.) Cool slightly; cut into sixteen 3×1-inch rectangles.

3 For the sundaes, scoop ice cream among eight dessert dishes. Tuck two shortbread strips into each dish.

Serve with dark chocolate ice cream topping. Makes 8 servings.

Nutrition Facts per serving: 374 cal., 19 g total fat (10 g sat. fat), 42 mg chol., 224 mg sodium, 48 g carbo., 1 g fiber, 4 g pro. **Daily Values:** 15% vit. A, 7% vit. C, 10% calcium, 6% iron.

A Billow of Berries 'n' Brownies

A dazzling dessert doesn't get much easier than this. Your biggest challenge will be whipping the cream. (See the photograph on page 44.)

Start to finish: 15 minutes

- 4 cups fresh red raspberries
- 4 to 5 Tbsp. sugar
- 2 tsp. finely shredded orange peel
- 2 cups whipping cream
- ¼ cup raspberry liqueur (Chambord) (optional)
- 4 3-inch squares bakery brownies, such as milk chocolate, blond, or marbled brownies, cut into irregular chunks

1 Set aside 8 to 10 of the berries. In a bowl combine remaining berries, the sugar, and orange peel. Place the berry mixture in a 1- to 1½-quart compote dish or serving bowl.

2 In a chilled mixing bowl combine whipping cream and liqueur (if using). Beat with chilled beaters of an electric mixer on medium speed until soft peaks form. Spoon on top of raspberry mixture. Top the whipped cream with the brownie chunks and the reserved raspberries. Serves 12.

Nutrition Facts per serving: 263 cal., 19 g total fat (10 g sat. fat), 69 mg chol., 63 mg sodium, 23 g carbo., 5 g fiber, 3 g pro. **Daily Values:** 18% vit. A, 27% vit. C, 5% calcium, 7% iron.

Raspberry Creme And Fruit Sundaes

It's simple indulgence when fluffy pink cream tops mountains of fresh fruit. Select the freshest of fruits to vary this dessert from season to season.

Start to finish: 20 minutes

- 1 10-oz. pkg. frozen red raspberries in syrup, thawed
- 1 8-oz. pkg. cream cheese, softened
- ½ cup whipping cream
- 1 Tbsp. orange juice concentrate
- 4 cups desired cut-up fresh fruit
- ¼ cup toasted coconut or chopped nuts

1 Place undrained raspberries in a blender container or food processor bowl. Cover and blend or process until smooth. Strain through a sieve. Discard seeds. Set aside.

2 In a large mixing bowl beat cream cheese with an electric mixer on medium speed until fluffy. Wash beaters. In a medium mixing bowl beat whipping cream with an electric mixer on medium speed to soft peaks. Gradually beat whipped cream and orange juice concentrate into cream cheese. Gradually beat in sieved raspberries.

3 To serve, arrange fruit in eight glass dessert dishes. Spoon cream mixture atop. Sprinkle with coconut or nuts. Makes 8 servings.

Nutrition Facts per serving: 243 cal., 16 g total fat (10 g sat. fat), 52 mg chol., 100 mg sodium, 22 g carbo., 3 g fiber, 3 g pro. **Daily Values:** 47% vit. C, 4% calcium, 6% iron.

To separate a yolk from the white, use an egg separator. Place the egg separator over a bowl and place the egg in the separator. The white will drain away from the yolk into the bowl. Avoid separating egg yolks from egg whites by passing the yolk from shell to shell; this is an unsafe practice. Be careful as you separate eggs—even tiny specks of fat, oil, or yolk in the bowl prevent the whites from whipping. For best results, separate eggs and let the whites sit at room temperature for 30 minutes before beating them.

PRIZE WINNER

Hearts and Cherries

TerryAnn Moore
Oaklyn, New Jersey
$200—Valentine Treats

Prep: 20 minutes **Bake:** 8 minutes

- 2 8- to 10-inch flour tortillas
   Butter-flavored nonstick cooking spray
- 2 Tbsp. sugar
- ½ tsp. unsweetened cocoa powder
- 1 15½-oz. can pitted dark sweet cherries, well drained
- ½ cup black cherry spreadable fruit
- 1 cup (½ of a pint) butter-pecan or butter-brickle ice cream (or other desired flavor)
- ½ cup whipping cream, whipped

1 Preheat oven to 350°F. Cut each tortilla into six wedges. Fold each tortilla wedge in half lengthwise; use scissors to trim the top edge to form a heart shape.

2 Open hearts and place them close together on an ungreased baking sheet. Coat hearts lightly with cooking spray; sprinkle with a mixture of sugar and cocoa powder. Bake for 8 to 10 minutes or until lightly browned. Cool on a wire rack.

3 For cherry sauce, combine drained cherries and spreadable fruit in a small saucepan or in a microwave-safe bowl. Heat through over low heat or in a microwave oven on 100% power (high) for 1 minute.

4 To serve, place one tortilla heart on each of four dessert plates. Spoon some cherry sauce on top. Top with several small scoops of ice cream, with another heart, and with a dollop of whipped cream. Cover with a third tortilla heart. Pass remaining cherry sauce. Makes 4 servings.

Nutrition Facts per serving: 716 cal., 37 g total fat (20 g sat. fat), 158 mg chol., 171 mg sodium, 95 g carbo., 3 g fiber, 5 g pro. **Daily Values:** 37% vit. A, 6% vit. C, 14% calcium, 11% iron.

LOW FAT

Chocolate Meringue Mountains

Fudgy topping spills over the top of a scoop of pink peppermint ice cream perched on a crispy chocolate meringue. (See the photograph on page 42.)

Prep: 20 minutes **Bake:** 35 minutes
Stand: 1½ hours

- 3 egg whites
- ¼ tsp. cream of tartar
- 1 cup sugar
- 2 Tbsp. unsweetened cocoa powder
- 1 pint pink peppermint ice cream
- ¼ cup fudge ice cream topping

1 Let egg whites stand in a large mixing bowl at room temperature for 30 minutes. Cover a baking sheet with clean plain brown paper or parchment paper. Draw eight 3-inch circles on the paper; set aside.

2 Preheat oven to 300°F. Add the cream of tartar to egg whites. In a small bowl stir together the sugar and cocoa powder; set aside. Beat egg white mixture with an electric mixer on medium speed until soft peaks form. Add the sugar mixture, one tablespoon at a time, beating about 7 minutes on high speed until stiff peaks form and sugar is almost dissolved.

3 Using a pastry bag, pipe the meringue onto the circles on the paper, building up the sides to form shells. (Or use the back of a spoon to spread the meringue over the circles, building up the sides.)

4 Bake for 35 minutes. Turn off oven. Let shells dry in oven, with door closed, for 1 hour. Remove from paper. Cool completely.

5 Place a scoop of ice cream in each shell. Drizzle each with fudge topping. Makes 8 servings.

Nutrition Facts per serving: 213 cal., 5 g total fat (3 g sat. fat), 16 mg chol., 101 mg sodium, 39 g carbo., 0 g fiber, 3 g pro. **Daily Values:** 5% calcium, 1% iron.

Chocolate-Topped Fruited Phyllo Tarts

Two bite-size tarts equal one serving. (See the photograph on page 43.)

Start to finish: 1 hour

- 6 oz. semisweet chocolate, cut up
- ¼ cup whipping cream
- ¼ cup snipped dried apricots

¼ cup snipped dried cherries
¼ cup brandy
½ cup finely chopped almonds
24 (1¾-inch) baked miniature
   phyllo shells

1 In a medium saucepan combine chocolate and whipping cream. Cook and stir over low heat until smooth. Remove from heat; cool.

2 In a small bowl combine apricots, cherries, and brandy. Cover and let stand 45 minutes or until softened; drain well. Stir in ¼ cup of the nuts.

3 Place about 1 teaspoon dried fruit in the bottom of each phyllo shell. Spoon about 1 teaspoon of chocolate mixture in each shell. Sprinkle with remaining nuts. Makes 24 tarts.

To Make Ahead:
Prepare tarts as directed. Cover and store in the refrigerator for up to 2 days. To serve, let stand at room temperature for 30 minutes.

Nutrition Facts per two tarts: 186 cal., 11 g total fat (4 g sat. fat), 7 mg chol., 22 mg sodium, 18 g carbo., 2 g fiber, 3 g pro. Daily Values: 2% calcium, 8% iron.

Rhubarb Surprise Crisp

You'll be surprised when you taste the licorice-like flavor brought forth from the basil in this old-fashioned baked fruit treat.

Prep: 20 minutes Bake: 30 minutes

2 cups chopped fresh rhubarb or
   frozen unsweetened sliced
   rhubarb, thawed
2 cups chopped strawberries

2 Tbsp. snipped fresh basil or
   1½ tsp. dried basil, crumbled
1 cup granulated sugar
1 Tbsp. cornstarch
¼ tsp. ground cinnamon
½ cup all-purpose flour
½ cup quick-cooking oats
¼ cup packed brown sugar
¼ tsp. salt
2 Tbsp. margarine or butter,
   melted

1 Preheat oven to 375°F. In a medium bowl combine the rhubarb, strawberries, and basil. Stir in the 1 cup granulated sugar, cornstarch, and cinnamon. Spoon into the bottom of an 8×8×2-inch baking pan; set aside.

2 In a medium bowl combine flour, oats, brown sugar, and salt. Stir in melted margarine or butter. Sprinkle over fruit mixture. Bake 30 to 35 minutes or until fruit is tender and topping is golden brown. Makes 6 servings.

Nutrition Facts per serving: 276 cal., 7 g total fat (4 g sat. fat), 16 mg chol., 167 mg. sodium, 52 g carbo., 3 g fiber, 3 g pro. Daily Values: 7% vit. A, 51% vit. C, 6% calcium, 7% iron.

PRIZE WINNER

Hazelnut Truffles

Colette Smith
Seattle, Washington
$400—Valentine Treats

Prep: 1¼ hours Chill: 3 hours

1 14-oz. can (1¼ cups) sweetened
   condensed milk
1 13-oz. jar (about 1¼ cups)
   chocolate-hazelnut spread

4 oz. unsweetened chocolate,
   chopped
1 Tbsp. Irish cream liqueur or
   vanilla
⅔ cup halved hazelnuts (filberts),
   toasted*
   Finely or coarsely chopped
     toasted hazelnuts (filberts)
   Unsweetened cocoa powder

1 In a heavy medium saucepan combine sweetened condensed milk, chocolate-hazelnut spread, and unsweetened chocolate. Cook over low heat until chocolate melts, stirring constantly. Remove saucepan from heat. Cool slightly. Stir in liqueur or vanilla until smooth. Transfer to a mixing bowl. Cover and chill about 3 hours or until firm.

2 Line a baking sheet with waxed paper. For each truffle, form about 1 teaspoon of the chocolate mixture around 1 toasted hazelnut half to make a ¾-inch ball. Roll in chopped toasted nuts or cocoa powder. Store in a tightly covered container in the refrigerator for several weeks or in the freezer for up to 3 months. Makes about 120 candies.

*Note: To toast hazelnuts, place nuts in a skillet. Cook over medium-low heat, stirring or shaking skillet often, for 7 to 10 minutes or until skins begin to flake and nuts are light golden brown. Watch carefully to avoid overbrowning. Remove nuts from skillet and place on a clean kitchen towel. When hazelnuts are cool enough to handle, rub the nuts together in the towel, removing as much of the brown skin as possible.

Nutrition Facts per candy: 46 cal., 3 g total fat (1 g sat. fat), 1 mg chol., 7 mg sodium, 4 g carbo., 0 g fiber, 1 g pro. Daily Values: 1% calcium, 1% iron.

Trifle-Style Red Raspberry Parfaits

If you're looking for an easy way to grate chocolate, try using your food processor.

Prep: 25 minutes **Chill:** 2 hours

- 2 cups fresh or frozen raspberries
- ¾ cup sugar
- 2 Tbsp. quick-cooking tapioca
- 1 Tbsp. raspberry liqueur (optional)
- 1 cup whipping cream
- 1 Tbsp. sugar
- ½ of a 10.75-oz. frozen pound cake, thawed, cut into ½-inch cubes, and toasted* (about 3 cups)
- ½ cup grated bittersweet chocolate (3 oz.)

1 Thaw the frozen raspberries, if using; do not drain. In a medium saucepan stir together the ¾ cup sugar and tapioca. Stir in the berries. Mash slightly. Let stand for 10 minutes. Bring mixture to boiling; reduce heat. Boil gently for 1 minute, stirring constantly. Remove from heat. Stir in raspberry liqueur, if desired. Cool slightly. Transfer mixture to a medium bowl. Cover and chill for 2 to 24 hours.

2 Before serving, in a chilled medium mixing bowl beat whipping cream and the 1 tablespoon sugar with an electric mixer on medium speed until stiff peaks form. Spoon half of the raspberry mixture in the bottoms of parfait glasses. Top with half of the pound cake cubes and half of the chocolate. Top with half of the whipped cream. Repeat layers. Cover and chill up to 1 hour. Makes 4 to 6 servings.

*Note: To toast pound cake cubes, spread out in a single layer in a shallow baking pan. Bake in a 350°F oven about 10 minutes or until lightly golden.

Nutrition Facts per serving: 674 cal., 37 g total fat (22 g sat. fat), 125 mg chol., 163 mg sodium, 84 g carbo., 6 g fiber, 5 g pro. Daily Values: 27% vit. C, 6% calcium, 11% iron.

NO FAT

Cranberry-Champagne Sparkler

Refrigerate the make-ahead cranberry syrup to be ready for company or for a family celebration. Then all it takes is some splishing and splashing to create this dressed-up drink.

Prep: 25 minutes **Stand:** 1 hour
Chill: 1 hour

- 1 12-oz. pkg. (3 cups) cranberries
- 1 lemon
- ¾ cup water
- ½ cup sugar
- 4 inches stick cinnamon, broken
- 5 whole cloves
- 1 Tbsp. snipped fresh sage or 1 tsp. dried sage, crushed
- ½ cup honey
- ¼ cup lemon juice
- 2 cups ice cubes
- 1 750 ml bottle Champagne or nonalcoholic Champagne, chilled
  Fresh sage leaves (optional)

1 Reserve ⅓ cup of the cranberries; set remainder aside. Use a vegetable peeler to remove strips of peel from lemon. In a medium saucepan combine water, sugar, strips of lemon peel, stick cinnamon, whole cloves, and snipped sage. Bring to boiling, stirring to dissolve sugar. Add the remaining 2⅔ cups cranberries.

Return just to boiling, stirring with a wooden spoon; reduce heat. Cover and simmer for 5 minutes.

2 Remove cranberry mixture from heat. Cool to room temperature, about 1 hour. Stir in honey and lemon juice. Press mixture through a sieve placed over a bowl. Discard solids. Cover and chill syrup until ready to use, at least 1 hour.

3 To serve, in a small punch bowl or pitcher combine the cranberry syrup and ice cubes. Slowly add Champagne. Stir gently. If desired, place a couple of reserved cranberries or a sage leaf into glasses or cups. Ladle the Champagne mixture into the glasses. Makes 8 servings.

To Make Ahead:

Prepare cranberry syrup as directed. Place in an airtight container and store it in the refrigerator for up to 3 days. Serve as directed.

Nutrition Facts per serving: 200 cal., 0 g total fat, 0 mg chol., 2 mg sodium, 38 g carbo., 2 g fiber, 0 g pro. **Daily Values:** 17% vit. C, 1% calcium, 1% iron.

march

IN THIS CHAPTER

30-minute recipes indicated in COLOR.
Low-fat and no-fat recipes indicated
with a ♥.
Photographs indicated in italics.
*Bonus recipe

Mandarin Apricot Chicken Wings

Line the roasting pan with foil for the easiest cleanup possible.

Prep: 15 minutes **Bake:** 25 minutes

- 2 lb. chicken wing drumettes (about 24)*
- ⅔ cup bottled sweet and sour sauce
- ½ cup snipped dried apricots
- ⅓ cup bottled hoisin sauce
- ¼ cup soy sauce
- 2 Tbsp. honey
- 2 cloves garlic, minced
- ¼ tsp. ground ginger
- ¼ tsp. five-spice powder
- 1 Tbsp. toasted sesame seed

1 Preheat oven to 400°F. Arrange drumettes in a single layer in a foil-lined baking pan or roasting pan. Bake drumettes for 20 minutes.

2 Meanwhile, in a small saucepan stir together the sweet and sour sauce, apricots, hoisin sauce, soy sauce, honey, garlic, ginger, and five-spice powder. Bring to boiling; reduce heat. Simmer, uncovered, for 5 minutes. Remove from heat.

3 Brush about ¼ cup of the sauce mixture over drumettes. Sprinkle with sesame seed. Bake about 5 minutes more or until drumettes are no longer pink in the center. Serve drumettes with remaining sauce. Makes 24 appetizer servings.

*Note: If you can't find drumettes, use 12 chicken wings. Cut off and discard wing tips or reserve them for making broth. Cut each wing into 2 sections (drumettes).

Nutrition Facts per serving: 86 cal., 5 g total fat (1 g sat. fat), 29 mg chol., 274 mg sodium, 7 g carbo., 0 g fiber, 5 g pro. Daily Values: 4% vit. A, 1% iron.

Carrot, Pineapple, And Mango Salad

With the new variety of purple carrots available at farmers' markets and grocery stores, try mixing them with familiar orange ones for added color.

Prep: 25 minutes **Chill:** 30 minutes

- ¼ cup cider vinegar
- 2 Tbsp. sugar
- 2 Tbsp. orange juice
- 2 Tbsp. salad oil or olive oil
- 3 cups very thinly sliced carrots (about 1 lb.)
- 1 cup cubed, peeled fresh pineapple or one 8-oz. can pineapple chunks (juice pack), drained
- 1 cup cubed, peeled, pitted fresh mango
- 2 Tbsp. snipped fresh cilantro
- ¼ cup coarsely chopped honey-roasted peanuts

1 In a medium bowl whisk vinegar, sugar, orange juice, and oil together. Add carrots; mix well. Cover and refrigerate at least 30 minutes or up to 8 hours, tossing occasionally.

2 Add fruit and cilantro to carrot mixture, tossing to mix. Transfer to a serving dish. Sprinkle with chopped nuts just before serving. Makes 6 servings.

Nutrition Facts per serving: 148 cal., 7 g total fat (1 g sat. fat), 0 mg chol., 38 mg sodium, 22 g carbo., 3 g fiber, 2 g pro. Daily Values: 185% vit. A, 37% vit. C, 2% calcium, 4% iron.

PRIZE WINNER

Mango-Broccoli Salad

Anita Price
Midlothian, Virginia
$400—Better-Than-Ever Broccoli

Start to finish: 25 minutes

- 4 cups chopped fresh broccoli
- 1 large ripe mango, peeled, pitted, and diced
- ½ cup cashews
- ½ cup finely chopped red onion
- ¾ cup bottled buttermilk ranch salad dressing
- 3 Tbsp. orange juice
- 1 Tbsp. prepared horseradish
- 1 11-oz. can mandarin orange sections, drained

1 In a large mixing bowl combine broccoli, mango, cashews, and onion. In another bowl combine ranch dressing, orange juice, and horseradish. Add dressing mixture to broccoli mixture, tossing to mix. Top with drained mandarin orange sections. Makes 8 servings.

Nutrition Facts per serving: 207 cal., 16 g total fat (3 g sat. fat), 1 mg chol., 284 mg sodium, 16 g carbo., 3 g fiber, 3 g pro. Daily Values: 109% vit. C, 4% calcium, 5% iron.

Pacific Rim Coleslaw

Chill this sesame-dressed slaw for as long as six hours—any longer and the veggies will lose their crunch.

Prep: 25 minutes **Chill:** 2 hours

- 2 **cups coarsely chopped broccoli florets and finely chopped stems**
- 2 **cups thinly sliced Napa cabbage**
- ½ **cup shredded carrots**
- ¼ **cup thinly sliced green onions**
- 2 **tsp. sesame seed, toasted**
- ¼ **cup canola oil or salad oil**
- 2 **Tbsp. red or white wine vinegar**
- 1½ **tsp. sugar**
- 1½ **tsp. reduced-sodium soy sauce**
- 1 **tsp. toasted sesame oil**
- ½ **tsp. ground ginger**
- ¼ **tsp. salt**
- ⅛ **tsp. pepper**

1 In a large bowl combine the broccoli, cabbage, carrots, onions, and sesame seed. Set aside.

2 For dressing, in a small bowl whisk together the oil, vinegar, sugar, soy sauce, sesame oil, ginger, salt, and pepper. Pour dressing over broccoli mixture, tossing to combine. Cover and chill for 2 to 6 hours. Makes 6 servings.

Nutrition Facts per serving: 115 cal., 10 g total fat (1 g sat. fat), 0 mg chol., 159 mg sodium, 5 g carbo., 2 g fiber, 2 g pro. **Daily Values:** 67% vit. A, 60% vit. C, 4% calcium, 3% iron.

---

30 MINUTE

Greek-Style Broccoli And Spinach Salad

Broccoli and ripe olives are tossed in a light lime and herb dressing, served on a bed of fresh spinach, and topped with feta cheese—a Greek favorite.

Start to finish: 20 minutes

- 1 **16-oz. pkg. frozen cut broccoli or 4 cups fresh broccoli florets**
- 1 **6-oz. can pitted ripe olives, drained and quartered**
- 3 **Tbsp. lime juice**
- 3 **Tbsp. olive oil**
- 2 **cloves garlic, minced**
- 1 **tsp. snipped fresh dillweed**
- 1 **tsp. snipped fresh parsley**
- ½ **tsp. salt**
- ¼ **tsp. pepper**
- 4 **cups shredded fresh spinach (8 oz.)**
- ¼ **cup crumbled feta cheese (1 oz.)**

1 Cook broccoli in a small amount of boiling water about 2 minutes or until just tender. Drain and rinse with cold water; drain well. In a large salad bowl combine drained broccoli and ripe olives; set aside.

2 For dressing, in a screw-top jar combine lime juice, olive oil, garlic, dillweed, parsley, salt, and pepper. Cover and shake well. Pour over broccoli and olives. Toss to coat.

3 To serve, spoon broccoli mixture atop a bed of shredded spinach; sprinkle with feta cheese. Serve immediately. Makes 6 servings.

Nutrition Facts per serving: 132 cal., 11 g total fat (2 g sat. fat), 4 mg chol., 537 mg sodium, 7 g carbo., 5 g fiber, 4 g pro. **Daily Values:** 54% vit. A, 64% vit. C, 11% calcium, 16% iron.

---

30 MINUTE

Broccoli and Peppers With Walnuts

This crunchy, walnut-topped stir-fry is a great Asian-style complement to grilled chicken and cooked rice. (See the photograph on page 82.)

Start to finish: 25 minutes

- ¼ **cup chicken broth**
- 2 **Tbsp. bottled oyster sauce**
- 1 **tsp. finely shredded lemon peel**
- ⅛ **tsp. ground red pepper**
- 4 **tsp. cooking oil**
- 1 **clove garlic, minced**
- ½ **cup coarsely chopped walnuts**
- 1 **lb. broccoli, cut into 1-inch pieces**
- 1 **medium red sweet pepper, cut into bite-size strips**

1 In a small bowl combine chicken broth, oyster sauce, lemon peel, and ground red pepper; set aside.

2 In a large nonstick skillet heat 2 teaspoons of the oil. Add garlic and walnuts; cook and stir for 2 to 3 minutes or until nuts are lightly toasted. Transfer to a bowl. Set aside.

3 Heat remaining oil in same skillet over medium-high heat. Add broccoli and red sweet pepper. Stir-fry 2 to 3 minutes or until crisp-tender.

4 Stir the sauce and add it to the skillet. Cook and stir 1 minute more. Transfer to a serving bowl. Sprinkle with the walnuts. Makes 6 side-dish servings.

Nutrition Facts per serving: 124 cal., 10 g total fat (1 g sat. fat), 0 mg chol., 199 mg sodium, 7 g carbo., 3 g fiber, 4 g pro. **Daily Values:** 43% vit. A, 151% vit. C, 52% calcium, 6% iron.

AWESOME ASPARAGUS

Tender spears of asparagus emerge through the soil and show up at the market for only a few weeks each year. Plan how to make the best use of this beautiful spring vegetable and enjoy its delicate flavor in one or several of this classic recipes while the selection is at its peak.

Asparagus Spring Rolls

Choose asparagus spears that are uniform in diameter so that they cook evenly for these fresh, appealing appetizers.

Start to finish: 45 minutes

   1   8-oz. pkg. reduced-fat cream
         cheese (Neufchâtel)
   2   Tbsp. snipped fresh chives
   2   Tbsp. milk
   1   to 2 Tbsp. snipped fresh dill
   1   clove garlic, minced
   1   tsp. lemon juice
   ½   tsp. freshly ground black
         pepper
   3   quarts water
   1   Tbsp. olive oil
   ¼   tsp. salt
   8   dried lasagna noodles
  24   fresh asparagus spears
   6   oz. thinly sliced smoked salmon
   8   long fresh chives

1 In a small mixing bowl stir together cream cheese, snipped chives, milk, dill, garlic, lemon juice, and pepper; set aside. In a 4-quart Dutch oven combine the water, oil, and salt. Bring to boiling; add lasagna noodles. Cook for 10 to 12 minutes or until noodles are nearly tender.

2 Meanwhile, snap off and discard woody bases of asparagus spears.

If necessary, trim asparagus to 5-inch lengths. Add asparagus to pasta; cook 3 minutes more. Drain; rinse with cold water. Drain again. Pat lasagna noodles dry with paper towels.

3 Spread about 2 tablespoons cream cheese mixture evenly over each noodle. Divide salmon evenly among the noodles, placing a single layer of salmon on each noodle. Place three asparagus spears on one end of each noodle, letting the tips extend beyond the edge. Roll up each noodle. Tie with a fresh chive. Stand spring rolls upright to serve. Makes 8 spring rolls.

Nutrition Facts per spring roll: 196 cal., 10 g total fat (5 g sat. fat), 27 mg chol., 350 mg sodium, 17 g carbo., 1 g fiber, 10 g pro. **Daily Values:** 13% vit. A, 14% vit. C, 3% calcium, 8% iron.

Asparagus and Tomato Salad

Popular in Europe and less common in the United States, creamy white asparagus spears are harvested when the tips just break through the soil (the lack of exposure to the sun keeps the stalks pale). If you're lucky enough to find white asparagus spears, combine them with the traditional green spears to dress up this salad.

Prep: 20 minutes

  12   oz. fresh white and/or green
         asparagus spears
   ¼   cup mayonnaise or salad
         dressing
   1   Tbsp. Dijon-style mustard
   1   tsp. vinegar
         Dash bottled hot pepper sauce
         Boston or Bibb lettuce leaves
   2   hard-cooked eggs, sliced
   8   red and/or yellow baby pear
         tomatoes, halved, or 2 red
         or yellow plum tomatoes,
         cut into wedges
   1   cup watercress (optional)

1 Snap off and discard woody bases of asparagus. Cook asparagus, covered, in a small amount of boiling water for 4 to 8 minutes or until crisp-tender. Drain; cool.

2 For dressing, in a small bowl stir together the mayonnaise or salad dressing, mustard, vinegar, and hot pepper sauce. Cover and chill for up to 24 hours.

3 To serve, line four salad plates with lettuce leaves. Top each plate with some of the asparagus, egg, tomatoes, and, if desired, watercress. Serve with the dressing. Makes 4 side-dish servings.

Nutrition Facts per serving: 164 cal., 14 g total fat (2 g sat. fat), 115 mg chol., 210 mg sodium, 5 g carbo., 2 g fiber, 5 g pro. **Daily Values:** 13% vit. A, 35% vit. C, 2% calcium, 6% iron.

Springtime Soup

Combine garden-fresh asparagus, snow peas, and spinach for a quick vegetarian treat. Use a vegetable peeler to remove asparagus scales.

Start to finish: 25 minutes

1	lb. fresh asparagus spears
½	cup chopped onion
3	cloves garlic, minced
1	Tbsp. olive oil
1	49½-oz. can chicken broth
½	cup dried orzo or tiny pasta
3	cups snow pea pods, ends and strings removed
6	cups torn fresh spinach
¼	tsp. pepper
¼	cup purchased pesto (optional)
¼	cup finely shredded Parmesan cheese

1 Snap off and discard woody asparagus bases. If desired, scrape off scales. Bias-slice the asparagus into 1-inch pieces; set aside.

2 Meanwhile, in a 4-quart Dutch oven cook the onion and garlic in hot oil until tender. Carefully add chicken broth; bring to boiling. Stir in pasta; reduce heat and boil gently for 5 minutes. Stir in asparagus and snow pea pods. Return soup to boiling; cook for 3 minutes more. Stir in spinach and pepper; cook for 1 minute more.

3 To serve, ladle soup into bowls. If desired, swirl some of the pesto into each bowl of soup. Sprinkle Parmesan cheese on top of each. Makes 8 side-dish servings.

Nutrition Facts per serving: 133 cal., 4 g total fat (1 g sat. fat), 3 mg chol., 634 mg sodium, 15 g carbo., 3 g fiber, 10 g pro. **Daily Values:** 31% vit. A, 59% vit. C, 8% calcium, 18% iron.

Turkey-Asparagus Brunch Bake

This classic asparagus-studded brunch dish was a big hit with our readers when it was published in 1989. Substituting frozen asparagus or broccoli when fresh asparagus is unavailable provides added appeal for the recipe.

Prep: 30 minutes **Bake:** 23 minutes

1	lb. fresh asparagus or one 10-oz. pkg. frozen cut asparagus or cut broccoli
1	lb. ground turkey
1	cup chopped onion
½	cup chopped red sweet pepper
3	eggs
2	cups milk
1	cup all-purpose flour
¼	cup grated Parmesan cheese
1	tsp. lemon-pepper seasoning
½	tsp. dried tarragon, basil, or thyme, crushed
1	cup shredded Swiss cheese (4 oz.)

1 Break off and discard woody bases of fresh asparagus. Cut asparagus into 1½-inch pieces. In a covered saucepan cook fresh asparagus in a small amount of boiling water for 4 to 6 minutes or until crisp-tender. (Cook frozen vegetables according to package directions; drain and set aside.)

2 Preheat oven to 425°F. In a large skillet cook turkey, onion, and sweet pepper until vegetables are just tender and no pink remains in the turkey. Remove from heat; drain. Set aside. Grease a 3-quart rectangular baking dish. Arrange meat mixture in dish; top with cooked asparagus.

3 In a large mixing bowl combine eggs, milk, flour, Parmesan cheese, lemon-pepper seasoning, and tarragon; beat until smooth with a wire whisk or rotary beater. (Or combine ingredients in a blender container; cover and blend for 20 seconds.)* Pour egg mixture evenly over layers in baking dish.

4 Bake about 20 minutes or until a knife inserted near the center comes out clean. Sprinkle with Swiss cheese; bake for 3 to 5 minutes more or until the cheese melts. Makes 6 servings.

To Make Ahead:
Prepare as directed to the asterisk (*). Pour egg mixture into a bowl; cover and refrigerate. Cover and refrigerate turkey and asparagus in the baking dish. To bake, stir egg mixture well and pour over turkey mixture. Bake, uncovered, in 425°F oven about 30 minutes or until a knife inserted near the center comes out clean. Continue as directed.

Nutrition Facts per serving: 388 cal., 18 g total fat (8 g sat. fat), 196 mg chol., 419 mg sodium, 26 g carbo., 2 g fiber, 30 g pro. **Daily Values:** 19% vit. A, 33% vit. C, 37% calcium, 16% iron.

Pick a Potato

More than likely, potatoes are often included on your grocery list. Do you ever wonder which bag of potatoes—red or white, round or oval—to put in your grocery cart? Although you can use a variety of potatoes in your favorite recipes, some potatoes are naturally better suited for certain dishes than others. Here are the Better Homes and Gardens® Test Kitchen recommendations:

Russet: The texture of these oblong, brown-skinned potatoes is described as floury when cooked. The texture and slightly thick skin make russets the first choice for baking. They also work well for mashed potatoes and french fries.

Round red: Also known as boilers, these potatoes have a thin red skin and a waxy texture. When red potatoes are cubed and cooked, they don't get mushy. They are the best choice for potato salad. Also, use round reds for baked potato wedges, oven-fried or skillet-fried potatoes, mashed potatoes, and in soups and stews.

Round white: All-purpose round whites are suitable for mashing, baking, frying, and boiling. Identify them by the round shape and thin, light brown skin. Round whites make delicious mashed potatoes and panfried potato slices because of their moist, creamy texture.

Long white: Use long whites as you would round red potatoes. Do not confuse them with russets; long whites have a waxy, moist texture that helps them hold their shape when cooked. Slice or cube them to use for scalloped potatoes, salads, soups, and stews.

---

30 MINUTE

Three-Way Mashed Potatoes

Here's what makes these mashers super delicious: Baking potatoes yield a mashed potato with light texture. Leave on some of the skin for added flavor and add sour cream for tartness.

Prep: 15 minutes **Cook:** 15 minutes

- 1½ lb. russet (baking) potatoes
- 1 tsp. salt
- 2 Tbsp. margarine or butter, softened
- ¼ tsp. pepper
- ⅓ cup milk, half-and-half, or light cream, warmed
- ⅓ cup dairy sour cream

1 Peel potatoes, leaving about half the skin on each potato. Cut potatoes into large chunks and place in a large saucepan. Add cold water to cover along with ½ teaspoon of the salt. Bring to boiling; reduce heat. Cover and cook for 15 to 20 minutes or until potatoes are tender. Drain.

2 Add margarine, pepper, and the remaining salt to potatoes. Using a potato masher, mash potatoes slightly, leaving some lumps, if desired. Gently mash in milk, about half at a time, then mash in the sour cream. With a wooden spoon, stir potatoes until evenly mixed. Season to taste with additional salt and pepper, if desired. Serve at once.* Serves 6.

*Note: To keep mashed potatoes warm before serving, transfer the prepared potatoes to a heat-proof serving bowl. Smooth top; pour 3 to 4 tablespoons of additional warmed milk or cream over potatoes to barely cover the surface. Cover the bowl with foil and place over a saucepan partially filled with hot water. Hold the bowl over low heat for up to 20 minutes. When ready to serve, stir in the milk to moisten the potatoes.

Nutrition Facts per serving: 148 cal., 7 g total fat (2 g sat. fat), 6 mg chol., 445 mg sodium, 19 g carbo., 2 g fiber, 4 g pro. **Daily Values:** 7% vit. A, 26% vit. C, 4% calcium, 5% iron.

Roasted Garlic Mashed Potatoes

1 Preheat oven to 350°F. Rub off most of the papery skin from a garlic head. With a sharp knife, slice off the top third of the garlic head. Place garlic in a small baking dish and drizzle with about 1 tablespoon of olive oil. Cover with foil. Bake for 20 to 25 minutes or until garlic is tender. Squeeze the roasted garlic cloves into a small bowl and mash with 1 tablespoon softened margarine.

2 Prepare potatoes as directed at left. Add the garlic-butter mixture to the potatoes along with the sour cream.

Parmesan-Basil Mashed Potatoes

1 Prepare potatoes as directed at left, except after adding milk, add ½ cup finely shredded Parmesan cheese and 1 tablespoon finely snipped fresh basil. Add sour cream. Top mashed potatoes with additional Parmesan.

Sautéed Spinach Mashed Potatoes

1 Prepare potatoes as directed at left. While the potatoes cook, coarsely chop one half of a 6-ounce package of baby spinach. In a large skillet cook ⅓ cup chopped onion in 1 tablespoon olive oil for 5 minutes or until onion is tender. Stir in the spinach. Cook for 1 to 2 minutes or just until spinach wilts, then stir the spinach mixture into the mashed potatoes. Add a dash of grated nutmeg, if desired. (Note: You may decrease the ⅓ cup warmed milk used in the original recipe to ¼ cup, using just enough to moisten.)

30 MINUTE

Potato-Cauliflower Chowder

Rye bread is a snappy complement to the nutty flavor of Jarlsberg cheese.

Prep: 20 minutes **Cook:** 10 minutes

  1 **cup chopped onion**
  2 **Tbsp. margarine or butter**
  4 **cups chicken broth**
  2 **cups diced, peeled Yukon gold or white potatoes**
  2½ **cups cauliflower florets**
  1 **cup half-and-half, light cream, or milk**
  2 **Tbsp. all-purpose flour**
  2½ **cups shredded Jarlsberg cheese (10 oz.)**
     Salt and pepper
  3 **slices dark rye or pumpernickel bread, halved crosswise (optional)**
  ½ **cup shredded Jarlsberg cheese (2 oz.) (optional)**
  2 **Tbsp. snipped fresh Italian parsley (optional)**

1 In a large saucepan or Dutch oven cook onion in margarine until tender. Carefully add chicken broth and potatoes. Bring to boiling; reduce

the heat. Cover and simmer for 6 minutes. Add cauliflower; return to boiling. Reduce heat. Simmer, covered, for 4 to 6 minutes or until vegetables are tender.

2 In a small bowl whisk half-and-half into flour until smooth; add to soup mixture. Cook and stir until mixture is thickened and bubbly. Reduce heat to low. Stir in the 2½ cups cheese until melted. Do not allow mixture to boil. Season to taste with salt and pepper.

3 Meanwhile, if using bread, preheat oven to 350°F. Trim crusts from bread, if desired. Place the halved bread slices on a baking sheet. Bake about 3 minutes or until crisp on top. Turn slices over. Sprinkle with the ½ cup cheese and the parsley. Bake for 5 minutes more or until cheese melts.

4 Ladle soup into bowls. Float one cheese-topped bread slice in each bowl. Makes 6 main-dish servings.

Nutrition Facts per serving: 267 cal., 17 g total fat (10 g sat. fat), 48 mg chol., 533 mg sodium, 14 g carbo., 2 g fiber, 15 g pro. **Daily Values:** 15% vit. A, 31% vit. C, 39% calcium, 5% iron.

30 MINUTE

Spicy Chili-Tomato Sauce

Serve this versatile spicy sauce with Corn-Stuffed Peppers (see recipe, page 56) or use it as pasta sauce, enchilada sauce, or in chili.

Start to finish: 20 minutes

  ½ **cup finely chopped onion**

SOUP SUPPER

■ **Potato-Cauliflower Chowder (see left)**

■ **Salad of fresh spinach, mandarin orange sections, sliced fresh strawberries, and poppy seed dressing**

■ **Giant Snickerdoodle Cookies (see recipe, page 60)**

  1 **clove garlic, minced**
  2 **Tbsp. cooking oil**
  2 **Tbsp. chili powder**
  1 **Tbsp. all-purpose flour**
  2 **tsp. ground cumin**
  1¼ **cups reduced-sodium chicken broth**
  1½ **cups canned crushed tomatoes in puree**
  1½ **tsp. sugar**
  1 **tsp. dried oregano, crushed**
  ½ **tsp. salt**

1 In a large skillet cook and stir onion and garlic in hot oil over medium heat until onion is tender. Stir in chili powder, flour, and cumin. Cook 1 minute. Slowly add broth. Cook and stir until thickened and bubbly.

2 Add undrained tomatoes, sugar, oregano, and salt. Simmer gently, uncovered, for 7 minutes, stirring occasionally. Use 1½ cups sauce for Corn-Stuffed Peppers (see recipe, page 56). Cover. Refrigerate or freeze remaining sauce. Makes 2¼ cups.

Nutrition Facts per ¼-cup serving: 60 cal., 3 g total fat (1 g sat. fat), 0 mg chol., 334 mg sodium, 6 g carbo., 2 g fiber, 1 g pro. **Daily Values:** 8% vit. A, 9% vit. C, 3% calcium, 3% iron.

MEATLESS MEAL

- Broccoli Lasagna
(see right)

- Salad of torn romaine, sliced fresh mushrooms, tomato wedges, and thinly sliced onion drizzled with bottled Caesar dressing

- Chocolate ice cream and coconut macaroons

Corn-Stuffed Peppers

Prep: 30 minutes **Bake:** 35 minutes

- 4 medium green and/or white sweet peppers
- 2¼ cups cold water
- ⅔ cup yellow cornmeal
- ½ tsp. salt
- 1½ cups loose-pack frozen corn, thawed
- 1¼ cups shredded Monterey Jack cheese or Monterey Jack cheese with jalapeño peppers (5 oz.)
- 1½ cups Spicy Chili-Tomato Sauce (see recipe, page 55)

1 Preheat oven to 375°F. In a Dutch oven heat ½ inch of water to boiling. Slice off tops of peppers. Remove stems; finely chop enough tops to equal ½ cup; set aside. Remove white ribs from whole peppers. Add peppers to water in Dutch oven; return to boiling. Cover and cook for 3 minutes. Carefully remove the peppers with tongs; invert and drain peppers on paper towels.

2 Prepare the Spicy Chili-Tomato Sauce. In a medium saucepan combine the 2¼ cups cold water, cornmeal, and salt. Bring to boiling over medium heat, stirring frequently. Cook and stir 10 minutes. Remove from heat. Stir in corn, 1 cup of the cheese, and reserved sweet pepper.

3 Spread Spicy Chili-Tomato Sauce in a 2-quart baking dish. Spoon cornmeal mixture into peppers (see photo, page 190); set filled side up in prepared dish. Bake, loosely covered with foil, 35 minutes. Remove foil; sprinkle tops with reserved ¼ cup of cheese. Serve peppers with some of the sauce. Makes 4 main-dish servings.

Nutrition Facts per serving: 380 cal., 17 g total fat (8 g sat. fat), 31 mg chol., 989 mg sodium, 46 g carbo., 7 g fiber, 15 g pro. **Daily Values:** 30% vit. A, 156% vit. C, 31% calcium, 15% iron.

PRIZE WINNER

Broccoli Lasagna

Christine McLaughlin
Methuen, Massachusetts
$200—Better-Than-Ever Broccoli

Prep: 30 minutes **Bake:** 30 minutes
Stand: 10 minutes

- 2 bunches broccoli, trimmed (about 8 cups)
- 12 dried lasagna noodles
- 1 15-oz. carton ricotta cheese
- ¼ cup grated Parmesan cheese
- 1 egg, slightly beaten
- 2 Tbsp. snipped fresh parsley
- 1 12-oz. jar roasted red sweet peppers, drained
- ¼ cup butter
- ¼ cup all-purpose flour
- 2 cloves garlic, minced
- 3 cups milk
- ½ tsp. salt
- ½ tsp. dried basil, crushed
- ¼ tsp. ground pepper
  Nonstick cooking spray
- 2 cups shredded Monterey Jack cheese (8 oz.)
- 3 Tbsp. grated Parmesan cheese

1 Preheat oven to 425°F. Place a steamer basket in a 4-quart Dutch oven. Add water to just below bottom of steamer basket; bring to boiling. Add broccoli to steamer basket. Cover and reduce heat. Steam for 4 to 5 minutes or until crisp-tender.

2 Cook 12 lasagna noodles according to package directions. Drain noodles; rinse with cold water. Drain well. In a bowl stir together ricotta cheese, grated Parmesan cheese, egg, and parsley; set aside.

3 For sauce, in a blender container puree roasted sweet peppers until almost smooth. In a large skillet melt butter. Stir in flour and garlic. Cook and stir for 1 minute. Gradually add milk and pureed peppers. Cook and stir until thickened and bubbly. Stir in salt, basil, and ground pepper.

4 Coat a 3-quart rectangular baking dish with nonstick cooking spray. Spread ¾ cup of the sauce in dish. Arrange three lasagna noodles over sauce. Carefully spread one-third of the ricotta mixture over noodles. Top with one-third of the broccoli. Sprinkle ½ cup of the Monterey Jack cheese over broccoli. Repeat layers two times, beginning with sauce. Top with remaining noodles and sauce.

5 Bake, covered, for 20 minutes. Uncover and sprinkle with the remaining ½ cup Monterey Jack cheese and the 3 tablespoons grated Parmesan cheese. Bake 10 minutes or until heated through. Let stand 10 minutes. Makes 10 servings.

Nutrition Facts per serving: 406 cal., 21 g total fat (13 g sat. fat), 84 mg chol., 460 mg sodium, 34 g carbo., 3 g fiber, 21 g pro. **Daily Values:** 198% vit. C, 45% calcium, 14% iron.

Rarebit Sauce with Roasted Veggies

Also referred to as Welsh rabbit, the term rarebit supposedly came into use when hunters failed to bring home a rabbit. (See the photo on page 80.)

Prep: 20 minutes **Roast:** 8 minutes

	Cooking oil
1	lb. asparagus spears
12	plum tomatoes, cored and halved lengthwise
2	Tbsp. olive oil
¾	cup milk
1	Tbsp. margarine or butter
2	egg yolks, beaten
2	tsp. Dijon-style mustard
	Dash ground red pepper
10	oz. extra-sharp cheddar cheese, finely shredded (2½ cups)
6	thick slices sourdough bread
2	cloves garlic, peeled and halved
	Fresh parsley sprigs

1 Preheat oven to 450°F. Line a 15×10×1-inch baking pan with foil; oil the foil well. Set aside.

2 Wash asparagus and break off woody bases where spears snap easily. Scrape off scales, if desired. Place tomato halves, cut sides up, and asparagus spears on prepared pan. Drizzle with the olive oil; sprinkle lightly with salt and pepper. Roast, uncovered, for 8 to 15 minutes or until asparagus is crisp-tender and tomatoes are heated through.

3 Meanwhile, for sauce, in medium saucepan heat milk and margarine over medium heat. Gradually add hot milk mixture into beaten egg yolks, stirring constantly. Stir in mustard and red pepper. Return mixture to saucepan. Continue to heat, stirring constantly, until mixture coats a metal spoon. Stir in cheese, a handful at a time, stirring until melted after each addition. Continue to heat and stir for 1 to 2 minutes more or until smooth. Do not boil.

4 Toast the bread; rub one surface of each slice with the cut side of a garlic clove. Transfer toast to serving plates, garlic side up. Top each toast slice with four tomato halves and several of the asparagus spears. Spoon hot rarebit sauce over tomatoes and top with a sprig of parsley. Serve immediately. Makes 6 servings.

Nutrition Facts per serving: 393 cal., 26 g total fat (12 g sat. fat), 123 mg chol., 539 mg sodium, 22 g carbo., 3 g fiber, 19 g pro. Daily Values: 28% vit. A, 57% vit. C, 42% calcium, 12% iron.

Weeknight Steak With Vegetables

(See the photograph on page 81.)

Prep: 15 minutes **Cook:** 15 minutes

2	Tbsp. olive oil
2	medium zucchini and/or yellow summer squash, cut into 1-inch chunks
1	large onion, cut into thick wedges
2	stalks celery, cut into 1-inch slices
3	cloves garlic, peeled
1	tsp. dried rosemary, crushed
1	lb. boneless beef sirloin steak, cut ¾ inch thick
½	cup Zinfandel or other fruity dry red wine
1	14½-oz. can diced tomatoes with basil, oregano, and garlic

1 In a large skillet heat 1 tablespoon of the oil. Cook the zucchini, onion, celery, garlic, and rosemary in the hot oil over medium heat for 6 to 7 minutes or until vegetables are just crisp-tender, stirring occasionally. Remove mixture from skillet.

2 Cut beef into 4 serving-size pieces. Add remaining oil to skillet. Add beef to hot skillet. Season with salt and pepper. Cook over medium-high heat for 4 to 6 minutes or until medium-rare, turning once. (The internal temperature will rise about five degrees with standing.) Remove meat from skillet; cover and keep warm.

3 Add wine to skillet, stirring up browned bits. Add the undrained tomatoes. Bring to boiling. Boil gently, uncovered, 5 minutes or until slightly thickened. Return vegetables to skillet. Cook and stir until mixture is just heated through. Spoon sauce over beef to serve. Makes 4 servings.

Nutrition Facts per serving: 388 cal., 23 g total fat (7 g sat. fat), 74 mg chol., 362 mg sodium, 16 g carbo., 3 g fiber, 24 g pro. Daily Values: 37% vit. C, 9% calcium, 22% iron.

TEST KITCHEN TIP

Squeaky Clean Fruits and Vegetables

When you bring produce home from the grocery store or farmer's market, use these tips for removing dirt and pesticide residues:

• Rinse all produce thoroughly under cold running water. Do not use soap or detergent on foods.

• Remove the outer leaves of greens, cabbage, and Brussels sprouts, and discard.

• Trim off any bruised, wilted, discolored, or tough parts.

• Peel firm vegetables and fruits such as carrots or potatoes or scrub them with a soft vegetable brush under running water.

Wine & Dine

Consider these particularly compatible food and wine pairings:

White Table Wines	Suggested Foods
Chardonnay (dry; medium to full-bodied)	Seafood, pork, tuna, chicken
Pinot Grigio (dry; light-bodied)	Seafood, fish, poultry, antipasto (Italian appetizers)
Riesling (dry to sweet; light-bodied)	Light chicken, pork
Sauvignon Blanc (dry and crisp; light- to medium-bodied)	Goat cheese, seafood
Red Table Wines	**Suggested Foods**
Cabernet Sauvignon (rich, dry; medium- to full-bodied)	Game, beef dishes, steak
Merlot (dry; light- to full-bodied)	Lamb, strong cheeses, steak
Pinot Noir (smooth; light-bodied)	Salmon, strong cheeses
Zinfandel (fruity; light- to strong-bodied)	Steak, pizza, pasta dishes

Country-Style Oven Ribs

The secret ingredient in the sweet dark basting sauce will keep your family guessing—it's root beer! For a complete meal, serve the ribs with a side dish of crisp, refreshing coleslaw or our Carrot, Pineapple, and Mango Salad (see recipe, page 50). (See the photograph on page 81.)

Prep: 15 minutes **Bake:** 2 hours

1½ tsp. salt
 1 tsp. ground cumin
 1 tsp. paprika
 ½ tsp. ground black pepper
 ½ tsp. ground cinnamon
 ¼ tsp. ground cloves
3½ lb. pork country-style ribs
 4 cups root beer (not low calorie)
 ⅓ cup bottled barbecue sauce
 2 Tbsp. tomato paste
 1 Tbsp. vinegar
 2 tsp. Dijon-style mustard
 1 tsp. Worcestershire sauce

1 Preheat oven to 350°F. In a small bowl combine the salt, cumin, paprika, pepper, cinnamon, and cloves.

Sprinkle ribs with the spice mixture, rubbing it over entire surface. Place ribs, bone side up, in a shallow roasting pan. Bake, covered, for 1¼ hours; drain.

2 Meanwhile, as ribs bake, in a large saucepan bring the root beer to boiling. Boil gently, uncovered, until root beer is reduced to 1¼ cups, about 20 to 25 minutes. Remove from heat. Stir in the barbecue sauce, tomato paste, vinegar, Dijon-style mustard, and Worcestershire sauce. Return sauce mixture to boiling. Boil gently, uncovered, for 1 minute. Remove from heat; set aside.

3 Turn the drained ribs meaty side up. Spoon about half of the root beer sauce over the ribs. Bake, uncovered, for 45 minutes more, basting once or twice with the remaining sauce. Spoon sauce over the ribs to serve. Makes 4 servings.

Nutrition Facts per serving: 549 cal., 24 g total fat (8 g sat. fat), 99 mg chol., 1,186 mg sodium, 32 g carbo., 1 g fiber, 49 g pro. **Daily Values:** 8% vit. A, 7% vit. C, 5% calcium, 15% iron.

Chicken Osso Buco

Tamara Bandstra
Grand Haven, Michigan
$200—Chicken Drumsticks, Wings, and Thighs

Start to finish: 1 hour

 8 medium chicken drumsticks (about 2 lb.)
 2 Tbsp. all-purpose flour
 2 Tbsp. olive oil
 ½ cup chopped carrot
 ½ cup chopped onion
 ½ cup chopped celery
 4 cloves garlic, minced
 ½ cup dry white wine or chicken broth
 1 8-oz. can tomato sauce
 ¼ cup chicken broth
 1 tsp. finely shredded lemon peel
 1 Tbsp. lemon juice
 1 sprig fresh thyme
 1 bay leaf
 2 cups dried penne pasta
    Snipped fresh parsley (optional)

1 Remove skin from chicken. Place flour in a plastic bag. Add chicken, a few pieces at a time, shaking to coat. In a 10-inch skillet brown chicken in hot oil over medium heat about 5 minutes per side or until golden. Remove chicken; set aside.

2 Add carrot, onion, celery, and garlic to the skillet. Cook and stir for 4 to 5 minutes or until lightly browned. Carefully add wine to skillet, scraping up any browned bits. Stir in tomato sauce, the ¼ cup chicken broth, the lemon peel, lemon juice, thyme, and bay leaf. Return chicken to skillet. Bring mixture to boiling; reduce heat. Cover and simmer for

35 to 40 minutes more or until chicken is done (180°F). Discard thyme and bay leaf.

3 Meanwhile, prepare pasta according to package directions. Drain well. To serve, spoon chicken and sauce over pasta. Garnish with snipped parsley, if desired. Makes 4 servings.

Nutrition Facts per serving: 457 cal., 12 g total fat (2 g sat. fat), 109 mg chol., 452 mg sodium, 43 g carbo., 3 g fiber, 36 g pro. Daily Values: 18% vit. C, 5% calcium, 19% iron.

Chicken, Pasta, and Mushrooms

The white wine-based sauce adds heavenly bistro flavor to this old-fashioned favorite.

Prep: 20 minutes **Cook:** 38 minutes

- 4 skinless chicken thighs (about 1 lb.)
- 1 Tbsp. olive oil
  Salt and pepper
- 2 cups thinly sliced fresh mushrooms, such as button, chanterelle, and/or shiitake
- 1 cup chopped onion
- 2 cloves garlic, minced
- 2 bay leaves
- ¾ cup chicken broth
- ¾ cup dry white wine or chicken broth
- 2 tsp. snipped fresh thyme or ½ tsp. dried thyme, crushed
- ¼ tsp. salt
- ⅔ cup half-and-half or light cream
- 2 Tbsp. all-purpose flour
- 8 oz. dried lemon-pepper or plain linguine or penne pasta
  Fresh thyme sprigs or snipped fresh thyme (optional)

1 In a large saucepan brown chicken in hot oil over medium heat for 3 to 4 minutes on each side. Sprinkle lightly with salt and pepper. Transfer chicken to a plate.

2 Add mushrooms, onion, and garlic to pan. Cook for 5 minutes, stirring occasionally. Return chicken to pan. Add the bay leaves, broth, wine, the 2 teaspoons thyme, and the ¼ teaspoon salt. Bring to boiling; reduce heat. Cover and simmer gently for 30 minutes. Remove chicken; cover and keep warm. Remove bay leaves and discard.

3 In small bowl whisk half-and-half and flour together until smooth. Add to liquid in pan. Cook and stir until thickened and bubbly; cook and stir 1 minute more. Add additional pepper to taste, if desired.

4 Meanwhile, cook the pasta according to the package directions; drain. To serve, place pasta in a serving dish and top with chicken. Spoon sauce over chicken and pasta. Top with fresh thyme, if desired. Makes 4 servings.

Nutrition Facts per serving: 565 cal., 16 g total fat (5 g sat. fat), 139 mg chol., 494 mg sodium, 53 g carbo., 3 g fiber, 43 g pro. Daily Values: 7% vit. A, 13% vit. C, 9% calcium, 23% iron.

PRIZE WINNER

Turkish Chicken Thighs

Janice Elder
Charlotte, North Carolina
$400—Chicken Drumsticks, Wings, and Thighs

Prep: 10 minutes **Grill:** 12 minutes

- ⅓ cup chutney
- 1 Tbsp. honey
- 1 Tbsp. lime juice
- 2 tsp. spicy brown mustard
- 1½ tsp. grated fresh ginger
- ¼ tsp. five-spice powder
- 8 skinless, boneless chicken thighs (about 2 lb.)
- 1 Tbsp. snipped fresh parsley
- 1 Tbsp. sesame seed, toasted
- 2 tsp. finely shredded orange peel

1 Snip large chutney pieces. In a small bowl combine chutney, honey, lime juice, mustard, ginger, and five-spice powder; set aside. Trim fat from chicken thighs.

2 Grill chicken on the rack of an uncovered grill directly over medium coals for 12 to 15 minutes or until chicken is done (180°F), turning once and brushing with chutney mixture during the last 4 to 5 minutes of grilling. (For a gas grill, preheat the grill. Add chicken, cover, and grill as above.)

3 In a small bowl combine parsley, sesame seed, and orange peel. To serve, place chicken on a serving platter. Sprinkle with the parsley mixture. Makes 4 to 6 servings.

To Broil:

Place chicken on rack of an unheated broiler pan. Broil 4 to 5 inches from heat for 12 to 15 minutes or until chicken is done (180°F), turning once and brushing with chutney mixture during last 4 to 5 minutes of broiling.

Nutrition Facts per serving: 384 cal., 11 g total fat (3 g sat. fat), 181 mg chol., 213 mg sodium, 24 g carbo., 1 g fiber, 46 g pro. Daily Values: 33% vit. C, 4% calcium, 14% iron.

- Grilled Citrus Chicken and Onions (see below)

- Cooked couscous or rice

- Salad of spring greens tossed with mixed fresh berries and champagne vinaigrette

- Rhubarb crisp or cobbler with vanilla ice cream

Grilled Citrus Chicken and Onions

Prep: 20 minutes **Marinate:** 2 to 24 hours
Grill: 40 minutes

8	chicken thighs (about 2½ lb.)
¾	cup orange juice
1	tsp. finely shredded lime peel
⅓	cup lime juice
2	Tbsp. snipped fresh cilantro
4	cloves garlic, minced
½	tsp. salt
½	tsp. dried oregano, crushed
½	tsp. ground cumin
¼	tsp. pepper
1	large red onion, sliced ¾ inch thick
2	tsp. olive oil
	Snipped fresh cilantro

1 Place chicken in a large self-sealing plastic bag set in a shallow dish. For marinade, stir together orange juice, lime peel, lime juice, the 2 tablespoons cilantro, garlic, salt, oregano, cumin, and pepper. Pour marinade over chicken in bag; seal bag. Marinate in refrigerator for 2 to 24 hours, turning the bag occasionally.

2 Drain chicken, reserving marinade. Arrange medium-hot coals around a drip pan. Test for medium heat above the pan. Place chicken on grill rack over drip pan. Cover and grill for 40 to 45 minutes or until chicken is tender and no longer pink (180°F); turn and brush with reserved marinade halfway through grilling. Brush the onion slices with the 2 teaspoons olive oil. Add onion slices to grill rack the last 15 to 20 minutes of grilling; turn and brush with reserved marinade halfway through cooking. Discard remaining marinade.

3 To serve, separate onion into rings and serve over chicken. Sprinkle with additional cilantro. Makes 4 servings.

Nutrition Facts per serving: 466 cal., 31 g total fat (8 g sat. fat), 165 mg chol., 272 mg sodium, 10 g carbo., 2 g fiber, 36 g pro. **Daily Values:** 40% vit. C, 5% calcium, 12% iron.

Giant Snickerdoodle Cookies

The name will make you giggle and the flavor will make you swoon. Because these big cookies need room to expand, place only five or six on a large baking sheet.

Prep: 20 minutes **Chill:** 4 hours
Bake: 12 minutes per batch

4½	cups all-purpose flour
2	tsp. baking powder
1	tsp. baking soda
¾	tsp. salt
1¼	cups shortening
2	cups sugar
2	eggs
1½	tsp. vanilla
½	tsp. lemon extract or 1 tsp. finely shredded lemon peel
1	cup buttermilk
½	cup sugar
2	Tbsp. ground cinnamon

1 In a bowl stir together flour, baking powder, baking soda, and salt; set aside. In a large mixing bowl beat shortening with an electric mixer on medium to high speed for 30 seconds. Add the 2 cups sugar. Beat mixture until combined, scraping sides of bowl. Beat in eggs, one at a time, beating well after each addition. Stir in vanilla and lemon extract or peel.

2 Add dry ingredients and buttermilk alternately to creamed mixture, scraping sides of bowl. Cover and chill dough for at least 4 hours. Meanwhile, combine the ½ cup sugar and the cinnamon; set aside.

3 Preheat oven to 375°F. Lightly grease baking sheets; set aside. For each cookie, use a ¼-cup measure or ¼-cup ice cream scoop*. Roll each scoop of dough in the sugar-cinnamon mixture to coat. Place 3 inches apart on baking sheet. Gently press down cookie to ½-inch thickness with the palm of your hand.

4 Bake cookies for 12 to 14 minutes or until bottoms are light golden. (Cookies bake more evenly if you bake just one batch at a time.) Transfer cookies to a wire rack to cool. Makes about 24 cookies.

***Note:** Lightly coat an ice cream scoop with nonstick cooking spray to prevent dough from sticking.

Nutrition Facts per cookie: 263 cal., 11 g total fat (3 g sat. fat), 18 mg chol., 175 mg sodium, 37 g carbo., 1 g fiber, 3 g pro. **Daily Values:** 1% vit. A, 4% calcium, 7% iron.

EDITOR'S TIP

The Moody Cues

When that chocolate chip cookie calls out your name, or a pile of mashed potatoes beckons—go ahead and help yourself. Those foods just might make you feel good, as long as you remember the moderation rule.

Think about the last time you had a wedge of homemade apple pie, still warm from the oven. For some, a few bites can induce euphoria. There are reasons for that feeling, says Elizabeth Somer, a registered dietitian and author of *Food and Mood: The Complete Guide to Eating Well and Feeling Your Best.* "Many people ignore the profound effects food can have on mood, intellect, and energy. When you make the right food choices, you're providing fuel for a healthy body, a good mood, an active mind, and a high energy level," Somer says.

Food can get you going in the morning, keep you alert at midday, and lull you to sleep at night. Take, for example, carbohydrates. They're linked to the brain chemical serotonin, which tends to soothe and calm. That may explain why high-carbo foods such as chicken potpie, mashed potatoes, pudding, and macaroni and cheese are at the top of the list of comfort foods. A little too much serotonin, however, may make you drowsy.

Carbo Planning

Strategic carbo-eating is key to preventing post-lunch slumps, as well as midafternoon munchies, says Judith Wurtman, Ph.D., program director of Triad Weight Management and research scientist at Massachusetts Institute of Technology. Carbohydrates in such foods as bananas, bread, milk, turkey, and tomatoes elevate serotonin levels, which tend to peak in late morning, then plummet a few hours later. That's when you rush to your refrigerator or the nearest vending machine.

To keep your mood stable throughout the day, Wurtman advises keeping meals and snacks small while focusing on complex carbohydrates, such as whole grains, starchy vegetables, or legumes. For breakfast, have whole grain cereal with low-fat milk (or yogurt) and fresh fruit. Pair multigrain bread with turkey (or chicken) breast and raw veggies for lunch. Serve brown rice (or beans) with broiled fish for dinner.

If you're still hungry, select fresh fruit to complete lunch and dinner. Skip the sugar-laden soft drinks, pastries, or candy bars at midday. Instead, snack on whole wheat pretzels or sip an unsweetened beverage. Other soothing carbohydrate-rich between-meals snacks include whole-grain crackers, brown-rice cakes, bran cereal, or bread. Wurtman's research showed that eating a 1- to 2-ounce slice of bread had a calming effect on most people.

The Energizers

Protein manipulates moods also. Tyrosine, an amino acid found in protein foods, boosts two brain chemicals, dopamine and norepinephrine. This duo stimulates the central nervous system, increases energy, and improves concentration, alertness, and performance. When sharpness counts, choose protein. Select 3- to 4-ounce servings of high-protein grilled chicken, fish, or beef. You'll reap benefits in two or three hours.

Selenium, essential fatty acids, and calcium may also affect mood. People who lack selenium show signs of anxiety, irritability, and depression. When selenium deficiency is corrected, mood improves. Although selenium may have a neurological function, scientists haven't pinpointed how it works in the brain.

The recommended daily allowance for selenium is easily found in food—55 micrograms. Just one Brazil nut contains 51 micrograms, a 4-ounce serving of seafood contains about 38 micrograms of selenium, and a 4-ounce serving of lean meat or chicken contains 23 micrograms. Selenium can be toxic at doses above 250 micrograms. Caution is advised regarding selenium supplements.

Adequate essential fatty acids (EFAs) may prevent depression. People who experience depression have 40 percent fewer EFAs in their brains than people who do not report feelings of depression. Two or three 3-ounce servings of fatty fish (salmon, herring, or mackerel) a week should be part of a healthful diet. Flaxseed and purslane are good sources of EFAs.

Other researchers believe calcium eases mood swings, depression, irritability, and nervousness in women who suffer from premenstrual syndrome (PMS). In a study by Dr. Susan Thys-Jacobs, Mt. Sinai Medical Center, New York, 75 percent of women with PMS who took a 1,000-milligram calcium supplement daily for three months reported fewer symptoms. Just 1 cup of nonfat milk, 1 cup of cooked spinach, or a container of yogurt works too.

The Feel-Good Food Facts

Nutrition experts agree that a balanced diet should keep you healthy. According to Elizabeth Somer, your daily diet should include five to nine servings of fruits and vegetables, six to eleven of whole grains, three glasses of low-fat milk, and two servings of extra-lean meat, chicken, fish, or legumes. Somer also suggests taking a balanced multiple vitamin and mineral supplement, along with extra calcium, magnesium, and vitamins C and E. Other nutrition experts advise meeting your nutritional needs strictly through food.

Chocolate Cake with Fluffy Icing

This is almost like the one Grandma used to make, maybe even a tad better; you be the judge. It makes one generous single layer. See note for a two-layer cake.

Prep: 30 minutes **Bake:** 30 minutes

- 1 cup all-purpose flour
- ½ cup unsweetened cocoa powder
- ¾ tsp. baking soda
- ½ tsp. baking powder
- 6 Tbsp. butter, softened
- 1 cup granulated sugar
- 2 eggs
- 1 tsp. vanilla
- ¾ cup milk
- 1 recipe Fluffy Icing (see right)

1 Preheat oven to 350°F. Lightly grease bottom of an 8×8×2-inch baking pan. Line bottom of pan with waxed paper. Grease and flour paper and sides of pan.

2 In a bowl stir together flour, cocoa powder, baking soda, and baking powder; set aside.

3 In a large mixing bowl beat butter with an electric mixer on medium to high speed for 30 seconds. Gradually add granulated sugar and beat on medium speed until well combined. Add eggs, one at a time, beating well after each addition. Beat in vanilla.

4 Add dry ingredients and milk alternately to beaten mixture, beating just until combined after each addition. Beat on medium to high speed for 20 seconds more. Spread batter evenly in the prepared pan.

5 Bake for 30 to 35 minutes or until a wooden toothpick inserted in the center comes out clean. Cool cake in pan for 10 minutes. Loosen sides with a knife and invert onto a wire rack. Peel off waxed paper. Cool completely on rack. Transfer to a serving plate.

6 Prepare Fluffy Icing. Spread over top and sides of cake. Cover and store cake in refrigerator. Makes 8 to 10 servings.

Note: To make a two-layer cake, double all of the cake ingredients. Divide batter between two 8×8×2-inch baking pans. Bake as directed. For icing, follow the same method using double the ingredients.

Fluffy Icing

Coarsely chop 3 ounces unsweetened chocolate. In a heavy small saucepan melt chocolate over low heat, stirring frequently. Remove from heat; cool to room temperature. In a medium mixing bowl beat 4 ounces softened cream cheese and 2 tablespoons softened butter with an electric mixer on medium speed about 30 seconds or until well combined. Beat in 2 cups sifted powdered sugar, half at a time, beating until smooth and fluffy. Beat in ½ teaspoon vanilla. Add cooled chocolate to the cream cheese mixture; beat for 30 seconds, scraping sides of bowl occasionally. Beat in 1 to 2 tablespoons milk, 1 or 2 teaspoons at a time, just until icing is soft and fluffy. Do not overbeat.

Nutrition Facts per serving: 512 cal., 26 g total fat (15 g sat. fat), 103 mg chol., 339 mg sodium, 67 g carbo., 2 g fiber, 7 g pro. **Daily Values:** 21% vit. A, 14% calcium, 13% iron.

april

IN THIS CHAPTER

**30-minute recipes indicated in COLOR.
Low-fat and no-fat recipes indicated
with a ♥.
Photographs indicated in italics.
*Bonus recipe**

Baked Grapefruit Halves

Prunes have a new name—dried plums—and they complement the flavor of grapefruit. (See the photograph on page 78.)

Prep: 15 minutes **Bake:** 12 minutes

- 3 red grapefruit
- 1 large orange, peeled and sectioned
- 1 medium banana, sliced
- ⅓ cup orange- or lemon-flavored or regular pitted dried plums (prunes), coarsely snipped
- 2 Tbsp. orange liqueur (optional)
- 1 Tbsp. margarine or butter, cut into small pieces
- 2 Tbsp. brown sugar
- ½ tsp. ground cinnamon

1 Preheat oven to 450°F. Halve each grapefruit. Cut a thin slice from the bottom of each half so the grapefruit will sit flat. Cut around the outer edges and between the membranes with a small knife or grapefruit knife to loosen the fruit from the peel.

2 In a bowl combine orange sections, banana slices, prunes, and, if using, liqueur. Place grapefruit halves in a 3-quart rectangular baking dish. Mound the orange mixture atop the grapefruit. Dot each half with margarine or butter. Combine brown sugar and cinnamon; sprinkle over fruit mixture. Bake, uncovered, about 12 minutes or until grapefruit is warm and topping is hot. Makes 6 servings.

Nutrition Facts per serving: 105 cal., 2 g total fat (0 g sat. fat), 0 mg chol., 23 mg sodium, 23 g carbo., 3 g fiber, 1 g pro. **Daily Values:** 65% vit. C, 3% calcium, 3% iron.

Pick-Your-Fruit Smoothie

For the best flavor and texture, chill the juice well before preparing. (See the photograph on page 78.)

Start to finish: 10 minutes

- 2 cups strawberry-flavored juice blend or strawberry drink, chilled
- 2 cups fresh or frozen, unsweetened strawberries
- 1 8-oz. carton plain yogurt
- 2 to 4 Tbsp. sugar or honey
- ½ tsp. vanilla
  Toasted wheat germ with brown sugar and honey (optional)

1 In a blender container combine strawberry juice blend, strawberries, yogurt, sugar, and vanilla. Cover and blend until nearly smooth, with small chunks of strawberry visible.

2 Divide among four glasses. Sprinkle with wheat germ, if desired. Makes 4 servings.

Nutrition Facts per serving: 142 cal., 1 g total fat (1 g sat. fat), 3 mg chol., 53 mg sodium, 30 g carbo., 2 g fiber, 3 g pro. **Daily Values:** 72% vit. C, 11% calcium, 3% iron.

Kiwi Smoothie

Substitute kiwi fruit juice blend for the strawberry juice blend and 1 cup peeled and cut-up kiwi fruit for the strawberries.

Melon Smoothie

Substitute orange or orange-tangerine juice for the strawberry juice blend and 1 cup cubed cantaloupe for the strawberries.

Ready-When-You-Are Granola

Keep this healthful breakfast mix on hand to stir into milk or yogurt for crunch and fiber.

Prep: 15 minutes **Cook:** 3 minutes

- 1 Tbsp. margarine or butter
- 1 Tbsp. brown sugar
- 1¾ cups unsalted or lightly salted mixed nuts
- ½ tsp. ground cinnamon
- 4 cups multigrain cereal with rolled rye, oats, barley, and wheat
- 1 cup regular rolled oats
- 1 cup toasted wheat germ
- 1 6- or 7-oz. package mixed dried fruit bits
- ½ cup unsalted shelled sunflower seeds or Grape Nuts cereal
  Milk or nonfat vanilla yogurt
  Sugar (optional)
  Coarsely cut-up Granny Smith apple (optional)

1 For skillet-roasted nuts, in a large skillet or saucepan heat margarine or butter over medium heat. Stir in brown sugar; add mixed nuts. Cook and stir about 3 minutes until sugar is dissolved and nuts are lightly glazed. Remove from heat. Sprinkle with cinnamon. Transfer to greased foil to cool. Set aside ¾ cup of the nuts. Transfer remainder to an airtight container; chill or freeze.

2 In a bowl stir together multigrain cereal, rolled oats, the ¾ cup roasted nuts, wheat germ, dried fruit bits, and sunflower seeds or Grape Nuts cereal. Cover the mixture tightly and refrigerate for up to 1 month.

3 For each serving, pour about ½ cup of the granola in a bowl and add milk. (To serve with yogurt: Combine ½ cup vanilla yogurt and ¼ cup granola; cover and chill for 4 hours or overnight. Stir in sugar to taste and milk to desired consistency.) If desired, sprinkle with sugar, apple, and additional skillet-roasted nuts. Makes 8 cups of mix (sixteen ½-cup servings).

Nutrition Facts per serving with ½ cup reduced-fat milk: 272 cal., 9 g total fat (2 g sat. fat), 0 mg chol., 16 mg sodium, 35 g carbo., 6 g fiber, 10 g pro. Daily Values: 1% vit. C, 6% calcium, 13% iron.

30 MINUTE

Grilled Muffins

Turn leftover muffins into a tasty treat using a breakfast trick borrowed from the Dream Cafe in Dallas.

Start to finish: 10 minutes

- 2 large or jumbo prepared fruit muffins
- 1 to 2 Tbsp. margarine or butter
- ¼ tsp. ground ginger or cinnamon
- ¼ cup marmalade, preserves, or jam

1 Slice the muffins in half vertically. In a large skillet melt margarine or butter over medium heat. Stir in ginger or cinnamon. Lay muffins, cut side down, in margarine mixture. Cook about 2 minutes or until golden brown. Transfer to a serving platter. Serve with marmalade, preserves, or jam. Makes 4 servings.

Nutrition Facts per serving: 169 cal., 8 g total fat (1 g sat. fat), 8 mg chol., 126 mg sodium, 22 g carbo., 1 g fiber, 2 g pro. Daily Values: 1% vit. C, 2% calcium, 2% iron.

Quick Whole Wheat Hot Cross Buns

The muffin-style batter is a speedy alternative to classic yeast dough.

Prep: 15 minutes **Bake:** 25 minutes

- 1 cup whole wheat flour
- 1 cup all-purpose flour
- 2 Tbsp. toasted wheat germ
- 2½ tsp. baking powder
- ¼ tsp. ground cinnamon
- ½ cup raisins
- ⅓ cup chopped almonds
- ¼ cup dried blueberries or snipped dried tart red cherries
- 1 egg, beaten
- 1 cup milk
- ½ cup sugar
- ⅓ cup cooking oil
- ⅓ cup purchased white frosting

1 Preheat oven to 400°F. Grease the bottom and ½ inch up the sides of a 9×9×2-inch baking pan; set aside. In a mixing bowl combine flours, wheat germ, baking powder, cinnamon, and ¾ teaspoon salt. Stir in raisins, nuts, and dried fruit until coated with flour. Make a well in the center; set aside.

2 In a mixing bowl combine the egg, milk, sugar, and oil. Add egg mixture all at once to flour mixture. Stir just until moistened (batter should be lumpy). Spoon batter into the prepared pan, spreading evenly. Bake about 25 minutes or until golden brown. Cool in pan on a wire rack for 20 minutes. Cut into 16 squares. Pipe a frosting X on top of each square. Serve warm. Makes 16 buns.

Nutrition Facts per bun: 195 cal., 8 g total fat (1 g sat. fat), 14 mg chol., 192 mg sodium, 29 g carbo., 2 g fiber, 4 g pro. Daily Values: 1% vit. A, 1% vit. C, 7% calcium, 5% iron.

Nutmeg Beignets

Use a deep saucepan and leave about 3 inches between the fat and the top of the pan to fry the beignets. (See the photograph on page 83.)

Prep: 40 minutes **Chill:** 4 hours
Stand: 30 minutes
Cook: 1 minute per batch

- 3 to 3¼ cups all-purpose flour
- 1 pkg. active dry yeast
- 1¼ tsp. grated fresh nutmeg or
     1 tsp. ground nutmeg
- 1 cup milk
- ¼ cup granulated sugar
- 2 Tbsp. shortening
- ½ tsp. salt
- 1 egg
  Shortening or cooking oil
  Sifted powdered sugar (optional)
  Honey

1 In a large mixing bowl stir together 1½ cups of the flour, the yeast, and nutmeg. In a small saucepan heat and stir milk, granulated sugar, shortening, and salt just until warm (120° to 130°F) and the shortening is almost melted.

2 Add milk mixture to the flour mixture. Add the egg. Beat the mixture with an electric mixer on low speed for 30 seconds, scraping bowl. Beat on high speed 3 minutes. Use a wooden spoon to stir in enough of the remaining flour to make a soft dough.

3 Place the dough in a greased bowl; turn once to grease the surface. Cover and refrigerate the dough for 4 to 24 hours.

4 Turn dough out onto a lightly floured surface. Cover; let rest 10 minutes. Roll into a 15×12-inch rectangle. Cut into thirty 3×2-inch rectangles. Cover; let rest 20 minutes.

5 In a deep saucepan heat 3 inches of shortening or oil to 375°F. Fry a few dough rectangles at a time about 1 minute or until beignets are golden brown on both sides, turning once. Drain on paper towels. Keep warm in a 300°F oven while frying remaining beignets. If desired, lightly sift powdered sugar over beignets. Serve warm, drizzled with honey. Makes 30 beignets.

Nutrition Facts per beignet: 111 cal., 5 g total fat (1 g sat. fat), 8 mg chol., 46 mg sodium, 16 g carbo., 0 g fiber, 2 g pro. Daily Values: 1% calcium, 3% iron.

<u>**30 MINUTE**</u>

Mango Hot Cakes

To peel a mango, cut through the fruit by sliding a sharp knife next to the seed along one side. Repeat with the other side, then remove the peel. Cut away fruit that clings to the seed.

Prep: 20 minutes
Cook: 4 minutes per batch

- 1 cup all-purpose flour
- 1 Tbsp. sugar
- 2 tsp. baking powder
- ¼ tsp. salt
- ⅛ tsp. ground allspice
- 1 egg, slightly beaten
- 1 cup milk
- 2 Tbsp. butter, melted
- ⅓ cup chopped macadamia nuts or
     almonds, toasted
- 1 tsp. finely shredded lime peel
- 2 large mangoes, peeled
     and cubed
  Vanilla yogurt or dairy sour
     cream (optional)
  Shredded coconut,
     toasted (optional)

1 In a large bowl stir together flour, sugar, baking powder, salt, and allspice. Make a well in the center of the flour mixture; set aside.

2 In another mixing bowl combine the egg, milk, and melted butter. Add egg mixture all at once to flour mixture. Stir just until moistened. Fold in toasted nuts and lime peel.

3 For each pancake, place several cubes of mango on a hot, lightly greased griddle or heavy skillet. Pour ¼ cup of the batter over the top (see photo, below). Cook over medium heat 2 minutes on each side or until pancakes are golden brown; turn over the pancakes when the surfaces are bubbly and the edges are slightly dry. Repeat with remaining batter.

4 Serve warm, topped with yogurt or sour cream and coconut, if desired, and any remaining mango. Makes 8 to 10 four-inch pancakes.

Nutrition Facts per pancake: 195 cal., 9 g total fat (2 g sat. fat), 30 mg chol., 241 mg sodium, 25 g carbo., 2 g fiber, 5 g pro. Daily Values: 25% vit. C, 14% calcium, 6% iron.

Use a measuring cup to make all the pancakes the same size.

Lemon Soufflé Pancakes

Use a rubber spatula to fold egg whites. Cut down through the middle of the mixture and sweep upward; give the bowl a quarter-turn and repeat. (See the photograph on pages 78–79.)

Prep: 20 minutes
Cook: 4 minutes per batch

- 2 **cups frozen lightly sweetened red raspberries**
- 1 **cup maple syrup**
- 1 **cup all-purpose flour**
- 2 **tsp. baking powder**
- 2 **tsp. finely shredded lemon peel**
- ¼ **tsp. salt**
- 1 **egg yolk**
- ¼ **cup butter, melted**
- ¾ **cup milk**
- 3 **egg whites**
  Butter (optional)
  Fresh raspberries (optional)

1 To make raspberry syrup, thaw berries but do not drain. Place the berries in a blender container or food processor bowl. Cover and blend or process until berries are smooth. Press berries through a fine-mesh sieve into a small saucepan. Discard seeds. Cook and stir juice over medium heat until heated through. Stir in maple syrup; set aside.

2 To make pancakes, in a medium mixing bowl stir together flour, baking powder, lemon peel, and salt. Make a well in the center of flour mixture; set aside. In a small mixing bowl slightly beat egg yolk. Stir in melted butter and milk. Add egg yolk mixture all at once to the flour mixture. Stir just until moistened (batter should be lumpy).

3 In another medium mixing bowl beat egg whites with an electric mixer on medium speed until stiff peaks form (tips stand straight). Gently fold egg whites into flour mixture, leaving a few fluffs of egg white. Do not overmix.

4 For standard-size pancakes, pour ¼ cup batter onto a hot, lightly greased griddle or heavy skillet. (For dollar-size pancakes, pour about 1 tablespoon batter onto a hot, lightly greased griddle or heavy skillet.) Cook over medium heat 2 minutes per side or until pancakes are golden brown. Turn over pancakes when the surfaces are bubbly and the edges are slightly dry. Repeat with remaining batter. Serve with raspberry syrup and, if desired, butter and fresh raspberries. Makes 8 four-inch pancakes or 20 two-inch pancakes.

Nutrition Facts per large pancake: 249 cal., 7 g total fat (4 g sat. fat), 45 mg chol., 271 mg sodium, 42 g carbo., 1 g fiber, 4 g pro. **Daily Values:** 2% vit. C, 12% calcium, 7% iron.

Passover Coffee Cake

Prep: 25 minutes **Bake:** 30 minutes
Cool: 30 minutes

- 5 **eggs**
- 1¼ **cups matzo cake meal**
- 2 **Tbsp. potato starch**
- 1¼ **cups sugar**
- ½ **cup cooking oil**
- 1 **Tbsp. finely shredded lemon peel (set aside)**
- 2 **Tbsp. lemon juice**
- ¾ **cup dried tart red cherries, snipped**
- 2 **Tbsp. sugar**

TEST KITCHEN TIP

Keep 'Em Hot

Piping hot—that's when pancakes are at their best. So keep the first ones warm while you cook the remaining batches. Place the pancakes hot from the griddle in an ovenproof container or on a baking sheet. Loosely cover the pancakes with aluminum foil and place them in a 300°F oven.

- 2 **Tbsp. finely chopped walnuts**
- ¼ **tsp. ground cinnamon**

1 Let eggs stand at room temperature for 30 minutes. Preheat oven to 325°F. Grease a 9×9×2- or an 11×7×1½-inch baking pan; set aside. In a small mixing bowl stir together matzo meal and potato starch; set aside.

2 In a large mixing bowl beat together eggs and the 1¼ cups sugar with an electric mixer on high speed for 4 to 5 minutes or until thickened and light in color. Gradually beat in oil on medium speed. Stir in lemon juice.

3 Add matzo meal mixture to egg mixture, beating on low speed just until combined. Stir in dried cherries and lemon peel. Spread batter into prepared pan. Sprinkle top with a mixture of 2 tablespoons sugar, the walnuts, and cinnamon.

4 Bake for 30 to 35 minutes or until a wooden toothpick inserted in the center comes out clean. Cool 30 minutes in the pan on a wire rack. Cut into 9 servings and serve warm.

Nutrition Facts per serving: 375 cal., 16 g total fat (3 g sat. fat), 118 mg chol., 37 mg sodium, 53 g carbo., 1 g fiber, 6 g pro. **Daily Values:** 4% vit. A, 5% vit. C, 3% calcium, 5% iron.

Chocolate Gravy

Grandmothers have delighted youngsters for more than a century by ladling this sauce over plates of Sweet Biscuits (see recipe, right).

Start to finish: 10 minutes

 ¼ cup sugar
 2 Tbsp. unsweetened cocoa powder
 1 Tbsp. all-purpose flour
 1 Tbsp. margarine or butter
 1¼ cups milk

1 In a small bowl stir together sugar, cocoa powder, and flour. In a medium saucepan melt the margarine or butter. Stir in the cocoa mixture until thoroughly mixed and no lumps are visible. Gradually add milk to saucepan, stirring constantly.

2 Cook and stir over medium heat until mixture is thickened and bubbly; cook and stir 1 minute more. Serve over Sweet Biscuits. Makes 1¼ cups (10 two-tablespoon servings).

*Note: Cover and chill leftover gravy for up to 2 days. To reheat ½ to ⅔ cup gravy, place in a microwave-safe bowl. Microcook on 100% power (high) for 1 to 2 minutes or until heated through, stirring once. Or place the gravy in a small saucepan. Heat gravy over medium-low heat, stirring constantly.

Nutrition Facts per serving: 52 cal., 2 g total fat (0 g sat. fat), 1 mg chol., 28 mg sodium, 7 g carbo., 0 g fiber, 1 g pro. **Daily Values:** 5% calcium, 1% iron.

Sweet Biscuits

Don't overknead the dough; a dozen or fewer strokes ensures the most tender biscuits.

Prep: 10 minutes **Bake:** 8 minutes

 1 cup all-purpose flour
 1½ tsp. baking powder
 1 tsp. granulated sugar
 ¼ cup butter
 ⅓ cup milk
 ½ cup sifted powdered sugar
 1 to 3 tsp. cherry or other fruit juice or milk
 ¼ cup chopped unsalted peanuts
 1 recipe Chocolate Gravy (see left)

1 Preheat oven to 450°F. Stir together flour, baking powder, and granulated sugar. Cut in butter until mixture resembles coarse crumbs. Make a well in center. Add the ⅓ cup milk all at once; stir until moistened.

2 Turn out dough onto a lightly floured surface. Knead dough, gently folding and pressing 10 to 12 strokes, until smooth. Pat dough to ¼-inch thickness. Cut dough with a floured donut cutter, dipping cutter into flour between cuts. (Or cut dough with a floured 2½-inch square or rectangular cutter, and cut out center of each larger biscuit using a floured 1-inch round cutter.) Separate biscuit rings and holes. If desired, reroll holes to make an eighth biscuit.

3 Gently place biscuit rings and holes 1 inch apart on an ungreased baking sheet. Bake about 8 minutes or until golden brown.

4 For glaze, in a bowl stir together powdered sugar and juice or milk to make of drizzling consistency.

5 Remove biscuit rings and holes from baking sheet. Cool slightly. Brush with glaze; sprinkle with peanuts. Serve with Chocolate Gravy. Makes 7 to 8 biscuits.

Nutrition Facts per biscuit with Chocolate Gravy: 226 cal., 11 g total fat (6 g sat. fat), 24 mg chol., 181 mg sodium, 27 g carbo., 0 g fiber, 4 g pro. **Daily Values:** 1% vit. C, 7% calcium, 5% iron.

Banana Easter Egg Rolls

Vi Pierce
Moreno Valley, California
$400—Festive Holiday Breads

Prep: 25 minutes **Rise:** 30 minutes (plus dough cycle time for bread machine)
Bake: 15 minutes

 ½ cup water
 ½ cup mashed banana (1 large)
 1 egg
 3 Tbsp. butter, cut up
 3¼ cups bread flour
 ½ cup granulated sugar
 1 tsp. salt
 1 pkg. active dry yeast or 2¼ tsp. bread machine yeast
 2 tsp. butter, melted
 1 Tbsp. cinnamon-sugar
 1 recipe Icing (see page 69)

1 Add first eight ingredients to bread machine according to manufacturer's directions. (See page 69 for conventional directions.) Select dough cycle.

2 When cycle is complete, remove dough from bread machine. Punch down dough; cover and let rest 10 minutes. Lightly grease baking sheets; set aside. On a lightly floured surface roll dough about ½ inch thick.

Cut and shape into eight to twelve 3- to 3½-inch-long egg shapes (reroll as needed). Place on prepared baking sheets. Brush with the melted butter and sprinkle with cinnamon-sugar.*

3 Cover; let rise in a warm place until nearly doubled (about 30 minutes). Preheat oven to 350°F. Bake rolls about 15 minutes or until golden brown. Cool on wire racks. Prepare Icing; pipe or drizzle onto rolls to resemble Easter eggs. Makes 8 to 12 rolls.

*Note: Combine 1 tablespoon granulated sugar and ¼ teaspoon ground cinnamon.

Icing

Stir together 2 cups sifted powdered sugar, ¼ teaspoon vanilla, and about 2 tablespoons milk to make of piping or drizzling consistency. Divide icing and tint with food coloring as desired.

Nutrition Facts per roll: 410 cal., 7 g total fat (4 g sat. fat), 42 mg chol., 360 mg sodium, 78 g carbo., 2 g fiber, 8 g pro. **Daily Values:** 3% vit. C, 2% calcium, 16% iron.

Conventional Method for Banana Easter Egg Rolls

If you don't have a bread machine, use this method to create the prize-winning rolls.

Prep: 25 minutes **Rise:** 1½ hours
Bake: 15 minutes

- **3** to 3½ cups all-purpose flour or bread flour
- **1** pkg. active dry yeast
- **½** cup water
- **¼** cup granulated sugar
- **3** Tbsp. butter, cut up
- **1** tsp. salt
- **1** egg
- **½** cup mashed banana (1 large)
- **2** tsp. butter, melted
- **1** Tbsp. cinnamon-sugar
- **1** recipe Icing (see bottom right)

1 In a large mixing bowl stir together 1½ cups of the flour and the yeast. In a medium saucepan combine the water, granulated sugar, the 3 tablespoons butter, and the salt. Heat and stir until warm (120° to 130°F) and butter almost melts. Add to flour mixture; add the egg and the banana. Beat with an electric mixer on medium to high speed for 30 seconds, scraping sides of bowl. Beat on high speed for 3 minutes. Using a wooden spoon, stir in as much of the remaining flour as you can.

2 On a lightly floured surface knead in enough remaining flour to make a moderately soft dough that is smooth and elastic (3 to 5 minutes). Place in a greased bowl, turning once to grease surface. Cover; let rise in a warm place until doubled (about 1 hour).

3 Punch down dough; cover and let rest 10 minutes. Lightly grease baking sheets; set aside. On a lightly floured surface roll dough about ½ inch thick. Cut and shape the dough into 3- to 3½-inch-long eggs (reroll dough as desired). Place on the prepared baking sheets. Brush with the melted butter; sprinkle with cinnamon-sugar.*

4 Cover and let rise in a warm place until nearly doubled (about 30 minutes). Preheat oven to 350°F.

Bake rolls about 15 minutes or until golden brown. Cool on wire racks. Prepare Icing; pipe or drizzle onto rolls to resemble Easter eggs. Makes 8 to 12 rolls.

*Note: Combine 1 tablespoon granulated sugar and ¼ teaspoon ground cinnamon.

Icing

In a mixing bowl stir together 2 cups sifted powdered sugar, ¼ teaspoon vanilla, and about 2 tablespoons milk to make of piping or drizzling consistency. Divide icing and tint with food coloring as desired.

Nutrition Facts per roll: 410 cal., 7 g total fat (4 g sat. fat), 42 mg chol., 360 mg sodium, 78 g carbo., 2 g fiber, 8 g pro. **Daily Values:** 3% vit. C, 2% calcium, 16% iron.

Whole Grains and Stroke Reduction

Eating more whole-grain foods, such as certain breads and cereals, may help women reduce their risk of the most common stroke—ischemic stroke—which happens when blood to the brain is blocked.

That's the finding of a recent study published in the *Journal of the American Medical Association*. Researchers at Brigham and Women's Hospital in Boston studied more than 75,000 women ages 38 to 63 and found that those who ate the most whole grains had the lowest rates of ischemic stroke.

Women who ate the equivalent of two or three pieces of whole-grain bread a day had a 30 to 40 percent lower risk of ischemic stroke than women who ate less than half a slice a day.

Some of the whole-grain foods the women also ate included cooked oatmeal, whole-grain breakfast cereal, popcorn, wheat germ, brown rice, and couscous.

PRIZE WINNER

Aunt Deia's Easter Bread

Karen and Joe Pietrantonio
Fogelsville, Pennsylvania
$200—Festive Holiday Breads

Prep: 30 minutes **Rise:** 3½ hours
Bake: 50 minutes

- 1 pkg. active dry yeast
- ½ tsp. sugar
- ½ cup warm water (105° to 115°F)
- 3 eggs
- ⅔ cup sugar
- 1 Tbsp. finely shredded orange peel
- ⅓ cup orange juice
- ¼ cup butter, melted

- ¼ cup cooking oil
- 2 tsp. anise seed
- 1 tsp. salt
- 4½ to 5 cups all-purpose flour

1 Dissolve yeast and the ½ teaspoon sugar in the warm water. Set aside. In a large mixing bowl beat eggs with an electric mixer until frothy; gradually beat in the ⅔ cup sugar. Beat in orange peel, orange juice, melted butter, oil, anise seed, and salt. Beat in 2 cups of the flour and the yeast mixture on high speed for 3 minutes. Using a wooden spoon, stir in as much of the remaining flour as you can.

2 Turn out dough onto a lightly floured surface. Knead in enough remaining flour to make a moderately soft dough that is smooth and elastic (3 to 5 minutes). Shape dough into a ball. Place in a lightly greased bowl, turning once to grease surface of dough. Cover; let rise in a warm place until doubled (about 2 hours).

3 Punch down dough; cover and let rest 10 minutes. Grease a 10-inch tube pan. Press dough evenly into the prepared pan. Cover; let rise in a warm place until almost doubled (1½ to 1¾ hours). Preheat oven to 300°F. Bake bread about 50 minutes or until top and sides are golden brown. Remove from pan; cool on wire rack. Makes 1 loaf (16 slices).

Nutrition Facts per slice: 225 cal., 8 g total fat (3 g sat. fat), 48 mg chol., 189 mg sodium, 34 g carbo., 1 g fiber, 5 g pro. **Daily Values:** 5% vit. C, 1% calcium, 10% iron.

Onion and Sage Ladder Loaf

Caramelized onions seasoned with sage peek through the braids on this sweet loaf.

Prep: 45 minutes **Rise:** 1¾ hours
Bake: 20 minutes

- 4 to 4½ cups all-purpose flour
- ¼ cup packaged instant mashed potatoes
- 1 pkg. active dry yeast
- 1¼ cups milk
- ½ cup butter
- ⅓ cup granulated sugar
- 1¼ tsp. salt
- 1 egg, beaten
- 3 large white or red onions, cut into thin wedges
- 3 Tbsp. butter
- 2 Tbsp. brown sugar
- 1 Tbsp. snipped fresh sage or ½ tsp. ground sage
- 2 Tbsp. butter, melted
    Sesame seed

1 In a large mixing bowl stir together 1½ cups of the flour, instant potatoes, and yeast; set aside. In a medium saucepan heat and stir milk, the ½ cup butter, the granulated sugar, and salt until just warm (120° to 130°F) and butter almost melts. Add milk mixture to flour mixture; add egg. Beat with an electric mixer on low to medium speed for 30 seconds, scraping sides of bowl. Beat on high speed for 3 minutes. Stir in as much of the remaining flour as you can.

2 Turn out the dough onto a lightly floured surface. Knead in enough of the remaining flour to make a moderately soft dough that is smooth and elastic (3 to 5 minutes total). Shape dough into a ball. Place in a lightly greased bowl, turning once to grease the surface of the dough. Cover; let rise in a warm place until doubled (45 to 60 minutes).

3 Meanwhile, for filling, in a large skillet cook onions, covered, in the 3 tablespoons hot butter over medium-low heat for 13 to 15 minutes or until onions are tender. Uncover; add brown sugar. Cook and stir over medium-high heat for 4 to 5 minutes or until onions are golden. Stir in sage. Set aside to cool slightly.

4 Punch down dough. Turn dough out onto a lightly floured surface. Divide dough in half. Cover; let rest 10 minutes. Lightly grease two baking sheets. Roll each portion of dough into a 12×9-inch rectangle. Transfer each dough rectangle to a prepared baking sheet. Spread half of the filling in a 3-inch-wide strip down the center of each rectangle.

5 On both long sides, make 3-inch cuts from the edges toward the center, spacing the cuts 1 inch apart. Starting at an end, alternately fold opposite strips of dough at an angle across the filling. Slightly press ends together in the center to seal. Brush loaves with the 2 tablespoons melted butter and sprinkle with sesame seed. Cover and let rise in a warm place until nearly doubled (about 1 hour).

6 Preheat oven to 350°F. Bake for 20 to 25 minutes or until golden. Transfer loaves to a wire rack and cool slightly. Serve warm. Makes 2 loaves (16 servings).

Nutrition Facts per serving: 252 cal., 11 g total fat (7 g sat. fat), 41 mg chol., 299 mg sodium, 33 g carbo., 2 g fiber, 5 g pro. Daily Values: 9% vit. A, 4% vit. C, 4% calcium, 9% iron.

Herbed Soft Breadsticks

Measure the olive oil or canola oil in the measuring spoon first; when you measure and pour the honey, it will slide out easily.

Prep: 30 minutes Rise: 1 hour 5 minutes
Bake: 20 minutes

    2¼ to 2¾ cups bread flour or
          all-purpose flour
    2 tsp. dried dillweed, dried
          oregano, dried parsley, dried
          cilantro, and/or dried basil,
          crushed
    1 pkg. active dry yeast
    1¼ cups milk
    2 Tbsp. olive oil or canola oil
    2 Tbsp. honey
    1 tsp. salt
    1 cup whole wheat flour
    2 tsp. olive oil or canola oil
    2 Tbsp. grated Parmesan cheese

1 In a large mixing bowl combine 1½ cups of the bread or all-purpose flour, desired herb, and yeast; set aside. In a medium saucepan heat and stir milk, the 2 tablespoons olive or canola oil, the honey, and salt just until warm (120° to 130°F). Add milk mixture to flour mixture. Beat with an electric mixer on low to medium speed for 30 seconds, scraping the sides of the bowl. Beat on high speed for 3 minutes. Using a wooden spoon, stir in the whole wheat flour and as much of the remaining bread flour or all-purpose flour as you can.

2 Turn out the dough onto a lightly floured surface. Knead in enough of the remaining flour to make a moderately stiff dough that is smooth

SOUP SUPPER

- **Chicken and tortellini soup**

- **Herbed Soft Breadsticks (see left)**

- **Salad of mixed greens, carrot shreds, sliced fresh mushrooms, and thinly sliced onion drizzled with creamy Italian dressing**

and elastic (6 to 8 minutes total). Shape the dough into a ball. Place in a lightly greased bowl, turning once to grease the surface. Cover; let rise in a warm place until doubled (45 to 60 minutes).

3 Punch down dough. Turn dough out onto a lightly floured surface. Divide dough in half. Cover; let rest 10 minutes. Lightly grease two baking sheets or one large baking sheet. Divide each half of dough into six pieces. Shape each piece into a 6-inch-long loaf by patting and gently pinching each portion into a loaf shape and tucking the edges underneath. Place on prepared baking sheet(s). Brush breadsticks with the 2 teaspoons olive or canola oil and cut four diagonal slits about ¼ inch deep in the top of each. Cover and let rise in a warm place until nearly doubled (about 20 minutes).

4 Preheat oven to 350°F. Sprinkle breadsticks with Parmesan cheese. Bake about 20 minutes or until breadsticks sound hollow when tapped. Makes 12 breadsticks.

Nutrition Facts per breadstick: 182 cal., 4 g total fat (1 g sat. fat), 3 mg chol., 224 mg sodium, 30 g carbo., 2 g fiber, 6 g pro. Daily Values: 1% vit. A, 1% vit. C, 5% calcium, 10% iron.

Spring Asparagus Slaw

Roxanne E. Chan
Albany, California
$400—Spring Salads

Start to finish: 25 minutes

- 1 lb. asparagus spears
- 4 cups shredded green cabbage
- 1 cup torn radicchio or red cabbage
- ½ cup finely shredded carrot
- ¼ cup snipped fresh mint
- ¼ cup snipped fresh parsley
- ¼ of a small red onion, thinly sliced
- 2 Tbsp. olive oil
- 2 Tbsp. balsamic vinegar
- ½ tsp. finely shredded lemon peel
- 1 Tbsp. lemon juice
- 1 clove garlic, minced
- ½ tsp. sugar (optional)
- ½ tsp. pepper
- 1 oz. shredded Parmesan cheese

1 Wash asparagus. Snap off and discard woody bases. In a medium saucepan bring 1 inch of water to boiling. Place asparagus in steamer basket. Cover; steam asparagus over the boiling water for 4 to 6 minutes or until crisp-tender. Drain. Gently rinse with cool water.

2 Meanwhile, in a large mixing bowl toss together green cabbage, radicchio or red cabbage, carrot, mint, parsley, and red onion. Divide asparagus spears among eight salad plates; top with cabbage mixture.

3 In a screw-top jar combine oil, vinegar, lemon peel, lemon juice, garlic, sugar (if using), and pepper.

EDITOR'S TIP

Cornmeal and Corn Bread Variations

In the grocery store you'll likely find a choice of two or three colors of cornmeal—yellow, white, and blue. All three taste about the same and bake the same. The only difference is the color of the finished product, so choose the color you prefer.

For variety, stir in other flavors. In general, don't add more than one cup of any ingredient to corn bread recipes. Avoid adding anything that drips; it may make the corn bread cook unevenly.

Start with these variations. Any of the following items can be gently folded into the batter:

● A 12-ounce can of whole kernel corn with sweet peppers, well drained

● 1 cup shredded cheddar or Monterey Jack cheese and one 4-ounce can of diced green chile peppers, well drained

● About ½ cup shredded cheddar cheese, ¼ cup finely shredded carrot, and ¼ cup finely shredded zucchini

● About ¼ cup chopped cooked crisp bacon

Cover and shake to combine. Pour over cabbage mixture. Sprinkle slaw with Parmesan cheese. Makes 8 to 10 side-dish servings.

Nutrition Facts per serving: 76 cal., 5 g total fat (1 g sat. fat), 3 mg chol., 56 mg sodium, 6 g carbo., 2 g fiber, 3 g pro. **Daily Values:** 45% vit. C, 6% calcium, 7% iron.

Skillet Corn Bread

The homemade whipped honey butter is worth the effort. For a quicker option, try purchased honey butter.

Prep: 15 minutes **Bake:** 20 minutes

- 1 Tbsp. butter
- 1 Tbsp. cooking oil
- 1 cup all-purpose flour
- 1 cup cornmeal
- 2 Tbsp. sugar
- 1 Tbsp. baking powder
- 1 tsp. cracked black pepper
- ½ tsp. salt
- 1 cup milk
- ¼ cup cooking oil or shortening, melted
- 2 eggs, slightly beaten
- ½ cup butter or margarine, softened (optional)
- 2 Tbsp. honey (optional)

1 Preheat oven to 425°F. Place 1 tablespoon each of butter and oil in a large ovenproof or cast-iron skillet. Preheat in oven for 5 minutes.

2 In a medium mixing bowl stir together the flour, cornmeal, sugar, baking powder, ½ teaspoon of the cracked black pepper, and salt. Make a well in the center of the dry mixture; set aside.

3 In another bowl blend together the milk, the ¼ cup cooking oil or melted shortening, and the eggs. Add egg mixture all at once to flour mixture. Stir just until moistened (the batter will be slightly lumpy).

4 Spoon the batter into the prepared skillet and spread it with a spoon. Sprinkle with the remaining ½ teaspoon cracked black pepper.

Bake 20 minutes or until a wooden toothpick inserted near the center comes out clean.

5 Meanwhile, if desired, in a medium bowl beat the ½ cup softened butter or margarine with an electric mixer on medium speed for 30 seconds. Add honey and beat on high speed for 1 minute more or until fluffy. To serve, place a dollop of honey butter in the center of the hot corn bread; pass remaining honey butter. Makes 8 servings.

Nutrition Facts per serving: 252 cal., 12 g total fat (3 g sat. fat), 60 mg chol., 340 mg sodium, 30 g carbo., 2 g fiber, 6 g pro. Daily Values: 5% vit. A, 1% vit. C, 7% calcium, 9% iron.

PRIZE WINNER

Mandarin-Berry Salad

Maureen Scully
Grand Rapids, Michigan
$200—Spring Salads

Start to finish: 20 minutes

- 6   cups torn mixed salad greens
- 1   cup fresh strawberries, hulled and quartered
- ½   cup sliced green onions
- ½   cup canned rice noodles
- ¼   cup sliced almonds, toasted
- 1   11-oz. can mandarin orange sections, drained
- ¼   cup flaked coconut
- 2   tsp. honey
- 2   tsp. salad oil
- 2   tsp. balsamic vinegar
- ½   tsp. ground ginger
- ½   tsp. salt
- ¼   tsp. pepper
- 2   oz. semi-soft goat cheese, crumbled

Salad Days

Children and salad are thought to be like oil and vinegar: They don't mix well without a little coaxing. It doesn't have to be that way though. Just as a dab of mustard can turn oil and vinegar into a smooth vinaigrette, the right ingredients—and an open-mind approach—can turn even the most salad-suspicious kids into ardent greens activists.

First order of business? Make salad days a family affair. Use these ideas to get you started. Involvement is the bridge to good salad relations.

Recruit all hands to wash the lettuce, peel the carrots, and slice the radishes or tomatoes. Assign jobs appropriate to the ages of the kids.

Ask your kids what they like. Lots of color, halved grapes, raisins, and cheese attract young children. Also ask what they don't like, such as onions, peppers, and strong-tasting dressings. (Creamy Orange Dressing, below, is smooth and mellow.) The kids may be pleasantly surprised at the fresh taste and appeal of the salads that they help to prepare.

Goes-With-Any-Salad Creamy Orange Dressing

Go ahead. Pick any combination of greens and vegetables. Thoroughly wash and dry them, then heap the whole fresh mix into a big bowl and get tossing. Drizzle with this fresh and fruity dressing for a taste you'll want to repeat with your next salad.

Start to finish: 10 minutes

- ½   cup plain yogurt
- ¼   cup buttermilk
- 1   Tbsp. frozen thawed orange juice concentrate
- 1   Tbsp. finely chopped red or green onion
- 1   Tbsp. snipped fresh parsley
- 1   tsp. sugar
- ⅛   tsp. salt
     Pinch of ground cinnamon

1 In a medium bowl or screw-top jar combine the yogurt, buttermilk, orange juice concentrate, red or green onion, parsley, sugar, salt, and cinnamon. Cover the jar and shake well to combine, or use a whisk to stir until the mixture is combined. Cover and refrigerate dressing until serving time. Makes about ¾ cup.

Nutrition Facts per 2 Tbsp. serving: 26 cal., 1 g total fat (1 g sat. fat), 2 mg chol., 74 mg sodium, 4 g carbo., 0 g fiber, 2 g pro. Daily Values: 1% vit. A, 9% vit. C, 5% calcium.

1 In a large salad bowl combine greens, strawberries, green onions, rice noodles, and almonds; set aside.

2 In a food processor bowl or blender container combine ½ cup of the mandarin oranges, the coconut, honey, oil, vinegar, ginger, salt, and pepper. Cover and process or blend until combined. Pour dressing over salad; toss to coat. Top with remaining oranges and goat cheese. Makes 6 side-dish servings.

Nutrition Facts per serving: 153 cal., 9 g total fat (3 g sat. fat), 4 mg chol., 308 mg sodium, 16 g carbo., 3 g fiber, 4 g pro. Daily Values: 53% vit. C, 5% calcium, 7% iron.

Lemon-Tarragon Asparagus Salad

Cook the asparagus for only 2 minutes—just long enough to turn it bright green and retain its crunch. (See the photograph on page 82.)

Prep: 20 minutes **Chill:** 2 hours

1½	lb. asparagus spears
1	cup sliced radishes
2	Tbsp. olive oil
1	Tbsp. thinly sliced green onion
2	tsp. snipped fresh tarragon or
	½ tsp. dried tarragon, crushed
1	tsp. finely shredded lemon peel
¼	tsp. salt
¼	cup slivered almonds, toasted
2	Tbsp. white balsamic vinegar or white wine vinegar

1 In a large saucepan bring a large amount of lightly salted water to boiling. Meanwhile, wash asparagus. Snap off and discard woody bases. Cut spears into 1-inch pieces. Add to boiling water; return to boiling. Cover and cook for 2 minutes. Drain and rinse with cold water.

2 Transfer asparagus to a salad bowl. Add radishes, olive oil, green onion, tarragon, lemon peel, and salt. Toss to combine. Cover and chill for 2 to 3 hours.

3 Just before serving, stir in the almonds and the vinegar. Makes 6 to 8 side-dish servings.

Nutrition Facts per serving: 100 cal., 8 g total fat (1 g sat. fat), 0 mg chol., 112 mg sodium, 6 g carbo., 3 g fiber, 4 g pro. Daily Values: 10% vit. A, 25% vit. C, 4% calcium, 6% iron.

SPRING LUNCH

- Stacked deli sandwiches
- Lemon-Tarragon Asparagus Salad (see left)
- Frosted chocolate brownies with raspberry sorbet
- Fresh-squeezed lemonade

Broccoli-Fennel Spanakopita

Traditional Greek spanakopita is filled with a mixture of sautéed spinach, onions, feta cheese, eggs, and seasonings. This version is Italian and filled with fennel, onions, broccoli, ricotta cheese, and seasonings. (See the photograph on page 82.)

Prep: 40 minutes **Bake:** 25 minutes

1	medium fennel bulb, trimmed, cored, and thinly sliced (¾ cup)
½	cup chopped onion
2	Tbsp. chopped shallot
2	Tbsp. olive oil
1	lb. broccoli, trimmed and finely chopped (about 5 cups)
1½	cups ricotta cheese
¼	cup finely shredded Parmesan cheese
1	tsp. salt
1	tsp. dried dillweed
1	tsp. dried basil, crushed
11	sheets frozen phyllo dough (18×14-inch rectangles), thawed
½	cup butter, melted

1 In a large skillet cook the fennel, onion, and shallot in hot oil about 10 minutes or until tender.

2 Meanwhile, in a large bowl combine the broccoli, ricotta cheese, Parmesan cheese, salt, dillweed, and basil. Stir in cooked fennel mixture.

3 Preheat oven to 375°F. Working on a flat surface, lightly brush a sheet of the phyllo with some of the melted butter. Place another sheet of phyllo on top; brush with butter. Repeat with four more sheets of phyllo and some of the butter. Keep remaining phyllo covered with plastic wrap to prevent it from becoming dry and brittle. Place phyllo stack lengthwise in a 15×10×1-inch baking pan, folding long edges of phyllo down, as desired. Top with the broccoli mixture, spreading evenly. Working on a flat surface, lightly brush a sheet of the phyllo with some of the melted butter. Place another sheet of phyllo on top; brush with butter. Repeat with three more sheets of phyllo and some of the butter. Place phyllo stack lengthwise over the broccoli mixture in the baking pan; trim phyllo to the edge of the pan.

4 Bake about 25 minutes or until phyllo is golden. Cut into rectangles and serve warm. Makes 12 appetizer or side-dish servings.

Nutrition Facts per serving: 222 cal., 16 g total fat (9 g sat. fat), 40 mg chol., 425 mg sodium, 13 g carbo., 3 g fiber, 7 g pro. Daily Values: 21% vit. A, 50% vit. C, 11% calcium, 6% iron.

Savory Mushroom Burgers

These great big burgers are a mushroom delight. Not only are mushrooms heaped on top as a tasty tease, they're also packed into each juicy ground turkey patty.

Prep: 30 minutes **Grill:** 14 minutes

- 7 oz. fresh wild mushrooms (chanterelle, porcini, shiitake, or button mushrooms)
- 2 cloves garlic, minced
- ¾ cup chicken broth
- 3 Tbsp. bulgur
- 12 oz. uncooked lean ground turkey breast
- 2 Tbsp. thinly sliced green onion
- 2 tsp. Worcestershire sauce
- ¼ tsp. pepper
  Nonstick cooking spray
- 4 hamburger buns or kaiser rolls, split and toasted
  Dijon-style mustard (optional)
  Grilled red onion slices (optional)

1 Remove stems and finely chop half of the mushrooms (1 cup); slice remainder and set aside. In a small saucepan cook the finely chopped mushrooms and garlic in ½ cup of the chicken broth for 4 to 5 minutes or until tender. Stir in bulgur. Return to boiling; reduce heat to low. Cover and simmer 10 minutes or until liquid is absorbed and bulgur is tender. Remove from heat; cool slightly.

2 Meanwhile, in a large mixing bowl combine ground turkey, green onion, Worcestershire sauce, and pepper. Add bulgur mixture; mix until combined. Shape into four ¾-inch-thick patties.

3 Lightly coat a cool grill rack with nonstick cooking spray. Grill patties on the rack of the uncovered grill directly over medium coals for 14 to 18 minutes or until burgers are firm and no pink remains, turning once halfway through grilling.

4 Meanwhile, in a small saucepan cook the sliced mushrooms in remaining broth, covered, about 4 to 5 minutes or until tender.

5 To serve, spread mustard on bottom halves of buns or rolls, if desired. Place patties, grilled onion slices (if using), and some of the sliced mushrooms on top. Makes 4 servings.

Nutrition Facts per serving: 292 cal., 10 g total fat (2 g sat. fat), 67 mg chol., 520 mg sodium, 30 g carbo., 3 g fiber, 21 g pro. **Daily Values:** 2% vit. C, 9% calcium, 17% iron.

Salmon and Bagel Bake

If onion bagels are not available, substitute plain bagels.

Prep: 15 minutes **Bake:** 35 minutes
Stand: 10 minutes

- 4 eggs
- 1 14½-oz. can reduced-sodium chicken broth
- ¼ cup thinly sliced green onions
- 2 cloves garlic, minced
- 1 Tbsp. snipped fresh dillweed or ¾ tsp. dried dillweed, crushed
- 4 onion bagels or 10 mini bagels (8 to 10 oz. total), split
- 1 7½-oz. can red salmon, drained, skin and bones removed, and broken into chunks
- 1 cup shredded Havarti cheese, shredded (4 oz.)

TEST KITCHEN TIP
Egg Substitutes

Refrigerated and frozen egg substitutes are easy to use, readily available, and enable people who are on cholesterol-restricted diets to enjoy great-tasting egg dishes. These products are based mostly on egg whites and contain less fat than whole eggs and no cholesterol. Use ¼ cup of either the refrigerated or frozen egg product for each whole egg called for in scrambled egg dishes, omelets, quiches, and stratas. To replace hard-cooked eggs in salads and other recipes, cook the product as you would cook an omelet and cut it up.

1 Preheat oven to 350°F. Grease a 2-quart baking dish; set aside. In a medium mixing bowl beat together eggs and broth. Stir in green onions, garlic, and dillweed; set aside. Cut split bagels in two or three pieces.

2 In a prepared baking dish place the bagel bottoms, cut sides up. Spoon salmon and cheese over top. Arrange bagel top pieces on the salmon mixture, cut sides down. Gradually pour egg mixture over all.

3 Bake, uncovered, for 35 to 40 minutes or until a knife inserted near the center comes out clean. Let stand 10 minutes before serving. Makes 6 servings.

To Make Ahead:
Assemble mixture as directed. Cover with plastic wrap and chill up to 24 hours. Uncover and bake in a 350°F oven for 40 to 45 minutes.

Nutrition Facts per serving: 325 cal., 15 g total fat (2 g sat. fat), 174 mg chol., 694 mg sodium, 27 g carbo., 1 g fiber, 20 g pro. **Daily Values:** 11% vit. A, 2% vit. C, 25% calcium, 15% iron.

- **Knife-and-Fork Breakfast Burrito (see below)**

- **Cooked chorizo patties**

- **Grapefruit and orange sections**

- **Tomato juice, other fruit juice, or coffee**

---

30 MINUTE, LOW FAT

Knife-and-Fork Breakfast Burrito

Mash the beans slightly so they absorb the flavors of the other ingredients. (See the photograph on page 77.)

Start to finish: 25 minutes

- 1 cup canned black beans, rinsed and drained
- ⅓ cup bottled chunky salsa
- 4 eggs, slightly beaten
- 2 Tbsp. milk
- ¼ tsp. pepper
- ⅛ tsp. salt
  Nonstick cooking spray or cooking oil
- 1 medium tomato, thinly sliced
- ½ cup crumbled queso fresco or shredded Monterey Jack cheese (2 oz.)
- ¼ cup dairy sour cream
- 4 tsp. snipped fresh mint
  Bottled chunky salsa (optional)

1 In a small saucepan slightly mash the beans. Stir in the ⅓ cup salsa. Heat through over low heat. Cover and keep warm while making the egg tortillas.

2 In a medium mixing bowl combine eggs, milk, pepper, and salt. Coat a 10-inch nonstick omelet pan (or skillet with flared sides) with nonstick cooking spray, or brush lightly with a little cooking oil. Preheat pan over medium heat until a drop of water sizzles.

3 For each of the egg tortillas, pour about ¼ cup of the egg mixture into the pan. Lift and tilt pan to spread egg mixture over bottom. Return to heat. Cook for 1½ to 2 minutes or until light brown on the bottom (do not turn).

4 To serve, loosen edges of egg tortilla with a spatula. Carefully slide it onto a serving plate, brown side down. On one half of the tortilla, spread one-fourth of the bean-salsa mixture. Top with tomato and half of the cheese, divided. Fold in half and then into quarters to form burritos. Keep warm while preparing remaining tortillas and burritos. Top with sour cream and remaining cheese; sprinkle with mint. Serve with additional salsa, if desired. Makes 4 servings.

Nutrition Facts per serving: 179 cal., 9 g total fat (4 g sat. fat), 223 mg chol., 389 mg sodium, 14 g carbo., 4 g fiber, 14 g pro. **Daily Values:** 14% vit. C, 12% calcium, 12% iron.

---

30 MINUTE

Windowpane Eggs

When grape or cherry tomatoes are not available, substitute a chopped roma or beefsteak tomato. (See the photograph on page 77.)

Prep: 15 minutes **Cook:** 6 minutes

- ½ cup fresh sugar snap pea pods, strings and tips removed
- ½ cup grape tomatoes and/or yellow cherry tomatoes, halved
- 1 tsp. cooking oil
- 2 tsp. snipped fresh dillweed or ½ tsp. dried dillweed
  Salt and pepper
- 2 Tbsp. margarine or butter
- 2 ½-inch-thick slices sourdough bread, approximately 5×4-inch rectangles
- 2 eggs

1 In a very large (12-inch) skillet cook and stir pea pods and tomatoes in hot oil for 2 minutes or until the peas are crisp-tender and heated through. Stir in dillweed. Season with salt and pepper. Remove from skillet. Cover and keep warm.

2 In the same skillet melt margarine or butter over medium heat. Cut or tear a hole in each slice of bread, leaving about ½ inch band of bread around the perimeter. Place bread slices in hot skillet. Crack egg into center of each bread slice. Sprinkle with salt and pepper. Cover and cook 3 minutes. Using a pancake turner, turn over bread; cook 1 minute more or until desired doneness.

3 To serve, place egg and bread on plates. Serve with pea pod-tomato mixture. Makes 2 servings.

Nutrition Facts per serving: 282 cal., 20 g total fat (4 g sat. fat), 213 mg chol., 499 mg sodium, 17 g carbo., 2 g fiber, 9 g pro. **Daily Values:** 30% vit. C, 6% calcium, 11% iron.

Left: Windowpane Eggs (page 76)
Below: Knife-and-Fork Breakfast Burrito (page 76)

Top: Baked Grapefruit Halves (page 64)
Above: Pick-Your-Fruit Smoothie (page 64)
Right: Lemon Soufflé Pancakes (page 67)

Page 80: Rarebit Sauce with Roasted
Veggies (page 57)
Top: Weeknight Steak with Vegetables
(page 57)
Right: Country-Style Oven Ribs (page 58)

Top: Broccoli and Peppers with Walnuts (page 51)
Bottom left: Lemon-Tarragon Asparagus Salad (page 74)
Bottom right: Broccoli-Fennel Spanakopita (page 74)
Page 83: Nutmeg Beignets (page 66)

Top: Sausage-Pineapple Scrapple (page 85)
Left: Weekend Scramble (page 85)

Sausage-Pineapple Scrapple

(See the photograph on page 84.)

Prep: 20 minutes **Cool:** 30 minutes
Refrigerate: 4 hours **Cook:** 16 minutes

- 4 oz. hot-and-spicy or regular pork sausage
- ½ cup finely chopped red or green sweet pepper
- 1 cup yellow cornmeal
- 2 Tbsp. cooking oil
- 1 recipe Pineapple Sauce (see right)

1 Coat an 8×4×2-inch loaf pan with cooking spray or lightly grease the bottom and sides with cooking oil; set aside. Remove casings from sausage, if present. In a large skillet cook sausage and sweet pepper over medium heat until sausage is brown and pepper is tender, stirring to break up the meat. Drain and set aside.

2 For scrapple, in a medium saucepan bring 2½ cups water to boiling. Meanwhile, stir together cornmeal, 1 cup cold water, and ½ teaspoon salt. Slowly add cornmeal mixture to boiling water, stirring constantly with a long-handled wooden spoon. Cook and stir until mixture returns to boiling. Reduce heat to low. Cook, uncovered, 10 to 15 minutes or until the mixture is very thick, stirring almost constantly. Remove from heat. Stir in sausage-pepper mixture. Spread the hot mixture evenly into the prepared loaf pan. Cool 30 minutes. Cover and refrigerate 4 hours or overnight.

3 Loosen edges of chilled cornmeal loaf with a metal spatula. Turn out the loaf onto a cutting board and cut it crosswise into ½-inch-thick slices, wiping the knife clean and moistening it with cold water after each cut.

4 In a large skillet heat cooking oil over medium heat. Cook slices 8 to 10 minutes on each side or until brown and crisp. Drain on paper towels. Serve with Pineapple Sauce. Makes 6 servings.

Pineapple Sauce

Coarsely chop enough peeled whole pineapple to make 2 cups. (Set aside remaining pineapple for another use.) In a medium saucepan combine chopped pineapple and 1 tablespoon sugar. Bring to boiling; reduce heat. Boil gently, uncovered, 15 minutes or until most of the liquid has evaporated and mixture is slightly thickened. Remove from heat. Stir in ¼ cup finely chopped red sweet pepper and 1 tablespoon chopped fresh cilantro.

Nutrition Facts per serving with 2 tablespoons pineapple sauce: 225 cal., 10 g total fat (4 g sat. fat), 16 mg chol., 315 mg sodium, 28 g carbo., 3 g fiber, 5 g pro. Daily Values: 64% vit. C, 1% calcium, 4% iron.

Weekend Scramble

(See the photograph on page 84.)

Start to finish: 30 minutes

- ½ of a 4- to 5-oz. round Brie or Camembert cheese
- 8 eggs
- 2 Tbsp. milk
- 1 Tbsp. snipped fresh chives
- 2 oz. sliced pancetta or 3 slices bacon
   Olive oil
- 1½ cups fresh morel mushrooms, chanterelles, and/or white button mushrooms, sliced
- 4½ cups fresh arugula or fresh baby spinach*, lightly steamed

1 Remove rind from cheese, if desired. Cut cheese into bite-size pieces; set aside. In a medium mixing bowl beat together eggs, milk, chives, ¼ teaspoon salt, and ⅛ teaspoon pepper; set aside. In a large skillet cook pancetta over medium heat until crisp. Drain on paper towels, reserving drippings in skillet. Crumble pancetta and set aside. Measure drippings in skillet; add oil, if necessary, to equal 2 tablespoons.

2 Add mushrooms to skillet; cook over medium-high heat 4 to 5 minutes or until tender. Reduce heat to medium. Return pancetta to skillet. Pour egg mixture over mushroom mixture in skillet. Cook, without stirring, until egg mixture begins to set on the bottom and around the edges. Use a large spatula to lift and fold the partially cooked eggs so the uncooked portion flows underneath. Continue cooking and stirring 2 to 3 minutes or until eggs are cooked through and glossy and moist. Top with cheese. Remove from heat. Cover; let stand 1 to 2 minutes to soften cheese.

3 To serve, place arugula on each plate; spoon egg mixture alongside. Makes 6 servings.

*Note: To steam spinach, place spinach in a steamer basket in a skillet over gently boiling water. Cover and steam about 1 minute or until spinach is just wilted. Drain well.

Nutrition Facts per serving: 203 cal., 16 g total fat (6 g sat. fat), 300 mg chol., 308 mg sodium, 3 g carbo., 1 g fiber, 13 g pro. Daily Values: 8% vit. C, 10% calcium, 9% iron.

EDITOR'S TIP

An Omelet in 45 Seconds

All it takes is two eggs, two tablespoons of water, and butter or cooking oil.

Easy Omelets

These omelets, developed by the American Egg Board, cook in just 45 seconds. For the best results, cook them in a nonstick skillet.

Step 1

In a medium bowl whisk together 2 eggs and 2 tablespoons water, completely blending the whites and the yolks (use the same ratio for additional omelets). For each omelet, cook about ½ cup of the egg mixture.

Step 2

In a 10-inch nonstick skillet melt butter or cooking oil over medium-high heat just until hot enough to sizzle when a drop of water is added. (Or coat with nonstick cooking spray.) Pour in egg mixture. The egg should set immediately.

Step 3

With an inverted pancake turner, carefully push the cooked portions at the edges toward the center to allow the uncooked portions to reach the hot surface, tilting pan and moving cooked portions as necessary.

Step 4

When top is thickened and no visible liquid egg remains, fill one half of the omelet, if desired, with about ½ cup of filling. Fold omelet in half over the filling, using the pancake turner. Invert the omelet onto a plate with a quick flip of the wrist.

---

30 MINUTE, LOW FAT

Soft-Cooked Eggs

Cooking eggs slightly longer than the 3-minute version ensures that they are safe to eat and nearly as tender.

Start to finish: 10 minutes

    4   eggs
        Cold water

1 Place eggs in shells in a single layer in a medium saucepan. Cover with 1 inch of cold water. Bring to boiling over high heat. Reduce heat so water is just below simmering. Cover and cook for 4 to 6 minutes; drain.

2 Fill the saucepan with cold water and let stand until the eggs are cool enough to handle. Cut off tops and serve in egg cups. Or cut the eggs in half and use a spoon to scoop the eggs into serving dishes. Makes 4 soft-cooked eggs.

Nutrition Facts per egg: 77 cal., 5 g total fat (2 g sat. fat), 213 mg chol., 62 mg sodium, 1 g carbo., 0 g fiber, 6 g pro. **Daily Values:** 8% vit. A, 2% calcium, 4% iron.

LOW FAT

Shades-of-Green Pasta

Baby artichokes don't have fuzzy centers, which means they have a lot of heart.

Prep: 45 minutes **Cook:** 10 minutes

    12 baby artichokes or one 9-oz. pkg.
            frozen artichoke hearts,
            thawed and quartered
    4   oz. dried spinach fettuccine or
            plain fettuccine
    1   cup sliced leeks
    2   cloves garlic, minced
    2   Tbsp. olive oil

1 cup shelled peas (about 12 oz. in the pod) or frozen peas
¾ cup chicken broth or vegetable broth
½ cup coarsely snipped fresh Italian parsley
2 Tbsp. coarsely snipped fresh mint
Thin slices of Parmesan cheese*

1 If using baby artichokes, remove outer leaves to the pale green or yellow leaves on the bottom half. Cut off dark green leaf portions and discard. Cut off stem; trim remaining green from base of artichoke. Quarter artichokes. Remove purple or pink leaves from inside, if present.

2 Meanwhile, cook fettuccine according to package directions or until tender but firm. Drain and return to pan to keep warm.

3 In a large skillet cook and stir quartered artichokes or artichoke hearts with leeks and garlic in hot oil over medium-high heat for 5 minutes. Carefully add peas and broth. Bring to boiling; reduce heat. Simmer, uncovered, about 5 minutes or until artichokes are tender.

4 Add artichoke mixture, parsley, and mint to fettuccine; toss gently to mix. Transfer to a serving dish. Top with Parmesan cheese slices. Makes 4 main-dish servings.

***Note:** Use a vegetable peeler to create thin slices of Parmesan cheese.

Nutrition Facts per serving: 303 cal., 10 g total fat (1 g sat. fat), 5 mg chol., 332 mg sodium, 44 g carbo., 9 g fiber, 13 g pro. Daily Values: 10% vit. A, 48% vit. C, 14% calcium, 30% iron.

Chocolate Brazil Nut Torte

Prep: 25 minutes Bake: 20 minutes

1 Tbsp. margarine, softened
⅓ cup Brazil nuts, finely ground
4 egg yolks
¼ cup granulated sugar
3 oz. bittersweet or semisweet chocolate, melted and cooled
1 tsp. instant espresso powder or 2 tsp. instant coffee crystals
2 Tbsp. hot water
4 egg whites
¼ cup granulated sugar
Powdered sugar
Chocolate curls (optional)

1 Preheat oven to 350°F. Generously spread margarine over the bottom and 1½ inches up the sides of a 9-inch springform pan. Reserve 1 or 2 tablespoons of the nuts. Set aside. Sprinkle remaining nuts evenly in pan.

2 In a medium mixing bowl beat the egg yolks with an electric mixer on high speed for 5 minutes or until thick and lemon color. Gradually beat in ¼ cup granulated sugar until eggs are slightly thickened. Beat in the melted chocolate on low speed. Dissolve instant espresso or coffee crystals in the 2 tablespoons hot water. Stir into chocolate mixture.

3 Wash the beaters. In a large mixing bowl beat the egg whites with an electric mixer on medium speed until soft peaks form. Gradually add ¼ cup granulated sugar. Beat on high speed until stiff peaks form. Gently fold egg whites into the chocolate mixture. Spread the mixture evenly into the prepared pan.

PASTA PARTY

- **Shades-of Green-Pasta (see page 86)**

- **Salad of mixed greens, thinly sliced beets, crumbled blue cheese, and sugared pecans tossed in balsamic vinaigrette**

- **Country-style Italian bread or French baguette with olive oil for dipping**

- **Dry white wine**

- **Fresh fruit tart topped with cinnamon ice cream**

4 Bake 20 to 25 minutes or until set. Cool on a wire rack 15 minutes. (Center will dip on cooling and crust edges will be crumbly.) Using a thin metal spatula, loosen torte from the sides of the pan. Remove sides of the pan; cool torte completely. Serve immediately or cover and chill for up to 24 hours. If chilled, allow torte to stand at room temperature 15 minutes before serving.

5 To serve, cut torte into wedges and place on dessert plates. Sift powdered sugar and sprinkle reserved ground nuts over each serving. Garnish with chocolate curls, if desired. Makes 10 servings.

Nutrition Facts per serving: 151 cal., 9 g total fat (3 g sat. fat), 85 mg chol., 39 mg sodium, 16 g carbo., 1 g fiber, 4 g pro. Daily Values: 14% vit. A, 1% calcium, 4% iron.

Golden Macaroons

Not quite a cookie and not quite a candy, macaroons are difficult to categorize. They are equally difficult to resist—whatever method is used to make them. The Better Homes and Gardens® Test Kitchen has experimented with these morsels to concoct an incredibly luscious confection.

Mixing two kinds of coconut—a regular flaked, sweetened coconut from the grocery store and unsweetened, finely shredded coconut from the health food store—yields a macaroon with pleasing texture and well-rounded flavor that's not overly sweet. A touch of honey promotes a golden brown crust of toasted coconut, deepening the flavor. For an even more incredible taste sensation, add chocolate (see below).

Chocolate Macaroon Sandwiches: Loosely pack a tablespoon with macaroon dough. Transfer the dough to a parchment-lined baking sheet; press gently to form flattened mounds. Bake in a 300°F oven for 20 to 22 minutes. Cool. In a small saucepan heat ¾ cup heavy cream to near boiling; remove from heat. Add 6 ounces chopped semisweet chocolate. Let stand 5 minutes and whisk until smooth. Completely cool. Spoon a mound of chocolate onto the bottom of one macaroon. Top with the second macaroon and gently press the sandwich together.

Golden Macaroons

Use two kinds of coconut and a hint of honey for these marvelous morsels.

Prep: 10 minutes **Chill:** 30 minutes
Bake: 17 minutes

- 2½ cups flaked sweetened coconut (about 7 oz.)
- 2 cups unsweetened finely shredded coconut
- 1 cup sugar
- 3 Tbsp. all-purpose flour
- ¼ tsp. salt
- 4 egg whites
- 1 Tbsp. honey
- 1 tsp. vanilla

1 Break flaked coconut into separate flakes with only a few very small clumps present. In a large mixing bowl combine flaked and shredded coconut until evenly mixed.

2 In a mixing bowl combine sugar, flour, and salt. Add egg whites, honey, and vanilla. Whisk rapidly until smooth. Pour egg white mixture over coconut mixture. Stir with a wooden spoon, then use hands and continue to blend until evenly mixed. Cover; chill 30 minutes.

3 Preheat oven to 300°F. Line a large baking sheet with parchment. Drop rounded tablespoons of macaroon batter onto the sheet about 2 inches apart. Gently pinch mounds into shaggy pyramids. Bake 17 to 19 minutes or until golden brown. Remove from oven. Immediately transfer macaroons to a wire rack. Makes about 24 cookies.

Nutrition Facts per cookie: 99 cal., 5 g total fat (4 g sat. fat), 0 mg chol., 36 mg sodium, 14 g carbo., 1 g fiber, 1 g pro. **Daily Values:** 2% iron.

Salted Peanut Bars

One bite of these pleasingly sweet and salty treats and kids of all ages will come back for more.

Prep: 20 minutes **Bake:** 25 minutes

- ½ cup butter, melted
- 1 pkg. 2-layer-size white or yellow cake mix
- 1 egg, beaten
- 1 10-oz. pkg. peanut butter-flavored pieces
- 1 cup chopped salted peanuts
- 2 cups miniature marshmallows

1 Preheat oven to 350°F. In a large mixing bowl stir melted butter into cake mix. Stir in the egg (dough will be stiff). Press dough into the bottom of an ungreased 13×9×2-inch baking pan. Sprinkle with peanut butter-flavored pieces and peanuts.

2 Bake about 20 minutes or until edges are light brown. Remove from oven. Sprinkle with marshmallows. Return to oven and bake about 5 minutes more or until marshmallows are puffed and just starting to brown.

3 Cool in pan on a wire rack for 1 hour. Cut into triangles or rectangles. Store in an airtight container for up to 3 days. Makes 32 bars.

Salted Cashew Bars

Prepare bars as directed, except substitute 1 cup chopped cashews for the chopped peanuts.

Nutrition Facts per bar: 178 cal., 9 g total fat (4 g sat. fat), 15 mg chol., 189 mg sodium, 21 g carbo., 1 g fiber, 3 g pro. **Daily Values:** 3% vit. A, 3% calcium, 3% iron.

may

IN THIS CHAPTER

30-minute recipes indicated in COLOR.
Low-fat and no-fat recipes indicated
with a ♥.
Photographs indicated in italics.
*****Bonus recipe**

TEST KITCHEN TIP

Shrimply Divine

Company coming? While the shrimp for Grilled-Shrimp Cocktail (see recipe, right) basks in a garlicky marinade, you'll have time to relax before placing the seafood on the grill. The shrimp grills to perfection in minutes.

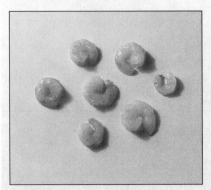

Popcorn or bay shrimp
Tasty in tacos and salads

Small tiger
Cook, peel, and eat

Medium
Perfect for pasta

Large
Favored size for shrimp cocktails

Jumbo prawn
Favored size for grilling

Colossal tiger
Super-size; eat whole or cut up

LOW FAT

Grilled-Shrimp Cocktail

Prep: 25 minutes **Marinate:** 30 minutes
Grill: 8 minutes

> 8 oz. fresh or frozen large shrimp in shells (10 to 16)
> 1 large tomato, seeded and coarsely chopped (about 1 cup)
> 2 Tbsp. fresh tarragon leaves
> 2 Tbsp. lemon juice
> 3 large cloves garlic
> ⅛ tsp. salt
> ⅛ tsp. pepper

1 Thaw shrimp, if frozen. Peel and devein shrimp, keeping tails intact. Rinse shrimp; pat dry with paper towels. Set aside.

2 In a small food processor bowl or a blender container combine tomato, tarragon, lemon juice, garlic, salt, and pepper. Cover and process or blend with several on and off turns until the mixture is coarsely chopped. Remove half of mixture (about ⅓ cup) to a small bowl and set aside. Process or blend the remaining mixture until nearly smooth.

3 In a large plastic bag combine shrimp and the smooth tomato mixture. Seal the bag. Marinate in refrigerator for 30 to 45 minutes.

4 On two long metal skewers, thread shrimp, spacing about ¼ inch apart to allow for even cooking. Grill on rack of an uncovered grill directly over medium coals for 8 to 10 minutes or until shrimp are opaque, turning once. Remove shrimp from skewers and place them in a bowl. Toss shrimp with the reserved coarsely chopped tomato mixture. Serve in cocktail glasses. Makes 4 appetizer servings.

Nutrition Facts per serving: 50 cal., 1 g total fat (0 g sat. fat), 65 mg chol., 147 mg sodium, 4 g carbo., 1 g fiber, 8 g pro. Daily Values: 6% vit. A, 26% vit. C, 1% calcium, 8% iron.

LOW FAT

Mounds-of-Mushrooms Pizza

Scientists have studied mushrooms, especially shiitake, for their ability to boost the immune system. Tossed with garlic and herbs, mushrooms make a tasty topper for a no-fuss pizza. (See the photograph on page 119.)

Prep: 30 minutes Bake: 20 minutes
Stand: 10 minutes

- 1 16-oz. loaf frozen bread dough, thawed
     Milk
- 6 cups sliced fresh mushrooms, such as shiitake, crimini, and/or oyster (about 1 lb.)
- ¼ cup snipped fresh herbs, such as oregano, basil, and/or parsley
- 1 clove elephant garlic or 3 cloves regular garlic, chopped
- ¼ cup olive oil
- ½ cup shredded provolone cheese (2 oz.)
- ¼ tsp. coarse salt or salt

1 Preheat oven to 425°F. Grease a 15×10×1-inch baking pan; set aside. Roll bread dough on a lightly floured surface to a 15×10-inch rectangle. Transfer dough to prepared baking pan. Prick dough generously with a fork. Let dough stand for 5 minutes. Brush with milk. Bake about 10 minutes or until lightly browned. Let cool for 5 minutes.

2 In a bowl combine mushrooms, herbs, and garlic. Drizzle olive oil over mixture. Toss to coat. Sprinkle cheese over prebaked crust. Top with mushroom mixture. Sprinkle with salt.

3 Bake for 10 to 12 minutes more or until edges are golden brown and pizza is heated through. Makes 16 appetizer servings.

Nutrition Facts per serving: 121 cal., 5 g total fat (1 g sat. fat), 2 mg chol., 69 mg sodium, 13 g carbo., 0 g fiber, 4 g pro. Daily Values: 1% vit. A, 1% vit. C, 5% calcium, 2% iron.

LOW FAT

On-the-Seedy-Side Breadsticks

Flax seed, high in protein and fiber, is available at health food stores and specialty markets. Serve the breadsticks with honey butter, made by stirring a little honey into softened butter. (See the photograph on page 119.)

Prep: 30 minutes   Rise: 1½ hours
Bake: 12 minutes

- ⅓ cup flax seeds
- 3¼ to 3¾ cups all-purpose flour
- 1 pkg. active dry yeast
- ½ cup warm water (120° to 130°F)
- 2 Tbsp. flax oil or olive oil
- 1 Tbsp. honey or 2 Tbsp. sugar
- 1¼ tsp. salt
- 2 to 3 Tbsp. flax seeds
     Honey butter (optional)

1 Heat a large skillet over medium-low heat. Add the ⅓ cup flax seeds; cook and stir with a wooden spoon for 5 to 7 minutes or until the seeds gently pop. Cool seeds. Place seeds in a blender container. Cover and process until seeds are finely ground (about ½ cup).

2 In a large mixing bowl stir together 2 cups of the flour and the yeast. Add warm water, flax oil or olive oil, honey or sugar, and salt. Beat with an electric mixer on low to medium speed for 30 seconds, scraping sides of bowl constantly. Beat on high speed for 3 minutes. Using a wooden spoon, stir in the ground flax seeds and as much of the remaining flour as you can.

3 Turn the dough onto a lightly floured surface. Knead in enough remaining flour to make a moderately stiff dough that is smooth and elastic (6 to 8 minutes). Shape dough into a ball. Place in a greased bowl. Turn once to grease surface of the dough. Cover; let dough rise until nearly double in size (about 1 hour).

4 Punch dough down. Cover; let rest 10 minutes. Grease two baking sheets; set aside. On a lightly floured surface, roll dough into a 16×8-inch rectangle. Brush generously with water. Sprinkle with the 2 to 3 tablespoons flax seeds. Gently pat flax seeds into dough. Cut dough crosswise into 1-inch strips. Place 1 inch apart on prepared baking sheets. Cover; let rise until nearly double (about 30 minutes).

5 Meanwhile, preheat oven to 425°F. Bake about 12 to 15 minutes or until breadsticks are golden brown. Remove from baking sheet. Cool on a wire rack. Serve with honey butter, if desired. Makes 16 breadsticks.

Nutrition Facts per breadstick: 132 cal., 4 g total fat (0 g sat. fat), 0 mg chol., 185 mg sodium, 21 g carbo., 2 g fiber, 4 g pro. Daily Values: 2% calcium, 8% iron.

May the Forks Be With You

Take a tip from the chef to the *Star Wars* visionaries: A satisfied appetite allows the mind to function on hyperdrive.

Chef Sherri Nichelman and her staff are in charge of feeding about 300 creative types each day at Lucasfilm's Skywalker Ranch near San Rafael, California. Miles from the nearest restaurant, the ranch is a self-contained creation station for George Lucas and his team, known for the *Star Wars* films and the *Indiana Jones* movies, among others. Three dining rooms keep the teams from going hungry.

The fresh fare Nichelman serves is similar to the food she feeds her family. It takes minimal effort to add special effects to meals at home, she says. Healthy cooking doesn't have to be an epic production. Roasting vegetables, for example, is as easy as tossing them in olive oil, salt, pepper, and herbs, then roasting them in a hot oven until tender.

Inspirational Food

Because fresh produce and herbs make a big flavor difference, Nichelman meets weekly with organic gardener Brian Flannery in Skywalker Ranch's 2½-acre herb and vegetable plot. The organic specialties, dependent on what's ready in the garden, include grilled halibut on braised lentils with arugula and mango-chili salsa; and summer potatoes, squash, and broccoli with black olives, saffron, ginger, and garlic.

If you're unsure of your culinary skills, use these recipes and add imagination to taste. For instance, Nichelman's Skywalker Ranch Salad goes vertical with a 4- to 5-inch-tall mold. She piles greens topped with Herbed Mushrooms (see recipe, right) into the mold to create a salad tower. These recipes have been tested and adjusted to make casual versions of her inspiration.

---

30 MINUTE

Skywalker Ranch Salad

Boston lettuce leaf cups make pretty little bowls to hold salads. If you don't have Boston lettuce, arrange the mixed greens on salad plates.

Prep: 20 minutes **Cook:** 3 minutes

- 1 recipe Lemon Vinaigrette (see right)
- 2 large shallots, peeled and thinly sliced lengthwise
- 2 Tbsp. extra virgin olive oil
- 16 cherry tomatoes, halved
- 6 cups torn mixed greens
- 4 large Boston lettuce leaf cups
- 1 recipe Herbed Mushrooms (see right)
- 4 tsp. snipped fresh parsley

1 Prepare the Lemon Vinaigrette recipe and set it aside.

2 In a skillet cook and stir shallots in hot oil over medium-high heat about 3 minutes or until crisp and golden brown. Using a slotted spoon, remove shallots from oil. Drain on paper towels. Set aside to cool.

3 In a medium bowl combine halved cherry tomatoes and 1 tablespoon of Lemon Vinaigrette. Toss to coat. Set aside.

4 In a large bowl combine torn greens and remaining dressing. Toss to coat. Divide greens among the lettuce cups. Spoon Herbed Mushrooms on top. Top with marinated tomatoes. Sprinkle salad with toasted shallots and snipped parsley. Makes 4 side-dish servings.

Lemon Vinaigrette:

In a screw-top jar combine 3 tablespoons extra virgin olive oil, 2 teaspoons lemon zest, 2 tablespoons lemon juice, 1 tablespoon snipped fresh tarragon, and 1 tablespoon Champagne or white wine vinegar. Cover and shake well. Add salt and pepper, if desired.

Nutrition Facts per serving: 309 cal., 26 g total fat (3 g sat. fat), 0 mg chol., 171 mg sodium, 19 g carbo., 3 g fiber, 6 g pro. Daily Values: 29% vit. A, 68% vit. C, 9% calcium, 17% iron.

---

30 MINUTE

Herbed Mushrooms

An earthy part of the Skywalker Ranch Salad (see recipe, left), these cooked mushrooms also make a tasty addition to grilled burgers or steak.

Prep: 15 minutes **Cook:** 15 minutes

- 2 large shallots, ends cut off, peeled, and thinly sliced
- 2 Tbsp. extra virgin olive oil
- 12 oz. fresh mushrooms, cleaned and chopped (about 4½ cups)
- 1 Tbsp. snipped fresh thyme
- ¼ tsp. salt
- ⅛ tsp. pepper

1 In a small saucepan cook shallots in olive oil over medium heat for 3 to 4 minutes or until tender, stirring frequently. Add mushrooms and thyme. Cook, uncovered, over medium heat for 12 to 15 minutes or until all the liquid has evaporated, stirring occasionally. Remove from heat. Season with salt and pepper. Set aside to cool.

Roasted Carrot Stick Snack

Best when served hot out of the oven, these healthful substitutes for french fries are loaded with vitamin A.

Prep: 20 minutes **Roast:** 10 minutes

- 6 **medium carrots (1 lb.)***
- 2 **to 3 tsp. olive oil**
- 2 **Tbsp. snipped fresh dillweed or basil**
  Coarse sea salt or salt

1 Preheat oven to 475°F. Peel carrots. Cut carrots into strips about 3 inches long and ½ inch wide.

2 In a large bowl combine olive oil and snipped dillweed or basil. Add carrots; toss to coat.

3 In a 15×10×1-inch baking pan spread carrots in a single layer. Roast, uncovered, about 10 minutes or until carrots are just tender, stirring once. Sprinkle with coarse salt. Makes 6 side-dish or snack servings.

*Note: Cut the prep time by substituting 1 pound of purchased carrot sticks.

Nutrition Facts per serving: 46 cal., 2 g total fat (0 g sat. fat), 0 mg chol., 27 mg sodium, 8 g carbo., 2 g fiber, 1 g pro. **Daily Values:** 383% vit. A, 9% vit. C, 2% calcium, 2% iron.

Creamy Borscht-Style Soup

Traditional borscht is served with a dollop of sour cream or a drizzle of light cream. This rich and creamy version has the sour cream stirred in.

Prep: 10 minutes **Cook:** 20 minutes

- ⅓ **cup chopped onion**
- ⅓ **cup chopped celery**
- ⅓ **cup finely chopped carrot**
- 1 **Tbsp. cooking oil**
- ½ **tsp. anise seed, crushed**
- 1 **16-oz. can thinly sliced beets, drained**
- 2 **cups shredded red cabbage**
- 1 **14½-oz. can beef broth**
- 1 **cup water**
- 1 **8-oz. carton dairy sour cream**
- 2 **Tbsp. all-purpose flour**
- 1 **Tbsp. sugar**
- 1 **Tbsp. vinegar**
- ⅛ **tsp. pepper**

1 In a large saucepan cook onion, celery, and carrot in hot oil over medium heat about 4 minutes or until vegetables are tender but not brown. Stir in the anise seed. Cook for 1 minute more.

2 Carefully add drained beets, cabbage, beef broth, and water. Bring to boiling; reduce heat. Cover and simmer for 10 minutes.

3 Meanwhile, in a small mixing bowl stir together sour cream, flour, sugar, vinegar, and pepper until smooth. Add sour cream mixture to soup. Cook and stir over medium heat until mixture returns to boiling. Cook and stir for 1 minute more. Remove from heat. To serve, ladle soup into bowls. Makes 4 side-dish servings.

Nutrition Facts per serving: 291 cal., 16 g total fat (8 g sat. fat), 25 mg chol., 583 mg sodium, 34 g carbo., 4 g fiber, 5 g pro. **Daily Values:** 66% vit. A, 43% vit. C, 11% calcium, 7% iron.

TEST KITCHEN TIP

Special Effects for Food Fixed at Home

Chef Sherri Nichelman at Lucasfilm's Skywalker Ranch offers four ideas to add special effects to the food you fix at home.

1. Sprinkle a favorite cut of chicken or beef with salt before cooking, then combine equal amounts of cracked black and white peppercorns, crushed fennel seed, and crushed lavender. Rub the mixture into the meat. The combination makes a flavorful dry marinade.

2. Toast spices before using them to bring out a rich nutlike flavor. In a medium skillet cook spice seeds or cinnamon sticks over medium-low heat for 3 to 4 minutes or until aromatic, stirring constantly. Watch closely to prevent overbrowning. Remove from heat. Cool. Use a spice grinder or a mortar and pestle to grind the spices to a fine powder.

3. Make low-fat yogurt spreads for sandwiches. Combine plain yogurt with a bit of lemon zest and fresh snipped herbs—dill, chives, or parsley. Add toasted mustard seed and chopped cucumber, if desired.

4. Perk up salads, vegetables, fish, poultry, and beef with a marinade or dressing consisting of this fabulous foursome: herbs or spices, salt, pepper, and a splash of lemon juice or vinegar.

Fava Beans and Greens

Favas are an excellent source of fiber and are rich in folate too. Fresh fava beans are available seasonally; canned and dried beans are available year-round. When using dried favas, combine 8 ounces beans with 4 cups of water. Bring to boiling and simmer for 15 to 30 minutes. Let stand 1 hour. Drain. Simmer in 8 cups of water for 45 minutes or until the beans are tender. Drain; cool. Peel if desired.

Start to finish: 20 minutes

- 3 **cups arugula and/or spinach**
- 3 **cups torn fresh greens**
- 1 **19-oz. can fava beans, drained and rinsed**
- ¼ **cup thinly sliced red onion**
- 2 **Tbsp. olive oil**
- 1 **to 2 Tbsp. lemon juice**
- 1 **Tbsp. snipped marjoram or 1 tsp. dried marjoram, crushed**
- 1¼ **tsp. salt**
- ¼ **to ½ tsp. coarsely ground black pepper**

1 In a large bowl toss together arugula and/or spinach, torn fresh greens, fava beans, and sliced onion.

2 For dressing, in a screw-top jar combine olive oil, lemon juice, marjoram, salt, and pepper. Cover and shake well.

3 Pour the dressing over the greens and toss lightly to coat. Makes 6 side-dish servings.

Nutrition Facts per serving: 108 cal., 5 g total fat (1 g sat. fat), 0 mg chol., 374 mg sodium, 12 g carbo., 8 g fiber, 5 g pro. **Daily Values:** 3% vit. A, 9% vit. C, 4% calcium.

EDITOR'S TIP

Fabulous Favas

Fava beans are culinary diplomats, moving freely among the cuisine styles of central Europe, the Mediterranean, and the Middle East. In some parts of the world—the Apulia region of Italy, for example—favas are indispensable staples of the local cuisine.

Scrumptious Soybeans

Find soybeans at major markets or health food stores—available fresh or frozen, in pods or shelled. Soy foods contain compounds that may lower cholesterol and reduce the risks of breast and prostate cancers. (See the photograph on page 123.)

Start to finish: 10 minutes

- 2 **tsp. butter or margarine**
- 3 **cups shelled fresh soybeans or frozen soybeans, thawed**
- 3 **Tbsp. fresh whole small mint leaves**
- 1 **Tbsp. snipped fresh basil Salt**

1 In a skillet melt 2 teaspoons butter or margarine over medium heat. Add shelled soybeans to skillet; cook and stir 5 minutes or until tender. Stir in mint, basil, and salt to taste. Makes 6 side-dish servings.

Nutrition Facts per serving: 140 cal., 7 g total fat (2 g sat. fat), 4 mg chol., 123 mg sodium, 10 g carbo., 4 g fiber, 11 g pro. **Daily Values:** 4% vit. A, 28% vit. C, 13% calcium, 15% iron.

Fresh Spinach Pasta Toss

The eyes have it. Spinach not only protects against age-related vision problems, it also tastes deliciously fresh in this brothy pasta dish. For a delicious meal, add a hearty salad and a crusty loaf of sourdough bread. (See the photograph on page 123.)

Prep: 35 minutes **Cook:** 8 minutes

- 1 **recipe Three-Step Homemade Pasta (see page 95)**
- 1 **cup thinly sliced onions**
- 1 **Tbsp. butter or margarine**
- 1 **14½-oz. can chicken broth or vegetable broth**
- ¼ **tsp. pepper**
- 6 **cups fresh baby spinach or torn spinach**
- ¼ **cup shaved Asiago cheese or Parmesan cheese**

1 Prepare Three-Step Homemade Pasta; set aside. In a 4-quart Dutch oven cook the onions in butter or margarine over medium heat about 7 minutes or until golden brown, stirring frequently.

2 Carefully add chicken or vegetable broth and pepper. Bring to boiling. Stir in the pasta. Top with spinach. Cover and cook for 1 to 2 minutes more or until spinach and pasta are tender.

3 To serve, ladle the pasta into a bowl. Top with cheese. Makes 4 main-dish servings.

Nutrition Facts per serving: 256 cal., 9 g total fat (4 g sat. fat), 69 mg chol., 756 mg sodium, 34 g carbo., 6 g fiber, 10 g pro. **Daily Values:** 54% vit. A, 15% vit. C, 12% calcium, 29% iron.

Three-Step Homemade Pasta

It's easier to make homemade pasta than you may imagine. No special equipment is required, and you'll discover that the half hour spent in preparation is time well spent.

Prep: 30 minutes **Stand:** 30 minutes

1⅓	cups all-purpose flour
¼	tsp. salt
1	egg, beaten
¼	cup very finely chopped, well-drained, cooked spinach
2	Tbsp. water
½	tsp. cooking oil or olive oil

1 In a large mixing bowl stir together 1 cup of the flour and the salt. Make a well in the center of the flour mixture. In a small bowl combine the beaten egg, spinach, water, and oil. Add to dry mixture; mix well.

2 Sprinkle kneading surface with the remaining flour. Turn dough out onto floured surface. Knead until dough is smooth and elastic (8 to 10 minutes total). Cover and let the dough rest for 10 minutes.

3 Divide dough in half. On a lightly floured surface, roll each half into an 11-inch square (about 1⁄16 inch thick). Let stand, uncovered, about 20 minutes. Cut each dough half into 1-inch-wide strips. Makes ½ pound fresh pasta (4 side-dish servings).

Food processor directions:

Place steel blade in food processor bowl. Add flour, salt, egg, and spinach to food processor bowl. Cover and process until mixture forms fine crumbs about the consistency of cornmeal. With the processor running, slowly pour water and oil through the feed tube. Continue processing just until the dough forms a ball. Transfer dough to a lightly floured surface. Cover; let dough rest for 10 minutes. Continue as directed in Step 3.

Nutrition Facts per serving: 163 cal., 2 g total fat (1 g sat. fat), 53 mg chol., 164 mg sodium, 29 g carbo., 1 g fiber, 6 g pro. **Daily Values:** 4% vit. A, 1% calcium, 11% iron.

Caramelized Onion Soup

See the photograph on page 123.

Prep: 25 minutes **Cook:** 30 minutes

3	lb. sweet onions, such as Vidalia, Walla Walla, or Maui
3	Tbsp. olive oil, margarine, or butter
12	medium shallots, halved
4	cups beef broth or reduced-sodium chicken broth
2	Tbsp. dry white wine (optional)
6	½-inch-thick slices sourdough or French bread (4 oz.)
6	oz. Gouda or Edam cheese, thinly sliced
	Green onion tops (optional)

1 Cut off about ½ inch from the tops of three whole onions. Peel off the papery outer leaves. Trim the root ends, leaving them intact. Turn one of the onions on its top. Cut two thin (¼ inch) slices from the center of the onion, cutting down from the root end to the onion top, keeping the slices intact. Repeat with remaining two onions for a total of six thin, center-cut onion slices. Set aside remaining onions.

2 For caramelized onions, in a large skillet heat 1 tablespoon of the olive oil. Carefully add the six onion slices in a single layer. Cook, uncovered, over medium heat for 3 to 4 minutes or until golden brown. Turn carefully with a wide metal spatula. Cook about 3 minutes more or until golden brown on second side. Carefully remove from skillet and drain on paper towels.

3 Halve and cut the remaining whole onions into thin slices. You should have 6 to 7 cups onion slices. In a 4- or 4½-quart Dutch oven heat the remaining 2 tablespoons oil over medium heat. Stir in the sliced onions and halved shallots. Cook, uncovered, over medium heat for 20 to 25 minutes or until onions are tender, stirring occasionally. Increase heat to medium-high and cook 5 minutes more or until onions are golden brown, stirring occasionally. Carefully stir broth and, if using, wine into onions in Dutch oven. Heat through. Season to taste with salt and pepper.

4 Meanwhile, place bread slices on rack of broiler pan. Broil 4 inches from heat about 1 minute or until lightly toasted. Turn over bread; top each piece with a slice of cheese. Broil for 1 to 2 minutes more or until cheese just begins to melt.

5 To serve, ladle soup into bowls. Top each with a piece of cheese toast. Add a caramelized onion slice and, if desired, green onion tops. Makes 6 main-dish servings.

Nutrition Facts per serving: 333 cal., 13 g total fat (6 g sat. fat), 32 mg chol., 998 mg sodium, 41 g carbo., 4 g fiber, 14 g pro. **Daily Values:** 17% vit. A, 28% vit. C, 26% calcium, 11% iron.

Creamy Penne and Mushrooms

Turn the heat to low before adding the sour cream to the sauce. Once the sour cream is added, the sauce will curdle if it gets too hot.

Prep: 10 minutes **Cook:** 15 minutes

- 8 oz. packaged dried penne pasta
- 3 cups sliced fresh button mushrooms (8 oz.)
- 1½ cups sliced fresh shiitake mushrooms (4 oz.)
- 4 cloves garlic, minced
- 1 Tbsp. butter
- ½ cup dry white wine
- 1 tsp. instant chicken bouillon granules
- ¼ tsp. coarse ground pepper
- ½ cup light dairy sour cream
- ¼ cup finely shredded Parmesan cheese

1 Cook pasta according to package directions; drain. Keep warm.

2 In a large skillet cook and stir sliced mushrooms and garlic in hot butter for 3 minutes. Stir in white wine, bouillon granules, and pepper. Bring to boiling; reduce heat. Simmer, uncovered, for 5 minutes. Reduce heat to low. Stir in sour cream; add hot cooked pasta. Cook and stir until heated through (do not let boil).

3 To serve, transfer pasta to shallow pasta bowls or dinner plates. Sprinkle each serving with Parmesan cheese. Makes 4 main-dish servings.

Nutrition Facts per serving: 360 cal., 9 g total fat (5 g sat. fat), 24 mg chol., 408 mg sodium, 51 g carbo., 2 g fiber, 14 g pro. **Daily Values:** 8% vit. A, 2% vit. C, 14% calcium, 13% iron.

Salmon with Apricot Sauce

Salmon contains a type of fat that may protect against heart disease and some cancers. Topping the fish with fruity hot pepper sauce provides a zap of flavor. (See the photograph on page 119.)

Prep: 25 minutes **Grill:** 6 minutes

- 4 fresh or frozen salmon or halibut steaks, ¾ inch thick (about 1¼ lb.)
- 4 fresh grilled apricots or 8 dried apricot halves
- ½ cup apricot nectar
- ⅓ cup apricot preserves
- 3 Tbsp. sliced green onions
- 1½ tsp. snipped fresh oregano or ½ tsp. dried oregano, crushed
- ⅛ tsp. salt
  Few dashes bottled hot pepper sauce
- 1 Tbsp. olive oil
- 1 to 2 tsp. bottled hot pepper sauce
  Salt and pepper
  Nonstick cooking spray
  Fresh oregano sprigs (optional)

1 Thaw fish, if frozen. Quarter grilled apricots; set aside. (Or cover dried apricots with boiling water. Let stand while sauce and fish are prepared.)

2 For sauce, in a small saucepan combine apricot nectar, preserves, green onions, oregano, and the ⅛ teaspoon salt. Bring just to boiling, stirring frequently; reduce heat. Boil gently, uncovered, about 8 minutes or until sauce thickens slightly. Remove from heat; reserve ¼ cup sauce to brush on fish. In a small bowl combine

remaining sauce, apricot quarters or halves, and a few dashes of hot pepper sauce. (If using dried apricots, drain well before adding.) Cover sauce and keep warm.

3 In a small bowl stir together the olive oil and the 1 to 2 teaspoons bottled hot pepper sauce. Brush both sides of the salmon or halibut with the oil mixture. Sprinkle lightly with salt and pepper.

4 Coat an unheated grill rack with cooking spray. Grill salmon on the rack of an uncovered grill directly over medium coals for 6 to 9 minutes or until fish just flakes easily, turning once halfway through grilling. Brush salmon with the reserved ¼ cup sauce during the last 2 to 3 minutes of grilling time.

5 Remove salmon to serving platter. Spoon chunky apricot sauce over salmon. Top with oregano sprigs, if desired. Makes 4 servings.

Nutrition Facts per serving: 304 cal., 8 g total fat (1 g sat. fat), 73 mg chol., 260 mg sodium, 27 g carbo., 2 g fiber, 29 g pro. **Daily Values:** 31% vit. A, 12% vit. C, 4% calcium, 10% iron.

Smoked Salmon and Spinach Salad

Welcome warm evenings when you have ingredients for this keep-the-kitchen-cool salad. No cooking required—just toss together!

Start to finish: 20 minutes

- 8 cups prewashed baby spinach
- 1 6-oz. piece smoked salmon, flaked, with skin and bones removed

2 plum tomatoes, chopped
½ cup cubed smoked Gouda
   cheese (2 oz.)
3 Tbsp. olive oil
2 Tbsp. white wine vinegar
1 Tbsp. lemon juice
1 Tbsp. snipped fresh dill or
   1 tsp. dried dillweed
1 clove garlic, minced
⅛ tsp. salt
⅛ tsp. pepper

1 In a large salad bowl combine the spinach, salmon, tomatoes, and the cheese.

2 For dressing, in a screw-top jar combine the olive oil, vinegar, lemon juice, dill, garlic, salt, and pepper. Cover and shake well. Pour dressing over spinach mixture, tossing to coat. Makes 4 main-dish servings.

Nutrition Facts per serving: 238 cal., 18 g total fat (5 g sat. fat), 40 mg chol., 527 mg sodium, 6 g carbo., 2 g fiber, 15 g pro. Daily Values: 88% vit. A, 42% vit. C, 16% calcium, 13% iron.

LOW FAT

Spring Chicken with Garlic Galore

Roasted garlic is sweet and mellow. Squeeze the cloves from the skin to eat with the chicken or to spread on bread. (See the photo on page 118.)

Prep: 25 minutes **Roast:** 1¼ hours
Stand: 15 minutes

3 heads garlic (about 40 cloves)
2 Tbsp. olive oil or cooking oil
1 Tbsp. snipped fresh lemon
   thyme, snipped fresh thyme,
   or 1 tsp. dried thyme, crushed
1 tsp. cracked black pepper
¼ tsp. salt

1 3- to 3½-lb. whole broiler/
   fryer chicken
1 medium onion, cut into wedges
2 cups fat-free half-and-half or
   half-and-half
2 Tbsp. all-purpose flour
1 tsp. snipped fresh lemon thyme,
   snipped fresh thyme, or
   ¼ tsp. dried thyme, crushed
¼ tsp. salt
⅛ tsp. pepper
   Fresh thyme sprigs (optional)

1 Preheat oven to 375°F. Peel away outer papery leaves from heads of garlic, leaving skin of garlic cloves intact. Separate the cloves. Peel and mince 4 of the cloves. Set aside remaining cloves.

2 In a small bowl combine minced garlic with 1 tablespoon of the olive oil, the 1 tablespoon snipped lemon thyme, the cracked black pepper, and ¼ teaspoon salt. Rub minced garlic mixture over chicken.

3 Place 6 garlic cloves into the cavity of the chicken. Tie legs to tail. Twist wing tips under back. Place onion wedges and remaining garlic cloves in the bottom of a shallow roasting pan. Drizzle onion and garlic with remaining olive oil.

4 Place chicken, breast side up, on top of the onion wedges and garlic cloves in roasting pan. Insert meat thermometer into center of an inside thigh muscle; do not allow the thermometer tip to touch bone. Roast, uncovered, for 1¼ to 1½ hours or until drumsticks move easily in their sockets and meat thermometer registers 180°F.

5 Remove chicken from oven. Using a slotted spoon, remove onion wedges and garlic cloves from pan.

SPRING SUPPER

- **Spring Chicken with Garlic Galore (see left)**

- **Mashed potatoes sprinkled with finely shredded fresh Parmesan cheese**

- **Buttered steamed green or wax beans**

- **Peasant-style Italian bread**

- **Tropical Fruit Pie (see page 107)**

Reserve two or three onion wedges for garnish. Cover chicken loosely with foil; let stand before carving.

6 For gravy, squeeze 10 cloves of roasted garlic from skins into a blender container or food processor bowl. Add remaining roasted onion wedges and ¼ cup of the half-and-half. Cover and blend or process the garlic mixture until smooth. Transfer to a small saucepan. Stir in flour. Add remaining half-and-half, the 1 teaspoon fresh lemon thyme, the ¼ teaspoon salt, and ⅛ teaspoon pepper to saucepan. Cook and stir over medium heat until slightly thickened and bubbly. Cook and stir for 1 minute more.

7 Serve the chicken with gravy, remaining roasted garlic cloves, reserved onion wedges, and, if desired, the fresh thyme sprigs. Serves 6.

Nutrition Facts per serving: 282 cal., 10 g total fat (2 g sat. fat), 67 mg chol., 343 mg sodium, 18 g carbo., 1 g fiber, 26 g pro. Daily Values: 1% vit. A, 13% vit. C, 10% calcium, 9% iron.

- **Chiles and Chicken in Cream Sauce** over hot cooked fettuccine (see below)

- **Mixed green salad** topped with shredded carrots, sliced avocado, thinly sliced onions, and lemon vinaigrette

- **Bolillos** or other hard rolls

- **Mexican beer** or ice water

---

30 MINUTE

Sweet and Sour Sausage Stir-Fry

Thick slices of fresh rye bread round out this one-dish meal.

Start to finish: 20 minutes

- 1 lb. fully cooked reduced-fat smoked sausage, sliced 1 inch thick
- 4 green onions, bias-sliced into 1-inch pieces
- 2 Tbsp. cooking oil
- 1 Tbsp. all-purpose flour
- 1 Tbsp. sugar
- ½ tsp. salt
- ½ tsp. celery seed
- ½ tsp. dry mustard
- ¼ tsp. pepper
- ⅔ cup water
- ¼ cup vinegar
- 1 10-oz. pkg. shredded red cabbage (5 cups)
- 2 cups packaged shredded carrot

1 In a 12-inch skillet cook and stir sliced sausage and green onions in hot oil for 5 minutes. Using a slotted spoon, remove sausage from skillet.

2 For dressing, stir the flour, sugar, salt, celery seed, dry mustard, and pepper into skillet drippings. Stir in the water and vinegar. Cook and stir until thickened and bubbly. Stir in the cabbage and carrot. Cover and simmer about 3 minutes or until cabbage is crisp-tender, stirring once. Top with sausage mixture. Cover and cook for 1 to 2 minutes more or until heated through. Transfer to a serving dish. Makes 4 main-dish servings.

Nutrition Facts per serving: 375 cal., 24 g total fat (10 g sat. fat), 50 mg chol., 1,344 mg sodium, 21 g carbo., 4 g fiber, 18 g pro. **Daily Values:** 280% vit. A, 86% vit. C, 8% calcium, 20% iron.

---

30 MINUTE

Chiles and Chicken In Cream Sauce

Anaheim chile peppers are long, green, and mild—it's the crushed red pepper that heats this creamy dish.

Prep: 15 minutes **Cook:** 14 minutes

- ¼ cup all-purpose flour
- ¼ tsp. salt
- ¼ tsp. black pepper
- 12 oz. skinless, boneless chicken breast halves, cut into bite-size strips
- 3 Tbsp. butter or margarine
- 2 fresh Anaheim chile peppers, seeded and sliced into rings (about 1½ cups)*
- 1 medium onion, sliced and separated into rings (½ cup)
- ¼ to ½ tsp. crushed red pepper
- ¾ cup half-and-half or light cream
- ⅓ cup shredded Monterey Jack cheese
  Hot cooked fettuccine

1 In a plastic bag combine the flour, salt, and black pepper. Add chicken strips, a few at a time, shaking to coat.

2 In a large skillet heat 2 tablespoons of the butter or margarine over medium heat until hot. Add coated chicken strips to hot butter. Cook about 8 minutes or until chicken is tender and no longer pink and coating is golden brown, stirring occasionally. Remove chicken from skillet; keep warm.

3 Heat remaining butter in skillet until hot. Add chile peppers, onion, and crushed red pepper. Cook and stir about 5 minutes or until tender but not browned, stirring up browned bits. Add half-and-half or light cream to skillet. Bring just to boiling. Return chicken to skillet; stir until combined. Simmer, uncovered, about 1 minute more or until sauce is slightly thickened.

4 Transfer chicken mixture to a serving dish. Sprinkle with cheese. Cover and let stand 2 to 3 minutes or until cheese is melted. To serve, spoon chicken mixture over hot cooked fettuccine. Makes 4 main-dish servings.

*Note: Hot peppers contain oils that can burn eyes, lips, and sensitive skin. Wear gloves while preparing them and thoroughly wash your hands afterward.

Nutrition Facts per serving: 392 cal., 19 g total fat (11 g sat. fat), 100 mg chol., 294 mg sodium, 28 g carbo., 1 g fiber, 27 g pro. **Daily Values:** 17% vit. A, 95% vit. C, 14% calcium, 12% iron.

Rosemary-Rubbed Chops with Apples

Flag this recipe for a fall cookout. Just-picked tart apples are perfect for the cooked apple topping.

Prep: 15 minutes **Grill:** 8 minutes

4	boneless pork loin chops, cut ¾ inch thick (about 1 lb.)
1	tsp. olive oil
½	tsp. dried rosemary, crushed
1½	cups peeled, sliced, cooking apples
⅓	cup apple juice
1	Tbsp. lemon juice
1½	tsp. cornstarch
¼	cup crumbled feta cheese (1 oz.)
¼	cup chopped toasted pecans

1 Rub both sides of chops lightly with olive oil. Sprinkle both sides of chops with rosemary, ½ teaspoon salt, and ¼ to ½ teaspoon pepper.

2 Grill chops on the rack of an uncovered grill directly over medium coals 8 to 10 minutes or until 160°F in the center, turning once.

3 Meanwhile, in a medium saucepan stir together apples, apple juice, and lemon juice. Bring to boiling; reduce heat. Cover and simmer for 3 minutes. In a small bowl combine the cornstarch and 1 tablespoon water. Add to apple mixture. Cook and stir until thickened and bubbly. Cook and stir 2 minutes more.

4 To serve, spoon apple mixture over each chop. Sprinkle with feta and pecans. Makes 4 main-dish servings.

Broiler Method:

Rub chops with oil and seasonings as directed. Place chops on the rack of a broiler pan. Broil 4 inches from the heat for 8 to 10 minutes or until 160°F in the center, turning once. Continue as directed in Step 3.

Nutrition Facts per serving: 272 cal., 13 g total fat (4 g sat. fat), 72 mg chol., 422 mg sodium, 11 g carbo., 2 g fiber, 26 g pro. Daily Values: 1% vit. A, 7% vit. C, 6% calcium, 7% iron.

Smoky Almond Pork Tenderloin

Nuts, a tasty source of protein and full of heart-healthy vitamins, add crunch to this tenderloin. (See the photograph on page 122.)

Prep: 10 minutes **Marinate:** 1 hour
Roast: 25 minutes **Stand:** 15 minutes

½	cup guava juice or apple juice
2	canned chipotle peppers in adobo sauce, chopped
2	Tbsp. honey
2	Tbsp. balsamic vinegar
1	12-oz. pork tenderloin
⅓	cup finely chopped smoked almonds or regular almonds
3	cups spring-mix salad greens
1	papaya, quartered lengthwise (optional)
¼	cup whole and/or chopped smoked almonds or regular almonds

1 In a small bowl combine guava or apple juice, chopped chipotle peppers, honey, and balsamic vinegar. Set aside ⅓ cup of the sauce. Place pork tenderloin in a shallow dish. Spoon the remaining sauce evenly over pork. Cover and refrigerate for 1 to 2 hours, turning pork once.

2 Preheat oven to 425°F. Remove pork from marinade; discard marinade. Coat pork evenly with the ⅓ cup finely chopped almonds. Place pork on a rack in a shallow roasting pan. Insert a meat thermometer so tip of thermometer is in the center of the meat. Roast for 25 to 30 minutes or until thermometer registers 160°F. Cover with foil and let stand 15 minutes before carving meat. Slice tenderloin into ¼-inch-thick slices.

3 To serve, divide greens and pork tenderloin evenly among four plates. If desired, place a papaya quarter on each plate. Stir 2 tablespoons of the remaining whole and/or chopped almonds into reserved sauce; drizzle greens and pork with the sauce. Sprinkle with remaining almonds. Makes 4 main-dish servings.

Nutrition Facts per serving: 346 cal., 17 g total fat (2 g sat. fat), 67 mg chol., 570 mg sodium, 19 g carbo., 3 g fiber, 29 g pro. Daily Values: 8% vit. A, 14% vit. C, 12% calcium, 15% iron.

TEST KITCHEN TIP
Pork Know-How

Choose from six preferred forms of pork available in the marketplace.

1. *Chops* are boneless or bone-in, thick or thin, cut from the center loin, sirloin, rib, or top loin.

2. *Ribs* can be cut back, spare, or country-style and will star in any barbecue dinner.

3. *Cutlets* are thin, boneless slices cut from the loin, leg, shoulder, or the tenderloin.

4. *Large-cut roasts* are perfect for roasting in the oven or for grilling over indirect heat.

5. *Strips* are a stir-fry favorite.

6. *Cubes* are just right for kabobs or for traditional stews.

■ Herbed Beef Pinwheels
(see right)

■ Green salad topped with
Caesar dressing, croutons, and
Parmesan cheese shavings

■ Italian bread or focaccia

■ Fresh berries with
custard sauce

PRIZE WINNER

Caliente Pot Roast

Mary Lou Cook
Welches, Oregon
$400—20-Minute Main Dishes

Start to finish: 20 minutes

- 1 16- or 17-oz. pkg. refrigerated
  cooked beef pot roast
  with juices
- 1½ cups purchased sliced
  fresh mushrooms
- 1 8-oz. bottle picante sauce
- 1 14½-oz. can reduced-sodium
  chicken broth
- 1 cup quick-cooking couscous
- 2 Tbsp. snipped fresh cilantro
  Dairy sour cream (optional)
  Chopped fresh tomato (optional)
  Sliced avocado (optional)
  Cilantro sprigs (optional)

1 Transfer liquid from pot roast
package to a large skillet; add
mushrooms and picante sauce. Cut pot
roast into 1- to 1½-inch cubes; add to
skillet. Bring to boiling; reduce heat.
Cover and simmer for 10 minutes.

2 Meanwhile, in a medium saucepan
bring chicken broth to boiling; stir
in couscous. Remove from heat. Cover
and let stand 5 minutes. Fluff with a
fork. Stir in snipped cilantro.

3 To serve, spoon pot roast mixture
over hot cooked couscous mixture.
If desired, serve with sour cream,
tomato, or avocado, and garnish with
cilantro sprigs. Makes 4 to 6 servings.

Nutrition Facts per serving: 479 cal.,
13 g total fat (4 g sat. fat), 120 mg chol.,
1,000 mg sodium, 43 g carbo., 3 g fiber,
46 g pro. Daily Values: 6% vit. A,
9% vit. C, 6% calcium, 31% iron.

Greek Beef

Greek cooking often flavors meat with
a hint of aromatic spices and fruity
sweetness. Cinnamon and currants add
Hellenic touches to this recipe. Keep
the Greek theme going with warm
pita bread and a green salad garnished
with onions, kalamata olives,
tomatoes, and feta cheese.

Prep: 15 minutes
Cook: 2 hours 10 minutes

- 1 2- to 2½-lb. boneless beef chuck
  pot roast
- 2 Tbsp. cooking oil
- ½ cup beef broth
- 3 cloves garlic, minced
- ¼ tsp. ground cinnamon
- ¼ tsp. cracked black pepper
- 8 carrots, peeled and bias-cut
  into 2-inch pieces
- 2 large onions, cut into wedges
- ¼ cup dried currants
- 1 14½-ounce can diced tomatoes
- 2 Tbsp. tomato paste
- 3 to 4 cups hot cooked fettuccine

1 Trim fat from pot roast. In a 4- to
6-quart Dutch oven heat oil.
Brown meat on all sides in hot oil.

Drain fat. In a measuring cup stir
together beef broth, garlic, cinnamon,
and pepper. Carefully pour over meat.
Bring to boiling; reduce heat. Cover
and simmer for 1¼ hours.

2 Add carrots, onions, and currants
to meat. Return to boiling; reduce
heat. Cover and simmer for 50 to
60 minutes or until meat and
vegetables are tender. Transfer meat
and vegetables to a serving platter;
reserve cooking liquid in pan. Cover
meat with foil to keep warm.

3 For sauce, stir undrained tomatoes
and tomato paste into pan liquids.
Bring to boiling; reduce heat. Simmer,
uncovered, about 5 minutes or until
slightly thickened. Pour some of the
sauce over meat and vegetables. Serve
with fettuccine. Pass remaining sauce.
Makes 6 to 8 servings.

Nutrition Facts per serving: 586 cal.,
30 g total fat (11 g sat. fat), 129 mg chol.,
308 mg sodium, 43 g carbo., 5 g fiber,
35 g pro. Daily Values: 179% vit. A,
31% vit. C, 9% calcium, 32% iron.

Herbed Beef Pinwheels

These pinwheels are a version of
braciola (brah-chee-OH-lah), an Italian
vegetable-stuffed meat roll. The
continental classic becomes a one-dish
meal when potatoes and onions are
roasted alongside the meat.

Prep: 25 minutes **Bake:** 1¼ hours

- 1 1- to 1¼-lb. beef flank steak
- 2 Tbsp. olive oil or cooking oil
- 2 medium leeks, sliced
  (⅔ cup total)
- 2 cloves garlic, minced

3 Tbsp. snipped fresh basil
¼ tsp. salt
⅛ tsp. pepper
2 Yukon gold potatoes, cut
    into eighths
1 large onion, cut into thin wedges
1 14½-oz. can diced tomatoes with
    basil, oregano, and garlic

1 Make shallow diamond cuts at 1-inch intervals on both sides of the meat. Place between two pieces of plastic wrap. Working from center to edges, use the flat side of a meat mallet to pound steak into a 12×8-inch rectangle. Remove wrap; set aside meat.

2 Preheat oven to 350°F. In a large skillet heat 1 tablespoon of the oil over medium-high heat. Add leeks and garlic. Cook for 3 to 5 minutes or until leek is tender. Stir in basil, salt, and pepper. Remove from heat. Spread leek mixture evenly on one side of steak. Starting at a short end, tightly roll meat into a spiral. Tie kitchen string around steak, evenly spaced in four places.

3 In the same large skillet heat the remaining 1 tablespoon oil over medium-high heat. Brown meat on all sides in the hot oil. Transfer meat to a 2-quart rectangular baking dish.

4 Arrange potatoes and onion wedges around meat in dish. Pour undrained tomatoes over beef and vegetables. Bake, uncovered, for 1¼ to 1½ hours or until beef is tender. Transfer meat to a cutting board. Slice into serving-size pieces. Remove the string. Serve with vegetables. Makes 4 servings.

To Make Ahead:

Prepare the beef roll through Step 2. Place the tightly wrapped spiral in the refrigerator for up to 24 hours. To cook, continue with Step 3.

Nutrition Facts per serving: 355 cal., 15 g total fat (4 g sat. fat), 53 mg chol., 722 mg sodium, 30 g carbo., 4 g fiber, 25 g pro. **Daily Values:** 7% vit. A, 49% vit. C, 6% calcium, 27% iron.

<u>**PRIZE WINNER**</u>

Saucy One-Pan Ravioli

Guido A. Tango
North Arlington, New Jersey
$200—20-Minute Main Dishes

Start to finish: 15 minutes

2 cups cherry tomatoes
1 clove garlic
¾ cup chicken broth
¼ tsp. salt
¼ tsp. pepper
1 9-oz. pkg. refrigerated ravioli
2 Tbsp. snipped fresh basil
1 Tbsp. snipped fresh
    Italian parsley
¼ cup shredded Romano or
    Parmesan cheese

1 In a blender container or food processor bowl place cherry tomatoes and garlic. Cover and blend or process until smooth. Transfer to a large saucepan. Add chicken broth, salt, and pepper. Bring to boiling.

2 Add ravioli to broth mixture; return to boiling. Reduce heat; cover and simmer for 6 to 8 minutes or until pasta is tender. Gently stir once or twice. Stir in basil and parsley.

3 To serve, spoon onto two plates. Sprinkle with Romano or Parmesan cheese. Makes 2 servings.

Nutrition Facts per serving: 502 cal., 21 g total fat (11 g sat. fat), 123 mg chol., 1,346 mg sodium, 56 g carbo., 3 g fiber, 25 g pro. **Daily Values:** 31% vit. A, 71% vit. C, 43% calcium, 19% iron.

<u>**30 MINUTE, LOW FAT**</u>

Spicy Sloppy Joes

Start to finish: 25 minutes

1 lb. lean ground beef
½ cup chopped onion
2 cloves garlic, minced
1 cup chopped zucchini
1 cup chopped yellow
    summer squash
1 cup sliced fresh mushrooms
¾ cup chopped green sweet pepper
1 oz. jarred salsa
1 tsp. dried basil, crushed
½ tsp. dried parsley flakes
½ tsp. dried rosemary, crushed
6 to 8 kaiser rolls, split and toasted

1 In a medium skillet cook beef, onion, and garlic over medium heat until meat is brown. Drain off fat. Stir in zucchini, yellow summer squash, mushrooms, and sweet pepper. Cover and cook over low heat for 5 to 7 minutes or until vegetables are tender. Stir in salsa, basil, parsley, and rosemary. Simmer, uncovered, about 10 minutes or until most of the liquid evaporates. Serve meat mixture on toasted rolls. Makes 6 to 8 servings.

Nutrition Facts per serving: 334 cal., 10 g total fat (3 g sat. fat), 48 mg chol., 668 mg sodium, 39 g carbo., 4 g fiber, 22 g pro. **Daily Values:** 14% vit. A, 50% vit. C, 10% calcium, 25% iron.

The Regal Pistachio Nut

Once a rare delicacy hoarded by royalty, the pistachio nut is abundant enough for year-round enjoyment. The mild, sweet flavor and light green color of pistachios are regal additions to recipes.

Here's a little pistachio lore to serve with dessert: During the Middle Ages on moonlit nights, lovers sat beneath pistachio trees hoping to hear the cracking of the ripening shells. The sound promised good fortune to all who heard it.

Because cracked shells indicate that nuts are ripe, avoid pistachios with closed shells. Buy pistachio nuts in the natural light-tan shells or in shells that have been colored red with vegetable dye. The flavor is the same either way. To save time when using the nuts in baking, purchase shelled pistachios.

NO FAT

Mandarin Orange Ice

Pop the fruit, cans and all, into the freezer to make this two-ingredient treat that is rich in vitamin C.

Prep: 10 minutes **Freeze:** 12 to 24 hours

    2 11-oz. cans mandarin orange
         sections
  1½ tsp. grated fresh ginger

1 Place unopened cans of mandarin oranges into the freezer. Freeze for 12 to 24 hours or until the fruit is frozen solid.

2 Place unopened cans of frozen fruit into a container of hot water for 1 to 2 minutes. (Avoid thawing too long to prevent the fruit from

becoming soft.) Remove cans from water; pat dry with paper towels. Open cans at both ends to push out the fruit into a small bowl. Pour thawed juice into a blender container or food processor bowl. Break frozen oranges into small chunks. Add orange chunks and ginger to blender container or food processor bowl. Cover and blend or process until nearly smooth, but not melted.

3 To serve, spoon mixture into glasses. Makes 4 or 5 servings.

To Make Ahead:
Transfer the blended smooth orange mixture to an 8×8×2-inch baking pan. Cover and freeze for up to 3 days or until ready to serve. Use a scraping motion to scoop sorbet.

Nutrition Facts per serving: 58 cal., 0 g total fat, 0 mg chol., 8 mg sodium, 15 g carbo., 1 g fiber, 4 g pro.
Daily Values: 27% vit. A, 89% vit. C, 2% calcium, 2% iron.

Rum-Pistachio Ice Cream

Play up the pistachios! For each serving, dip the rim of a stemmed dessert dish into melted white baking bar, semisweet chocolate, or bittersweet chocolate. Allow the excess baking bar or chocolate to drip off, and dip the rim of the dish into finely chopped pistachio nuts. Let the dessert dishes stand until dry.

Prep: 20 minutes **Cool:** 30 minutes
Freeze: 25 minutes **Ripen:** 4 hours

    1 Tbsp. rum
   ⅔ cup raisins

    2 cups milk
   ½ cup sugar
    6 egg yolks
   ½ cup sugar
    1 cup whipping cream
    1 tsp. finely shredded orange peel
   ⅓ cup coarsely chopped
         pistachio nuts

1 In a small mixing bowl pour rum over raisins; set aside.

2 Meanwhile, in a large saucepan stir together milk and ½ cup sugar. Cook and stir over medium heat until mixture almost boils and sugar dissolves. Remove from heat; set aside.

3 In a blender container or food processor bowl place egg yolks and ½ cup sugar. Cover and blend or process about 2 minutes or until mixture thickens. With the blender or food processor running, gradually add about 1 cup of the warm milk mixture. (Or in a medium mixing bowl beat egg yolks and the ½ cup sugar with an electric mixer on medium to high speed about 4 minutes or until thick. Gradually beat in about 1 cup of the warm milk mixture.)

4 Return the egg yolk mixture to the remaining milk mixture in saucepan. Bring to boiling, stirring constantly. Immediately pour mixture into a large mixing bowl. Stir in whipping cream, orange peel, and undrained raisins. Cool thoroughly by placing the bowl in a larger bowl or sink filled with icewater or by placing it overnight in the refrigerator.

5 Stir the pistachio nuts into the cream mixture. Freeze in a 2-quart ice cream freezer according to the manufacturer's directions. Makes about 1 quart (6 servings).

Nutrition Facts per serving: 431 cal., 25 g total fat (12 g sat. fat), 274 mg chol., 64 mg sodium, 46 g carbo., 1 g fiber, 8 g pro. Daily Values: 22% vit. A, 3% vit. C, 16% calcium, 6% iron.

Lemon-Pistachio Bread

Prep: 15 minutes **Bake:** 50 minutes

- 1¾ cups all-purpose flour
- ¾ cup sugar
- 2 tsp. baking powder
- ¼ tsp. salt
- 1 cup milk
- 1 egg, beaten
- ¼ cup cooking oil
- 2 tsp. finely shredded lemon peel
- 1 Tbsp. lemon juice
- ½ cup chopped pistachio nuts
- 2 Tbsp. lemon juice
- 1 Tbsp. sugar

1 Preheat oven to 350°F. Grease the bottom and ½ inch up the sides of an 8×4×2-inch loaf pan; set aside.

2 In a medium bowl stir together flour, the ¾ cup sugar, baking powder, and salt. Make a well in the center of flour mixture; set aside.

3 In another medium mixing bowl combine milk, egg, cooking oil, lemon peel, and the 1 tablespoon lemon juice. Add egg mixture all at once to the flour mixture. Stir just until moistened (batter will be lumpy). Fold in the pistachios.

4 Spoon batter into the prepared pan. Bake for 50 to 55 minutes or until a wooden toothpick inserted near

center comes out clean. Meanwhile, stir together the 2 tablespoons lemon juice and the 1 tablespoon sugar. While bread is in the pan, brush lemon-sugar mixture over the loaf. Cool in pan on a wire rack for 10 minutes. Remove loaf from pan; cool on wire rack. Wrap and store overnight before serving. Makes 1 loaf (16 servings).

To Make Ahead:

Prepare and bake bread as directed. Cool completely. Wrap loaf in foil or clear plastic wrap. Store in the refrigerator up to 1 week. To freeze, place loaf in a freezer container or bag. Freeze for up to 3 months. Thaw the loaf overnight in the refrigerator.

Nutrition Facts per serving: 152 cal., 6 g total fat (1 g sat. fat), 14 mg chol., 91 mg sodium, 22 g carbo., 1 g fiber, 3 g pro. Daily Values: 1% vit. A, 3% vit. C, 5% calcium, 6% iron.

30 MINUTE

Fast and Fruity Banana Split Tarts

Start to finish: 10 minutes

- 1 8-oz. tub cream cheese with pineapple
- ¼ cup strawberry preserves
- 1 banana, thinly sliced
- 1 2.1-oz. pkg. (15) miniature phyllo dough shells
- ⅓ cup chocolate ice cream topping

1 For filling, in a small mixing bowl beat the cream cheese and preserves until light and fluffy. Spoon filling into each shell.

2 To serve, divide banana slices among shells. Drizzle with ice cream topping. Serve immediately. Makes 15 tarts.

To Make Ahead:

Spoon filling into tarts as directed. Cover and refrigerate for up to 4 hours. Just before serving, add banana slices and drizzle with ice cream topping.

Nutrition Facts per tart: 115 cal., 6 g total fat (3 g sat. fat), 13 mg chol., 63 mg sodium, 14 g carbo., 0 g fiber, 1 g pro. Daily Values: 2% vit. A, 1% vit. C, 1% calcium, 2% iron.

30 MINUTE

Dessert Waffles With Berry Coulis

Coulis (koo-LEE), a thick fruit sauce, and ice cream turn breakfast favorites into dashing desserts.

Start to finish: 10 minutes

- 1 10-oz. pkg. frozen raspberries in syrup, thawed
- ¼ cup sifted powdered sugar
- 2 tablespoons crème de cassis (optional)
- 6 frozen waffles, toasted
- 3 cups vanilla ice cream
  Sifted powdered sugar (optional)

1 For coulis, press raspberries and syrup through a fine-mesh sieve; discard seeds. In a small bowl combine sieved berries, the ¼ cup powdered sugar, and, if desired, crème de cassis.

2 To serve, diagonally cut waffles in half. Place two waffle halves on each of six dessert plates; top with ice cream. Drizzle with coulis. Dust with additional powdered sugar, if desired. Makes 6 servings.

Nutrition Facts per serving: 300 cal., 11 g total fat (4 g sat. fat), 29 mg chol., 310 mg sodium, 48 g carbo., 3 g fiber, 5 g pro. Daily Values: 17% vit. A, 13% vit. C, 10% calcium, 14% iron.

ROSY RHUBARB

Rosy red rhubarb stalks are a gardening treat each spring. Also referred to as "pie plant," raw rhubarb is tart. When sweetened and cooked, however, the taste is reminiscent of apricot, strawberry, and lemon. Try these classic recipes when you look for delicious ways to enjoy rhubarb.

Rhubarb-Glazed Pork Roast

For a bright ruby glaze, select rhubarb stalks that are light to cherry pink.

Prep: 45 minutes **Grill:** 1¼ hours
Stand: 15 minutes

- 12 oz. fresh or frozen rhubarb, sliced (about 2 cups)
- 1 6-oz. can (⅔ cup) frozen apple juice concentrate
- Several drops of red food coloring (optional)
- 2 Tbsp. honey
- 1 3-lb. pork loin center rib roast (backbone loosened)

1 For glaze, in a saucepan combine rhubarb, juice concentrate, and, if desired, red food coloring. Bring to boiling; reduce heat. Cover and simmer for 15 to 20 minutes or until rhubarb is very tender. Strain, pressing liquid out of pulp. Discard pulp. Return liquid to pan. Bring to boiling; reduce heat. Simmer, uncovered, about 15 minutes or until reduced to about ½ cup. Remove from heat. Stir in honey. Reserve ¼ cup glaze; set aside.

2 Meanwhile, trim fat from meat. Insert a meat thermometer into the center of meat without it touching the bone.

3 Arrange coals around a drip pan on lower rack of grill. Test for medium-low heat above pan. Place meat, bone side down, on grill rack over pan. Cover; grill for 1¼ to 1¾ hours or until meat thermometer registers 155°F, occasionally brushing with reserved glaze the last 15 minutes of grilling.

4 Remove meat from grill. Cover; let stand 15 minutes before carving. (The temperature will rise 5°F during standing.) In a saucepan cook remaining glaze over medium-low heat until heated through. Pass with meat. Makes 4 to 8 servings.

Nutrition Facts per serving: 391 cal., 15 g total fat (5 g sat. fat), 102 mg chol., 93 mg sodium, 30 g carbo., 2 g fiber, 33 g pro. **Daily Values:** 1% vit. A, 13% vit. C, 7% calcium, 12% iron.

Applesauce-Rhubarb Muffins

Use fresh rhubarb—frozen rhubarb will make the muffins soggy.

Prep: 20 minutes **Bake:** 18 minutes

- 2 cups all-purpose flour
- 1 cup whole wheat flour
- 2 tsp. baking powder
- 2 tsp. ground cinnamon
- ½ tsp. baking soda
- ½ tsp. salt
- 2 eggs, beaten
- 1⅓ cups packed brown sugar
- 1⅓ cups applesauce
- ½ cup cooking oil
- 1½ cups chopped fresh rhubarb
- Cinnamon-sugar

1 Preheat oven to 400°F. Lightly grease twenty-four 2½-inch muffin cups or line with paper bake cups.

2 In a large bowl stir together the all-purpose flour, whole wheat flour, baking powder, cinnamon, baking soda, and salt. Make a well in the center of the mixture; set aside.

3 In a medium bowl combine eggs, brown sugar, applesauce, and oil. Add egg mixture all at once to flour mixture. Using a spoon, stir just until moistened (batter should be lumpy). Gently fold in rhubarb.

4 Spoon batter into prepared muffin cups, filling each cup two-thirds full. Sprinkle with cinnamon-sugar.

5 Bake for 18 to 20 minutes or until a wooden toothpick inserted in center comes out clean. Cool in muffin cups on a wire rack for 5 minutes. Remove from muffin cups; serve warm. Makes 24 muffins.

Nutrition Facts per muffin: 361 cal., 13 g total fat (2 g sat. fat), 43 mg chol., 265 mg sodium, 59 g carbo., 3 g fiber, 6 g pro. **Daily Values:** 2% vit. A, 3% vit. C, 10% calcium, 17% iron.

Rhubarb-Pineapple Crumble

This irresistible crumble is equally delicious with fresh or frozen rhubarb. To freeze rhubarb, wash and slice fresh-picked stalks, cook the rhubarb in boiling water for 1 minute, and cool it quickly in cold water. Drain, and place rhubarb into freezer containers or bags, leaving ½-inch space. Freeze for up to 6 months.

Prep: 10 minutes **Stand:** 1 hour
Bake: 45 minutes

7	cups fresh or frozen rhubarb, cut into 1-inch pieces
1	8-oz. can crushed pineapple (juice pack), drained
1	cup packed brown sugar
2	Tbsp. cornstarch
2	tsp. finely shredded lemon peel
⅔	cup all-purpose flour
¼	cup packed brown sugar
1	Tbsp. granulated sugar
1	Tbsp. chopped crystallized ginger
	Dash salt
⅓	cup butter
	Vanilla ice cream (optional)

1 Preheat oven to 350°F. Thaw rhubarb, if frozen; drain well. In a large bowl combine the rhubarb, pineapple, and the 1 cup brown sugar. Let stand for 1 hour. Drain mixture, reserving juices. If necessary, add water to the reserved juices to equal ⅔ cup liquid.

2 Place juices in a small saucepan. Stir in cornstarch. Cook and stir over medium heat until thickened and bubbly. Remove from heat. Stir into rhubarb mixture; stir in lemon peel. Spoon into a 2-quart square baking dish; set aside.

3 For topping, in a small bowl stir together the flour, the ¼ cup brown sugar, the granulated sugar, ginger, and salt. Using a pastry blender, cut in butter until mixture resembles coarse crumbs. Spoon topping over fruit.

4 Bake for 45 to 50 minutes or until lightly browned and bubbly. Serve warm. If desired, serve with ice cream. Makes 6 to 8 servings.

Nutrition Facts per serving: 391 cal., 11 g total fat (7 g sat. fat), 29 mg chol., 158 mg sodium, 73 g carbo., 3 g fiber, 3 g pro. Daily Values: 12% vit. A, 27% vit. C, 17% calcium, 11% iron.

Rhubarb Custard Pie

This homey lattice-top pie has old-time charm and flavor. It's been a favorite for years.

Prep: 35 minutes **Bake:** 50 minutes
Cool: 1 hour

1½	cups sugar
¼	cup all-purpose flour
¼	tsp. ground nutmeg or ground cinnamon
	Dash salt
3	eggs, slightly beaten
4	cups sliced fresh rhubarb*
1	recipe Pastry for Lattice-Top Pie (see page 106)
2	Tbsp. butter

1 In a large mixing bowl stir together sugar, flour, nutmeg or cinnamon, and salt. Add the eggs, stirring until smooth. Stir in the rhubarb; set aside.

2 Preheat oven to 375°F. On a lightly floured surface roll out one ball of pastry to a 12-inch circle; carefully transfer pastry to a 9-inch pie plate. Trim pastry to ½ inch beyond edge of pie plate. Transfer rhubarb mixture to the pastry-lined pie plate. Dot the mixture with butter; set aside.

3 For lattice top, roll out remaining pastry as above. Using a knife or fluted pastry wheel, cut into ½-inch-wide strips. Weave strips on top of filling to make a lattice. Press ends of strips into rim of bottom crust. Fold bottom pastry over strips; seal and crimp edge. Cover the edge of pie with foil.

4 Bake for 25 minutes. Remove foil. Bake for 25 to 30 minutes more or until knife inserted near the center comes out clean. Cool for 1 to 2 hours on a wire rack. Refrigerate within 2 hours; cover for longer storage. Makes 8 servings.

*Note: Substitute one 16-ounce package frozen unsweetened sliced rhubarb for fresh rhubarb. Thaw, but do not drain, rhubarb. Add fruit and liquid to egg mixture.

Nutrition Facts per serving: 480 cal., 22 g total fat (7 g sat. fat), 88 mg chol., 207 mg sodium, 65 g carbo., 2 g fiber, 6 g pro. Daily Values: 6% vit. A, 8% vit. C, 5% calcium, 12% iron.

Confetti Carrot Cake

This glorious show-off has sweet spring carrots stirred into buttermilk cake batter and is topped with thick lemon icing and walnut chunks. (See the photograph on page 119.)

Prep: 25 minutes **Bake:** 30 minutes
Cool: 1 hour

2	cups all-purpose flour
1	tsp. baking powder
½	tsp. baking soda
⅛	tsp. salt
½	cup shortening
1¾	cups granulated sugar
1	tsp. vanilla
4	egg whites
1	cup buttermilk or sour milk*
2½	cups shredded carrots
1	recipe Thick and Lemony Icing (see right)
1	cup chopped walnuts
	Walnut halves (optional)
	Carrot curls (optional)

1 Preheat oven to 350°F. Grease and lightly flour two 8×1½-inch or 9×1½-inch round baking pans; set aside. In a medium bowl stir together flour, baking powder, baking soda, and salt; set aside.

2 In a large mixing bowl beat shortening with an electric mixer on medium to high speed for 30 seconds. Add granulated sugar and vanilla; beat until well combined. Add egg whites, one at a time, beating well after each. Add flour mixture and buttermilk alternately to beaten mixture, beating on low speed after each addition until just combined. Using a wooden spoon, fold in carrots, stirring until combined. Divide batter evenly between prepared pans.

3 Bake for 35 to 40 minutes for 8-inch pans or 30 to 35 minutes for 9-inch pans or until a wooden toothpick inserted near center comes out clean. Cool cakes in pans on wire racks for 10 minutes. Remove from pans. Cool thoroughly on racks.

4 Meanwhile, prepare Thick and Lemony Icing. Place one cake layer on serving plate. Spoon about three-fourths of the icing (about ⅔ cup) on top of the first cake layer. Sprinkle with half of the chopped nuts. Place the second cake layer, top side up, on top of the first layer. Spoon remaining icing over cake. Sprinkle with remaining chopped nuts. If desired, add walnut halves and carrot curls. Makes 12 servings.

Thick and Lemony Icing

In a small bowl combine 3 cups sifted powdered sugar and enough lemon juice (about 3 tablespoons) to make a thick glaze.

*Note: To prepare sour milk, place 1 tablespoon lemon juice or vinegar in a glass measuring cup. Add enough milk to make 1 cup total liquid; stir. Let stand for 5 minutes.

Nutrition Facts per serving: 444 cal., 15 g total fat (3 g sat. fat), 1 mg chol., 160 mg sodium, 73 g carbo., 2 g fiber, 6 g pro. **Daily Values:** 128% vit. A, 6% vit. C, 7% calcium, 7% iron.

PRIZE WINNER
Triple-Delicious Pie

Paula Marchesi
Lenhartsville, Pennsylvania
$400—Glorious Spring Pies

Prep: 30 minutes **Bake:** 45 minutes

1½	cups sliced fresh or frozen rhubarb
1	cup sugar
3	Tbsp. quick-cooking tapioca
1½	cups fresh blueberries
1	cup sliced fresh strawberries
1	Tbsp. lemon juice
½	tsp. vanilla
	Dash ground mace or ground nutmeg
1	recipe Pastry for Lattice-Top Pie (see below)

1 If using frozen rhubarb, thaw but do not drain. In a large mixing bowl stir together sugar and tapioca. Add the rhubarb, blueberries, strawberries, lemon juice, vanilla, and mace or nutmeg. Gently toss to coat fruit. Let mixture stand 15 minutes, stirring once.

2 Meanwhile, preheat oven to 375°F. On a lightly floured surface roll out one ball of pastry to a 12-inch circle; carefully transfer pastry to a 9-inch pie plate. Trim pastry to ½ inch beyond edge of pie plate. Transfer fruit mixture to the pastry-lined pie plate.

3 For lattice top, roll out remaining pastry. Using a knife or fluted pastry wheel, cut into ½-inch-wide strips. Weave strips on filling to make a lattice. Press ends of strips into rim of bottom crust. Fold bottom pastry over strips; seal and crimp edge. Cover edge of pie with foil. Bake for 25 minutes. Remove foil. Bake for 20 to 25 minutes more or until top is golden brown and juices are bubbly. Cool on a wire rack. Makes 8 servings.

Pastry for Lattice-Top Pie

In a medium bowl stir together 2 cups all-purpose flour and ½ teaspoon salt. Using a pastry blender, cut in ⅔ cup shortening until pieces are the size of small peas. Using a total of 6 to 7 tablespoons cold water, sprinkle 1 tablespoon water over part of mixture. Toss with fork. Push to side of bowl; repeat until all is moistened. Divide in half and form each half into a ball.

Nutrition Facts per serving: 390 cal., 18 g total fat (4 g sat. fat), 0 mg chol., 137 mg sodium, 56 g carbo., 2 g fiber, 3 g pro. Daily Values: 1% vit. A, 27% vit. C, 3% calcium, 8% iron.

Tropical Fruit Pie

Elaine R. Zelinski
Brookfield, Illinois
$200—Glorious Spring Pies

Prep: 30 minutes **Bake:** 18 minutes
Cool: 1 hour **Chill:** 1 hour

1¼	cups all-purpose flour
3	Tbsp. granulated sugar
¼	tsp. salt
6	Tbsp. butter
1	egg yolk
3 to 4	Tbsp. cold water
1½	8-oz. pkg. cream cheese (12 oz.), softened
⅔	cup sifted powdered sugar
¼	cup whipping cream
1	Tbsp. orange liqueur or orange juice
1	tsp. vanilla
2 to 2½	cups assorted fruits (peeled and cut-up kiwi fruit, raspberries, peeled and chopped papaya, and/or cut-up strawberries)
2	Tbsp. apricot preserves
½	tsp. orange liqueur or orange juice

1 Preheat oven to 400°F. For pastry, in a medium bowl stir together flour, granulated sugar, and salt.

Using a pastry blender, cut in butter until mixture resembles coarse crumbs. Stir in egg yolk and enough cold water to moisten. Knead gently until mixture forms a ball.

2 On a lightly floured surface roll pastry to a 12-inch circle. Transfer to a 9-inch pie plate. Trim pastry to ½ inch beyond edge of pie plate. Fold under pastry. Crimp edge. Generously prick pastry bottom and sides with a fork. Line pastry with a double layer of foil. Bake 8 minutes; remove foil. Bake 10 minutes more or until golden. Cool on a wire rack.

3 For filling, in a medium mixing bowl beat cream cheese and powdered sugar with an electric mixer on medium speed until combined. Add whipping cream, the 1 tablespoon liqueur, and vanilla. Beat until combined. Spoon filling into pastry shell. Cover and chill 1 to 4 hours.

4 To serve, arrange fruit on top of filling. Heat preserves and the ½ teaspoon liqueur until melted. Drizzle over pie. Makes 8 servings.

Nutrition Facts per serving: 427 cal., 28 g total fat (17 g sat. fat), 108 mg chol., 298 mg sodium, 38 g carbo., 3 g fiber, 6 g pro. Daily Values: 24% vit. A, 56% vit. C, 6% calcium, 9% iron.

Berries 'n' Cream Meringue Torta

Prep: 30 minutes **Bake:** 45 minutes
Stand: 1 hour **Chill:** up to 2 hours

3	egg whites
1	tsp. vanilla
1	cup granulated sugar
1	8-oz. pkg. reduced-fat cream cheese, softened (Neufchâtel)

½	cup lemon curd
3	cups large strawberries, hulled
¼	cup apple jelly

1 Let egg whites stand at room temperature for 30 minutes. Preheat oven to 300°F. Cover a baking sheet with parchment paper. Draw a 9-inch circle on the paper. In a large mixing bowl beat egg whites and vanilla until soft peaks form. Gradually add sugar and beat until stiff peaks form. Spread meringue over circle on paper, building up sides taller than the center to form a shell.

2 Bake for 45 minutes. Turn off oven. Let meringue dry in oven, door closed, for 1 hour (do not open oven). Remove baking sheet from oven. Lift meringue; carefully peel off paper. Transfer to a serving platter.

3 For filling, beat cream cheese until fluffy. Beat in lemon curd. Spread into meringue shell. Arrange berries, with points up, on cream cheese mixture. Melt jelly; brush on berries. Cover; chill up to 2 hours. Serves 8.

Nutrition Facts per serving: 282 cal., 8 g total fat (5 g sat. fat), 36 mg chol., 151 mg sodium, 37 g carbo., 3 g fiber, 4 g pro. Daily Values: 7% vit. A, 51% vit. C, 3% calcium, 2% iron.

Fruity Tofu Shakes

Start to finish: 10 minutes

1½   cups fresh or frozen fruit
     (strawberries, raspberries,
     blueberries, peeled and
     cut-up peaches or mangoes,
     or cut-up nectarines)
1½   cups orange juice
1   10½-oz. pkg. light tofu, cut up
2   Tbsp. honey

1 Partially thaw the fruit, if frozen. In a blender container combine the fruit, orange juice, tofu, and honey. Cover and blend until nearly smooth. Pour into glasses. Makes 3 servings.

Nutrition Facts per serving: 250 cal., 3 g total fat (0 g sat. fat), 0 mg chol., 38 mg sodium, 51 g carbo., 8 g fiber, 8 g pro. **Daily Values:** 2% vit. A, 168% vit. C, 4% calcium, 12% iron.

Blueberries with Shortcake Drops

In addition to the health benefits (see Editor's Tip, right), blueberries are bursts of sweetness that are especially tasty with petite shortcakes. (See the photograph on page 123.)

Prep: 20 minutes **Bake:** 10 minutes

1½   cups all-purpose flour
2   Tbsp. sugar
1   tsp. baking powder
¼   tsp. baking soda
¼   tsp. ground cardamom (optional)
⅓   cup cold butter
1   egg, beaten
¼   cup plain low-fat yogurt
3   Tbsp. milk

4   cups fresh blueberries
1   recipe Blueberry-Cardamom
     Syrup (see below)

1 Preheat oven to 400°F. Grease a baking sheet; set aside. For shortcake drops, in a medium bowl stir together flour, the 2 tablespoons sugar, the baking powder, baking soda, and cardamom, if using. Using a pastry blender, cut in butter until mixture resembles coarse crumbs.

2 In a small bowl combine egg, yogurt, and milk. Add to flour mixture, stirring just until moistened. Drop dough by teaspoons into small 1-inch mounds onto the prepared baking sheet. Bake about 10 minutes or until golden brown. Remove shortcake drops from baking sheet; cool slightly on a wire rack.

3 Divide shortcake drops and blueberries among six dessert dishes. Drizzle with Blueberry-Cardamom Syrup. Makes 6 servings.

Nutrition Facts per serving: 338 cal., 12 g total fat (7 g sat. fat), 66 mg chol., 257 mg sodium, 52 g carbo., 4 g fiber, 6 g pro. **Daily Values:** 12% vit. A, 27% vit. C, 6% calcium, 9% iron.

Blueberry-Cardamom Syrup

Make this gently spiced sauce up to one week in advance and store it in the refrigerator to drizzle it on ice cream, pancakes, or waffles.

Prep: 15 minutes **Cool:** 1 hour

1   cup fresh blueberries
½   cup water
¼   cup sugar
2   tsp. lime juice or lemon juice
¼   tsp. ground cardamom

EDITOR'S TIP

Big on Blueberries

Two-thirds of a cup of blueberries yields the antioxidant capacity of 1,773 IU of vitamin E (60 times the recommended daily allowance) and 1,270 mg of vitamin C (21 times the recommended daily allowance).

"The antioxidant anthocyanin not only gives blueberries color, but also discourages blood clots, thus warding off heart attacks," says May Ann Lila Smith, Ph.D., professor of in vitro technology at the University of Illinois. Her studies indicate blueberries may strengthen tiny blood vessels in the back of the eye, improving night vision and slowing macular degeneration. In addition, blueberries contain compounds that may hold off age-related memory loss and also may prevent urinary tract infections.

According to a recent *Journal of Neuroscience* concerning a trial at Boston's Tufts University, aged rats fed blueberries for two months were faster, more coordinated, and better able to run mazes.

1 In a small saucepan combine blueberries, water, sugar, lime or lemon juice, and cardamom. Bring to boiling, stirring to dissolve sugar; reduce heat. Simmer the mixture, uncovered, about 10 minutes or until slightly thickened, stirring occasionally. Remove from heat; cool slightly. Strain the syrup through a fine-mesh sieve. Discard the solids.

2 Cool syrup completely. Cover and refrigerate for up to 1 week. Makes ¾ cup.

Nutrition Facts per 1 Tbsp. serving: 22 cal., 0 g total fat, 0 mg chol., 1 mg sodium, 6 g carbo., 0 g fiber, 0 g pro. **Daily Values:** 3% vit. A.

june

IN THIS CHAPTER

30-minute recipes indicated in COLOR.
Low-fat and no-fat recipes indicated
with a ♥.
Photographs indicated in italics.
*Bonus recipe

Flatbread Wedges And Ginger Dip

Tandoori naan (flatbread) is a traditional Indian bread. It is sold in large supermarkets and in markets that specialize in Indian foods.

Prep: 10 minutes **Bake:** 18 minutes

- 1 recipe Ginger Dip (see right)
  Nonstick cooking spray
- 4 loaves tandoori naan or other flatbread (8-inch rounds or 10×5-inch ovals)
- 2 Tbsp. margarine or butter, melted
- 1 egg yolk
- 2 tsp. water
- ¼ cup shelled unsalted sunflower seeds
- 1 Tbsp. white or black sesame seeds
- 1 Tbsp. poppy seeds
- 1 tsp. ground coriander
- ½ tsp. salt
- ½ tsp. coarsely ground black pepper
- ⅛ to ¼ tsp. ground red pepper

1 Prepare Ginger Dip; cover and chill. Preheat oven to 350°F. Lightly coat two baking sheets with nonstick cooking spray.

2 Cut each flatbread round into eight wedges, or cut ovals into 1½-inch-wide strips. Arrange bread wedges or strips on prepared baking sheets. Brush bread wedges with the melted margarine or butter.

3 In a small bowl stir together egg yolk and water; set aside. In another small bowl combine sunflower

Sprinkle seeds evenly, covering the entire surface of the bread.

seeds, sesame seeds, poppy seeds, ground coriander, salt, black pepper, and ground red pepper.

4 Brush bread wedges with egg yolk mixture; sprinkle seed mixture (see photo, above) on bread and gently press the seeds into the bread with your fingers.

5 Bake for 18 to 20 minutes or until crisp and golden brown. Cool. Serve wedges with Ginger Dip. Makes 16 servings.

Ginger Dip

In a medium bowl stir together one 8-ounce carton plain low-fat yogurt; ½ cup dairy sour cream; 2 tablespoons grated fresh ginger; 2 teaspoons coriander seed, slightly crushed; and ¼ teaspoon salt. Mix until well combined. Cover and chill until serving time. Add 1½ cups coarsely chopped red radishes to the dip just before serving. Makes 2¼ cups.

Nutrition Facts per serving: 73 cal., 5 g total fat (2 g sat. fat), 21 mg chol., 158 mg sodium, 5 g carbo., 1 g fiber, 2 g pro. **Daily Values:** 3% vit. A, 5% vit. C, 6% calcium, 15% iron.

Cheese-Filled Squash Boats

The cheese filling, which is stiff before it is baked, will soften in the oven.

Prep: 25 minutes **Bake:** 25 minutes

- 4 medium yellow summer squash or zucchini
- ½ of an 8-oz. pkg. reduced-fat cream cheese (Neufchâtel), softened
- ⅓ cup crumbled blue cheese (about 1½ oz.)
- ⅓ cup shredded carrot
- ¼ cup thinly sliced green onions
- ¼ cup dairy sour cream
- 3 Tbsp. fine dry bread crumbs
- ⅛ tsp. salt
- ⅛ tsp. pepper
- ¼ cup chopped walnuts

1 Preheat oven to 400°F. Grease a 3-quart rectangular baking dish. Rinse squash; cut in half lengthwise. Remove seeds with a spoon, leaving a ¼-inch shell; discard seeds. Place squash halves, cut side down, in prepared dish. Bake, uncovered, 10 minutes. Turn cut side up.

2 Meanwhile, stir together the cream cheese, blue cheese, shredded carrot, green onion, sour cream, bread crumbs, salt, and pepper.

3 Spoon mixture evenly into squash shells. Bake, uncovered, for 10 minutes. Sprinkle walnuts over filling in each squash shell. Bake about 5 minutes more or until squash is tender and filling is heated through. Makes 8 side-dish servings.

Nutrition Facts per serving: 113 cal., 9 g total fat (4 g sat. fat), 17 mg chol., 224 mg sodium, 5 g carbo., 1 g fiber, 4 g pro. **Daily Values:** 38% vit. A, 13% vit. C, 7% calcium, 4% iron.

Smoky Rice and Bean Bake

One little chipotle pepper contributes subtle smoky flavor to this Mexican-style casserole. Look for chipotle peppers at the supermarket in the Mexican foods section.

Prep: 20 minutes **Bake:** 20 minutes

- ¾ cup uncooked long grain rice
- 3 medium zucchini and/or yellow summer squash, sliced (about 3½ cups)
- ½ of a 15½-oz. can (¾ cup) small red or pinto beans, rinsed and drained
- ¾ cup bottled picante sauce or salsa
- 1 canned chipotle pepper in adobo sauce, drained and finely chopped
- 2 cloves garlic, minced
- 1 cup Mexican-blend shredded cheese (4 oz.)

1 Preheat oven to 350°F. In a medium saucepan combine the uncooked rice, 1½ cups water, and ⅛ teaspoon salt. Bring to boiling; reduce heat. Simmer, covered, for 18 to 20 minutes or until rice is tender and liquid is absorbed.

2 Meanwhile, in a large bowl combine sliced squash, beans, picante sauce, chipotle pepper, and garlic. Stir in cooked rice. Transfer mixture to a 2-quart rectangular baking dish. Sprinkle with cheese. Bake, uncovered, about 20 minutes or until heated through. Makes 6 to 8 side-dish servings.

Nutrition Facts per serving: 210 cal., 7 g total fat (3 g sat. fat), 17 mg chol., 601 mg sodium, 29 g carbo., 3 g fiber, 9 g pro. **Daily Values:** 7% vit. A, 12% vit. C, 15% calcium, 11% iron.

LOW FAT

Zucchini Stuffed With Polenta

Prep: 25 minutes **Bake:** 20 minutes

- 4 large zucchini (about 2 lb. total) Nonstick cooking spray
- 1 egg, beaten
- ½ of a 16-oz. tube refrigerated cooked plain polenta, crumbled
- ½ cup grated Parmesan cheese
- ⅓ cup finely chopped red or green sweet pepper
- 1 Tbsp. butter, softened
- 1 tsp. dried marjoram, crushed
- 1 tsp. bottled minced roasted garlic
- 2 Tbsp. grated Parmesan cheese

1 Preheat oven to 400°F. Rinse zucchini and trim ends. Cut in half lengthwise. Remove seeds with a spoon; discard seeds. Remove pulp with a spoon, leaving a ¼-inch shell. Chop zucchini pulp. Measure 1½ cups; set aside. Place zucchini halves, cut side up, in a shallow baking pan. Lightly coat insides of shells with nonstick cooking spray; set aside.

2 In a medium bowl combine the egg, polenta, chopped zucchini pulp, the ½ cup Parmesan cheese, sweet pepper, butter, marjoram, garlic, and a dash black pepper. Spoon into the zucchini halves. Sprinkle with the 2 tablespoons Parmesan cheese.

3 Bake, uncovered, for 20 to 25 minutes or until zucchini is tender. Makes 8 servings.

Nutrition Facts per serving: 97 cal., 5 g total fat (3 g sat. fat), 37 mg chol., 276 mg sodium, 9 g carbo., 2 g fiber, 6 g pro. **Daily Values:** 15% vit. A, 28% vit. C, 12% calcium, 3% iron.

30 MINUTE

Baby Squash in Tomato Cream

Start to finish: 15 minutes

- ½ cup water
- 1½ lb. assorted baby squash, such as baby zucchini, baby sunburst, and/or pattypan squash (about 6 cups)
- ⅓ cup tomato sauce
- ¼ cup whipping cream
- ½ of a jalapeño pepper, seeded if desired, and finely chopped*
- ½ tsp. finely shredded lime peel
- ⅛ tsp. ground cumin
- 2 Tbsp. snipped fresh cilantro

1 In a large skillet bring the water to boiling; add squash. Cook, covered, for 5 to 7 minutes or until squash is crisp-tender. Drain well. Cover to keep warm; set aside.

2 Meanwhile, in a small saucepan combine the tomato sauce, whipping cream, jalapeño pepper, lime peel, and cumin. Cook and stir over medium heat until boiling. Cook, stirring occasionally, about 3 minutes more or until thickened.

3 To serve, divide the sauce evenly among four plates. Top with squash and sprinkle with cilantro. Serve immediately. Makes 4 servings.

*Note: Hot peppers contain oils that can burn eyes, lips, and sensitive skin. Wear gloves while preparing hot peppers and wash your hands thoroughly afterward.

Nutrition Facts per serving: 85 cal., 6 g total fat (4 g sat. fat), 21 mg chol., 134 mg sodium, 7 g carbo., 2 g fiber, 3 g pro. **Daily Values:** 22% vit. A, 28% vit. C, 4% calcium, 5% iron.

- ■ **Grilled lamb chops or pork chops**
- ■ **Rice pilaf**
- ■ **Apple-Mint Beets (see below)**
- ■ **Multigrain dinner rolls with butter**
- ■ **Red wine**

NO FAT

Apple-Mint Beets

Behind the unassuming appearance of beets dwell enchanting velvety texture and luscious sweetness. Boil, roast, or turn beets into soup—their succulence will shine through.

Prep: 10 minutes **Cook:** 26 minutes

- 4 medium beets (about 12 oz.)
- ½ cup apple cider or apple juice
- 2 to 3 tsp. snipped fresh mint leaves

1 Wash beets well. Cut off and discard root tails and all except 1 inch of stems. Do not peel. Cook the beets, covered, in lightly salted boiling water for 20 minutes. Drain. Let cool until easy to handle.

2 Slip skins off beets under running water. Carefully slice each beet crosswise into ¼-inch-thick slices, removing and discarding remaining stem ends.

3 In a medium saucepan combine beet slices, apple cider or juice, and half of the mint. Bring mixture to boiling over medium heat; reduce heat. Cover and simmer for 6 to 8 minutes or until just tender.

Sprinkle with the remaining mint. Serve immediately. Makes 4 to 6 servings.

Nutrition Facts per serving: 61 cal., 0 g total fat, 0 mg chol., 84 mg sodium, 11 g carbo., 3 g fiber, 2 g pro. **Daily Values:** 1% vit. A, 7% vit. C, 2% calcium, 5% iron.

Orange-Beet Salad

In addition to a wonderful orange flavor, this salad gets a boost from toasted walnuts and walnut oil. Walnut oil is golden in color with a pronounced nut flavor and rich aroma. Look for it at specialty foods stores and large supermarkets.

Prep: 15 minutes **Cook:** 40 minutes

- 3 medium beets (about 9 oz.)
- 3 Tbsp. walnut oil or salad oil
- 1 tsp. shredded orange peel
- 2 Tbsp. orange juice
- 1 Tbsp. white wine vinegar or white vinegar
- 2 Tbsp. broken walnuts, toasted
- 3 Tbsp. crumbled feta cheese
- ¼ tsp. coarsely ground pepper

1 Wash beets well. Cut off and discard root tails and all except 1 inch of stems. Do not peel. Cook, covered, in lightly salted boiling water for 40 to 50 minutes or until just tender. Drain. Let cool until easy to handle.

2 Slip skins off beets under running water. Carefully slice each beet into ¼-inch-thick slices, removing and discarding remaining stem ends.

3 Meanwhile, for dressing, in a screw-top jar combine walnut oil or salad oil, orange peel, orange juice, and vinegar. Cover and shake well.

4 In a medium mixing bowl gently toss the beet slices with the dressing. Cover and chill for 2 to 24 hours.

5 To serve, let mixture come to room temperature. Gently stir walnuts into beets. Sprinkle with feta cheese and pepper. Serve with a slotted spoon. Makes 4 servings.

Nutrition Facts per serving: 171 cal., 14 g total fat (2 g sat. fat), 5 mg chol., 122 mg sodium, 10 g carbo., 2 g fiber, 3 g pro. **Daily Values:** 1% vit. A, 12% vit. C, 5% calcium, 5% iron.

Mustard and Curry Potato Salad

Two treasured flavors from India—mustard and curry powder—season this fragrant potato salad. (See the photograph on page 120.)

Prep: 30 minutes **Cook:** 13 minutes

- 2 lb. tiny new potatoes, halved (about 24 potatoes)
- 2 cups coarsely shredded cabbage
- ⅓ cup olive oil
- 1 Tbsp. curry powder
- 3 Tbsp. vinegar
- 1 Tbsp. coarse-grain brown mustard
- 1 tsp. salt
- ½ tsp. coarsely ground black pepper
- ¾ cup sliced celery

1 In a Dutch oven cook potatoes, covered, in a small amount of boiling salted water for 12 to 15 minutes or until just tender; add cabbage the last 1 to 2 minutes of cooking time. Drain; cool.

2 For dressing, in a medium skillet heat the olive oil over medium heat. Stir in curry powder. Cook and stir for 1 minute. Carefully stir in the vinegar, mustard, salt, and black pepper until combined. Remove from heat; cool slightly.

3 In a large bowl combine cooked potato mixture and celery. Pour dressing over potato mixture; toss gently to coat. Makes 8 to 10 servings.

Nutrition Facts per serving: 133 cal., 9 g total fat (1 g sat. fat), 0 mg chol., 588 mg sodium, 12 g carbo., 2 g fiber, 1 g pro. Daily Values: 1% vit. A, 22% vit. C, 3% calcium, 4% iron.

LOW FAT

Go Anywhere Garlic Green Beans

Toast slices of fresh coconut to combine with garlic and green beans for a tropical vegetable dish.

Prep: 35 minutes **Bake:** 10 minutes
Cook: 9 minutes

- 1 fresh coconut or ½ cup unsweetened coconut chips
- 1 Tbsp. olive oil, divided
- 2 cloves garlic, sliced
- 1 lb. green beans, trimmed
- 1 Tbsp. soy sauce

1 If using fresh coconut, choose a coconut full of liquid and heavy for its size. Preheat oven to 375°F. Using a hammer and nail, punch three holes through the coconut eyes and invert the coconut over a glass to drain (the coconut water or juice should smell fresh, not fermented).

2 Place coconut in a shallow baking pan. Bake for 10 minutes. Wrap coconut in a towel or foil and pound it to crack the shell and to separate flesh from shell. Remove brown portions with a vegetable peeler. Peel the

Cut coconut strips from large sections of fresh coconut, drawing a peeler blade toward you.

coconut into 2- to 3-inch-long strips (see photo, above). Measure enough for ½ cup. (Tightly wrap the remaining coconut and store it in the refrigerator for up to 5 days.)

3 In a large skillet or wok with a lid heat 1½ teaspoons of the olive oil over medium-high heat. Cook and stir the coconut for 2 to 3 minutes or until slightly brown. Add the garlic. Cook 30 seconds more. Remove mixture from skillet; set aside.

4 Add remaining olive oil to the skillet or wok. Add green beans. Cook and stir for 1 minute. Carefully add ⅓ cup water. Bring to boiling; reduce heat. Cover and simmer for 5 to 7 minutes. Stir in the soy sauce and the reserved coconut mixture. Cook and stir until heated through. Makes 6 servings.

Nutrition Facts per serving: 76 cal., 5 g total fat (3 g sat. fat), 0 mg chol., 156 mg sodium, 7 g carbo., 2 g fiber, 2 g pro. Daily Values: 7% vit. A, 1% vit. C, 3% calcium, 6% iron.

Marinated Carrots With Pistachios

Pound a few cardamom seeds, using a mortar and pestle, to add magic to this carrot side dish. (See the photograph on page 120.)

Prep: 10 minutes **Cook:** 7 minutes
Chill: 4 hours

- 1¼ lb. small whole carrots with tops or 1 lb. carrots
- 2 Tbsp. lemon juice
- ⅛ tsp. crushed cardamom seeds or ground cardamom
- 1 Tbsp. olive oil
- ¼ cup coarsely chopped, shelled unsalted pistachios

1 Peel the carrots. If present, trim all except ½ to 1 inch of the green stems from small, whole carrots. Cut long carrots in half lengthwise; halve crosswise.

2 Place a steamer basket in a large saucepan. Add water to just below the basket. Bring to boiling. Add carrots to basket. Cover and steam for 7 to 9 minutes or until tender.

3 In a small bowl stir together the lemon juice, cardamom, ¼ teaspoon salt, and ¼ teaspoon pepper. Whisk in the olive oil. Transfer to a shallow bowl. Add the carrots; toss to coat. Cover and chill for 4 to 24 hours.

4 To serve, place carrots in a serving bowl. Sprinkle with pistachios. Makes 4 to 6 servings.

Nutrition Facts per serving: 133 cal., 8 g total fat (1 g sat. fat), 0 mg chol., 188 mg sodium, 15 g carbo., 1 g fiber, 3 g pro. Daily Values: 1% vit. A, 25% vit. C, 4% calcium, 2% iron.

Creating Croutons

Make flavorful croutons from bread that's too old for sandwiches and too good to feed to the birds.

Perched on a bounty of summer's sweetest greens (or a sea of chicken and noodles in the winter), garlicky, crunchy bread chunks capitalize on the kitchen dilemma of making the best use of leftover bread.

Go slow when making croutons. Use medium-low heat so you won't have to admit "I looked away for a minute, and when I turned back they were burned."

Stir gently, as well. Wait to turn the croutons until they reach the brownness and crispness you want.

Choose from herb blends that complement the recipes you prepare. Freely substitute your favorite combinations or use a single preferred herb (when you use rosemary, reduce the amount to about ½ teaspoon).

Helpful tips:

1. Cut or tear bread into medium-size cubes—just about a bite or two big. If possible, use sturdy French or Italian bread because they hold together better than sandwich slices.

2. Spice merchants continually concoct new combinations of herbs, flavorings, and spices. Sprinkle a teaspoon or two on croutons to taste-test the flavors.

3. Drizzle the melted herb butter from the skillet over the bread cubes. Toss the cubes with a large spoon to distribute the coating.

4. Stir and turn the bread cubes as they brown on each side. Most of them will brown; a few will remain only slightly brown.

Real Homemade Croutons

Compare the fresh flavor and crunch of homemade croutons to store-bought versions. You'll be willing to take the time to make them yourself.

Prep: 10 minutes **Cook:** 7 minutes

- 2 cups 1- to 1½-inch cubes French or Italian bread (about 2 oz.)
- 1 Tbsp. cooking oil
- 1 Tbsp. margarine or butter
- 2 large cloves garlic, minced
- 1 tsp. dried seasoning, crushed (such as Italian herbs, Greek seasoning, herbes de Provence, bouquet garni seasoning, or desired spice blend)

1 Place bread cubes in a bowl. In a large skillet heat oil and margarine or butter over medium-low heat. Add garlic and dried seasoning. Cook and stir 30 seconds. Drizzle over bread cubes, tossing to coat well.

2 Pour cubes into skillet. Cook, stirring occasionally, over medium-low heat for 6 to 8 minutes or until cubes are lightly brown and crisp. Remove from pan. Drain on paper towels. Store tightly covered at room temperature for up to 1 week. Makes about 2 cups.

Nutrition Facts per 2-tablespoon serving: 24 cal., 2 g total fat (0 g sat. fat), 0 mg chol., 30 mg sodium, 2 g carbo., 0 g fiber, 0 g pro. **Daily Values:** 1% vit. A, 1% iron.

California Club Sandwich

Use the leftover cream cheese to spread on toasted bagels.

Start to finish: 25 minutes

- 1 8-oz. tub cream cheese
- 2 Tbsp. honey mustard
- 1 6½-oz. jar marinated artichoke hearts, drained and chopped
- ¼ cup chopped pitted ripe olives, pitted green olives, or pitted Greek black olives
- 1 16-oz. loaf crusty French bread
- 2 cups loosely packed fresh spinach leaves, stems removed
- 2 cups sliced fresh mushrooms
- 1 small red onion, thinly sliced
- 8 oz. thinly sliced cooked turkey breast
- 4 slices bacon, crisp-cooked, drained, and crumbled
- ¼ cup dry roasted and salted shelled sunflower seeds

1 In a small bowl stir together cream cheese and honey mustard. Gently stir in chopped artichokes and olives; set aside.

2 Cut bread loaf in half lengthwise. Hollow out bottom half of bread loaf, leaving a ½-inch shell (reserve bread crumbs for another use). Spread hollowed bottom half of bread with ⅔ cup of the cream cheese mixture. Layer spinach leaves, sliced mushrooms, sliced red onion, and sliced turkey into bottom half of loaf. Sprinkle with crumbled bacon and sunflower seeds.

3 Spread another ⅔ cup cream cheese mixture onto cut side of top half of bread. Reserve remaining cream cheese mixture for another use. Place top half of bread, cream cheese mixture side down, over the bottom half. Cut into 4 serving-size pieces.

To Make Ahead:

Prepare sandwich. Wrap in clear plastic wrap. Chill in the refrigerator for up to 4 hours. To tote, place the wrapped sandwich in an insulated cooler with an ice pack.

Nutrition Facts per serving: 665 cal., 34 g total fat (16 g sat. fat), 85 mg chol., 1,941 mg sodium, 62 g carbo., 5 g fiber, 31 g pro. Daily Values: 32% vit. A, 25% vit. C, 15% calcium, 23% iron.

Zucchini Bread Pudding

Kay Krause
Sioux Falls, South Dakota
$400—Summer Squash Fix-Ups

Prep: 25 minutes **Bake:** 35 minutes
Stand: 10 minutes

- 2 medium zucchini, sliced ¼ inch thick
- ½ cup frozen whole kernel corn
- 2 Tbsp. olive oil
- ½ cup chopped roasted red sweet peppers
- 6 cloves garlic, minced
- 1 Tbsp. snipped fresh basil or 1 tsp. dried basil, crushed
- 1 Tbsp. snipped fresh parsley or 1 tsp. dried parsley
- 1 Tbsp. snipped fresh sage or 1 tsp. dried sage, crushed
- 5 cups 1-inch sourdough or Italian bread cubes (about 13 oz.)
- 1 cup shredded Swiss cheese, shredded (4 oz.)
- 3 Tbsp. chopped toasted pecans
- 5 eggs, slightly beaten
- 2 cups half-and-half or light cream
- 1 tsp. salt
- ¼ tsp. black pepper

1 Preheat oven to 350°F. Grease a 2-quart rectangular or oval baking dish; set aside.

2 In a large skillet cook the zucchini and corn in hot oil for 3 minutes. Stir in roasted sweet peppers, garlic, basil, parsley, and sage. Cook and stir about 2 minutes more or until zucchini is tender. Remove from heat. Stir in bread cubes.

3 Place half of the mixture in the prepared dish. Sprinkle with half of the cheese. Repeat layers. Sprinkle with nuts. In a medium mixing bowl whisk together eggs, half-and-half, salt, and black pepper. Carefully pour over bread mixture.

4 Bake, uncovered, for about 35 minutes or until a knife inserted near the center comes out clean. Let stand 10 minutes before serving. Makes 6 main-dish servings.

To Make Ahead:

Layer mixture. Cover and refrigerate for up to 24 hours. Preheat oven to 350°F. Bake, uncovered, about 45 minutes or until a knife inserted near the center comes out clean. Let stand for 10 minutes.

Nutrition Facts per serving: 502 cal., 26 g total fat (11 g sat. fat), 224 mg chol., 886 mg sodium, 47 g carbo., 1 g fiber, 22 g pro. Daily Values: 17% vit. A, 90% vit. C, 30% calcium, 15% iron.

Zucchini with Shrimp

Randolph C. Bush
Bridgeport, Connecticut
$200—Summer Squash Fix-Ups

Start to finish: 30 minutes

- 8 oz. fresh or frozen peeled, deveined medium shrimp (12 oz. in shells)
- 5 zucchini (about 1¼ lb.)
- 8 oz. fresh asparagus spears
- 1 fresh jalapeño pepper, seeded and finely chopped*
- 1 Tbsp. grated fresh ginger
- 2 cloves garlic, minced
- 2 Tbsp. cooking oil
- 2 Tbsp. snipped fresh cilantro
- 1 Tbsp. toasted sesame seeds
- 2 tsp. toasted sesame oil

1 Thaw shrimp, if frozen. Halve each zucchini lengthwise. Place each half, cut side down, on a board and cut into long, thin strips. Set aside. Snap off and discard woody bases from asparagus. Cut asparagus diagonally into 1-inch pieces.

2 Place asparagus in a steamer basket over gently boiling water. Cover and steam 2 minutes; add zucchini and steam 2 to 3 minutes more or until vegetables are just crisp-tender (don't overcook). Drain well; keep warm.

3 Meanwhile, in a large skillet cook jalapeño, ginger, and garlic in cooking oil over medium-high heat for 30 seconds. Add shrimp. Cook over medium-high heat for 2 to 3 minutes or until shrimp turn pink, stirring often. Stir in cilantro, sesame seeds, sesame oil, and ¼ teaspoon each salt and black pepper. Add zucchini and asparagus to skillet; toss gently to

coat. Transfer to a serving platter. If desired, sprinkle with additional cilantro and/or sesame seeds. Makes 4 servings.

*Note: Hot peppers contain oils that can burn eyes, lips, and sensitive skin. Wear gloves while preparing hot peppers and wash your hands thoroughly afterward.

Nutrition Facts per serving: 197 cal., 12 g total fat (2 g sat. fat), 86 mg chol., 239 mg sodium, 8 g carbo., 1 g fiber, 17 g pro. Daily Values: 7% vit. A, 112% vit. C, 9% calcium, 12% iron.

BBQ Shrimp on Pineapple Planks

(See the photograph on page 117.)

Prep: 40 minutes **Marinate:** 30 minutes
Grill: 6 minutes

- 8 jumbo or 24 large fresh or frozen shrimp (about 1 lb.)
- 1 medium fresh pineapple, crown removed and peeled
- 3 Tbsp. margarine or butter, melted
- ¼ cup bottled barbecue sauce
- 1 to 2 Tbsp. chopped canned chipotle peppers in adobo sauce
- 2 cloves garlic, minced
- ½ cup chopped, seeded cucumber
- ½ cup chopped, peeled jicama
- 1 Tbsp. lime or lemon juice
- ¼ cup snipped fresh cilantro

1 Soak eight 6- to 8-inch wooden skewers in enough water to cover for 30 minutes; drain. Thaw shrimp, if frozen.

2 Cut pineapple lengthwise into ½-inch-thick slices. Chop one of the slices to measure ½ cup; set aside

for relish. Halve each pineapple slice crosswise to equal eight pineapple planks. Using one tablespoon of the melted margarine or butter, brush the pineapple planks on both sides; set aside.

3 Peel fresh shrimp, if using, leaving tail intact, if desired. Devein shrimp. In a medium mixing bowl combine barbecue sauce, chipotle peppers, garlic, and the remaining 2 tablespoons melted margarine or butter. Stir in shrimp. Cover and let stand at room temperature for 30 minutes, stirring occasionally. Remove shrimp; discard marinade. Thread one jumbo or three large shrimp onto each skewer; set aside.

4 For relish, combine the reserved ½ cup chopped pineapple, the chopped cucumber, jicama, lime or lemon juice, and ¼ teaspoon salt. Cover and set aside until serving time.

5 Grill shrimp kabobs and pineapple planks on the rack of an uncovered grill directly over medium coals until shrimp are opaque and pineapple is heated through, turning once halfway through grilling time. (Allow 10 to 12 minutes for jumbo shrimp, 6 to 10 minutes for large shrimp, and 6 to 8 minutes for pineapple planks.) If desired, brush each shrimp kabob with additional bottled barbecue sauce during the last 1 minute of grilling.

6 To serve, stir snipped cilantro into the relish mixture. Place pineapple planks onto a serving platter. Spoon some of the relish over the pineapple planks; top each with a shrimp skewer. Makes 8 servings.

Nutrition Facts per serving: 135 cal., 6 g total fat (3 g sat. fat), 98 mg chol., 288 mg sodium, 8 g carbo., 1 g fiber, 12 g pro. Daily Values: 10% vit. A, 19% vit. C, 4% calcium, 9% iron.

Above: BBQ Shrimp on Pineapple Planks
(page 116)
Left: Beef Steak with Avocado Sauce (page 126)

Page 118: Spring Chicken with Garlic Galore (page 97)
Top left: On-the-Seedy-Side Breadsticks (page 91)
Top right: Confetti Carrot Cake (page 106)
Left: Salmon with Apricot Sauce (page 96)
Above: Mounds-of-Mushrooms Pizza (page 91)

Left: Triple-Dipster Strawberries (page 134)
Below left: Mustard and Curry Potato Salad (page 112)
Below right: Marinated Carrots with Pistachios (page 113)
Page 121: Pulled Chicken Sandwiches (page 127)

Page 122: Smoky Almond Pork Tenderloin (page 99)
Left: Caramelized Onion Soup (page 95)
Below: Blueberries with Shortcake Drops (page 108)
Below left: Fresh Spinach Pasta Toss (page 94)
Below right: Scrumptious Soybeans (page 94)

Right: Melon and Salami on Rye (page 125)
Below: Pork with Mango, Mint, and Basil (page 125)

Pork with Mango, Mint, and Basil

Enhance the sweet-sour flavor of tropical tamarind with honey and ginger to make a marinade and sauce for this charcoal-grilled tenderloin. Tamarind pulp, which usually contains seeds, is inexpensive and available in Asian and Latin specialty foods stores. (See the photograph on page 124.)

Prep: 30 minutes **Marinate:** 1 hour
Grill: 20 minutes **Stand:** 10 minutes

- ⅓ cup tamarind pulp (about 2 oz.)
- 1 cup boiling water
- 2 Tbsp. honey
- 1 Tbsp. minced or grated fresh ginger
- ¼ tsp. salt
- 2 12-oz. whole pork tenderloins
- 2 firm ripe mangoes, seeded, peeled, and cut into 1- to 1½-inch slices or cubes
- ¼ cup finely shredded fresh basil
- ¼ cup finely shredded fresh mint
  Coarsely cracked black pepper

1 For marinade, separate the tamarind pulp into small pieces. In a medium bowl combine pulp, boiling water, and honey, stirring and mashing until cool. Strain through a medium sieve, forcing pulp through and scraping bottom of sieve. Discard seeds. Stir in ginger and salt. Remove and reserve ½ cup of the marinade; cover and chill. Pour remaining tamarind mixture into a large self-sealing plastic bag set in a bowl.

2 Prick tenderloins all over, about 30 times, with a knife tip. Place pork in the bag; seal and marinate in the refrigerator for 1 to 3 hours.

3 Drain meat; discard marinade. Place pork on grill rack directly over medium coals. Grill for 20 to 30 minutes or until meat thermometer inserted in center registers 160°F, turning frequently to brown evenly. Remove pork from heat to a cutting board; cover with foil and let rest 10 to 15 minutes before slicing.

4 To serve, cut tenderloin across the grain into ½-inch-thick slices. Arrange pork on a platter with mango. Drizzle reserved tamarind sauce over the pork. Sprinkle with basil, mint, and cracked black pepper. Makes 6 servings.

Nutrition Facts per serving: 216 cal., 3 g total fat (1 g sat. fat), 73 mg chol., 147 mg sodium, 22 g carbo., 2 g fiber, 24 g pro. **Daily Values:** 55% vit. A, 38% vit. C, 3% calcium, 13% iron.

Melon and Salami On Rye

Debbie Spenda
Temecula, California
$400—Take-Along Sandwiches
(See the photograph on page 124.)

Start to finish: 20 minutes

- 4 slices rye bread and/or pumpernickel bread
- 2 tsp. Dijon-style mustard
- 2 to 3 oz. thinly sliced Jarlsberg cheese

PICNIC LUNCH

- Melon and Salami on Rye (see below)
- Home-style potato chips
- Mixed fresh berries
- Iced tea or lemonade
- Sugar or ginger cookies

- 2 oz. thinly sliced prosciutto
- 4 to 8 thin slices honeydew melon, peeled
- 2 tsp. light dairy sour cream
- 2 oz. thinly sliced salami
- 2 to 3 oz. thinly sliced Gouda cheese
- 2 romaine lettuce leaves, ribs removed (optional)

1 Lightly spread one side of the bread slices with mustard. On two of the bread slices layer the Jarlsberg cheese, prosciutto, and melon on the mustard. Spread a thin layer of sour cream over the melon slices. Add salami, Gouda, and, if desired, romaine. Top with remaining two bread slices, mustard side down. Makes 2 sandwiches.

To Make Ahead:

Wrap prepared sandwiches in clear plastic wrap. Chill in the refrigerator for 1 to 6 hours. To tote, place the wrapped sandwiches in an insulated cooler with an ice pack.

Nutrition Facts per sandwich: 627 cal., 30 g total fat (14 g sat. fat), 96 mg chol., 2,137 mg sodium, 56 g carbo., 5 g fiber, 36 g pro. **Daily Values:** 18% vit. A, 108% vit. C, 52% calcium, 17% iron.

The Right Avocado

For neat avocado cubes or slices, choose firm, not hard, fruits that give to gentle pressure when pressed between a thumb and finger. If you plan to mash avocado for guacamole, choose fruits that feel soft to your fingers. Very firm avocados will ripen in three to four days stored at room temperature. Speed ripening by placing avocados in a brown paper bag or in a fruit ripening bowl. Place them in the refrigerator after they ripen, and use them within a few days.

---

30 MINUTE

Decked-Out Deli Sandwiches

Start to finish: 20 minutes

- ¼ cup dairy sour cream
- 2 tsp. prepared horseradish
- 8 slices marble rye bread
- ½ cup drained jarred roasted red sweet peppers, chopped
- ¼ cup sliced green onions
- 1 cup lightly packed fresh basil leaves
- 2 Roma tomatoes, thinly sliced
- 4 oz. thinly sliced pastrami or cooked roast beef
- 4 oz. thinly sliced provolone or mozzarella cheese

1 In a small bowl stir together sour cream and horseradish. Spread one side of four bread slices with the horseradish mixture; sprinkle with chopped roasted red peppers and sliced onions. Top each with a layer of basil leaves, tomato slices, pastrami or roast beef, and provolone or mozzarella cheese. Top with remaining bread slices. To serve, cut each sandwich in half diagonally. Makes 4 sandwiches.

To Make Ahead:

Wrap prepared sandwiches in clear plastic wrap. Chill in the refrigerator for up to 2 hours. To tote, place the wrapped sandwiches in an insulated cooler with an ice pack.

Nutrition Facts per sandwich: 390 cal., 20 g total fat (10 g sat. fat), 51 mg chol., 952 mg sodium, 34 g carbo., 4 g fiber, 18 g pro. **Daily Values:** 19% vit. A, 100% vit. C, 30% calcium, 18% iron.

Beef Steak with Avocado Sauce

Latin America inspired the chili rub for steak and creamy gravy made from avocado and tomatillos. (See the photograph on page 117.)

Prep: 25 minutes **Stand:** 30 minutes
Grill: 14 minutes

- 2 12-oz. beef ribeye steaks or top loin steaks, cut 1¼ to 1½ inches thick
- 1 Tbsp. brown sugar
- 1 tsp. chili powder
- ½ tsp. garlic salt
- ½ tsp. black pepper
- 6 medium fresh tomatillos, husked and quartered (8 oz.)
- ¼ cup water
- 2 oz. cream cheese
- 1 avocado, halved, seeded, peeled, and cut up
- ¼ cup sliced green onions
- ½ tsp. salt
- 8 to 12 green onions, trimmed to 6-inch lengths
- 4 to 6 jalapeño peppers* Cooking oil
- 1 large tomato, chopped

1 Trim fat from around the edges of beef ribeye steaks. In a small bowl combine the brown sugar, chili powder, garlic salt, and black pepper. Pat onto both sides of the steaks. Let the steaks stand at room temperature for 30 minutes.

2 Meanwhile, for sauce, in a small saucepan combine the quartered tomatillos and water. Bring to boiling; reduce heat. Cover and simmer for 5 to 7 minutes or until soft. Stir the cream cheese into tomatillo mixture until melted; cool mixture slightly.

3 In a food processor bowl or blender container combine the tomatillo mixture, the avocado, the sliced green onions, and salt. Cover and process or blend until the sauce mixture is smooth. Transfer sauce to a serving bowl.

4 Grill steaks on the rack of an uncovered grill directly over medium coals to desired doneness, turning halfway through. (Allow 14 to 18 minutes for medium rare and 18 to 22 minutes for medium.) If desired, brush the whole green onions and jalapeños lightly with oil. Grill green onions about 5 minutes and jalapeños about 10 minutes or until soft and lightly charred, turning occasionally.

5 To serve, slice steaks. Serve with sauce and the grilled green onions and jalapeños. Sprinkle with chopped tomato. Makes 4 to 6 servings.

*Note: Hot peppers contain oils that can burn eyes, lips, and sensitive skin. Wear gloves while preparing them and thoroughly wash your hands afterward.

Nutrition Facts per serving: 415 cal., 24 g total fat (8 g sat. fat), 96 mg chol., 559 mg sodium, 11 g carbo., 4 g fiber, 40 g pro. **Daily Values:** 19% vit. A, 29% vit. C, 4% calcium, 24% iron.

Pulled Chicken Sandwiches

Pull the meat from store-bought rotisserie chicken—how simple! Bread-and-butter pickles and a spicy-sweet sauce make this sandwich a big hero. (See the photograph on page 121.)

Start to finish: 30 minutes

- 1   1¾- to 2-lb. purchased roasted chicken
- 1   Tbsp. olive oil
- 1   medium onion, cut into ¼-inch-thick slices
- ⅓   cup apple cider vinegar or white wine vinegar
- ½   cup tomato sauce
- 3 to 4 Tbsp. seeded and finely chopped fresh red and/or green hot chile peppers*
- 2   Tbsp. snipped fresh thyme
- 2   Tbsp. molasses
- 2   Tbsp. water
- ½   tsp. salt
- 4   kaiser rolls or hamburger buns, split
    Bread-and-butter pickle slices

1 Using two forks or your fingers, pull the meat from the chicken into shreds, discarding skin, if desired, and bones. If desired, use a sharp knife to chop some of the seasoned skin and add it to the chicken.

2 In a large skillet heat the olive oil over medium heat. Add onion; cook about 5 minutes or until tender, stirring occasionally to separate into rings. Add vinegar. Cook and stir 1 minute more.

3 Stir in tomato sauce, hot peppers, thyme, molasses, water, and salt. Bring to boiling. Add the chicken; toss gently to coat. Heat through. Serve on split rolls with pickle slices. Makes 6 sandwiches.

*Note: Hot peppers contain oils that can burn eyes, lips, and sensitive skin. Wear gloves while preparing them and thoroughly wash your hands afterward.

Nutrition Facts per sandwich: 445 cal., 12 g total fat (3 g sat. fat), 84 mg chol., 990 mg sodium, 51 g carbo., 2 g fiber, 33 g pro. **Daily Values:** 6% vit. A, 13% vit. C, 9% calcium, 17% iron.

Tomato-Turkey Wrap

Shelley Worden
Ann Arbor, Michigan
$200—Take-Along Sandwiches

Start to finish: 20 minutes

- 1   7-oz. container prepared hummus
- 3   9- to 10-inch tomato-basil-flavored flour tortillas or plain flour tortillas
- 8   oz. thinly sliced cooked, peppered turkey breast
- 6   romaine lettuce leaves, center ribs removed
- 3   small tomatoes, thinly sliced
- 3   thin slices red onion, separated into rings

1 Spread hummus evenly over tortillas. Layer turkey breast, romaine, tomatoes, and red onion on each tortilla; roll them into spirals. Cut each tortilla in half; secure with wooden toothpicks. Makes 6 servings.

To Make Ahead:

Wrap prepared sandwiches in clear plastic wrap. Chill in the refrigerator for up to 4 hours. To tote, place the wrapped sandwiches in an insulated cooler with an ice pack.

Nutrition Facts per serving: 221 cal., 6 g total fat (1 g sat. fat), 16 mg chol., 926 mg sodium, 29 g carbo., 3 g fiber, 14 g pro. **Daily Values:** 19% vit. A, 28% vit. C, 6% calcium, 13% iron.

Turkey, Cheese, and Chutney Sandwiches

Start to finish: 20 minutes

- 8   ½-inch-thick slices sourdough bread
- 1   5- to 6.5-oz. container semi-soft cheese with herbs or French onion
- 8   oz. thinly sliced cooked, smoked turkey breast
- 4   large leaves romaine lettuce, center ribs removed
- ⅓   cup mango chutney (snip any large pieces)

1 Spread one side of four bread slices with the semi-soft cheese. Top each with a layer of smoked turkey and romaine. Spread one side of the remaining bread slices with the chutney and place them, chutney side down, over the romaine. Makes 4 sandwiches.

To Make Ahead:

Wrap prepared sandwiches in clear plastic wrap. Chill in the refrigerator for up to 4 hours. To tote, place the wrapped sandwiches in an insulated cooler with an ice pack.

Nutrition Facts per sandwich: 404 cal., 17 g total fat (11 g sat. fat), 26 mg chol., 1,107 mg sodium, 46 g carbo., 2 g fiber, 19 g pro. **Daily Values:** 23% vit. A, 22% vit. C, 5% calcium, 11% iron.

NEW POTATOES

Although small, round red potatoes are often referred to as new potatoes, technically "new" refers to freshly dug potatoes that have not reached maturity. The fresh and tender skins of new potatoes require no peeling, and the cooked white centers are smooth and almost creamy. Delicious boiled and drizzled with a stream of butter, their freshness is equally delectable in a range of dishes—from salads to gratin-style casseroles.

Dill-Artichoke Potato Salad

Select new potatoes that are small and uniform in size so that they cook evenly.

Prep: 25 minutes **Cook:** 20 minutes
Chill: 4 hours

- 3   lb. whole tiny new potatoes
- 1   cup mayonnaise or salad dressing
- 2   Tbsp. red wine vinegar
- 2   Tbsp. Dijon-style mustard
- 1   Tbsp. lemon-pepper seasoning
- 1   Tbsp. snipped fresh dill or 2 to 3 tsp. dillweed, crushed
- 4   hard-cooked eggs, chopped
- 2   6-oz. jars marinated artichoke hearts, drained and sliced
- ¾   cup chopped onion
- 2   Tbsp. chopped dill pickle

1 Scrub potatoes with a vegetable brush under running water. In a covered Dutch oven cook unpeeled potatoes in lightly salted boiling water about 20 minutes or just until tender. Drain. Cool potatoes; cut into bite-size pieces.

2 In a large bowl stir together mayonnaise or salad dressing, vinegar, mustard, lemon-pepper seasoning, and dill. Gently fold in cooked potatoes, eggs, artichoke hearts, onion, and pickle. Cover and chill in the refrigerator for 4 to 24 hours. Stir the mixture gently before serving. Makes 16 servings.

Nutrition Facts per serving: 206 cal., 14 g total fat (2 g sat. fat), 58 mg chol., 396 mg sodium, 16 g carbo., 2 g fiber, 4 g pro. Daily Values: 2% vit. A, 28% vit. C, 2% calcium, 6% iron.

Roasted New Potato Salad

Retain nutritional value and add color to the salad by leaving the skins on the new potatoes.

Prep: 25 minutes **Roast:** 35 minutes
Chill: up to 24 hours

- 1½   lb. whole tiny new potatoes, quartered
- 3   Tbsp. olive oil or cooking oil
- 2   cloves garlic, minced
- 4   tsp. snipped fresh rosemary or 1¼ tsp. dried rosemary, crushed
- ½   tsp. salt
- ¼   tsp. pepper
- 1   9¼-oz. can chunk white tuna (water pack), drained and broken into chunks
- 1   6-oz. can pitted ripe olives
- 1   large green sweet pepper, cut into bite-size pieces
- 12   tiny pear-shaped red and/or yellow tomatoes, halved; or cherry tomatoes, halved
- 1   recipe Herb Vinaigrette (see below) or ¾ cup bottled Italian salad dressing
   Fresh rosemary sprigs (optional)

1 Preheat oven to 450°F. Place potatoes in a 13×9×2-inch pan. Combine oil, garlic, rosemary, salt, and pepper. Drizzle over potatoes; toss gently to coat. Roast, uncovered, for 35 to 40 minutes or until tender and brown on the edges, stirring every 10 minutes. Cool slightly.

2 Meanwhile, in a large bowl combine tuna, olives, green pepper, and tomatoes. Add the potatoes. Toss with the Herb Vinaigrette or bottled Italian salad dressing. Cover; chill for up to 24 hours. Serve in a lettuce-lined bowl. Garnish with fresh rosemary sprigs, if desired. Makes 8 servings.

Herb Vinaigrette
In a screw-top jar combine ⅓ cup olive oil or salad oil; ⅓ cup white wine vinegar; 1 tablespoon snipped fresh thyme or basil or 1 teaspoon

dried thyme or basil, crushed; 1 teaspoon sugar; 1 teaspoon coarse-grain brown mustard or Dijon-style mustard; ¼ teaspoon salt; and ¼ teaspoon pepper. Cover and shake well. Store in the refrigerator for up to 2 weeks. Shake before serving.

Nutrition Facts per serving: 288 cal., 17 g total fat (3 g sat. fat), 14 mg chol., 544 mg sodium, 23 g carbo., 2 g fiber, 11 g pro. Daily Values: 3% vit. A, 42% vit. C, 18% iron.

Scalloped New Potatoes

Store potatoes in a cool, dark place to prevent sprouts from developing.

Prep: 25 minutes Bake: 20 minutes

    Nonstick cooking spray
  2 lb. whole tiny new
        potatoes, sliced
  3 Tbsp. margarine or butter
  1 cup chopped onion
  3 cloves garlic, minced
  3 Tbsp. all-purpose flour
  1¼ tsp. dried rosemary, crushed
  1 tsp. dried parsley
  ½ tsp. salt
  ¼ tsp. ground black pepper
  1¾ cups milk
  6 cups torn spinach or 4 cups
        broccoli rabe, cut into
        1½-inch pieces
  1 small red sweet pepper, cut
        into thin bite-size strips
  ¾ cup shredded white
        cheddar cheese (3 oz.)
  ¼ cup fine dry bread crumbs

1 Preheat oven to 375°F. Coat a 2-quart oval or rectangular baking dish with cooking spray; set aside. In a large saucepan cook potatoes, covered, in a moderate amount of boiling salted water about 5 minutes or just until tender. Drain and transfer to an extra-large bowl.

2 For sauce, in same saucepan melt 2 tablespoons of the margarine or butter over medium heat; add onion and garlic and cook about 5 minutes or just until tender. Stir in flour, rosemary, parsley, salt, and black pepper. Stir in milk all at once. Cook and stir over medium heat until thickened and bubbly.

3 Add spinach or broccoli rabe and sweet pepper to potatoes. Toss gently to combine. Pour sauce over potato mixture. Stir gently until coated. Spoon potato mixture into prepared baking dish (dish will be very full). Set baking dish on a baking sheet.

4 Sprinkle with cheese. Melt the remaining margarine or butter. Add bread crumbs, tossing to coat. Sprinkle over cheese. Bake about 20 minutes or until edges are bubbly and crumbs are golden brown. Makes 10 to 12 servings.

Nutrition Facts per serving: 214 cal., 8 g total fat (3 g sat. fat), 12 mg chol., 274 mg sodium, 30 g carbo., 2 g fiber, 8 g pro. Daily Values: 35% vit. A, 54% vit. C, 14% calcium, 16% iron.

30 MINUTE, LOW FAT
New Potatoes Gruyère

Start to finish: 25 minutes

  2 lb. whole tiny new potatoes
  1 small onion, sliced and
        separated into rings
  1 Tbsp. all-purpose flour
  ⅛ tsp. garlic powder
  ⅛ tsp. ground white pepper
  ½ cup milk
  ¼ cup chicken broth
  ½ cup shredded Gruyère cheese
        Snipped fresh parsley (optional)

1 Peel a strip around the center of each potato with a vegetable peeler. In a large saucepan cook the potatoes and onion, covered, in a small amount of boiling salted water for 5 minutes or until potatoes are just tender. Drain.

2 Meanwhile, for cheese sauce, in a small saucepan combine the flour, garlic powder, and pepper. Stir in the milk and the broth all at once. Cook and stir over medium heat until thickened and bubbly. Cook and stir for 1 minute more. Reduce heat to low. Add the cheese; cook and stir just until cheese melts. Add the cheese sauce to the potatoes; heat through. Transfer to a serving bowl. Sprinkle with parsley, if desired.

Nutrition Facts per serving: 168 cal., 4 g total fat (2 g sat. fat), 12 mg chol., 78 mg sodium, 26 g carbo., 3 g fiber, 8 g pro. Daily Values: 3% vit. A, 35% vit. C, 13% calcium, 7% iron.

Dieting Myths

By Michelle Meyer

Achieving and maintaining a healthy weight may seem like a losing battle to the one in three American adults who diet and spend more than $30 billion a year on diet programs, products, potions, and pills. Knowing the facts dispels the myths behind unhealthy and risky weight-loss schemes.

Myth: Feast on steak; cut the carbs

Eating lots of high-fat foods—such as steaks, burgers, cheeses, and eggs—and eliminating or severely restricting carbohydrate-containing foods is too good to be true.

"You don't lose weight because you give up carbs," says Kenneth H. Cooper, M.D., founder and president of Cooper Clinic and Cooper Aerobics Center in Dallas. "The real reason you lose weight is because you cut calories, generally to 1,200 from the average American consumption of 2,000."

A high-protein diet, such as Atkins, promotes water loss more than fat loss, says Cooper. Water loss is temporary—and these diets are dangerous. Your body doesn't function normally. You may develop ketosis, an unhealthy state in which your body burns off muscle mass because you run out of starches in your energy stores. Your body's uric acid levels rise, which may lead to headaches, lightheadedness, irritability, and potentially serious kidney problems as well as gout. Your body also leaches calcium from the bones, which can induce osteoporosis.

Lawrence Cheskin, M.D., director of the Johns Hopkins Weight Management Center in Baltimore, notes other health risks. "You won't get long-lasting results with an off-balance diet, and you shortchange yourself in the long run. Meat diets, for instance, are high in saturated fat, a risk factor for heart disease and other medical problems."

"A diet rich in fruits and vegetables has been shown to not only make dieting easier but to lower cancer risks," says Cooper. "I'd recommend five to nine servings a day."

Myth: Fat-burning foods work really fast

"No food stimulates your body to burn fat," says Kristi Fuller, registered dietitian and editor of Better Homes and Gardens® *The Smart Diet.* "At first, these diets seem to work as you eat unlimited quantities and lose weight." You lose weight because you eat fewer total calories, not because the food is magically burning body fat, she says. These diets are nutritionally unbalanced and risky for your health.

To keep weight off, "take it off slowly—at most two pounds a week," says Cooper. More rapid weight loss usually results in equal weight regained. Use the weight-loss formula: Burn more calories than you consume. A pound equals 3,500 calories. If you cut caloric intake by 250 calories a day, you'll lose half a pound a week; if you reduce by 500 calories a day, expect to lose one pound a week.

Cooper says that eating during the day—when you most need it—produces even better results. He recommends 25 percent of calories for breakfast, 50 percent for lunch, and 25 percent for the evening meal. "Eat before 7 p.m. when possible and eliminate high-calorie snacks," he says.

"To lose weight and keep it off, stay on a nutritional plan for the rest of your life," says Xavier Pi-Sunyer, M.D., director of the Obesity Research Center at New York's St. Luke's-Roosevelt Hospital Center. He suggests 25 to 30 percent fat, 15 to 20 percent protein, and the rest carbohydrates.

Why diets fail

1. People often view diets as temporary situations to endure while they lose weight. Then they go off the diet and back to the eating patterns that caused them to gain weight.

2. Diets can override inborn hunger and fullness signals. "Chronic dieters are used to eating when, what, and how much their current diet dictates, not because they're hungry or full," says registered dietitian Evelyn Tribole, a California-based weight management and eating disorders specialist.

3. Eventually dieters break the rigid food rules, which often results in rebound overeating.

4. Many diets, especially those that produce fast weight loss, cause the loss of muscle mass along with fat stores. When those pounds are regained, they come back mostly as fat.

"If your current weight is more than your body naturally is programmed to be, you will probably lose weight until you settle at your natural weight," says registered dietitian Monika Woolsey, president of A Better Way Health Consulting, Inc., in Glendale, Arizona, and publisher of *After the Diet,* a newsletter for health professionals who specialize in weight and eating issues.

"If you think you're overweight when you're not, your weight will either stay the same, or you might even gain until you reach your natural weight," says Woolsey. If you lose weight, odds are you'll shed it slowly, which means you're apt to keep it off.

Remember a positive body image

"A person does not live life on diet alone," Fuller says. "Having a positive body image is so important. If you realize that your body image was shaped by people and outside influences, as an adult you can refute those messages and use positive thoughts to shape your body image."

Respecting your body enough to let it take its genetic shape is a critical step toward developing a relaxed and enjoyable relationship with food and with yourself.

Tahini and Smoked Salmon Sandwiches

Tahini, commonly used to flavor Middle Eastern recipes, is a paste made from ground sesame seeds. Find it in specialty foods stores and markets.

Start to finish: 20 minutes

- ¼ cup mayonnaise or salad dressing
- 2 Tbsp. tahini
- 1 Tbsp. lemon juice
- 1 medium carrot
- 4 6-inch Italian sesame seed rolls, halved and toasted
- 4 oz. smoked salmon (lox-style)
- ½ of a small red onion, thinly sliced
- 4 leaves red-tipped or green leaf lettuce

1 In a bowl stir together mayonnaise, tahini, and lemon juice; set aside. Using a vegetable peeler, peel the carrot into long, thin ribbons.

2 To assemble, top the toasted side of roll bottoms with smoked salmon, onion slices, carrot ribbons, and lettuce leaves. Spread the toasted side of roll tops with the mayonnaise mixture. Place roll tops, mayonnaise side down, on leaf lettuce. Makes 4 sandwiches.

To Make Ahead:
Wrap prepared sandwiches in clear plastic wrap. Chill in the refrigerator for up to 4 hours. To tote, place the wrapped sandwiches in an insulated cooler with an ice pack.

Nutrition Facts per sandwich: 374 cal., 20 g total fat (3 g sat. fat), 24 mg chol., 556 mg sodium, 35 g carbo., 3 g fiber, 14 g pro. **Daily Values:** 99% vit. A, 16% vit. C, 9% calcium, 14% iron.

Kielbasa and Squash Stir-Fry

Start to finish: 35 minutes

- ½ cup reduced-sodium chicken broth
- ½ cup sliced green onions
- 2 Tbsp. soy sauce
- 2 tsp. cornstarch
- 2 cloves garlic, minced
- 1 tsp. Cajun seasoning
- ½ tsp. grated fresh ginger
- 1 lb. cooked kielbasa or cooked smoked sausage, sliced ½ inch thick
- 2 cups sliced zucchini
- 2 cups sliced yellow summer squash
- 2 cups fresh pea pods, ends trimmed and strings removed
- 1 cup sliced fresh mushrooms
- 1 medium red sweet pepper, stemmed, seeded, and cut into bite-size strips
- 3 cups hot cooked brown rice

1 For sauce, in a bowl combine chicken broth, green onions, soy sauce, cornstarch, garlic, Cajun seasoning, and ginger; set aside.

2 In a 12-inch skillet cook kielbasa over medium heat 5 minutes or until browned, stirring and turning occasionally. Add zucchini, yellow squash, pea pods, mushrooms, and red pepper strips. Cook and stir for 5 minutes. Stir sauce mixture and add it to skillet. Cook and stir until sauce is thickened and bubbly. Cook and stir for 2 minutes more. Serve with hot cooked brown rice. Makes 6 servings.

Nutrition Facts per serving: 412 cal., 24 g total fat (8 g sat. fat), 51 mg chol., 1,142 mg sodium, 35 g carbo., 5 g fiber, 17 g pro. **Daily Values:** 27% vit. A, 101% vit. C, 5% calcium, 11% iron.

Pasta with Arugula And Sausage

Arugula, also known as rocket, has a peppery mustard flavor and is somewhat bitter. If you have delicate taste buds, substitute mild spinach.

Start to finish: 25 minutes

- 4 oz. cooked smoked turkey sausage or chicken sausage
- 1 large leek, cut into ¼-inch slices
- 2 cloves garlic, minced
- 1 tsp. olive oil
- ⅔ cup reduced-sodium chicken broth
- ½ of a 7-oz. jar roasted red sweet peppers, drained and cut into bite-size strips
- 8 cups torn fresh arugula or spinach
- 6 oz. dried medium bow tie pasta
- ¼ cup snipped fresh basil
- ¼ cup finely shredded Parmesan cheese
- ½ tsp. coarsely cracked black pepper

1 Cut sausage lengthwise into quarters; cut into ¼-inch pieces. In a large skillet cook leek and garlic in hot oil until tender. Stir in sausage pieces, broth, and red peppers. Bring to boiling; reduce heat. Add arugula or spinach; cook 1 to 2 minutes or until greens are wilted. Remove from heat.

2 Meanwhile, cook pasta according to package directions; drain. Toss pasta with sausage mixture, basil, cheese, and black pepper. Serves 4.

Nutrition Facts per serving: 270 cal., 7 g total fat (2 g sat. fat), 66 mg chol., 446 mg sodium, 36 g carbo., 3 g fiber, 15 g pro. **Daily Values:** 23% vit. A, 99% vit. C, 16% calcium, 17% iron.

Pat-a-Cake, Pat-a-Cake

Kids love scones—especially pat-together scones that are marked with a "D" for delicious.

Roll or pat the dough, cut it, and because the recipe is streamlined with whipping cream replacing the butter and egg, you and your little baker can indeed bake 'em as fast as you can.

Play with tradition to make scones, filling them with such favorites as raisins, dried cherries, or currants; or top them with yummy seeds. Cut them in wedges to bake.

Serve warm scones from a cloth-lined basket with tea, hot chocolate, cider, or coffee. A fresh batch is a thoughtful gift for moms, dads, teachers, grandparents, and friends.

Should you roll the dough or pat it? Either way works with this flexible method, and it is forgiving of small, uncertain hands. If the top of the dough is uneven, the variations will puff up and bake to a smooth finish. Likewise, your little baker will puff up with pride when the first batch of mouthwatering scones is served.

Pat-a-Cake Scones

Prep: 15 minutes **Bake:** 18 minutes

- 1½ cups all-purpose flour
- ⅓ cup sugar
- 2 tsp. baking powder
- ½ tsp. salt
- ¾ cup whipping cream
- 2 tsp. finely shredded lemon peel
-   Whipping cream
-   Sugar

1 Preheat oven to 375°F. In a large mixing bowl combine the flour, the ⅓ cup sugar, baking powder, and salt. Make a well in the center of the flour mixture. Add the ¾ cup whipping cream and lemon peel.

2 Stir until the mixture is crumbly. Coat hands with a little flour and use them to gently knead the dough in the mixing bowl until the dough can be formed into a ball. Turn dough out onto a lightly floured surface.

3 Gently roll or pat the dough into a 7½-inch circle. Using a table knife, cut the dough into 6 or 8 wedges to make scones. Place scones about 1 inch apart on an ungreased baking sheet.

4 Lightly brush scones with additional cream; sprinkle with additional sugar. Bake about 18 minutes or until scones are golden brown on top and bottom. Use a wide metal spatula to remove the scones from cookie sheet. Serve warm. Makes 6 to 8 scones.

Fruit Scones

Stir ¾ cup raisins, snipped dried cherries, currants, or other chopped dried fruit into flour mixture before adding cream. Continue as directed.

Poppy Seed-Topped Scones

Prepare scones as directed except after brushing wedges with cream, sprinkle with 2 teaspoons poppy seeds or sesame seeds, instead of the sugar. Continue as directed.

Nutrition Facts per serving: 261 cal., 12 g total fat (7 g sat. fat), 43 mg chol., 340 mg sodium, 35 g carbo., 1 g fiber, 4 g pro. **Daily Values:** 9% vit. A, 2% vit. C, 11% calcium, 7% iron.

Lemon-Berry Crumb Cake

This tender lemon cake bursts with blueberries and is crowned with buttery crumbs—just right for breakfast or a snack.

Prep: 30 minutes **Bake:** 45 minutes

-   Nonstick cooking spray
- 1 cup all-purpose flour
- 1 tsp. baking powder
- ¼ cup butter, softened
- ¾ cup sugar
- 2 tsp. finely shredded lemon peel
- 2 Tbsp. lemon juice
- 2 eggs
- 2 Tbsp. milk
- 1½ cups fresh blueberries
- ½ cup all-purpose flour
- ½ cup sugar
- 1 tsp. ground coriander
- ¼ cup cold butter

1 Preheat oven to 350°F. Coat bottom and sides of an 8×8×2-inch baking pan with cooking spray; set aside. Combine the 1 cup flour and the baking powder; set aside.

2 In a large mixing bowl beat the ¼ cup softened butter with an electric mixer on medium to high speed for 30 seconds. Add the ¾ cup sugar, lemon peel, and lemon juice; beat until well combined. Add eggs, one at a time, beating well after each. Add the flour mixture and milk alternately to beaten mixture, beating on low speed after each addition until just combined. Pour batter into prepared pan; spread evenly. Sprinkle with blueberries.

3 In a small bowl combine the ½ cup flour, ½ cup sugar, and coriander. Cut in butter until mixture resembles coarse crumbs. Sprinkle over the berries. Bake for 45 to 50 minutes or until a wooden toothpick inserted near center comes out clean. Serve warm. Serves 9.

Nutrition Facts per serving: 312 cal., 12 g total fat (7 g sat. fat), 75 mg chol., 162 mg sodium, 47 g carbo., 1 g fiber, 4 g pro. Daily Values: 11% vit. A, 8% vit. C, 4% calcium, 8% iron.

Strawberry Ripple Tea Cake

Prep: 30 minutes Bake: 30 minutes

- 1 10-oz. pkg. frozen, sweetened, sliced strawberries or red raspberries, thawed
- 1 Tbsp. cornstarch
- 2¼ cups all-purpose flour
- ¾ cup sugar
- ¾ cup butter
- ½ tsp. baking powder
- ½ tsp. baking soda
- ⅛ tsp. salt
- 1 egg, beaten
- ¾ cup buttermilk or sour milk

1 Preheat oven to 350°F. Grease and flour a 10×2-inch round removable bottom tart pan or an 11×7×1½-inch baking pan; set aside.

2 For filling, in a small saucepan stir together undrained strawberries or raspberries and the cornstarch until well combined. Cook and stir until thickened and bubbly. Remove from heat. Sieve the mixture. Discard seeds and pulp. Set aside to cool slightly.

3 In a large mixing bowl stir together flour and sugar. Cut in butter until mixture resembles coarse crumbs. Set ½ cup of the flour mixture aside for crumb topping. Into the remaining flour mixture stir baking powder, baking soda, and salt; mix well. Make a well in the center of the flour mixture.

4 In a small bowl combine egg and buttermilk or sour milk. Add the egg mixture all at once to the flour mixture. Stir just until moistened.

5 Spread two-thirds of the batter over the bottom and about 1 inch up the sides of the prepared pan. Carefully spread the filling on top of the batter in pan. Spoon remaining batter in small mounds on the surface. Sprinkle with the crumb topping.

6 Bake for 30 to 35 minutes or until a wooden toothpick inserted near center comes out clean. Cool in pan on a rack for 15 minutes. Remove cake from tart pan (leave in baking pan). Cut into wedges or squares and serve warm. Cover leftovers and store at room temperature or in the refrigerator for up to 3 days. Serves 8.

Nutrition Facts per serving: 406 cal., 19 g total fat (12 g sat. fat), 77 mg chol., 360 mg sodium, 54 g carbo., 2 g fiber, 5 g pro. Daily Values: 15% vit. A, 25% vit. C, 6% calcium, 10% iron.

Peanut Butter Coffee Cake

Prep: 30 minutes Bake: 25 minutes

- ¼ cup all-purpose flour
- ¼ cup packed brown sugar
- 2 Tbsp. peanut butter
- 1 Tbsp. butter
- ¼ cup miniature semisweet chocolate pieces
- ¼ cup peanut butter
- 2 Tbsp. butter
- 1 cup all-purpose flour
- ½ cup packed brown sugar
- ½ cup milk
- 1 egg
- 1 tsp. baking powder
- ¼ tsp. baking soda
- ¼ tsp. salt
- ¼ cup miniature semisweet chocolate pieces

1 Preheat oven to 375°F. Grease an 8×8×2-inch baking pan; set aside. For streusel topping, in a small mixing bowl combine the ¼ cup flour, the ¼ cup brown sugar, the 2 tablespoons peanut butter, and the 1 tablespoon butter. Stir together until crumbly. Stir in the ¼ cup miniature chocolate pieces; set aside.

2 In a large mixing bowl beat the ¼ cup peanut butter and the 2 tablespoons butter with an electric mixer on medium to high speed for 30 seconds or until combined. Add about half of the 1 cup flour, the ½ cup brown sugar, half of the milk, the egg, baking powder, baking soda, and salt. Beat with an electric mixer on low speed until thoroughly combined, scraping the bowl constantly. Add the remaining flour and remaining milk. Beat on low to medium speed just until combined. Stir in the remaining ¼ cup miniature chocolate pieces.

3 Spread batter evenly into prepared pan. Sprinkle with the streusel topping. Bake for 25 to 30 minutes or until a wooden toothpick inserted near the center comes out clean. Cool in pan on a wire rack for 15 minutes. Cut into squares and serve warm. Cover leftovers and store at room temperature or in the refrigerator for up to 3 days. Makes 9 servings.

Nutrition Facts per serving: 269 cal., 13 g total fat (4 g sat. fat), 35 mg chol., 243 mg sodium, 36 g carbo., 1 g fiber, 6 g pro. Daily Values: 5% vit. A, 6% calcium, 10% iron.

Triple-Dipster Strawberries

When children are in the serving group, set out a bowl of miniature semisweet chocolate pieces as an alternate to the chocolate-covered coffee beans. (See the photograph on page 120.)

Start to finish: 20 minutes

- 4 cups large strawberries with stems
- 1 8-oz. carton dairy sour cream
- ½ tsp. ground cinnamon
- ½ cup coarsely chopped toasted macadamia nuts
- ½ cup raw sugar* or packed brown sugar
- ¼ cup chocolate-covered coffee beans, coarsely chopped

1 Wash strawberries; drain well on paper towels. Place in a serving bowl; set aside.

2 In a small bowl stir together the sour cream and the cinnamon. In separate small serving dishes or bowls place the sour cream mixture, macadamia nuts, raw or brown sugar, and coffee beans.

3 To serve, dip strawberries first in sour cream mixture, then in the toasted macadamia nuts, sugar, and coffee beans, as desired. Serves 4.

*Note: Raw sugar is usually available in the supermarket baking products aisle, and often comes granulated.

Nutrition Facts per serving: 415 cal., 27 g total fat (10 g sat. fat), 25 mg chol., 87 mg sodium, 45 g carbo., 5 g fiber, 4 g pro. Daily Values: 10% vit. A, 137% vit. C, 13% calcium, 10% iron.

TEST KITCHEN TIP

Keeping Spices Nice

Avoid ruining a great recipe by using spices that have been stored too long in the pantry. Spice flavors come from volatile oils, which begin to fade as soon as the whole spice is ground. Spices that have lost their punch can give baked goods a bitter or medicinal taste. Follow these tips for storing and using spices:

- Store spices sealed in airtight containers in a cool, dry place.

- Buy small amounts of spices and throw out spices that are older than six months.

- Grind whole spices just before using them to ensure the most intense flavors.

Creamy Three-Spice Ice Cream

Special spices from India and the Spice Islands star in this ice cream.

Prep: 15 minutes **Chill:** 2 hours
Freeze: 25 minutes **Ripen:** 4 hours

- 2½ cups half-and-half, light cream, and/or milk
- ¾ cup sugar
- ½ tsp. grated fresh nutmeg
- ¼ tsp. ground cardamom
- ¼ tsp. saffron threads, slightly crushed
- 1½ cups whipping cream
- 1 Tbsp. vanilla

1 In a saucepan combine 1½ cups of half-and-half, light cream, and/or milk; the sugar; nutmeg; cardamom; and saffron. Bring mixture just to a simmer, stirring often. Remove from heat. Let cool to room temperature. Cover and chill in the refrigerator for two hours or overnight.

2 Combine chilled spice mixture with whipping cream; remaining half-and-half, light cream, and/or milk; and vanilla. Freeze mixture in a 4- or 5-quart ice cream freezer according to manufacturer's directions. Ripen for 4 hours according to manufacturer's directions. Makes 10 servings.

Nutrition Facts per serving: 263 cal., 20 g total fat (13 g sat. fat), 71 mg chol., 38 mg sodium, 18 g carbo., 0 g fiber, 3 g pro. Daily Values: 16% vit. A, 1% vit. C, 9% calcium.

Strawberry Gelato-Style Dessert

This irresistible sweet and creamy Italian frozen dessert is especially good with fresh strawberries.

Prep: 25 minutes **Chill:** 6 hours
Freeze: 25 minutes

- 2 cups reduced-fat milk
- 1 cup refrigerated or frozen egg product, thawed
- ½ cup sugar
- 4 cups strawberries
- 1 tsp. lemon juice
  Fresh strawberries (optional)
  Fresh oregano (optional)

1 In a medium saucepan combine milk, egg product, and sugar. Cook and stir over medium heat about 10 minutes or until the custard mixture is thickened. Do not boil. Remove saucepan from heat.

2 Place saucepan in a sink or bowl of ice water for 1 to 2 minutes, stirring constantly. Pour custard mixture into a bowl; set aside.

3 Place the 4 cups strawberries in a blender container or food processor bowl. Cover and blend or process until nearly smooth. Stir the pureed strawberries and lemon juice into custard mixture. Cover the surface of custard with plastic wrap. Chill in the refrigerator for several hours or overnight until completely chilled. (To chill quickly, place bowl in a sink of ice water.)

4 Freeze mixture in a 2- or 3-quart ice cream freezer according to the manufacturer's directions. If desired, serve with additional fresh strawberries and garnish with oregano. Makes 14 servings.

Peach Gelato-Style Dessert

Prepare gelato mixture as directed, except substitute 4 cups cut-up, pitted, and peeled peaches (5 to 6 peaches) for the strawberries.

Nutrition Facts per serving: 65 cal., 1 g total fat (0 g sat. fat), 3 mg chol., 41 mg sodium, 12 g carbo., 1 g fiber, 3 g pro. Daily Values: 41% vit. C.

NO FAT

Passion Fruit Frozen Pops

Cool, wet, and refreshing, these tropical ice pops are inspired by popular Latino cocktails.

Prep: 10 minutes **Freeze:** 3 hours

- 3 Tbsp. sugar
- 3 Tbsp. water
- 1 cup guava nectar or pineapple juice
- ½ cup passion fruit juice blend
- 2 Tbsp. lime juice
- 1 Tbsp. rum (optional)
- ½ tsp. vanilla

1 In a bowl combine sugar and water; stir until sugar is dissolved. Stir in guava nectar or pineapple juice, passion fruit juice blend, lime juice, rum (if using), and vanilla.

2 Pour into eight 3- to 4-ounce ice-pop molds, or pour into 3-ounce plastic cups. Cover cups with foil. With a sharp knife make a slit in the foil of each. Add sticks or plastic spoons for handles. Freeze for 3 to 4 hours or until firm. Makes 8 pops.

Nutrition Facts per pop: 46 cal., 0 g total fat, 0 mg chol., 2 mg sodium, 12 g carbo., 0 g fiber, 0 g pro. Daily Values: 2% vit. A, 18% vit. C.

Chocolate Chip Ice Cream Cake

Prep: 20 minutes **Freeze:** 6 hours

- 1 3-oz. pkg. cream cheese, softened
- 1 Tbsp. sugar
- 1½ cups chocolate chip, strawberry, or vanilla ice cream
- 1 8- or 9-inch purchased angel food cake (15 or 16 oz.)
- ⅓ cup sliced strawberries
- ⅓ cup chocolate fudge or strawberry ice cream topping

1 For filling, in a small bowl stir together cream cheese and sugar. In a medium bowl stir ice cream just until it begins to soften; fold cream cheese mixture into ice cream. Place in freezer while preparing the cake.

2 Use a serrated knife to cut off the top ½ inch of the cake; set aside. Hold the knife parallel to the center hole of the cake and cut around the hole, leaving about ¾-inch thickness of cake around the hole. Cut around the outer edge of the cake, leaving an outer cake wall about ¾ inch thick. Use a spoon to remove center of cake, leaving about a ¾-inch base. (Reserve scooped-out cake for another use.)

3 Spoon filling into hollowed cake. Arrange sliced strawberries on the filling. Replace the top of the cake. Cover and freeze for several hours or overnight.

4 To serve, in a small saucepan heat ice cream topping to drizzling consistency; drizzle over cake. Slice cake with a serrated knife. Makes 10 to 12 servings.

Nutrition Facts per serving: 219 cal., 7 g total fat (4 g sat. fat), 18 mg chol., 265 mg sodium, 37 g carbo., 0 g fiber, 5 g pro. Daily Values: 6% vit. A, 4% vit. C, 6% calcium, 2% iron.

Clove-Laced Watermelon Cooler

This is like putting a whole watermelon in a glass! Clove-accented brown sugar syrup delightfully boosts the flavor of summer watermelon.

Prep: 20 minutes **Stand:** 1 hour
Chill: at least 2 hours

- 5 cups cubed and seeded watermelon (about one 5-lb. piece)
- ⅔ cup water
- ¼ cup packed light brown sugar
- 1 tsp. whole cloves (about 20 to 25 cloves)
- ¼ cup lemon juice
- 1¼ cups chilled club soda

1 Place watermelon cubes in a food processor bowl or blender container; cover and process or blend until smooth. Press mixture through a fine-mesh sieve. Discard pulp. (You should have 2 cups juice.) Cover and chill until ready to use.

2 In a small saucepan combine water, brown sugar, and cloves. Bring just to boiling. Remove from heat. Cover and let stand about 1 hour. Strain syrup, discarding cloves. Cover and chill for at least 2 hours or until ready to use.

3 To serve, combine watermelon juice, brown sugar syrup, and lemon juice. Gently stir into chilled club soda. Serve in glasses over ice cubes. Makes 6 servings.

Nutrition Facts per serving: 78 cal., 1 g total fat (0 g sat. fat), 0 mg chol., 17 mg sodium, 19 g carbo., 1 g fiber, 1 g pro. Daily Values: 9% vit. A, 28% vit. C, 2% calcium, 2% iron.

Spiced Lemon and Lime Ade

Prep: 25 minutes **Stand:** 1 hour
Chill: 1 hour

- 8 6-inch fresh rosemary sprigs
- 3 Tbsp. whole allspice, coarsely cracked
- 1¼ cups sugar
- ½ cup fresh lemon juice
- ½ cup fresh lime juice
- 2 lemons and/or limes, sliced or cubed (optional)
  Ice cubes

1 In a medium saucepan combine 2 cups water, rosemary, and allspice. Bring to boiling; remove from heat. Cover and let stand 1 hour or until cool. Remove two rosemary sprigs; rinse, wrap, and chill to use to garnish the pitcher. Strain liquid through a fine-mesh sieve. Discard solids. Stir sugar into strained liquid until dissolved. Cover and chill 1 to 24 hours.

2 To serve, in large pitcher or punch bowl combine 7 cups cold water, herb-spice liquid and lemon and lime juices. If desired, float lemon and/or lime slices and reserved rosemary sprigs in pitcher. Serve in tall glasses over ice. Makes 7 servings.

Nutrition Facts per serving: 142 cal., 0 g total fat, 0 mg chol., 10 mg sodium, 37 g carbo., 0 g fiber, 0 g pro. Daily Values: 22% vit. C, 1% calcium.

Hawaiian Lemonade

Start to finish: 10 minutes

- ½ of a 12-oz. can (¾ cup) frozen lemonade concentrate, thawed

EDITOR'S TIP

Hawaiian Improvisation

Cooks across the U.S. have heard the call of the Hawaiian Islands since the early 20th century. During the '20s and '30s, any recipe that contained pineapple was labeled as Hawaiian—even pineapple placed on baked ham. In the '40s and '50s, such well-known restaurants as Don the Beachcomber's and Trader Vic's presented Americanized blends of Polynesian and Chinese foods that were dubbed Hawaiian. By the late '50s tourists flocked to the islands, *South Pacific* was a popular movie, and Hawaiian parties and luaus were fashionable entertainment. Rather than featuring authentic Hawaiian cuisine, however, party menus had a Polynesian influence, with rumaki, shrimp tempura, and Hawaiian Lemonade, *below.*

- 1 12-oz. can (1½ cups) apricot nectar, chilled
- 1 12-oz. can (1½ cups) unsweetened pineapple juice, chilled
  Ice cubes
  Chilled ginger ale (1¼ cups)
  Lemon slices (optional)

1 In a pitcher stir together ¾ cup water and lemonade concentrate. Stir in the apricot nectar and pineapple juice.

2 To serve, place ice cubes in six 12-ounce glasses. Pour juice mixture over ice cubes. Fill glasses with ginger ale. If desired, garnish with lemon slices. Makes 6 servings.

Nutrition Facts per serving: 138 cal., 0 g total fat, 0 mg chol., 8 mg sodium, 35 g carbo., 1 g fiber, 1 g pro. Daily Values: 9% vit. A, 20% vit. C, 2% calcium, 4% iron.

july

IN THIS CHAPTER

30-minute recipes indicated in COLOR.
Low-fat and no-fat recipes indicated
with a ♥.
Photographs indicated in italics.
*Bonus recipe

30 MINUTE, LOW FAT

Cherry Bruschetta

A spin on the traditional tomato relish-topped appetizer, these sweet and spicy fruit-topped appetizers make a great afternoon snack. (See the photograph on page 164.)

Start to finish: 10 minutes

- 1 cup coarsely chopped, pitted light or dark sweet cherries
- 2 Tbsp. red or green jalapeño jelly or currant jelly
- 4 to 6 French bread slices and/or butterhead or Boston lettuce leaves
- 2 Tbsp. crumbled blue cheese
- 1 to 2 Tbsp. slivered almonds

1 In a small mixing bowl stir together cherries and red or green jalapeño or currant jelly. Mound mixture on French bread slices or butterhead or Boston lettuce leaves. Top each bruschetta with crumbled blue cheese and sprinkle with slivered almonds. Makes 4 appetizer servings.

Nutrition Facts per serving: 146 cal., 3 g total fat (1 g sat. fat), 3 mg chol., 204 mg sodium, 26 g carbo., 2 g fiber, 4 g pro. **Daily Values:** 2% vit. A, 4% vit. C, 5% calcium, 5% iron.

---

30 MINUTE

Wind-Down Dip

Scoop this "can't-stop-eating-it" dip onto large corn chips. Or spoon some on crackers or pita bread wedges.

Start to finish: 25 minutes

- 1 15-oz. can chickpeas (garbanzo beans)
- 5 cups torn fresh spinach
- 3 Tbsp. olive oil
- 2 cloves garlic, minced
- ¼ tsp. salt
    Corn chips, crackers, or pita bread wedges

1 Drain the chickpeas, reserving 2 tablespoons of liquid. Rinse and drain again. In a medium saucepan stir together the chickpeas, the reserved liquid, spinach, olive oil, garlic, and salt. Cook over medium heat for 5 minutes. Remove from heat; cool.

2 Transfer the cooled mixture to a blender container or a food processor bowl. Blend or process until smooth. Transfer to a serving bowl. Serve dip with corn chips, crackers, or pita bread wedges. Makes 6 appetizer servings.

To Make Ahead:

Prepare dip; cover with clear plastic wrap. Chill in the refrigerator for up to 2 days. To serve, let stand at room temperature for 1 hour.

Nutrition Facts per serving: 105 cal., 7 g total fat (1 g sat. fat), 0 mg chol., 280 mg sodium, 8 g carbo., 4 g fiber, 4 g pro. **Daily Values:** 24% vit. A, 9% vit. C, 4% calcium, 13% iron.

LOW FAT

Icy Shrimp Cocktail

Cool down on a hot evening with a bowl of Mediterranean-style shrimp. Serve it as individual servings or from a large bowl. (See the photograph on page 158.)

Prep: 15 minutes **Chill:** 1 hour

- 2 medium oranges
- 20 cooked, peeled, and deveined large shrimp
- 2 Tbsp. snipped fresh cilantro
- ⅛ tsp. salt
- ⅛ tsp. pepper
    Whole pitted green olives
    Bottled hot pepper sauce

1 Peel, section, and coarsely chop one orange. In a medium mixing bowl combine the chopped orange, shrimp, cilantro, salt, and pepper. Lightly toss to coat shrimp. Cover and chill in the refrigerator for 1 to 2 hours.

2 To serve, arrange shrimp mixture in each of four cocktail glasses or bowls. Cut the remaining orange into eight wedges. Arrange orange wedges in glasses with shrimp. Skewer three olives onto each of four short wooden skewers and place one in each glass. Serve with hot pepper sauce. Makes 4 appetizer servings.

Nutrition Facts per serving: 123 cal., 3 g total fat (0 g sat. fat), 129 mg chol., 402 mg sodium, 7 g carbo., 1 g fiber, 18 g pro. **Daily Values:** 8% vit. A, 46% vit. C, 7% calcium, 12% iron.

SHORT-ORDER APPETIZERS

Last-minute entertaining goes full speed ahead with these eight easy front-runners. Make as many appetizers as you wish, using your creativity and a few fresh ingredients.

1. Belgian endive leaves transport mascarpone cheese, taramasalata (salmon roe dip), capers, and lemon peel, blended in equal proportions.

2. Layer mini-bagel crisps with bite-size slices of smoked salmon. Top the tower with sour cream and snipped fresh dill.

3. Skewer fresh basil leaves, red grape tomatoes, and fresh mozzarella on fancy cocktail picks.

4. Fill hollowed cucumber cups with a mixture of chopped honey-roasted peanuts, cilantro, and ground red pepper. Top with a carrot quill.

5. Butterflied shrimp hold a food processor blend of leftover rice and a smidge of Thai curry paste. Green onion shreds add Asian appeal.

6. Sprinkle blue cheese crumbles on Italian bread brushed with olive oil; broil until cheese melts. Top with slivers of red onion.

7. Wrap ribbons of seedless cucumber (cut with a vegetable peeler) around cubes of cantaloupe. Cap with sweet pepper squares.

8. Anchor spirals of rolled smoked deli turkey, bottled chutney, and snipped fresh parsley to baguette slices spread with honey mustard.

EDITOR'S TIP

Making Crab Cakes

You know you are eating a great crab cake when chunks of meaty crab, accented by fresh ingredients, bring out the delicate sweet and briny flavor of the crustacean.

Practice this method with the recipe, *right,* for the delightful cakes to reach the impeccable balance between tender center and crunchy exterior. Toss the ingredients, shape and pat the cakes, and fry in a hot skillet. No overmixing allowed.

Combine and mix all the ingredients except the crab. Carefully toss the crabmeat with the mayonnaise mixture just to moisten the crabmeat.

Heat a skillet. With the bowl of crab cake ingredients at the cooktop, scoop the crabmeat mixture into your hand with a half-cup measure, or use your hand to scoop an amount that looks right to you. Pat the mixture into a patty about ½ inch thick for uniform size and to allow the cakes to cook through by the time they brown. Press on bread crumbs and gently lower the cake into the hot skillet. Cook as directed.

When the cakes are fried to a toasty color (about the shade of a pancake), serve them with the Tartar Sauce recipe on page 141, your favorite cocktail sauce, mustard, or a wedge of fresh lemon.

1. To keep big savory chunks of crab intact, add it last, and lightly toss with the other ingredients.

2. Gently pat into shapes. Cakes will be crumbly at this stage, but cooking firms them.

3. The crabmeat is precooked, but the eggs are raw, so keep the cakes on the heat until they are golden brown. An instant-read thermometer, with the tip of the probe inserted sideways into the cake, should reach 160°F.

Crab Cakes

(See the photograph on page 162.)

Start to finish: 30 minutes

- 1 6- to 8-oz. pkg. frozen lump crabmeat or one 6-oz. can crabmeat, drained, flaked, and cartilage removed
- 1 egg, slightly beaten
- 6 Tbsp. fine dry bread crumbs
- 2 Tbsp. finely chopped carrot
- 2 Tbsp. finely chopped celery
- 1 Tbsp. finely chopped green onion (green part only; chop and set aside the white part for the Tartar Sauce)
- 2 Tbsp. mayonnaise or salad dressing
- ¾ tsp. dry mustard
- ¼ tsp. salt*
- ¼ tsp. bottled hot pepper sauce
- 2 Tbsp. cooking oil
   Lemon wedges (optional)
- 1 recipe Tartar Sauce (see right)

1 Thaw crabmeat in refrigerator, if frozen; drain. Combine the egg, 4 tablespoons of the bread crumbs, the carrot, celery, green onion, mayonnaise or salad dressing, dry mustard, salt, and hot pepper sauce. Gently stir in crabmeat just until combined. With wet hands, gently shape the mixture into four 3½-inch diameter patties, about ½ inch thick.

2 Place remaining bread crumbs in a shallow dish. Coat both sides of patties with crumbs. In a large skillet heat oil over medium heat. Add crab cakes. Cook 3 minutes on each side or until golden brown and heated through. Serve with lemon wedges, if desired, and Tartar Sauce. Serves 4.

*Note: When using canned crabmeat, omit the ¼ teaspoon salt.

Tartar Sauce

Stir together ½ cup mayonnaise, 1 tablespoon chopped celery leaves, 1 tablespoon sweet or dill pickle relish, 1 tablespoon capers, and 1 tablespoon chopped white portions of green onion.

Nutrition Facts per serving: 298 cal., 26 g total fat (4 g sat. fat), 119 mg chol., 560 mg sodium, 7 g carbo., 1 g fiber, 11 g pro. Daily Values: 25% vit. A, 3% vit. C, 7% calcium, 5% iron.

30 MINUTE

Lime and Thyme Potato Salad

(See the photograph on page 162.)

Prep: 30 minutes **Chill:** 6 hours

- 4 medium potatoes, peeled and cubed
- ⅓ cup mayonnaise or salad dressing
- ¼ cup dairy sour cream
- ½ tsp. finely shredded lime peel
- 2 Tbsp. lime juice
- 1 Tbsp. snipped fresh thyme
- ¼ tsp. salt
- ¼ tsp. pepper
  milk (optional)
  Snipped fresh thyme (optional)
- 1 lime, sliced (optional)

1 Cook potatoes, covered, in a small amount of boiling salted water for 10 to 12 minutes or until just tender; drain. In a bowl combine mayonnaise or salad dressing, sour cream, lime peel, juice, fresh thyme, salt, and pepper. Add cooked potatoes; gently stir. Cover and chill for 6 to 24 hours.

2 To serve, if salad seems too stiff after chilling, stir in a little milk. Garnish with additional fresh thyme and lime slices, if desired. Serves 4.

Nutrition Facts per serving: 264 cal., 17 g total fat (4 g sat. fat), 12 mg chol., 255 mg sodium, 23 g carbo., 3 g fiber, 4 g pro. Daily Values: 2% vit. A, 38% vit. C, 3% calcium, 7% iron.

NO FAT

Sunrise Salad

This salad is named for the red and yellow fruits and vegetables arranged to resemble the sun.

Prep: 15 minutes **Marinate:** 4 to 24 hours
Assemble: 15 minutes

- 2 sweet yellow peppers, cut into rings
- ½ tsp. finely shredded orange peel
- 3 Tbsp. orange juice
- 2 tsp. snipped fresh chives
- ½ tsp. honey
- ⅛ tsp. salt
- ⅛ tsp. freshly ground pepper
  Lettuce leaves
- 6 to 9 plum tomatoes or 2 to 3 medium tomatoes, sliced
- 1 medium orange, sliced
- 1 cup red cherry tomatoes, halved
- ½ cup yellow cherry tomatoes, halved (optional)
  Freshly ground pepper (optional)

1 In a covered large skillet cook yellow pepper rings in a small amount of boiling water for 1 to 2 minutes or until crisp-tender; drain and cool.

2 For marinade, in a small mixing bowl stir together orange peel, orange juice, chives, honey, salt, and the ⅛ teaspoon pepper. Set aside.

3 Place pepper rings in a plastic bag set in a bowl. Add marinade; close bag. Rotate bag to coat pepper rings with marinade. Chill for 4 to 24 hours, turning bag occasionally.

4 To serve, line a large platter with lettuce leaves. Arrange tomato and orange slices around the edge of the platter. Drain pepper rings, reserving marinade. Arrange pepper rings in an overlapping circle inside tomato and orange slices. Fill center with red cherry tomatoes. If desired, garnish with yellow cherry tomatoes and sprinkle with additional pepper. Drizzle with reserved marinade. Makes 4 to 6 servings.

Nutrition Facts per serving: 72 cal., 0 g total fat, 0 mg chol., 87 mg sodium, 17 g carbo., 2 g fiber, 2 g pro. Daily Values: 21% vit. A, 360% vit. C, 3% calcium, 6% iron.

SUMMER SUPPER

- Chili Pepper Potato Salad (see below)

- Sliced grilled flank steak

- Soft breadsticks or corn bread squares

- Berry pie with vanilla ice cream

Chile Pepper Potato Salad

If you're counting calories, use reduced-calorie ranch-style salad dressing on this potato combo.

Prep: 30 minutes **Chill:** 6 hours

- 1   lb. whole tiny new potatoes, cut into ¼-inch-thick slices
- ¼   cup bottled ranch with cucumber salad dressing or bottled ranch with bacon salad dressing
- 1   4-oz. can diced green chile peppers, drained
- ⅛   tsp. black pepper
- 1   clove garlic, minced
- 1   cup frozen peas
- ½   cup coarsely chopped yellow and/or red sweet pepper

1 Cook potatoes, covered, in a small amount of boiling salted water for 10 to 12 minutes or until just tender; drain well. Cool potatoes slightly.

2 Meanwhile, for dressing, in a small mixing bowl stir together bottled dressing, green chile peppers, black pepper, and garlic.

3 In a large mixing bowl combine dressing, peas, and yellow or red sweet pepper. Add potatoes, tossing lightly to coat. Cover and chill for 6 to 24 hours. Makes 4 to 6 servings.

Nutrition Facts per serving: 201 cal., 8 g total fat (1 g sat. fat), 1 mg chol., 305 mg sodium, 29 g carbo., 4 g fiber, 5 g pro. Daily Values: 8% vit. A, 98 vit. C, 4% calcium, 8% iron.

Southwestern Vegetable Slaw

Sweet peppers in three colors give this crunchy salad confetti appeal. You may choose to use just one color of sweet pepper. (See the photograph on page 158.)

Prep: 30 minutes **Chill:** 1 hour

- 2   cups shredded red cabbage
- 2   cups jicama, peeled and cut into thin matchstick strips (about 6½ oz.)
- ½   cup chopped red sweet pepper
- ½   cup chopped yellow sweet pepper
- ½   cup chopped green sweet pepper
- 1   recipe Cilantro Dressing (see right)
- 1   6-inch corn tortilla
- 2   tsp. cooking oil

1 In a large salad bowl combine shredded red cabbage, jicama, and sweet peppers. Prepare Cilantro Dressing. Pour dressing over vegetable mixture, tossing to coat. Cover and chill for 1 to 4 hours, stirring occasionally.

2 Meanwhile, preheat oven to 400°F. Brush each side of tortilla with the cooking oil. Cut tortilla into thin strips. Place strips in a single layer on a cookie sheet. Bake, uncovered, about 4 minutes or until tortilla strips are golden and crisp. Cool; set aside until ready to serve.

3 To serve, using a slotted spoon, divide vegetable mixture among six small glasses or bowls. Top each salad with tortilla strips. Serves 6.

Cilantro Dressing

In a screw-top jar combine ⅓ cup snipped fresh cilantro; ¼ cup cooking oil; 2 tablespoons finely chopped red onion; 2 tablespoons vinegar; 2 tablespoons lime juice; 1 tablespoon snipped fresh mint; 1 tablespoon honey; 2 cloves garlic, minced; and a dash each of salt, black pepper, and ground red pepper. Cover; shake well.

Nutrition Facts per serving: 163 cal., 11 g total fat (2 g sat. fat), 0 mg chol., 31 mg sodium, 16 g carbo., 2 g fiber, 2 g pro. Daily Values: 23% vit. A, 158% vit. C, 3% calcium, 7% iron.

30 MINUTE, LOW FAT

Fresh Corn-Rice Salad

Juice from the tomatoes and green chiles serves as the dressing for this fresh salad. (See the photograph on page 162.)

Start to finish: 25 minutes

- 4   fresh ears of corn
- 1½ cups cooked rice, cooled
- 1   10- to 14½-oz. can undrained diced tomatoes and green chile peppers
     Shredded radish, chopped red sweet pepper, and/or sliced green onion

1 Remove husks from ears of corn. Scrub corn with a stiff brush to remove silks; rinse. Cut kernels from cob (you should have about 2 cups of kernels).* Cook corn, covered, in a small amount of boiling salted water for 4 minutes. Drain.

2 In a bowl stir together the corn and cooked rice. Stir in undrained diced tomatoes and green chile peppers. Sprinkle with shredded radish, chopped red sweet pepper, and/or sliced green onion. Serve at room temperature. Makes 4 servings.

*Note: To remove corn kernels, hold the top of the cob and slice downward with a sharp knife, turning the cob to capture every kernel.

Nutrition Facts per serving: 123 cal., 1 g total fat (0 g sat. fat), 0 mg chol., 332 mg sodium, 28 g carbo., 2 g fiber, 3 g pro. **Daily Values:** 12% vit. A, 16% vit. C, 2% calcium, 6% iron.

PRIZE WINNER

Pacific Very Cherry Salad

Susan Asanovic
Wilton, Connecticut
$200—Cherries, Sweet and Sour

Prep: 30 minutes
Stand: 3 days (Cherry Vinegar)

- ¼ **cup olive oil**
- 3 **Tbsp. Cherry Vinegar* (see right) or white wine vinegar**
- 2 **Tbsp. minced shallot**
- 2 **tsp. wasabi powder or prepared horseradish**
- 1 **tsp. sugar**
- 1 **tsp. fish sauce (optional)**
- ¼ **tsp. sea salt or salt**
- ⅛ **tsp. pepper**
- 1 **lb. fresh sweet cherries, pitted**
- 8 **cups mixed greens, such as shredded napa cabbage, torn romaine, and/or torn spinach**

- 1 **avocado, halved, seeded, peeled, and thinly sliced**
- ½ **cup slivered almonds, toasted**
- ½ **cup small fresh basil leaves or larger basil leaves, shredded**

1 For dressing, in a screw-top jar combine olive oil, Cherry Vinegar or wine vinegar, shallot, wasabi or horseradish, sugar, fish sauce (if desired), salt, and pepper. Cover and shake well; set aside.

2 Halve cherries, if desired; set aside ¼ cup of the cherries. In a large salad bowl combine the greens, remaining cherries, and the avocado. Shake dressing and drizzle over greens mixture, tossing to coat. Top salad with almonds, basil, and reserved ¼ cup cherries. Makes 4 to 6 servings.

Cherry Vinegar

Mash ½ cup pitted sweet cherries. Place mashed cherries in a clean, heatproof jar. In a small stainless steel saucepan heat ¾ cup white wine vinegar to boiling. Pour over cherries in jar. Cool slightly; cover with a nonmetallic lid. Let stand at room temperature 3 to 5 days. Strain out cherries; cover and store vinegar in a cool place up to 3 months.

Nutrition Facts per serving: 392 cal., 31 g total fat (4 g sat. fat), 0 mg chol., 181 mg sodium, 28 g carbo., 9 g fiber, 8 g pro. **Daily Values:** 73% vit. A, 65% vit. C, 11% calcium, 18% iron.

Red Pepper and Two-Grain Salad

Prep: 30 minutes **Chill:** 4 hours

- ½ **cup bulgur**
- ½ **cup quick-cooking couscous**

- 1 **2¼-oz. can (⅔ cup) sliced pitted ripe olives**
- ½ **cup shredded carrot**
- ¼ **cup sliced green onions**
- ¼ **cup olive oil or salad oil**
- ½ **tsp. finely shredded lime peel**
- ¼ **cup lime juice**
- 2 **tsp. sugar**
- ½ **to 1 tsp. crushed red pepper**
- ¼ **tsp. salt**
  Radicchio leaves and/or romaine leaves
  Carrots, julienne strips (optional)
  Green onion curls (optional)

1 In a medium saucepan combine 2 cups water and bulgur. Bring to boiling; reduce heat. Cover and simmer for 10 to 15 minutes or until bulgur is almost tender. Remove from heat; stir in the couscous. Cover and let grain mixture stand for 5 minutes. Drain mixture. Rinse with cold water; drain again.

2 In a large mixing bowl combine the cooked grain mixture, olives, shredded carrot, and sliced green onions; set salad mixture aside.

3 For dressing, in a screw-top jar combine olive oil or salad oil, lime peel, lime juice, sugar, red pepper, and salt. Cover and shake well. Pour dressing over salad mixture, tossing lightly to coat. Cover and chill for 4 to 24 hours.

4 To serve, line salad plates with radicchio and/or romaine leaves. Divide salad mixture among plates. Garnish each serving with julienne strips of carrot and a green onion curl, if desired. Makes 6 to 8 servings.

Nutrition Facts per serving: 212 cal., 11 g total fat (1 g sat. fat), 0 mg chol., 238 mg sodium, 26 g carbo., 4 g fiber, 4 g pro. **Daily Values:** 57% vit. A, 12% vit. C, 4% calcium, 7% iron.

Ginger-Tomato Salad

This lightly dressed fresh tomato compote is a perfect companion to grilled chicken or pork. (See the photograph on page 158.)

Prep: 15 minutes **Chill:** 1 hour

- 2 Tbsp. rice vinegar
- 1 Tbsp. finely minced fresh ginger
- 1 Tbsp. honey
- ⅛ tsp. salt
- 2 cups cherry, grape, and/or yellow pear tomatoes, halved

1 For dressing, in a screw-top jar or large mixing bowl combine rice vinegar, fresh ginger, honey, and salt. Cover and shake or whisk until combined.

2 Add tomatoes to jar or bowl. Cover and gently turn to mix or gently stir. Cover and chill for 1 to 4 hours. Makes 4 servings.

Nutrition Facts per serving: 40 cal., 0 g total fat, 0 mg chol., 91 mg sodium, 9 g carbo., 2 g fiber, 1 g pro. Daily Values: 20% vit. A, 32% vit. C, 1% calcium, 6% iron.

Garlic-Marinated Tomato Wedges

Braised garlic gives a nutty, sweet taste to the herb dressing.

Prep: 20 minutes **Marinate:** 2 hours

- 4 or 5 large cloves garlic
- 1 tsp. margarine or butter
- ¼ cup salad oil
- ¼ cup white wine vinegar or white vinegar

- 2 Tbsp. thinly sliced green onion
- 1 Tbsp. snipped fresh dill or 1 tsp. dried dillweed
- 1 Tbsp. snipped fresh basil or 1 tsp. dried basil, crushed
- 1 Tbsp. mayonnaise or salad dressing
- ¼ tsp. salt
- ⅛ tsp. pepper
- 4 medium tomatoes, cut into wedges
  Leaf lettuce

1 To braise garlic, in a covered small saucepan cook garlic cloves in hot margarine or butter over low heat about 15 minutes or until golden and soft, stirring frequently. Remove from heat and mash with a fork until the garlic is well combined with the margarine or butter.

2 For marinade, in a screw-top jar combine braised garlic, salad oil, vinegar, green onion, dill, basil, mayonnaise or salad dressing, salt, and pepper. Cover and shake well.

3 Place tomato wedges in a large mixing bowl. Pour marinade over tomato wedges. Cover and chill for 2 to 4 hours, stirring occasionally.

4 To serve, line a salad bowl with lettuce leaves. Using a slotted spoon, transfer tomato wedges from marinade to lettuce-lined bowl. Discard remaining marinade. Makes 4 to 6 servings.

Nutrition Facts per serving: 107 cal., 9 g total fat (1 g sat. fat), 1 mg chol., 101 mg sodium, 7 g carbo., 2 g fiber, 1 g pro. Daily Values: 20% vit. A, 44% vit. C, 2% calcium, 5% iron.

Peach-Basil Delight

Using the back of a spoon, slightly crush the basil sprigs to release the flavor. (See the photograph on page 160.)

Start to finish: 35 minutes

- 9 peaches or nectarines
- 1 cup sweet white wine
- 3 sprigs fresh basil, slightly crushed
- 2 tsp. snipped fresh basil

1 Peel, pit, and chop three of the peaches or nectarines. In a medium saucepan combine the chopped peaches or nectarines, the sweet wine, and basil sprigs. Bring to boiling; reduce heat. Boil gently for 12 to 15 minutes or until slightly thickened. Remove from heat and cool slightly. Remove the basil sprigs.

2 Transfer cooked peach mixture to a food processor bowl or blender container. Cover and process or blend until smooth.

3 To serve, halve and pit the remaining peaches or nectarines. Place three peach halves in each of four dessert bowls. Spoon warm peach sauce atop. Sprinkle with snipped fresh basil. Makes 4 servings.

Nutrition Facts per serving: 205 cal., 1 g total fat (0 g sat. fat), 0 mg chol., 5 mg sodium, 35 g carbo., 5 g fiber, 2 g pro. Daily Values: 30% vit. A, 23% vit. C, 2% calcium, 3% iron.

TEST KITCHEN TIP

Salad Math

Many recipes call for cup measures of greens, vegetables, and fruits. To know how much to buy when planning your grocery list, refer to these charts.

Greens	Weight as Purchased	Measure After Preparation
Arugula	1 ounce	1½ cups torn
Belgian Endive	4 ounces (1 head)	20 leaves
Bok Choy	1¼ pounds (1 head)	7 cups coarsely chopped
Butterhead (Boston or Bibb)	12 ounces (1 head)	4 cups torn
Cabbage	2 pounds (1 head)	12 cups shredded
Chinese Cabbage	2 pounds (1 head)	10 cups coarsely chopped
Collard Greens	8 ounces	4 cups torn
Curly Endive	12 ounces (1 head)	10 cups torn
Dandelion Greens	8 ounces	6 cups torn
Escarole	8 ounces (1 head)	7 cups torn
Iceberg Lettuce	1¼ pounds (1 head)	10 cups torn; 12 cups shredded
Kale	12 ounces (1 head)	7 cups torn
Leaf Lettuce	12 ounces (1 head)	8 cups torn
Mustard Greens	8 ounces	12 cups torn
Radicchio	8 ounces (1 head)	5½ cups torn
Romaine	1 pound (1 head)	6 cups torn
Sorrel	1 ounce	1 cup torn
Spinach	1 pound	12 cups torn, stems removed
Watercress	4 ounces	2⅓ cups, stems removed

Vegetables and Fruits	Amount Before Preparation	Approximate Measure After Preparation
Apple	1 medium	¾ cup chopped
Asparagus	1 pound	2 cups cut or snapped
Banana	3 medium (1 pound)	2¼ cups sliced
Beans, Green	1 pound	4 cups cut or snapped
Beet	4 medium (1 pound)	2 cups diced (without tops)
Broccoli	1 pound	3½ cups florets
Carrot	2 medium (5 ounces)	1 cup sliced, chopped, or shredded
Cauliflower	1 medium head (1½ pounds)	4 cups florets
Celery	1 stalk	½ cup sliced
Cherries	1 cup	1 cup chopped
Corn	1 ear	½ cup kernels
Cranberries	1 pound (4 cups)	4 cups chopped
Cucumber	1 medium (8 ounces)	1¾ cups sliced; 1¼ cups chopped
Green Onion with Top	1 bunch (6 to 8 medium)	¾ cup sliced
Green or Red Sweet Pepper	1 large	1 cup chopped; 1½ cups thin strips
Lemon	1 medium or large	3 tablespoons juice/2 teaspoons grated peel
Mushroom	16 large (8 ounces)	3 cups sliced
Onion	1 large	1 cup chopped
Orange	1 medium	¼ to ⅓ cup juice/4 teaspoons grated peel
Peach	4 medium (1 pound)	2 cups sliced
Potato	3 medium (1 pound)	2 cups cooked, cubed
Radish	12 medium (4 ounces)	1 cup sliced
Raspberries	1 pint	2¾ cups whole berries
Strawberries	1 quart	4 cups sliced
Tomato	1 medium (6 ounces)	1 cup chopped
Tomato, Cherry	12 whole	1 cup halved; 1 cup chopped
Zucchini or Summer Squash	1 medium (8 ounces)	2 cups sliced

PRIZED PEACHES

Sinking your teeth into a juicy ripe peach plucked fresh from the tree is heavenly. If you don't have a peach tree in the backyard, fresh peaches are usually available between June and September in grocery stores and markets. Choose one or more of these recipe options to use the bounty while it lasts.

Honey-Peach Sauce

To easily remove peach peel, use a slotted spoon to dip the peach into boiling water for 20 seconds. Remove from water and use a knife to peel off the skin, working from the stem to the bottom of the fruit. If the skin doesn't peel off easily, dip it into the boiling water a few seconds longer.

Start to finish: 25 minutes

- 4 medium peaches, peeled (if desired) and pitted, or nectarines, pitted
- 2 Tbsp. lemon juice
- 2 Tbsp. honey
- ½ tsp. cracked black pepper
- 1 to 2 tsp. snipped fresh thyme or ¼ to ½ tsp. dried thyme, crushed

1 For sauce, cut up three of the peaches or nectarines. In a blender container or food processor bowl combine cut-up fruit, lemon juice, honey, and pepper. Cover and blend or process until smooth. Transfer blended fruit mixture to a saucepan. Bring to boiling; reduce heat. Simmer, uncovered, about 15 minutes or until slightly thickened, stirring occasionally.

2 Meanwhile, finely chop the remaining peach or nectarine; stir into sauce with thyme. Brush sauce onto pork chops, pork roast, or chicken the last 15 minutes of grilling. Heat remaining sauce just until bubbly; serve with meat. Makes about 1¾ cups sauce, enough for 2 to 3 pounds of meat, or 8 servings.

To Make Ahead:

Cover and chill sauce for up to 24 hours. To serve, reheat the sauce in a small saucepan over low heat, stirring occasionally.

Nutrition Facts per serving: 50 cal., 0 g total fat, 0 mg chol., 0 mg sodium, 13 g carbo., 2 g fiber, 1 g pro., Daily Values: 8% vit. A, 12% vit. C, 1% calcium, 1% iron.

Peach-Blueberry Bread

Select peaches that are well-shaped and firm to slightly soft when pressed. Skin color varies from golden yellow to dark reddish brown; the skin should have no green tinges.

Prep: 20 minutes **Bake:** 55 minutes

- ⅔ cup chopped almonds
- 1 Tbsp. sugar
- 1½ cups all-purpose flour
- ¾ cup sugar
- 2 tsp. baking powder
- ½ tsp. ground allspice
- ¼ tsp. baking soda
- ¼ tsp. salt
- ⅓ cup margarine or butter, softened
- 1 tsp. finely shredded orange peel
- ¼ cup orange juice
- 2 eggs
- ⅔ cup coarsely chopped peeled peach or unpeeled nectarine
- ½ cup blueberries

1 Preheat oven to 350°F. Grease an 8×4×2-inch loaf pan; set aside. For topping, in a small bowl stir together ¼ cup of the almonds and the 1 tablespoon sugar; set aside.

2 In a large mixing bowl stir together 1 cup of the flour, the ¾ cup sugar, the baking powder, allspice, baking soda, and salt. Add margarine or butter, orange peel, and juice. Beat with an electric mixer on low to medium speed about 30 seconds or until combined. Beat on high speed for 2 minutes. Add the eggs and the remaining flour. Beat on low speed just until combined. Carefully fold in the peach or nectarine, blueberries, and remaining almonds. Pour into prepared loaf pan and sprinkle with topping.

3 Bake in the preheated oven for 55 to 60 minutes or until a wooden toothpick inserted near the center comes out clean. Cover with foil the last 15 minutes, if necessary to prevent overbrowning. Cool in pan for 10 minutes. Remove from pan; cool completely on a wire rack. Wrap and store the loaf overnight before slicing. Makes 1 loaf (about 16 servings).

To Make Ahead:
Make, bake, and cool the loaf completely. Place the completely cooled loaf in a freezer container or bag and freeze for up to 3 months. Thaw the wrapped loaf overnight in the refrigerator.

Nutrition Facts per serving: 128 cal., 7 g total fat (1 g sat. fat), 27 mg chol., 151 mg sodium, 16 g carbo., 1 g fiber, 2 g pro. Daily Values: 6% vit. A, 5% vit. C, 5% calcium, 3% iron.

Peach-Praline Cobbler

If you purchase firm peaches, place them in a small, clean paper bag, loosely close the bag, and store it at room temperature. Check the fruit daily and remove peaches that are slightly soft when gently pressed. When ripe, eat the peaches or transfer them to the refrigerator to stop further ripening.

Prep: 25 minutes **Bake:** 25 minutes

- 8 cups sliced, peeled fresh peaches or frozen peaches, thawed
- 1 cup granulated sugar
- 1 cup water
- 2 Tbsp. cornstarch
- 1 tsp. ground cinnamon
- ¾ cup packed brown sugar
- ¼ cup margarine or butter, melted
- 1½ cups chopped pecans
- 2 cups self-rising flour*
- 2 tsp. granulated sugar
- ½ cup shortening
- ¾ cup buttermilk
  Half-and-half or light cream (optional)

1 In a Dutch oven combine the peaches, the 1 cup granulated sugar, the water, cornstarch, and cinnamon. Cook and stir until thickened and bubbly. Transfer to a 3-quart rectangular baking dish.

2 Meanwhile, for filling, stir together the brown sugar and melted margarine or butter. Add pecans; toss to coat. Set aside.

3 Preheat oven to 400°F. For biscuit dough, in a large mixing bowl stir together the self-rising flour and the 2 teaspoons granulated sugar. Using a pastry blender, cut in the shortening until mixture resembles coarse crumbs. Make a well in the center of the dry mixture. Add buttermilk all at once. Using a fork, stir until dough clings together.

4 Turn out dough onto a lightly floured surface. Quickly knead dough by gently folding and pressing for 10 to 12 strokes. Roll to a 12×8-inch rectangle; spread with the filling. Roll up, starting from one long side. Cut into twelve 1-inch slices. Place biscuit slices, cut sides down, on the hot peach mixture.

5 Bake, uncovered, in the preheated oven for 25 to 30 minutes or until biscuits are golden brown. Serve warm. If

desired, serve with half-and-half or light cream. Makes 12 servings.

*Note: To substitute for the 2 cups self-rising flour, use 2 cups all-purpose flour plus 2 teaspoons baking powder, ½ teaspoon baking soda, and ½ teaspoon salt.

Nutrition Facts per serving: 453 cal., 22 g total fat (4 g sat. fat), 1 mg chol., 331 mg sodium, 63 g carbo., 4 g fiber, 5 g pro. Daily Values: 54% vit. A, 284% vit. C, 12% calcium, 12% iron.

30 MINUTE
Just Peachy Shake

Start to finish: 5 minutes

- 1 pint frozen vanilla yogurt
- 1 medium peach, peeled, pitted, and cut up, or ½ cup frozen sliced peaches
- 1 Tbsp. honey
- 1 Tbsp. creamy peanut butter
  Peach slices (optional)
  Finely chopped peanuts (optional)

1 In a blender container combine frozen yogurt, fresh or frozen peach, honey, and peanut butter. Cover and blend until smooth.

2 To serve, pour mixture into two glasses. Garnish each with a peach slice and finely chopped peanuts, if desired. Makes 2 servings.

Nutrition Facts per serving: 320 cal., 10 g total fat (5 g sat. fat), 30 mg chol., 208 mg sodium, 54 g carbo., 2 g fiber, 10 g pro. Daily Values: 5% vit. A, 6% vit. C, 17% calcium, 2% iron.

Pork Ribs

Use this helpful review to buy pork ribs:

Country-Style Ribs, the meatiest of pork ribs, are cut from the rib end of the loin. These ribs usually have more meat than bone and can be eaten with a knife and fork.

Pork Loin Back Ribs are cut from the blade and center section of the loin. These ribs are meaty between the bones and are easier to handle than spareribs.

Spareribs come from the belly or side of the hog, have the least amount of meat, and are less tender than other ribs.

PRIZE WINNER

Peppery Pork Sandwiches

Micky Strang
McKinleyville, California
$200—Sizzle and Spice Entrées

Prep: 30 minutes **Bake:** 2½ hours

- 1 large onion, thinly sliced
- 1 2- to 2½-lb. boneless pork shoulder roast
- 1 Tbsp. hot paprika
- 2 14½-oz. cans chunky chile-style tomatoes
- 1 4½-oz. can diced green chile peppers
- 2 tsp. dried oregano, crushed
- 1 tsp. black pepper
- ¼ tsp. salt
- 8 or 9 (6-inch) French-style rolls, split and toasted*

1 Preheat oven to 325°F. In a 4-quart Dutch oven arrange onion slices in bottom of pan. Sprinkle pork roast evenly with paprika. Place roast on top of onion. In a medium bowl combine undrained tomatoes, undrained chile peppers, oregano, black pepper, and salt. Pour over roast in pot. Cover and bake in the preheated oven for 2½ to 3 hours or until roast is very tender.

2 Remove pork to cutting board, reserving mixture in pot. Using two forks, pull pork into shreds. Skim fat from pan juices. Add shredded meat to pan juices; stir until combined. Heat through.

3 To serve, spoon pork mixture onto toasted rolls. Makes 8 or 9 sandwiches.

*Note: To toast, arrange buns, cut side up, on the unheated rack of a broiler pan. Broil 4 to 5 inches from heat 1 to 2 minutes or until toasted.

Nutrition Facts per sandwich: 383 cal., 18 g total fat (6 g sat. fat), 79 mg chol., 964 mg sodium, 29 g carbo., 3 g fiber, 25 g pro. **Daily Values:** 19% vit. A, 25% vit. C, 10% calcium, 18% iron.

Pepper-Rubbed Pork Ribs

For a mouthwatering taste sensation, dip each bite of pepper-crusted ribs into the mustardy peach sauce.

Prep: 20 minutes **Bake:** 1¼ hours

- 2 Tbsp. brown sugar
- 1 Tbsp. paprika
- 2 tsp. garlic powder
- 2 tsp. coarsely ground black pepper
- ¾ tsp. salt
- 3 lb. pork loin back ribs or meaty spareribs, cut into serving-size pieces
- ½ cup chopped onion
- 1 clove garlic, minced
- 1 Tbsp. cooking oil
- ¾ cup peach preserves
- 2 Tbsp. cider vinegar
- 1 Tbsp. coarse-grain brown mustard

1 Preheat oven to 450°F. For rub, in a small bowl combine brown sugar, paprika, garlic powder, coarsely ground black pepper, and salt. Sprinkle rub evenly over ribs; rub in with your fingers.

2 Place ribs, meaty side down, in a shallow roasting pan. Bake in the preheated oven, uncovered, for 30 minutes. Remove meat from oven; drain off excess fat. Turn ribs meaty side up. Reduce oven temperature to 350°F. Continue baking for 45 to 60 minutes more or until tender.

3 Meanwhile, for sauce, in a small saucepan cook onion and garlic in hot cooking oil until onion is tender but not brown. Stir in peach preserves, vinegar, and coarse-grain mustard. Bring to boiling; reduce heat. Boil gently, uncovered, for 5 minutes, stirring occasionally. Serve as a dipping sauce with ribs. Makes 4 to 5 servings.

Nutrition Facts per serving: 608 cal., 26 g total fat (8 g sat. fat), 100 mg chol., 606 mg sodium, 52 g carbo., 2 g fiber, 43 g pro. **Daily Values:** 19% vit. A, 14% vit. C, 6% calcium, 13% iron.

Thai-Coconut Ribs

These grilled ribs marinate in a spicy coconut-milk sauce reminiscent of the flavors of Thailand.

Prep: 15 minutes **Marinate:** 8 hours
Grill: 1¼ hours

- 4 lb. pork loin back ribs
- 1 cup coconut milk
- 3 Tbsp. brown sugar
- 3 Tbsp. soy sauce
- 1 Tbsp. grated fresh ginger
- 1 tsp. finely shredded lime peel
- 1 Tbsp. lime juice
- 4 cloves garlic, minced
- 1 tsp. crushed red pepper

1 Trim fat from ribs. Cut ribs into six serving-size pieces. Place ribs in a plastic bag set in a shallow dish.

2 For marinade, in a small bowl combine coconut milk, brown sugar, soy sauce, ginger, lime peel, lime juice, garlic, and red pepper. Pour over ribs; seal bag. Marinate in the refrigerator for 8 to 24 hours, turning the bag occasionally. Drain ribs, reserving marinade.

3 To grill, arrange medium-hot coals around a drip pan. Test for medium heat above the pan. Place ribs, bone side down, on grill rack over drip pan. Cover and grill for 1¼ to 1½ hours or until ribs are tender, brushing frequently with marinade during the first hour of grilling. Discard marinade.

4 To serve, place ribs on a serving platter. Makes 6 servings.

Nutrition Facts per serving: 431 cal., 32 g total fat (16 g sat. fat), 99 mg chol., 607 mg sodium, 9 g carbo., 0 g fiber, 25 g pro. **Daily Values:** 2% vit. A, 8% vit. C, 4% calcium, 15% iron.

Melt-in-Your-Mouth Short Ribs

Boil then broil these beefy ribs for a fall-off-the-bone tender delight.

Prep: 15 minutes **Cook:** 1½ hours
Broil: 10 minutes

- 3 to 4 lb. boneless beef short ribs
- 2 cups water
- ½ cup vinegar
- ½ cup bottled barbecue sauce
- ⅓ cup catsup
- ¼ cup honey
- 1 to 2 Tbsp. prepared horseradish
- 1 Tbsp. Dijon-style mustard
- 3 cloves garlic, minced
- ¼ tsp. pepper
- 1 Tbsp. olive oil
- 2 large onions, sliced (2 cups)
- 1 Tbsp. Dijon-style mustard
- ½ tsp. paprika
- ¼ tsp. salt
- ⅛ tsp. pepper

1 Trim fat from ribs. Cut ribs into serving-size pieces, if necessary. Place ribs in a 4- to 6-quart pot or Dutch oven. Add water and vinegar. Bring to boiling; reduce heat. Simmer, covered, about 1½ hours or until tender; drain. Discard the cooking liquid.

2 For sauce, in a small saucepan combine barbecue sauce, catsup, honey, horseradish, 1 tablespoon Dijon-style mustard, garlic, and the ¼ teaspoon pepper. Bring to boiling; reduce heat. Simmer, covered, for 5 minutes. Remove from heat.

3 Place ribs on the unheated rack of a broiler pan. Brush with some of the sauce. Broil 4 to 5 inches from the heat for 10 to 15 minutes or until heated through, turning often and brushing with sauce.

4 Meanwhile, in a large skillet heat the olive oil over medium heat. Add onions. Cook and stir for 8 to 10 minutes or until onions are tender and lightly golden brown. Stir in 1 tablespoon Dijon-style mustard, the paprika, salt, and the ⅛ teaspoon pepper. Cook and stir for 1 minute more. Remove from heat.

5 To serve, place ribs on a serving platter. Top with onions. Heat any remaining sauce and pass with ribs. Makes 8 servings.

Nutrition Facts per serving: 366 cal., 17 g total fat (6 g sat. fat), 79 mg chol., 477 mg sodium, 19 g carbo., 1 g fiber, 35 g pro. **Daily Values:** 7% vit. A, 9% vit. C, 5% calcium, 20% iron.

- Berries and Melon Chicken Salad (see below, right)

- Croissants or poppy seed muffins with butter

- Fruit-flavored iced tea

- Ice cream pie with fudge sauce

30 MINUTE, LOW FAT

Spiced Jerk Turkey With Mango Salsa

Start to finish: 25 minutes

    4   tsp. Jamaican jerk seasoning
    1   tsp. ground cumin
    ½   tsp. salt
    ½   tsp. ground ginger
    ⅛   tsp. ground red pepper
    1   Tbsp. olive oil
    2   cloves garlic, minced
    8   ¼- to ⅜-inch-thick turkey
        breast slices or cutlets
        (about 1 lb.)
    1   ripe medium mango, seeded,
        peeled, and chopped; or
        ¾ cup pitted, chopped
        nectarines or peeled peaches
    ¼   cup finely chopped red
        sweet pepper
    ¼   cup finely chopped red onion
    2   Tbsp. snipped fresh cilantro
    1   Tbsp. lime juice
    1   fresh serrano chile pepper,
        seeded and finely chopped*
    1   Tbsp. olive oil

1 For seasoning mixture, in a small bowl combine Jamaican jerk seasoning, cumin, salt, ginger, and ground red pepper. Set aside 1 teaspoon of the seasoning mixture

for salsa. Add 1 tablespoon olive oil and the garlic to remaining seasoning mixture. Use your fingers to rub mixture over both sides of turkey breast slices. Set aside.

2 For salsa, in a small bowl stir together the mango, nectarines, or peaches; sweet pepper; red onion; cilantro; lime juice; serrano pepper; and reserved seasoning mixture. Cover and chill until ready to serve.

3 In a large skillet cook turkey, half at a time, in 1 tablespoon hot oil (add more oil if necessary) over medium heat for 4 to 6 minutes or until turkey is tender and no pink remains, turning once. Serve with the salsa. Makes 4 servings.

*Note: Hot peppers contain oils that can burn eyes, lips, and sensitive skin. Wear gloves while preparing them and wash your hands thoroughly afterward.

Nutrition Facts per serving: 232 cal., 8 g total fat (1 g sat. fat), 70 mg chol., 637 mg sodium, 11 g carbo., 2 g fiber, 29 g pro. **Daily Values:** 55% vit. A, 36% vit. C, 3% calcium, 8% iron.

30 MINUTE

Berries and Melon Chicken Salad

Bright and colorful, cool and fresh, this fruited salad is perfect for a hot summer day. Serve the dressing alongside the salad rather than toss it with the greens to avoid giving the salad a muddy appearance.

Start to finish: 30 minutes

    2   cups fresh raspberries
    3   Tbsp. olive oil
    3   Tbsp. balsamic vinegar
    1   Tbsp. finely chopped red onion
    2   cloves garlic, minced
    ½   tsp. sugar
    ¼   tsp. salt
    ¼   tsp. pepper
    6   cups torn mixed baby greens
    1   6-oz. pkg. refrigerated grilled
        chicken breast strips,
        6 oz. thinly sliced cooked
        ham, or 4 oz. very thinly
        sliced prosciutto
    ½   of a small cantaloupe melon,
        peeled, seeded, and
        thinly sliced
    ½   of a small honeydew melon,
        peeled, seeded, and
        thinly sliced
    ⅓   cup chopped toasted pecans

1 For dressing, place 1 cup of the raspberries in a small bowl. Use a potato masher to mash the raspberries. Transfer mashed berries to a fine-mesh sieve. Strain raspberries; discard seeds. Return raspberry puree to the small bowl. Whisk in the olive oil, vinegar, red onion, garlic, sugar, salt, and pepper until well combined. Cover and chill until ready to serve.

2 To serve, arrange greens on four serving plates. If using ham or prosciutto, roll up each slice. Arrange chicken, ham, or prosciutto; melon slices; and remaining raspberries over greens. Sprinkle each with toasted pecans. Serve dressing with salads. Makes 4 main-dish servings.

Nutrition Facts per serving: 309 cal., 18 g total fat (2 g sat. fat), 24 mg chol., 672 mg sodium, 31 g carbo., 7 g fiber, 12 g pro. **Daily Values:** 59% vit. A, 125% vit. C, 5% calcium, 11% iron.

Chicken Antipasti Salad

These classic antipasti ingredients—tortellini, artichokes, kalamata olives, tomatoes, and Parmesan cheese—tossed together and herb-dressed make a perfect picnic dish. To tote, place the salad bowl on ice in an insulated cooler. (See the photograph on page 161.)

Prep: 25 minutes **Chill:** 1 hour

- 1 9-oz. pkg. refrigerated cheese tortellini
- ⅓ cup olive oil
- ¼ cup red wine vinegar
- 1 Tbsp. sugar
- 1 Tbsp. snipped fresh basil or ½ tsp. dried basil, crushed
- 1 Tbsp. Dijon-style mustard
- 2 cloves garlic, minced
- ¼ tsp. salt
- ⅛ tsp. pepper
- 1 9-oz. pkg. sliced smoked chicken breast strips or 2 cups sliced cooked chicken breast strips
- 1 15-oz. can chickpeas (garbanzo beans), rinsed and drained
- 1 14-oz. can artichoke hearts, drained and quartered
- ½ cup pitted whole kalamata olives or other ripe olives, drained
- 1 small red onion, thinly sliced
- 1 large tomato, coarsely chopped (about 1 cup)
    Finely shredded Parmesan cheese (optional)

1 Cook tortellini according to package directions; drain. Rinse with cold water and drain well. Place in a large bowl; set aside.

2 Meanwhile, for dressing, in a screw-top jar combine the olive oil, red wine vinegar, sugar, basil, Dijon-style mustard, garlic, salt, and pepper. Cover and shake well.

3 Add chicken strips, chickpeas, artichokes, olives, and onion to pasta in bowl. Gently stir to mix. Add the dressing, tossing gently to coat. Cover and chill at least 1 hour or up to 6 hours, stirring occasionally.

4 Just before serving, gently stir in the tomato. Sprinkle with Parmesan cheese, if desired. Makes 6 main-dish servings.

Nutrition Facts per serving: 455 cal., 19 g total fat (3 g sat. fat), 60 mg chol., 861 mg sodium, 45 g carbo., 6 g fiber, 26 g pro. **Daily Values:** 7% vit. A, 18% vit. C, 14% calcium, 23% iron.

---

30 MINUTE

Three Corner Chicken Salad

(See the photograph on page 161.)

Start to finish: 25 minutes

- 1 10-oz. pkg. refrigerated pizza dough
- 1 9- or 10-oz. pkg. frozen cooked chicken strips
- 6 cups torn mixed salad greens
- ⅓ cup bottled salad dressing

1 Preheat oven to 400°F. Unroll refrigerated pizza dough on a cutting board. Shape into a 10-inch square. Cut the square into four triangles. Drape each triangle over a well-greased, inverted 10-ounce custard cup (see photo, below).

2 Place cups on a shallow baking pan. Bake in the preheated oven about 15 minutes or until deep golden brown. Remove from cups; cool.

3 Prepare frozen cooked chicken strips as directed on the package. To serve, divide the mixed salad greens and the chicken among bread "bowls." Drizzle with dressing. Makes 4 main-dish servings.

Nutrition Facts per serving: 419 cal., 21 g total fat (4 g sat. fat), 43 mg chol., 1,333 mg sodium, 37 g carbo., 2 g fiber, 21 g pro. **Daily Values:** 16% vit. A, 9% vit. C, 4% calcium, 14% iron.

Jamaican Plum Chicken Kabobs

(See the photograph on page 161.)

Prep: 25 minutes **Grill:** 10 minutes

- 1 lb. skinless, boneless chicken breasts, cut into 1-inch pieces
- 1 tsp. Jamaican jerk seasoning
- 1 cup sugar snap or snow pea pods, cut in half crosswise (if large)
- 1 cup cubed fresh pineapple
- 1 medium red sweet pepper, cut into 1-inch pieces
- ½ cup plum preserves or jam
- ½ tsp. Jamaican jerk seasoning

1 In a medium mixing bowl combine chicken cubes and the 1 teaspoon jerk seasoning, tossing gently to coat all surfaces. Thread the chicken cubes alternately with the pea pods, pineapple cubes, and red pepper pieces onto four long or eight short metal skewers, leaving about ¼ inch between pieces.

2 For brush-on sauce, in a small saucepan stir together the plum preserves and the ½ teaspoon jerk seasoning. Cook and stir until preserves are just melted; set aside.

3 Grill kabobs on the rack of an uncovered grill directly over medium coals for 10 to 12 minutes or until an instant read thermometer registers 170°F and vegetables are tender, turning once and brushing often with sauce during the last 5 minutes of grilling. Serves 4.

Nutrition Facts per serving: 287 cal., 2 g total fat (0 g sat. fat), 66 mg chol., 192 mg sodium, 39 g carbo., 3 g fiber, 28 g pro. Daily Values: 4% vit. A, 78% vit. C, 5% calcium, 10% iron.

PRIZE WINNER

Mango-Chile Chicken

Shobhana Venugopalan
San Jose, California
$400—Sizzle and Spice Entrées

Start to finish: 25 minutes

- ⅓ cup mango chutney, snipped
- 2 tsp. hot chile garlic sauce
- 1 tsp. minced fresh ginger
- 1 tsp. minced garlic
- 2 tsp. cooking oil
- 1 to 3 small dried hot chile peppers
- 1 lb. skinless, boneless chicken breasts, cut into ¾- to 1-inch pieces
- 1 red sweet pepper, cut into 1- to 2-inch strips
- 1 mango, seeded, peeled, and cut into thin strips
- 2 cups hot cooked rice

1 For sauce, in a small bowl stir together chutney, garlic sauce, ginger, and garlic; set aside.

2 Heat oil in a large wok or 12-inch nonstick skillet over medium-high heat. Add chile peppers; cook and stir for 10 seconds.* Add chicken; cook and stir for 3 to 4 minutes or until chicken is no longer pink. Push chicken from center of wok. Add sweet pepper; cook and stir 1 minute. Stir in sauce and heat through.

3 To serve, spoon mixture into individual bowls or onto dinner plates. Top with mango and serve with rice. Makes 4 servings.

*Note: Cook hot peppers in a well-ventilated area.

Nutrition Facts per serving: 367 cal., 5 g total fat (1 g sat. fat), 66 mg chol., 124 mg sodium, 52 g carbo., 3 g fiber, 29 g pro. Daily Values: 65% vit. A, 89% vit. C, 4% calcium, 12% iron.

Garlicky Grilled Chicken

Ground coffee adds intriguing crunch to this garlic-crusted entrée. (See the photograph on page 163.)

Prep: 15 minutes **Grill:** 1 hour

- 1 2½- to 3-pound roasting chicken
- 1 Tbsp. cooking oil
- 2 cloves garlic, minced
- ⅛ tsp. salt
- ⅛ tsp. freshly ground pepper
- 1 tsp. dark roast ground coffee

1 Skewer neck skin to the back of the chicken. Twist wing tips under the back. Stir together cooking oil and garlic. Brush mixture onto chicken. Sprinkle with salt and freshly ground pepper. Rub ground coffee evenly onto chicken.

2 Arrange medium-hot coals around a drip pan. Test for medium heat above the pan. Place chicken, breast side up, on grill rack over drip pan. Cover and grill for 1 to 1¼ hours until chicken is no longer pink and a meat thermometer registers 180°F. Makes 4 servings.

Nutrition Facts per serving: 200 cal., 12 g total fat (3 g sat. fat), 66 mg chol., 110 mg sodium, 0 g carbo., 0 g fiber, 20 g pro. Daily Values: 1% vit. C, 1% calcium, 5% iron.

Jalapeño Chicken Spirals

The creamy, peppery-hot filling resembles the flavors of a popular appetizer—jalapeño poppers. If you're a fan of dark green chile peppers filled with creamy cheese, you'll love this dish.

Prep: 30 minutes Bake: 35 minutes

    4 skinless, boneless chicken breast
         halves (1 lb. total)
       Salt and black pepper
    2 oz. cream cheese, softened
   ⅓ cup chopped, seeded fresh
         jalapeño peppers*
   ⅓ cup chopped red sweet pepper
   ½ tsp. paprika
   ½ tsp. garlic powder
    2 Tbsp. butter or
         margarine, melted
   ¼ cup garlic-seasoned fine dry
         bread crumbs
   ¼ to ½ tsp. ground red pepper
    1 small tomato, chopped

1 Preheat oven to 350°F. Place each chicken breast half between two pieces of plastic wrap. Using the flat side of a meat mallet, pound lightly into a rectangle about ⅛ inch thick. Remove plastic wrap. Sprinkle chicken with salt and black pepper; set aside.

2 In a small bowl stir together softened cream cheese, jalapeño peppers, sweet pepper, paprika, and garlic powder. Spread filling evenly over each breast half. Fold in the bottom and sides; roll into a spiral. Secure with wooden toothpicks.

3 Brush chicken rolls with melted butter. In a shallow dish combine bread crumbs and ground red pepper. Coat chicken rolls with crumb mixture. Place rolls, seam side down, in a 2-quart rectangular baking dish. Drizzle with remaining butter. Bake for 35 minutes or until an instant read thermometer registers 170°F.

4 To serve, transfer chicken rolls to a serving platter. Sprinkle with chopped tomato. Makes 4 servings.

*Note: Hot peppers contain volatile oils that can burn eyes, lips, and sensitive skin. Wear plastic gloves while working with peppers and wash your hands thoroughly afterward.

Nutrition Facts per serving: 266 cal., 13 g total fat (7 g sat. fat), 98 mg chol., 443 mg sodium, 8 g carbo., 1 g fiber, 29 g pro. Daily Values: 29% vit. A, 51% vit. C, 4% calcium, 9% iron.

Cherry-Glazed Chicken

Start to finish: 35 minutes

   ¼ cup all-purpose flour
   ½ tsp. salt
   ¼ tsp. pepper
    4 skinless, boneless chicken breast
         halves (about 1¼ lb. total)
    2 Tbsp. cooking oil
   ⅓ cup chopped onion
    1 cup apple juice
   ½ cup dried tart red cherries
   ¼ cup cherry preserves
   ¼ cup peeled (if desired), chopped
         red cooking apple
  1½ tsp. cornstarch
   ⅛ tsp. ground cinnamon
   ⅓ cup chopped toasted walnuts
    2 cups hot cooked couscous

1 In a plastic bag combine flour, salt, and pepper. Add chicken breast halves; shake the bag to coat chicken.

2 In a large skillet cook chicken in hot oil over medium heat about 8 minutes or until lightly browned, turning once. Using a slotted spoon, remove chicken from skillet; set aside.

3 In the same skillet cook onion in drippings over medium heat until tender, not brown (add more oil, if necessary). Carefully stir ½ cup of the apple juice, the dried cherries, cherry preserves, and chopped apple into skillet. Return chicken to skillet. Bring to boiling; reduce heat. Cover and simmer for 5 minutes or until chicken is no longer pink and registers 170°F on an instant read thermometer. Use a slotted spoon to remove chicken to a serving platter. Keep warm.

4 Meanwhile, in a small mixing bowl combine the remaining ½ cup apple juice, cornstarch, and cinnamon. Stir apple juice mixture into skillet. Cook and stir until thickened and bubbly. Cook and stir for 2 minutes more.

5 To serve, spoon sauce over chicken. Sprinkle with toasted walnuts. Serve with hot cooked couscous. Makes 4 servings.

Nutrition Facts per serving: 530 cal., 15 g total fat (2 g sat. fat), 82 mg chol., 232 mg sodium, 59 g carbo., 3 g fiber, 38 g pro. Daily Values: 1% vit. A, 9% vit. C, 5% calcium, 12% iron.

Whether the sauce is store-bought or homemade, here are a few ideas to put extra sauce to good use:

- as pizza or spaghetti sauce

- instead of catsup for burgers, fries, and meat loaf

- mixed with ground meats, cheese, and sour cream to use as taco filling or potato stuffing

- to spice up tomato juice and Bloody Marys

- blended with cream cheese or sour cream for vegetable and chip dips

- as potato, corn, and bean salad dressing

- to spice up baked beans and bean dip

- to add smoky flavor to chili

---

30 MINUTE

BBQ Burgers

Use this zingy homemade barbecue sauce as a marinade while grilling and as a condiment when serving.

Prep: 15 minutes **Grill:** 14 minutes

  1 clove garlic, minced
  ¼ cup catsup
  2 Tbsp. steak sauce
  1 Tbsp. water
  1 tsp. sugar
  1 tsp. vinegar
     Few dashes bottled hot pepper
       sauce (optional)
  1 lb. lean ground beef

  ¼ tsp. salt
  ¼ tsp. black pepper
  4 hamburger buns, split
       and toasted*
     American cheese slices, lettuce
       leaves, tomato slices, onion
       slices, pickle slices (optional)

1 For sauce, in a small saucepan combine garlic, catsup, steak sauce, water, sugar, vinegar, and, if desired, hot pepper sauce. Bring to boiling; reduce heat. Simmer, uncovered, for 3 minutes. Remove from heat; set aside.

2 In a medium bowl combine beef, salt, and black pepper. Shape mixture into four ¾-inch-thick patties.

3 Grill burgers on the rack of an uncovered grill directly over medium coals for 14 to 18 minutes or until an instant read thermometer registers 160°F, turning once halfway through grilling and brushing with sauce once or twice during the last 5 minutes. Remove from the grill.

4 To serve, place burgers on buns. Spoon remaining sauce over burgers. If desired, top burgers with cheese, lettuce, tomato, onion, and pickles. Makes 4 servings.

*Note: To toast buns on the grill, place bun halves, cut side down, on the rack of an uncovered grill directly over coals. Grill 1 minute or until lightly toasted.

Nutrition Facts per serving: 332 cal., 13 g total fat (5 g sat. fat), 71 mg chol., 713 mg sodium, 29 g carbo., 1 g fiber, 24 g pro. Daily Values: 1% vit. A, 4% vit. C, 3% calcium, 21% iron.

---

30 MINUTE

BLT Steak

A loaf of crusty bread and a bottle of red wine complete this bistro-style dinner. (See the photograph on page 159.)

Start to finish: 30 minutes

  2 12-oz. boneless beef top loin
       steaks, cut 1¼ inches thick
  2 slices bacon
  ½ cup bottled balsamic vinaigrette
       salad dressing
  8 slices red and/or yellow tomato
  2 cups mixed baby greens

1 Trim fat from steaks. Grill steaks on the rack of an uncovered grill over medium coals until desired doneness, turning once halfway through grilling. (Allow 14 to 18 minutes for medium-rare or 18 to 22 minutes for medium doneness.)

2 Meanwhile, in a large skillet cook bacon over medium heat until crisp-cooked. Remove bacon and drain on paper towels. Crumble bacon and set aside. Drain fat, reserving 1 tablespoon drippings in skillet. Add the balsamic vinaigrette salad dressing to the skillet. Cook and stir over high heat about one minute, scraping up browned bits. Remove from heat.

3 To serve, halve the steaks. Place a piece of steak on each of four dinner plates. Top each with two tomato slices, some cooked bacon, some mixed greens, and a splash of dressing from the skillet. Makes 4 servings.

Nutrition Facts per serving: 556 cal., 42 g total fat (14 g sat. fat), 122 mg chol., 636 mg sodium, 5 g carbo., 1 g fiber, 38 g pro. Daily Values: 6% vit. A, 12% vit. C, 2% calcium, 17% iron.

Beef Steaks with Tomato-Garlic Butter

Beef steaks take kindly to butter, especially this tangy, garlic-infused blend. Double the butter recipe to spread it on warm bread.

Prep: 12 minutes **Grill:** 8 minutes

- ½ cup butter, softened
- 1 Tbsp. snipped oil-packed dried tomatoes, drained
- 1 Tbsp. chopped pitted kalamata olives
- 1 Tbsp. finely chopped green onion
- 1 clove garlic, minced
- 4 boneless beef top loin steaks, cut 1 inch thick
  Salt and pepper (optional)

1 For garlic butter, in a small bowl stir together the butter, drained tomatoes, kalamata olives, green onion, and garlic. Set aside.

2 Trim fat from steaks. Grill steaks on the rack of an uncovered grill directly over medium coals until desired doneness, turning once halfway through grilling. (Allow 8 to 12 minutes for medium-rare and 12 to 15 minutes for medium doneness.)

3 If desired, sprinkle steaks with salt and pepper. To serve, spread 1 tablespoon of the butter mixture over each steak. Cover and chill the remaining butter mixture for another use (also can be used as a spread for bread). Makes 4 servings.

Nutrition Facts per serving: 383 cal., 22 g total fat (11 g saturated fat), 161 mg chol., 227 mg sodium, 0 g carbo., 0 g fiber, 45 g pro.
Daily Values: 10% vit. A, 1% vit. C, 1% calcium, 32% iron.

Mediterranean Steak 'n' Vegetables

In Greece and in Turkey, where grilling on skewers originated, kabobs are the most popular street food. The marinade for these kabobs infuses sirloin with Mediterranean herbs and zest. The cucumber-yogurt sauce, tzatziki, is simply delicious.

Prep: 30 minutes **Marinate:** 2 hours
Grill: 5 minutes

- 1 boneless beef top sirloin steak, cut 1 inch thick (about 1½ lb.)
- 2 medium red or green sweet peppers, cut into 1-inch pieces
- 1 medium onion, cut into wedges
- ½ cup bottled clear Italian salad dressing
- 2 tsp. dried oregano, crushed
- ½ tsp. ground black pepper
- ½ cup chopped cucumber
- ½ cup plain yogurt
- 1 clove garlic, minced
- ⅛ tsp. salt
- 4 large pita bread rounds, warmed*

1 Trim fat from steak. Cut steak across the grain into ¼-inch-thick strips. Place the beef strips, sweet pepper pieces, and onion wedges in a plastic bag set in a shallow dish.

2 For marinade, in a glass measure or small mixing bowl combine salad dressing, oregano, and black pepper. Pour over beef and vegetables, tossing to coat. Close bag. Marinate in refrigerator for at least 2 hours or up to 8 hours.

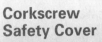
3 Meanwhile, for sauce, in a small serving bowl stir together the cucumber, yogurt, garlic, and salt. Cover and chill sauce in the refrigerator until serving time.

4 Drain the beef and vegetables, discarding marinade. On six metal skewers, thread the beef strips, sweet pepper pieces, and onion wedges, leaving space between pieces. Grill on the rack of an uncovered grill directly over medium coals to desired doneness, turning occasionally. (Allow 5 to 6 minutes for medium doneness.) Serve kabobs with pita rounds and yogurt sauce. Makes 6 servings.

***Note:** To warm pita bread, place rounds on the rack of an uncovered grill directly over coals. Grill for 1 to 2 minutes or until warm, turning once halfway through grilling.

Nutrition Facts per serving: 327 cal., 10 g total fat (3 g sat. fat), 56 mg chol., 411 mg sodium, 29 g carbo., 2 g fiber, 29 g pro., **Daily Values:** 44% vit. A, 109% vit. C, 9% calcium, 21% iron.

30 MINUTE

Portobello Pizzas

Portobellos, the titans of the fungi world, serve as the crust for these single-serving gourmet pizzas. Though they look exotic, portobellos are a variety of brown mushroom that is allowed to grow until the cap is three or more inches wide. (See the photograph on page 157.)

Prep: 15 minutes **Grill:** 8 minutes

- 4 large portobello mushroom caps
- 2 tsp. olive oil
   Salt and pepper
- 1 4½-oz. Brie round, thinly sliced
- ¼ cup small fresh arugula leaves
- 1 Tbsp. olive oil
- 8 thin slices red and/or yellow tomato

1 Clean and remove the stems from the portobello mushrooms. Brush both sides of caps with the 2 teaspoons olive oil. Season with salt and pepper.

2 Place the caps, rounded side down, on the grill rack directly over medium coals. Cover with lid and grill for 8 to 10 minutes or until mushrooms are tender and heated through, turning once. Remove caps from grill.

3 Top each mushroom cap with cheese slices and arugula leaves. Drizzle some of the 1 tablespoon olive oil over each. Top with tomato slices. Serve immediately. Makes 4 appetizer servings.

Oven Method

Preheat oven to 400°F. Prepare mushroom caps as directed, except do not grill. Instead, place on a foil-lined baking sheet. Bake, uncovered, for 8 to 10 minutes or until tender, turning once. Continue as directed.

Nutrition Facts per serving: 181 cal., 16 g total fat (6 g sat. fat), 28 mg chol., 257 mg sodium, 5 g carbo., 1 g fiber, 10 g pro. Daily Values: 8% vit. A, 10% vit. C, 6% calcium, 5% iron.

30 MINUTE

Ginger Beer Float

Start to finish: 5 minutes

- ¼ cup pineapple juice, chilled
- ½ cup pineapple-coconut or vanilla ice cream
- ½ of a 12-ounce bottle ginger beer
   Fresh pineapple spear and/or toasted coconut shavings (optional)

1 In a tall glass pour the chilled pineapple juice. Add the pineapple-coconut or vanilla ice cream. Carefully pour the ginger beer into the glass. Garnish with a fresh pineapple spear or toasted coconut shavings, if desired. Serve with a straw and long-handled spoon. Makes 1 serving.

Nutrition Facts per serving: 270 cal., 12 g total fat (7 g sat. fat), 45 mg chol., 81 mg sodium, 42 g carbo., 1 g fiber, 3 g pro. Daily Values: 10% vit. A, 26% vit. C, 9% calcium, 1% iron.

30 MINUTE, NO FAT

Mosaic Cooler

Use your blender to mix this fruity concoction of sweet and tart flavors. (See the photograph on page 157.)

Start to finish: 10 minutes

- 1½ cups peeled, seeded, and coarsely chopped fruits, such as mango, strawberries, kiwi fruit, pineapple, and carambola (star fruit)
- 1 cup chilled piña colada mix
- 1 cup ice
- ¼ cup light rum
- 1 Tbsp. lime juice
- 1 fresh basil sprig

1 In a glass pitcher place your choice of chopped fruits. Set aside.

2 In a blender container combine the piña colada mix, ice, light rum, and lime juice. Cover and blend until smooth. Pour over fruits in pitcher. Garnish with fresh basil, if desired.

3 To serve, pour into chilled glasses. Serve with straws and long-handled spoons. Makes 4 servings.

Nutrition Facts per serving: 134 cal., 0 g total fat, 0 mg chol., 58 mg sodium, 23 g carbo., 1 g fiber, 4 g pro. Daily Values: 53% vit. C, 1% calcium, 1% iron.

Right: Mosaic Cooler (page 156)
Below: Portobello Pizzas (page 156)

Above left: Ginger-Tomato Salad (page 144)
Above right: Icy Shrimp Cocktail (page 138)
Right: Southwestern Vegetable Slaw (page 142)
Page 159: BLT Steak (page 154)

Page 160: Peach-Basil Delight (page 144)
Left: Three Corner Chicken Salad (page 151)
Below Left: Chicken Antipasti Salad (page 151)
Below Right: Jamaican Plum Chicken Kabobs (page 152)

Left: Lime and Thyme Potato Salad (page 141)
Below left: Crab Cakes (page 140)
Below right: Fresh Corn-Rice Salad (page 142)
Page 163: Garlicky Grilled Chicken (page 152)

Right: Cherry Bruschetta (page 138)
Below: Banana Split Trifles (page 165)

Banana Split Trifles

A duo of hot fudge topping and strawberry preserves makes these sundaes yummy. Substitute any combination of ice cream toppings or preserves, such as caramel and marshmallow, butterscotch and chocolate, or fudge and raspberry. (See the photograph on page 164.)

Prep: 15 minutes **Freeze:** up to 1 hour

- 2 to 3 cups tin roof sundae, chocolate chunk, or vanilla ice cream
- 4 soft-style oatmeal or chocolate chip cookies, about 3 inches in diameter, crumbled
- ⅔ cup hot fudge ice cream topping and/or strawberry preserves
- ½ cup whipped cream
- 2 small bananas, halved lengthwise and sliced into 1- to 2-inch pieces

1 In a medium mixing bowl use a wooden spoon to stir the ice cream to soften. In each of four glasses layer cookie crumbs, softened ice cream, hot fudge topping and/or preserves, layering ingredients to the top of the glasses.

2 Top each trifle with whipped cream, banana slices, and more hot fudge topping and cookie crumbs. Cover and freeze up to 1 hour. Makes 4 servings.

Nutrition Facts per serving: 524 cal., 23 g total fat (12 g sat. fat), 48 mg chol., 161 mg sodium, 73 g carbo., 3 g fiber, 6 g pro. Daily Values: 14% vit. A, 21% vit. C, 15% calcium, 7% iron.

COOKING WITH KIDS

Wish Kabobs

Children relish the thrill of backyard cookouts as much as adults. Let kids assist in the meal preparation by helping with the grilled fruit kabobs. Let them build on the skills they have already mastered toasting marshmallows around the campfire.

Here are a few pointers to follow in allowing children close to the grill:

Age and size matter. When children are chest high to the grilling surface, they can be allowed to assemble food on wooden skewers and to carry supplies.

Dress for the occasion. Teach children to wear snug-fitting, long-sleeve T-shirts to protect arms from splatters. Don't allow billowy sleeves or loose clothing that can be hazardous around the grill.

---

30 MINUTE, LOW FAT
Happy Fruit Kabobs

Start to finish: 20 minutes

- 8 12-inch wooden skewers
- ½ cup apple jelly
- 1 Tbsp. lemon juice
- ⅛ tsp. ground cinnamon
- ½ of a medium fresh pineapple, peeled and cored (about 9 oz.)
- 2 cups large fresh strawberries
- 1 nectarine, seeded and cut into wedges
- ½ of a 10-oz. loaf frozen pound cake, cut into 1½-inch cubes
- 8 small, firm kiwi fruit, peeled and cut in half crosswise

1 Soak wooden skewers in water for 1 hour. In a grill with a cover have an adult arrange preheated coals around drip pan for indirect grilling.

2 For sauce, in a saucepan combine apple jelly, lemon juice, and cinnamon. Cook over low heat, stirring occasionally, until smooth and bubbly. Remove from heat; set aside.

3 Cut pineapple into 1½-inch pieces. Thread pineapple, strawberries, nectarine wedges, and cake cubes alternately onto skewers, placing kiwi fruit halves on each end. Leave space (about ¼ inch) between each piece to heat evenly. Transfer kabobs to a baking sheet or tray to carry to the grill.

4 Place kabobs on grill rack over drip pan. Cover grill. Grill kabobs for 2 minutes. Carefully turn over skewers, using oven mitts to protect hands.

5 Use a long-handled brush to brush some of the sauce over kabobs. Grill for 1 to 2 minutes more or until heated through. Turn. Brush with sauce. Remove kabobs from grill. Makes 8 servings.

Nutrition Facts per serving: 216 cal., 5 g total fat (2 g sat. fat), 20 mg chol., 73 mg sodium, 42 g carbo., 4 g fiber, 3 g pro. Daily Values: 6% vit. A, 170% vit. C, 4% calcium, 5% iron.

Sweet Cherry Trifles

Prep: 20 minutes **Chill:** Up to 8 hours

- 1 8-oz. carton plain low-fat yogurt
- ¼ cup cherry preserves
- 2 Tbsp. cherry liqueur (optional)
- ½ of a 10¾-oz. frozen loaf pound cake
- 1 cup halved and pitted dark or light sweet cherries
- ¼ cup sliced, toasted almonds

1 In a small mixing bowl stir together yogurt, half of the cherry preserves, and cherry liqueur, if using, until smooth. Set aside.

2 Cut the pound cake in half again. Spread the cut sides of each cake half with remaining cherry preserves. Cut each half into ½-inch cubes.

3 In four parfait glasses or deep dessert dishes, place half of the cake cubes. Layer half of the cherries, half of the yogurt mixture, and half of the nuts atop cake cubes in glasses. Repeat layers using remaining ingredients. Cover and chill up to 8 hours. Makes 4 servings.

Nutrition Facts per serving: 278 cal., 10 g total fat (5 g sat. fat), 43 mg chol., 177 mg sodium, 42 g carbo., 2 g fiber, 6 g pro. **Daily Values:** 6% vit. A, 8% vit. C, 13% calcium, 5% iron.

Cherry-Chocolate Chunk Mousse

Prep: 20 minutes **Chill:** 3½ hours

- ¾ cup whipping cream
- ½ cup dairy sour cream
- ⅓ cup sugar
- 1½ tsp. unflavored gelatin
- 2 Tbsp. cold water
- 1 Tbsp. cherry brandy (optional)
- 1 cup fresh or frozen pitted dark sweet cherries, chopped
- ½ of a 4-oz. pkg. sweet baking chocolate, chopped

1 In a medium mixing bowl beat together whipping cream and sour cream until soft peaks form. Stir in sugar; set aside.

2 In a small heat-proof bowl soften gelatin in cold water. Place bowl in saucepan of boiling water, stirring to dissolve. Gradually stir gelatin mixture into whipped cream mixture along with cherry brandy, if using. Fold in cherries and chocolate. Chill until mixture mounds (about 30 minutes). Spoon mousse into dessert dishes. Cover and chill about 3 hours or until set. Serves 5 or 6.

Nutrition Facts per serving: 297 cal., 22 g total fat (11 g sat. fat), 58 mg chol., 27 mg sodium, 26 g carbo., 1 g fiber, 3 g pro. **Daily Values:** 15% vit. A, 4% vit. C, 5% calcium, 2% iron.

Sweet Glazed Cherry Pie

Carolyn Blakemore
Fairmont, West Virginia
$400—Cherries, Sweet and Sour

Prep: 20 minutes **Bake:** 1 hour 20 minutes **Stand:** 1 hour

- ½ cup granulated sugar
- 3 Tbsp. cornstarch
- 1 16-oz. pkg. frozen unsweetened pitted dark sweet cherries
- ½ tsp. vanilla
- 1 purchased or homemade pastry for double-crust 9-inch pie
- ¾ cup sliced, toasted almonds
- 1 21-oz. can cherry pie filling
- ¼ cup sifted powdered sugar
- 1 to 1½ tsp. milk

TEST KITCHEN TIP
Choosing Cherries

Shop for fresh cherries that are plump, even-colored, firm, smooth-skinned, and brightly colored for the variety. Avoid bruised, split, or very soft fruit.

1 In a bowl stir together granulated sugar and cornstarch. Add frozen cherries and vanilla; toss. Let stand at room temperature about 1 hour or until a syrup forms; stir occasionally.

2 Preheat oven to 375°F. Prepare pastry. On a lightly floured surface, roll half of the pastry into a 12-inch circle. Line a 9-inch pie plate with pastry. Place ½ cup of the almonds in bottom of pastry-lined pie plate. Stir cherry mixture; spoon on top of almonds. Spoon pie filling over sweet cherry mixture; spread evenly.

3 Trim bottom pastry to edge of pie plate. For top crust, roll remaining pastry into a 12-inch circle. Cut slits in top crust. Place on filling; trim ½ inch beyond edge of plate. Fold top pastry under bottom pastry; seal. Flute edge; cover edge with foil to prevent overbrowning. Bake for 50 minutes. Remove foil. Bake about 30 minutes more or until top is golden brown and filling is bubbly. Remove from oven; cool on a wire rack for 1 to 1½ hours.

4 For icing, in a small bowl stir together powdered sugar and enough milk to make of drizzling consistency. Drizzle over pie. Sprinkle remaining almonds on top of pie. Cool completely. Makes 8 servings.

Nutrition Facts per serving: 524 cal., 24 g total fat (5 g sat. fat), 0 mg chol., 148 mg sodium, 72 g carbo., 4 g fiber, 7 g pro. **Daily Values:** 6% vit. A, 11% vit. C, 5% calcium, 13% iron.

august

IN THIS CHAPTER

30-minute recipes indicated in COLOR.
Low-fat and no-fat recipes indicated with a ♥.
Photographs indicated in italics.
*Bonus recipe

LOW FAT

Berry Breakfast Rolls

See the photograph on page 200.

Prep: 15 minutes **Bake:** 12 minutes
Cool: 10 minutes

- 1   11½-oz. pkg. (8) refrigerated cinnamon rolls with icing
- 1   cup fresh blueberries
- ⅓   cup blueberry preserves
- 1   tsp. finely shredded lemon peel
- ¼   cup chopped pecans

1 Preheat oven to 375°F. Lightly grease sixteen 2½-inch muffin cups. Cut each cinnamon roll in half crosswise. Press each roll in bottom and halfway up sides of a muffin cup.

2 Stir together berries, preserves, and lemon peel. Spoon mixture over the rolls. Sprinkle with pecans. Bake 12 minutes or until golden. Cool 10 minutes; remove from cups. Stir a little milk into icing to make of drizzling consistency. Drizzle over rolls. Serve warm. Makes 16 rolls.

Nutrition Facts per roll: 110 cal., 4 g total fat (1 g sat. fat), 0 mg chol., 173 mg sodium, 18 g carbo., 0 g fiber, 1 g pro. **Daily Values:** 3% vit. C, 3% iron.

PRIZE WINNER

French Toast Gets Dilly

Lynn Boynton
Columbia, Missouri
$200—Fresh Herb Ideas

Start to finish: 25 minutes

- 4   eggs
- ¼   cup dairy sour cream
- 3   Tbsp. snipped fresh dillweed
- 1   Tbsp. Dijon-style mustard
- 6   ¾-inch-thick slices sourdough or French bread
- 1   Tbsp. margarine, butter, or cooking oil
- 6   thin slices cheddar cheese
- 6   thin slices tomato
- 1   to 2 Tbsp. snipped fresh chives
      Salt and pepper (optional)

1 In a shallow bowl beat together eggs, sour cream, dillweed, and Dijon-style mustard. Dip bread slices, one at a time, into egg mixture, allowing bread to soak in egg mixture about 15 seconds on each side.

2 In a skillet or on a griddle cook bread in hot margarine over medium heat for 2 to 3 minutes or until bottom is golden brown. Turn slices over. Place a cheese slice on top of each bread slice. Top each with a tomato slice and sprinkle with chives. Season with salt and pepper, if desired. Cook for 2 to 3 minutes more or until bottom is golden brown, adding more margarine as needed. Serve warm. Makes 6 slices.

Nutrition Facts per slice: 221 cal., 14 g total fat (7 g sat. fat), 165 mg chol., 311 mg sodium, 13 g carbo., 0 g fiber, 11 g pro. **Daily Values:** 13% vit. A, 5% vit. C, 17% calcium, 7% iron.

30 MINUTE

Sage Biscuits

Prep: 15 minutes **Bake:** 12 minutes

- 1⅓   cups all-purpose flour
- ⅔   cup whole wheat flour
- 1   Tbsp. baking powder
- ¼   tsp. baking soda
- ¼   tsp. salt
- ⅓   cup butter
- ½   cup finely shredded smoked Gouda or smoked cheddar cheese (2 oz.)
- 2   Tbsp. finely snipped fresh sage
- 2   cloves garlic, minced
- 1   cup buttermilk

1 Preheat oven to 425°F. Grease a large baking sheet; set aside. In a medium bowl combine flours, baking powder, baking soda, and salt. Using a pastry blender, cut in butter until mixture resembles coarse crumbs. Stir in cheese, sage, and garlic. Make a well in center of dry mixture.

2 Add buttermilk all at once to the dry mixture. Using a fork, stir just until moistened. Drop dough from a tablespoon into mounds 1 inch apart onto prepared baking sheet.

3 Bake in the preheated oven for 12 to 14 minutes or until golden. Remove biscuits from baking sheet. Serve warm. Makes 10 biscuits.

To Make Ahead:

Prepare and bake biscuits as directed; cool completely. Place biscuits in a freezer container or bag; freeze up to 3 months. To serve, wrap frozen biscuits in foil. Heat in a 300°F oven for 20 to 25 minutes or until warm.

Nutrition Facts per biscuit: 171 cal., 8 g total fat (5 g sat. fat), 25 mg chol., 347 mg sodium, 19 g carbo., 1 g fiber, 5 g pro. **Daily Values:** 6% vit. A, 1% vit. C, 15% calcium, 6% iron.

Spicy Shrimp Appetizer

French bread for dipping is a welcome accompaniment to the flavorful sauce.

Prep: 30 minutes **Bake:** 10 minutes
Cool: 10 minutes

- 1¼ lb. fresh or frozen medium shrimp, peeled and deveined
- ¼ cup snipped fresh parsley
- 2 Tbsp. finely chopped fresh garlic
- 2 tsp. snipped fresh rosemary
- ⅓ cup dry white wine
- 1 Tbsp. olive oil
- 1 Tbsp. Worcestershire sauce
- 2 tsp. lemon juice
- ⅛ tsp. ground red pepper
- 2 Tbsp. butter or margarine
  Sliced French bread

1 Thaw shrimp, if frozen. Preheat oven to 375°F. In a medium bowl stir together the uncooked shrimp, parsley, garlic, and rosemary. Divide the shrimp mixture evenly among six individual 8-ounce casseroles or small au gratin dishes.

2 In a small mixing bowl whisk together the white wine, olive oil, Worcestershire sauce, lemon juice, and ground red pepper. Carefully pour the wine mixture evenly over shrimp mixture in each dish. Dot each with some of the butter or margarine.

3 Bake, uncovered, in the preheated oven for 10 to 12 minutes or until shrimp turn pink, stirring casseroles once. Remove from oven; cool for 10 minutes. Serve with French bread slices for dipping. Makes 6 servings.

Nutrition Facts per serving: 192 cal., 8 g total fat (3 g sat. fat), 110 mg chol., 338 mg sodium, 15 g carbo., 1 g fiber, 13 g pro. Daily Values: 8% vit. A, 11% vit. C, 5% calcium, 15% iron.

30 MINUTE

Herbed Goat Cheese Crostini

Start to finish: 30 minutes

- 16 ½-inch slices French bread (10 oz.)
- 2 Tbsp. olive oil
- 2 cups sliced leeks
- 4 cloves garlic, minced
- 2 Tbsp. butter or margarine
- 2 tsp. snipped fresh rosemary or ½ tsp. dried rosemary, crushed
- 2 tsp. snipped fresh basil or ½ tsp. dried basil, crushed
- 2 tsp. snipped fresh thyme or ½ tsp. dried thyme, crushed
- 1 tsp. fennel seed, crushed
- ½ tsp. coarsely cracked black pepper
- ½ tsp. brown sugar
- 6 oz. soft goat cheese (chévre)
  Snipped fresh herbs (optional)

1 Preheat oven to 425°F. Lightly brush both sides of each slice of bread with olive oil. Place on an ungreased baking sheet. Bake in the prepared oven about 10 minutes or until crisp and light brown; set aside.

2 Meanwhile, in a medium skillet cook sliced leeks and garlic, covered, in hot butter over medium-low heat for 10 to 12 minutes or until leeks are very tender, stirring occasionally. Uncover and stir in the rosemary, basil, thyme, fennel seed, pepper, and brown sugar. Cook and stir over medium-high heat for 3 to 4 minutes or until leeks are golden.

3 In a small mixing bowl stir together the goat cheese and leek mixture. Spread each piece of toast with some of the goat cheese mixture. Return slices to the baking sheet. Bake

in the preheated oven about 3 minutes more or until heated through. Sprinkle with additional fresh herbs, if desired. Serve warm. Makes 16 appetizers.

Nutrition Facts per appetizer: 114 cal., 6 g total fat (3 g sat. fat), 9 mg chol., 165 mg sodium, 11 g carbo., 1 g fiber, 4 g pro. Daily Values: 2% vit. A, 2% vit. C, 4% calcium, 5% iron.

30 MINUTE

Squished Tomato Catsup

Catsup doesn't get any fresher than this! Start with a just-picked tomato, mash it, add a little olive oil and balsamic vinegar, and season it with salt and pepper for the best summer condiment around. (See the photograph on page 201.)

Start to finish: 10 minutes

- 1 ripe red tomato
- 1 tsp. olive oil
- 1 tsp. balsamic vinegar
  Salt and pepper

1 Make a shallow X on the bottom of the tomato. Using a slotted spoon, dip the tomato into a pan of boiling water for 15 seconds. Remove tomato; rinse in cold water. Peel off skin.

2 Cut tomato in half. Gently squeeze each half to remove seeds. In a small bowl coarsely mash tomato with a fork. If desired, drain to remove excess juice. Stir in olive oil and balsamic vinegar. Season with salt and pepper. Spread on a grilled hamburger or chicken breast. Makes 1 serving.

Nutrition Facts per serving: 69 cal., 5 g total fat (1 g sat. fat), 0 mg chol., 156 mg sodium, 6 g carbo., 1 g fiber, 1 g pro. Daily Values: 15% vit. A, 39% vit. C, 1% calcium, 3% iron.

Purple Thai rice, purchased at Asian markets, adds rich color and subtle nutty flavor to recipes. Although the deep-color rice is a long grain variety, it takes a little longer to cook than white long grain rice. Either rice works well with the refreshing mint and mango flavors of Mango-Rice Salad (see recipe, right).

PRIZE WINNER

Perky Pistachio Torta

Margaret Berry
Lincoln, Nebraska
$400—Fresh Herb Ideas

Start to finish: 20 minutes

- 4 cubes Pistachio Pesto (see recipe, right)
- 1 8-oz. package cream cheese
  Roasted red pepper strips
  Chopped pistachio nuts

1 Thaw four cubes of Pistachio Pesto. Equally divide cream cheese into four portions. On four pieces of waxed paper, spread each portion of cream cheese into a 4-inch round.

2 Invert one cream cheese round on a plate; remove waxed paper. Spread one of the pesto cubes on a cheese round. Layer remaining cheese rounds and pesto. (If cheese is too soft, chill until it can easily be removed from paper.) Sprinkle top with pepper strips and pistachio nuts. Makes 8 appetizer servings.

Nutrition Facts per serving: 143 cal., 14 g total fat (7 g sat. fat), 32 mg chol., 135 mg sodium, 2 g carbo., 1 g fiber, 3 g pro. **Daily Values:** 12% vit. A, 10% vit. C, 5% calcium, 4% iron.

30 MINUTE

Pistachio Pesto

The flavorful combination of mint and basil works wonders in this brilliant green pesto. Layer it on the Perky Pistachio Torta (see recipe, left), toss it with long strands of pasta, or spoon it over grilled lamb chops or grilled fish.

Start to finish: 20 minutes

- 2 cups firmly packed fresh basil leaves
- 1 cup firmly packed fresh parsley, stems removed
- ½ cup grated Parmesan cheese
- ½ cup pistachio nuts
- 2 Tbsp. fresh mint leaves
- 1 clove garlic, quartered
- ½ tsp. salt
- ½ cup olive oil

1 In a food processor bowl combine fresh basil leaves, fresh parsley sprigs, Parmesan cheese, pistachio nuts, fresh mint leaves, garlic, salt, and olive oil. Cover and process with several on-off turns until a paste forms. Stop the machine several times and scrape sides. Process to the consistency of soft butter.

2 Transfer pesto to an ice cube tray; cover and freeze. Release cubes into a freezer bag. Seal and return to freezer. Freeze for up to 3 months. Thaw before using. Makes 1⅓ cups.

Blender Directions:

Process half of the ingredients and 1 to 2 tablespoons of the olive oil at a time. Cover and blend with several on-off turns until a paste forms. Stop blender several times and scrape sides. With machine running, gradually add remaining olive oil and blend to consistency of soft butter. Freeze and use as directed.

Nutrition Facts per tablespoon: 76 cal., 7 g total fat (1 g sat. fat), 2 mg chol., 102 mg sodium, 1 g carbo., 1 g fiber, 2 g pro. **Daily Values:** 8% vit. A, 8% vit. C, 5% calcium, 3% iron.

LOW FAT

Mango-Rice Salad

The flavors of citrus, fruit, and mint provide a delicate fresh taste to the salad, whether you use colorful Thai rice or long grain rice.

Prep: 15 minutes **Cook:** 25 minutes
Stand: 10 minutes

- 1 cup uncooked purple Thai rice, rinsed and drained, or 1 cup long grain rice
- ½ cup orange juice
- 1 tsp. margarine or butter
- ½ tsp. salt
- 1 cup chopped, peeled mango
- ½ cup bottled roasted red sweet pepper, drained and chopped
- ¼ cup snipped fresh mint
- 2 Tbsp. lime juice
- 1 Tbsp. olive oil

1 In a medium saucepan combine 1½ cups water, the uncooked rice, orange juice, margarine, and salt. Bring to boiling. Cover and simmer 25 minutes (20 minutes for long grain rice) or until most of the liquid is absorbed and rice is tender. Remove from heat; let stand 10 minutes. Place rice in a colander. Rinse with cool water; drain well.

2 In a serving bowl combine rice, mango, red pepper, mint, lime juice, and olive oil. Serve immediately. Makes 6 side-dish servings.

To Make Ahead:

Prepare salad as directed. Cover and chill for up to 24 hours. Let stand at room temperature for 30 minutes before serving.

Nutrition Facts per serving: 175 cal., 3 g total fat (1 g sat. fat), 2 mg chol., 189 mg sodium, 34 g carbo., 2 g fiber, 3 g pro. Daily Values: 96% vit. C, 1% calcium, 14% iron.

Seared Vegetable Medley

Romano beans are wider and flatter than green beans. They make a wonderful addition to this casserole or make a tasty side dish. Cook them as you do fresh green beans. (See the photograph on page 202.)

Prep: 25 minutes **Broil:** 20 minutes

- 3 cups cauliflower florets (about 12 oz.)
- 2 medium yellow, orange, and/or red sweet peppers, seeded and cut into strips or squares
- 12 oz. green beans or Romano beans, trimmed and cut into 2-inch pieces (3½ cups)
- 2 medium onions, cut into wedges or chunks
- 3 Tbsp. olive oil or cooking oil
- 4 cloves garlic, minced
- ½ tsp. salt
- ¼ tsp. black pepper
- 2 tsp. finely shredded lemon peel
- 2 tsp. lemon juice

1 In the bottom of a broiler pan combine the cauliflower, sweet peppers, green beans or Romano beans, and onions. In a small bowl stir together the olive oil or cooking oil, garlic, salt, and black pepper. Drizzle the oil mixture over the vegetables, tossing to coat.

2 Broil 5 to 6 inches from heat for 20 to 25 minutes or until the vegetables are just tender and browned, stirring every 5 minutes. Watch carefully the last 5 to 10 minutes and stir more frequently, if needed, to prevent burning. Remove the pan from the oven. Sprinkle the vegetables with lemon peel and lemon juice, tossing gently to coat. Makes 6 to 8 side-dish servings.

Nutrition Facts per serving: 121 cal., 7 g total fat (1 g sat. fat), 0 mg chol., 215 mg sodium, 14 g carbo., 4 g fiber, 3 g pro. Daily Values: 10% vit. A, 213% vit. C, 5% calcium, 7% iron.

30 MINUTE

Teeny Zucchini With Onions

Start to finish: 20 minutes

- 1 lb. baby zucchini or 3 medium zucchini
- 1 Tbsp. olive oil
- 1 small onion, cut into thin wedges
- ¼ cup chopped walnuts
- ½ tsp. dried oregano, crushed
- ¼ tsp. salt
- ¼ tsp. pepper

1 Rinse and trim zucchini. If using medium zucchini, cut each in half lengthwise, then into ½-inch slices.

2 In a large nonstick skillet heat olive oil over medium heat. Add zucchini and onion. Cook for 6 to 8 minutes or until vegetables are just tender, stirring occasionally. Add walnuts, oregano, salt, and pepper to mixture in skillet. Cook and stir for 1 minute more. Makes 4 to 6 servings.

Nutrition Facts per serving: 106 cal., 9 g total fat (1 g sat. fat), 0 mg chol., 146 mg sodium, 6 g carbo., 1 g fiber, 4 g pro. Daily Values: 67% vit. C, 3% calcium, 2% iron.

30 MINUTE, LOW FAT

Summer S'ghetti

Three main ingredients and 20 minutes of preparation reward you with a magnificent main dish. (See the photograph on page 200.)

Start to finish: 20 minutes

- 2 cups mixed vegetables, such as sliced yellow summer squash, halved baby sunburst squash, chopped carrots, and sliced green onions
- 8 oz. packaged dried spaghetti
- 2 Tbsp. butter or olive oil
- ¼ cup finely shredded Asiago or Parmesan cheese
- ⅛ tsp. freshly ground pepper

1 Place the vegetables in a colander. Cook pasta according to package directions. Pour over vegetables in colander; drain.

2 Transfer pasta and vegetable mixture to a serving bowl. Drizzle with butter or olive oil, tossing to coat. Sprinkle with cheese and pepper. Makes 4 side-dish servings.

Nutrition Facts per serving: 320 cal., 10 g total fat (6 g sat. fat), 24 mg chol., 152 mg sodium, 48 g carbo., 3 g fiber, 10 g pro. Daily Values: 135% vit. A, 19% vit. C, 7% calcium, 12% iron.

ZILLIONS OF ZUCCHINI

It takes only one season of growing zucchini to discover that one little plant delivers an abundance of long, slender green squash. Plentiful gardens over the years have challenged cooks to discover ways to use zucchini in casseroles, relishes, and baked goods. Experiment with the mild flavor of this versatile vegetable in these treasured favorites.

Vegetable Relish

To freeze rather than can this relish, cool the hot mixture by setting the Dutch oven into ice water. Ladle the relish into wide-top freezer containers, leaving ½-inch of space at the top. Freeze for up to 12 months.

Prep: 30 minutes **Chill:** 8 hours
Process: 10 minutes

    8   medium tomatoes
          (about 2¾ lb.)
    6   medium zucchini
          (about 3 lb.)
    3   large red sweet peppers
    3   large green sweet peppers
    2   medium onions
    4   cloves garlic
    ¼   cup pickling salt
  2½   cups vinegar
    2   cups sugar
    1   tsp. dried thyme, crushed
    ½   tsp. pepper

1 Wash tomatoes, zucchini, and sweet peppers. Peel, core, and quarter the tomatoes. Cut the zucchini lengthwise into quarters. Remove stems and seeds from the peppers; cut into chunks. Cut onions into quarters. Using the coarse blade of a food grinder, grind tomatoes, zucchini, sweet peppers, onions, and garlic. Place in a colander to drain excess liquid. Measure 8 cups of the vegetable mixture.

2 Place the vegetable mixture in a large nonmetallic container; sprinkle with pickling salt. Cover and refrigerate overnight. Transfer the vegetable mixture to a colander. Rinse and drain well.

3 In an 8- or 10-quart Dutch oven combine vinegar, sugar, thyme, and pepper. Bring to boiling, stirring to dissolve sugar. Stir in vegetable mixture. Return mixture to boiling; remove from heat.

4 Ladle into hot, sterilized pint or half-pint canning jars, leaving ½-inch headspace. Remove air bubbles, wipe jar rims, and adjust lids. Process the filled jars in a boiling-water canner for 10 minutes for pints and 5 minutes for half-pints, starting the timing when the water begins to boil. Remove jars from canner; cool on racks. Makes 4 pints or 8 half-pints.

Nutrition Facts per tablespoon: 20 cal., 0 g total fat, 0 mg chol., 116 mg sodium, 5 g carbo., 0 g fiber, 0 g pro. **Daily Values:** 3% vit. A, 15% vit. C, 1% iron.

Stuffed Zucchini

Prep: 30 minutes **Bake:** 25 minutes

    6   medium zucchini
  1½   cups soft bread crumbs
    ¼   cup finely shredded cheddar
          cheese or Parmesan
          cheese (1 oz.)
    ¼   cup finely chopped onion
    1   Tbsp. snipped fresh parsley
    ¼   tsp. salt
    ⅛   tsp. pepper
    1   egg, slightly beaten
    ¼   cup finely shredded cheddar
          cheese or Parmesan
          cheese (1 oz.)

1 Preheat oven to 350°F. Wash zucchini and trim ends. Do not peel. In a covered Dutch oven cook whole zucchini in lightly salted boiling water for 5 minutes; drain and cool slightly. Cut a lengthwise slice off the top of each zucchini. Carefully remove the pulp with a spoon, leaving about a ¼-inch shell.

2 Chop enough of the pulp to measure 2 cups. Place chopped pulp in a medium bowl. (Save remaining pulp for another use.) Stir the bread crumbs, ¼ cup cheddar or Parmesan cheese, the onion, parsley, salt, pepper, and egg into chopped pulp until well mixed. Fill zucchini shells with pulp mixture. Place in a shallow baking pan.

3 Bake in the preheated oven for 20 minutes. Sprinkle with ¼ cup cheddar or Parmesan cheese. Bake for 5 to 10 minutes more or until golden brown and heated through. Makes 6 side-dish servings.

Nutrition Facts per serving: 93 cal., 4 g total fat (2 g sat. fat), 45 mg chol., 229 mg sodium, 8 g carbo., 1 g fiber, 5 g pro. Daily Values: 7% vit. A, 13% vit. C, 10% calcium, 5% iron.

30 MINUTE

Zucchini Frittata

The tender skin of zucchini blemishes and bruises easily. Select small, firm zucchini that are spot-free.

Start to finish: 25 minutes

 1 **cup thinly sliced zucchini (1 small)**
 ½ **cup thinly sliced leek**
 1 **Tbsp. margarine or butter**
 6 **eggs**
 2 **Tbsp. snipped fresh parsley**
 2 **Tbsp. water**
 ½ **tsp. snipped fresh rosemary or ⅛ tsp. dried rosemary, crushed**
 ½ **tsp. salt**
 ⅛ **tsp. pepper**
 ½ **of a 4½-oz. pkg. Camembert cheese or 2 Tbsp. freshly shredded Parmesan cheese**

1 Preheat oven to 400°F. In an omelet pan or 10-inch oven-safe skillet cook zucchini and leek in hot margarine or butter just until tender.

2 Meanwhile, in a medium mixing bowl beat together eggs, parsley, water, rosemary, salt, and pepper. Pour egg mixture over vegetables. Cook over medium-low heat. As mixture sets, run a spatula around skillet edge, lifting egg mixture to

allow uncooked portion to flow underneath. Continue cooking and lifting until egg mixture is almost set (surface will be moist).

3 Place pan in the preheated oven. Bake, uncovered, for 4 minutes or until top is set. Cut the half-circle of Camembert horizontally (if using); cut each half into 2 wedges and place on the frittata, or sprinkle frittata with Parmesan cheese. Allow cheese to melt slightly before serving. Makes 4 servings.

Nutrition Facts per serving: 197 cal., 14 g total fat (5 g sat. fat), 331 mg chol., 557 mg sodium, 4 g carbo., 1 g fiber, 13 g pro. Daily Values: 19% vit. A, 10% vit. C, 11% calcium, 9% iron.

Carrot and Zucchini Bars

When zucchini are picked fresh from the garden, store them in plastic bags for up to 2 weeks in the refrigerator. If they're not so fresh, store them for up to 5 days. Blot the moisture from the vegetables before placing them in plastic storage bags—zucchini keep better when they are dry.

Prep: 30 minutes **Bake:** 25 minutes

 1½ **cups all-purpose flour**
 ¾ **cup packed brown sugar**
 1 **tsp. baking powder**
 ½ **tsp. ground ginger**
 ¼ **tsp. baking soda**
 2 **eggs, slightly beaten**
 1½ **cups shredded carrot**

 1 **cup shredded zucchini (1 medium)**
 ½ **cup raisins**
 ½ **cup chopped walnuts**
 ½ **cup cooking oil**
 ¼ **cup honey**
 1 **tsp. vanilla**
 1 **recipe Citrus-Cream Cheese Frosting (see below)**

1 Preheat oven to 350°F. In a large bowl stir together flour, brown sugar, baking powder, ginger, and baking soda. In another large bowl stir together eggs, carrot, zucchini, raisins, walnuts, cooking oil, honey, and vanilla. Add carrot mixture to flour mixture, stirring just until combined. Spread batter into an ungreased 13×9×2-inch baking pan.

2 Bake in the preheated oven for 25 minutes or until a wooden toothpick inserted in the center comes out clean. Cool in pan on a wire rack. Frost with Citrus-Cream Cheese Frosting. Store, covered, in the refrigerator. Cut into bars. Makes 36 bars.

Citrus-Cream Cheese Frosting

In a medium mixing bowl beat one 8-ounce package cream cheese, softened, and 1 cup sifted powdered sugar with an electric mixer on medium speed until fluffy. Stir in 1 teaspoon finely shredded lemon peel or orange peel.

Nutrition Facts per bar: 125 cal., 7 g total fat (2 g sat. fat), 19 mg chol., 46 mg sodium, 16 g carbo., 0 g fiber, 2 g pro. Daily Values: 17% vit. A, 2% vit. C, 2% calcium, 3% iron.

30 MINUTE, LOW FAT

Veggie-Stuffed Veggies

See the photograph on page 200.

Start to finish: 30 minutes

2	or 3 medium zucchini
1½	cups cooked chopped vegetables (sweet peppers, eggplant, zucchini, and/or onion)
1	cup chopped cooked chicken
½	cup hot cooked rice
½	cup chopped tomato
1	tsp. Mediterranean seasoning or other herb seasoning
¼	cup finely shredded Parmesan cheese

1 Preheat oven to 400°F. Wash zucchini and trim ends. Do not peel. In a covered Dutch oven cook whole zucchini in lightly salted boiling water for 5 minutes; drain and cool slightly. Cut a lengthwise slice from the top of each zucchini. Carefully remove the pulp with a spoon, leaving about ¼-inch shell. Use part of the pulp for filling or save for another use.

2 For filling, in a medium mixing bowl stir together the chopped vegetables, cooked chicken, rice, tomato, and the seasoning. Spoon filling into zucchini shells. Place in a shallow baking pan. Sprinkle with Parmesan cheese.

3 Bake, uncovered, in the preheated oven for 15 to 20 minutes or until heated through. Season to taste. Cut into serving-size pieces. Makes 4 main-dish servings.

Nutrition Facts per serving: 152 cal., 5 g total fat (2 g sat. fat), 36 mg chol., 372 mg sodium, 11 g carbo., 2 g fiber, 15 g pro. **Daily Values:** 40% vit. A, 94% vit. C, 11% calcium, 8% iron.

Herb-Marinated Eggplant

Marinate the absorbent flesh of eggplant by brushing on fresh herbs or seasonings.

Prep: 15 minutes **Marinate:** 30 minutes
Bake: 20 minutes

¼	cup lightly packed fresh oregano leaves, snipped
¼	cup olive oil
2	Tbsp. snipped fresh thyme leaves
4	to 5 cloves garlic, minced
1	Tbsp. lemon juice
½	tsp. coarse salt
1	medium eggplant (1 lb.) Freshly ground black pepper Coarse salt

1 In a small bowl stir together the oregano, olive oil, thyme, garlic, lemon juice, and ½ teaspoon salt. Set aside mixture.

2 Trim and discard ends from eggplant. Cut eggplant in half lengthwise. Score the cut side of the eggplant in a diamond pattern at 1-inch intervals. Place cut side up in a shallow baking pan. Brush with the herb mixture. Season with freshly ground black pepper. Let stand at room temperature for 30 minutes.

3 Meanwhile, preheat oven to 450°F. Bake eggplant in the preheated oven for 20 minutes or until tender. To serve, cut baked eggplant halves into serving-size portions. Season to taste with coarse salt. Makes 4 side-dish servings.

Nutrition Facts per serving: 157 cal., 14 g total fat (2 g sat. fat), 0 mg chol., 330 mg sodium, 9 g carbo., 3 g fiber, 1 g pro. **Daily Values:** 4% vit. A, 12% vit. C, 3% calcium, 4% iron.

30 MINUTE, LOW FAT

Baby Potato Kabobs

See the photograph on page 201.

Start to finish: 25 minutes

1	lb. small potatoes, such as baby Dutch yellow, fingerlings, baby purple, and/or new red potatoes
4	6-inch fresh rosemary sprigs
2	tsp. olive oil
½	tsp. snipped fresh rosemary
½	tsp. coarse salt

1 Wash potatoes. In a medium saucepan cook the potatoes, covered, in a small amount of boiling salted water for 12 to 15 minutes or until tender. Drain and cool slightly.

2 Skewer the potatoes onto rosemary sprigs or short metal skewers. In a small bowl stir together olive oil and snipped rosemary. Brush oil mixture over potatoes. Sprinkle with coarse salt.

3 Grill potato kabobs on the rack of an uncovered grill directly over medium coals about 5 minutes or until potatoes are lightly browned, turning once. Makes 4 side-dish servings.

Nutrition Facts per serving: 104 cal., 2 g total fat (1 g sat. fat), 0 mg chol., 298 mg sodium, 19 g carbo., 2 g fiber, 2 g pro. Daily Values: 24% vit. C, 1% calcium, 8% iron.

30 MINUTE, LOW FAT

Grilled Sweet Potato Slices

Lightly glazed sweet potato slices are a good late-summer dinner accompaniment. At the height of sweet potato season, look for two varieties—creamy yellow or bright orange flesh.

Prep: 10 minutes Microcook: 8 minutes
Grill: 5 minutes

2	lb. sweet potatoes, peeled
1	cup water
2	Tbsp. Dijon-style mustard
2	Tbsp. honey
2	Tbsp. olive oil
1	Tbsp. snipped fresh rosemary
⅛	tsp. freshly ground black pepper

1 Slice peeled sweet potatoes lengthwise into ½-inch slices. Place sweet potato slices and water in a microwave-safe baking dish. Cover with vented plastic wrap. Microcook on 100% power (high) for 8 to 10 minutes or until nearly tender, rearranging potatoes halfway through cooking time. Drain well.

2 Meanwhile, in a small mixing bowl stir together Dijon-style mustard, honey, olive oil, rosemary, and pepper; set aside.

3 Grill precooked potato slices on the lightly greased rack of an uncovered grill directly over medium coals for 3 to 4 minutes or until golden brown. Carefully turn potato slices using a metal spatula. Brush with mustard mixture. Grill for 2 to 3 minutes more or until potatoes are just tender. Transfer to a serving platter. Makes 6 side-dish servings.

Nutrition Facts per serving: 227 cal., 5 g total fat (1 g sat. fat), 0 mg chol., 47 mg sodium, 43 g carbo., 5 g fiber, 3 g pro. Daily Values: 546% vit. A, 37% vit. C, 4% calcium, 6% iron.

Farmer's Tomato Pie

One bite of this pie equals the bliss of eating a sun-warmed tomato straight from the garden. Bits of garlic and melted cheese enhance the taste, and a handful of fresh basil makes a fragrant exclamation. (See the photograph on page 200.)

Prep: 30 minutes Bake: 32 minutes
Stand: 10 minutes

½	of a 15-oz. pkg. (1 crust) folded refrigerated unbaked piecrust
1⅓	cups shredded Italian-blend cheese or shredded mozzarella cheese (5½ oz.)
4	cloves garlic, minced
2	Tbsp. fine dry bread crumbs
2	lb. ripe tomatoes, cut into wedges (about 6 cups)
6	oz. cherry tomatoes, halved (1 cup)
½	tsp. salt
¼	to ½ cup loosely packed small fresh basil leaves or ¼ cup shredded fresh basil leaves

1 Preheat oven to 450°F. Unfold piecrust according to package directions. On a lightly floured surface

roll crust into a 12-inch circle. Place in a 9- to 9½-inch quiche dish or 9-inch pie plate. Trim edges, if necessary. Fold under extra pastry. If using pie plate, crimp edge as desired.

2 Line the unpricked pastry with a double thickness of foil. Bake in the preheated oven for 8 minutes. Remove foil. Bake for 4 to 5 minutes more or until pastry is set and dry. Remove from oven.

3 Reduce oven temperature to 375°F. Sprinkle ⅓ cup of the cheese evenly over baked pie shell. Sprinkle minced garlic evenly over cheese. Sprinkle with 2 teaspoons of the bread crumbs. Top with one-third of the tomato wedges, one-third of the cherry tomatoes, and ⅓ cup of the remaining cheese. Sprinkle with 2 teaspoons bread crumbs.

4 Repeat with another one-third of the tomato wedges, one-third of the cherry tomatoes, and ⅓ cup of the cheese. Sprinkle with remaining bread crumbs. Top with remaining tomato wedges, cherry tomatoes, and cheese. Sprinkle with salt. (The pie shell will be quite full.)

5 Bake for 20 to 25 minutes more or until pastry is golden brown and tomatoes just start to brown on top. Remove from oven to a wire rack and sprinkle tomatoes with basil leaves. Let stand only 10 minutes before serving. (If held longer, tomatoes tend to release their juices, which may make the pastry slightly soggy.) Makes 8 side-dish servings.

Nutrition Facts per serving: 216 cal., 12 g total fat (6 g sat. fat), 19 mg chol., 413 mg sodium, 21 g carbo., 2 g fiber, 7 g pro. Daily Values: 18% vit. A, 44% vit. C, 12% calcium, 4% iron.

Great Food and a Love of Garlic Are Inseparable

A passion for garlic fills the hearts of the world's greatest cooks. The very essence of favorite dishes, from Italian spaghetti sauces to Asian noodle bowls, centers on the earthy goodness of garlic.

Foods with garlic nurture and comfort. Savoring a favorite garlic-rich meal is compared to a warm, motherly embrace. Eating garlic does more than make you feel good—it's also a way to be good to yourself.

Garlic stimulates the palate and adds to the enjoyment of many foods. Its rich flavor can replace much of the fat and salt in cooking, making it invaluable to lighten recipes. Some cooks use garlic discriminately, while other cooks use garlic with abandon, rationalizing that prudence has no place in the kitchen. Learn to use this popular seasoning to enhance your favorite foods.

Like most of Mother Nature's bounty, garlic tastes best fresh. You don't have to adhere to the common grocery-store variety either. As your appreciation for garlic deepens, you'll be encouraged to join millions of cooks around the world who grow more than 400 varieties of garlic. Learn more and get started by contacting seed suppliers and garlic clubs, and by reading garlic cookbooks and newsletters. Even when you start small, you can grow enough varieties for yourself and to share.

---

30 MINUTE, LOW FAT

Garlic Pilaf with Cajun Eggplant

Native to the Americas, protein-packed quinoa (KEEN-wah) is an ancient grain that has recently been reintroduced to North American tables. It cooks like rice and has a mild flavor and slightly chewy texture. Purchase it at natural food stores and large supermarkets.

Start to finish: 30 minutes

- ½   cup chopped onion
- 1   tsp. olive oil
- 6   cloves garlic, minced
- 1   cup quinoa, rinsed and drained, or long grain rice
- 1   cup coarsely shredded carrot
- 1   tsp. Cajun seasoning
- ½   tsp. salt
- 1   15-oz. can hominy, rinsed and drained
- 1   Tbsp. snipped fresh basil, rosemary, chives, thyme, or oregano
- 1   medium eggplant, cut into ½-inch slices
- 2   tsp. olive oil
     Cajun seasoning

1 In a medium saucepan cook the onion in 1 teaspoon hot olive oil over medium heat for 3 minutes. Add garlic; cook 1 minute more. Carefully stir in 2 cups water, the quinoa, carrot, 1 teaspoon Cajun seasoning, and salt.

2 Bring mixture to boiling; reduce heat. Cover and simmer about 15 minutes or until quinoa is tender and liquid is absorbed. Stir in hominy and the desired herb. Cover and let stand for 1 minute.

3 Meanwhile, lightly brush eggplant slices with the 2 teaspoons oil; sprinkle with additional Cajun

seasoning. Place on the unheated rack of a broiler pan. Broil 4 to 5 inches from the heat for 2½ to 3 minutes on each side or just until tender.

4 To serve, divide the eggplant slices among four plates. Top with the quinoa mixture. Makes 4 main-dish servings.

Nutrition Facts per serving: 296 cal., 7 g total fat (1 g sat. fat), 0 mg chol., 499 mg sodium, 52 g carbo., 7 g fiber, 8 g pro. **Daily Values:** 87% vit. A, 7% vit. C, 5% calcium, 34% iron.

---

30 MINUTE, LOW FAT

Peppery Artichoke Pitas

No time to shop? These pitas, filled with ingredients typically stocked in the pantry—tender artichokes, cooked beans, and bottled garlic dressing—put a premium on convenience and great flavor.

Start to finish: 20 minutes

- 1   15-oz. can Great Northern beans, rinsed and drained
- 1   13¾- to 14-oz. can artichoke hearts, drained and coarsely chopped
- ½   cup torn arugula or spinach
- ¼   cup bottled creamy garlic salad dressing
- ¼   tsp. cracked black pepper
- 3   large pita bread rounds, halved crosswise

1 In a medium mixing bowl combine beans, artichoke hearts, arugula, salad dressing, and pepper. Spoon into pita bread halves to serve. Serves 6.

Nutrition Facts per serving: 227 cal., 5 g total fat (1 g sat. fat), 3 mg chol., 269 mg sodium, 38 g carbo., 6 g fiber, 10 g pro. **Daily Values:** 1% vit. A, 8% vit. C, 7% calcium, 16% iron.

Portobello Flats

Broiled or grilled, the portobello mushroom adds substance to this no-meat sandwich.

Start to finish: 20 minutes

⅔ **cup chopped tomato**
2 **tsp. snipped fresh basil, thyme, and/or oregano**
⅛ **tsp. salt**
2 **medium fresh portobello mushrooms (about 4 inches in diameter)**
1 **tsp. balsamic vinegar or red wine vinegar**
½ **tsp. olive oil**
½ **of a 12-inch Italian flat bread (focaccia), quartered, or ½ of a 12-inch thin-crust Italian bread shell (Boboli)**
   Finely shredded Parmesan cheese (optional)

1 In a small bowl stir together the tomato, desired herb, and salt; set aside. Cut the mushroom stems even with the caps; discard stems. Rinse mushroom caps; gently pat dry.

2 In a small bowl stir together balsamic or red wine vinegar and olive oil. Gently brush mixture over the mushrooms. Place mushrooms on the unheated rack of a broiler pan. Broil 4 to 5 inches from the heat for 6 to 8 minutes or until mushrooms are just tender, turning once halfway through broiling. Drain the mushrooms on paper towels; thinly slice the mushrooms.

3 Place bread on a baking sheet. Broil for 2 to 3 minutes or until heated through.

4 To serve, top bread with mushrooms and tomato mixture. If desired, sprinkle with Parmesan cheese. Makes 4 sandwiches.

Grill Directions:
Prepare mushrooms as directed, except grill mushrooms on the rack of an uncovered grill directly over medium coals for 6 to 8 minutes or until mushrooms are just tender, turning once halfway through grilling.

Nutrition Facts per serving: 157 cal., 3 g total fat (1 g sat. fat), 0 mg chol., 80 mg sodium, 28 g carbo., 4 g fiber, 7 g pro. **Daily Values:** 4% vit. A, 10% vit. C, 7% calcium, 3% iron.

Broccoli with Ginger Tofu

Enjoy an iron-rich meatless meal when you serve this dish of rice, broccoli, tofu, and cashews.

Start to finish: 25 minutes

1 **cup short grain rice**
2 **stalks fresh broccoli (12 oz.)**
⅓ **cup reduced-sodium chicken broth**
3 **Tbsp. reduced-sodium soy sauce**
1 **Tbsp. dry sherry**
1 **Tbsp. grated fresh ginger**
2 **tsp. cornstarch**
1 **Tbsp. peanut oil**
4 **cloves garlic, minced**
1 **medium red sweet pepper, cut into thin bite-size strips**
8 **oz. extra-firm tofu (fresh bean curd), drained and cut into ½-inch cubes**
2 **Tbsp. coarsely chopped cashews**

EDITOR'S TIP

Arugula (a.k.a. Rocket or Roquette)

Whatever you call it, arugula (ah-ROO-guh-lah) is a peppery salad green that is often mistaken for dandelion. Mature leaves are large and very pungent—tasty accents to mild greens in a mixed salad. Less assertive young leaves can be used alone. Rinse leaves well in cold water, pat dry, and chill in a plastic bag for up to 2 days.

1 Cook rice according to package directions; keep warm.

2 Remove florets from broccoli stalks and cut, as necessary, into smaller florets. Peel broccoli stems; cut crosswise into thin rounds. Set broccoli (4 to 4½ cups) aside.

3 In a small bowl combine chicken broth, soy sauce, dry sherry, ginger, and cornstarch. Set aside.

4 Pour peanut oil into a large skillet or wok. Preheat over medium-high heat. Stir-fry garlic in hot oil for 30 seconds. Add broccoli and sweet pepper; stir-fry for 4 to 5 minutes or until vegetables are crisp-tender. Push vegetables to the side of skillet. Stir chicken broth mixture; add to the center of skillet. Cook and stir until thickened and bubbly. Gently stir in tofu. Cook and stir for 1 to 2 minutes more or until heated through. Serve over rice; sprinkle with cashews. Makes 4 main-dish servings.

Nutrition Facts per serving: 348 cal., 9 g total fat (2 g sat. fat), 0 mg chol., 513 mg sodium, 52 g carbo., 5 g fiber, 14 g pro. **Daily Values:** 58% vit. A, 195% vit. C, 9% calcium, 24% iron.

LOW FAT

Garden Chicken Soup

Look for white, red, or purple carrots at the market. Although the deep colors tend to fade to standard orange when cooked, it's so much fun to eat colorful raw carrots.

Prep: 25 minutes **Cook:** 11 minutes

- 1 Tbsp. cooking oil
- 12 oz. packaged skinless, boneless chicken breast strips
- 3 cups reduced-sodium chicken broth
- 12 tiny whole carrots with ½-inch tops (about 6 oz.)
- 2 medium onions, cut in thin wedges (1 cup)
- 2 cloves garlic, minced
- 1 large yellow summer squash, halved lengthwise and sliced (about 2 cups)
- 2 cups shredded Swiss chard
- 1 Tbsp. snipped fresh lemon-thyme or thyme
  Asiago cheese curls or Parmesan cheese curls*

1 In a very large skillet heat oil over medium-high heat. Cook and stir chicken in hot oil for 3 minutes.

2 Carefully add broth, carrots, onions, and garlic. Bring to boiling; reduce heat. Cover and simmer for 5 minutes. Add squash and chard. Cook, covered, about 3 minutes more or until vegetables are just tender. Stir in lemon-thyme. Top each serving with Asiago cheese curls. Makes 4 main-dish servings.

*Note: Make thin curls of cheese using a vegetable peeler on a wedge of cheese.

Nutrition Facts per serving: 217 cal., 8 g total fat (3 g sat. fat), 57 mg chol., 643 mg sodium, 12 g carbo., 3 g fiber, 26 g pro. **Daily Values:** 231% vit. A, 25% vit. C, 11% calcium, 9% iron.

30 MINUTE

Zesty Chicken and Pasta Salad

Although the name offers no clue, this lively, low-fuss salad hails from the blazing Southwest, where fiery peppers rule. The bold, cilantro-flecked dressing radiates with the region's signature flavor. Adjust the heat with more or less jalapeño pepper.

Start to finish: 25 minutes

- 1 cup tricolor rotini or gemelli
- 1 cup frozen whole kernel corn
- 8 oz. smoked cooked chicken or turkey breast, cut into bite-size strips (1½ cups)
- 1 cup thinly sliced carrots or bite-size jicama strips
- ½ cup pitted ripe olives, halved
- 1 recipe Zesty Lime Dressing (see right)
- 4 cups torn mixed salad greens

1 Cook pasta according to package directions, adding corn the last 2 minutes of cooking; drain. Rinse with cold water; drain again.

2 In a large bowl combine the pasta mixture, chicken, carrots, and olives. Pour Zesty Lime Dressing over pasta mixture, tossing lightly to coat. Serve immediately or cover and chill up to 24 hours.

3 To serve, divide salad greens among four plates. Top with pasta mixture. Makes 4 servings.

Zesty Lime Dressing

In a screw-top jar combine ¼ cup lime juice; ¼ cup snipped fresh cilantro; ¼ cup finely chopped red onion; 3 tablespoons olive oil or salad oil; 1 fresh or canned jalapeño pepper, seeded and finely chopped;* and 1 clove garlic, minced. Cover and shake well.

*Note: Hot peppers contain oils that can burn eyes, lips, and sensitive skin. Wear gloves while preparing them and thoroughly wash your hands afterward.

Nutrition Facts per serving: 358 cal., 21 g total fat (4 g sat. fat), 41 mg chol., 450 mg sodium, 31 g carbo., 2 g fiber, 15 g pro. **Daily Values:** 10% vit. A, 47% vit. C, 3% calcium, 14% iron.

30 MINUTE

Cool-as-a-Cucumber Chicken Salad

Start to finish: 25 minutes

- 2 cups cubed cantaloupe and/or honeydew melon
- 1 cup very finely chopped cucumber
- 1 cup very finely chopped zucchini
- ¼ cup thinly sliced green onions

⅓ cup lime juice
2 Tbsp. salad oil
2 Tbsp. water
2 Tbsp. snipped fresh cilantro
   or mint
1 Tbsp. sugar
⅛ tsp. ground white pepper
4 cups shredded leaf lettuce
2 cups shredded cooked
   chicken (10 oz.)

1 In a large bowl toss together the melon, cucumber, zucchini, and onions. Set aside.

2 For dressing, in a screw-top jar combine lime juice, salad oil, water, cilantro, sugar, and white pepper. Cover and shake well. Drizzle ½ cup of the dressing over the melon mixture, tossing lightly to coat.

3 Divide lettuce among four plates. Top with melon mixture. Arrange chicken around edges of plates. Drizzle remaining dressing over chicken. Makes 4 servings.

Nutrition Facts per serving: 268 cal., 13 g total fat (3 g sat. fat), 68 mg chol., 79 mg sodium, 15 g carbo., 2 g fiber, 24 g pro. **Daily Values:** 41% vit. A, 94% vit. C, 6% calcium, 17% iron.

---

30 MINUTE, LOW FAT
Chicken Caribbean

Experience the islands without venturing off your patio. Fresh basil (try cinnamon basil if you can find it) infuses aroma and peppery-clove flavor into the slightly sweet coconut-orange sauce—perfect with the spicy jerk-seasoned chicken.

Start to finish: 25 minutes

4 medium skinless, boneless
   chicken breast halves
   (about 1 lb. total)

½ tsp. Jamaican jerk seasoning
½ cup canned coconut milk
¼ cup orange juice
2 Tbsp. snipped fresh basil
1 tsp. finely shredded orange
   peel (optional)
2 cups hot cooked rice

1 Rub both sides of chicken with jerk seasoning. Grill chicken on the rack of an uncovered grill directly over medium coals for 12 to 15 minutes or until chicken is no longer pink and registers 170°F on an instant-read thermometer, turning once.

2 Meanwhile, for sauce, in a small saucepan combine coconut milk, orange juice, and 1 tablespoon of the basil. Bring to boiling; reduce heat. Simmer, uncovered, about 5 minutes or until reduced to ½ cup.

3 If desired, stir the orange peel into cooked rice. Serve chicken and sauce over rice. Sprinkle with the remaining basil. Makes 4 servings.

Nutrition Facts per serving: 287 cal., 9 g total fat (6 g sat. fat), 59 mg chol., 85 mg sodium, 25 g carbo., 0 g fiber, 24 g pro. **Daily Values:** 2% vit. A, 13% vit. C, 2% calcium, 13% iron.

---

30 MINUTE, LOW FAT
Asian Primavera Stir-Fry

Start to finish: 30 minutes

1 oz. dried shiitake mushrooms
1 Tbsp. cornstarch
6 oz. packaged dried fettuccine
12 oz. skinless, boneless chicken
   breast halves, cut into
   bite-size pieces
2 Tbsp. dry sherry
2 Tbsp. light soy sauce
1 Tbsp. grated fresh ginger

2 cloves garlic, minced
   Nonstick cooking spray
1 cup sugar snap peas (strings
   and tips removed)
8 oz. tiny whole carrots with tops
   (about 12), trimmed
4 green onions, bias-sliced into
   1-inch pieces

1 In a small bowl combine dried mushrooms and 1 cup warm water; let stand for 15 minutes. Drain mushrooms, squeezing out excess liquid; reserve liquid. Slice mushroom caps; discard stems. Stir cornstarch into reserved mushroom liquid.

2 Meanwhile, cook pasta according to package directions. Drain and keep warm. Set aside.

3 In a bowl stir together the chicken, sherry, soy sauce, ginger, and garlic; set aside.

4 Lightly coat a wok or large skillet with nonstick cooking spray. Heat wok or skillet over medium-high heat. Stir-fry sugar snap peas and carrots for 3 to 4 minutes or until crisp-tender. Add green onions and stir-fry for 1 minute more. Remove vegetables from wok; set aside. Add chicken mixture to wok. Stir-fry for 2 to 4 minutes or until chicken is no longer pink. Push chicken from center of wok. Stir cornstarch mixture; add to center of wok. Cook and stir until thickened and bubbly.

5 Return vegetables to wok. Add mushrooms and pasta. Stir to coat with sauce. Cook and stir for 1 minute or until heated through. Serves 4.

Nutrition Facts per serving: 334 cal., 2 g total fat (1 g sat. fat), 49 mg chol., 360 mg sodium, 49 g carbo., 4 g fiber, 28 g pro. **Daily Values:** 289% vit. A, 27% vit. C, 6% calcium, 16% iron.

PRIZE WINNER

Turkey Salad Platter

Lauri Knox
Golden, Colorado
$400—Easy Turkey Suppers

Start to finish: 20 minutes

1 lb. chopped cooked smoked turkey breast
2 stalks celery, sliced ½ inch thick (1 cup)
½ cup mayonnaise or salad dressing
¼ tsp. cracked black pepper
8 cups mixed baby salad greens
1 medium orange, cut into wedges
½ of a small red onion, thinly sliced and separated into rings (¼ cup)
½ cup bottled raspberry vinaigrette
½ cup dried cranberries
½ cup broken walnuts, toasted

1 In a medium mixing bowl combine turkey, celery, mayonnaise or salad dressing, and pepper. Cover and chill until serving time, if desired.

2 To assemble, spoon turkey mixture onto one-half of a large serving platter. Place salad greens and orange wedges next to turkey mixture on platter. Top greens with red onion rings. Drizzle raspberry vinaigrette over greens. Sprinkle dried cranberries and toasted walnuts atop the turkey mixture and greens. Makes 6 servings.

Nutrition Facts per serving: 400 cal., 30 g total fat (4 g sat. fat), 39 mg chol., 880 mg sodium, 17 g carbo., 3 g fiber, 19 g pro. **Daily Values:** 7% vit. A, 27% vit. C, 4% calcium, 8% iron.

Italian-Style Turkey Hero

Prep: 30 minutes **Bake:** 5 minutes
Chill: 2 hours

1 16-oz. loaf unsliced French bread
¼ cup purchased basil pesto
¼ cup pine nuts, toasted
1 tsp. cracked black pepper
4 oz. thinly sliced cooked smoked turkey breast
4 oz. thinly sliced prosciutto
1½ cups shredded radicchio
1 cup torn baby or other mixed salad greens
¾ cup thinly sliced cucumber
½ cup thinly sliced Vidalia or other sweet onion
¼ cup mayonnaise or salad dressing

1 Preheat oven to 450°F. Cut the bread loaf in half horizontally. Hollow out bread loaf, leaving a ½-inch shell. Set bread pieces aside for another use. Place bread halves, hollow sides up, on a baking sheet. Bake in the preheated oven about 5 minutes or until toasted. Set aside to cool.

2 Spread the inside bottom half of the bread loaf with the pesto. Sprinkle with pine nuts and pepper. Layer turkey, prosciutto, radicchio, greens, cucumber, and onion over nuts. Spread the inside top half of the bread loaf with the mayonnaise. Replace top of bread. Cover and chill for 2 to 8 hours. Slice to serve. Makes 8 servings.

Nutrition Facts per serving: 320 cal., 15 g total fat (3 g sat. fat), 21 mg chol., 955 mg sodium, 33 g carbo., 2 g fiber, 15 g pro. **Daily Values:** 1% vit. A, 4% vit. C, 9% calcium, 14% iron.

Fiesta Tostados

Prep: 30 minutes **Bake:** 5 minutes

½ cup canned black beans, rinsed and drained
¼ cup frozen whole kernel corn, thawed
¼ cup red or green sweet pepper, seeded and chopped
¼ cup chopped tomatillos or tomato
¼ cup thinly sliced green onions
2 Tbsp. sliced pitted ripe olives
1 cup shredded taco or Mexican-blend cheese (4 oz.)
1 Tbsp. snipped fresh cilantro
1 tsp. ground cumin
½ tsp. finely shredded lime peel
¼ tsp. crushed red pepper
12 tostada shells
¾ cup canned enchilada sauce or bottled taco sauce
1 cup shredded cooked chicken or turkey
    Dairy sour cream

1 Preheat oven to 375°F. In a bowl combine beans, corn, sweet pepper, tomatillos or tomato, green onions, and olives. In another bowl toss together taco cheese, cilantro, cumin, finely shredded lime peel, and crushed red pepper.

2 Spread one side of each tostada with 1 tablespoon of the enchilada or taco sauce. Place six of the tostadas, sauce side up, on a large baking sheet;

set aside remaining tostada shells. Sprinkle chicken or turkey evenly over each tostada on baking sheet. Top each with some of the bean mixture and cheese mixture. Place remaining tostada shells, sauce side down, over cheese mixture.

3 Bake in the preheated oven for 5 to 7 minutes or until cheese is melted and filling is heated through. If desired, cut into wedges to serve. Serve warm with sour cream. Makes 6 servings.

Nutrition Facts per serving: 310 cal., 16 g total fat (7 g sat. fat), 80 mg chol., 486 mg sodium, 26 g carbo., 2 g fiber, 15 g pro. **Daily Values:** 17% vit. A, 28% vit. C, 20% calcium, 8% iron.

30 MINUTE, LOW FAT

Sweet and Spicy Turkey Skillet

Start to finish: 30 minutes

2	8-oz. whole turkey tenderloins
½	cup apple juice
¼	cup bottled hoisin sauce
1	tsp. grated fresh ginger
¼	tsp. salt
⅛	tsp. ground red pepper
2	small red, green, and/or yellow sweet peppers, cut into bite-size strips
1	medium onion, cut into thin wedges
2	Tbsp. cooking oil
1	Tbsp. water
2	tsp. cornstarch
1	small apple or pear, cored and cut into wedges

1 Cut each turkey tenderloin in half horizontally to form two ½-inch-thick steak slices. Set aside. In a small mixing bowl stir together apple juice, hoisin sauce, ginger, salt, and ground red pepper; set aside.

2 In a large skillet cook sweet peppers and onion in hot oil over medium-high heat for 4 to 5 minutes or until nearly tender. Remove vegetables, reserving oil in skillet. Add turkey tenderloin steaks to skillet. Cook about 2 minutes on each side or until browned.

3 Return vegetables to skillet. Add apple juice mixture. Bring to boiling; reduce heat. Simmer, covered, for 8 to 10 minutes or until turkey is tender and no pink remains. Using a slotted spoon, remove turkey and vegetables to serving platter, reserving liquid in skillet. Keep warm.

4 In a small bowl stir together water and cornstarch. Add to liquid in skillet. Cook and stir until thickened and bubbly. Add apple or pear to skillet. Cover and cook about 3 minutes or until fruit is just slightly softened. Serve over turkey and vegetables. Makes 4 servings.

Nutrition Facts per serving: 289 cal., 9 g total fat (2 g sat. fat), 68 mg chol., 534 mg sodium, 22 g carbo., 2 g fiber, 27 g pro. **Daily Values:** 41% vit. A, 105% vit. C, 3% calcium, 10% iron.

LOW FAT

Bacon-Wrapped Turkey with Veggies

Prep: 25 minutes **Bake:** 35 minutes

4	slices bacon
4	4- to 6-oz. turkey tenderloin steaks*
¾	cup bottled Mediterranean-style or herb-and-garlic marinade
½	cup finely shredded Asiago or Parmesan cheese
6	small red potatoes, cut up (about 1 lb.)
2	medium onions, cut into wedges
¼	tsp. pepper
1	lb. asparagus spears, trimmed and cut into 2-inch pieces

1 Preheat oven to 375°F. Cook bacon until done but not crisp. Drain on paper towels. Set aside.

2 Place tenderloin steaks between two pieces of plastic wrap. Pound with the flat side of a meat mallet to flatten to ½-inch thickness. Spread each tenderloin with 1 tablespoon of the marinade; sprinkle each with about 2 tablespoons of the cheese. Starting from a short side, roll turkey into a spiral; wrap a strip of partially cooked bacon around each roll. Secure with a wooden toothpick.

3 Place turkey rolls in one-half of a 13×9×2-inch baking pan. Drizzle each with about 1 tablespoon more of the marinade.

4 Cook potatoes, covered, in a small amount of boiling water for 5 minutes. Drain well. Add onion, remaining marinade, and pepper to the potatoes; toss to coat. Add vegetable mixture next to the turkey in the baking pan.

5 Bake, uncovered, in the preheated oven for 20 minutes. Stir asparagus into potato mixture. Bake 15 to 20 minutes more or until turkey registers 170°F with an instant read thermometer and vegetables are tender. Makes 4 servings.

*Note: If tenderloin steaks are not available, slice two 8 to 12 oz. turkey breast tenderloins in half horizontally to make 4 steaks.

Nutrition Facts per serving: 289 cal., 9 g total fat (2 g sat. fat), 68 mg chol., 534 mg sodium, 22 g carbo., 2 g fiber, 27 g pro. **Daily Values:** 41% vit. A, 105% vit. C, 3% calcium, 10% iron.

How to Pick a Dreamy Peach

To find the lushest, juiciest peaches, look for the ripest, most mature, and freshest fruit.

Ripeness. Peaches sweeten only when allowed to fully ripen on the tree. The longer they remain on the tree, the sweeter they become; therefore, peaches picked late in the season are the sweetest. Although peaches are available from May to October, late-summer peaches are the most flavorful.

The best indicator of ripeness is a delectable sweet, warm aroma. Sniff the peaches until you find the enticing ripe peach scent. Ripeness also can be detected by color. Rather than look for the blush of the peach, look for yellow background with no hint of green.

Maturity. The largest peaches are those picked after reaching full maturity—they'll have a distinct seam on one side.

Freshness. Juicy peaches feel firm, yield to gentle thumb pressure, and never feel mushy. Avoid hard, bruised peaches or peaches covered with shriveled or wrinkled skin. Tan-color patches on the skin usually mean decay inside. Also avoid cold peaches; although they may look and feel fresh, they may be damaged by chilling, deteriorate quickly, and have a woody texture.

PRIZE WINNER

Triple Turkey-Rice Skillet

Rita Maduell
New Orleans, Louisiana
$200—Easy Turkey Suppers

Start to finish: 1 hour

- ⅓ cup chopped onion
- ½ of a medium yellow, green, or red sweet pepper, seeded and cut into 1-inch pieces
- 6 slices turkey bacon, chopped
- 1 Tbsp. cooking oil
- 3¼ cups water
- 6 oz. cooked smoked turkey sausage links, cut into ½-inch slices
- 1½ cups uncooked regular brown rice
- 2 tsp. bottled hot pepper sauce
- 1 tsp. dried rosemary, crushed
- ½ to 1 tsp. ground black pepper
- ¼ tsp. salt
- 2 cups cubed cooked turkey
  Warm buttered French bread slices (optional)
  Bottled hot pepper sauce (optional)

1 In a large saucepan cook onion, sweet pepper, and turkey bacon in hot oil over medium-high heat until vegetables are tender. Carefully add the water, turkey sausage, uncooked rice, the 2 teaspoons hot sauce, the rosemary, black pepper, and salt. Bring to boiling; reduce heat. Cover and simmer for 45 to 50 minutes or until the rice is tender and most of the liquid is absorbed.

2 Stir the cubed cooked turkey into the rice mixture; heat through. To serve, spoon the rice mixture into five or six shallow bowls. Serve with buttered French bread slices and additional hot sauce, if desired. Makes 5 or 6 servings.

Nutrition Facts per serving: 390 cal., 12 g total fat (3 g sat. fat), 69 mg chol., 730 mg sodium, 46 g carbo., 2 g fiber, 24 g pro. **Daily Values:** 1% vit. A, 52% vit. C, 4% calcium, 12% iron.

Sizzling Catfish with Pepper-Mint Slaw

Watch the heat levels in your pick of peppers. The poblanos called for in the recipe are mild; however, other peppers can be scorching. Ask the produce aisle manager before you buy. (See the photograph on page 203.)

Prep: 30 minutes **Cook:** 8 minutes

- 1 to 1¼ lb. fresh or frozen catfish fillets, ½ to ¾ inch thick
- 1 recipe Pepper-Mint Slaw (see page 183)
- 1 egg, beaten
- 2 Tbsp. water
- ¼ cup yellow cornmeal
- ½ of a medium fresh poblano pepper, seeded and finely chopped* (⅓ cup)
- 2 Tbsp. fine dry bread crumbs
- 2 Tbsp. grated Parmesan cheese
- ¼ tsp. salt
- ¼ cup all-purpose flour
- 3 Tbsp. cooking oil
  Lemon wedges

1 Thaw fish, if frozen. Cut into four serving-size pieces, if necessary. Set aside. Prepare Pepper-Mint Slaw up to 30 minutes before serving time. Cover and chill.

2 In a shallow dish combine egg and water. In another shallow dish combine the cornmeal, poblano pepper, bread crumbs, Parmesan cheese, and salt. Place flour in a third shallow dish. Dip each piece of fish in flour, then in egg mixture, then coat evenly with cornmeal mixture.

3 In a large skillet heat the oil over medium heat. Add the fish and fry for 4 to 5 minutes on each side or until golden brown and fish flakes easily with a fork. Serve fish fillets with Pepper-Mint slaw and lemon wedges. Makes 4 servings.

Pepper-Mint Slaw

Remove seeds, stem, and membranes from half of a medium poblano pepper.* Cut into thin, bite-size strips. In a large bowl combine 3 cups shredded cabbage with ¼ cup bottled coleslaw dressing. Gently stir in pepper strips, ¼ cup snipped fresh Italian parsley, and 2 tablespoons snipped fresh mint.

***Note:** Hot peppers contain oils that can burn eyes, lips, and sensitive skin. Wear gloves while preparing them and thoroughly wash your hands afterward.

Nutrition Facts per serving: 446 cal., 29 g total fat (6 g sat. fat), 110 mg chol., 738 mg sodium, 22 g carbo., 2 g fiber, 23 g pro. Daily Values: 14% vit. A, 177% vit. C, 10% calcium, 19% iron.

30 MINUTE

Garden Greens with Swordfish

Complement strips of swordfish or tuna and fresh mixed greens with an assertive salad dressing. This convenient dressing is made with roasted sweet peppers from a jar.

Start to finish: 30 minutes

- 1 lb. swordfish or tuna steaks, cut 1 inch thick
- 1 Tbsp. lemon juice
- 1 tsp. dried Italian seasoning, crushed
- ¼ tsp. garlic salt
- ⅛ tsp. pepper
- 6 cups torn mixed salad greens
- 12 red and/or yellow pear tomatoes or cherry tomatoes, halved
- 1 recipe Roasted Pepper Dressing (see below)

1 Rinse fish; pat dry. Brush fish with lemon juice. Stir together the Italian seasoning, garlic salt, and pepper; rub over fish. Place fish on the greased, unheated rack of a broiler pan.

2 Broil 4 inches from heat for 5 minutes. Using a wide spatula, carefully turn fish over. Broil 3 to 7 minutes more or until fish flakes easily with a fork. Cool; cut fish into thin, bite-size strips.

3 Divide the salad greens among four plates. Top with fish strips and halved tomatoes. Drizzle Roasted Pepper Dressing over salads. Makes 4 servings.

Roasted Pepper Dressing

In a blender container or food processor bowl combine one half of a 7-ounce jar roasted red sweet peppers, drained (½ cup); ¼ cup salad oil; 3 tablespoons vinegar; ¼ teaspoon salt; and dash ground red pepper. Cover and blend or process until nearly smooth. Cover and chill for up to 24 hours.

Nutrition Facts per serving: 282 cal., 18 g total fat (3 g sat. fat), 45 mg chol., 374 mg sodium, 6 g carbo., 2 g fiber, 24 g pro. Daily Values: 17% vit. A, 104% vit. C, 2% calcium, 13% iron.

30 MINUTE

Peachy Lobster Pasta Salad

Herbs make this sunny afternoon salad a standout. If you don't care for the basil, dillweed, and thyme combo, use your favorite herbs. Accompany the salad with garlic bread or crusty sourdough rolls and iced tea.

Start to finish: 30 minutes

- 2 cups medium shell macaroni
- ½ cup snipped mixed fresh herbs, such as basil, dillweed, and thyme
- ¼ cup olive oil
- 1 tsp. finely shredded lime peel
- 3 Tbsp. lime juice
- 3 Tbsp. orange juice
- 2 cloves garlic, minced
- 1 Tbsp. honey
- 3 medium peaches, peeled, pitted, and sliced
- 2 cups cut-up, cooked lobster or crabmeat (cartilage removed) or flake-style imitation lobster (12 oz. cooked)
- 1 cup watercress

1 Cook pasta according to package directions. Drain. Rinse with cold water and drain well again.

2 Meanwhile, in a large salad bowl combine herbs, olive oil, lime peel, lime juice, orange juice, garlic, honey, ¼ teaspoon salt, and ¼ teaspoon pepper. Add peach slices, tossing gently to combine. Add pasta, lobster, and watercress, tossing gently to combine. Season with additional salt and pepper. Makes 4 servings.

Nutrition Facts per serving: 422 cal., 15 g total fat (2 g sat. fat), 61 mg chol., 509 mg sodium, 49 g carbo., 3 g fiber, 24 g pro. Daily Values: 22% vit. A, 33% vit. C, 9% calcium, 11% iron.

- Salad of fresh arugula or mixed greens, sliced fresh mushrooms, and sliced onions, drizzled with dried tomato vinaigrette

- Sage-Brushed Cowboy Steak (see right)

- Semolina bread or crusty garlic-herb bread

- Cantaloupe and honeydew melon wedges topped with minted crème fraîche

30 MINUTE

Curried Beef Spirals On Spinach

Pick up roast beef sliced to your liking at the deli, and the work is half finished for this protein-rich entrée. Fresh asparagus is a crisp counterpoint to the curry and chutney cream filling that is spread on the beef slices.

Start to finish: 30 minutes

1	lb. asparagus spears
⅓	of an 8-oz. tub (about ⅓ cup) cream cheese
3	Tbsp. peach or mango chutney, snipped
2	Tbsp. finely chopped green onion
¼	tsp. curry powder
8	oz. lean cooked beef, thinly sliced (about 8 slices)
6	cups torn fresh spinach or torn mixed salad greens
2	Tbsp. lemon juice
1	Tbsp. olive oil
2	Tbsp. chopped peanuts

1 Snap off and discard woody bases from asparagus. Cook asparagus spears, covered, in a small amount of boiling water for 4 to 6 minutes or until crisp-tender. Drain; set aside.

2 Meanwhile, in a small bowl stir together cream cheese, chutney, green onion, and curry powder. Spread about 1 tablespoon of the cream cheese mixture over each beef slice. Roll up each beef slice, starting from a short side; cut each beef spiral in half.

3 Divide spinach among four plates. Arrange asparagus spears on spinach. Stir together the lemon juice and olive oil; drizzle over spinach and asparagus. Arrange four of the beef spirals on each plate; sprinkle with the peanuts. Makes 4 servings.

Nutrition Facts per serving: 317 cal., 19 g total fat (6 g sat. fat), 71 mg chol., 213 mg sodium, 16 g carbo., 4 g fiber, 24 g pro. Daily Values: 66% vit. A, 76% vit. C, 10% calcium, 31% iron.

Sage-Brushed Cowboy Steak

A cloudless night, a blanket on the ground, and a steak on the grill. What cowboy could ask for more? Pile skillet-toasted corn and grilled sweet peppers on a platter for a savory side dish. Test the steak for doneness with a meat thermometer. (See the photograph on page 201.)

Prep: 40 minutes **Cook:** 10 minutes
Grill: 8 minutes

3	cups fresh corn kernels
1	Tbsp. olive oil
¼	tsp. salt
2	beef T-bone or porterhouse steaks, cut 1 inch thick
	Salt and pepper (optional)
1	small red or yellow sweet pepper, halved and seeded
¼	cup snipped fresh sage
2	Tbsp. melted butter or margarine
3	or 4 large fresh sage leaves
⅓	cup queso fresco or farmer cheese, crumbled

1 In a large skillet cook the corn in hot olive oil over medium-high heat about 10 minutes or until the corn is tender and golden brown, stirring often. Stir in the ¼ teaspoon salt. Remove from heat. Cover and keep warm.

2 If desired, sprinkle the steaks with salt and pepper. Grill the steaks and sweet pepper halves on the rack of an uncovered grill directly over medium coals to desired doneness, turning once. (For steak, allow 8 to 12 minutes for medium-rare doneness or until temperature reaches 145°F. For medium doneness allow 12 to 15 minutes or until temperature reaches 160°F. For sweet pepper, allow 8 to 10 minutes, turning once.)

3 Meanwhile, stir 2 tablespoons of the snipped fresh sage into melted butter. Make a sage brush by tying 3 or 4 fresh sage leaves together with a clean kitchen string at the base of the leaves, and tie again closer to the leaves to make a sturdier brush. After turning steaks, brush with melted butter using sage brush or a pastry brush. Remove the steaks and sweet pepper halves from grill.

4 Chop grilled sweet pepper. Stir chopped sweet pepper and remaining 2 tablespoons snipped sage into corn. Just before serving, sprinkle corn with crumbled cheese. Serve corn mixture with steaks. Makes 4 servings.

Indirect Grill Method:

To grill steaks with indirect heat, in a grill with a cover arrange preheated coals around a drip pan. Test for medium heat above pan. Place steaks over drip pan. Place sweet pepper halves in a grill basket or rack directly over coals. Cover and grill steaks and sweet pepper to desired doneness. After turning steaks, brush them with melted butter using sage brush or pastry brush. (For steaks, allow 16 to 20 minutes for medium-rare doneness or until temperature reaches 145°F. Allow 20 to 24 minutes for medium doneness or until temperature reaches 160°F. For sweet pepper, allow 8 to 10 minutes, turning once.)

Broiler Method:

To broil, place the steaks and sweet pepper halves on the unheated rack of a broiler pan. Broil, surfaces of steak and sweet pepper halves 3 to 4 inches from the heat, to desired doneness, turning once. (For steaks, allow 15 to 20 minutes for medium-rare to medium doneness. For sweet pepper, allow 8 to 10 minutes.) After turning steaks, brush with melted butter using a sage or pastry brush.

Nutrition Facts per serving: 483 cal., 22 g total fat (9 g sat. fat), 111 mg chol., 317 mg sodium, 29 g carbo., 4 g fiber, 44 g pro. **Daily Values:** 31% vit. A, 60% vit. C, 5% calcium, 28% iron.

Mushroom-Stuffed Pork Chops

For a ready-made glaze, use a jar of ginger jelly or orange marmalade. (See the photograph on page 202.)

Prep: 25 minutes **Grill:** 35 minutes

- ½ cup coarsely chopped fresh mushrooms, such as button, chanterelle, or shiitake
- ¼ cup chopped onion
- 1 Tbsp. margarine or butter
- 1 tsp. grated fresh ginger
- ¼ tsp. salt
- ¼ tsp. pepper
- 1 cup coarsely chopped fresh spinach leaves
- ¼ cup soft sourdough or white bread crumbs
- 4 pork loin chops or pork rib chops, cut 1¼ inches thick (about 3 lb.)
  Salt and pepper
- ¼ cup ginger jelly or preserves or orange marmalade
- 12 green onions
- 2 tsp. olive oil

1 For stuffing, in a saucepan cook the mushrooms and onion in margarine or butter until the onion is tender. Remove from the heat. Stir in the ginger, the ¼ teaspoon salt, and the ¼ teaspoon pepper. Add spinach and bread crumbs, tossing gently to combine.

2 Trim fat from meat. Make a pocket in each chop by cutting horizontally from the fat side almost to the bone. Spoon one-fourth of the stuffing into each pocket. Secure the opening with wooden toothpicks. Sprinkle chops with salt and pepper.

3 In a grill with a cover arrange preheated coals around a drip pan for indirect grilling. Test for medium heat above the pan. Place chops on the grill rack over the drip pan. Cover; grill for 35 to 40 minutes or until center of meat reaches a temperature of 160°F, turning once and brushing occasionally with ginger jelly during the last 5 minutes of grilling.

4 Meanwhile, trim roots and tops of the green onions. Heat olive oil in a medium skillet. Add green onions and cook, uncovered, for 1 to 3 minutes until slightly softened. To serve, place chops and green onions on dinner plates. Makes 4 servings.

Oven Method:

To bake stuffed chops, after stuffing and sprinkling chops with salt and pepper, brown them in a small amount of olive oil or cooking oil in a large skillet. Transfer to a baking dish. Bake, uncovered, in a 375°F oven for 35 to 45 minutes or until center of meat reaches a temperature of 160°F, brushing with ginger jelly during the last 5 minutes of baking.

Nutrition Facts per serving: 442 cal., 17 g total fat (5 g sat. fat), 132 mg chol., 355 mg sodium, 19 g carbo., 2 g fiber, 50 g pro. **Daily Values:** 15% vit. A, 20% vit. C, 7% calcium, 16% iron.

30 MINUTE

Caper Butter

Turn a simple grilled fish steak into a something-special dish by topping it with this simple stir-together butter.

Start to finish: 5 minutes

- ¼ cup butter, softened
- 1 Tbsp. capers, drained and finely chopped
- 1 clove garlic, minced
  Pepper

1 In small bowl stir together the butter, capers, and garlic. Season to taste with pepper. Serve with grilled fish, such as salmon or halibut. Makes about ¼ cup.

Nutrition Facts per tablespoon: 109 cal., 12 g total fat (8 g sat. fat), 33 mg chol., 188 mg sodium, 0 g carbo., 0 g fiber, 0 g pro. **Daily Values:** 9% vit. A, 1% vit. C, 1% calcium, 1% iron.

The Real Face of Diabetes

The future is brighter every day for people with diabetes. Researchers are learning more about this disease and developing innovative treatments that make it easier to manage. Yet more Americans than ever—a diverse group of 16 million—have diabetes. And the number continues to grow.

A Preventable Epidemic

Diabetes has risen at a startling rate—30 percent in the past decade. More than 90 percent of people who have diabetes are classified as type 2 (see "The Basics of Diabetes, opposite), which until several years ago mostly occurred in overweight adults older than 45. The disease does not discriminate now, however. Women, men, children, and adolescents of all races and ethnic groups are developing type 2 diabetes.

The epidemic of type 2 diabetes seems linked to a major risk factor: obesity, or being overweight by about 30 or more pounds. The rate of obesity in the United States has increased by 57 percent since 1991. Simply put, Americans sit too much and eat too many fatty foods. They pay a heavy price: spiraling health-care costs and, for those with diabetes, a lifetime of potential complications, including blindness, kidney failure, heart attack, and stroke.

The statistics seem grim. But they are reversible. Type 2 diabetes is preventable and certainly treatable, especially with exercise and a low-fat diet.

Some diabetes risk factors, such as heredity, cannot be controlled, says David S.H. Bell, M.D., of the University of Alabama at Birmingham. These factors include having a close relative with diabetes, such as a father, mother, sister, or brother; or being of African-American, Latino, Native American, or Asian descent. Or you might have high blood pressure, good (HDL) cholesterol that is too low (less than 40 mg/dl), or triglycerides (another type of fat in the blood) that are high (more than 259 mg/dl).

Special Concerns for Women

About 8.1 million women and about 7.5 million men have diabetes. There is a higher incidence of type 2 diabetes in women than in men probably because females tend to be more overweight, Bell says.

Women are vulnerable to other risk factors, such as having given birth to a large baby. "By that, I mean a baby weighing more than 10 pounds," Bell says.

Some women develop gestational diabetes, which occurs in 2 to 5 percent of all pregnancies. However, it disappears when a pregnancy is over. A registered dietitian, working with the doctor, can plan a diet that provides the baby with adequate nutrition while omitting foods that increase blood sugar levels in the mother. Women with gestational diabetes may avoid insulin injections if they do not eat certain foods, such as table sugar, honey, brown sugar, corn syrup, maple syrup, molasses, soft drinks, fruit drinks, fruit packed in syrup, cake, cookies, ice cream, candy, jams, and doughnuts. It is also recommended that fruit juices be limited to 6 ounces and taken with meals.

About one-third of women with gestational diabetes will develop type 2 diabetes later on, Bell says. Many of these women can prevent this from happening if they keep their weight down—after pregnancy—by following a diet low in fat and calories and by exercising.

If you are a diabetic woman who wants to bear children, seek expert medical advice before getting pregnant. "Generally, it's better for pregnancy to occur when you're young and in the early controlled stages of diabetes," Bell says. "However, you'll need high-risk pregnancy management that may include an endocrinologist working with your obstetrician."

Women with diabetes, especially type 2, are at risk for heart problems. "Women who are not diabetic typically do not get heart disease until they're in their 60s," Bell says. "However, with diabetic women, this can occur a lot earlier. "That's why it's essential that their doctors apply what Bell calls the Big Three: (1) Treat the blood sugar problems associated with diabetes; (2) treat lipids—the cholesterol and triglycerides; and (3) keep blood pressure under control.

Crisis: Children and Type 2 Diabetes

Type 1 diabetes has been called "juvenile diabetes" and type 2 "adult-onset diabetes." Traditionally, pediatricians have treated type 1 (not type 2) diabetes in children. However, those lines are blurring because of an increase of type 2 diabetes in children and adolescents. This crisis is an indictment of lifestyles—too much junk food and television and too little exercise, says James R. Gavin III, M.D., of the Howard Hughes Medical Institute in Chevy Chase, Maryland, and former president of the American Diabetes Association.

Parents can fight this epidemic by exercising with their children and minimizing fast-food junkets. Stock the refrigerator with fruits and vegetables, and put beans, grains, cereals, low-fat dairy foods, lean meats, chicken, and fish on the family menu.

If your children have diabetes, ensure they get cholesterol and other blood fat tests, a yearly dilated eye exam, a foot exam to check circulation and nerves, a urine test to check kidney function, and regular dental checkups. They need to have their blood pressure checked regularly; if elevated, it should be treated.

Better Tools

"There now are tremendous drugs to treat type 2 diabetes," says Bell. The hemoglobin A1c test, a valuable but underused tool, also makes a big difference in treatment. The test can tell doctors how high the patient's blood sugar has been on average over the last two to three months. This provides a better picture of the degree to which the kidneys, heart, nerves, and eyes have been exposed to high blood sugar.

Surprisingly, only 40 percent of patients with diabetes get the hemoglobin A1c test once a year, Bell says. If you are diabetic, talk to your doctor about taking the test.

Painless Possibilities

For those who must take insulin, the chore of injection has become quicker and less painful with inventive gadgets. For example, a disposable penlike injector that contains insulin and small needles can be tucked into a pocket.

The insulin pump, an improved insulin-delivery method used mainly by type 1 diabetic patients, is available in sizes as small as a pager.

All patients with diabetes must measure blood glucose with finger-stick tests—on a daily basis or even hour by hour—so they know how food, exercise, and medication affect their blood sugar. Thanks to new testers, the days of numerous pricks and sore fingers may end soon. The Food and Drug Administration has approved a meter that resembles a wristwatch and uses low-frequency electrical current to measure glucose. Other products under development include a patch that continuously monitors glucose levels, and a self-monitoring device with a laser to draw blood.

The insulin inhaler is another innovation. However, more studies are needed to investigate how inhaling insulin directly into the lungs affects lung tissue, Bell says. Gavin does not believe these inhalers will replace insulin injections for most patients over the long term.

For now, medications, regular checkups, nutrition, and exercise are the best methods to manage diabetes and live a full life.

The Basics of Diabetes

The technical term for diabetes is *diabetes mellitus,* which is characterized by the body's problems with insulin, a hormone produced in the pancreas. Insulin plays a vital role in metabolism—in helping glucose (sugar) to move out of the blood into cells, which use the glucose for fuel. In type 1 and type 2 diabetes, there's a need to control glucose levels in the blood.

Type 1

About 10 percent of all people with diabetes have type 1, or juvenile diabetes, in which the insulin-producing beta cells in the pancreas have been destroyed. Most people with type 1 diabetes develop it before age 30.

Symptoms

May include high levels of blood sugar, high levels of sugar in the urine, frequent urination, extreme hunger, extreme thirst, extreme weight loss, weakness and fatigue, moodiness and irritability, or nausea and vomiting.

Treatment

Insulin is received via injections or insulin pumps.

Complications

Kidney disease; eye damage; heart problems; compromised nerve function in the arms, hands, legs, and feet that can set the stage for ulcers and amputations; coma; and death.

Type 2

About 90 percent of all people with diabetes have type 2. The pancreas may be producing insulin; however, there are insulin-resistance problems in the body that interfere with the ability of insulin to do its job.

Symptoms

May include increased thirst; frequent urination; increased appetite accompanied by weight loss; edginess; fatigue; nausea; repeated hard-to-heal infections; tingling or numbness in the hands or feet; high levels of sugar in the urine; dry, itchy skin.

Treatment

Ten percent of type 2 patients rely on diet and exercise to manage their disease. Fifty percent are treated with oral medications, 30 percent with a combination of insulin and oral medications, and 10 percent with insulin alone.

Complications

Same as type 1.

For more information

- American Diabetes Association (ADA): 800/342-2383 or visit www.diabetes.org.
- Juvenile Diabetes Research Foundation International (JDRF): 800/533-2873 or visit www.jdrf.org.

Juicy Goodness

Go ahead. Put the squeeze on fruit. Drinking fruit juice is an easy way to get vitamins and minerals. Health experts agree that increasing the intake of fruits and vegetables cuts the risk of stroke, cancer, and heart disease. Still, many people don't eat the recommended amounts.

Boosting daily intake to at least five servings of fruits and vegetables may reduce risk of cancer by 20 percent, says Melanie Polk, registered dietitian and spokesperson for the American Institute for Cancer Research (AICR). "It would be great if everyone could eat 10 servings of fruits and vegetables. The more the better," Polk says.

Getting Juiced

Juice typically lacks the fiber of whole fruit, but fruit juice can still pack nutritional punch in your diet. Polk recommends blending juice by combining whole fruits, such as berries and melons, with orange juice. Use a citrus juicer to juice oranges, lemons, limes, and grapefruits. To go beyond citrus, use a juice extractor. A whirling disk chops food into tiny pieces that are rapidly spun to separate juice from pulp. It works well on fruits and vegetables, such as apples and carrots.

Promoters in Your Pantry

Cranberry juice—Drinking 10 ounces of cranberry juice each day reduces the chance of getting urinary tract infections, according to a study published in the *Journal of the American Medical Association.* New lab studies indicate cranberry components —flavonoids—may be useful in battling cancer and gum disease.

Orange juice—One 8-ounce glass of orange juice provides 25 percent of the recommended daily level of folic acid, which women need to prevent certain birth defects. That same amount of juice supplies 100 percent of the recommended daily amount for vitamin C. Some fortified juices boost vitamin C levels even more; others contain calcium.

Grape juice—Beverages from red grapes contain resveratrol, a cancer-fighting substance that seems to work as an anti-inflammatory agent and may also keep early cancer cells from growing. Like red wine, grape juice has some heart-protecting benefits.

Look at the Label

The word "juice" on a label may not mean 100 percent fruit juice.

• Check the ingredient list. The terms "beverage," "cocktail," "drink," and "punch" indicate a beverage is not 100 percent fruit juice.

• Choose from a variety of citrus juices to drink frequently. They are important sources of vitamin C, potassium, folic acid, and, when fortified, calcium.

---

2 In a blender container combine cranberry juice and reserved raspberry juice. With blender running, add ice through opening in lid. Blend until slushy.

3 Transfer juice to a pitcher. Slowly pour in carbonated beverage; stir. Serve over ice. Add fresh raspberries and a lemon slice, if desired. Serves 5.

Nutrition Facts per serving: 97 cal., 0 g total fat, 0 mg chol., 11 mg sodium, 24 g carbo., 3 g fiber, 0 g pro. Daily Values: 1% vit. A, 65% vit. C, 2% calcium, 3% iron.

---

30 MINUTE, NO FAT

Herbed Pineapple Refresher

Start to finish: 15 minutes

> 1 4-inch piece fresh peeled ginger, finely chopped
> 3 cups pineapple juice, chilled
> 1 cup orange juice, chilled
> 3 Tbsp. lime juice
> ¼ cup finely chopped fresh cilantro leaves
> Fresh cilantro sprigs

1 Place the ginger, a little at a time, in a garlic press to extract juice; reserve juice (should have about 1½ teaspoons juice).

2 In a blender container or food processor bowl combine ginger juice, pineapple juice, orange juice, lime juice, and cilantro leaves. Cover and blend or process until nearly smooth. Garnish with fresh cilantro sprigs. Serve immediately. Serves 6.

Nutrition Facts per serving: 98 cal., 0 g total fat, 0 mg chol., 5 mg sodium, 24 g carbo., 1 g fiber, 1 g pro. Daily Values: 3% vit. A, 63% vit. C, 3% calcium, 3% iron.

NO FAT

Cranberry-Raspberry Freeze

Prep: 5 minutes **Chill:** 1 hour

> 2 cups fresh raspberries or one 12-oz. pkg. frozen raspberries, thawed
> ½ cup boiling water
> 1½ cups cranberry juice, chilled
> 1 cup ice cubes

> 1 12-oz. can lemon-lime flavored carbonated beverage, chilled
> Fresh raspberries (optional)
> Lemon slices (optional)

1 Put 2 cups raspberries in a fine-mesh strainer placed over a large glass measure or pitcher. Pour boiling water over raspberries. With the back of a spoon, press berries to release juice. Discard berry pulp; reserve juice (about 1 cup). Chill.

Berry Patch Ice Cream Dessert

This recipe makes an extra brownie layer that can be popped in the freezer for another day.

Prep: 15 minutes **Bake:** 25 minutes
Freeze: 4 hours

- 1   19- to 22-oz. pkg. fudge brownie mix
- 1   quart vanilla ice cream
- 2½ cups desired berries, such as raspberries, blueberries, and/or halved strawberries
- ¼   cup chocolate ice cream topping or raspberry syrup

1 Preheat oven to 325°F. Lightly grease two 8×1½-inch round baking pans; line bottoms with waxed paper. Grease the waxed paper and set pans aside. Prepare the brownie mix according to package directions; divide batter and spread into prepared pans.

2 Bake in the preheated oven for 25 minutes. Cool in pans on wire rack for 10 minutes. Loosen edges, invert, and carefully remove brownie rounds from pans. Peel off waxed paper. Cool completely. Wrap each of the brownies in plastic wrap. Place one of the brownie rounds in an airtight freezer container and freeze for up to 2 months. Store remaining brownie at room temperature for several hours or overnight while berry-ice cream layer is being frozen.

3 Line an 8×1½-inch round baking pan with plastic wrap, allowing excess to extend over edges; set aside. In a large mixing bowl stir ice cream just to soften. Carefully fold in 1 cup of the berries. Spread berry-ice cream mixture evenly into prepared pan. Cover and freeze for 4 to 24 hours.

CLEVER COOK

Frozen Flower Cubes

To brighten drinks and punches, use ice cubes decorated with flowers, herbs, and berries. Rose petals, violas, and nasturtium are my favorites for summer. Choose fresh, blemish-free edible flowers that have not been treated with chemical fertilizers or pesticides. Rinse the flowers before placing a single petal, a whole flower, or a sprig in each ice-cube compartment. Cover with water and freeze.

Jere Cockrell
Missoula, Montana

4 To serve, place brownie round on a serving plate. Lift ice cream and plastic wrap from pan. Invert ice cream layer onto brownie; peel off plastic wrap. Top with remaining 1½ cups of berries. Drizzle with chocolate topping or raspberry syrup. Let dessert stand 15 minutes before serving. Makes 10 servings.

Nutrition Facts per serving: 350 cal., 19 g total fat (8 g sat. fat), 58 mg chol., 141 mg sodium, 44 g carbo., 3 g fiber, 4 g pro. **Daily Values:** 9% vit. A, 14% vit. C, 8% calcium, 8% iron.

30 MINUTE

Plum Soaking Syrup

This rosy-colored fruit syrup is delicious for a morning meal served over French toast. For dessert, try it spooned over slices of toasted pound cake. (See the photograph on page 201.)

Start to finish: 20 minutes

- 1   vanilla bean
- 2   cups sliced, pitted plums and/or sliced peeled, pitted peaches
- ¼   cup sugar
- 4   slices prepared French toast

1 With a knife, halve vanilla bean lengthwise. In a small saucepan combine vanilla bean, 1 cup of the fruit, sugar, and ¼ cup water. Bring to boiling, stirring to dissolve sugar; reduce heat. Simmer, uncovered, about 10 minutes or until slightly thickened, stirring occasionally. Remove from heat.

2 Carefully remove vanilla bean and discard. Using a potato masher, mash the fruit. Stir in the remaining sliced fruit. Return to heat and heat through. Serve over French toast. Makes 4 servings.

Nutrition Facts per serving: 241 cal., 8 g total fat (2 g sat. fat), 75 mg chol., 312 mg sodium, 39 g carbo., 3 g fiber, 6 g pro. **Daily Values:** 12% vit. A, 13% vit. C, 7% calcium, 7% iron.

30 MINUTE

Melon Calling, Baby

Start to finish: 10 minutes

- ½   cup whipping cream
- 2   Tbsp. honey
- 2   small cantaloupe melons, halved and seeded
- 2   Tbsp. chopped toasted hazelnuts

1 In a chilled small mixing bowl beat together whipping cream and 1 tablespoon of the honey with chilled beaters of an electric mixer on medium speed until soft peaks form.

2 To serve, spoon whipped cream into each melon half. Drizzle with the remaining honey and sprinkle with hazelnuts. Makes 4 servings.

Nutrition Facts per serving: 232 cal., 14 g total fat (7 g sat. fat), 41 mg chol., 30 mg sodium, 27 g carbo., 2 g fiber, 3 g pro. **Daily Values:** 138% vit. A, 142% vit. C, 5% calcium, 4% iron.

My Berry, Your Berry

Put a twinkle in a child's eye with fresh berries—summer's jewels of fresh fruit. Berries are colorful gems that mark time from the beginning of summer through to the finish. Fortunately, berries rate high on nearly every kid's list of summer favorites: strawberry shortcake, blueberry muffins, raspberry jam, and blackberry ice cream.

Whether you grow them, pick your own, or shop at a farm stand or supermarket, fresh berries are a ripe subject. Keep a supply on hand and you'll discover that youngsters are intuitive berry masters. Opportunity seldom escapes them. When you fix pancakes during the summer, tumble a container of blueberries into the batter. Or place a border of raspberries around cakes or puddings.

Berry experts or not, parents can teach kids how to select the freshest and best berries or how to make an old-fashioned berry fool dessert (see the recipe, right).

Berry Perfect

• Buy fresh berries at the height of their season for best value. Peak supplies often bring lower prices.

• Plan a choose-a-berry party, with an all-berry menu that includes berry parfaits or smoothies.

• Avoid berry containers with excess juice in the bottom, overly soft fruit, and other telltale signs of age, such as bruises, mold, and unhealthy color.

• Refrigerate berries in a single layer, loosely covered, in a shallow dish so they won't crush.

• Rinse berries just prior to using, not before. Blot dry on paper towels if needed. Invert raspberries to drain.

• Freeze whole berries by spreading them out on a baking sheet. When they're frozen solid, place them in tight-sealing freezer bags.

Are You Berry Smart?

Can you match these rhymes to the berries in the pictures below? We bet you can.

1. I'm not the sad berry that my name would imply. My skin's a dark shade of the clear morning sky.

2. I taste yummy with rhubarb; with shortcakes I'm swell. If you snitch one too many, blushing fingers will tell.

3. I look like a thimble, rosy colored and sweet, but please handle me gently, as I'm a delicate treat.

4. I've a thorny reputation, but I'm delicious indeed. Big, dark, and plump, and full of small seeds.

ANSWERS: 1) B, Blueberry 2) A, Strawberry 3) D, Raspberry 4) C, Blackberry

30 MINUTE

Fresh Strawberry Fool

Prep: 10 minutes

½ cup whipping cream
⅓ cup powdered sugar
½ tsp. vanilla
1 8-oz. carton lemon yogurt
3 cups sliced fresh strawberries
   or 2 cups fresh blueberries
½ cup coarsely crumbled
   shortbread cookies
   (about 5)

1 In a chilled medium mixing bowl beat whipping cream, powdered sugar, and vanilla with chilled beaters of an electric mixer on medium speed or a chilled rotary beater until soft peaks form. By hand, fold in the yogurt and half of the berries.

2 Spoon some of the whipped cream mixture into the bottoms of four 10-ounce glasses. Top each with some of the remaining berries, the rest of the whipped cream mixture, and the rest of the berries. Serve immediately or cover and chill up to 2 hours. Before serving, sprinkle with the crumbled cookies. Makes 4 servings.

Nutrition Facts per serving: 272 cal., 15 g total fat (8 g sat. fat), 47 mg chol., 98 mg sodium, 32 g carbo., 3 g fiber, 4 g pro. **Daily Values:** 11% vit. A, 103% vit. C, 14% calcium, 4% iron.

september

IN THIS CHAPTER

30-minute recipes indicated in COLOR.
Low-fat and no-fat recipes indicated
with a ♥.
Photographs indicated in italics.
*Bonus recipe

Garden Veggie Burgers

Two toppings—sharp red onion and a tangy spinach-feta combination—complement these meatless grilled burgers. (See the photograph on page 199.)

Prep: 10 minutes **Grill:** 15 minutes

2 medium red onions
4 refrigerated or frozen meatless
    burger patties
¼ cup bottled vinaigrette salad
    dressing (room temperature)
4 cups fresh spinach leaves
1 clove garlic, minced
1 Tbsp. olive oil
½ cup crumbled feta cheese (2 oz.)
4 hamburger buns

1 For onion topping, cut onions into ½-inch-thick slices. On the rack of an uncovered grill, grill onions directly over medium coals for 15 to 20 minutes or until tender, turning once. Grill patties directly over coals alongside onions 4 to 5 minutes per side or until heated through. Brush grilled onions with salad dressing.

2 Meanwhile, for spinach topping, in a large skillet cook and stir the spinach and garlic in hot olive oil over medium-high heat 30 seconds or until spinach is just wilted. Remove from heat. Stir in the feta cheese. To serve, place the onion slices on bottom of buns. Top with grilled burger patties, spinach mixture, and bun tops. Makes 4 servings.

Nutrition Facts per serving: 350 cal., 14 g total fat (4 g sat. fat), 17 mg chol., 920 mg sodium, 37 g carbo., 7 g fiber, 21 g pro. **Daily Values:** 42% vit. A, 21% vit. C, 24% calcium, 21% iron.

A to Z Vegetable Soup

Start to finish: 45 minutes

1 Tbsp. cooking oil or olive oil
2 cups mixed, cut-up fresh
    vegetables, such as sliced
    small zucchini, carrots, celery,
    and chopped red onions
2 14½-oz. cans reduced-sodium
    chicken broth
2 cloves garlic, minced
1 15-oz. can cannellini or Great
    Northern beans, rinsed
    and drained
½ cup packaged dried alphabet-
    shape pasta or tiny shells
2 Tbsp. fresh small oregano leaves
1 oz. Parmesan cheese, thinly
    sliced (optional)

1 In a large saucepan heat oil over medium-high heat. Add mixed vegetables. Cook, uncovered, about 10 minutes or until vegetables are crisp-tender, stirring occasionally. Remove half the vegetables; set aside.

2 Stir chicken broth and garlic into remaining vegetables in saucepan. Bring to boiling. Stir in beans and pasta. Return to boiling; reduce heat. Simmer, covered, about 10 minutes or until pasta is just tender. Stir in fresh oregano leaves.

3 To serve, ladle soup into four bowls. Top each with reserved vegetables. Sprinkle each serving with Parmesan cheese slices, if desired. Makes 4 servings.

Nutrition Facts per serving: 188 cal., 4 g total fat (1 g sat. fat), 0 mg chol., 717 mg sodium, 33 g carbo., 6 g fiber, 12 g pro. **Daily Values:** 79% vit. A, 9% vit. C, 5% calcium, 12% iron.

Rich and Creamy Pasta Bake

Prep: 35 minutes **Bake:** 30 minutes

10 oz. packaged dried mostaccioli
     or rotini pasta
 1 Tbsp. olive oil
 2 cloves garlic, minced
 1 15-oz. can tomato sauce
 1 14½-oz. can diced tomatoes,
     undrained
 1 tsp. dried Italian
     seasoning, crushed
¼ cup butter
 1 clove garlic, minced
 3 Tbsp. all-purpose flour
1½ cups half-and-half or light cream
     or one 12-oz. can (1½ cups)
     evaporated milk
 2 cups shredded provolone or
     mozzarella cheese (8 oz.)

1 Preheat oven to 350°F. Cook pasta according to package directions; drain and set aside.

2 For red sauce, in a medium saucepan heat olive oil over medium-high heat. Add 2 cloves of the garlic; cook and stir 30 seconds. Stir in the tomato sauce, undrained tomatoes, Italian seasoning, and ¼ teaspoon pepper. Bring to boiling; reduce heat. Simmer, covered, for 10 minutes. Remove from heat.

3 For white sauce, in a small saucepan melt butter over medium heat. Add the 1 clove garlic. Cook and stir for 30 seconds. Stir in the flour, ¼ teaspoon salt, and ⅛ teaspoon pepper. Add half-and-half all at once. Cook and stir until thickened and bubbly. Remove from heat.

4 To assemble, spread a small amount (about ⅓ cup) of the red sauce in the bottom of a 3-quart rectangular baking dish. Sprinkle half of the pasta evenly over sauce in dish. Spoon half of the remaining red sauce over pasta. Spoon on half of the white sauce. Top with half of the cheese. Top with the remaining pasta, red sauce, white sauce, and cheese.

5 Cover dish loosely with foil. Bake for 20 minutes. Uncover and bake about 10 minutes more or until bubbly. Makes 8 servings.

Nutrition Facts per serving: 382 cal., 19 g total fat (11 g sat. fat), 48 mg chol., 712 mg sodium, 37 g carbo., 2 g fiber, 14 g pro. Daily Values: 12% vit. A, 12% vit. C, 29% calcium, 11% iron.

Pasta and Veggies In Tomato Cream

Start to finish: 45 minutes

- 12 oz. packaged dried penne pasta
- 1 small eggplant, peeled and cut into 1-inch cubes (about 1 lb.)
- 1 large onion, cut into thin wedges
- 2 cups sliced portobello mushrooms
- 4 cloves garlic, minced
- 2 tsp. snipped fresh oregano or ½ tsp. dried oregano, crushed
- ¼ cup olive oil
- 1 12-oz. jar roasted red sweet peppers, drained and coarsely chopped
- 1 28-oz. jar pasta sauce Dash ground red pepper
- ⅓ cup whipping cream Snipped fresh oregano (optional)

1 Preheat oven to 400°F. Cook pasta according to package directions; drain and set aside.

2 Meanwhile, in a shallow roasting pan combine eggplant, onion, mushrooms, garlic, 1 teaspoon of the

fresh or ¼ teaspoon of the dried oregano, and the olive oil. Toss to coat vegetables. Roast, uncovered, for 20 to 25 minutes or until vegetables are tender, stirring once. Remove from oven. Stir in cooked pasta and roasted red peppers. Set aside.

3 Meanwhile, in a medium saucepan combine pasta sauce, remaining 1 teaspoon fresh or ¼ teaspoon dried oregano, the ground red pepper, and ¼ teaspoon black pepper. Bring to

boiling; reduce heat. Simmer, uncovered, 10 minutes. Remove from heat. Stir in whipping cream.

4 Pour sauce over pasta mixture, tossing gently to coat. Arrange mixture on a large serving platter. Sprinkle with additional fresh snipped oregano, if desired. Serves 6.

Nutrition Facts per serving: 433 cal., 17 g total fat (4 g sat. fat), 18 mg chol., 428 mg sodium, 61 g carbo., 6 g fiber, 12 g pro. Daily Values: 14% vit. A, 129% vit. C, 12% calcium, 18% iron.

Upside-Down Pizza Pie

Make the lattice crust from the center of the bowl outward, cutting or piecing pastry strips to fit. (See the photograph on page 198.)

Prep: 20 minutes **Bake:** 25 minutes
Stand: 5 minutes

- 1   14½-oz. can undrained diced tomatoes with basil, garlic, and oregano
- 2   cups cubed cooked chicken
- 1   8-oz. can pizza sauce
- 1½ cups quartered fresh mushrooms, such as brown, white, or button
- 1   cup shredded pizza cheese (4 oz.)
- ¼   cup grated Parmesan cheese
- 1   11-oz. pkg. (12) refrigerated breadsticks
      Milk
- 1   Tbsp. grated Parmesan cheese
      Desired toppings, such as sliced green onions, snipped fresh chives, sliced pitted black or green olives, chopped green or yellow sweet pepper, and/or shredded pizza cheese

1 Preheat oven to 375°F. In a medium bowl stir together the undrained tomatoes, chicken, pizza sauce, and mushrooms. Spoon mixture into four greased 12- to 16-ounce individual baking dishes. Sprinkle the pizza cheese evenly over the tomato mixture. Sprinkle with the ¼ cup Parmesan cheese.

2 Unroll the breadstick dough. Separate along perforations to form 12 strips. Weave strips over filling to form a lattice crust on each baking dish. Depending on the width of your bowls, you may need to cut strips to length or piece strips together. Brush dough with a little milk. Sprinkle with remaining 1 tablespoon of Parmesan cheese.

3 Bake in the preheated oven about 25 minutes or until breadsticks are golden brown and filling is bubbly. Let stand 5 minutes. Serve in dishes or loosen edges and invert onto plates; remove dishes. Sprinkle with desired toppings. Makes 4 servings.

Nutrition Facts per serving: 562 cal., 20 g total fat (8 g sat. fat), 88 mg chol., 1,865 mg sodium, 52 g carbo., 3 g fiber, 40 g pro. **Daily Values:** 21% vit. A, 33% vit. C, 40% calcium, 29% iron.

30 MINUTE

Cheesy Pasta and Vegetables

Start to finish: 25 minutes

- 12   oz. packaged dried rotini pasta
- 1   16-oz. pkg. loose-pack frozen broccoli stir-fry vegetables (broccoli, carrots, onions, water chestnuts, and mushrooms)
- ¼   cup margarine or butter
- ¼   cup all-purpose flour
- ⅛   tsp. black pepper
- 2¼   cups milk
- 1½   cups shredded smoked cheddar cheese (6 oz.)
- ¼   cup grated Parmesan cheese
- 2   cups chopped cooked chicken
- 1   Tbsp. snipped fresh basil

1 In a 4-quart Dutch oven, cook pasta according to package directions, except 5 minutes before pasta is done, add frozen vegetables to Dutch oven. Return to boiling; reduce heat. Cook 5 minutes more or until pasta and vegetables are just tender. Drain and return to Dutch oven.

2 Meanwhile, in a medium saucepan melt butter over medium heat. Stir in the flour and pepper until smooth. Add milk all at once. Cook and stir until thickened and bubbly. Reduce heat. Add the smoked cheddar cheese and Parmesan cheese. Stir over low heat until cheese is melted. Stir in chicken and basil; heat through. Add sauce to pasta; stir until combined. Transfer to a serving platter. Serves 6.

Nutrition Facts per serving: 588 cal., 24 g total fat (10 g sat. fat), 81 mg chol., 449 mg sodium, 56 g carbo., 3 g fiber, 34 g pro. **Daily Values:** 46% vit. A, 20% vit. C, 41% calcium, 17% iron.

PRIZE WINNER

Cajun Chicken Lasagna

Ann Peterson
Reno, Nevada
$400—Pasta Bakes

Prep: 25 minutes **Bake:** 1 hour
Stand: 15 minutes

- 16   packaged dried lasagna noodles
- 1   lb. andouille sausage or smoked pork sausage, quartered lengthwise and sliced
- 1   lb. skinless, boneless chicken breast halves, cut into ¾-inch cubes
- 2   to 3 tsp. Cajun seasoning

- 1 tsp. dried sage, crushed
- ½ cup chopped onion
- ½ cup chopped celery
- ¼ cup chopped green sweet pepper
- 1 Tbsp. finely chopped garlic
- 2 10-oz. containers refrigerated light Alfredo sauce
- ½ cup grated Parmesan cheese Nonstick cooking spray
- 1½ cups shredded mozzarella cheese

1 Preheat oven to 325°F. Cook lasagna noodles according to package directions. Drain; rinse.

2 In a large skillet combine sausage, chicken, Cajun seasoning, and sage. Cook over medium-high heat about 8 minutes or until chicken is no longer pink. Using a slotted spoon, remove meat mixture from skillet, reserving drippings in skillet. Set meat mixture aside; keep warm. In the same skillet cook onion, celery, sweet pepper, and garlic in drippings until vegetables are tender. Remove from heat. Stir meat mixture, one container of the Alfredo sauce, and Parmesan cheese into the vegetables.

3 Lightly coat a 3-quart rectangular baking dish with nonstick spray. Arrange four noodles in bottom of dish. Spread with 2 cups of the meat-vegetable mixture. Sprinkle with ½ cup of the mozzarella. Repeat layers, ending with noodles. Carefully spread remaining Alfredo sauce over top (if sauce is too thick, heat slightly).

4 Cover and bake in the preheated oven about 1 hour or until heated through. Let stand 15 to 20 minutes before carefully cutting. Serves 12.

Nutrition Facts per serving: 469 cal., 24 g total fat (11 g sat. fat), 79 mg chol., 1,187 mg sodium, 34 g carbo., 1 g fiber, 29 g pro. Daily Values: 4% vit. A, 8% vit. C, 29% calcium, 10% iron.

Spice-Grilled Chicken

The aromas of jasmine rice and spice-laden chicken will tempt everyone to dinner.

Prep: 20 minutes Grill: 1 hour for whole chicken; 50 minutes for drumsticks

- 2 tsp. brown sugar
- 1½ tsp. ground cinnamon
- 1 tsp. smoked paprika or paprika
- ½ tsp. salt
- ½ tsp. pepper
- ½ tsp. ground allspice
- 1 3-lb. whole broiler-fryer chicken or 12 chicken drumsticks
- 4 tsp. cooking oil
- 2 cups chicken broth or 2 cups water plus ½ tsp. salt
- 1 cup uncooked jasmine or long grain rice
- ¼ cup snipped dried apricots
- ¼ cup golden raisins
- 4 lemon wedges (optional) Swiss chard (optional) Halved fresh apricots, broiled* (optional)
- 2 Tbsp. chopped peanuts

1 In a small bowl combine the brown sugar, cinnamon, paprika, salt, pepper, and allspice. Set aside 1½ teaspoons of the mixture. Remove the neck and giblets from the whole chicken. Pat chicken dry with paper towels. Skewer the neck skin to the back. Twist wing tips under the back. Brush chicken with the cooking oil; gently rub remaining cinnamon mixture onto chicken.

2 In a grill with a cover, arrange preheated coals around a drip pan. Test for medium heat above pan. Place whole chicken, breast side up,

on the grill rack over drip pan. Cover and grill 1 to 1¼ hours or until meat thermometer registers 180°F, the chicken is no longer pink, and drumsticks move easily in their sockets. (Or, grill drumsticks on grill rack for 50 to 60 minutes or until tender and no longer pink. A thermometer inserted in thickest part of drumstick should register 170°F.)

3 Meanwhile, in a medium saucepan combine the broth or water plus ½ teaspoon salt, uncooked rice, and the 1½ teaspoons reserved cinnamon mixture. Bring to boiling; reduce heat. Simmer, covered, for 15 minutes. Remove from heat. Stir in apricots and raisins. Let stand, covered, 5 minutes before serving.

4 Spoon rice onto a serving platter; top with chicken. Garnish with lemon wedges, Swiss chard, and broiled apricots, if desired.

5 To serve, carve the whole chicken or cut it into 4 to 6 pieces using kitchen shears. Divide rice among serving plates. Top with chicken; sprinkle with chopped peanuts. Makes 4 to 6 servings.

*Note: For broiled apricots, preheat broiler. Halve and pit fresh apricots. Brush cut sides lightly with melted margarine or butter. Place cut side up on the unheated rack of a broiler pan. Broil 3 inches from the heat for 3 to 6 minutes or until lightly browned.

Nutrition Facts per serving: 646 cal., 23 g total fat (6 g sat. fat), 207 mg chol., 1,012 mg sodium, 54 g carbo., 2 g fiber, 58 g pro. Daily Values: 18% vit. A, 2% vit. C, 11% calcium, 49% iron.

Bail-Out Beef Stroganoff

Follow this quick-prep method to make a classic Old World recipe. The horseradish-sour cream is an imperial touch. (See the photograph on page 197.)

Start to finish: 30 minutes

     3 cups packaged dried
           wide noodles
     3 cups broccoli florets (12 oz.)
     ½ cup light dairy sour cream
    1½ tsp. prepared horseradish
     ½ tsp. snipped fresh dill
     1 lb. beef rib-eye steak
     1 small onion, cut into
           ½-inch slices
     1 clove garlic, minced
     1 Tbsp. cooking oil
     4 tsp. all-purpose flour
     ½ tsp. pepper
     1 14½-oz. can beef broth
     3 Tbsp. tomato paste
     1 tsp. Worcestershire sauce

1 Cook noodles according to package directions, adding broccoli the last 5 minutes of cooking; drain and keep warm.

2 Meanwhile, in a small serving bowl stir together the sour cream, horseradish, and dill. Cover and chill until serving time.

3 Trim fat from beef. Cut into bite-size strips. In a large skillet cook half of the beef, the onion, and garlic in hot oil until onion is tender and beef is desired doneness. Remove from skillet. Add remaining beef, and cook and stir until beef is desired doneness. Return all meat to skillet; sprinkle flour and pepper over meat. Stir to coat.

4 Stir in the beef broth, tomato paste, and Worcestershire sauce. Cook and stir until thickened and bubbly. Cook and stir for 1 minute more. Remove from heat.

5 To serve, divide noodle-broccoli mixture among four bowls. Spoon beef mixture on top of noodle mixture. Top with a spoon or two of the horseradish-sour cream mixture. Makes 4 servings.

Nutrition Facts per serving: 368 cal., 15 g total fat (5 g sat. fat), 81 mg chol., 454 mg sodium, 32 g carbo., 4 g fiber, 29 g pro. **Daily Values:** 21% vit. A, 83% vit. C, 9% calcium, 21% iron.

CLEVER COOK

Pumped-Up Tomato Sauces

Add a handful of chopped dried tomatoes to tomato sauces. Use them to thicken sauces made with fresh-picked tomatoes or use them to add sweet, fresh flavor to canned or jarred tomato sauces.

L. A. Wilson
Fort Worth, Texas

Sauté-and-Serve Pasta Toss

Green tomatoes, red onion, and sweet peppers provide this quick dish with piquant flavor and color. (See the photograph on page 197.)

Start to finish: 25 minutes

     8 oz. packaged dried fusilli
           or spaghetti
     2 Tbsp. olive oil or cooking oil
    1½ oz. Italian bread, torn into small
           pieces (1½ cups)
     8 oz. uncooked Italian sweet or
           hot sausage, or ground beef
     2 medium green tomatoes,
           cut into wedges
     1 medium red onion,
           coarsely chopped
     1 medium red, green, or yellow
           sweet pepper, cut into
           bite-size pieces
     1 26-oz. jar pasta sauce with olives

1 Cook pasta according to package directions; drain.

2 Meanwhile, in a large skillet heat the olive oil or cooking oil over medium-high heat. Add bread pieces. Cook and stir for 2 to 3 minutes or until bread is toasted. Remove from skillet; set aside.

3 Remove casings, if present, from sausages. In the same skillet cook and stir the sausage or ground beef, tomatoes, onion, and pepper over medium heat for 6 to 8 minutes or until vegetables are tender and sausage is browned. Drain off fat. Stir in pasta sauce. Cook and stir until heated through.

4 To serve, divide the hot-cooked pasta among four shallow pasta bowls. Spoon sauce over pasta and sprinkle with toasted bread pieces. Makes 4 servings.

Nutrition Facts per serving: 595 cal., 23 g total fat (6 g sat. fat), 38 mg chol., 1,023 mg sodium, 71 g carbo., 6 g fiber, 20 g pro. **Daily Values:** 55% vit. A, 121% vit. C, 13% calcium, 22% iron.

Left: Sauté-and-Serve Pasta Toss
(page 196)
Below: Bail-Out Beef Stroganoff
(page 196)

Page 198, top: Salmon Shortcakes (page 207)
Page 198, bottom: Upside-Down Pizza Pie (page 194)

Top left: Garden Veggie Burgers (page 192)
Top right: Vegetable Bread (page 208)
Bottom left: Banana-Apple Butter Bread (page 208)
Bottom right: Coconut-Topped Mango-Berry Pie (page 214)

Summer S'Ghetti (page 171)   Berry Breakfast Rolls (page 168)   Veggie-Stuffed Veggies (page 174)

Farmer's Tomato Pie (page 175)

Plum Soaking Syrup (page 189)   Baby Potato Kabobs (page 174)   Squished Tomato Catsup (page 169)

Sage-Brushed Cowboy Steak (page 184)

Top left: Mushroom-Stuffed
Pork Chops (page 185)
Left: Seared Vegetable
Medley (page 171)
Page 203: Sizzling Catfish
with Pepper-Mint Slaw
(page 182)

Left: Provolone and Ham Melt (page 205)
Below: Molasses-Glazed Pork Tenderloin (page 205)

Molasses-Glazed Pork Tenderloin

Old-fashioned corn bread is an appetizing dinner partner for this Southern-inspired dish. (See the photograph on page 204.)

Start to finish: 30 minutes

- ¼ cup finely chopped prosciutto or 2 slices bacon, coarsely chopped
- 1 16-oz. pkg. frozen lima beans or two 9-oz. pkg. frozen Italian green beans
- ½ cup chopped onion
- ¾ cup water
- 1 Tbsp. olive oil
- 12 oz. pork tenderloin, cut into ½-inch-thick slices (11 to 12 slices)
- ½ cup orange juice
- 3 Tbsp. molasses
- 1 tsp. cornstarch
- ½ tsp. salt
- ¼ tsp. pepper
  Steamed spinach or turnip greens (optional)
- 2 Tbsp. snipped fresh parsley

1 In a large skillet cook prosciutto or bacon over medium heat until crisp-cooked; drain and set aside. In the same skillet cook beans and onion in the water according to lima bean package directions. Drain the beans; set aside.

2 Add the olive oil to same skillet; cook tenderloin in hot oil over medium-high heat 4 to 5 minutes or until just barely pink in center, turning once.

3 Meanwhile, in a small bowl stir together orange juice, molasses, cornstarch, salt, and pepper. Add to meat in skillet. Cook and stir until thickened and bubbly. Cook and stir about 2 minutes more. Stir beans into skillet mixture; heat through.

4 To serve, divide steamed spinach, if desired, among four plates. Spoon meat and bean mixture over steamed spinach, if desired. Top with bacon or prosciutto and sprinkle with parsley. Makes 4 servings.

Nutrition Facts per serving: 324 cal., 6 g total fat (1 g sat. fat), 52 mg chol., 460 mg sodium, 38 g carbo., 7 g fiber, 29 g pro. Daily Values: 7% vit. A, 44% vit. C, 8% calcium, 24% iron.

Provolone and Ham Melt

This sandwich will satisfy children and adults. Try cheese, ham, and fruit, or red sweet pepper and prosciutto. (See the photograph on page 204.)

Prep: 15 minutes   **Cook:** 8 minutes

- 8 slices thick-cut multi-grain, whole wheat, poppy seed, white, or pumpernickel bread
  Margarine or butter, softened
- 4 tsp. mayonnaise or salad dressing
- 4 oz. provolone and/or cheddar cheese, thinly sliced
- ½ of a 7-oz. jar roasted red sweet peppers, well drained
- ½ of a small pear or apple, thinly sliced or 2 canned pineapple rings, well drained and patted dry
- 4 oz. thinly sliced cooked ham or prosciutto

SIMPLE LUNCH

- **Provolone and Ham Melt (see below)**
- **Cottage cheese sprinkled with fresh snipped herbs**
- **Marinated vegetable salad**
- **Candy Bar Peanut Butter Cookies (see page 210)**

- 2 Tbsp. mango chutney
  Fresh fruit, such as sliced pears and apples, pineapple wedges, or grapes (optional)

1 Spread one side of each bread slice with margarine or butter. Place four bread slices, buttered sides down, on griddle. Spread mayonnaise on the four slices on the griddle. Top with provolone cheese. Top two of the bread slices with red sweet peppers; top two with slices of fruit. Top all four with ham or prosciutto.

2 Cut up large pieces of chutney. Spread the unbuttered sides of four remaining bread slices with chutney. Place over bread slices on griddle, buttered sides up.

3 Cook sandwiches over medium heat about 4 minutes each side or until bread is toasted and cheese is melted, turning once halfway through cooking. Serve with additional fruit slices, if desired. Makes 4 servings.

Nutrition Facts per serving: 398 cal., 22 g total fat (10 g sat. fat), 53 mg chol., 970 mg sodium, 35 g carbo., 3 g fiber, 17 g pro. Daily Values: 16% vit. A, 82% vit. C, 27% calcium, 13% iron.

Pasta Rustica Bake

Prep: 20 minutes **Bake:** 20 minutes
Stand: 10 minutes

- 8 oz. fresh or frozen medium shrimp in shells, peeled and deveined
- 1 lb. packaged dried gemelli or penne pasta
- 8 oz. bulk mild Italian sausage
- 8 oz. skinless, boneless chicken breast, cut into bite-size strips
- 2 oz. prosciutto, chopped
- 2 cloves garlic, minced
- 2 cups whipping cream
- 1 8-oz. can tomato sauce
- 1 cup finely shredded Parmesan cheese
- ½ tsp. salt
- ½ tsp. coarsely ground pepper

1 Thaw shrimp, if frozen. Cook pasta according to package directions. Drain; return pasta to pan.

2 Meanwhile, preheat oven to 400°F. In a large skillet cook sausage until browned, stirring to break up. Add shrimp, chicken, prosciutto, and garlic. Cook and stir until chicken is no longer pink and shrimp is just opaque. Stir in the whipping cream. Stir in tomato sauce, ⅓ cup of the Parmesan cheese, the salt, and pepper. Stir into pasta. Transfer to a 3-quart rectangular baking dish. Sprinkle with the remaining ⅔ cup Parmesan cheese.

3 Bake, uncovered, in the preheated oven about 20 minutes or until cheese begins to brown. Let stand for 10 minutes before serving. Serves 8.

Nutrition Facts per serving: 520 cal., 37 g total fat (19 g sat. fat), 197 mg chol., 979 mg sodium, 21 g carbo., 1 g fiber, 26 g pro. **Daily Values:** 27% vit. A, 9% vit. C, 20% calcium, 13% iron.

---

30 MINUTE
Linguine in Gorgonzola Cream

Start to finish: 25 minutes

- 8 oz. packaged dried linguine or fettuccine pasta
- ¾ cup crumbled Gorgonzola cheese (3 oz.)
- ¼ cup shredded mozzarella or provolone cheese (1 oz.)
- 2 tsp. all-purpose flour
- 1 Tbsp. olive oil
- 1 medium onion, cut into thin wedges
- 1 medium red or orange sweet pepper, seeded and cut into bite-size strips
- 3 oz. prosciutto, chopped
- 2 cloves garlic, minced
- 1 cup whipping cream
- 1 14½-oz. can artichoke hearts, drained and quartered
- 2 Tbsp. slivered fresh basil

1 Cook pasta according to package directions; drain and set aside.

2 Meanwhile, in a small mixing bowl combine Gorgonzola cheese, mozzarella cheese, and flour; toss to coat. Set aside cheese mixture. In a large skillet cook the onion, sweet pepper, prosciutto, and garlic in hot olive oil over medium heat for 4 to 5 minutes or until onion is tender but not brown.

3 Stir the whipping cream into the onion mixture in the skillet. Add the cheese mixture. Cook and stir until the sauce thickens and bubbles slightly. Stir in the artichoke hearts; heat through.

4 To serve, transfer pasta to a serving platter. Pour sauce over pasta; sprinkle with basil. Toss gently to coat. Serve immediately. Serves 4.

Nutrition Facts per serving: 649 cal., 37 g total fat (21 g sat. fat), 120 mg chol., 1,332 mg sodium, 55 g carbo., 6 g fiber, 24 g pro. **Daily Values:** 57% vit. A, 82% vit. C, 28% calcium, 25% iron.

PRIZE WINNER
Tortellini Emilia

Geoff Rudaw
Nanuet, New York
$200—Pasta Bakes

Prep: 25 minutes **Bake:** 20 minutes
Stand: 10 minutes

- 2 8-oz. pkg. dried cheese-filled tortellini
- 3 Tbsp. finely chopped red onion
- 2 Tbsp. finely chopped shallots
- 1 Tbsp. margarine or butter
- 2 cups half-and-half or light cream
- ½ cup milk
- 2 egg yolks
- ¼ cup grated Parmesan cheese
- 1 Tbsp. snipped fresh sage or 1 tsp. dried sage, crushed
- ½ cup shredded Gruyère or Swiss cheese (2 oz.)
- ½ cup walnut pieces
- 2 oz. prosciutto, finely snipped, or cooked ham, finely chopped

1 Preheat oven to 400°F. Prepare tortellini according to package directions; drain and set aside.

2 Meanwhile, in a medium saucepan cook onion and shallots in hot margarine or butter over medium heat until tender. Stir in half-and-half or light cream and milk. Bring just to boiling; remove from heat.

3 In a small bowl lightly beat egg yolks. Slowly add about 1 cup of hot mixture to yolks, beating until combined. Return all to saucepan. Cook and stir over medium-low heat about 10 minutes or until slightly thickened and just bubbly. Remove from heat. Stir in Parmesan cheese, sage, and ¼ teaspoon pepper.

4 Transfer half of the tortellini to a 2-quart rectangular baking dish. Sprinkle with the Gruyére or Swiss cheese. Pour half of the sauce over tortellini. Top with remaining pasta, the walnuts, prosciutto, and remaining sauce. Bake, uncovered, in the preheated oven about 20 minutes or until top is lightly browned and mixture is bubbly. Let stand for 10 minutes before serving. Serves 8.

Nutrition Facts per serving: 455 cal., 25 g total fat (8 g sat. fat), 96 mg chol., 824 mg sodium, 38 g carbo., 1 g fiber, 21 g pro. Daily Values: 12% vit. A, 2% vit. C, 39% calcium, 7% iron.

30 MINUTE
Tuna Alfredo Casserole

For convenience, and good taste, make this easy casserole, substituting any pesto you please.

Prep: 20 minutes Bake: 10 minutes

- 3 cups packaged dried rigatoni or penne pasta
- 1 10-oz. container refrigerated Alfredo (or four-cheese pasta sauce, or 1¼ cups bottled Alfredo or four-cheese pasta sauce)
- 2 Tbsp. purchased dried tomato pesto
- 3 Tbsp. milk
- 1 12-oz. can water-pack solid white tuna, drained and broken into chunks
- ¼ cup finely shredded Parmesan cheese

1 Preheat oven to 425°F. In a Dutch oven cook pasta according to package directions. Drain well and return to pan.

2 Meanwhile, in a bowl stir together the Alfredo sauce, dried tomato pesto, and milk. Add sauce mixture to pasta; stir gently to coat. Gently fold in tuna.

3 Transfer pasta mixture to a 2-quart oval baking dish. Sprinkle with shredded Parmesan cheese. Bake, uncovered, in the preheated oven for 10 to 15 minutes or until heated through and cheese is just melted. Makes 6 servings.

Nutrition Facts per serving: 453 cal., 24 g total fat (4 g sat. fat), 53 mg chol., 587 mg sodium, 35 g carbo., 2 g fiber, 24 g pro. Daily Values: 4% vit. A, 5% vit. C, 11% calcium, 16% iron.

30 MINUTE
Salmon Shortcakes

Handle the salmon mixture gently and cook the cakes only until browned. (See the photograph on page 198.)

Prep: 15 minutes Cook: 9 minutes

- 1 recipe Herbed Mayonnaise (see right)
- 1 egg, beaten
- 1 14¾-oz. can salmon, drained, flaked, and skin and bones removed
- ¾ cup soft bread crumbs
- 2 Tbsp. mayonnaise or salad dressing
- 1 green onion, chopped
- 1 Tbsp. margarine or butter
- 4 purchased buttermilk biscuits or one 10.8-oz. pkg. (5) refrigerated large flaky biscuits, baked

WEEKNIGHT MEAL

- Salad of fresh spinach leaves, thin red onion slices, coarsely chopped fresh pineapple, toasted almonds, and poppy seed dressing

- Salmon Shortcakes (see below)

- Assorted roasted vegetables

- Fruit pie à la mode

1 Prepare Herbed Mayonnaise; set aside.

2 In a medium mixing bowl stir together the egg, salmon, bread crumbs, mayonnaise or salad dressing, and green onion. Form the mixture into eight patties.

3 In a large skillet melt margarine or butter over medium heat. Cook salmon patties about 9 minutes or until brown, turning once.

4 Split biscuits. (Warm already-baked biscuits slightly in the oven or microwave before serving.) Top a biscuit half with 2 salmon patties; spoon on Herbed Mayonnaise, and top with remaining biscuit half. Makes 4 servings.

Herbed Mayonnaise

In a small bowl stir together ¼ cup mayonnaise, 1 tablespoon snipped fresh dillweed, and 1 tablespoon milk. Add additional milk to make of drizzling consistency.

Nutrition Facts per serving: 528 cal., 37 g total fat (8 g sat. fat), 121 mg chol., 1,129 mg sodium, 23 g carbo., 1 g fiber, 26 g pro. Daily Values: 11% vit. A, 3% vit. C, 32% calcium, 17% iron.

Vegetable Bread

See the photograph on page 199.

Prep: 30 minutes **Rise:** 1½ hours
Bake: 25 minutes

- ¼ cup dried tomato pieces (not oil pack)
- ½ cup chopped green sweet pepper
- ½ cup chopped onion
- 3 Tbsp. cooking oil
- 3½ to 4 cups bread flour or all-purpose flour
- 1 pkg. active dry yeast
- 1 cup water
- 1 Tbsp. sugar
- 1 tsp. dried Italian seasoning, crushed
- 1½ tsp. salt
- 1 egg

1 Place dried tomato pieces in a small bowl. Pour enough boiling water over tomato pieces to cover. Let stand for 15 minutes. Drain tomatoes well.

2 In a small skillet cook the green pepper and onion in 1 tablespoon of the oil until vegetables are tender. Set aside and cool completely.

3 Meanwhile, in a large mixing bowl combine 1½ cups of the flour and the yeast; set aside. In a medium saucepan heat and stir water, the remaining 2 tablespoons oil, the sugar, Italian seasoning, and salt until warm (120° to 130°F). Add to flour mixture. Add egg. Beat with an electric mixer on low speed for 30 seconds, scraping the sides of the bowl constantly. Beat on high speed for 3 minutes more. Using a wooden spoon, stir in the drained tomatoes, cooked vegetables, and as much of the remaining flour as you can.

4 Turn dough out onto a lightly floured surface. Knead in enough remaining flour to make a moderately stiff dough that is smooth and elastic (6 to 8 minutes). Shape the dough into a ball. Place dough in a lightly greased bowl; turn to grease surface of dough. Cover and let rise in warm place until double in size (about 60 minutes). Punch down dough. Turn out dough onto a lightly floured surface. Cover and let rest for 10 minutes.

5 Lightly grease a 9×5×3-inch loaf pan. Shape the dough into a loaf. and place into prepared loaf pan. Cover and let rise in a warm place until nearly double (30 to 40 minutes). Preheat oven to 350°F.

6 Bake for 25 to 30 minutes or until bread sounds hollow when tapped. Cover loosely with foil the last 5 minutes of baking to prevent overbrowning, if necessary. Remove from pan immediately and cool on a wire rack. Makes 1 loaf (16 servings).

Nutrition Facts per serving: 145 cal., 3 g total fat (1 g sat. fat), 13 mg chol., 241 mg sodium, 24 g carbo., 1 g fiber, 4 g pro. **Daily Values:** 1% vit. A, 7% vit. C, 1% calcium, 9% iron.

Banana-Apple Butter Bread

See the photograph on page 199.

Prep: 25 minutes **Bake:** 45 minutes

- 1½ cups all-purpose flour
- 1½ tsp. baking powder
- ½ tsp. ground cinnamon
- ¼ tsp. baking soda
- ¼ tsp. salt
- ⅛ tsp. ground nutmeg
- 2 eggs, slightly beaten
- ¾ cup sugar

Fiber Quiz

Which has more fiber?

1 pear	vs.	4 stalks of celery
1 cup popcorn	vs.	1 oz. whole wheat pretzels
6 oz. steak	vs.	1 cup cooked noodles
1 apple	vs.	1 banana

Answers:
Pear, 4 g fiber (4 celery stalks, 2.7 g)
Pretzels, 2 g fiber (popcorn, 1.2 g)
Noodles, 2.4 g fiber (meat, 0 fiber)
Apple 3.7 g fiber (banana, 2.8 g)

- ½ cup mashed ripe banana
- ½ cup apple butter
- ¼ cup cooking oil

1 Preheat oven to 350°F. Grease and flour the bottom and ½ inch up sides of 9×5×3-inch loaf pan; set aside. In a large mixing bowl stir together flour, baking powder, cinnamon, baking soda, salt, and nutmeg. Make a well in the center of the dry mixture; set aside.

2 In another bowl combine the eggs, sugar, banana, apple butter, and oil. Add egg mixture all at once to dry mixture. Stir just until moistened. Spoon batter into the prepared pan.

3 Bake for 45 minutes or until a wooden toothpick inserted near center comes out clean. Cool in pan on a wire rack 10 minutes. Remove from pan; cool completely on a wire rack. Wrap and store overnight. Makes 1 loaf (16 servings).

Nutrition Facts per serving: 168 cal., 4 g total fat (1 g sat. fat), 27 mg chol., 103 mg sodium, 31 g carbo., 1 g fiber, 2 g pro. **Daily Values:** 2% vit. A, 1% vit. C, 3% calcium, 5% iron.

Fiber Contributes to Good Health

Although there is still evidence to be gathered concerning the role of fiber in preventing colon cancer, studies clearly show that high-fiber diets have health benefits. An abundance of evidence attests to dietary fiber as one of the most valuable substances to include in your diet.

The role of fiber in heart health is well established. Other bonuses of a high-fiber diet include keeping cholesterol levels in the normal range, reducing the risk of developing diabetes, and assisting in weight loss. Eating fiber prevents constipation and possibly diverticulosis, a painful inflammation of the colon. Reducing cholesterol and the risk of heart disease are key reasons to boost your fiber intake.

"Fiber is the most practical dietary measure for lowering cholesterol," says Dr. James W. Anderson, Professor of Medicine and Clinical Nutrition at the University of Kentucky in Lexington. "Dietary fiber can lower cholesterol from 6 to 10 percent, twice what you get from dietary restrictions if you have high cholesterol," Anderson says. Dietary restrictions typically include limiting high-cholesterol foods.

Soluble fiber latches onto harmful cholesterol and bile acids, pulls them along the digestive tract, and moves them out of the body. Higher cholesterol experiences greater reduction.

Impact on Diabetes

A high-fiber diet also helps to prevent and control diabetes. In a recent study at the University of Texas Southwestern Medical Center in Dallas, a small group of people who have diabetes ate daily servings of fruits and vegetables containing 50 grams of fiber. The payoff was a 10 percent reduction of glucose levels and a reduced risk of heart disease.

Dietary fiber in the meals of these diabetics may have increased the speed at which the food moved through their bodies, possibly reducing the glucose absorbed from the small intestine. Study participants also had lowered levels of cholesterol.

"We're concerned [with cholesterol] because coronary heart disease is a primary killer among people with diabetes," says Dr. Abhimanyu Garg, Professor of Internal Medicine at UT Southwestern and principal author of the study.

How Much Is Enough?

Most experts recommend consuming 20 to 35 grams of fiber every day. Children over age 2 should get enough fiber to equal their age plus 5 grams. A healthy day's menu for a 7-year-old contains 12 grams of fiber.

The average American gets only about 15 grams of fiber a day. Although people should look for easy ways to get more fiber in their diets, they need to be aware that fibrous textures don't necessarily indicate that a food is high in fiber. A stringy celery stalk has only 0.7 grams of fiber. By contrast, a carrot has

Fiber Content of Foods

FOOD	AMOUNT	FIBER
100% bran cereal	½ cup	12 g
Beans, baked	½ cup	9.3 g
Blackberries	½ cup	5.3 g
Corn	½ cup	4.7 g
Lentils, cooked	½ cup	3.7 g
Whole-grain bread	1 slice	2.1 g
Lettuce	½ cup	0.8 g
White bread	1 slice	0.7 g

2.2 grams. As for meat, there is no fiber from animal sources. The chart, above, lists examples of food and fiber content. The labels on packaged foods generally provide fiber information per serving.

Soluble and Insoluble Fiber

Plant foods contain two types of fiber: soluble fiber, which dissolves in water; and insoluble fiber, which doesn't. Both offer health benefits, and both are found in many grains, fruits, and vegetables.

To get 6 to 10 grams of soluble fiber daily, which is within the recommended range for heart health, it is necessary to consume 25 grams of fiber from fruits, vegetables, whole grains, and legumes.

Fiber and Colon Cancer

As good as it is, dietary fiber is not the single solution to health problems. Some controversy surrounded the positive results of fiber when two major reports showed that a high-fiber diet didn't offer protection against colon cancer, as once believed. In the Polyp Prevention Trial and the Wheat Bran Study, both funded by the National Cancer Institute (NCI), there was no evidence that fiber reduced the risk of developing colorectal polyps, the precursors to colorectal cancer.

"The jury is still out on fiber [for colon cancer prevention]," said Dr. Arthur Schatzkin, chief of the Nutritional Epidemiological branch of NCI. "We followed people for three or four years. You may need a longer period on a high-fiber diet. We are aware of other fiber studies showing a protective effect for colorectal cancer."

In the Polyp Prevention Trial headed by Schatzkin, 2,079 people ate meals rich in vegetables, beans, legumes, and grains, with only 20 percent of calories from fat. "There are other [than colon cancer] reasons to eat a diet high in vegetables and grains," said Dr. Schatzkin.

Fig Muffins

Prepare these sweet, moist muffins the evening before and look forward to rising early to enjoy them.

Prep: 15 minutes **Bake:** 20 minutes
Cool: 5 minutes

2½	cups all-purpose flour
1	Tbsp. baking powder
1½	tsp. ground cinnamon
¼	tsp. baking soda
¼	tsp. salt
2	eggs, slightly beaten
1	cup buttermilk
⅔	cup packed brown sugar
½	cup butter, melted
¾	cup chopped dried figs

1 Preheat oven to 375°F. Lightly grease eighteen 2½-inch muffin cups or line with paper bake cups; set aside. In a large mixing bowl stir together the flour, baking powder, cinnamon, baking soda, and salt. Make a well in the center of the dry mixture.

2 In a medium mixing bowl stir together the eggs, buttermilk, brown sugar, and melted butter. Add egg mixture all at once to dry mixture. Stir just until moistened. (Batter should be slightly lumpy.) Gently fold in figs. Fill prepared muffin cups about two-thirds full.

3 Bake in the preheated oven about 20 minutes or until golden and a wooden toothpick inserted in center comes out clean. Cool in muffin cups on a wire rack for 5 minutes. Remove from muffin cups; serve warm, if desired. Makes 18 muffins.

To Make Ahead:

Prepare and bake muffins as directed; cool completely. Wrap the muffins tightly in heavy foil or place them in a freezer bag and freeze for up to 3 months. To reheat frozen muffins, wrap them in heavy foil. Heat muffins in a 300°F oven for 15 to 18 minutes or until warm.

Nutrition Facts per muffin: 160 cal., 6 g total fat (3 g sat. fat), 38 mg chol., 184 mg sodium, 24 g carbo., 1 g fiber, 3 g pro. **Daily Values:** 6% vit. A, 1% vit. C, 7% calcium, 8% iron.

Candy Bar Peanut Butter Cookies

Use this idea to wrap almost any small candy in the dough.

Prep: 30 minutes **Bake:** 12 minutes

1½	cups all-purpose flour
1½	cups sugar
¼	tsp. baking soda
⅛	tsp. salt
½	cup cold butter
½	cup creamy peanut butter
¼	cup honey
1	Tbsp. milk
½	of a 12-oz. pkg. chocolate-covered peanut clusters or 1⅓ cups (8 oz.) candy-coated peanut butter pieces

1 Preheat oven to 350°F. In a large mixing bowl stir together the flour, sugar, baking soda, and salt. Using a pastry blender, cut in the butter and peanut butter until mixture resembles coarse crumbs. In a small bowl stir together honey and milk; drizzle over flour mixture. Using a wooden spoon, stir until combined.

2 For each cookie, shape a well-rounded tablespoon of dough into a ball. Flatten in the palm of your hand. Place an approximate 1-inch peanut cluster* or a slightly rounded teaspoon of small candy-coated peanut

butter pieces in the center of the dough. Shape dough up and around candy, rolling into a ball (see photo, below). Place 2 inches apart on an ungreased cookie sheet.

Nestle the candy in the middle of the cookie; fold dough around the candy.

3 Bake about 12 minutes or until the bottoms of cookies are lightly browned. Let stand for 1 minute on cookie sheet before removing. Transfer cookies to a wire rack and let cool. Makes 20 to 24 cookies.

*Note: If peanut clusters are larger than 1 inch, cut them into two pieces, using one piece per cookie.

To Make Ahead:

Prepare and bake cookies as directed. Cool completely. Place cookies in a freezer container or freezer bag and freeze for up to 3 months. To serve, thaw about 15 minutes.

Nutrition Facts per cookie: 190 cal., 11 g total fat (5 g sat. fat), 14 mg chol., 114 mg sodium, 21 g carbo., 1 g fiber, 4 g pro. **Daily Values:** 4% vit. A, 2% calcium, 4% iron.

COOKING WITH KIDS

Lemonade Stand 101

Children know that lemonade stops traffic. On a hot sunny day, passersby rarely resist buying refreshing drinks from young entrepreneurs.

Lemonade stands are the first business ventures for many children. They can have as much fun with planning and production as with the exchange of cold drinks for cold cash.

Moms and dads can plan to serve as venture capitalists and quality control supervisors with a fruity homemade lemonade. An excellent product always ensures repeat sales.

Squeezing the Profit Margin

Math class story problems are more fun when they're about the project at hand. Try these:

1. When the recipe uses 4 lemons plus sugar and water to make 6 cups of lemonade, and 1 cup equals 8 ounces, how many ounces of lemonade will the recipe make?

2. If you use 3-ounce cups at the stand, how many servings will there be from each batch of Fruit Power Lemonade?

3. The lemons cost $1, the fruit cost $2, the sugar cost 25 cents, and the supplies were donated. How much profit will you make if you sell all the lemonade for 50 cents a cup?

Answers:
1. 6 cups × 8 ounces per cup = 48 ounces of lemonade.

2. 48 ounces lemonade ÷ 3-ounce cups = 16 servings.

3. 16 servings × 50 cents per serving = $8 projected gross profit. Gross profit ($8) – costs ($1 + $2 + 25 cents) = projected net profit ($4.75).

Lemonade Stand Checklist:

✔ Start with a great product (see recipe, right)
✔ Invest weekly allowance for capital
✔ Set the right price
✔ Stock up on supplies
✔ Make signs that have curb appeal
✔ Sell…Sell…Sell

Helpful Parent Tips to Keep Things Sweet

● Choose medium-size lemons that small hands can hold and press onto a lemon reamer or citrus juicer.

● Supervise preparation: Pre-cut the lemons and fruit, and let the kids help with the mixing and stirring.

● Encourage older kids to help out with younger ones to pour, strain, and remove the seeds from the lemon juice.

● Help with choosing a location, stand construction, sign hanging, and sales.

● Have plenty of change on hand.

● Stay nearby to offer security, while letting the kids have a little space to feel independent.

30 MINUTE, NO FAT

Fruit Power Lemonade

Think big! Triple the recipe to avoid running out during peak sales time.

Start to finish: 15 minutes

4	medium lemons, halved
4½	cups water
¾	cup sugar
2	cups assorted sliced fresh fruit, such as star fruit, mango, strawberries, kiwi fruit, nectarines, peaches, and/or limes
	Ice cubes

1 Grip one lemon half firmly; press and twist onto lemon reamer until all juice is released. Repeat with remaining lemon halves. Discard empty halves. If necessary, strain juice through strainer to remove lemon seeds. You should have about ¾ cup freshly squeezed lemon juice.

2 In a large jar or pitcher combine the freshly squeezed lemon juice, water, and sugar. Stir well until sugar is dissolved. Add assorted fruits. Immediately ladle into disposable cups filled with ice cubes, or chill several hours. Makes 6 cups.

Nutrition Facts per cup: 123 cal., 0 g total fat, 0 mg chol., 7 mg sodium, 32 g carbo., 1 g fiber, 0 g pro.
Daily Values: 9% vit. A, 57% vit. C, 1% calcium, 1% iron.

Simple Two-Bite Treats

Make mealtime endings memorable by impressing party guests with these sweet and simple two-bite treats.

Cookies and Cream Bites
Combine half of an 8-ounce tub of cream cheese, 2 tablespoons sour cream, 1 tablespoon sifted powdered sugar, and ½ teaspoon finely shredded orange peel. Spread mixture onto 2-inch-square shortbread cookies. Top with assorted fruits, such as sliced small strawberries, raspberries, blueberries, quartered and thinly sliced kiwi fruits, green grapes, or mandarin orange sections.

Berry-Pound Cake Bites
Cut 1-inch rounds from purchased pound cake slices; top with whipped cream, a fresh raspberry, and a mint leaf.

Cake and Dip
Dip cubes of pound cake or angel food cake into a mixture of equal parts softened cream cheese and a favorite flavor of low-fat yogurt.

Lemon-Blueberry Tarts
Fill baked miniature phyllo dough shells with lemon yogurt or lemon curd; top with blueberries.

Miniature Tropical Trifles
Drizzle rounds of pound cake with sherry or orange juice. Top with whipped cream and a mixture of crushed pineapple and coarsely chopped toasted macadamia nuts.

Brownie Bites
Cut a purchased pan of brownies into miniature diamond or triangle shapes. Pipe cream cheese frosting onto each serving; sprinkle chopped toasted walnuts over the frosting.

Bite-Size Boston Cream Pies
Cut thick slices of pound cake into rounds; split each in half horizontally. Fill with vanilla pudding and top with fudge topping.

Chocolate-Cinnamon Roll-Ups
Brush milk on an unfolded refrigerated pie crust; sprinkle with cinnamon-sugar and semisweet chocolate pieces. Cut into narrow wedges; roll from a wide edge. Bake in a 375°F oven for 8 minutes or until golden.

Layered Cakes
Spread split ladyfingers with raspberry jam, fill with sweetened whipped cream, and drizzle with melted white chocolate.

LOW FAT

Raspberry Fudge Pudding Cake

Prep: 30 minutes **Bake:** 40 minutes
Cool: 1 hour

The raspberries and syrup spooned over the cake batter descend to the bottom, forming a delicious puddinglike fruit layer.

- 2 10-oz. pkg. frozen red raspberries in syrup, thawed
- ½ cup all-purpose flour
- 1 Tbsp. unsweetened cocoa powder
- 1 tsp. baking powder
- 2 Tbsp. butter, softened
- ½ cup packed brown sugar
- 1 tsp. vanilla
- ¼ cup milk
- ⅓ cup packed brown sugar
- 2 Tbsp. unsweetened cocoa powder
- 1 recipe Sweetened Whipped Cream (see below) or vanilla ice cream (optional)

1 Preheat oven to 350°F. Drain thawed berries, reserving ¾ cup syrup. Set aside.

2 In a bowl stir together flour, the 1 tablespoon cocoa powder, and the baking powder; set aside. In a medium mixing bowl beat butter with an electric mixer on medium speed for 30 seconds. Add the ½ cup brown sugar and the vanilla; beat until well combined. Alternately add flour mixture and milk, beating until smooth after each addition.

3 Spread batter in a greased 2-quart square baking dish. Spoon drained raspberries over batter. Pour raspberry syrup atop. In a small bowl stir together the remaining ⅓ cup brown sugar and the 2 tablespoons cocoa powder. Sprinkle the mixture evenly over batter.

4 Bake in the preheated oven about 40 minutes or until a wooden toothpick inserted about ½ inch into cake portion comes out clean. Cool about 1 hour on a wire rack. Serve warm with Sweetened Whipped Cream or vanilla ice cream, if desired. Makes 6 servings.

Sweetened Whipped Cream

In a small chilled mixing bowl combine ⅔ cup whipping cream,

2 tablespoons granulated sugar, and 1 teaspoon vanilla. Beat with chilled beaters of an electric mixer on medium speed until soft peaks form. Do not overbeat.

Nutrition Facts per serving: 362 cal., 5 g total fat (3 g sat. fat), 12 mg chol., 152 mg sodium, 78 g carbo., 3 g fiber, 3 g pro. Daily Values: 3% vit. A, 14% vit. C, 12% calcium, 15% iron.

LOW FAT

Tiny Apricot Cheesecake Tarts

Prep: 25 minutes **Chill:** 2 hours
Stand: 30 minutes

- 3 oz. bittersweet or semisweet chocolate, cut up
- ½ tsp. shortening (no substitutes)
- 1 2.1-oz. pkg. baked miniature phyllo shells (fifteen 1¾-inch shells)
- 1 3-oz. pkg. cream cheese, softened
- 2 Tbsp. dairy sour cream
- 2 Tbsp. powdered sugar
- 2 tsp. apricot brandy or apricot nectar
- 2 or 3 dried apricots, cut into thin strips
  Bittersweet or semisweet chocolate, grated (optional)

1 In a small saucepan stir the cut up chocolate and shortening over low heat until melted. Remove from heat. Brush the bottom and inside edges of each phyllo shell evenly with the melted chocolate mixture. Place phyllo shells in refrigerator about 20 minutes or until chocolate is set.

2 Meanwhile, in a small bowl stir together the cream cheese, sour cream, and powdered sugar until smooth. Stir in apricot brandy or nectar. Spoon 1 rounded teaspoon of cream cheese mixture into each shell. Place a strip of dried apricot atop each. Cover loosely; chill 2 to 4 hours.

3 Remove tarts from refrigerator and allow to stand at room temperature about 30 minutes before serving. Sprinkle with grated chocolate, if desired. Makes 15 tarts.

Nutrition Facts per tart: 82 cal., 5 g total fat (3 g sat. fat), 7 mg chol., 28 mg sodium, 7 g carbo., 0 g fiber, 1 g pro. Daily Values: 3% vit. A, 1% calcium, 2% iron.

Crème Mousse and Fruit Parfaits

Preserves hint at the peach flavor of the light and airy mousse filling, layered with colorful fresh fruits.

Prep: 30 minutes **Chill:** 2 hours

- ⅓ cup sugar
- 1 Tbsp. cornstarch
- ¼ tsp. salt
- ⅛ tsp. ground ginger
- 1 cup milk
- 1 egg yolk, beaten
- ¼ tsp. vanilla
- ⅓ cup peach preserves
- 1 tsp. finely shredded lime peel
- 1 cup whipping cream
- 4 cups peeled, pitted, and thinly sliced peaches and/or mangoes; peeled and sliced kiwi fruits; and/or raspberries
- ⅓ cup flake coconut, toasted
  Strips of lime peel (optional)

1 In a heavy medium saucepan combine the sugar, cornstarch, salt, and ginger. Stir in the milk. Cook and stir over medium heat until the mixture is thickened and bubbly. Cook and stir for 2 minutes more. Remove from heat.

2 Gradually whisk about half of the milk mixture into the beaten egg yolk. Return egg mixture to saucepan. Bring to a gentle boil; reduce heat. Cook and stir for 2 minutes more. Remove from heat. Stir in vanilla. Pour mixture into a medium bowl; cover surface with plastic wrap. Place in the refrigerator about 2 hours or until thoroughly chilled.

3 Stir peach preserves and the 1 teaspoon shredded lime peel into the chilled egg mixture. In a chilled medium mixing bowl beat the whipping cream with the chilled beaters of an electric mixer on medium speed until soft peaks form. Gently fold whipped cream into the chilled egg mixture.

4 Divide half of the mousse mixture among six parfait glasses or goblets. Spoon half of the fruit evenly atop mousse mixture in each glass. Repeat layers with remaining mousse mixture and fruit. Serve immediately or chill until serving time. Before serving, sprinkle each with some of the toasted coconut. Garnish each with strips of lime peel, if desired. Makes 6 servings.

Nutrition Facts per serving: 333 cal., 18 g total fat (11 g sat. fat), 93 mg chol., 140 mg sodium, 42 g carbo., 2 g fiber, 4 g pro. Daily Values: 65% vit. A, 287% vit. C, 9% calcium, 4% iron.

Cutting a Mango

To cut a mango, first observe its shape. The broad, flat side reveals the shape of the seed.

Use a sharp knife to slice all the way through the mango next to the seed. (In the photo above, the seed, toward the center of the fruit, is next to the knife.) Slice on the opposite side of the seed, resulting in two large pieces of fruit.

Cut away the fruit from around the seed. Remove the peel and slice, chop, or puree the fruit.

Coconut-Topped Mango-Berry Pie

(See the photograph on page 199.)

Prep: 30 minutes **Bake:** 12 minutes for crust, 50 minutes for pie **Cool:** 1 hour

- 1   recipe Pastry for Single-Crust Pie (see right)
- ½   cup packed brown sugar
- 4   tsp. cornstarch
- 2   cups chopped mangoes (about 2)
- 1½ cups fresh raspberries
- ¾   cup shredded coconut
- ½   cup coarsely chopped macadamia nuts or almonds
- 2   Tbsp. granulated sugar
- 2   Tbsp. butter, melted

1 Preheat oven to 450°F. Prepare Pastry for Single-Crust Pie. On a lightly floured surface, roll out dough to a 12-inch circle. Line a 9-inch pie plate with pastry. Trim to ½ inch beyond edge of plate. Fold under extra pastry and flute edge. Using the tines of a fork, prick all around where bottom and sides meet. Line pastry with a double thickness of foil. Bake in the preheated oven for 8 minutes. Remove foil. Bake for 4 to 5 minutes more or until set and dry. Remove from oven. Reduce oven temperature to 375°F.

2 For filling, in a large mixing bowl stir together the brown sugar and the cornstarch. Add the mangoes and raspberries, tossing gently to coat fruit. Spoon filling into crust. Cover edge of pie with foil. Bake in the preheated oven for 35 minutes.

3 Meanwhile, in a small mixing bowl stir together the coconut, macadamia nuts or almonds, the granulated sugar, and melted butter. Remove foil from pie. Sprinkle coconut mixture atop pie. Bake for 15 to 20 minutes more or until topping is golden. Cool on a wire rack about 1 hour. Serve slightly warm or cool. Makes 8 servings.

Pastry for Single-Crust Pie

In a medium mixing bowl stir together 1¼ cups all-purpose flour and ¼ teaspoon salt. Use a pastry blender to cut in ⅓ cup shortening until the pieces are the size of small peas. Using a total of 4 to 5 tablespoons of cold water, sprinkle 1 tablespoon water over part of the mixture; gently toss with a fork. Push moistened dough to the side of the bowl. Repeat until all the dough is moistened. Form into a ball.

Nutrition Facts per serving: 387 cal., 22 g total fat (9 g sat. fat), 8 mg chol., 160 mg sodium, 47 g carbo., 4 g fiber, 4 g pro. **Daily Values:** 35% vit. A, 29% vit. C, 3% calcium, 8% iron.

Lemon Cream Tart

Add a few extras to a packaged lemon bar mix—the result is a fancy tart.

Prep: 30 minutes **Bake:** 10 minutes for crust, 25 minutes for tart **Cool:** 1 hour **Chill:** 2 hours

- 1   16.5-oz. pkg. lemon bar mix
- ½   cup finely chopped macadamia nuts
- 1   8-oz. pkg. cream cheese, softened
- ½   tsp. vanilla
- 1   tsp. finely shredded lemon peel
- 1   8-oz. container dairy sour cream
- 1   Tbsp. sugar
- ½   tsp. vanilla
- 1½ to 2 cups fresh berries, such as blueberries, raspberries, and/or blackberries
     Fresh mint leaves, cut into long, thin strips (optional)

1 Preheat oven to 350°F. Prepare lemon filling mixture according to package directions; set aside. Press the packaged crust mixture into the bottom of a 10-inch springform pan or a 9×9×2-inch baking pan. Sprinkle macadamia nuts evenly over crust;

press gently into crust. Bake about 10 minutes or until lightly browned. Set aside to cool.

2 Meanwhile, in a medium mixing bowl beat cream cheese and ½ teaspoon vanilla with an electric mixer on medium to high speed until smooth. Add lemon filling mixture; beat until combined. Stir in lemon peel. Pour cream cheese mixture evenly over the crust in the pan. Bake about 25 minutes or until set. Cool on wire rack for 1 hour. Cover and chill at least 2 hours before serving.

3 Just before serving, in a small mixing bowl combine sour cream, 1 tablespoon sugar, and ½ teaspoon vanilla. Spread sour cream mixture over top of tart. Sprinkle fresh berries and, if desired, mint leaf strips, evenly over the top. Makes 12 to 16 servings.

Nutrition Facts per serving: 190 cal., 16 g total fat (8 g sat. fat), 82 mg chol., 109 mg sodium, 7 g carbo., 5 g fiber, 4 g pro. **Daily Values:** 10% vit. A, 6% vit. C, 5% calcium, 3% iron.

PRIZE WINNER

Hazelnut Cream Cassata

Gloria T. Bove
Bethlehem, Pennsylvania
$400—Quick Desserts

Prep: 35 minutes **Bake:** 15 minutes
Chill: up to 24 hours

- **1** pkg. 2-layer-size white cake mix or lemon-flavor cake mix
- **1** Tbsp. finely shredded lemon peel (only if using white cake mix)
- ⅓ cup chocolate-hazelnut spread
- ⅓ cup ricotta cheese
- ⅓ cup seedless red raspberry jam

- 1½ cups whipping cream
- **2** Tbsp. sifted powdered sugar
  Halved toasted hazelnuts

1 Preheat oven to 350°F. Grease and flour three 9×1½-inch round cake pans; set aside. Prepare cake mix according to package directions using the water, oil, and eggs called for. (If using white cake mix, stir in the 1 tablespoon lemon peel.) Divide batter among prepared pans. (For two 9-inch cake pans, cover and chill one-third of the batter to bake after the other layers are out of the pans.) Bake about 15 minutes or until a toothpick inserted near the center comes out clean. Let cool in pans on a wire rack for 10 minutes. Remove cakes from pans. Cool completely.

2 For filling, in a small bowl stir together the chocolate-hazelnut spread and ricotta cheese. Place one layer of cake on a serving platter; spread top with half of the jam. Spread half of the chocolate mixture over jam. Top with another layer of cake. Spread with remaining jam and remaining chocolate mixture. Top with remaining layer of cake.

3 In a large chilled mixing bowl beat whipping cream and powdered sugar with chilled beaters of an electric mixer on medium speed until stiff peaks form. Spread whipped cream over top and sides of cake. Top with hazelnuts. Cover and chill up to 24 hours. Makes 12 servings.

Nutrition Facts per serving: 413 cal., 23 g total fat (10 g sat. fat), 45 mg chol., 310 mg sodium, 47 g carbo., 1 g fiber, 5 g pro. **Daily Values:** 10% vit. A, 3% vit. C, 4% calcium, 4% iron.

LOW FAT

Pour-and-Bake Pear Pudding

To prevent leaks, use a pan without a removable bottom.

Prep: 15 minutes **Bake:** 25 minutes
Stand: 30 minutes

- **2** 15-oz. cans pear halves in light syrup
- ⅓ cup all-purpose flour
- ¼ cup granulated sugar
- ½ cup plain low-fat or fat-free yogurt
- **2** eggs
- **1** tsp. vanilla
- **3** Tbsp. brown sugar

1 Preheat oven to 375°F. Drain pear halves, reserving ¾ cup syrup. Score round side of pear halves with shallow crosswise cuts. Set aside pears and syrup.

2 In a blender container or food processor bowl place flour and granulated sugar. Cover and blend or process until combined (to prevent flour from clumping). Add yogurt, eggs, vanilla, and reserved pear syrup. Cover; blend or process until smooth.

3 Grease a 9½- or 10×1½-inch-deep quiche dish. Arrange pear halves, cut side down, in bottom of the dish. Pour batter over fruit. Sprinkle with brown sugar. Bake for 25 to 30 minutes or until center is just set when gently shaken. Cool on a wire rack about 30 minutes. Spoon into dessert dishes; serve warm. Serves 6.

Nutrition Facts per serving: 192 cal., 2 g total fat (1 g sat. fat), 72 mg chol., 44 mg sodium, 40 g carbo., 2 g fiber, 4 g pro. **Daily Values:** 2% vit. A, 2% vit. C, 6% calcium, 6% iron.

Measuring Up

Making desserts that look and taste their best is achieved by correctly and consistently measuring ingredients. Follow these hints to measure ingredients that are commonly used in dessert recipes:

Flour

Proper measuring of flour is critical. Too much flour can cause baked goods to be dry or sauces to become too thick. To measure flour, stir it in the bag or canister to lighten it. Gently spoon flour into a dry measuring cup or a measuring spoon, filling it to overflowing. Scrape a metal spatula across the edge of the measure to level the flour. (With the exception of cake flour, sifting is not necessary.)

Sugar

Spoon granulated or powdered sugar into a dry measuring cup to overflowing; level it using the method for flour. Press brown sugar firmly into a dry measure until it holds the shape of the cup, then turn out the brown sugar.

Shortening

Measure solid shortening by pressing it firmly into a dry measuring cup or spoon with a rubber scraper. Level the shortening with the straight edge of a knife.

Liquids

Use a glass or clear plastic liquid measuring cup on a level surface. Bend over so your eye is level with the marking on the cup. To measure liquid in a measuring spoon, fill the spoon to the top without letting it spill over. Avoid measuring liquid ingredients over other ingredients in case you spill.

Butter or margarine

Sticks of butter and margarine often have tablespoon and cup markings on the wrapping. Use a sharp knife to cut through the stick at designated marks. When wrappers are unmarked, measure as for shortening.

PRIZE WINNER

Cinnamon-Seared Cake

Debbi Bracker
Carl Junction, Missouri
$200—Quick Desserts

Prep: 20 minutes **Grill:** 2 minutes

- 1 16-oz. carton frozen sliced strawberries in syrup, thawed
- 1 10¾-oz. frozen pound cake, thawed
- 2 Tbsp. butter, softened
- ½ tsp. ground cinnamon
- ⅓ cup whipping cream, whipped
  Ground cinnamon
  Toasted slivered almonds

1 Place undrained strawberries in a blender container. Cover; blend until smooth. Chill.

2 Cut thin slices off each end of pound cake. Cut remaining cake into six thick slices. Stir together the butter and ½ teaspoon cinnamon. Spread butter-cinnamon mixture over one side of each cake slice.

3 Grill cake slices, buttered side down, on the rack of an uncovered grill directly over medium coals 1 to 2 minutes or until golden brown. Turn and grill 1 to 2 minutes more. (Or cook cake on a griddle over medium heat 1 to 2 minutes per side.)

4 To serve, divide strawberries among six dessert dishes. Top each with a pound cake slice, buttered side up. Spoon on whipped cream and sprinkle with additional cinnamon. Top with almonds. Makes 6 servings.

Nutrition Facts per serving: 360 cal., 20 g total fat (12 g sat. fat), 84 mg chol., 223 mg sodium, 44 g carbo., 2 g fiber, 3 g pro. **Daily Values:** 13% vit. A, 53% vit. C, 3% calcium, 7% iron.

---

30 MINUTE

Toffee Crunch Sundaes

Start to finish: 20 minutes

- ¼ cup granulated sugar
- ¾ cup whipping cream
- 2 Tbsp. light-colored corn syrup
- 1 Tbsp. butter
- ⅓ cup chocolate-covered toffee pieces
- 1 Tbsp. powdered sugar
- ½ tsp. vanilla
- ⅛ tsp. ground cinnamon
- 2 to 3 cups desired ice cream
- ¼ cup chopped toasted pecans

1 For sauce, in a saucepan combine granulated sugar, ¼ cup whipping cream, corn syrup, and butter. Cook and stir over medium heat until boiling. Boil 1 minute. Remove from heat. Stir in toffee. Set aside to cool.

2 For whipped cream, beat the remaining ½ cup whipping cream, powdered sugar, vanilla, and cinnamon with an electric mixer on medium speed until soft peaks form. To serve, spoon sauce over ice cream. Top with whipped cream and pecans. Serves 4.

Nutrition Facts per serving: 549 cal., 38 g total fat (20 g sat. fat), 106 mg chol., 192 mg sodium, 51 g carbo., 1 g fiber, 4 g pro. **Daily Values:** 21% vit. A, 1% vit. C, 12% calcium, 2% iron.

october

IN THIS CHAPTER

30-minute recipes indicated in COLOR.
Low-fat and no-fat recipes indicated
with a ♥.
Photographs indicated in italics.
*Bonus recipe

PRIZE WINNER

Feta Cheese Appetizers

Laurie Balcom
Lynden, Washington
$200—Cheese Appetizers

Start to finish: 20 minutes

⅓ cup finely chopped onion
3 cloves garlic, minced
2 tsp. olive oil or cooking oil
1 tsp. toasted sesame oil
1 8-oz. pkg. cream cheese, cut up
1 cup crumbled feta cheese (4 oz.)
½ cup chopped pitted kalamata olives or ripe olives
¼ cup chopped roasted red sweet pepper
1 tsp. dried dillweed
3 large pita bread rounds

1 Preheat broiler. In a medium skillet cook onion and garlic in olive oil and sesame oil over medium heat for 4 to 5 minutes or until onion is tender. Remove from heat. Add cream cheese and feta cheese; stir until

mixture is nearly smooth. Stir in the olives, sweet peppers, and dillweed. Set aside.

2 Using a long serrated knife, split pita rounds to form six circles. Place pita rounds, cut side up, on a large ungreased baking sheet. Broil 3 inches from heat about 1 minute or until pita rounds are lightly toasted.

3 Spread each pita round with ⅓ cup of the cheese mixture. Broil about 1 minute more or until the cheese is hot and melted.

4 To serve, using a sharp knife or kitchen scissors, cut each round into six wedges. Serve immediately. Makes 36 appetizers.

Nutrition Facts per appetizer: 51 cal., 4 g total fat (2 g sat. fat), 10 mg chol., 101 mg sodium, 4 g carbo., 0 g fiber, 1 g pro. **Daily Values:** 2% vit. A, 5% vit. C, 3% calcium, 1% iron.

LOW FAT

Blue Cheese and Pear Crostini

Because blue cheese is typically salty, use unsalted butter when you make this easy appetizer.

Prep: 20 minutes **Stand:** 30 minutes
Broil: 2 minutes

1 cup crumbled blue cheese (4 oz.)
2 Tbsp. unsalted butter
2 Tbsp. brandy
¼ cup coarsely chopped walnuts
16 ¼-inch-thick toasted French bread slices
1 medium ripe pear, cored and thinly sliced

1 In a small bowl combine the blue cheese and unsalted butter. Let stand at room temperature about

30 minutes to soften. Using a fork, mash the blue cheese and butter together until well combined. Stir in the brandy and chopped walnuts.

2 To assemble, top each bread slice with a pear slice. Top each pear slice with 1 tablespoon of the blue cheese mixture. Place bread slices on a baking sheet.

3 Broil 4 to 5 inches from heat about 2 minutes or until the cheese is melted and bubbly. Transfer to a serving platter. Serve immediately. Makes 16 appetizers.

Nutrition Facts per appetizer: 105 cal., 5 g total fat (2 g sat. fat), 10 mg chol., 204 mg sodium, 9 g carbo., 0 g fiber, 3 g pro. **Daily Values:** 2% vit. A, 1% vit. C, 6% calcium, 3% iron.

PRIZE WINNER

Smoked Cheese Pizza Squares

Suzanne Goddyn
Portland, Oregon
$400—Cheese Appetizers

Prep: 25 minutes **Bake:** 8 minutes
Stand: 5 minutes

2 medium onions, thinly sliced
1 Tbsp. butter or margarine
1 Tbsp. olive oil
¼ cup pitted whole dates, snipped
1 Tbsp. brown sugar
1 Tbsp. balsamic vinegar
¼ cup pine nuts or slivered almonds
½ cup shredded mozzarella cheese (2 oz.)
½ cup shredded smoked Gouda cheese (2 oz.)
½ cup shredded smoked cheddar cheese (2 oz.)
1 16-oz. Italian bread shell (Boboli)

1 Preheat oven to 450°F. In a large skillet cook onions in butter or margarine and olive oil over medium heat for 10 minutes, stirring occasionally. Stir in dates, brown sugar, and balsamic vinegar. Cook and stir about 5 minutes more or until onions are golden brown. Remove from heat. Stir in the pine nuts or almonds.

2 Meanwhile, in a medium bowl combine the mozzarella, smoked Gouda, and smoked cheddar cheeses. Sprinkle cheese mixture evenly over bread shell. Top with onion mixture.

3 Carefully place the bread shell on an ungreased baking sheet. Bake in the preheated oven about 8 minutes or until cheese is melted. Let stand for 5 minutes.

4 To serve, using a sharp knife or kitchen scissors, cut into 2-inch squares. Makes about 30 appetizers.

Nutrition Facts per appetizer: 81 cal., 4 g total fat (1 g sat. fat), 6 mg chol., 139 mg sodium, 9 g carbo., 0 g fiber, 3 g pro. **Daily Values:** 1% vit. A, 6% calcium, 3% iron.

30 MINUTE, LOW FAT

Sweet and Spicy Cheese Dip

Naan is a lightly leavened flatbread, which is made with white flour and is common to East Indian cuisine. Look for it at specialty markets or bakeries.

Start to finish: 15 minutes

- 1 **8-oz. pkg. reduced-fat cream cheese (Neufchâtel), softened**
- ¼ **cup mango chutney, snipped**
- 1 **tsp. grated fresh ginger or finely chopped crystallized ginger**
- ¼ **tsp. curry powder**
- ¼ **tsp. ground cumin**
- ¼ **tsp. finely shredded orange peel**
- ⅛ **tsp. ground red pepper**
- 2 **Tbsp. toasted flaked coconut**
- 2 **Tbsp. dry roasted shelled sunflower seeds**
  Naan or assorted crackers

1 In a medium mixing bowl beat the cream cheese with an electric mixer on medium speed about 30 seconds or until smooth. Using a wooden spoon, stir in chutney, fresh or crystallized ginger, curry powder, cumin, orange peel, and red pepper; mix well.

2 Transfer to a serving bowl. Sprinkle with toasted coconut and sunflower seeds. Serve with Naan or crackers. Makes 20 appetizer servings.

To Make Ahead:

Prepare dip, except do not top with coconut or sunflower seeds. Cover and chill in the refrigerator for up to 24 hours. Before serving, let stand 30 minutes at room temperature. Sprinkle with the toasted coconut and sunflower seeds. Serve as directed.

Nutrition Facts per serving: 49 cal., 3 g total fat (2 g sat. fat), 9 mg chol., 51 mg sodium, 4 g carbo., 0 g fiber, 1 g pro. **Daily Values:** 5% vit. A, 3% vit. C, 1% calcium, 1% iron.

Sweet Cheese with Amaretto Fruit Salsa

Prep: 25 minutes **Chill:** 8 hours

- 2 **8-oz. pkg. cream cheese, softened**
- 1 **cup sifted powdered sugar**
- 3 **Tbsp. orange marmalade**
- 2 **Tbsp. amaretto**
- 1 **Tbsp. finely chopped crystallized ginger**
- 2 **kiwi fruits, peeled, halved lengthwise, and sliced**
- 1 **cup fresh strawberries, chopped**
- ½ **cup kumquats, quartered and seeded**
- 1 **Tbsp. granulated sugar**
- ¼ **cup sliced almonds, toasted**
- 16 **shortbread fingers or cinnamon graham crackers**

1 In a medium mixing bowl beat the cream cheese with an electric mixer on medium speed until smooth. Beat in the powdered sugar, 2 tablespoons of the marmalade, and 1 tablespoon of the amaretto until combined. Using a wooden spoon, stir in the chopped crystallized ginger.

2 Line a small bowl with plastic wrap. Spoon cream cheese mixture into bowl. Cover surface of cheese mixture with plastic wrap; chill in the refrigerator for 8 hours or overnight.

3 For fruit salsa, in a small mixing bowl gently stir together the kiwi fruits, strawberries, kumquats, granulated sugar, the remaining 1 tablespoon orange marmalade, and remaining 1 tablespoon amaretto.

4 To serve, uncover cheese. Carefully unmold cream cheese mixture and place it in the center of a rimmed serving platter. Remove plastic wrap. Spoon fruit salsa around the cream cheese mixture. Sprinkle the toasted almonds over the fruit. Serve with shortbread fingers or cinnamon graham crackers. Makes 8 appetizer servings.

Nutrition Facts per serving: 417 cal., 26 g total fat (14 g sat. fat), 65 mg chol., 247 mg sodium, 39 g carbo., 3 g fiber, 7 g pro. **Daily Values:** 18% vit. A, 58% vit. C, 8% calcium, 9% iron.

Of Cabbage and Things

Cabbage doesn't deserve its stinky reputation. Eating just 1 cup of cooked cabbage provides the recommended daily dose of vitamin C and only 32 calories.

In addition to that good news, a decade or so ago scientists found that cabbage and other cruciferous vegetables contain compounds that may prevent cancer—particularly estrogen-related breast and uterine cancers. Cruciferous vegetables include arugula, bok choy, broccoli, broccoli sprouts, Brussels sprouts, cabbage, cauliflower, collards, chard, kale, kohlrabi, mustard greens, radishes, rutabaga, turnips, turnip greens, and watercress.

According to the American Cancer Society, eating cabbage may protect against esophagus, stomach, and colon cancers. Also, the high fiber content of cabbage helps to lower cholesterol, prevent constipation, and reduce hemorrhoids.

To cook cabbage so that it doesn't smell up the kitchen, use low to medium temperatures and cook it until just crisp-tender. You'll be rewarded with a subtle aroma, a mildly sweet flavor, and plenty of nutritional value.

30 MINUTE

Mustard-Glazed Cabbage

A mustard glaze that's studded with pecans turns ordinary cooked cabbage into a dish that's special enough for company. The bonus—it's super easy.

Start to finish: 15 minutes

- ¼ cup water
- 1 tsp. instant beef bouillon granules

- 5 cups coarsely shredded cabbage*
- 1 cup coarsely shredded carrots*
- ½ cup sliced green onions
- ¼ tsp. salt
- ¼ tsp. pepper
- ⅓ cup chopped pecans
- 2 Tbsp. butter or margarine, melted
- 1 tsp. prepared mustard
  Paprika

1 In a large saucepan combine the water and beef bouillon granules. Cook over high heat until dissolved. Add the shredded cabbage, shredded carrots, sliced green onions, salt, and pepper. Toss to mix. Cover and cook over medium-low heat about 5 minutes or until vegetables are crisp-tender, stirring once or twice during cooking. Remove from heat. Drain, if necessary.

2 In a small bowl stir together the pecans, melted butter or margarine, and mustard. Pour pecan mixture over vegetables, gently tossing to mix. Carefully spoon mixture into a serving dish. Sprinkle with paprika. Makes 6 servings.

*Note: If you wish, substitute 6 cups packaged shredded cabbage with carrot (coleslaw mix) for the shredded cabbage and carrots.

Nutrition Facts per serving: 103 cal., 8 g total fat (3 g sat. fat), 11 mg chol., 311 mg sodium, 7 g carbo., 3 g fiber, 2 g pro. **Daily Values:** 51% vit. A, 31% vit. C, 4% calcium, 4% iron.

30 MINUTE, LOW FAT

Rosy Tangerine-Scented Cabbage

Brighten up dinner plates with this citrusy side dish. It's a natural complement for roasted pork.

Start to finish: 20 minutes

- 2 tangerines
- 1 Tbsp. lemon juice
- 1 tsp. olive oil
- 4 cups shredded red cabbage
- 1 large red onion, cut into thin slivers (1 cup)
- 1 Tbsp. sugar
- ½ tsp. salt
- ¼ tsp. coarsely ground peppercorn blend
- 1 Tbsp. minced fresh cilantro

1 Finely shred ½ teaspoon peel from one of the tangerines. Set aside the peel. Peel, seed, and section the tangerines over a bowl to catch the juice. Set aside.

2 In a large nonstick skillet combine 1 tablespoon of the tangerine juice, lemon juice, and olive oil. Bring to boiling. Add cabbage and onion; reduce heat. Cook, covered, over medium heat for 3 to 5 minutes or until cabbage is slightly wilted but crisp, stirring occasionally. Remove from heat.

3 Stir in the sugar, salt, and coarsely ground peppercorn blend. Gently stir in the tangerine peel, the fruit sections, and the cilantro. Carefully spoon mixture into a serving bowl. Makes 4 servings.

Nutrition Facts per serving: 72 cal., 1 g total fat (0 g sat. fat), 0 mg chol., 300 mg sodium, 15 g carbo., 3 g fiber, 2 g pro. **Daily Values:** 10% vit. A, 85% vit. C, 5% calcium, 3% iron.

Pesto and Prosciutto Portobello Pizzas

Speed up the preparation time by substituting ¾ cup purchased pesto for the homemade version.

Prep: 30 minutes **Bake:** 10 minutes

- 4 large portobello mushroom caps, stems removed
- 2 Tbsp. olive oil
- 1 cup snipped fresh parsley
- ½ cup smoked almonds or toasted walnuts
- ⅓ cup olive oil
- 2 Tbsp. snipped fresh chives
- 2 cloves garlic
- 1 Tbsp. red wine vinegar
- 1½ cups red and/or yellow cherry tomatoes, quartered
- 1 6- to 6½-oz. jar marinated artichoke hearts, drained and quartered
- ½ tsp. cracked black pepper
- ¼ cup chopped prosciutto or crisp-cooked bacon
- ¼ cup finely shredded Asiago cheese (1 oz.)
- ¼ cup shredded provolone cheese (1 oz.)

1 Preheat oven to 400°F. Line a baking sheet with foil. Grease the foil; set aside. Use a spoon to remove the gills from the underside of the mushroom caps. Brush both sides of the mushroom caps with some of the 2 tablespoons olive oil. Set aside remaining olive oil. Place mushrooms, rounded side down, on the prepared baking sheet.

2 For pesto, in a food processor bowl or blender container combine snipped parsley, almonds or walnuts, the ⅓ cup olive oil, chives, garlic, and red wine vinegar. Cover and process or blend with several on-off turns until smooth. Spread about 3 tablespoons of the pesto on each mushroom cap.

3 In a small mixing bowl combine the red or yellow tomatoes, artichokes, cracked black pepper, and reserved olive oil. Toss to coat evenly. Divide tomato mixture evenly among the mushroom caps. Sprinkle with the prosciutto or bacon, Asiago cheese, and provolone cheese.

4 Bake, uncovered, in the preheated oven about 10 minutes or until cheese is melted and mushrooms are heated through. Cool slightly before serving. Makes 4 main-dish servings.

Nutrition Facts per serving: 503 cal., 45 g total fat (8 g sat. fat), 12 mg chol., 423 mg sodium, 15 g carbo., 7 g fiber, 13 g pro. Daily Values: 16% vit. A, 39% vit. C, 21% calcium, 11% iron.

LOW FAT

Curried Pepper and Bean Stew

Sweet mango tops this spunky vegetarian stew that has colorful sweet peppers and a bean duo.

Start to finish: 1 hour

- 1 medium onion, cut into wedges
- 4 cloves garlic, minced
- 1 Tbsp. olive oil
- 1 15-oz. can tomato sauce
- ½ tsp. curry powder
- ¼ tsp. salt
- ¼ tsp. ground allspice
- ¼ tsp. ground red pepper
- ¼ tsp. ground ginger
- 2 medium green and/or yellow sweet peppers, cut into bite-size strips
- 1 medium red sweet pepper, cut into bite-size strips
- 1 15- to 15½-oz. can red kidney beans, rinsed and drained
- 1 15-oz. can chickpeas (garbanzo beans), rinsed and drained
- ½ cup water
- 3 cups hot cooked basmati rice or brown rice
- 1 medium mango, peeled, seeded, and chopped

1 In a large saucepan cook and stir onion and garlic in hot olive oil over medium heat about 5 minutes or until onion is tender. Carefully add the tomato sauce, curry powder, salt, allspice, ground red pepper, and ginger. Cook and stir for 1 minute.

2 Stir in the sweet peppers, kidney beans, chickpeas, and water. Bring to boiling; reduce heat. Simmer, covered, about 30 minutes or until sweet peppers are tender, stirring stew occasionally.

3 To serve, spoon hot cooked rice into shallow bowls or onto plates. Ladle stew mixture over rice. Sprinkle with the chopped mango. Makes 6 servings.

Nutrition Facts per serving: 308 cal., 4 g total fat (0 g sat. fat), 0 mg chol., 860 mg sodium, 61 g carbo., 10 g fiber, 12 g pro. Daily Values: 66% vit. A, 131% vit. C, 7% calcium, 19% iron.

- Salad of mixed greens, orange and grapefruit slices, thin red onion slices, and toasted pecans drizzled with a sweet dressing

- Moroccan Chicken Stew (see below, right)

- Warm pita bread wedges

- Cheddar-Rosemary-Crusted Pear Pie (see page 236)

Autumn Vegetable And Chicken Stew

Butternut squash, sweet potatoes, Brussels sprouts, and red sweet pepper give this delectable stew the hues of autumn. Serve a mixed green salad and cracked wheat rolls to complete the menu.

Start to finish: 1 hour

- 2 medium Vidalia onions or other sweet onions, cut into thin wedges
- 3 Tbsp. butter or olive oil
- 2 cloves garlic, minced
- ½ cup all-purpose flour
- ½ tsp. dried marjoram, crushed
- ⅛ tsp. ground white pepper
- 2 14½-oz. cans chicken broth
- 1 cup half-and-half, light cream, or milk
- 2 cups cubed, peeled butternut squash
- 2 cups cubed, peeled sweet potato and/or sliced carrots
- 1½ cups small Brussels sprouts, quartered
- 1 medium red sweet pepper, seeded and cut into bite-size strips
- 3 cups chopped cooked chicken

- 2 Tbsp. orange juice
    Cracked black pepper

1 In a 4-quart Dutch oven cook onion wedges in hot butter or olive oil over medium heat for 3 minutes. Add the garlic. Cook and stir for 1 minute more.

2 Add flour, marjoram, and white pepper to pan. Cook and stir until onion is coated. Add chicken broth and half-and-half, light cream, or milk all at once. Cook and stir until thickened and bubbly.

3 Stir in butternut squash and sweet potato or carrots. Bring to boiling; reduce heat. Simmer, covered, for 15 minutes. Stir in Brussels sprouts and red sweet pepper. Cover and cook for 10 to 15 minutes more or until vegetables are tender. Stir in the chopped cooked chicken and orange juice; heat through.

4 To serve, ladle stew into soup bowls. Sprinkle with cracked black pepper. Makes 6 servings.

Nutrition Facts per serving: 385 cal., 17 g total fat (8 g sat. fat), 93 mg chol., 588 mg sodium, 30 g carbo., 4 g fiber, 28 g pro. **Daily Values:** 223% vit. A, 103% vit. C, 10% calcium, 14% iron.

PRIZE WINNER

Moroccan Chicken Stew

Yocheved Schwartz
Brooklyn, New York
$200—Stew for All

Start to finish: 35 minutes

- 1 Tbsp. all-purpose flour
- 1 tsp. ground coriander
- 1 tsp. ground cumin
- 1 tsp. ground paprika

- ½ tsp. salt
- ½ tsp. ground cinnamon
- 1 lb. skinless, boneless chicken thighs, cut into 1-inch pieces
- 2 medium onions, cut into wedges
- 3 cloves garlic, minced
- 1 Tbsp. olive oil
- 1 28-oz. can crushed tomatoes
- 1 15-oz. can chickpeas (garbanzo beans), rinsed and drained
- 1½ cups water
- ½ cup raisins
- ⅓ cup small pitted ripe olives
- 3 cups hot cooked couscous
- ¼ cup snipped fresh cilantro

1 In a small bowl stir together the flour, coriander, cumin, paprika, salt, and cinnamon. Place chicken in a large bowl. Sprinkle the flour mixture over the chicken, tossing to coat pieces. Set aside.

2 In a 4-quart Dutch oven cook onions and garlic in hot olive oil over medium heat about 5 minutes or until tender. Remove from Dutch oven, reserving oil in pan. Add chicken pieces to pan, half at a time. Cook quickly until lightly browned, stirring frequently. Return all chicken and the onion mixture to pan.

3 Add crushed tomatoes, drained chickpeas, water, raisins, and ripe olives to pan. Bring to boiling; reduce heat. Simmer, covered, for 10 minutes or until chicken is tender, stirring occasionally.

4 To serve, spoon couscous into soup bowls. Ladle stew over the couscous. Sprinkle with cilantro. Makes 6 servings.

Nutrition Facts per serving: 394 cal., 7 g total fat (1 g sat. fat), 60 mg chol., 858 mg sodium, 57 g carbo., 8 g fiber, 24 g pro. **Daily Values:** 10% vit. A, 35% vit. C, 10% calcium, 19% iron.

Gingersnap Stew

Suzanne Goddyn
Portland, Oregon
$400—Stew for All

Start to finish: 45 minutes

3	medium carrots, cut into ¾-inch pieces
3	medium stalks celery, cut into ½-inch pieces
¼	cup chopped onion
2	tsp. cooking oil
8	oz. cooked smoked sausage, halved lengthwise and cut into 1-inch pieces
1½	cups water
½	of a 15- or 15½-oz. can kidney beans, rinsed and drained (about ¾ cup)
1	Tbsp. chili powder
1	Tbsp. Worcestershire sauce
1	14½-oz. can stewed tomatoes
6	gingersnaps, crushed* (about ⅓ cup)
	Sliced pumpernickel bread, toasted (optional)

1 In a large saucepan cook carrots, celery, and onion in hot cooking oil over medium heat about 5 minutes or until onion is nearly tender. Remove vegetables from pan.

2 Add sausage pieces to pan. Cook over medium heat until lightly browned. Return vegetables to pan. Carefully add the water, drained kidney beans, chili powder, and Worcestershire sauce. Bring to boiling; reduce heat. Simmer, covered, about 20 minutes or until vegetables are tender. Stir in undrained tomatoes. Add crushed gingersnaps.

Cook and stir until mixture thickens and bubbles.

3 To serve, ladle stew into shallow bowls. If desired, serve with slices of toasted pumpernickel bread. Makes 4 servings.

*Note: To crush gingersnaps, place cookies in a self-sealing plastic bag. Seal and use a rolling pin or the flat side of a meat mallet to gently crush.

Nutrition Facts per serving: 410 cal., 23 g total fat (7 g sat. fat), 39 mg chol., 1,302 mg sodium, 35 g carbo., 7 g fiber, 19 g pro. **Daily Values:** 302% vit. A, 19% vit. C, 11% calcium, 19% iron.

EDITOR'S TIP

Bye-Bye Kitchen Clutter

It happens in nearly every kitchen: a jumbled utensil drawer, condiments in the refrigerator years past their prime, and forgotten canned goods at the back of the cabinet.

Bid farewell to clutter. Focus on three areas of the kitchen to get organized and to stay organized.

Conquer the Drawer War

• Cut down on utensils. Give away or toss out gadgets that you haven't used for a year or more.

• Store utensils close to the area of the kitchen in which they are used. Use decorative canisters or crocks to hold frequently used utensils, such as spoons, spatulas, whisks, and tongs. Wall-mounted utility rods can free valuable counter space.

• Use drawer dividers to combine items that have similar functions—a potato peeler with a citrus zester, a can opener with a corkscrew, and spatulas with kitchen tongs, for example.

Open the Cabinets

• Organize pantry foods into groups: soups, broths, and canned tomatoes; pasta, rice, and beans; cereals; and beverages. It will be easy to see what you have and what you need to buy.

• Write dates of purchase on spice jars and packages of flour, cereals, grains, and crackers. Rotate these products for optimum freshness.

• Organize spices alphabetically. Throw out spices after six months.

• Pack away appliances, glassware, or china that you seldom use. Store them in a basement or attic or donate them to charity. Eliminate duplicates—wash mixing bowls or measuring cups to reuse as you cook, rather than store several sets.

• Use glass or plastic bins to organize bulk food items or small items such as spice envelopes and tea bags.

A Place for Everything and Everything in Its Place

• Clean out the refrigerator every time you put away groceries, tossing out everything past its prime. Wipe the drawers and shelves before putting away fresh fruits and vegetables and milk and beverage containers.

• Use inexpensive plastic turntables to keep small jars accessible.

• Liberate refrigerator drawer space. Use small stackable plastic bins to organize meats, cheeses, jams, jellies, condiments, pickles, and relishes.

• Keep a running grocery list posted on the refrigerator with a magnet or on a tablet stored near the refrigerator. Also post menu ideas, matching ingredients to the ingredients on hand or on the shopping list.

MEXICAN MEAL

- Tortilla chips, guacamole

- Salad of torn leaf lettuce, chopped tomatoes, jicama strips, and ripe olives, drizzled with citrus vinaigrette

- Pork and Salsa Verde Stew (see below)

- Mexican beer or ice water with lime wedges

- Rice pudding

Pork and Salsa Verde Stew

Use leftover salsa verde to spoon over grilled fish, to stir into sour cream, to top a baked potato, or as a dip for tortilla chips.

Prep: 25 minutes **Cook:** 65 minutes

1¾	lb. lean, boneless pork stew meat (such as shoulder or sirloin), cut into 1-inch cubes
1	Tbsp. olive oil
1	cup sliced green onions
2	cloves garlic, minced
2½	cups beef broth
1	cup bottled salsa verde
1	fresh jalapeño pepper, seeded and finely chopped*
½	tsp. dried thyme, crushed
¼	tsp. ground red pepper
1	lb. sweet potatoes, peeled and cut into 1-inch cubes (3 cups)
½	cup dairy sour cream
3	Tbsp. all-purpose flour
1	cup frozen whole kernel corn
	Snipped fresh cilantro
	Corn tortillas, warmed**

1 In a 4-quart Dutch oven cook half the pork in hot olive oil over medium-high heat until browned. Remove pork from pan. Repeat with remaining pork. Remove pork from pan. Add green onions and garlic to pan, adding more oil if necessary. Cook and stir about 2 minutes or until green onions are tender.

2 Return pork to pan. Add beef broth, salsa verde, jalapeño pepper, thyme, and ground red pepper. Bring to boiling; reduce heat. Simmer, covered, for 30 minutes. Stir in sweet potatoes. Cover and cook about 30 minutes more or until meat and sweet potatoes are tender.

3 Meanwhile, in a small bowl stir together the sour cream and flour. Gradually stir ½ cup of the hot stew mixture into the sour cream mixture. Return entire mixture to saucepan. Cook and stir until thickened and bubbly. Cook and stir 1 minute more. Stir in corn; heat through.

4 To serve, ladle stew into soup bowls. Sprinkle each serving with cilantro. Serve with warmed corn tortillas. Makes 4 servings.

*Note: Hot peppers contain oils that can burn eyes, lips, and sensitive skin. Wear gloves while preparing them and wash your hands thoroughly afterward.

**Note: To warm corn tortillas, tightly wrap a stack of tortillas in foil. Heat in a 350°F oven until heated through.

Nutrition Facts per serving: 589 cal., 23 g total fat (8 g sat. fat), 143 mg chol., 676 mg sodium, 47 g carbo., 5 g fiber, 48 g pro. **Daily Values:** 419% vit. A, 57% vit. C, 12% calcium, 24% iron.

Oven-Style Beef and Vegetable Stew

The small amount of molasses adds a subtle flavor to this hearty, full-of-vegetables stew. Round out the meal with a spinach salad and rye bread.

Prep: 30 minutes **Bake:** 2½ hours

2	lb. boneless beef chuck roast, cut into 1-inch cubes
2	medium red onions, cut into thin wedges
4	carrots, cut into ½-inch slices (2 cups)
3	cloves garlic, minced
¼	cup butter or margarine
⅓	cup all-purpose flour
1	14½-oz. can beef broth
1	cup water
½	cup dry red wine
1¼	cups dried porcini and/or shiitake mushrooms (1 oz.)
½	cup snipped dried tomatoes (not oil-packed)
½	cup snipped fresh parsley
1	Tbsp. molasses
¾	tsp. dried thyme, crushed
½	tsp. caraway seed, crushed
1	bay leaf
¼	tsp. salt
¼	tsp. pepper
	Parsley sprigs (optional)

1 Preheat oven to 350°F. In a 2½- to 3-quart casserole combine the beef, onions, carrots, and garlic. Set aside.

2 In a medium saucepan melt the butter or margarine over medium-low heat. Stir in the flour; cook and stir for 1 minute. Add the beef broth, water, and red wine all at once. Cook and stir until mixture is thickened and just bubbly. Stir in dried mushrooms, snipped dried tomatoes, the ½ cup parsley, molasses, thyme, caraway seed, bay leaf, salt, and pepper until combined. Pour mixture over beef mixture.

3 Bake, covered, in the preheated oven for 1½ hours. Stir mixture. Bake, uncovered, about 1 hour more or until meat and vegetables are tender, stirring occasionally. Remove bay leaf before serving.

4 To serve, ladle stew into bowls. Garnish each serving with a parsley sprig, if desired. Makes 6 servings.

Nutrition Facts per serving: 394 cal., 18 g total fat (8 g sat. fat), 118 mg chol., 593 mg sodium, 22 g carbo., 3 g fiber, 34 g pro. Daily Values: 218% vit. A, 23% vit. C, 7% calcium, 31% iron.

Beef Stew with Tarragon Dumplings

Spoon eight mounds of dumpling dough onto the bubbly stew—each serving will have a light, fluffy morsel.

Prep: 20 minutes
Cook: 1 hour, 40 minutes

 2 lb. boneless beef chuck roast, cut into 1-inch cubes
 1 Tbsp. cooking oil
 1 cup chopped onion
 1 28-oz. can tomatoes, cut up
 ½ cup water
 ½ cup dry red wine
 ¼ cup coarse-grain Dijon-style mustard
 2 cloves garlic, minced
 1 tsp. instant beef bouillon granules

 1 tsp. sugar
 1 tsp. dried tarragon, crushed
 ½ tsp. dried oregano, crushed
 ½ tsp. pepper
 3 cups cubed potatoes
 12 tiny whole carrots or 1 cup packaged peeled baby carrots
 1 9-oz. pkg. frozen Italian green beans
 1 recipe Tarragon Dumplings (see below)

1 In a 4-quart Dutch oven cook half the beef in hot oil over medium-high heat until browned. Remove beef from pan. Repeat with remaining beef, adding the onion.

2 Return all beef to pan. Add undrained tomatoes, water, red wine, coarse-grain Dijon-style mustard, garlic, beef bouillon granules, sugar, tarragon, oregano, and pepper. Bring to boiling; reduce heat. Simmer, covered, for 1 hour.

3 Add potatoes and carrots to stew mixture. Return to boiling; reduce heat. Simmer, covered, 20 minutes.

4 Stir in the frozen green beans. Drop the dumplings from a tablespoon into eight small mounds onto simmering stew. Cover and cook about 20 minutes more or until a wooden toothpick inserted in a dumpling comes out clean.

5 To serve, ladle stew into soup bowls. Top each serving with a dumpling. Makes 8 servings.

Tarragon Dumplings

In a medium mixing bowl stir together 1 cup all-purpose flour, ½ cup shredded cheddar cheese (2 ounces), 2 teaspoons baking powder, 1 teaspoon crushed dried tarragon, and ¼ teaspoon salt. Add ⅔ cup milk and 3 tablespoons cooking oil all at once. Stir just until moistened.

To Make Ahead:

Prepare stew through Step 3. Cool; cover and chill in the refrigerator for up to 2 days. To serve, return stew mixture to boiling; reduce heat. Continue with Step 4.

Nutrition Facts per serving: 510 cal., 19 g total fat (6 g sat. fat), 123 mg chol., 787 mg sodium, 32 g carbo., 3 g fiber, 44 g pro. Daily Values: 6% vit. A, 35% vit. C, 19% calcium, 36% iron.

Just about any firm apple is a candidate for caramel coating. Petite apples, also known as pocket or lunch box apples, are fully mature, wonderfully sweet, and are good for dipping into caramel. One well-known petite variety, the lady apple, is a diminutive beauty. Give the caramel-coated apples a second coating of nuts, granola, coconut, or cereal (see recipe, below).

Petite Caramel Apples

These pretty treats will be a party hit and a tasty snack for the kids.

Prep: 20 minutes **Cook:** 25 minutes

- 8 to 10 small apples, such as lady apples
- 8 to 10 wooden craft sticks
- 2 cups coarsely chopped toasted nuts, toasted coconut, ready-to-eat sweetened cereal, and/or granola
- 1 cup whipping cream
- ¾ cup granulated sugar
- ½ cup light corn syrup
- ¼ cup packed dark brown sugar
- 1 Tbsp. butter
- ½ tsp. vanilla

1 Lightly grease a large baking sheet; set aside. Wash apples; pat dry. Remove stems. Insert a wooden stick into stem end of each apple; set aside. Place chopped nuts, coconut, cereal, and/or granola in separate shallow dishes or pie plates; set aside.

2 In a medium saucepan combine whipping cream, granulated sugar, corn syrup, brown sugar, and butter.

Cook and stir over medium-high heat until mixture just boils. Reduce heat to medium.

3 Attach a candy thermometer to the side of the pan (the tip of the thermometer should not touch the bottom of the pan). Boil mixture at a steady moderate rate, stirring frequently until thermometer reaches 248°F, firm-ball stage (about 25 minutes). Remove from heat. Remove thermometer. Stir in vanilla.

4 Working quickly, dip each apple into the hot caramel, turning to coat all but the top inch or so. Lift apple out of caramel and twirl gently to allow excess caramel to run into the saucepan. (If caramel thickens, return saucepan to low heat. Stir in a teaspoon or two of milk.) Using a table knife, remove excess caramel.

5 Roll apple in desired topping, coating bottom half of apple. Place coated apple on prepared baking sheet. Serve warm. Or let cool, then cover loosely with plastic wrap and store in the refrigerator for several hours. Makes 8 to 10 apples.

Nutrition Facts per apple: 488 cal., 26 g total fat (10 g sat. fat), 45 mg chol., 56 mg sodium, 67 g carbo., 5 g fiber, 3 g pro. Daily Values: 15% vit. A, 11% vit. C, 5% calcium, 6% iron.

Chocolate-Drizzled Petite Caramel Apples

Prepare Petite Caramel Apples as directed above. Let stand to cool. Meanwhile, in a small saucepan melt together 3 ounces chocolate- or vanilla-flavored candy coating and 1 teaspoon shortening over low heat, stirring often. Drizzle over caramel-coated apples. Place on waxed paper. Let dry. Store in the refrigerator.

LOW FAT

Strudel Triangles With Apples

Garner rave reviews when you serve thin, crisp layers of oven-toasted phyllo topped with slices of spiced caramel apples.

Prep: 30 minutes **Bake:** 6 minutes

- ¼ cup low-fat cinnamon graham cracker crumbs
- 1 Tbsp. granulated sugar
- 2 sheets frozen phyllo dough (18×14-inch rectangles), thawed
  Nonstick spray coating
- 1 Tbsp. margarine or butter
- 1 Tbsp. brown sugar
- 3 medium apples, peeled, cored, and thinly sliced
- ¼ cup raisins or dried cherries
- 1 Tbsp. apple brandy or water
- ¼ tsp. ground cinnamon
- ⅛ tsp. ground nutmeg
- ⅓ cup fat-free caramel ice cream topping
  Ground cinnamon (optional)
  Fresh mint (optional)

1 Preheat oven to 375°F. In a small bowl combine graham cracker crumbs and sugar; set aside.

2 Cut phyllo sheets in half crosswise. Lightly coat phyllo halves with nonstick cooking spray. Sprinkle one-fourth of the crumb mixture on one phyllo half. Top with a phyllo sheet and one-fourth of the crumb mixture; repeat with remaining phyllo and crumb mixture. Cut the four-layer stack into nine 2¾×4-inch rectangles. Cut each rectangle diagonally in half to form two triangles (18 triangles total).

3 Lightly coat a large baking sheet with nonstick cooking spray. Carefully place triangles on baking sheet. Bake in the preheated oven for 6 to 8 minutes or until golden brown.

4 Meanwhile, in a large skillet melt margarine or butter; stir in brown sugar. Stir in apples, raisins or dried cherries, brandy or water, cinnamon, nutmeg, and 3 tablespoons of the ice cream topping. Cook, uncovered, about 5 minutes or until apples are tender, stirring occasionally.

5 To serve, place a strudel triangle on each of six dessert plates. Spoon one-third of apple mixture over each triangle. Add a second strudel triangle. Top with half of the remaining apple mixture. Repeat with remaining triangles and apple mixture. Drizzle with remaining ice cream topping. If desired, sprinkle with cinnamon; garnish with mint. Serve immediately. Makes 6 servings.

Nutrition Facts per serving: 185 cal., 2 g total fat (0 g sat. fat), 0 mg chol., 121 mg sodium, 38 g carbo., 2 g fiber, 1 g pro. Daily Values: 2% vit. A, 3% vit. C, 2% calcium, 3% iron.

30 MINUTE

Berry-Apple Slump

Dumplings dropped onto hot, sweetened fruit is a slump—or a grunt for folks in Cape Cod. Both are part of the extended family of pastry-topped desserts also known as cobblers, betties, and pandowdies.

Start to finish: 30 minutes

- 1 cup water
- 1 cup chopped, peeled cooking apples
- 1 cup fresh or frozen blueberries
- ¾ cup cranberries

- ⅔ cup sugar
- ¾ cup all-purpose flour
- ¼ cup sugar
- 1 tsp. baking powder
- ¼ tsp. ground cinnamon
- ⅛ tsp. ground nutmeg
- ¼ tsp. salt
- 3 Tbsp. margarine or butter
- ⅓ cup milk
   Half-and-half (optional)

1 In a 3-quart saucepan combine water, apples, blueberries, cranberries, and the ⅔ cup sugar. Bring to boiling; reduce heat. Simmer, covered, for 5 minutes.

2 Meanwhile, for topping, in a small mixing bowl stir together the flour, the ¼ cup sugar, baking powder, cinnamon, nutmeg, and salt. Using a pastry blender, cut in margarine or butter until the mixture resembles coarse crumbs. Add milk to flour mixture, stirring just to moisten.

3 Drop topping into six mounds onto hot filling. Cover and simmer about 15 minutes or until a wooden toothpick inserted in the topping comes out clean. Serve warm. If desired, top with half-and-half. Makes 6 servings.

Nutrition Facts per serving: 263 cal., 6 g total fat (1 g sat. fat), 1 mg chol., 240 mg sodium, 51 g carbo., 3 g fiber, 2 g pro. Daily Values: 6% vit. A, 9% vit. C, 7% calcium, 5% iron.

Dutch Apple Cake

Prep: 20 minutes **Bake:** 35 minutes
Cool: 2 hours

- 2 cups all-purpose flour
- 1½ cups granulated sugar
- 1 tsp. baking powder
- 1 tsp. baking soda
- 1 tsp. ground cinnamon

- ¼ tsp. ground nutmeg
- ¼ tsp. ground cloves
- ¼ tsp. ground ginger
- 1 cup applesauce
- ¼ cup buttermilk
- ¼ cup margarine or butter, softened
- ¼ cup shortening
- ½ tsp. vanilla
- 3 eggs
- 2 cups chopped, peeled apples
- 1 recipe Apple Brandy Glaze (see below)

1 Preheat oven to 350°F. Grease a 13×9×2-inch baking pan; set aside. In a large mixing bowl stir together the flour, sugar, baking powder, baking soda, cinnamon, nutmeg, cloves, and ginger. Add applesauce, buttermilk, softened margarine or butter, shortening, and vanilla. Beat with an electric mixer on low to medium speed until combined. Beat on medium to high speed for 2 minutes. Add eggs; beat 2 minutes more. Fold in chopped apples. Pour batter into the prepared baking pan.

2 Bake in the preheated oven for 35 to 40 minutes or until a wooden toothpick inserted near the center comes out clean. Cool on a wire rack. Drizzle with Apple Brandy Glaze. Cover and store in the refrigerator. Makes 12 servings.

Apple Brandy Glaze

In a small bowl stir together 1 cup sifted powdered sugar, 1 tablespoon apple brandy or apple juice, and ¼ teaspoon vanilla. Stir in additional brandy or juice, 1 teaspoon at a time, until mixture is drizzling consistency.

Nutrition Facts per serving: 331 cal., 9 g total fat (2 g sat. fat), 53 mg chol., 205 mg sodium, 57 g carbo., 1 g fiber, 4 g. pro. Daily Values: 5% vit. A, 1% vit. C, 5% calcium, 8% iron.

If the pastry doesn't turn out well, determine possible problems and solutions from the following:

Pastry is crumbly and difficult to roll:

• Add more water, 1 teaspoon at a time.

• Toss the flour mixture and water together evenly while moistening the mixture.

Pastry is tough:

• Use a pastry blender to cut in the shortening or lard so that the mixture resembles small peas.

• Use less water when moistening the flour.

• Toss the flour mixture and water together only until the flour mixture is moistened.

• Use less flour to roll the pastry.

Crust has shrunk excessively:

• Mix in the water only until the dough is evenly moistened.

• Let the pastry rest for 5 minutes if it is difficult to roll.

• Don't stretch the pastry when transferring it.

Bottom crust is soggy:

• Use a dull finish metal or a glass pie plate rather than a shiny metal pie plate.

• Patch cracks in the pastry with leftover pieces of pastry before pouring in the filling.

• Test to ensure accurate oven temperature. The bottom crust will not bake properly when the oven temperature is too low.

Flaky Spiced Pastry

Mace, which is ground from the dried membrane that surrounds the nutmeg seed, resembles the taste of nutmeg.

Start to finish: 10 minutes

- 1¼ **cups all-purpose flour**
- ½ **tsp. ground mace**
- ¼ **tsp. salt**
- ⅓ **cup shortening**
- 4 **to 5 Tbsp. cold water**

1 In a medium mixing bowl stir together flour, mace, and salt. Using a pastry blender, cut in shortening until pieces are pea-size. Sprinkle 1 tablespoon of the water over part of the mixture; gently toss with a fork. Push moistened dough to side of the bowl. Repeat moistening dough, using 1 tablespoon of the water at a time, until all the dough is moistened. Form dough into a ball.

2 Fill and bake as directed in Walnut-Molasses Pie (see recipe, page 232) or other desired pie. Makes 1 single-crust pastry to serve 8.

Nutrition Facts per serving: 115 cal., 7 g total fat (2 g sat. fat), 0 mg chol., 59 mg sodium, 12 g carbo., 0 g fiber, 2 g pro. **Daily Values:** 1% vit. A, 1% calcium, 5% iron.

Pastry for Single-Crust Pie

Use a lightly floured rolling pin sock and pastry cloth to roll pastry that doesn't stick.

Start to finish: 10 minutes

- 1¼ **cups all-purpose flour**
- ¼ **tsp. salt**
- ⅓ **cup shortening**
- 4 **to 5 Tbsp. cold water**

1 In a medium mixing bowl stir together flour and salt. Using a pastry blender, cut in shortening until pieces are pea-size. Sprinkle 1 tablespoon of the water over part of the mixture; gently toss with a fork. Push moistened dough to the side of the bowl. Repeat moistening dough, using 1 tablespoon of the water at a time, until all the dough is moistened. Form dough into a ball.

2 On a lightly floured surface, slightly flatten dough with your hands. Roll the dough from the center to the edges into a circle about 12 inches in diameter.

3 To transfer pastry, wrap it around the rolling pin. Unroll pastry into a 9-inch pie plate. Ease the pastry into the pie plate, being careful not to stretch the pastry.

4 Trim pastry to ½ inch beyond edge of pie plate. Fold under extra pastry. Crimp edge as desired. Do not prick pastry. Fill and bake as directed in individual pies. Makes 1 single-crust pastry to serve 8.

Food Processor Directions:

Place the steel blade in a food processor bowl. Add flour, salt, and shortening. Cover and process with on-off turns until most of the mixture resembles cornmeal, but a few larger pieces remain. With food processor running, quickly add ¼ cup water through feed tube. Stop processor as soon as all water is added; scrape down sides. Process with two on-off turns (mixture may not all be moistened). Remove dough from bowl; shape into a ball.

Nutrition Facts per serving: 144 cal.,
8 g total fat (2 g sat. fat), 0 mg chol.,
73 mg sodium, 15 g carbo., 1 g fiber,
2 g pro. **Daily Values:** 1% vit. A,
1% calcium, 6% iron.

Baked Pastry Shell

Preheat oven to 450°F. Prepare and
roll out pastry as directed (see page
228), except generously prick the
bottom and sides of pastry in pie plate
with a fork. Prick all around where
bottom and sides meet. Line pastry
with a double thickness of foil. Bake
in the preheated oven for 8 minutes.
Remove foil. Bake for 5 to 6 minutes
more or until golden. Cool on a
wire rack.

Cheddar-Rosemary Pastry

To make this pastry for a deep-dish
pie, measure your ingredients
accurately. Too much flour or too
much water can make the pastry
tough. This rich pastry is used for the
Cheddar-Rosemary-Crusted Pear Pie
(see recipe, page 236). It's equally
delicious for making apple pie.

Start to finish: 20 minutes

2½ cups all-purpose flour
1½ tsp. snipped fresh rosemary
 ½ tsp. salt
 ⅔ cup shortening
 ½ cup finely shredded white
      cheddar cheese (2 oz.)
 7 to 8 Tbsp. cold water

1 In a large mixing bowl stir
together flour, rosemary, and salt.
Using a pastry blender, cut in
shortening until pieces are pea-size.
Stir in cheese. Sprinkle 1 tablespoon

of the water over part of the mixture;
gently toss with a fork. Push
moistened dough to side of bowl.
Repeat moistening dough, using
1 tablespoon of the water at a time,
until all the dough is moistened.
Divide dough in half. Form each half
into a ball.

2 Fill and bake as directed in
Cheddar-Rosemary-Crusted
Pear Pie (see recipe, page 236) or
other desired pie. Makes 1 double-
crust pastry to serve 8.

Nutrition Facts per serving: 316 cal.,
19 g total fat (6 g sat. fat), 7 mg chol.,
191 mg sodium, 30 g carbo., 1 g fiber,
6 g pro. **Daily Values:** 2% vit. A,
1% vit. C, 7% calcium, 12% iron.

Cream Cheese Pastry

This rich, buttery flavor pastry provides
the base for the Caramel-Nut Tart (see
recipe, page 231).

Start to finish: 20 minutes

1¼ cups all-purpose flour
 ⅛ tsp. salt
 1 3-oz. pkg. cold cream cheese
 ¼ cup cold butter (no substitutes)
 2 to 3 Tbsp. ice water
 1 tsp. cider vinegar

1 In a medium mixing bowl stir
together the flour and salt. Using
a pastry blender, cut in cream cheese
and butter until pieces are pea-size.
Using a fork, stir in the ice water and
vinegar until all dough is moistened.
Use your fingers to gently knead the
dough just until a ball forms. Flatten
the dough into a disc. Makes one
10-inch pastry to serve 8.

Nutrition Facts per serving: 130 cal.,
8 g total fat (5 g sat. fat), 22 mg chol.,
104 mg sodium, 12 g carbo., 0 g fiber,
2 g pro. **Daily Values:** 6% vit. A,
1% calcium, 5% iron.

Ever-So-Easy Pastry

Heidi Downen Pollock of Indianola,
Iowa, tipped us off to this dough. Just
toss the ingredients together with a
fork and press it in the pan with your
fingers. This one-pan pastry is about as
easy as it gets. For evenly browned
pastry, use a glass pie plate or dull
metal pie pan.

Start to finish: 10 minutes

1¼ cups all-purpose flour
 1 Tbsp. sugar
 ¼ tsp. salt
 ¼ cup cooking oil
 3 Tbsp. milk

1 In a 9-inch pie pan or plate stir
together flour, sugar, and salt. Add
oil and milk all at once to flour
mixture. Stir lightly with a fork. Form
into a ball.

2 Press dough firmly onto bottom
and up sides of pie pan or plate.
Fill and bake as directed in individual
recipe. Makes 1 single-crust pastry to
serve 8.

Nutrition Facts per serving: 40 cal.,
7 g total fat (1 g sat. fat), 0 mg chol.,
76 mg sodium, 17 g carbo., 1 g fiber,
2 g pro. **Daily Values:** 1% vit. C,
1% calcium, 6% iron.

The Edges Have It—Finish Your Pie with Flair

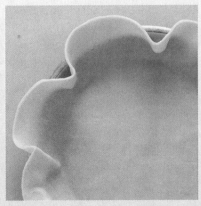

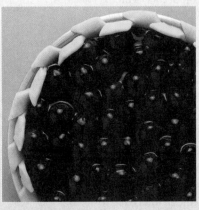

The Classic
Fold under edge as directed in recipe. Place your thumb against the inside rim of the pastry, and press the dough around your thumb with the thumb and index finger of the opposite hand.

Free Form
Trim pastry ¾ inch wider than the pan; lift and form the pastry into shape, allowing it to fall over the pie pan edge. Use only for pies baked less than 20 minutes; the pastry burns easily.

Up and Down
Fold under edge as directed in recipe. Use scissors to snip dough about every inch, folding every other section toward the center of the pie.

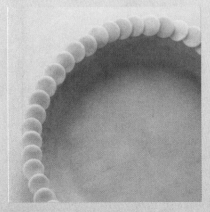

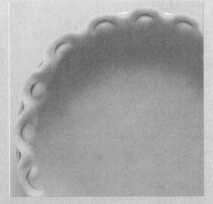

Coins
Trim pastry flush to the edge of the pie plate. Use a melon baller or cookie cutter to cut small circles from pastry to cover the rim. Use a little water to affix the pastry circles along the pie plate edge.

Beginner's Pride
After folding under the edge as directed in recipe, use a spoon to press a design into the rim of the crust.

Flute Variation
Fold under edge as directed in recipe. Loosely pinch dough around your thumb to form scallops. Use the edge of a spoon to make indentations along the inside of the scallop.

Pastry for Lattice-Top Pie

Use this standard, nearly fail-safe crust for lattice-topped or double-crust pies.

Start to finish: 15 minutes

- 2 **cups all-purpose flour**
- ½ **tsp. salt**
- ⅔ **cup shortening**
- 6 **to 7 Tbsp. cold water**

1 In a medium mixing bowl stir together flour and salt. Using a pastry blender, cut in shortening until pieces are pea-size.

2 Sprinkle 1 tablespoon of the water over part of the mixture; gently toss with a fork. Push moistened dough to side of bowl. Repeat, using 1 tablespoon water at a time, until all the dough is moistened. Divide in half. Form each half into a ball.

3 On a lightly floured surface, flatten one dough ball. Roll from center to edge into a 12-inch circle.

4 Transfer pastry by wrapping it around a rolling pin to ease and unroll into a 9-inch pie plate, being careful to avoid stretching pastry. Fill pastry-lined pie plate. Trim pastry even with rim of pie plate.

5 Roll remaining dough into a circle about 12 inches in diameter. For lattice top, cut pastry into ½-inch-wide strips. Weave strips over the filling as desired. Press ends of strips into crust rim. Fold bottom pastry over strips. Seal and crimp edge. Makes 1 lattice-crust pastry to serve 8.

Pastry for Double-Crust Pie

Prepare as above, except roll second half of dough into a circle about 12 inches in diameter. Cut slits to allow steam to escape. Place remaining pastry on filling; trim ½ inch beyond edge of plate. Fold top pastry under bottom pastry. Crimp edge as desired. Bake as directed.

Food Processor Directions:

Place steel blade in food processor bowl. Add flour, salt, and shortening. Cover; process with on-off turns until most of the mixture resembles cornmeal, but with a few larger pieces. With processor running, quickly add 6 tablespoons water through feed tube. Stop processor when all water is added; scrape down sides. Process with two on-off turns (all of mixture may not be moistened). Remove dough from bowl; shape each half into a ball.

Nutrition Facts per serving: 259 cal., 16 g total fat (4 g sat. fat), 0 mg chol., 146 mg sodium, 24 g carbo., 1 g fiber, 3 g pro. **Daily Values:** 1% vit. C, 2% calcium, 9% iron.

Caramel-Nut Tart

See the photograph on page 240.

Prep: 25 minutes **Bake:** 38 minutes

- 1 **recipe Cream Cheese Pastry (see page 229)**
- ⅓ **cup butter**
- ⅓ **cup packed brown sugar**
- 2 **Tbsp. light-colored corn syrup**
- 1½ **cups unsalted mixed nuts**
- ½ **tsp. vanilla**

1 Preheat oven to 450°F. Prepare Cream Cheese Pastry. On a lightly floured surface, slightly flatten the pastry dough. Roll dough from center to edge into a 16×6-inch rectangle. Wrap pastry around rolling pin. Unroll into an ungreased 13¾×4-inch tart pan with a removable bottom.

Ease pastry into tart pan, being careful not to stretch pastry. (Or roll dough from center to edge into a 10-inch circle. Wrap pastry around rolling pin. Unroll into an ungreased 9-inch tart pan with removable bottom.) Press pastry into fluted sides of pan. Trim edge. Line pastry with a double thickness of foil. Bake in preheated oven 10 minutes. Remove foil; bake 8 minutes more. Cool on a wire rack. Decrease oven temperature to 375°F.

2 In a heavy small saucepan combine butter, brown sugar, and corn syrup. Bring to boiling over medium heat; remove from heat. Stir in mixed nuts and vanilla. Pour filling into cooled crust, spreading evenly. Place tart pan on a baking sheet. Bake in the 375°F oven for 20 minutes. Cool on a wire rack 15 minutes; remove sides of pan. Cool completely. Serves 10.

Nutrition Facts per serving: 357 cal., 26 g total fat (11 g sat. fat), 40 mg chol., 180 mg sodium, 27 g carbo., 3 g fiber, 6 g pro. **Daily Values:** 11% vit. A, 4% calcium, 9% iron.

Walnut-Molasses Pie

Make this recipe using one bowl and two spoons. Although the filling may remind you of pecan pie, the walnuts in this pie rise during baking, providing a crunchy topper for the old-fashioned molasses filling.

Prep: 25 minutes **Bake:** 45 minutes
Cool: 2 hours

- 1   recipe Flaky Spiced Pastry (see page 228)
- 3   eggs, slightly beaten
- ¾   cup light-colored corn syrup
- ⅔   cup sugar
- ⅓   cup margarine or butter, melted
- ¼   cup molasses
- 1   tsp. vanilla
- 1½   cups walnut pieces
      Vanilla ice cream (optional)

1 Prepare Flaky Spiced Pastry. On a lightly floured surface use your hands to slightly flatten dough. Roll dough from center to edges into a circle about 12 inches in diameter. To transfer pastry, wrap it around the rolling pin. Unroll pastry into a 9-inch pie plate. Ease pastry into pie plate, being careful not to stretch pastry. Trim pastry to ½ inch beyond edge of pie plate. Fold under extra pastry. Crimp edge as desired. Set aside.

2 Preheat oven to 350°F. For filling, in a large mixing bowl combine eggs, corn syrup, sugar, margarine or butter, molasses, and vanilla. Mix well. Stir in walnut pieces.

3 Place the pastry-lined pie plate on the oven rack. Carefully pour the filling into the pastry shell. To prevent overbrowning, cover edge of the pie with foil.

4 Bake in the preheated oven for 25 minutes. Remove foil. Bake for 20 to 25 minutes more or until a knife inserted near the center comes out clean. Cool on a wire rack. Refrigerate pie within 2 hours. Cover pie for longer storage.

5 To serve, using a sharp knife, cut pie into wedges. Serve with vanilla ice cream, if desired. Cover and store any leftovers in the refrigerator. Makes 10 to 12 servings.

Nutrition Facts per serving: 448 cal., 26 g total fat (4 g sat. fat), 64 mg chol., 180 mg sodium, 51 g carbo., 2 g fiber, 6 g pro. **Daily Values:** 7% vit. A, 1% vit. C, 5% calcium, 11% iron.

Loverly Lemon Meringue Pie

Follow these two suggestions for successful meringue. Put the meringue on a warm filling; if the filling is cool, the bottom of the meringue might undercook, causing a weepy layer between the filling and meringue. Bake only about 15 minutes; if the meringue cooks too long, little sugary beads of moisture will form on top. (See the photograph on page 242.)

Prep: 40 minutes **Bake:** 15 minutes
Cool: 1 hour **Chill:** 3 hours

- 1   recipe Pastry for Single-Crust Pie (see page 228)
- 3   eggs
- 1   cup sugar
- 3   Tbsp. all-purpose flour
- 3   Tbsp. cornstarch
      Dash salt
- 1½   cups water
- ½   cup lemon curd
- 2   Tbsp. margarine or butter
- 2   tsp. finely shredded lemon peel
- ½   tsp. vanilla
- ¼   tsp. cream of tartar
- 5   Tbsp. sugar

1 Prepare and bake the Pastry for Single-Crust Pie. Set aside.

2 Separate egg yolks from whites. Set whites aside for meringue, allowing egg whites to stand at room temperature for 30 minutes.

3 Meanwhile, for filling, in a medium saucepan combine the 1 cup sugar, flour, cornstarch, and salt. Gradually stir in the 1½ cups water. Cook and stir over medium-high heat until thickened and bubbly; reduce heat. Cook and stir for 2 minutes more. Remove from heat.

4 Slightly beat egg yolks with a rotary beater or fork. Gradually stir about 1 cup of the hot filling into yolks. Pour egg yolk mixture into remaining hot filling in saucepan. Bring to a gentle boil. Cook and stir 2 minutes more. Remove from heat. Stir in lemon curd, margarine or butter, and lemon peel. Keep filling warm. Preheat oven to 350°F.

5 For meringue, in a large mixing bowl combine egg whites, vanilla, and cream of tartar. Beat with an electric mixer on medium speed about 1 minute or until soft peaks form (tips curl). Gradually add the 5 tablespoons sugar, 1 tablespoon at a time, beating on high speed for about 4 minutes more or until mixture forms stiff, glossy peaks (tips stand straight) and sugar dissolves.

6 Pour warm lemon filling into Baked Pastry Shell. Using a large star tip, pipe meringue in rows over warm filling, sealing to edge. Bake in the preheated oven for 15 minutes. Cool on wire rack 1 hour. Chill 3 to 6 hours before serving. Cover pie for longer storage.

7 To serve, using a sharp knife, cut pie into wedges. Cover and store any leftovers in the refrigerator. Makes 8 servings.

Nutrition Facts per serving: 410 cal., 14 g total fat (4 g sat. fat), 95 mg chol., 140 mg sodium, 54 g carbo., 3 g fiber, 5 g pro. Daily Values: 5% vit. A, 1% vit. C, 1% calcium, 7% iron.

Sour Cream Harvest Pie

The pastry for this pie is mixed and patted right in the pie pan. Then fill with the yummy peaches and sour cream filling.

Prep: 15 minutes **Bake:** 58 minutes
Cool: 1 hour

- 1 recipe Ever-So-Easy Pastry (see page 229)
- 1 6-oz. pkg. dried peach or apricot halves
- 1 cup peach or apricot nectar
- 2 8-oz. cartons dairy sour cream
- ½ cup sugar
- 3 Tbsp. all-purpose flour

- ¼ tsp. ground nutmeg
- ⅛ tsp. ground cloves
- ½ cup milk
- 2 eggs, slightly beaten

1 Preheat oven to 450°F. Prepare Ever-So-Easy Pastry. Press into a 9-inch pie pan or plate as directed. Line pastry with a double thickness of foil. Bake in the preheated oven for 8 minutes. Remove foil. Bake for 5 to 6 minutes more or until golden; remove and set aside on a wire rack. Reduce oven to 375°F.

2 Snip enough of the peach or apricot halves to make ¾ cup snipped dried fruit. Cut remaining peach or apricot halves into slivers and place in a small bowl; set aside.

3 For filling, in a small saucepan combine peach or apricot nectar and snipped peaches or apricots. Bring to boiling; reduce heat. Simmer, covered, for 10 minutes. Remove from heat; drain well, reserving juice. Pour reserved juice over dried fruit slivers in bowl. Cover and set aside.

4 In a medium mixing bowl stir together the sour cream, sugar, flour, nutmeg, and cloves. Stir in milk and eggs until smooth. Stir in drained snipped fruit. Pour the mixture into the pastry-lined pie pan or plate.

5 Bake in the 375°F oven for 45 to 50 minutes or until top is golden brown and puffed and filling appears set in center when gently shaken. Cool pie for 1 hour on a wire rack (filling will fall as it cools). Cover and chill until serving time.

TEST KITCHEN TIP
Pie Safe

Follow these storage rules whether you make pies ahead of time or store a few servings:

- **Fruit pies** may stand at room temperature for 24 hours. Cover and refrigerate for longer storage.

- **Custard and cream pies** should be served as soon as they are cool, or covered lightly with plastic wrap and refrigerated for up to 2 days. Don't freeze cream or custard pies.

- **To freeze unbaked fruit pies,** treat light-color fruit with ascorbic acid color keeper. Assemble the pie in a metal or freezer-to-oven pie plate. Place the pie in a labeled freezer bag; seal and freeze. Use frozen pies within 2 to 4 months. To bake a frozen pie, unwrap it and cover it with foil. Bake in a 450°F oven for 15 minutes; reduce the temperature to 375°F and bake for another 15 minutes. Uncover and continue baking for 55 to 60 minutes or until crust is golden and filling is bubbly.

- **To freeze fruit pies that have been completely baked,** cool the pie. Place it in a labeled freezer bag; seal and freeze for up to 8 months. To serve, thaw the pie, covered, at room temperature. If desired, reheat the pie, covered, in a 325°F oven until warm.

6 To serve, using a sharp knife, cut pie into wedges. Transfer each serving to a dessert plate. Spoon some reserved dried fruit slivers and juice atop each serving. Cover and store any leftovers in the refrigerator. Makes 10 servings.

Nutrition Facts per serving: 327 cal., 17 g total fat (7 g sat. fat), 64 mg chol., 106 mg sodium, 40 g carbo., 2 g fiber, 6 g pro. Daily Values: 17% vit. A, 4% vit. C, 9% calcium, 10% iron.

One-Handed Fried Pies

Gussie Ann Stanford—a transplant to Columbus, Ohio, from Mississippi—shares her secret for making classic Southern filled pastry treats. (Her grandchildren love the chocolate-filled version.) She suggests cooking the pies slowly in a nearly dry skillet over medium-low heat. (See the photograph on page 239.)

Prep: 35 minutes
Cook: 20 minutes plus 8 minutes per batch

- 1½ cups dried peaches, apricots, and/or apples (6 oz.)
- 1¼ cups apple cider
- 2 cups all-purpose flour
- 2 tsp. baking powder
- 2 tsp. granulated sugar
- ¼ tsp. salt
- ¼ tsp. baking soda
- ½ cup shortening
- ⅔ cup buttermilk or
   - ⅓ cup buttermilk and
   - ⅓ cup whipping cream
- Water
- 4 Tbsp. shortening
- Sifted powdered sugar

1 For the filling, in a medium saucepan combine the dried fruit and apple cider. Bring to boiling; reduce heat. Simmer, covered, for 20 to 25 minutes or until fruit is tender (cider should be cooked down). Mash slightly; cool.

2 Meanwhile, for the pastry, in a medium mixing bowl combine flour, baking powder, granulated sugar, salt, and baking soda. Using a pastry blender, cut in the ½ cup shortening until pieces are pea-size.

3 Sprinkle 1 tablespoon of the buttermilk or buttermilk mixture over part of the flour mixture; gently toss with a fork. Push the moistened dough to the side of the bowl. Repeat, using 1 tablespoon of the buttermilk at a time, until all the dough is moistened. If pastry seems dry, add a little water, 1 tablespoon at a time. (Do not overhandle.) Form dough into a ball.

4 Pat or lightly roll dough into a 15-inch circle. Using a 4-inch round cutter, cut the dough into 12 circles, re-rolling dough as needed. Place about 1 tablespoon fruit filling on half of each circle. Moisten edges of pastry circles with water. Fold over into half-moon shapes; seal edges with tines of a fork.

5 In a 12-inch nonstick skillet heat 2 tablespoons of the shortening over medium-low heat. Fry half of the pies for 8 to 10 minutes or until golden brown, turning once. Drain on paper towels. Add the remaining shortening to the skillet. Fry remaining pies. Serve warm. Sprinkle with powdered sugar before serving. Makes 12 individual pies.

Nutrition Facts per pie: 258 cal., 13 g total fat (3 g sat. fat), 0 mg chol., 158 mg sodium, 34 g carbo., 2 g fiber, 3 g pro. **Daily Values:** 7% vit. A, 3% vit. C, 8% calcium, 11% iron.

Chocolate Fried Pies

Omit the fruit filling. Prepare pastry as directed at left. For chocolate filling, in a small bowl combine ½ cup sifted powdered sugar and ¼ cup unsweetened cocoa powder. Stir in 4 tablespoons melted butter. Spread a scant 2 teaspoons of mixture onto each pastry circle. Fry pies as directed.

Mom's Apple Pie

To take fresh apple-pie season to the sweetest limit, double this recipe. Make one for immediate eating and place the other in the freezer to bake on a wintry day when you're longing for apple season. (See the photograph on page 241.)

Prep: 30 minutes **Bake:** 50 minutes

- 1 recipe Pastry for Single-Crust Pie (see page 228)
- ¼ cup granulated sugar
- 2 Tbsp. all-purpose flour
- ½ tsp. ground cinnamon
- ⅛ tsp. salt
- 6 cups thinly sliced, peeled tart cooking apples (about 2¼ lb.)
- 1 recipe Crumb Topping (see page 235)

1 Prepare and roll out Pastry for Single-Crust Pie. Line a 9-inch pie plate with the pastry. Trim pastry to ½ inch beyond edge of pie plate. Fold under extra pastry. Crimp edge as desired. Do not prick pastry; set aside.

2 Preheat oven to 375°F. In a large mixing bowl stir together granulated sugar, flour, cinnamon, and salt. Add apple slices. Gently toss to combine.

3 Transfer apple mixture to the pastry-lined pie plate. Prepare Crumb Topping and sprinkle over apple mixture. Gently pat mixture down over apples. Place pie on a baking sheet. Cover entire pie loosely with foil.

4 Bake in the preheated oven for 15 minutes. Remove foil. Bake for 35 to 40 minutes more or until top is brown and apples are tender. Cool on a wire rack. Makes 8 servings.

Crumb Topping

In a small mixing bowl stir together ¾ cup packed brown sugar, ½ cup all-purpose flour, and ½ teaspoon ground cinnamon. Using a pastry blender, cut in ⅓ cup butter until the mixture resembles coarse crumbs. Stir in 1 cup chopped walnuts.

To Make Ahead:

Prepare pie as directed on page 234, except after sprinkling with Crumb Topping, wrap entire pie tightly in foil. Freeze for up to 3 months.

To bake frozen pie, remove foil wrapping and place frozen pie on a baking sheet. Cover entire pie loosely with foil. Bake in a 350°F oven for 40 minutes. Remove foil. Bake for 35 to 40 minutes more or until top is brown and apples are tender. Cool on a wire rack.

Nutrition Facts per serving: 521 cal., 27 g total fat (8 g sat. fat), 22 mg chol., 201 mg sodium, 69 g carbo., 6 g fiber, 6 g pro. **Daily Values:** 7% vit. A, 2% vit. C, 6% calcium, 15% iron.

Grape Mini Pies

This recipe makes four mini pies or one 9-inch pie. To make a 9-inch pie, spoon the grape mixture into one unbaked pie crust, cover the edge with foil, and bake for 25 minutes. Remove the foil and bake for 25 to 30 minutes more or until filling is bubbly. Top with baked leaf cutouts.

Prep: 40 minutes **Bake:** 25 minutes

- **5 cups large seedless red and/or green grapes, halved**
- **⅓ cup packed brown sugar**
- **¼ cup all-purpose flour**
- **1 Tbsp. port wine or grape juice**
- **1 15-oz. package folded refrigerated unbaked piecrust (2 crusts)**
- **1 egg white**
- **1 Tbsp. water**
- **Coarse sugar**

1 Preheat oven to 400°F. For filling, in a large mixing bowl stir together grapes, brown sugar, flour, and port wine or grape juice. Set aside.

2 Let refrigerated piecrust stand at room temperature according to package directions. On a lightly floured surface, roll each crust into a 13-inch circle. Cut two 6- to 6½-inch circles from each crust. Line four 4-inch pie pans with the pastry circles. Trim pastry to ¾ inch beyond edge of pie pans (do not fold under). Crimp edge as desired. Transfer filling to the pastry-lined pie pans.

3 Bake in the preheated oven about 25 minutes or until pastry is golden brown and filling is bubbly. Cool on a wire rack.

4 Meanwhile, use a leaf cookie cutter to cut designs from the remaining pastry. Combine egg white and water. Brush leaf cutouts with egg white mixture. Sprinkle with coarse sugar. Place cutouts on a cookie sheet. Bake for 7 to 8 minutes or until golden brown.

5 To serve, using a sharp knife, cut each pie in half. Transfer each half to a dessert plate. Place a leaf cutout on each serving. Makes 8 servings.

Nutrition Facts per serving: 365 cal., 14 g total fat (6 g sat. fat), 10 mg chol., 209 mg sodium, 57 g carbo., 1 g fiber, 2 g pro. **Daily Values:** 1% vit. A, 18% vit. C, 2% calcium, 3% iron.

TEST KITCHEN TIP

Fruit Pies 101

Pair a plain pastry and a sweet fruit filling to make a delicious pie. Whichever fruit you use, here are a few tips to make each creation a winning combination:

- Use either a double-crust or lattice-top as the recipe specifies. Don't substitute one for the other; some fillings require the venting that the lattice provides, while others, such as apples, benefit from steaming under a top crust.

- To make a pie with frozen fruit, mix the frozen fruit with a sugar-flour mixture. Let the mixture thaw for 15 to 30 minutes, until the fruit is partially thawed and still icy. Transfer the mixture to a pastry-lined plate. Pies made with frozen fruit take longer to bake. Cover the pie with foil and bake it in a 375°F oven for about 50 minutes. Remove the foil and continue to bake until the pie is done, usually from 20 to 30 minutes longer.

- Make several cuts in the top of double-crust pies before baking to allow the steam to escape and to prevent excessive bubbling.

- For attractive glazed crusts, brush the top crust with milk and sprinkle on granulated sugar before baking.

- Place a pizza pan or baking sheet under a double-crust fruit pie when you put it in the oven to catch any filling that bubbles over.

- Fruit pies need to bubble in the center to cook properly. Otherwise, the thickener (flour, cornstarch, or tapioca) will be cloudy. To see whether the pie is done, make a small hole in the top crust and spoon out some of the juice. If the juice is clear, the pie is done. If it's cloudy, bake the pie a little longer.

- Let pies cool for 3 to 4 hours to serve them at their flavorful best and to prevent slices from falling apart when the pie is cut.

Cheddar-Rosemary-Crusted Pear Pie

Herbs provide mellow taste for dessert recipes paired with fruit and cheese. The sweetness of the pears complements the assertive flavor of rosemary in the pastry. Cheddar bonds these three flavorful foods. (See the photograph on page 237.)

Prep: 50 minutes **Bake:** 50 minutes

- ¾ cup sugar
- 3 Tbsp. cornstarch
- 2 Tbsp. pear nectar, orange juice, or apple juice
- 8 cups thinly sliced, peeled pears
- 1 recipe Cheddar-Rosemary Pastry (see page 229)
  White cheddar cheese (optional)
  Fresh rosemary sprigs (optional)

1 For filling, in a large mixing bowl stir together sugar and cornstarch. Stir in pear nectar or fruit juice. Add pear slices, gently tossing to coat. Set aside.

2 Preheat oven to 375°F. Prepare Cheddar-Rosemary Pastry. On a lightly floured surface, flatten one dough ball. Roll from center to edges into a 13-inch circle. To transfer pastry, wrap it around the rolling pin; unroll into a 9- or 9½-inch deep-dish pie plate. Ease pastry into pie plate, being careful not to stretch pastry. Spoon the pear filling into pastry-lined pie plate.

3 Roll remaining dough into a 12-inch circle. Place remaining pastry on filling; trim ½ inch beyond edge of plate. Fold pastry top under bottom pastry. Crimp edge as desired. With a small, sharp knife cut slits in the top pastry to allow the steam to escape. To prevent overbrowning, cover edge of pie with foil. Place pie on baking sheet.

4 Bake pie in the preheated oven for 25 minutes. Remove foil. Bake for 25 to 35 minutes more or until top is golden brown and filling is bubbly. Cool on a wire rack.

5 To serve, using a sharp knife, cut pie into wedges. Serve with white cheddar cheese and garnish with fresh rosemary sprigs, if desired. Serves 8.

Nutrition Facts per serving: 496 cal., 19 g total fat (6 g sat. fat), 7 mg chol., 191 mg sodium, 76 g carbo., 5 g fiber, 6 g pro. Daily Values: 2% vit. A, 16% vit. C, 9% calcium, 14% iron.

Apricot-Cherry Slab Pie

Perfect to take to a potluck or large gathering, this giant pie is similar to fruit-filled bars.

Prep: 30 minutes **Bake:** 40 minutes

- 3¼ cups all-purpose flour
- 1 tsp. salt
- 1 cup shortening
- 1 egg yolk
  Milk
- ½ cup sugar
- 3 Tbsp. cornstarch
- 3 15¼-oz. cans apricot halves, drained and cut into quarters
- 1 16-oz. can pitted tart red cherries, drained
- 1 recipe Vanilla Glaze (see right)

1 For pastry, in a large mixing bowl stir together the flour and salt. Using a pastry blender, cut in shortening until mixture resembles coarse crumbs. Lightly beat egg yolk in a glass measuring cup. Add enough milk to the egg yolk to make ¾ cup total liquid; mix well. Stir egg yolk mixture into flour mixture; mix well. Divide dough into two-thirds and one-third portions.

2 On a lightly floured surface, roll the two-thirds portion of the dough into an 18×12-inch rectangle. To transfer pastry, wrap it around the rolling pin; unroll into a 15×10×1-inch baking pan (pastry will hang over edges of pan).

3 Preheat oven to 375°F. For filling, in a large mixing bowl stir together the sugar and cornstarch. Stir in apricots and cherries. Spoon into prepared crust.

4 Roll the one-third dough portion into a 16×11-inch rectangle. Carefully place dough rectangle over fruit. Bring bottom pastry up and over top pastry. Seal edges with the tines of a fork. Using the tines of a fork, prick top pastry over entire surface.

5 Bake in the preheated oven about 40 minutes or until golden brown. Cool in pan on a wire rack. Serve warm or cool. Drizzle with Vanilla Glaze. Cut into 2×3-inch bars. Makes 25 bars.

Vanilla Glaze

In a small bowl stir together 1¼ cups sifted powdered sugar, ½ teaspoon vanilla, and enough milk (approximately 5 to 6 teaspoons) to make of drizzling consistency.

Nutrition Facts per bar: 230 cal., 8 g total fat (2 g sat. fat), 9 mg chol., 104 mg sodium, 37 g carbo., 1 g fiber, 2 g pro. Daily Values: 16% vit. A, 3% vit. C, 2% calcium, 8% iron.

Cheddar-Rosemary-Crusted Pear Pie (page 236)

Left: Extreme Chocolate Pie (page 246)
Above: One-Handed Fried Pies (page 234)

Above: Caramel-Nut Tart (page 231)
Page 241: Mom's Apple Pie (page 234)

Top: Loverly Lemon Meringue Pie (page 232)
Above: Pumpkin Mascarpone Pie (page 246)
Right: Caramelized Quince Skillet Tart (page 245)

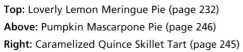

Pucker-Up Lemon-Cranberry
Pie (page 245)

Pucker-Up Lemon-Cranberry Pie

Fresh cranberry pie is a colorful favorite. Sliced lemons are added to this recipe to give it even more pucker power. There's plenty of sugar to make this pie a tart-sweet specialty. (See the photograph on page 244.)

Prep: 25 minutes **Bake:** 55 minutes

- 1 recipe Pastry for Lattice-Top Pie (see page 231)
- 1¼ to 1⅓ cups granulated sugar
- 2 Tbsp. all-purpose flour
- 3 cups cranberries
- 2 lemons, peeled (with white membrane removed), halved lengthwise, and thinly sliced
- 1 egg white, beaten
- 1 Tbsp. water
- 1 Tbsp. coarse sugar

1 Prepare and roll out Pastry for Lattice-Top Pie. Line a 9-inch pie plate with half of the pastry. Set aside.

2 Preheat oven to 375°F. For filling, in a large mixing bowl stir together granulated sugar and flour. Add cranberries and lemon slices, gently tossing to coat.

3 Transfer fruit mixture to pastry-lined pie plate. Top with a lattice crust. Seal and trim pastry.

4 In a small bowl stir together egg white and water. Brush onto pastry. Sprinkle with coarse sugar. To prevent overbrowning, cover edge of pie with foil.

5 Bake in the preheated oven for 25 minutes. Remove foil. Bake for 30 to 35 minutes more or until the top is golden and filling is bubbly. Cool slightly on a wire rack; serve warm. Or cool completely on wire rack. Makes 8 servings.

Nutrition Facts per serving: 411 cal., 18 g total fat (4 g sat. fat), 0 mg chol., 142 mg sodium, 61 g carbo., 3 g fiber, 4 g pro. **Daily Values:** 22% vit. C, 1% calcium, 9% iron.

Caramelized Quince Skillet Tart

Quince, which tastes like a cross between an apple and a pear, must be peeled and cooked to bring out its best flavor. Apples are a wonderful substitute in this tart, but the finished dessert won't have the same golden caramel color as when quince is used. (See the photograph on page 243.)

Prep: 20 minutes **Cook:** 20 minutes
Bake: 30 minutes **Stand:** 20 minutes

- ½ cup butter
- 6 cups thickly sliced, peeled quince or cooking apples (5 to 6 quince or apples)
- ⅔ cup sugar
- 1 recipe Buttery Pastry (see right)

1 Preheat oven to 375°F. In a 10-inch ovenproof skillet melt the butter over medium heat. Stir in the quince or apples and sugar. Cook over medium heat, stirring occasionally, until bubbly. Reduce heat to medium-low. Cook, uncovered, about 20 minutes more or until quince or apples are very tender (if using quince, mixture will thicken and turn deep golden brown), stirring occasionally. Remove from heat.

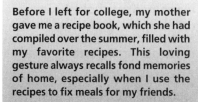
2 Prepare Buttery Pastry. On a lightly floured surface, use your hands to slightly flatten dough. Roll dough from center to edge, forming a 10-inch circle. Cut slits in the pastry. Wrap pastry around rolling pin. Unroll pastry over the quince mixture in the skillet, being careful not to stretch the pastry. If necessary, carefully fold under edges of pastry.

3 Bake in the preheated oven about 30 minutes or until the pastry is golden brown and filling is bubbly. Cool in skillet on a wire rack for 5 minutes. Invert onto a large serving plate. Lift off the skillet. Allow to stand about 20 minutes more. Makes 12 servings.

Buttery Pastry
In a medium mixing bowl stir together 1½ cups all-purpose flour and 3 tablespoons sugar. Using a pastry blender, cut in ½ cup butter until pieces are pea-size. Using a fork, stir in 1 slightly beaten egg and 1 to 2 tablespoons cold water until all dough is moistened. Form into a ball.

Nutrition Facts per serving: 289 cal., 17 g total fat (10 g sat. fat), 61 mg chol., 173 mg sodium, 33 g carbo., 1 g fiber, 3 g pro. **Daily Values:** 13% vit. A, 13% vit. C, 2% calcium, 7% iron.

- Salad of mixed greens, marinated artichoke hearts, red pear tomatoes, and fresh mozzarella drizzled with balsamic vinaigrette

- Fettuccine with chicken and wild mushrooms in a light cream sauce

- Crusty Italian bread

- Extreme Chocolate Pie (see below, right)

Pumpkin Mascarpone Pie

The mascarpone cheese mixture is heavier than the pumpkin mixture and needs to be coaxed with a spatula or knife to swirl through the filling. (See the photograph on page 242.)

Prep: 25 minutes **Bake:** 50 minutes
Cool: 1 hour **Chill:** 2 hours

- 1   recipe Pastry for Single-Crust Pie (see page 228)
- 1   8-oz. pkg. mascarpone or cream cheese, softened
- 1   egg yolk, slightly beaten
- 2   Tbsp. honey
- ½   tsp. vanilla
- 1   cup canned pumpkin
- 1   5-oz. can (⅔ cup) evaporated milk
- 2   eggs, slightly beaten
- ⅓   cup packed brown sugar
- 1   tsp. ground cinnamon
- ¼   tsp. ground nutmeg

1 Preheat oven to 375°F. Prepare and roll out Pastry for Single-Crust Pie. Line a 9-inch pie plate with the pastry. Trim and crimp a high edge crust.

2 In a medium mixing bowl beat mascarpone or cream cheese, egg yolk, honey, and vanilla with an electric mixer on low to medium speed until smooth. Set aside.

3 In another medium mixing bowl stir together pumpkin, evaporated milk, the 2 whole eggs, brown sugar, cinnamon, and nutmeg. Pour into pastry-lined pie plate. Drop the mascarpone mixture over the pumpkin mixture by tablespoons. Pull a thin metal spatula through mascarpone to swirl fillings.

4 Bake in the preheated oven about 50 minutes or until puffed and a knife inserted near the center comes out clean. Cool on a wire rack for 1 hour. Cover and chill at least 2 hours before serving. Serves 8.

Nutrition Facts per serving: 377 cal., 25 g total fat (11 g sat. fat), 121 mg chol., 124 mg sodium, 33 g carbo., 2 g fiber, 11 g pro. Daily Values: 138% vit. A, 3% vit. C, 8% calcium, 10% iron.

Extreme Chocolate Pie

A sliver of this deep, dark dessert will keep chocolate fans smiling for hours. Make the pie a day early, and you'll be relaxed when it's time to serve dessert. (See the photograph on page 238.)

Prep: 35 minutes **Bake:** 20 minutes
Chill: 4 hours

- 1   8-oz. pkg. brownie mix
- 1   cup sugar
- ¾   cup butter
- 6   oz. unsweetened chocolate, melted and cooled
- 1   tsp. vanilla
- ¾   cup refrigerated or frozen egg product, thawed, or ¾ cup pasteurized eggs
- 1   1.45-oz. bar dark sweet chocolate, coarsely chopped
- 1   recipe Chocolate Whipped Cream (see below) (optional)

1 Preheat oven to 350°F. For crust, prepare brownie mix according to package directions. Spread in the bottom of a greased 9-inch pie plate. Bake in the preheated oven for 20 to 25 minutes or until a wooden toothpick comes out clean. Cool on a wire rack.

2 For filling, in a medium mixing bowl beat sugar and butter with an electric mixer on medium speed about 4 minutes or until fluffy. Stir in the melted and cooled chocolate and the vanilla. Gradually add egg product, beating on low speed until combined. Beat on medium to high speed about 1 minute or until light and fluffy, scraping sides of bowl.

3 Transfer filling to brownie-mix crust. Cover and chill for 4 to 24 hours. Before serving, sprinkle with coarsely chopped chocolate bar. Serve with Chocolate Whipped Cream, if desired. Makes 10 servings.

Nutrition Facts per serving: 428 cal., 29 g total fat (16 g sat. fat), 61 mg chol., 285 mg sodium, 45 g carbo., 3 g fiber, 5 g pro. Daily Values: 13% vit. A, 8% calcium, 13% iron.

Chocolate Whipped Cream
In a chilled small mixing bowl combine ½ cup whipping cream, 1 tablespoon sugar, and 1½ teaspoons unsweetened cocoa powder. Beat with chilled beaters of an electric mixer (or a rotary beater) on medium speed until soft peaks form.

november

IN THIS CHAPTER

30-minute recipes indicated in COLOR.
Low-fat and no-fat recipes indicated
with a ♥.
Photographs indicated in italics.
***Bonus recipe**

Baked Oatmeal

Cynthia Knudsen
Rockford, Michigan
$200—Holiday Breakfasts

Prep: 15 minutes **Bake:** 40 minutes

2½ cups regular rolled oats
¼ cup oat bran
¼ cup steel-cut oats
2 tsp. baking powder
½ tsp. salt
½ tsp. ground cinnamon
2 cups milk
1 egg, beaten
⅓ cup applesauce
¼ cup cooking oil
¼ cup granulated sugar
¼ cup packed brown sugar
2 cups fresh fruit (such as
  blueberries; peeled, cored,
  and chopped pears or apples;
  or chopped strawberries)
  Plain or vanilla low-fat yogurt,
  milk, or light cream (optional)

1 Preheat oven to 400°F. Lightly grease a 2-quart soufflé dish or casserole. In a large mixing bowl stir together rolled oats, oat bran, steel-cut oats, baking powder, salt, and cinnamon; set aside.

2 In a medium bowl stir together milk, egg, applesauce, oil, granulated sugar, and brown sugar. Add liquid mixture to oat mixture, stirring until combined. Turn into the prepared soufflé dish or casserole.

3 Bake, uncovered, in the preheated oven for 20 minutes. Stir mixture. Gently fold in fruit. Bake, uncovered, about 20 minutes more or until top is lightly browned.

4 To serve, spoon into bowls. If desired, serve with yogurt, milk, or light cream. Makes 6 to 8 servings.

Nutrition Facts per serving: 431 cal., 15 g total fat (3 g sat. fat), 42 mg chol., 387 mg sodium, 66 g carbo., 7 g fiber, 12 g pro. **Daily Values:** 5% vit. A, 12% vit. C, 22% calcium, 12% iron.

Biscuits with Lingonberry Cream

These fancy, flaky biscuits are pretty enough to serve for holiday brunch and sweet enough to serve for afternoon tea.

Prep: 25 minutes **Bake:** 10 minutes

1½ cups all-purpose flour
⅓ cup packed brown sugar
¼ cup cornmeal
2 tsp. baking powder
1 tsp. baking soda
½ tsp. pumpkin pie spice
⅓ cup butter or margarine
⅓ cup chopped toasted pecans
⅓ cup quick-cooking or regular
  rolled oats
1 tsp. finely shredded orange peel
1 egg, slightly beaten
¾ cup buttermilk
¾ cup whipping cream
2 Tbsp. maple syrup
2 Tbsp. powdered sugar
  Dash pumpkin pie spice
1 14½-oz. jar lingonberries,
  drained
1 cup fresh or frozen raspberries,
  thawed
  Chopped toasted pecans
  (optional)

1 Preheat oven to 400°F. Grease a large baking sheet; set aside.

2 In a large mixing bowl stir together flour, brown sugar, cornmeal, baking powder, baking soda, and the ½ teaspoon pumpkin pie spice. Using a pastry blender cut in butter or margarine until mixture resembles coarse crumbs. Stir in the ⅓ cup chopped nuts, oats, and orange peel. Make a well in the center of the dry mixture; set aside.

3 In a medium bowl combine egg and buttermilk. Add egg mixture to the dry mixture all at once. Using a fork, stir just until moistened. Drop dough from a tablespoon into 12 mounds, 1½ inches apart, onto the prepared baking sheet.

4 Bake in the preheated oven for 10 to 12 minutes or until golden. Remove biscuits from baking sheet and cool slightly on a wire rack.

5 Meanwhile, in a medium chilled mixing bowl combine the whipping cream, maple syrup, powdered sugar, and a dash of pumpkin pie spice. Beat with the chilled beaters of an electric mixer on medium speed until soft peaks form (tips curl). Gently fold the drained lingonberries into the whipped cream mixture.

6 To serve, place a biscuit on each serving plate. Spoon some of the whipped cream mixture onto each biscuit. Top each with raspberries. Garnish with additional pecans, if desired. Makes 12 biscuits.

Nutrition Facts per biscuit: 312 cal., 14 g total fat (7 g sat. fat), 53 mg chol., 261 mg sodium, 44 g carbo., 3 g fiber, 4 g pro. **Daily Values:** 10% vit. A, 5% vit. C, 9% calcium, 7% iron.

Sour Cream Danish Dough

This flaky and rich dough is similar to croissant dough, but it's substantially quicker to make and requires less chilling time.

Prep: 25 minutes **Chill:** 1 hour

- 2 cups all-purpose flour
- ¼ tsp. salt
- 1 cup cold butter, cut up
- ½ cup dairy sour cream
- 1 to 2 Tbsp. cold water

1 In a medium mixing bowl stir together flour and salt. Using a pastry blender, cut cold butter into flour until mixture resembles coarse meal, leaving some pieces of butter the size of small peas.

2 In a small bowl stir together the sour cream and 1 tablespoon of the water. Add to the flour mixture and stir with a fork until the mixture starts to clump together. Add the remaining water, if necessary, to moisten. Form into a ball. Shape the dough into a rectangle. Place between two pieces of waxed paper or plastic wrap. Roll to an 18×9-inch rectangle.

3 Peel off top sheet of waxed paper or plastic wrap. Turn the dough onto a lightly floured surface and peel off remaining paper or wrap. Fold the dough crosswise into thirds, forming a 6×9-inch rectangle. Fold the dough in thirds again, forming a thick piece about 3×6 inches. Wrap the dough and chill it in the refrigerator for 1 to 24 hours or until firm. Let stand at room temperature until easily rolled. Use the dough as directed in Apricot-Almond Breakfast Pastries (see page 250) and Sunrise Apple Tartlets (see right).

To Make Ahead:
Prepare dough as directed, except wrap dough in heavy foil. Seal, label, and freeze for up to 3 months. Thaw the dough, covered, overnight in the refrigerator before using.

Sunrise Apple Tartlets

These pastries are likely to pop open a bit during baking, revealing the buttery apple filling.

Prep: 30 minutes plus dough
Bake: 25 minutes

- ½ recipe Sour Cream Danish Dough (see left)
- ⅓ cup sugar
- 1 tsp. cornstarch
- 3 large baking apples, peeled, cored, and sliced ⅛ inch thick (about 4 cups)
- 2 Tbsp. butter
- 1 Tbsp. lemon juice

1 Prepare and chill the Sour Cream Danish Dough as directed. Line a baking sheet with parchment paper or foil; set aside.

2 For filling, in a large skillet stir together sugar and cornstarch. Add apple slices, butter, and lemon juice. Cook over medium heat about 8 minutes or until apples are tender, stirring occasionally. Place in a bowl to cool completely.

3 Preheat oven to 400°F. On a lightly floured surface roll dough to a 12-inch square. Cut into four 6-inch squares. Place pastry squares on prepared baking sheet.

4 Divide apple mixture among the pastry squares, spooning about ½ cup in the center of each square. Fold corners up over the apple mixture to center of tarts (they should just meet).

5 Bake in the preheated oven about 25 minutes or until golden brown. Remove tartlets from baking sheet. Cool slightly on a wire rack. Serve warm. Makes 4 tartlets.

Nutrition Facts per tartlet: 518 cal., 32 g total fat (20 g sat. fat), 83 mg chol., 365 mg sodium, 57 g carbo., 3 g fiber, 4 g pro. Daily Values: 30% vit. A, 13% vit. C, 3% calcium, 10% iron.

EDITOR'S TIP

Onions, Apples, And Grapefruit May Fight Cancer

More than just a savory flavoring for recipes, onions contain helpful chemical compounds, flavonoids, which may help suppress the growth of cancer cells. Apples and white grapefruits also are rich in these substances. Research shows that eating these three foods may offer protection against lung cancer.

"People who had the highest intake (of the foods) had 40 to 50 percent less risk of lung cancer than people with the lowest intake," says Suzanne Murphy, Ph.D., a registered dietitian at the Cancer Research Center of Hawaii. Scientists there reached these conclusions after studying two groups of volunteers, one group with lung cancer and one without. Researchers saw protective benefits from a slice of onion or half an apple a day or half a grapefruit a week, according to Dr. Murphy.

Apricot-Almond Breakfast Pastries

Ease into the morning by preparing the dough and the almond filling a day ahead, and storing them in the refrigerator overnight.

Prep: 50 minutes plus dough
Bake: 25 minutes

- 1 recipe Sour Cream Danish Dough (see page 249)
- 1 cup sliced almonds
- 3 Tbsp. sugar
- 3 Tbsp. honey
- 1 egg
- 1 Tbsp. water
- 1 8-oz. pkg. cream cheese, softened
- ½ cup snipped dried apricots
- ½ cup apricot preserves
- 4 tsp. sugar
- ¼ cup sliced almonds

1 Prepare and chill the Sour Cream Danish Dough as directed.

2 For filling, in a food processor bowl combine the 1 cup sliced almonds, the 3 tablespoons sugar, and the honey. Cover and process until the almonds are ground and the mixture begins to form a ball. (If the mixture seems dry, add 1 teaspoon of water.) Divide into 8 equal portions; roll each portion on a lightly floured surface to a 3½-inch circle. Cover and set aside.

3 On a lightly floured surface roll dough to about ⅛ inch. Cut into eight 4½-inch circles. Cut the pastry scraps into ½-inch-wide strips. Beat egg and water using a fork; use to brush top edges of pastry circles. Arrange the pastry strips around the top edge of each pastry circle,

trimming as needed. Place pastry circles on an ungreased baking sheet. Place almond circle in center of each pastry circle.

4 Preheat oven to 375°F. Place the softened cream cheese in a small self-sealing plastic food storage bag. Snip off one corner of the bag and pipe cream cheese in dots over almond mixture. In a small bowl combine dried apricots and preserves. Spoon over the cream cheese. Brush the pastry-strip edges of the circles with egg mixture and lightly sprinkle with the 4 teaspoons sugar. Sprinkle the preserves with the ¼ cup almonds.

5 Bake in the preheated oven about 25 minutes or until golden. Remove from baking sheet; cool on a wire rack. Serve warm or at room temperature. Makes 8 pastries.

Nutrition Facts per pastry: 689 cal., 47 g total fat (24 g sat. fat), 126 mg chol., 406 mg sodium, 60 g carbo., 3 g fiber, 11 g pro. **Daily Values:** 43% vit. A, 1% vit. C, 9% calcium, 21% iron.

French Chocolate Coffee Cake

Everyone will come running when you pull this tempting cake from the oven. Delight in the tastes of this morning cake, from the chocolate-walnut streusel topping to the crowning buttery dough that's rolled around a luscious chocolate filling.

Prep: 25 minutes **Rise:** 2½ hours
Bake: 45 minutes **Cool:** 45 minutes

- 4 to 4½ cups all-purpose flour
- 2 pkg. active dry yeast
- ¾ cup sugar
- ⅔ cup water
- ½ cup butter, cut up
- 1 5-oz. can (⅔ cup) evaporated milk
- 4 egg yolks
- 1 cup semisweet chocolate pieces (6 oz.)
- 2 Tbsp. sugar
- ½ tsp. ground cinnamon
- ¼ cup all-purpose flour
- ¼ cup sugar
- 1 tsp. ground cinnamon
- ¼ cup butter
- ¼ cup chopped walnuts or pecans

1 In a large mixing bowl stir together 1½ cups of the flour and the yeast; set aside. In a medium saucepan heat and stir the ¾ cup sugar, the water, the ½ cup butter, ⅓ cup of the evaporated milk, and ½ teaspoon salt just until warm (120° to 130°F) and butter almost melts. Add milk mixture to flour mixture; add egg yolks. Beat with an electric mixer on low to medium speed for 30 seconds, constantly scraping the sides of the bowl. Beat on high speed for 3 minutes. Using a wooden spoon, stir in as much remaining flour as you can.

2 Turn dough out onto a lightly floured surface. Knead in enough of the remaining flour to make a moderately soft dough that is smooth and elastic (3 to 5 minutes total). Shape dough into a ball. Place in a lightly greased bowl, turning once to grease surface. Cover and let rise in a warm place until double (about 1½ hours). Punch down dough. Turn dough out onto a lightly floured surface. Cover; let rest for 10 minutes.

3 Meanwhile, in a small saucepan combine ¾ cup of the chocolate pieces, the remaining evaporated milk, the 2 tablespoons sugar, and the

½ teaspoon cinnamon. Cook and stir over low heat until chocolate is melted. Remove from heat; cool.

4 Grease a 10-inch tube pan; set aside. Roll dough into an 18×10-inch rectangle. Spread chocolate mixture to within 1 inch of the edges. Starting from a long side, roll up dough. Pinch seam to seal. Place, seam side down, in prepared pan. Pinch ends together.

5 In a small bowl combine the ¼ cup flour, the ¼ cup sugar, and the 1 teaspoon cinnamon. Using a pastry blender, cut in the ¼ cup butter until mixture resembles coarse crumbs. Stir in remaining chocolate pieces and the chopped nuts. Sprinkle over dough in pan. Cover; let rise in a warm place until nearly double (about 1 hour). Preheat oven to 350°F.

6 Bake in the preheated oven for 45 to 50 minutes or until coffee cake sounds hollow when lightly tapped. Cool in pan on a wire rack for 15 minutes. Remove from pan; cool on a wire rack for 30 to 45 minutes. Serve warm. Makes 12 to 16 servings.

Nutrition Facts per serving: 455 cal., 21 g total fat (11 g sat. fat), 108 mg chol., 240 mg sodium, 56 g carbo., 4 g fiber, 7 g pro. **Daily Values:** 15% vit. A, 1% vit. C, 6% calcium, 13% iron.

Vienna Brioche Loaf

Six eggs make this bread dough rich and similar to European-style sweet breads—while a spiral of caramel-nut filling makes the loaf delicious.

Prep: 45 minutes **Rise:** 3 hours
Chill: 6 hours to overnight
Bake: 35 minutes

1 pkg. active dry yeast
½ cup warm water (120° to 130°F)
1 cup butter, softened
4 cups granulated sugar
1 tsp. finely shredded lemon peel
1 tsp. salt
4¼ cups all-purpose flour
6 eggs
⅔ cup packed brown sugar
2 egg yolks, beaten
6 Tbsp. butter, melted
2 Tbsp. milk
¼ tsp. vanilla
2 cups chopped walnuts
Sifted powdered sugar (optional)

1 In a small bowl stir yeast into warm water; let stand for 5 to 10 minutes to soften. In a large mixing bowl beat the 1 cup butter, the granulated sugar, lemon peel, and salt with an electric mixer on medium to high speed until fluffy. Add 1 cup of the flour, the whole eggs, and softened yeast. Beat well. Stir in remaining flour. Place dough in a greased bowl; turn once to grease surface. Cover; let rise in a warm place until double (about 2 hours). Chill dough for 6 hours. (Or omit the 2-hour rise; chill dough overnight.)

2 Grease two 9×5×3-inch loaf pans; set aside. For filling, in a medium bowl combine brown sugar, egg yolks, and 3 tablespoons of the melted butter. Stir in the milk and vanilla; set aside.

3 Punch down dough. Divide dough in half. Return half of dough to refrigerator. Turn out other half onto a floured surface. Roll into a 14×9-inch rectangle. Brush with 1 tablespoon of the melted butter; spread with half of the filling. Sprinkle with half of the walnuts. Starting from each of the short sides, roll sides up

into a spiral to center. Seal each end of the loaf.

4 Repeat with remaining dough, 1 tablespoon of the melted butter, remaining filling, and remaining walnuts. Place loaves, rolled sides up, in prepared pans. Brush with the remaining melted butter. Cover and let rise in a warm place until double (about 1 hour). Preheat oven to 350°F.

5 Bake in the preheated oven about 35 minutes or until bread sounds hollow when lightly tapped. (If necessary to prevent overbrowning, cover with foil for the last 15 minutes of baking.) Cool in pans on wire racks for 10 minutes. Remove from pans. Serve warm, or cool on wire racks. If desired, sprinkle with powdered sugar. Makes 2 loaves (32 servings).

To Make Ahead:
Prepare dough as directed through Step 1, except omit the 2-hour rise and chill the dough overnight. Proceed as directed.

Nutrition Facts per serving: 223 cal., 14 g total fat (6 g sat. fat), 76 mg chol., 174 mg sodium, 20 g carbo., 1 g fiber, 4 g pro. **Daily Values:** 10% vit. A, 1% vit. C, 2% calcium, 7% iron.

HOLIDAY BRUNCH

- Eggs scrambled with diced ham and sliced green onions
- Assorted fresh fruits
- Vienna Brioche Loaf (see left)
- Coffee and fruit juice

Camembert Soufflé

Outstanding! You won't find a finer soufflé to serve for breakfast or as a side dish to roasted beef.

Prep: 35 minutes **Bake:** 40 minutes

- 5 egg yolks
- 7 egg whites
- ¼ cup chopped celery
- 2 Tbsp. thinly sliced green onion
- 1 small clove garlic, minced
- 3 Tbsp. butter or margarine
- 3 Tbsp. all-purpose flour
- 1 tsp. dry mustard
- ¼ tsp. salt
   Dash pepper
- 1 cup milk
- 5 oz. Camembert cheese, rind removed, and cut up (½ cup)
- ½ cup grated Parmesan cheese or Romano cheese (2 oz.)

1 Allow egg yolks and egg whites to stand at room temperature for 30 minutes. Meanwhile, in a medium saucepan cook celery, green onion, and garlic in butter or margarine about 5 minutes or until tender. Stir in flour, dry mustard, salt, and pepper. Stir in milk all at once. Cook and stir until thickened and bubbly. Reduce heat; add Camembert and Parmesan or Romano cheeses, a little at a time, stirring until melted. Remove from heat; set aside.

2 Preheat oven to 350°F. In a medium mixing bowl beat egg yolks with an electric mixer on high speed about 5 minutes or until thick and lemon color. Gradually beat in cheese mixture. Wash beaters with warm, soapy water; dry beaters.

3 In a large mixing bowl beat egg whites with the clean, dry beaters until stiff peaks form (tips stand straight). Gently fold 1 cup of the stiffly beaten egg whites into the egg yolk-cheese mixture. Gradually pour over remaining egg whites, folding to combine. Turn into an ungreased 2- to 2½-quart soufflé dish.

4 Bake in the preheated oven about 40 minutes or until a knife inserted near center comes out clean. Serve immediately. Makes 6 servings.

Nutrition Facts per serving: 269 cal., 20 g total fat (11 g sat. fat), 220 mg chol., 608 mg sodium, 6 g carbo., 0 g fiber, 17 g pro. **Daily Values:** 24% vit. A, 2% vit. C, 28% calcium, 5% iron.

PRIZE WINNER

Crab and Swiss Strata

Aubrey Corcoran
Beaufort, South Carolina
$400—Holiday Breakfasts

Prep: 25 minutes **Chill:** 8 hours
Bake: 50 minutes **Stand:** 10 minutes

- 6 English muffins, split
- 3 Tbsp. butter, softened
- 2 6½-oz. cans crabmeat, drained, flaked, and cartilage removed, or 12 oz. frozen cooked crabmeat, thawed
- ¾ cup shredded Swiss cheese (3 oz.)
- ¾ cup shredded cheddar cheese
- 2 Tbsp. capers, drained
- ½ cup finely chopped onion
- 1 Tbsp. butter
- ¼ cup dry sherry
- ½ tsp. Worcestershire sauce
- 6 eggs, beaten
- 1 cup milk
- 1 Tbsp. Dijon-style mustard
- 1 Tbsp. snipped fresh parsley
   Dash salt
   Dash pepper

1 Spread English muffin halves with the 3 tablespoons butter. Line a greased 2-quart rectangular baking dish with half the muffins, buttered side up. In a medium bowl combine crabmeat, Swiss cheese, and cheddar cheese. Layer crab mixture over muffins in dish; sprinkle with capers. Top with remaining muffins, buttered side up.

2 In a large skillet cook onion in the 1 tablespoon butter over medium heat about 5 minutes or until tender. Stir in sherry and Worcestershire sauce. Bring just to boiling; remove from heat.

3 In a medium mixing bowl combine eggs, milk, Dijon-style mustard, parsley, salt, and pepper. Stir in onion mixture. Carefully pour over layers in baking dish. Press muffins lightly with back of a large spoon to moisten muffins on top. Cover and chill in the refrigerator for 8 hours or overnight.

4 Preheat oven to 350°F. Bake, uncovered, about 50 minutes or until muffins are browned and a knife inserted near center comes out clean. Let stand for 10 minutes before serving. Makes 8 to 10 servings.

Nutrition Facts per serving: 361 cal., 18 g total fat (10 g sat. fat), 255 mg chol., 654 mg sodium, 24 g carbo., 2 g fiber, 22 g pro. **Daily Values:** 15% vit. A, 3% vit. C, 34% calcium, 10% iron.

Autumn Pork with Mushroom Sauce

Make this one for company—they'll be impressed by thyme-rubbed pork slices adorned with tender cooked apples and a creamy mushroom sauce.

Prep: 35 minutes **Roast:** 1½ hours

- 2 Tbsp. snipped fresh thyme or 2 tsp. dried thyme, crushed
- ½ tsp. salt
- ¼ tsp. pepper
- 1 3- to 4-lb. boneless pork loin roast (double loin, tied)
- ⅓ cup apple cider or apple juice
- 2 cups whipping cream
- 1 cup chicken broth
- ¼ cup dry sherry
- 2 Tbsp. margarine or butter
- 3 or 4 small cooking apples, peeled, cored, and cut into wedges
- 2 cups sliced fresh mushrooms

1 Preheat oven to 325°F. In a small bowl combine thyme, salt, and pepper. Rub pork roast with thyme mixture. Place roast on a rack in a shallow roasting pan. Insert a meat thermometer. Roast in the preheated oven for 1½ to 2½ hours or until the meat thermometer registers 160°F. Transfer meat to a platter; keep warm.

2 For sauce, skim fat from pan juices. Place roasting pan over medium heat; add apple cider or apple juice, stirring to scrape up any browned bits. Pour into a large saucepan. Stir in whipping cream, chicken broth, and dry sherry. Bring to boiling. Cook over medium-high heat about 20 minutes or until reduced to 1½ cups, stirring mixture occasionally.

3 Meanwhile, in a large skillet melt the margarine or butter. Add apple wedges; cook and stir until golden. Using a slotted spoon, remove apple wedges from skillet, reserving drippings; keep warm.

4 In the same skillet; add the mushrooms to reserved drippings and cook until tender. Stir mushrooms into thickened cream mixture.

5 To serve, place slices of pork roast and apples wedges on individual plates. Spoon sauce over meat. Makes 12 to 14 servings.

Nutrition Facts per serving: 330 cal., 21 g total fat (11 g sat. fat), 125 mg chol., 264 mg sodium, 6 g carbo., 0 fiber, 25 g pro. Daily Values: 14% vit. A, 5% vit. C, 5% calcium, 7% iron.

Potato-Topped Meatball Casserole

For an easy shortcut, substitute 20 purchased, frozen cooked Italian meatballs, thawed, for the homemade meatballs called for in this recipe.

Prep: 45 minutes **Bake:** 60 minutes
Stand: 10 minutes

- 1 egg, beaten
- ½ cup fine dry bread crumbs
- ½ cup finely chopped onion
- 1 Tbsp. snipped fresh oregano or 1 tsp. dried oregano, crushed
- 2 cloves garlic, minced
- ½ tsp. salt
- ½ tsp. black pepper
- 1 lb. lean ground lamb or beef
- 4 medium russet potatoes, peeled and quartered (about 1½ lb.)
- 2 Tbsp. margarine or butter
- ½ cup grated Parmesan cheese
- ½ cup dairy sour cream
- 2 cloves garlic, minced
- ¼ tsp. salt
- 3 cups torn fresh spinach
- 1 cup crumbled feta cheese (4 oz.)
- ½ cup bottled roasted red sweet peppers, drained and chopped

1 Preheat oven to 350°F. For meatballs, in a large mixing bowl combine the egg, bread crumbs, onion, oregano, the 2 cloves garlic, the ½ teaspoon salt, and black pepper. Add ground lamb or beef; mix well. Shape into twenty 1½-inch meatballs. Arrange meatballs in a single layer in a shallow baking pan. Bake in the preheated oven about 25 minutes or until done (160°F on an instant-read thermometer). Place meatballs in the bottom of a 2-quart square baking dish; set aside.

2 Meanwhile, cook potatoes, covered, in a small amount of boiling lightly salted water for 20 to 25 minutes or until tender; drain. Using a potato masher or an electric mixer on low speed, mash the potatoes. Add the 2 tablespoons margarine or butter and mash until melted. Stir in Parmesan cheese, sour cream, the 2 cloves garlic, and the ¼ teaspoon salt.

3 Stir spinach, feta cheese, and roasted red peppers into mashed potato mixture. Spoon atop meatballs, spreading evenly. Bake, uncovered, in the preheated oven for 35 to 40 minutes or until heated through. Let stand for 10 minutes before serving. Makes 8 to 10 servings.

Nutrition Facts per serving: 363 cal., 23 g total fat (11 g sat. fat), 92 mg chol., 764 mg sodium, 21 g carbo., 2 g fiber, 18 g pro. Daily Values: 23% vit. A, 58% vit. C, 24% calcium, 12% iron.

- Salad of mixed greens tossed in balsamic vinaigrette and topped with candied nuts, dried cranberries, and crumbled blue cheese

- Sausage-and-Apple-Stuffed Pork Chops (see right)

- Mashed sweet potatoes drizzled with butter

- Steamed broccoli

- Whole wheat or multigrain bread or rolls

---

30 MINUTE

Gemelli with Sausage and Beans

When the holidays get hectic, turn to this easy recipe for dinner. With pasta, vegetables, and meat all in one dish, all you need to add is a salad and a loaf of crusty bread.

Start to finish: 30 minutes

- ¼ cup snipped dried tomatoes (not oil-pack)
- ½ cup boiling water
- ⅔ cup purchased pesto
- 8 oz. packaged dried gemelli, farfalle, or rotini pasta
- 8 oz. fresh green beans, trimmed and cut into 2-inch pieces
- 8 oz. fresh sweet Italian sausage links, sliced diagonally into ¾-inch pieces
- 2 oz. shaved Parmesan or Romano cheese

1 Place snipped dried tomatoes in a bowl. Pour boiling water over tomatoes. Cover and let stand for 5 minutes. Drain tomatoes. Stir the drained tomatoes into pesto; set aside.

2 In a 4-quart Dutch oven cook the pasta according to package directions. Add the green beans the last 8 minutes of cooking time. Drain; return to pan. Cover to keep warm.

3 Meanwhile, in a large skillet cook sausage over medium heat about 10 minutes or until juices run clear, stirring frequently. Using a slotted spoon, remove sausage from skillet and add to the pasta mixture. Stir in pesto mixture. Cook and stir over medium heat about 2 minutes or until heated through.

4 To serve, transfer pasta to a serving platter. Top with shaved cheese. Serve immediately. Makes 4 or 5 servings.

Nutrition Facts per serving: 753 cal., 45 g total fat (8 g sat. fat), 55 mg chol., 957 mg sodium, 57 g carbo., 4 g fiber, 28 g pro. **Daily Values:** 9% vit. A, 15% vit. C, 24% calcium, 17% iron.

Sausage-and-Apple-Stuffed Pork Chops

A shiny apple jelly glaze coats the outside of these super-thick chops, while hints of sweet apple flavor the corn bread stuffing inside.

Prep: 25 minutes   **Bake:** 40 minutes

- 4 pork loin rib chops, cut 1¼ inches thick (about 2 lb. total)
- 8 oz. bulk pork sausage
- 1 cup chopped onions
- 1 cup corn-bread stuffing mix
- ⅔ cup shredded apple
- 2 tsp. snipped fresh thyme or ½ tsp. dried thyme, crushed
- ¼ tsp. pepper
- ⅓ cup apple cider or apple juice
- ⅓ cup apple jelly
- 1 Tbsp. lemon juice
 Apple wedges (optional)

1 Preheat oven to 375°F. Trim fat from chops. Cut a pocket in each chop by cutting a slit the length of the fat side almost to the bone. Set aside the pork.

2 For stuffing, in a large skillet cook sausage and onions until sausage is brown and onion is tender; drain well. Stir in stuffing mix, shredded apple, thyme, and pepper. Drizzle with 2 tablespoons of the apple cider to moisten, tossing lightly.

3 Spoon about 2 tablespoons of the stuffing into each pork chop pocket. Secure pockets with wooden toothpicks. Stir remaining apple cider into remaining stuffing.

4 Place stuffed pork chops on a rack in a shallow roasting pan. Place remaining stuffing in a greased 1-quart oven-safe casserole. Cover stuffing and refrigerate until ready to bake.

5 For glaze, in a small saucepan combine apple jelly and lemon juice. Cook and stir until jelly melts; brush chops with some of the glaze.

6 Bake chops, uncovered, in the preheated oven for 20 minutes. Brush again with glaze. Place covered casserole of stuffing in oven beside pork chops. Bake about 20 minutes more or until no pink remains in chops and stuffing is heated through. If desired, garnish with apple wedges. Makes 4 servings.

Nutrition Facts per serving: 558 cal., 24 g total fat (9 g sat. fat), 102 mg chol., 499 mg sodium, 40 g carbo., 2 fiber, 37 g pro. **Daily Values:** 1% vit. A, 12% vit. C, 6% calcium, 13% iron.

Southwestern Breakfast Bake

This puffy egg-topped dish is delicious served as a light dinner as well as breakfast. For a complete meal, serve with a mixed green salad topped with tomato wedges, chopped avocado, and sliced onions.

Prep: 20 minutes **Bake:** 45 minutes
Stand: 15 minutes

- 1   **15-oz. can black beans, rinsed and drained**
- ¾ **cup canned enchilada sauce**
- 2   **4-oz. cans diced green chile peppers**
- ½ **cup thinly sliced green onions**
- 2   **cloves garlic, minced**
      Several dashes bottled hot pepper sauce (optional)
- 1   **cup shredded sharp cheddar cheese and/or shredded Monterey Jack cheese with jalapeño peppers (4 oz.)**
- 3   **egg whites**
- 3   **egg yolks**
- 2   **Tbsp. all-purpose flour**
- ¼ **tsp. salt**
- ½ **cup milk**
- 1   **Tbsp. snipped fresh cilantro**
      Dairy sour cream (optional)
      Salsa (optional)
      Additional snipped fresh cilantro (optional)

1 Preheat oven to 325°F. In a greased 2-quart square baking dish combine the black beans, enchilada sauce, green chile peppers, green onions, garlic, and, if desired, hot pepper sauce. Sprinkle with the sharp cheddar cheese and/or the Monterey Jack cheese.

2 In a medium mixing bowl beat egg whites with an electric mixer on medium speed until soft peaks form (tips curl); set aside. In a large mixing bowl combine egg yolks, flour, and salt. Using a wire whisk, beat mixture until combined (mixture will be stiff). Gradually whisk in milk until smooth. Fold egg whites and the 1 tablespoon snipped cilantro into the yolk mixture. Carefully pour the egg mixture over the bean mixture in the baking dish.

3 Bake in the preheated oven about 45 minutes or until egg mixture appears set when gently shaken. Let stand for 15 minutes before serving. If desired, serve with sour cream, salsa, and additional snipped fresh cilantro. Makes 8 servings.

Nutrition Facts per serving: 163 cal., 8 g total fat (4 g sat. fat), 96 mg chol., 488 mg sodium, 15 g carbo., 4 g fiber, 11 g pro. **Daily Values:** 37% vit. A, 18% vit. C, 20% calcium, 11% iron.

Mediterranean Vegetable Strata

Hot, spicy flavor comes from the tomatoes with green chiles and the Monterey Jack cheese with jalapeño peppers. For a milder version, use plain Monterey Jack cheese.

Prep: 30 minutes **Chill:** 4 hours
Bake: 50 minutes **Stand:** 10 minutes

- 2   **cups sliced fresh mushrooms**
- 1   **cup chopped onions**
- 2   **Tbsp. margarine or butter**
- 1   **10-oz. pkg. frozen chopped spinach, thawed and well drained**
- 1   **2½-oz. can pitted ripe olives, drained and sliced**
- 1   **10-oz. can diced tomatoes with green chiles, drained**
- 1   **clove garlic, minced**
      Nonstick cooking spray
- 5   **cups seasoned croutons**
- 2   **cups shredded Monterey Jack cheese with jalapeño peppers (8 oz.)**
- ½ **cup grated Parmesan cheese**
- ½ **cup crumbed feta cheese (2 oz.)**
- 6   **eggs**
- 2½ **cups milk**
      Sliced green onion (optional)
      Snipped fresh cilantro (optional)

1 In a large skillet cook mushrooms and onions in hot margarine or butter until onion is tender. Stir in the drained spinach, drained olives, drained tomatoes with chiles, and the garlic.

2 Lightly coat a 3-quart rectangular baking dish with cooking spray. Layer half of the croutons and half of the spinach mixture in the baking dish. In a bowl combine Monterey Jack cheese, Parmesan cheese, and feta cheese. Sprinkle half of the cheese mixture over the layers in the baking dish. Repeat layers. In a large bowl combine eggs and milk; slowly pour over the mixture in the dish. Press lightly with the back of a large spoon to moisten the croutons. Cover and chill for 4 to 24 hours.

3 Preheat oven to 350°F. Bake the casserole, covered, for 25 minutes. Uncover and continue baking for 25 to 30 minutes or until a knife inserted off center comes out clean. Let stand for 10 minutes before serving. Top with sliced green onions and snipped fresh cilantro, if desired. Makes 12 servings.

Nutrition Facts per serving: 285 cal., 17 g total fat (8 g sat. fat), 135 mg chol., 683 mg sodium, 18 g carbo., 2 g fiber, 15 g pro. **Daily Values:** 51% vit. A, 10% vit. C, 36% calcium, 10% iron.

Beef Potpie with Cornmeal Crust

The crust contains finely shredded cheddar cheese for extra flavor.

Prep: 40 minutes **Cook:** 1 hour
Bake: 20 minutes **Stand:** 5 minutes

- 1 lb. boneless beef chuck, cut into ¼-inch pieces
- 1 Tbsp. cooking oil
- 1⅓ cups chopped green sweet pepper
- ½ cup chopped onion
- 1 14½-oz. can diced tomatoes, undrained
- 1 8¾-oz. can whole kernel corn, drained
- ⅔ cup water
- ¼ cup tomato paste
- 1 or 2 fresh jalapeño peppers, seeded and chopped*
- 1 Tbsp. chili powder
- 1 tsp. sugar
- ¼ tsp. salt
- 1 recipe Cornmeal Crust (see right)
- ½ cup shredded cheddar cheese (2 oz.) (optional)

1 In a large saucepan brown the beef, half at a time, in hot oil. Using a slotted spoon, remove beef. Cook sweet pepper and onion in drippings until tender. Add beef, undrained tomatoes, corn, water, tomato paste, jalapeño peppers, chili powder, sugar, and salt. Bring to boiling; reduce heat. Cover and simmer about 1 hour or until meat is tender, stirring twice.

2 Meanwhile, preheat oven to 425°F. Prepare Cornmeal Crust. On a lightly floured surface, roll dough for crust into a 12×8-inch rectangle. Spoon beef mixture into a 2-quart rectangular baking dish. Carefully top with the crust, fluting extra crust against the sides of the dish. Cut slits in the top of the crust for steam to escape.

3 Bake, uncovered, in the preheated oven about 20 minutes or until crust is golden brown. If desired, sprinkle with cheddar cheese; let stand for 5 minutes. Makes 6 servings.

Cornmeal Crust

In a medium bowl combine 1 cup all-purpose flour, ½ cup yellow cornmeal, and ½ teaspoon salt. Using a pastry blender or two knives, cut in ½ cup butter and ¼ cup finely shredded cheddar cheese until mixture resembles coarse crumbs. Sprinkle with ¼ cup cold water, 1 tablespoon at a time, tossing gently until the dough is moistened. Form into a ball.

*Note: Hot peppers contain oils that may burn eyes, lips, and sensitive skin. Wear gloves while preparing peppers and wash your hands thoroughly afterward.

Nutrition Facts per serving: 528 cal., 33 g total fat (16 g sat. fat), 98 mg chol., 747 mg sodium, 39 g carbo., 5 g fiber, 21 g pro. **Daily Values:** 31% vit. A, 80% vit. C, 7% calcium, 22% iron.

Tortellini Salad with Greens

Apricot nectar provides fruit flavor to the dressing and complements this deli-style salad.

Prep: 30 minutes **Chill:** up to 4 hours

- 1 9-oz. pkg. refrigerated cheese tortellini
- ¼ cup apricot nectar
- ¼ cup rice vinegar
- 2 Tbsp. salad oil
- 1 tsp. toasted sesame oil
- 2 cloves garlic, minced
- ⅛ to ¼ tsp. crushed red pepper or ⅛ tsp. ground red pepper
- 1 cup cherry or grape tomatoes, halved
- ⅓ cup dried light figs (Calimyrna), cut into strips, or golden raisins
- 1 10-oz. pkg. baby spinach or romaine blend torn mixed salad greens
- ⅓ cup coarsely chopped hazelnuts (filberts) or pecans, toasted

1 Cook pasta according to package directions; drain. Rinse in cool water and drain again.

2 Meanwhile, for dressing, in a screw-top jar combine apricot nectar, rice vinegar, salad oil, toasted sesame oil, garlic, and red pepper. Cover and shake well.

3 In a very large bowl combine the cooked pasta, tomatoes, and dried figs or raisins. Add dressing, tossing gently to coat. Cover and chill for up to 4 hours.

4 Just before serving, toss spinach or romaine and toasted nuts into the pasta mixture. Makes 4 to 6 main-dish servings.

Nutrition Facts per serving: 421 cal., 20 g total fat (4 g sat. fat), 34 mg chol., 312 mg sodium, 50 g carbo., 8 g fiber, 15 g pro. **Daily Values:** 106% vit. A, 50% vit. C, 23% calcium, 26% iron.

TEST KITCHEN TIP

Basic Turkey Roasting

1. Buy

To ensure that you have plenty of meat, buy 1 to 1½ pounds of turkey per person. Although it may seem like too much, about half of the weight is lost in cooking and carving.

To buy a fresh turkey, check the "sell-by" date. An unopened turkey will taste best and be safe to use for 1 or 2 days after the date on the wrapper. For frozen turkeys, look for clean, undamaged, and frost-free packaging.

2. Thaw

Plan to thaw a frozen turkey according to the weight and number of days until it is prepared. Place a wrapped frozen turkey on a tray or pan in the refrigerator for 3 to 5 days. Allow one day thawing for every 5 pounds, not counting the day it is roasted. For example, a 15-pound turkey should start thawing on Sunday to be ready for Thursday Thanksgiving dinner. Thawed turkeys will keep for 1 or 2 days in the refrigerator. When the giblets and neck can easily be removed and there are no ice crystals in the body cavity, the turkey has thawed adequately.

Remove the giblets and neck (wrapped in plastic or paper). Turkey drumsticks usually are held in place by a band of skin or a metal or plastic clamp. Unhook the legs. Rinse the skin and inside the turkey cavities, and pat the skin with several sheets of paper towels. If you plan to make stuffing, do it at this stage.

If the turkey has not completely thawed, place it in a clean sink full of cold water. Change the water every 30 minutes. Do not thaw turkeys on a kitchen counter, in a microwave oven, or in warm water. In those environments, bacteria can grow to dangerous levels.

3. Stuff

Allowing ¾ cup per pound of turkey, measure the stuffing that will go into the turkey (11 cups for 15 pounds). Spoon some stuffing loosely into the neck cavity, pull the neck skin over the stuffing, and fasten the skin to the back of the turkey with a short skewer.

Loosely spoon stuffing into the body cavity; don't pack it in or it may not fully cook by the time the turkey is done. Spoon the remaining stuffing into a baking dish. Cover and chill the dressing until about 1 hour before the turkey is done, then bake it in the oven.

Use an accurate meat thermometer when cooking turkey, especially when it is stuffed. If you do not have an accurate meat thermometer, cook the stuffing in a covered dish rather than in the turkey.

As an alternative to stuffing the turkey and to provide flavor to the drippings for making gravy, place quartered onions and celery in the body cavity. Pull the neck skin to the back as for stuffing.

Tuck the drumsticks under the band of skin that crosses the tail or tie the drumsticks together with thick cotton kitchen twine. Twist the wing tips under the back to provide a stable resting base while the turkey roasts.

4. Roast and serve

Place the oven rack in the lowest position. Preheat the oven to 325°F. Place the turkey, breast side up, on a rack in a shallow pan, such as the foil pans sold at supermarkets (the sides should be no deeper than 2 inches). Brush the turkey with cooking oil to enhance browning. Insert a meat thermometer into the center of an inside thigh muscle without touching bone. Loosely cover the turkey with foil, pressing it over the drumsticks and neck. Roast the turkey following the table, below, as a guide. Because most turkeys are self-basting, it is not necessary to baste as it roasts.

When the turkey has been in the oven for two-thirds of the roasting time, cut the skin or string holding the drumsticks. Remove the foil during the last 30 to 45 minutes to brown the skin. Test for doneness by inserting a meat thermometer deep into the thigh; the temperature should register 180°F. The stuffing should register at least 165°F.

When the turkey is done, the drumsticks will easily move in the sockets and the thickest parts will feel soft when pressed. Juices from the thigh should run clear when pierced deeply with a long-tined fork. Remove the turkey from the oven; loosely cover it with foil and let stand for 20 minutes. Remove stuffing before carving.

Turkey can remain at room temperature for up to 2 hours after being taken from the oven. After that, it must be refrigerated. Separately cover and refrigerate cooked turkey and stuffing for up to 2 days.

Turkey questions?

Get answers to turkey roasting questions, a holiday planner, and recipes. Visit our Internet site at www.bhg.com/extra or AOL keyword "Food." Or call the following hot lines during the holidays: Meat and Poultry Hot Line, 800/535-4555 (in Washington, D.C., 202/720-3333)—on Thanksgiving day, food safety experts will answer questions from 8 a.m. to 2 p.m. EST; Butterball Turkey-Talk Line, 800/288-8372; and the Reynolds Turkey Tips Line, 800/745-4000.

Stuffed Whole Turkey

Ready-to-Cook Turkey Weight	Oven Roasting Temp.	Time
8 to 12 lbs.	325°	3 to 3¾ hours
12 to 14 lbs.	325°	3¼ to 4½ hours
14 to 18 lbs.	325°	4 to 5 hours
18 to 20 lbs.	325°	4½ to 5¼ hours
20 to 24 lbs.	325°	4¾ to 5¾ hours

For unstuffed turkeys, reduce the cooking time by 15 to 45 minutes. The turkey is done when a meat thermometer inserted into the thigh registers 180°F. The stuffing is done when the thermometer registers 165°F.

Mixed Bean and Jicama Salad

Prep: 20 minutes **Chill:** 4 hours

- 1 15-oz. can black beans, rinsed and drained
- 1 15-oz. can garbanzo beans, rinsed and drained
- 1 15-oz. can hominy, rinsed and drained
- 1 cup peeled jicama, cut into thin strips (about 6 oz.)
- 1 small red onion, halved and thinly sliced (⅓ cup)
- ¼ cup white balsamic vinegar
- 3 Tbsp. olive oil
- 4 cloves garlic, minced
- 1 to 2 fresh serrano pepper(s), seeded and finely chopped*
- 1 tsp. finely shredded lemon peel
- 1 tsp. honey

1 In a large mixing bowl combine the black beans, garbanzo beans, hominy, jicama, and red onion. In a small mixing bowl stir together the balsamic vinegar, olive oil, garlic, serrano pepper, lemon peel, and honey. Pour over bean mixture, tossing gently to coat. Cover and chill bean mixture for 4 to 24 hours.

2 Stir salad before serving. Serve with a slotted spoon. Makes 10 servings.

*Note: Hot peppers contain oils that may burn eyes, lips, and sensitive skin. Wear gloves while preparing them and thoroughly wash your hands afterward.

Nutrition Facts per serving: 159 cal., 5 g total fat (1 g sat. fat), 0 mg chol., 322 mg sodium, 25 g carbo., 6 g fiber, 6 g pro. **Daily Values:** 9% vit. C, 4% calcium, 8% iron.

Fruit and Broccoli Salad

Rosemarie Adair
Tallahassee, Florida
$200—Surefire Potluck Dishes

Start to finish: 20 minutes

- 1 16-oz. pkg. shredded broccoli (broccoli slaw mix)
- 2 cups seedless red and/or green grapes, halved
- 2 medium apples, cored and chopped
- ⅔ cup bottled citrus salad dressing (such as tangerine vinaigrette)
- 1 cup coarsely chopped pecans or walnuts, toasted if desired*

1 In a very large bowl combine shredded broccoli, grapes, and apples. Up to 1 hour before serving, pour salad dressing over broccoli mixture, tossing to coat. Cover and chill. Transfer to a serving bowl. Sprinkle with nuts; toss again. Makes 12 to 16 servings.

*Note: To toast nuts, preheat oven to 350°F. Spread nuts in a single layer in a shallow baking pan. Bake for 5 to 10 minutes or until light golden brown, stirring once or twice.

Nutrition Facts per serving: 219 cal., 15 g total fat (2 g sat. fat), 6 mg chol., 131 mg sodium, 21 g carbo., 2 g fiber, 3 g pro. **Daily Values:** 8% vit. A, 32% vit. C, 3% calcium, 5% iron.

Orange-Fennel Autumn Salad

Save some of the feathery fronds from the fennel stalk to garnish the salad dressing. (See the photograph on page 278.)

Start to finish: 30 minutes

- 4 oz. fresh baby spinach, washed and stems removed (about 3 cups lightly packed)
- 3 cups torn radicchio
- 1 medium fennel bulb, cored and thinly sliced (about 2½ cups)
- 3 seedless oranges or clementines, peeled and thinly sliced
- 1 recipe Citrusy-Yogurt Dressing (see below)

1 In a straight-side large glass compote or trifle bowl arrange the spinach, radicchio, fennel, and oranges. Serve the salad with Citrusy-Yogurt Dressing. Makes 8 servings.

Citrusy-Yogurt Dressing

In a small bowl stir together ⅓ cup mayonnaise, light mayonnaise, or salad dressing; ⅓ cup yogurt; 2 tablespoons thawed frozen orange juice concentrate; and 1 tablespoon Pernod or thawed frozen orange juice concentrate. Spoon dressing into a small bowl; garnish with fennel leaves, if desired.

Nutrition Facts per serving: 109 cal., 8 g total fat (1 g sat. fat), 4 mg chol., 91 mg sodium, 8 g carbo., 9 g fiber, 2 g pro. **Daily Values:** 16% vit. A, 43% vit. C, 6% calcium, 5% iron.

Marinated Baby Beets

Prep: 20 minutes **Roast:** 40 minutes
Marinate: 30 minutes

- 2 lb. trimmed red and/or yellow baby beets or small beets (about 3½ lb. untrimmed with tops)
- 2 Tbsp. olive oil
- ¼ tsp. salt
- ¼ tsp. freshly ground pepper
- 1 large orange
- 3 Tbsp. white wine vinegar
- 2 Tbsp. thinly sliced shallots
- 2 tsp. Dijon-style mustard

1 Preheat oven to 425°F. If using small beets, cut into 1- to 1½-inch wedges. Place beets in a single layer in a shallow baking pan. Drizzle with 1 tablespoon of the olive oil; toss to coat. Season with salt and pepper; toss again. Cover with foil and roast for 25 minutes. Uncover and roast about 15 minutes more or until fork-tender. Cool; peel the small beets, if using. (Baby beets do not need to be peeled.)

2 Meanwhile, using a small knife or citrus tool, shred 2 tablespoons peel from the orange without removing pith. Squeeze juice from the orange to measure ⅓ cup juice.

3 In a serving dish, whisk together the orange juice, remaining oil, vinegar, shallots, and mustard. Add beets and orange peel; toss to mix. Let stand at room temperature for 30 minutes or chill for up to 8 hours before serving. Makes 8 servings.

Nutrition Facts per serving: 90 cal., 4 g total fat (0 g sat. fat), 0 mg chol., 169 mg sodium, 13 g carbo., 3 g fiber, 2 g pro. **Daily Values:** 2% vit. A, 22% vit. C, 3% calcium, 6% iron.

Green Beans with Vermouth Butter

Prep: 20 minutes **Chill:** 1 hour
Cook: 10 minutes

- 2 Tbsp. finely chopped shallots
- 2 tsp. olive oil
- ½ cup butter, softened
- 2 Tbsp. dry vermouth
- 1 lb. green beans

1 For vermouth butter, cook shallots in olive oil over medium-low heat for 10 to 12 minutes or until shallots are golden. Remove from heat; cool. Combine cooled shallot mixture with softened butter; stir in vermouth, 1 tablespoon at a time.

2 Transfer butter mixture onto a piece of plastic wrap. Shape into a 6-inch log by rolling the plastic wrap around the butter and rolling the wrapped butter back and forth between your hands. Tightly twist the ends of the wrap. Chill in the refrigerator at least 1 hour or freeze until ready to use.

3 Wash beans; remove ends and strings, if necessary. Leave whole or cut into 1-inch pieces. Cook, covered, in a small amount of boiling, salted water for 10 to 15 minutes or until crisp-tender; drain.

4 To serve, transfer the hot beans to a serving bowl. Top with 3 tablespoons of the vermouth butter. Makes 6 side-dish servings.

To Make Ahead:
Prepare butter as directed. Wrap butter tightly in plastic wrap, then wrap in aluminum foil. Store in the refrigerator for up to 1 week or in the freezer for up to 1 month. Proceed as directed in Step 3.

EDITOR'S TIP

Simple Compound Butter for Flavor

Compound butter is a fancy name for butter that has ingredients that flavor it. This simple fix-up can make ordinary foods extraordinary. As a pat of compound butter melts over hot vegetables, grilled meats, poultry, or seafood, it transforms into a delicious sauce. Compound butters also complement freshly baked breads.

If you haven't tasted a compound butter, try the vermouth, whiskey, or jalapeño-lime butters, below. Or experiment with hot peppers, pepper jelly, edible flowers, coarse ground black pepper, citrus peel, liqueurs, onions, garlic, shallots, spices, cheeses, toasted nuts, and snipped fresh herbs.

Nutrition Facts per serving: 78 cal., 6 g total fat (3 g sat. fat), 15 mg chol., 60 mg sodium, 6 g carbo., 3 g fiber, 1 g pro. **Daily Values:** 10% vit. A, 16% vit. C, 3% calcium, 4% iron.

Whiskey Butter

In a medium bowl combine ½ cup softened butter with 1 tablespoon dark brown sugar and 1 tablespoon bourbon whiskey. Mold and store butter as directed in Step 2 at left.

Jalapeño-Lime Butter

In a medium bowl combine ½ cup softened butter with 2 teaspoons seeded and finely chopped fresh jalapeño pepper,* 2 teaspoons finely shredded lime peel, and 1 clove garlic, minced. Mold and store butter as directed in Step 2 at left.

*Note: Hot peppers contain oils that may burn eyes, lips, and sensitive skin. Wear gloves while preparing them and thoroughly wash your hands afterward.

Sautéed Brussels Sprouts

Most of the cooking liquid evaporates, leaving a light glaze on the sprouts.

Prep: 15 minutes **Cook:** 18 minutes

- 1 lb. Brussels sprouts
- 3 Tbsp. butter or margarine
- ¼ cup finely chopped shallots
- 2 cloves garlic, minced
- 1¼ cups chicken broth
- ½ cup walnut pieces, toasted
- ¼ tsp. freshly ground pepper

1 Trim stems, remove wilted outer leaves, and wash the Brussels sprouts. Cut large sprouts in half.

2 In a large skillet melt butter or margarine. Cook shallots and garlic in melted butter or margarine over medium heat for 4 to 5 minutes or until tender and golden. Add Brussels sprouts; cook for 2 minutes more. Carefully stir in chicken broth. Bring to boiling; reduce heat. Simmer, uncovered, for 12 to 14 minutes or until liquid is almost evaporated and sprouts are crisp-tender. Transfer to a serving dish; sprinkle with walnuts and pepper. Makes 4 servings.

Nutrition Facts per serving: 248 cal., 19 g total fat (7 g sat. fat), 25 mg chol., 367 mg sodium, 15 g carbo., 5 g fiber, 8 g pro. **Daily Values:** 19% vit. A, 140% vit. C, 7% calcium, 13% iron.

Cauliflower Cheese Bake

Get a head start on the day's cooking by microwaving and slicing the cauliflower early in the day. Store it, covered, in the refrigerator. (See the photograph on page 279.)

Prep: 25 minutes **Bake:** 10 minutes

- 1 medium head cauliflower (about 2 lb.)
- ½ cup regular mayonnaise, light mayonnaise dressing, or salad dressing
- 1 Tbsp. country-style Dijon-style mustard
- 1 Tbsp. milk
- ¼ tsp. coarsely ground black pepper
- 1 cup dry firm-textured white bread or sourdough bread cubes*
- 1 Tbsp. butter or margarine, melted
- 1 cup shredded smoked Gruyère or cheddar cheese (4 oz.)

1 Preheat oven to 400°F. Remove leaves from cauliflower; trim core even with floret stems so the head will stand evenly. Place cauliflower in a 9-inch glass pie plate or a 2-quart microwave-safe baking dish. Add ½ cup water. Cover with vented plastic wrap. Microwave on high power (100%) for 7 to 10 minutes or until just tender, turning dish after 4 minutes. Transfer cauliflower to a cutting board; cool slightly.

2 Using a long, thin-blade knife, cut the cauliflower head into 1-inch slices. Arrange slices and any florets in a 1½-quart au gratin dish or a 10-inch quiche dish. For sauce, in a small bowl stir together mayonnaise or salad dressing, Dijon-style mustard, milk, and pepper. Spoon sauce over cauliflower.

3 For topping, toss together bread cubes and melted butter or margarine; sprinkle over cauliflower and sauce. Top with cheese.

4 Bake, uncovered, in the preheated oven about 10 minutes or until heated through and topping is golden brown. Makes 6 servings.

*Note: To dry bread cubes, spread cubes in a shallow baking pan. Bake, uncovered, in a 350°F oven about 10 minutes or until dry, stirring once.

To Make Ahead:

Prepare and microwave cauliflower as directed. Cover and chill for up to 24 hours. Prepare sauce; cover and chill. To serve, bake cauliflower, covered, in a 400°F oven for 20 minutes. Top with sauce, topping, and cheese. Bake about 10 minutes more or until heated through and topping is golden brown.

Nutrition Facts per serving: 271 cal., 23 g total fat (7 g sat. fat), 37 mg chol., 329 mg sodium, 8 g carbo., 4 g fiber, 9 g pro. **Daily Values:** 8% vit. A, 141% vit. C, 23% calcium, 5% iron.

Parsnip Potato Mash

The slightly sweet parsnip flavor balances the earthiness of the russet potatoes. (See the photograph on page 279.)

Prep: 20 minutes   **Cook:** 20 minutes

- 1½ lb. russet potatoes
       (4 to 5 medium)
- 8 oz. parsnips
- 4 Tbsp. butter or margarine,
       softened
- ¼ tsp. salt
- ⅛ tsp. pepper
- ¾ to 1 cup buttermilk,
       warmed slightly
- ¼ cup coarsely chopped
       flat-leaf parsley

1 Peel and quarter the potatoes. Peel and cut the parsnips into large chunks. Cook potatoes and parsnips in a small amount of boiling lightly salted water for 20 to 25 minutes or until tender; drain.

2 Mash potatoes and parsnips with a potato masher or beat with an electric mixer on low speed. Add butter or margarine, salt, and pepper. Gradually beat in enough buttermilk to make a light and fluffy consistency. Spoon into a serving bowl. Sprinkle with parsley. Makes 8 servings.

Nutrition Facts per serving: 149 cal., 7 g total fat (4 g sat. fat), 17 mg chol., 165 mg sodium, 20 g carbo., 3 g fiber, 3 g pro. Daily Values: 7% vit. A, 30% vit. C, 5% calcium, 5% iron.

Holiday Scalloped Potatoes

Choose red, Yukon Gold, or sweet potatoes to layer any way you choose, maintaining a total of 2¼ pounds of potatoes. (See the photograph on page 282.)

Prep: 40 minutes   **Bake:** 70 minutes

- 1½ lb. round red potatoes or Yukon
       Gold potatoes
- ¾ lb. sweet potatoes
- ½ cup chopped onion
- ¼ cup butter or margarine
- 3 Tbsp. all-purpose flour
- 2¼ cups milk
- ½ cup grated Parmesan cheese
- 1 Tbsp. snipped fresh tarragon
       or ½ tsp. dried tarragon,
       crushed
     Fresh tarragon (optional)

1 Preheat oven to 350°F. Thinly slice the red or Yukon Gold potatoes (do not peel). Peel and thinly slice the sweet potatoes.

2 In a medium saucepan cook onion in butter or margarine about 5 minutes or until tender. Stir in flour; cook and stir for 1 minute. Add milk all at once. Cook and stir until thickened and bubbly. Stir in the Parmesan cheese, tarragon, ½ teaspoon salt, and ½ teaspoon freshly ground black pepper.

3 Arrange half of the potatoes in a greased 2-quart baking dish, alternating rows, if desired. Spoon half of the sauce over the potatoes. Arrange remaining potatoes over sauce. Top with remaining sauce.

4 Bake, covered, in the preheated oven for 40 minutes. Uncover and bake about 30 minutes more or until potatoes are tender and sauce is golden. Garnish with fresh tarragon, if desired. Makes 8 servings.

Nutrition Facts per serving: 237 cal., 10 g total fat (6 g sat. fat), 26 mg chol., 366 mg sodium, 30 g carbo., 3 g fiber, 8 g pro. Daily Values: 170% vit. A, 33% vit. C, 19% calcium, 7% iron.

LOW FAT

Maple-Glazed Sweet Potatoes

Freshly ground black pepper spices up these sweet potatoes. (See the photograph on page 283.)

Prep: 20 minutes   **Bake:** 30 minutes

- 2 lb. sweet potatoes (6 medium)
- ⅓ cup pure maple syrup or
       maple-flavored syrup
- 2 Tbsp. cooking oil
- 3 Tbsp. country-style Dijon-style
       mustard
- ½ tsp. salt
- ½ tsp. freshly ground black pepper
- ½ cup cranberries

1 Preheat oven to 400°F. Peel and cut sweet potatoes into 1- to 1½-inch chunks. In a large bowl combine the maple syrup, cooking oil, mustard, salt, and pepper. Add sweet potatoes and cranberries; toss to coat. Transfer mixture to a 13×9×2-inch baking pan, spreading evenly.

2 Bake, uncovered, in the preheated oven for 30 to 35 minutes or until potatoes are glazed and tender, stirring twice. Makes 8 servings.

Nutrition Facts per serving: 169 cal., 4 g total fat (4 g sat. fat), 0 mg chol., 293 mg sodium, 32 g carbo., 3 g fiber, 2 g pro. Daily Values: 346% vit. A, 17% vit. C, 3% calcium, 4% iron.

Getting Into Squash

Winter squash comes with a life lesson: Even the toughest problems yield to persistence. In the case of squash, a hard shell gives way to the slow, steady pressure of a sharp knife to reveal sweet pumpkin-like flesh.

Acorn squash, which is available year-round, is a common squash variety. Its flesh varies from bright orange to off-white and the skin color ranges from green to orange or white to gold. Butternut squash is another year-round choice.

1. To safely halve most squashes, use a rocking motion with a carving or chef's knife that is longer than the squash. Push down with the palm of your hand, keeping your fingers well away from the blade. If the skin is very tough, lightly tap the back of the knife with a meat mallet or hammer. Additional tips: • Use a cutting board • Cut slowly and steadily • Steady the squash with one rolled kitchen towel and a second towel beneath the cutting board to keep it from slipping.

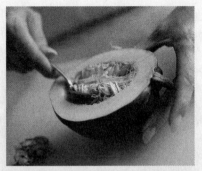

2. Use a large spoon to scoop out the seeds and strings from the squash. Remove all the strings—cooking does not make them tender.

3. Preheat the oven to 350°F. Place the split and seeded squash, cut sides down, on a baking sheet. Bake for 30 minutes. Turn cut sides up and bake for 20 to 25 minutes more or until tender. After cooking, squash offers many serving possibilities. Cut it into wedges, brush the flesh lightly with butter or margarine, and sprinkle it with salt, pepper, and brown sugar. Or use squash halves as vessels to serve chili, soup, or dips.

LOW FAT

Spiced Vegetable-Stuffed Squash

For a fancy touch, use a pastry bag fitted with a large star tip to pipe the vegetable mixture into the squash quarters.

Prep: 20 minutes **Bake:** 65 minutes

> 2 medium acorn squash
> (about 1 lb. each)
> 2 small turnips, chopped (1½ cups)
> 2 medium carrots, chopped (1 cup)
> 1 Tbsp. butter or margarine
> 1 Tbsp. brown sugar
> ½ tsp. ground cinnamon
> ¼ tsp. salt
> ¼ tsp. ground nutmeg
> 1 cup coarsely shredded,
> peeled apple

1 Preheat oven to 350°F. Quarter squash; remove seeds and strings. Place squash, cut sides down, in a 13×9×2-inch baking pan. Cover lightly with foil. Bake in the preheated oven for 30 minutes. Turn cut sides up; bake, covered, for 20 to 25 minutes more or until tender. Carefully scoop pulp out of each squash quarter, keeping shells intact and leaving a thin layer of squash in shells. Set shells aside. Place the cooked squash pulp in a large bowl.

2 Meanwhile, in a covered saucepan cook turnips and carrots in boiling lightly salted water about 20 minutes or until tender. Drain well. Add turnips and carrots to the squash pulp in bowl. Coarsely mash vegetables with a potato masher.

3 Add butter or margarine, brown sugar, cinnamon, salt, and nutmeg to mashed vegetables; stir to combine.

Fold in apple. Spoon vegetable-apple mixture evenly into squash shells. Return to baking pan. Bake for 15 to 20 minutes more or until heated through. Makes 8 servings.

Nutrition Facts per serving: 86 cal., 2 g total fat (1 g sat. fat), 4 mg chol., 114 mg sodium, 17 g carbo., 3 g fiber, 2 g pro. Daily Values: 84% vit. A, 29% vit. C, 5% calcium, 5% iron.

Cream of Squash And Garlic Soup

An entire head of garlic, oven-roasted with the other vegetables, provides perfection in its mellow flavor.

Prep: 30 minutes   **Bake:** 2 hours

  2 **medium acorn squash (about 3 lb. total)**
  2 **to 4 Tbsp. pure maple syrup or maple-flavored syrup**
  4 **tsp. margarine or butter**
  1 **head garlic, cloves separated and peeled**
  1 **carrot, cut into 1-inch pieces**
  1 **onion, cut into wedges**
  4 **cups chicken broth**
  1 **cup whipping cream**
     Whole or snipped fresh basil leaves or Italian parsley sprigs (optional)

1 Preheat oven to 350°F. Cut each squash in half lengthwise. Scoop out and discard seeds and strings. Place squash halves, cut sides up, in a shallow roasting pan. Place one-fourth of the maple syrup and 1 teaspoon margarine or butter in the cavity of each squash half. Arrange garlic, carrot, and onion around squash. Pour 2 cups of the chicken broth in pan; cover tightly with aluminum foil. Bake in the preheated oven for 2 hours or until vegetables are very tender.

2 Remove pan from oven; let vegetables cool slightly. Scoop pulp from squash shells and stir into vegetable mixture.

3 Place half of the squash mixture in a blender container or food processor bowl. Cover and blend or process until smooth. Repeat with remaining squash mixture.

4 Transfer squash mixture to a large saucepan; stir in remaining chicken broth. Heat and stir until boiling. Stir in whipping cream; remove from heat. Season to taste with salt and pepper.

5 To serve, ladle soup into bowls. Garnish each serving with basil or parsley, if desired. Makes 6 side-dish servings.

Nutrition Facts per serving: 285 cal., 18 g total fat (10 g sat. fat), 54 mg chol., 722 mg sodium, 28 g carbo., 3 g fiber, 4 g pro. Daily Values: 77% vit. A, 33% vit. C, 10% calcium, 8% iron.

Cumin Butternut Squash Soup

If you don't have blood oranges, select any thin-skinned orange to float on this velvety soup. (See the photograph on page 280.)

Prep: 30 minutes   **Cook:** 19 minutes

  1 **to 2 tsp. cumin seeds**
  ¼ **cup butter or margarine**
  ½ **cup chopped onion**
  ½ **cup chopped carrot**
  ½ **cup chopped celery**
  2 **lb. butternut squash, peeled and coarsely chopped (5 cups)**
  1 **tsp. ground cumin**
  3 **cups reduced-sodium chicken broth**
  1⅓ **cups buttermilk**
  ½ **tsp. salt**
  ⅛ **tsp. pepper**
     Blood oranges or oranges, thinly sliced (optional)

1 In a small skillet cook cumin seeds over medium heat about 1 minute or until seeds become fragrant and turn a shade darker, stirring frequently. Immediately remove seeds from skillet; set aside.

2 In a large saucepan melt butter or margarine. Stir in onion, carrot, and celery. Cook over medium heat for 5 minutes, stirring occasionally. Stir in squash and ground cumin. Cook and stir for 5 minutes more. Carefully add chicken broth. Bring to boiling; reduce heat. Simmer, covered, for 8 to 10 minutes or until vegetables are very tender. Allow mixture to cool slightly.

3 Place small batches of vegetable mixture at a time in a food processor bowl or blender container. Cover and process or blend until smooth. Return the pureed mixture to the saucepan. Stir in buttermilk, salt, and pepper. Heat through.

4 To serve, ladle soup into bowls. Top with orange slices, if desired, and toasted cumin seeds. Makes 8 side-dish servings.

Nutrition Facts per serving: 125 cal., 7 g total fat (4 g sat. fat), 18 mg chol., 497 mg sodium, 15 g carbo., 2 g fiber, 4 g pro. Daily Values: 180% vit. A, 34% vit. C, 10% calcium, 5% iron.

LOW FAT

Cranberry-Apple Dressing

Dry the bread cubes the day before, and store them in a tightly covered container at room temperature. (See the photograph on page 280.)

Prep: 30 minutes **Bake:** 40 minutes

- 12 oz. baguette-style French bread, cut into ½-inch cubes (about 11 cups)
- 8 slices bacon
- 1 cup chopped onion
- 1 large clove garlic, minced
- 1 large tart apple, cored and coarsely chopped (1½ cups)
- ½ cup dried cranberries
- ½ cup apple cider or juice
- ¼ cup snipped flat-leaf parsley
- 3 Tbsp. snipped fresh thyme or 2 tsp. dried thyme, crushed
- ½ tsp. freshly ground pepper
- ¼ tsp. salt
- ⅓ to ½ cup chicken broth
  Apple wedges (optional)
  Fresh thyme (optional)

1 Preheat oven to 350°F. Place bread cubes in a large roasting pan. Bake in the preheated oven about 10 minutes or until dry, stirring once. Transfer bread cubes to a very large mixing bowl; set aside. Reduce oven temperature to 325°F.

2 Meanwhile, in a large skillet cook bacon until crisp. Drain bacon, reserving drippings in skillet. Crumble bacon and set aside. Add onion and garlic to bacon drippings. Cook and stir over medium heat until onion is tender. Remove from heat. Stir in chopped apple, cranberries, apple cider or juice, parsley, thyme, pepper, and salt.

3 Add apple mixture and bacon to bread cubes, tossing gently to mix. Drizzle with enough of the chicken broth to moisten, tossing lightly. Place dressing in a 3-quart casserole.

4 Cover and bake in the preheated oven for 30 to 40 minutes or until heated through. Garnish with apple wedges and fresh thyme, if desired. Serve immediately. Makes 16 servings.

To Make Ahead:

Prepare dressing as directed, except turn into a 3-quart casserole but do not bake. Cover and chill for up to 4 hours. Bake, covered, in a 325°F oven for 45 to 55 minutes or until heated through.

Nutrition Facts per serving: 103 cal., 2 g total fat (1 g sat. fat), 3 mg chol., 234 mg sodium, 18 g carbo., 1 g fiber, 3 g pro. **Daily Values:** 2% vit. A, 5% vit. C, 2% calcium, 5% iron.

30 MINUTE

Sage-Sweet Pepper Couscous Dressing

Israeli couscous, also known as pearl pasta, is available in some specialty food stores and supermarkets. (See the photograph on page 280.)

Start to finish: 30 minutes

- 1½ cups Israeli couscous
- 1 Tbsp. olive oil
- 2½ cups vegetable broth
- 2 cups coarsely chopped red, orange, and/or yellow sweet peppers
- 1½ cups coarsely chopped celery
- 1 cup thinly sliced green onions or finely chopped onion
- 2 Tbsp. olive oil, butter, or margarine
- 3 Tbsp. snipped fresh sage or 1 Tbsp. dried sage, crushed
- 1 tsp. finely shredded orange peel
- ½ tsp. poultry seasoning
- ½ tsp. freshly ground black pepper
- ¼ tsp. salt
  Fresh sage (optional)

1 In a large saucepan cook and stir couscous in the 1 tablespoon olive oil about 5 minutes or until golden. Carefully add vegetable broth. Bring to boiling; reduce heat. Simmer, covered, for 8 to 10 minutes or until couscous is tender and most of the liquid is absorbed. Remove from heat; set aside.

2 Meanwhile, in a large skillet cook the sweet peppers, celery, and finely chopped onion (if using) in the 2 tablespoons olive oil, butter, or margarine for 5 to 6 minutes or until tender, stirring occasionally. Stir in green onions (if using), sage, orange peel, poultry seasoning, black pepper, and salt. Cook and stir 1 minute more.

3 Add vegetable mixture to couscous, tossing to combine. Transfer to a serving bowl. Garnish with fresh sage, if desired. Serve immediately. Makes 8 servings.

Nutrition Facts per serving: 193 cal., 6 g total fat (1 g sat. fat), 0 mg chol., 382 mg sodium, 32 g carbo., 3 g fiber, 5 g pro. **Daily Values:** 42% vit. A, 106% vit. C, 3% calcium, 5% iron.

Lemon-Parsley Stuffing

Prep: 35 minutes **Bake:** 40 minutes

10	cups dry bread cubes (about 15 slices)*
1	cup finely chopped onion
¾	cup snipped fresh parsley
2	eggs, slightly beaten
½	cup butter or margarine, melted
4	tsp. finely shredded lemon peel
3	Tbsp. lemon juice
2	tsp. dried marjoram, crushed
1	tsp. dried thyme, crushed
½	tsp. salt
½	tsp. pepper
2	cloves garlic, minced
½	to ¾ cup chicken broth

1 Preheat oven to 325°F. In a very large bowl combine dry bread cubes, onion, and parsley. In a small bowl combine eggs, melted butter or margarine, lemon peel, lemon juice, marjoram, thyme, salt, pepper, and garlic. Add to bread mixture. Add enough of the chicken broth to moisten, tossing gently.

2 Spoon stuffing into a 2-quart casserole. Bake, covered, in the preheated oven for 30 minutes. Uncover and bake for 10 to 15 minutes more or until an instant-read thermometer inserted in center of stuffing registers 165°F. Makes about 8 cups of stuffing.

*Note: To dry bread cubes, cut bread into cubes and place in a large shallow roasting pan. Bake, uncovered, in a 325°F oven about 20 minutes or until dried, stirring once or twice.

Nutrition Facts per cup: 134 cal., 8 g total fat (4 g sat. fat), 43 mg chol., 254 mg sodium, 13 g carbo., 1 g fiber, 3 g pro. **Daily Values:** 9% vit. A, 11% vit. C, 4% calcium, 6% iron.

Swiss Chard and Corn Bread Dressing

This dressing, with definite Southern appeal, will play well in any region of the country. (See the photograph on page 280.)

Prep: 50 minutes **Bake:** 50 minutes

1	recipe Country Skillet Corn Bread (see right)
1	large red onion, cut into wedges (1 cup)
3	Tbsp. butter or margarine
8	cups coarsely chopped Swiss chard or Ruby Swiss chard leaves
1	Tbsp. snipped fresh thyme or 1 tsp. dried thyme, crushed
1½	tsp. poultry seasoning
½	tsp. salt
½	tsp. coarse ground black pepper
	Dash ground red pepper
2½	to 3 cups chicken broth

1 Prepare Country Skillet Corn Bread; cool. Preheat oven to 325°F. Cut cooled corn bread into ¾-inch cubes (about 8 cups). Spread corn bread cubes in one or two shallow baking pans. Bake for 15 to 20 minutes or until lightly toasted, stirring once. Cool; transfer to a very large mixing bowl.

2 In a very large skillet cook red onion in butter or margarine about 4 minutes or just until tender, stirring frequently. Add Swiss chard; cook and stir about 3 minutes or until wilted and softened. Stir in thyme, poultry seasoning, salt, black pepper, and ground red pepper. Cook and stir for 2 minutes more.

3 Add chard mixture to corn bread cubes, tossing to mix. Drizzle with enough chicken broth to moisten. Place corn-bread mixture in a 2-quart casserole. Bake, covered, in a 325°F oven for 30 minutes. Uncover and bake 20 to 25 minutes more or until heated through and top is lightly browned. Makes 8 servings.

Country Skillet Corn Bread

Pour 2 tablespoons cooking oil into a 9-inch cast-iron skillet or a 9×1½-inch round baking pan. Place pan in oven while preheating oven to 450°F. Meanwhile, in a large bowl combine 3 eggs and 1 cup buttermilk with a wire whisk. Mix in 1½ teaspoons baking powder, ¼ teaspoon baking soda, and ½ teaspoon salt. Pour hot oil from pan into batter; mix well. Stir in 1½ cups yellow cornmeal. Pour batter into prepared skillet. Bake for 15 to 20 minutes or until a wooden toothpick comes out clean. Cool in skillet for 5 minutes. Loosen edges. Carefully invert to remove from skillet. Turn bread browned side up; cool on a wire rack.

Nutrition Facts per serving: 152 cal., 8 g total fat (3 g sat. fat), 62 mg chol., 596 mg sodium, 17 g carbo., 2 g fiber, 5 g pro. **Daily Values:** 21% vit. A, 9% vit. C, 8% calcium, 8% iron.

Guilt-Free Feasting

A typical American puts on slightly less than a pound from Thanksgiving through New Year's Day.

Myth: Feast on steak; cut the carbs

If your love affair with the Thanksgiving feast is thwarted because you're counting calories and fat grams, put away your pocket calculator and relax. Don't obsess about gaining weight. According to a study published in the New England Journal of Medicine, typical Americans put on slightly less than a pound from Thanksgiving through New Year's—not the 5 to 10 pounds you may feel as though you've gained.

Additionally, turkey-day menus contribute a wealth of nutrients for overall good health. You probably already know that turkey, pumpkin pie, and cranberries have nutritious components, and it's OK to eat those foods in moderation.

The following wholesome foods that you might consider including in a Thanksgiving feast contain many of the ingredients you already serve.

1. Fish. Although the turkey is the star, start the meal with a smoked salmon, sardine, or mackerel appetizer. You will put valuable omega-3 fatty acids to work to lower your blood pressure, raise your good cholesterol (HDL), and possibly improve your eyesight, says Barbara Levine, Ph.D., and director of nutrition for Rockfeller University in New York City.

2. Oranges. Go for the peel and the juice to get all the glory of this glowing citrus. Growers tout the fact that oranges are rich in folic acid, which can help prevent birth defects and protect against heart disease. Research suggests that folic acid may reduce the risk of breast cancer in women who regularly drink alcoholic beverages, according to Beverly Clevidence, Ph.D., research nutritionist with the U.S. Department of Agriculture. In addition, the perfumed oil in the rind of an orange has chemicals that may help your body create anticancer enzymes. Stir chopped fresh oranges into cranberry relish for bonus health benefits.

3. Brussels sprouts. Indulge in this cruciferous vegetable. Brussels sprouts contain compounds that may lower chances of developing cataracts and age-related macular degeneration, a condition that leads to blindness. Add flavor to the tiny cabbage-shape vegetables by simmering them in chicken broth just long enough to bring out the bright green color (about 7 to 10 minutes).

4. Onions. The potent-smelling allium family of onions, leeks, shallots, and garlic are rich in beneficial compounds. Add a few handfuls of chopped onion to your daily diet, and you're likely to lower your bad (LDL) cholesterol—which is a

good thing. There also is evidence that substances in onions offer animals protection against cancer.

5. Whole grains. Along with each bite of sweet, chewy whole wheat or rye bread, you get a generous supply of zinc. Experts say that seniors, vegetarians, and frequent dieters may not get enough of this mineral. Zinc, which helps the immune system function, is plentiful in brown rice, rye, triticale, and whole wheat flours. Or choose a whole-grain bread with sunflower or pumpkin seeds—both are high in vitamin E.

6. Carrots. Harvest a wealth of beta-carotene from these golden nuggets—whether eaten raw or cooked. Scientists believe beta-carotene has antioxidant qualities and more. "Evidence [for beta-carotene's effectiveness] goes beyond its being an antioxidant. Beta-carotene may help cells communicate with each other. When one cell goes awry [becomes cancerous] the normal cell gives the correct signals to cancer cells to become normal," Clevidence says.

7. Beans. By all means, add a side of old-fashioned baked beans to the feast. The soluble dietary fiber in beans is heart-healthy and helps maintain blood sugar levels. Beans may support cancer-fighting agents with two protective substances. One binds bile acids to prevent the body from exposure to toxic compounds. The other may boost the immune system, according to Melanie Polk, registered dietitian and director of nutrition education for the American Institute of Cancer Research in Washington, D.C.

8. Water. An unappreciated treasure that doesn't have to be prepared. And there's minimal cleanup after serving it. That's just the beginning. Everyone needs water. If you feel tired, have a headache, or feel constipated during the Thanksgiving rush, maybe you haven't been drinking enough water, Levine says. Drink eight glasses of water every day. Drinking a glass during meals means you're less likely to be hungry for second or third helpings.

Light weight

Apparently it's easy to get used to those extra ounces gained during the holidays, however, because most of the 195 study participants did not lose the added weight by March, said Dr. Susan Yanovski, executive director of an obesity task force for the National Institute of Diabetes and Digestive and Kidney Diseases. "The 10 pounds people gain per decade may be caused by the fact that they never lose that eight-tenths of a pound they gain during the holidays," said Yanovski, who coauthored the study. People who gained the least weight during the holidays reported being physically active. Take a brisk walk or add exercise to your daily routine during the holiday season to help prevent weight from creeping on.

Lemon-Pepper Butter

To serve on a butter plate, roll this butter in a tube of waxed paper and chill it in the refrigerator just until hardened. Unroll just before serving.

Start to finish: 5 minutes

- ½ **cup butter, softened**
- 2 **tsp. finely shredded lemon peel**
- 2 **tsp. lemon juice**
- 1 **tsp. cracked or coarsely ground black pepper**

1 In a food processor bowl combine the butter, lemon peel, juice, and pepper. Cover and process until blended. (Or combine ingredients in a mixing bowl; beat with an electric mixer on medium speed until smooth.)

2 Use immediately or chill for up to 2 days. To serve, let stand at room temperature until soft enough to spread. Serve with Cornmeal Skillet Rolls (see recipe, right) or other favorite bread. Makes ½ cup.

Nutrition Facts per tablespoon: 109 cal., 12 g total fat (8 g sat. fat), 33 mg chol., 124 mg sodium, 0 g carbo., 0 g fiber, 0 g pro. **Daily Values:** 1% calcium, 1% iron.

Kumquat Butter

This tangy, sweet butter is just as delicious drizzled over steamed green vegetables.

Start to finish: 10 minutes

- 4 **oz. kumquats (about 10)**
- ½ **cup butter, softened**

- 2 **Tbsp. finely shredded orange peel**
- 1 **Tbsp. honey**

1 Halve kumquats crosswise; remove and discard any seeds. Place kumquats in the bowl of a food processor. Cover and process until finely chopped. Add butter, orange peel, and honey. Process until fluffy. (Or using a sharp knife, finely chop kumquats and place in a medium mixing bowl. Add butter, orange peel, and honey; stir with a wire whisk until fluffy.)

2 Use immediately or chill for up to 2 days. To serve, let stand at room temperature until soft enough to spread. Serve with Cornmeal Skillet Rolls (see recipe, below) or other favorite bread. Makes ¾ cup.

Nutrition Facts per tablespoon: 84 cal., 8 g total fat (5 g sat. fat), 22 mg chol., 83 mg sodium, 3 g carbo., 1 g fiber, 0 g pro. **Daily Values:** 7% vit. A, 8% vit. C, 1% calcium.

Cornmeal Skillet Rolls

To easily shape this sticky dough, coat your hands well with flour. (See the photograph on page 283.)

Prep: 30 minutes **Rise:** 40 minutes
Bake: 30 minutes

- ½ **cup yellow cornmeal**
- 1 **cup boiling water**
- ¼ **cup molasses**
- 1 **Tbsp. butter or margarine**
- 1 **tsp. salt**
- 1 **egg**
- 1 **pkg. active dry yeast**
- ¼ **cup lukewarm water (105° to 115°F)**
- 3 **cups all-purpose flour**

  Yellow cornmeal
- 1 **recipe Lemon-Pepper Butter and/or Kumquat Butter (see left)**

1 Grease a 9-inch cast-iron skillet or 9-inch round baking pan. In a small bowl place the ½ cup cornmeal; add boiling water. Stir until combined. Add molasses, butter or margarine, and salt, stirring until butter melts. Stir in egg until combined; set aside.

2 In a small bowl dissolve yeast in the lukewarm water. Let stand until foamy, about 5 minutes.

3 In a large mixing bowl place the flour. Add cornmeal mixture and yeast mixture. Using a wooden spoon, beat until a soft dough forms. (Dough will be soft and sticky.)

4 With well-floured hands, pinch off sixteen 2-inch pieces of dough. Shape each piece into a ball. Place balls, touching each other, in the prepared skillet or baking pan, flouring hands as necessary. Cover and let rise in a warm place until double in size (40 to 45 minutes). Sprinkle with additional cornmeal.

5 Meanwhile, preheat oven to 375°F. Bake for 30 to 35 minutes or until golden brown on top and rolls sound hollow when gently tapped. Cool slightly. Serve warm directly from the skillet or pan. Or, to serve at room temperature, remove rolls from skillet or pan and cool on a wire rack. Serve with Lemon-Pepper Butter and/or Kumquat Butter. Makes 16 rolls.

Nutrition Facts per roll: 128 cal., 1 g total fat (0 g sat. fat), 15 mg chol., 160 mg sodium, 25 g carbo., 1 g fiber, 3 g pro. **Daily Values:** 1% vit. A, 2% calcium, 9% iron.

- **Waldorf salad or other apple salad served on leaf lettuce**

- **Pot roast with roasted carrots and onions**

- **Garlic mashed potatoes**

- **Green Onion Parker House Biscuits (see right)**

- **Pumpkin or custard pie**

Spinach Cheese Puff

Resembling soufflé—only less temperamental—this puff has the consistency of Southern-style spoon bread. (See the photograph on page 283.)

Prep: 30 minutes **Bake:** 40 minutes

- 6 egg yolks
- 6 egg whites
- 2 Tbsp. grated Parmesan cheese
- ¼ cup finely chopped shallots
- 2 cloves garlic, minced
- 3 Tbsp. butter or margarine
- ¼ cup finely snipped dried tomatoes (not oil-pack)
- ¼ cup all-purpose flour
- ¼ tsp. salt
- ⅛ tsp. ground red pepper
- 1 cup milk
- 1 cup shredded Swiss or Gruyère cheese (4 oz.)
- 8 oz. fresh spinach, cooked, well drained, and finely chopped (¾ cup)*, or one 10-oz. pkg. frozen chopped spinach, thawed and well drained
- ¼ cup finely chopped prosciutto
- 5 to 6 dried tomato slices

1 Allow egg yolks and egg whites to stand at room temperature for 30 minutes. Preheat oven to 375°F. Grease the bottom and sides of a 1½-quart soufflé dish. Sprinkle the inside of the dish with 1 tablespoon of the Parmesan cheese; set aside.

2 In a medium saucepan cook shallots and garlic in butter or margarine for 1 minute. Stir in snipped dried tomatoes, flour, salt, and ground red pepper. Cook and stir for 1 minute. Add milk all at once. Cook and stir until thickened and bubbly. Remove from heat. Add Swiss or Gruyère cheese and the remaining 1 tablespoon Parmesan, a little at a time, stirring until melted.

3 In a small bowl beat egg yolks with a fork until combined. Slowly add about half of the cheese sauce to yolks, stirring constantly. Return yolk mixture to the saucepan. Stir in spinach and prosciutto; set aside.

4 In a large mixing bowl beat egg whites with an electric mixer on medium to high speed until stiff peaks form (tips stand straight). Gently fold about one-third of the whites into the spinach sauce to lighten; fold spinach mixture into remaining egg whites.

5 Pour into prepared dish. Bake in the preheated oven for 40 to 45 minutes or until puffed and a knife inserted near the center comes out clean. Soak dried tomato slices in hot water about 5 minutes before puff is done. Drain well. Arrange tomato slices atop puff and serve immediately. Makes 6 to 8 servings.

*Note: To cook spinach, place the spinach leaves in a steamer basket over boiling water. Cover and steam for 2 minutes or until wilted. Drain in a colander, pressing with a spoon to squeeze out liquid. Finely chop.

Nutrition Facts per serving: 272 cal., 18 g total fat (10 g sat. fat), 252 mg chol., 477 mg sodium, 12 g carbo., 2 g fiber, 17 g pro. Daily Values: 67% vit. A, 19% vit. C, 32% calcium, 14% iron.

30 MINUTE

Green Onion Parker House Biscuits

Refrigerated biscuit dough and softened herb-blend cheese make these biscuits quick to prepare and tasty. (See the photograph on page 281.)

Prep: 10 minutes **Bake:** 8 minutes

- 1 5.2-oz. container boursin cheese with garlic and herb
- ¼ cup sliced green onions
- 1 12-oz. pkg. (10) refrigerated biscuits
- 1 egg yolk
- 1 Tbsp. water
- 2 Tbsp. grated Parmesan cheese
  Sliced green onions

1 Preheat the oven to 400°F. In a small bowl stir together the cheese and the ¼ cup green onions; set aside.

2 Unwrap biscuits. Using your fingers, gently split the biscuits horizontally. Place the biscuit bottoms on a greased cookie sheet. Spread about 1 tablespoon of the cheese mixture over each biscuit bottom. Replace biscuit tops.

3 In a small bowl use a fork to beat together egg yolk and water. Brush biscuit tops with yolk mixture. Sprinkle with Parmesan cheese and additional sliced green onions.

4 Bake in the preheated oven for 8 to 10 minutes or until golden brown. Serve warm. Makes 10 biscuits.

Nutrition Facts per biscuit: 149 cal., 8 g total fat (5 g sat. fat), 23 mg chol., 394 mg sodium, 16 g carbo., 0 g fiber, 4 g pro. **Daily Values:** 1% vit. A, 1% vit. C, 2% calcium, 6% iron.

---

30 MINUTE
Coffee Candied Nuts

These candy-coated nuts, with just a hint of coffee flavor, make a tasteful hostess gift. For a simple presentation, place the nuts in a small plastic pastry bag and tie the top with a pretty fabric ribbon.

Prep: 5 minutes **Bake:** 25 minutes

- 1 egg white
- 1 Tbsp. water
- 2 tsp. instant espresso coffee powder or 4 tsp. instant coffee crystals
- ½ cup sugar
- 3 cups salted mixed nuts (no peanuts)

1 Preheat oven to 300°F. Line a 15×10×1-inch baking pan with foil; grease the foil. Set pan aside. In a large bowl beat together the egg white, water, and espresso powder or coffee crystals with a fork until espresso powder is dissolved. Stir in sugar. Add nuts; stirring to coat. Spread the nut-syrup mixture in the prepared pan.

2 Bake in the preheated oven for 25 to 30 minutes, stirring occasionally, or until coating becomes stiff and mixture is somewhat difficult to stir. Spread nut mixture onto a large piece of lightly greased foil; cool. Break into pieces. Store in an airtight container. Makes 14 servings.

Nutrition Facts per serving: 218 cal., 17 g total fat (3 g sat. fat), 0 mg chol., 220 mg sodium, 14 g carbo., 2 g fiber, 5 g pro. **Daily Values:** 3% calcium, 4% iron.

Chocolate Fruit-Nut Torte

Brandy Ice Cream Sauce is a fitting finish for this chocolate cross between a brownie and a fudgy cake.

Prep: 20 minutes **Bake:** 20 minutes

- 1 cup all-purpose flour
- ½ tsp. ground cinnamon
- ¼ tsp. baking powder
- ⅛ tsp. salt
- ¾ cup snipped dried tart red cherries or dried cranberries
- ¾ cup snipped dried apricots
- ½ cup chopped walnuts
- ½ cup butter
- 4 oz. unsweetened chocolate, chopped
- 1½ cups sugar
- 1 tsp. vanilla
- 3 eggs
- 1 recipe Brandy Ice Cream Sauce (see right)

1 Preheat oven to 350°F. Grease and flour an 11×8-inch tart pan with removable bottom, a 9×9×2-inch square baking pan, or a 9-inch round cake pan. Set aside.

2 In a medium mixing bowl stir together the flour, cinnamon, baking powder, and salt. Stir in dried cherries or cranberries, dried apricots, and walnuts. Set aside.

3 In a large saucepan melt the butter and chocolate over low heat, stirring frequently. Remove from heat. Add the sugar, stirring until sugar is dissolved. Stir in vanilla. Beat in the eggs. Add flour mixture and stir until combined. Spread in prepared pan.

4 Bake in the preheated oven for 20 to 25 minutes (25 to 30 minutes if using round pan) or until the edges are firm and top looks dry. Cool in pan on a wire rack for 15 minutes. Remove sides of tart pan, if desired, or remove torte from square or round pan; cool completely. Wrap in foil. Let stand at room temperature or in the refrigerator overnight before serving.

5 To serve, cut torte into thin slices. Spoon Brandy Ice Cream Sauce over each serving. Makes 12 servings.

Brandy Ice Cream Sauce
Place 1 pint extra-rich vanilla or eggnog ice cream in a medium mixing bowl. Stir to soften slightly. Stir in 2 tablespoons brandy, cherry brandy, or bourbon whiskey until thick and creamy. Serve immediately with Chocolate Fruit-Nut Torte or return to freezer. Stir frozen sauce until desired consistency before serving.

Nutrition Facts per serving: 445 cal., 24 g total fat (13 g sat. fat), 115 mg chol., 162 mg sodium, 54 g carbo., 3 g fiber, 7 g pro. **Daily Values:** 23% vit. A, 8% calcium, 10% iron.

CHRISTMAS COOKIES

As you anticipate the wafting scent of freshly baked cookies filling your home during the holidays and you bring out recipes to make your family's favorites, you relive memories of cookie-baking through the years. Whether the cookies you like best are sprinkled with candy, drizzled with chocolate, or at their delicious best served plain, here are a few of the most treasured and requested Christmas cookie recipes from years past to add to your collection.

Chocolate Melt-Aways

A layer of chocolate sandwiches two cookies together, then colorful preserves glisten on top.

Prep: 40 minutes **Chill:** 1 hour
Bake: 7 minutes per batch

- ¾ cup butter, softened
- 1 cup granulated sugar
- 2 eggs
- 1 tsp. baking powder
- ½ tsp. salt
- ½ tsp. ground cinnamon
- ½ tsp. almond extract
- 2⅓ cups all-purpose flour
- 1 cup semisweet chocolate pieces (6 oz.)
-   Powdered sugar
- ½ cup preserves, jam, or jelly (such as cherry, mint, peach, apricot, or raspberry)

1 In a large mixing bowl beat butter with an electric mixer on medium to high speed for 30 seconds. Add granulated sugar; beat until fluffy. Beat in eggs, baking powder, salt, cinnamon, and almond extract. Gradually beat in as much of the flour as you can. Using a wooden spoon, stir in any remaining flour.

Divide dough in half. Cover; chill dough for 1 hour or until firm.

2 Preheat oven to 375°F. On a lightly floured surface, roll half of the dough to ⅛-inch thickness. (Keep remaining dough in refrigerator until ready to roll.) Using a 2- to 2½-inch cookie cutter, cut into desired shapes. Place on ungreased cookie sheets. With a 1-inch cookie cutter, cut out centers from half of the unbaked cookies.

3 Bake in the preheated oven about 7 minutes or until edges are firm and bottoms are very light brown. Transfer cookies to a wire rack; let cool. Repeat with dough scraps and remaining chilled dough.

4 In a heavy, small saucepan melt chocolate pieces over low heat, stirring constantly. Spread about 1 teaspoon of the melted chocolate on the bottom of each cookie with cutout center. Immediately place each chocolate-coated cookie, chocolate side down, on an uncut cookie to form a sandwich. Sift powdered sugar over cookies. Spoon about ½ teaspoon preserves, jam, or jelly into the center cutout of each cookie sandwich. Makes about 40 sandwich cookies.

Nutrition Facts per cookie: 111 cal., 5 g total fat (3 g sat. fat), 20 mg chol., 81 mg sodium, 14 g carbo., 1 g fiber, 1 g pro. Daily Values: 4% vit. A, 1% vit. C, 1% calcium, 2% iron.

Lime Zingers

These tangy treats became an immediate hit when they were prize winners in a *Better Homes and Gardens*® magazine cookie contest in 1994.

Prep: 40 minutes
Bake: 8 minutes per batch

- 1 cup butter
- ½ cup granulated sugar
- 2 tsp. finely shredded lime peel
- ¼ cup lime juice (2 limes)
- 1 tsp. vanilla
- 2¼ cups all-purpose flour
- ¾ cup finely chopped Brazil nuts or hazelnuts (filberts)
- ½ of an 8-oz. pkg. cream cheese, softened
- 1 cup sifted powdered sugar
- 1 Tbsp. lemon or lime juice
- 1 tsp. vanilla
-   Food coloring

1 Preheat oven to 350°F. In a large mixing bowl beat butter with an electric mixer on medium speed for 30 seconds. Beat in granulated sugar until combined. Beat in lime peel, the ¼ cup lime juice, and 1 teaspoon vanilla. Beat in as much flour as you can with the mixer. Using a wooden spoon, stir in any remaining flour. Stir in nuts. Divide dough in half.

2 On a lightly floured surface, roll half of the dough at a time to about ¼-inch thickness. Using 1- or 2-inch cookie cutters, cut into desired shapes. Place on an ungreased cookie sheet.

3 Bake in the preheated oven for 8 to 10 minutes or until edges are lightly browned. Transfer cookies to a wire rack; let cool.

4 For frosting, beat the cream cheese, powdered sugar, the 1 tablespoon lemon or lime juice, and 1 teaspoon vanilla with an electric mixer on medium speed until smooth. Tint frosting as desired with food coloring. Frost cooled cookies. Makes 72 one-inch cookies.

Nutrition Facts per cookie: 62 cal., 4 g total fat (2 g sat. fat), 9 mg chol., 31 mg sodium, 6 g carbo., 0 g fiber, 1 g pro. **Daily Values:** 3% vit. A, 1% iron.

Big Soft Ginger Cookies

This recipe, shared by a *Better Homes and Gardens*® reader, first appeared in a holiday sweets story titled "With Love From Grandma's Kitchen" in the magazine's December 1989 issue.

Prep: 25 minutes
Bake: 10 minutes per batch

2¼   **cups all-purpose flour**
2   **tsp. ground ginger**
1   **tsp. baking soda**
¾   **tsp. ground cinnamon**
½   **tsp. ground cloves**
¾   **cup butter**
1   **cup sugar**
1   **egg**
¼   **cup molasses**
2   **Tbsp. sugar**

1 Preheat oven to 350°F. In a medium bowl stir together the flour, ginger, baking soda, cinnamon, and cloves; set aside.

2 In a large mixing bowl beat butter with an electric mixer on medium speed for 30 seconds. Beat in the 1 cup sugar. Add egg and molasses; beat well. Using a wooden spoon, stir the flour mixture into the egg mixture.

3 Shape dough into 1½–inch balls, using about 1 heaping tablespoon of dough for each ball. Roll balls in the 2 tablespoons sugar to coat. Place balls about 2½ inches apart on an ungreased cookie sheet.

4 Bake in the preheated oven about 10 minutes or until light brown and still puffed. (Do not overbake.) Cool cookies on cookie sheet for 2 minutes. Transfer cookies to a wire rack; let cool. Makes 24 large cookies.

Nutrition Facts per cookie: 138 cal., 6 g total fat (4 g sat. fat), 24 mg chol., 114 mg sodium, 20 g carbo., 0 g fiber, 1 g pro. **Daily Values:** 5% vit. A, 4% iron.

Hickory Nut Macaroons

Prep: 20 minutes
Bake: 15 minutes per batch

This recipe was first published in *Better Homes and Gardens*® magazine in 1925, and it has been an all-time favorite ever since.

4   **egg whites**
4   **cups sifted powdered sugar**
2   **cups chopped hickory nuts, black walnuts, or toasted pecans**

1 Preheat oven to 325°F. Grease a cookie sheet; set aside. In a large mixing bowl beat egg whites with an electric mixer on high speed until stiff, but not dry, peaks form. Gradually add powdered sugar, about ¼ cup at a time, beating on medium speed just until combined. Beat for 1 to 2 minutes more or until combined. Using a wooden spoon, fold in nuts. Drop mixture by rounded teaspoons 2 inches apart on the prepared cookie sheet.

2 Bake in the preheated oven about 15 minutes or until edges are very lightly browned.* Transfer cookies to a wire rack and let cool. Makes 36 cookies.

***Note:** These cookies split around the edges as they bake.

Nutrition Facts per cookie: 86 cal., 4 g total fat (0 g sat. fat), 0 mg chol., 6 mg sodium, 12 g carbo., 1 g fiber, 1 g pro.

Brown Sugar-Hazelnut Rounds

These nutty sweets are one of our top picks from more than 75 years of publishing recipes. If you like, roll the log of dough in chopped toasted nuts before chilling, or dip half of each baked, cooled cookie in melted chocolate and sprinkle with chopped toasted nuts.

Prep: 40 minutes **Chill:** 4 hours
Bake: 10 minutes per batch

- ½ **cup shortening**
- ½ **cup butter**
- 1¼ **cups packed brown sugar**
- ½ **tsp. baking soda**
- ½ **tsp. salt**
- 1 **egg**
- 1 **tsp. vanilla**
- 2½ **cups all-purpose flour**
- ¾ **cup ground toasted hazelnuts or pecans**

1 In a large mixing bowl beat shortening and butter with an electric mixer on medium to high speed for 30 seconds. Add the brown sugar, baking soda, and salt. Beat until combined. Beat in egg and vanilla until combined. Beat in as much of the flour as you can with the mixer. Using a wooden spoon, stir in any remaining flour and the ground nuts.

2 On waxed paper shape dough into two 10-inch rolls. Wrap each in waxed paper or plastic wrap. Chill for 4 to 48 hours or until firm enough to slice.

3 Preheat oven to 375°F. Using a thin-blade knife, cut dough into ¼-inch-thick slices. Place cookie slices 1 inch apart on ungreased baking sheets.

4 Bake in the preheated oven about 10 minutes or until edges are firm. Transfer the cookies to a wire rack and let cool. Makes 80 cookies.

Nutrition Facts per cookie: 70 cal., 4 g total fat (1 g sat. fat), 8 mg chol., 37 mg sodium, 7 g carbo., 0 g fiber, 1 g pro. Daily Values: 1% vit. A, 2% iron.

Fairy Drops

Since this recipe was first submitted by a food editor for the "Delicious Memories" story that appeared in the magazine in December 1992, it has become a well-known favorite.

Prep: 30 minutes **Chill:** 30 minutes
Bake: 10 minutes per batch

- 1 **cup butter**
- 1 **cup sifted powdered sugar**
- 1 **cup granulated sugar**
- 1 **tsp. baking soda**
- 1 **tsp. cream of tartar**
- 1 **tsp. salt**
- 1 **cup cooking oil**
- 2 **eggs**
- 2 **tsp. almond extract**
- 4½ **cups all-purpose flour**
- 1 **recipe Almond Frosting (see right)**
  Crushed hard candies (optional)

1 In a large mixing bowl beat the butter with an electric mixer on medium to high speed for 30 seconds. Add powdered sugar, granulated sugar, baking soda, cream of tartar, and salt; beat on medium-high speed until fluffy. Add cooking oil, eggs, and almond extract; beat just until combined. Gradually beat in as much of the flour as you can with the mixer. Stir in any remaining flour. Cover and chill dough about 30 minutes or until needed.

2 Preheat oven to 350°F. Working with one-fourth of the dough at a time, shape dough into 1¼-inch balls. (The dough will be soft; keep it chilled as you work with a portion.) Arrange balls 2 inches apart on an ungreased cookie sheet. With the palm of your hand or, if desired, the bottom of a glass or a patterned cookie stamp dipped in granulated sugar, gently flatten balls to about ¼ inch thick. Sprinkle with sugar (unless flattened with sugared glass or stamp) or leave plain for frosting.

3 Bake in the preheated oven for 10 to 12 minutes or until edges just begin to brown. Transfer cookies to a wire rack and let cool. Frost with Almond Frosting and sprinkle with crushed candy. Place cookies in a single layer in an airtight container and store at room temperature for up to 3 days. Makes 84 cookies.

Almond Frosting

In a small mixing bowl beat ½ cup butter with an electric mixer on medium speed until fluffy. Beat in ½ teaspoon almond extract and ½ teaspoon vanilla. Alternately add 2½ to 3½ cups sifted powdered sugar and 3 tablespoons half-and-half, light cream, or milk, beating until smooth and easy to spread. To tint, if desired, stir in a few drops food coloring.

Nutrition Facts per cookie: 77 cal., 5 g total fat (2 g sat. fat), 10 mg chol., 61 mg sodium, 8 g carbo., 0 g fiber, 1 g pro. Daily Values: 2% vit. A, 1% iron.

Jam Thumbprints

Bake and cool these thumbprint cookies to have on hand for drop-in company during the holidays. Fill them just before serving.

Prep: 30 minutes **Chill:** 1 hour
Bake: 10 minutes per batch

- ⅔ **cup butter**
- ½ **cup sugar**
- 2 **egg yolks**
- 1 **tsp. vanilla**
- 1½ **cups all-purpose flour**
- 2 **egg whites, slightly beaten**
- 1 **cup finely chopped walnuts**
- ⅓ **to ½ cup strawberry, cherry, or apricot jam or preserves**

1 Preheat oven to 375°F. Grease a baking sheet; set aside. In a large mixing bowl beat butter with an electric mixer on medium to high speed for 30 seconds. Add the sugar and beat until combined, scraping sides of bowl occasionally. Beat in egg yolks and vanilla until combined. Beat in as much of the flour as you can with mixer. Stir in any remaining flour. Cover and chill dough about 1 hour or until easy to handle.

2 Shape dough into 1-inch balls. Roll balls in egg whites; roll in

walnuts. Place balls 1 inch apart on the prepared cookie sheet. Press your thumb into the center of each ball.

3 Bake in the preheated oven for 10 to 12 minutes or until edges are lightly browned. Transfer cookies to a wire rack and let cool. Place cookies in an airtight container and store at room temperature for up to 3 days.

4 Just before serving, spoon jam or preserves into the center of the cookies. Makes 42 cookies.

Nutrition Facts per cookie: 79 cal., 5 g total fat (2 g sat. fat), 18 mg chol., 33 mg sodium, 8 g carbo., 0 g fiber, 1 g pro. Daily Values: 4% vit. A, 2% iron.

Toffee Triangles

Prep: 25 minutes **Bake:** 33 minutes

- ¾ **cup butter**
- ¾ **cup packed brown sugar**
- 1 **egg yolk**
- 1½ **cups all-purpose flour**
- ¼ **tsp. salt**
- 1 **14½-oz. can (1¼ cups) sweetened condensed milk**
- 2 **Tbsp. butter**
- 2 **tsp. vanilla**
- 1 **12-oz. pkg. (2 cups) semisweet chocolate pieces**
- 1 **cup almond brickle pieces or toasted chopped pecans**

1 Preheat oven to 350°F. Grease a 13×9×2-inch baking pan; set aside. In a large mixing bowl beat the ¾ cup butter and brown sugar with an electric mixer on medium to high speed until combined. Add egg yolk;

beat well. Using a wooden spoon, stir in flour and salt; mix well. With floured hands, press the dough into the prepared pan.

2 Bake in the preheated oven about 20 minutes or until light brown. Transfer pan to a wire rack.

3 For filling, in a heavy medium saucepan heat condensed milk and the 2 tablespoons butter over medium heat until bubbly, stirring constantly. Cook and stir for 5 minutes more. (Mixture will thicken and become smooth.) Remove from heat. Stir in vanilla. Spread filling over baked layer. Bake for 12 to 15 minutes more or until top layer is golden.

4 Sprinkle filling layers evenly with chocolate pieces. Bake for 1 to 2 minutes more or until pieces are shiny and melted. Remove from oven; transfer to a wire rack. Immediately spread chocolate evenly over filling layer. Sprinkle with brickle pieces or pecans. Cool. Cover and chill until chocolate is set.

5 To serve, cut into 3×2-inch rectangles; cut diagonally into triangles. Place bars in an airtight container and store in the refrigerator for up to 3 days. Makes 36 bars.

Nutrition Facts per bar: 180 cal., 9 g total fat (3 g sat. fat), 23 mg chol., 109 mg sodium, 24 g carbo., 0 g fiber, 2 g pro. Daily Values: 6% vit. A, 4% calcium, 3% iron.

Ornament Cookies

Lots of giggles, flour everywhere, and plenty of hugs—all evoke memories of childhood holiday baking sessions. The recipes for these ornament cookies were developed to help you recapture delicious memories and to encourage you to share them with the youngsters in your life. The colorful cookie treats are adorable by the bucketful and easy on a crunched holiday schedule. All you will need is 60 minutes, four ingredients, and a few tubes of ready-made icing. Just use the fun and easy shortbread recipe below.

Shortbread Ornaments

Prep: 15 minutes
Bake: 12 minutes per batch

1	cup butter, softened
1	tsp. vanilla
2½	cups all-purpose flour
⅓	cup sugar
3	4.25-oz. tubes decorating icing, such as red, kelly green, and lemon yellow

1 Preheat oven to 325°F. In a large mixing bowl beat butter with an electric mixer on medium speed for 30 seconds. Add vanilla. Beat until combined.

2 In a medium mixing bowl combine flour and sugar. Add flour mixture to butter mixture in thirds, beating on low speed after each addition. Mixture will seem dry and crumbly. Use hands to press mixture until it forms a smooth ball.

3 Divide dough into thirds. Roll one-third of dough at a time between two sheets of waxed paper to ¼ inch thick.

4 Using a 3-inch ornament-shape or round cutter, cut some of the dough into large shapes. Reroll scraps. Chill dough, if necessary. Using a 1½-inch ornament-shape or round cutter, cut some of the dough into small shapes. Place 1 inch apart on a cookie sheet.

5 Bake in the preheated oven for 15 to 18 minutes for large ornaments or 12 to 14 minutes for small ornaments or until edges start to brown. Cool on cookie sheet for 2 minutes. Carefully transfer cookies to a wire rack and let cool completely.

6 Using red, kelly green, and lemon yellow decorating icing, decorate cookies with decorating tips, adding dots, stripes, and squiggles. Let cookies stand until icing is set. Makes about 18 large cookies and 22 small cookies.

Nutrition Facts per large cookie: 168 cal., 11 g total fat (7 g sat. fat), 29 mg chol., 110 mg sodium, 16 g carbo., 0 g fiber, 2 g pro. Daily Values: 10% vit. A, 1% calcium, 4% iron.

Chocolate Sandwich Cookies

These elegant cream cheese-filled chocolate-pastry wedges have only five ingredients to go together beautifully.

Prep: 20 minutes
Bake: 10 minutes per batch

1	pkg. piecrust mix (for 2 crusts)
½	cup sugar
¼	cup unsweetened cocoa powder
6	Tbsp. water
1	8-oz. tub cream cheese with strawberries

1 Preheat oven to 375°F. In a medium mixing bowl combine piecrust mix, sugar, and cocoa powder. Mix well. Sprinkle 1 tablespoon of the water over part of the mixture; gently toss with a fork. Push moistened dough to the side of the bowl. Repeat moistening dough, using 1 tablespoon of the water at a time, until all the dough is moistened. Form dough into a ball. Divide dough into thirds.

2 On a floured surface, roll each portion of dough into a 6-inch circle about ¼ inch thick. Cut each dough circle into 10 wedges. Using a fork, prick dough in a decorative design. Transfer wedges to ungreased baking sheets.

3 Bake in the preheated oven about 10 minutes or just until set. Transfer pastry wedges to a wire rack and let cool.

4 To assemble, spread about 2 teaspoons cream cheese over the bottom surface of half of the pastry wedges. Top with remaining wedges, bottom surface down, pressing together lightly. Placed filled cookies in an airtight container and store in the refrigerator. Makes 15 sandwich cookies.

Nutrition Facts per cookie: 200 cal., 12 g total fat (4 g sat. fat), 11 mg chol., 207 mg sodium, 19 g carbo., 0 g fiber, 1 g pro. Daily Values: 3% vit. A, 3% calcium, 3% iron.

Holiday Snowmen

Decorate these kid-friendly snowmen cookies with a glaze of powdered sugar icing, miniature chocolate chip eyes and buttons, and a gumdrop piece for a nose.

Prep: 30 minutes
Bake: 8 minutes per batch

    1   18-oz. roll refrigerated chocolate
        chip, sugar, or peanut butter
        cookie dough
    1   cup sifted powdered sugar
    ¼   tsp. vanilla
    1   to 2 Tbsp. milk
        Gumdrops
        Miniature semisweet
        chocolate pieces

1 Preheat oven to 375°F. Cut cookie dough into 18 equal pieces. Divide each dough piece into three balls: one large (about 1¼ inches in diameter), one medium (about 1 inch in diameter), and one small (about ¾ inch in diameter). Assemble each set of balls ¼ inch apart in a snowman shape on an ungreased cookie sheet, placing the largest balls 2 inches apart so the snowmen don't bake together.

2 Bake for 8 to 10 minutes or until edges are very lightly browned. Cool on cookie sheet 3 minutes. Transfer cookies to a rack; let cool.

3 For glaze, in a small mixing bowl stir together powdered sugar, vanilla, and 1 tablespoon of the milk. Stir in additional milk, 1 teaspoon at a time, to make glaze of drizzling consistency. Spoon glaze over snowmen. Decorate as desired with gumdrops and chocolate pieces. Makes 18 snowmen.

Nutrition Facts per snowman: 148 cal., 5 g total fat (2 g sat. fat), 6 mg chol., 59 mg sodium, 23 g carbo., 0 g fiber, 1 g pro. Daily Values: 1% calcium, 4% iron.

Tree-Topped Brownies

Prep: 15 minutes
Bake: Follow package directions

    1   19- to 22-oz. pkg. fudge
        brownie mix
   20   holiday marshmallows or
        ½ cup (about 50) miniature
        marshmallows
        Purchased frosting (optional)
        Nonpareils or other small candies
        for decorating (optional)

1 Grease a 13×9×2-inch baking pan (or use a foil pan for gift giving); set aside. Prepare brownie mix according to package directions; spread into the prepared pan.

2 Bake as directed, adding holiday marshmallows in a tree shape the last 4 to 5 minutes of baking. Cool in pan on a wire rack. Decorate with frosting and nonpareils or other small candies, if desired. Cut into bars. Makes 36 bars.

Nutrition Facts per bar: 98 cal., 5 g total fat (1 g sat. fat), 12 mg chol., 49 mg sodium, 12 g carbo., 0 g fiber, 1 g pro. Daily Values: 1% calcium, 2% iron.

Decorated Christmas Balls

Prep: 45 minutes Chill: 4 hours
Bake: 8 minutes per batch

    ¾   cup butter, softened
    1   3-oz. package cream
        cheese, softened
    ¾   cup granulated sugar
    ½   tsp. baking powder
    1   egg
    1   tsp. vanilla
   2½   cups all-purpose flour
        Small multicolored decorative
        candies, sprinkles, gumdrops,
        and assorted colored sugars

1 Beat butter and cream cheese for 30 seconds. Add granulated sugar, baking powder, and ¼ teaspoon salt. Beat until combined, scraping sides of bowl occasionally. Beat in egg and vanilla until combined. Beat in as much of the flour as you can. Using a wooden spoon, stir in any remaining flour.

2 Divide dough in half. Shape each half into a 7-inch-long roll. Wrap each roll in plastic wrap. Chill for 4 to 24 hours or until easy to handle.

3 Preheat oven to 375°F. Cut dough into ¼-inch-thick slices. Place slices about 2 inches apart on an ungreased cookie sheet. Decorate slices using decorative candies, sprinkles, colored sugars, and/or gumdrop pieces.

4 Bake for 8 to 10 minutes or until edges are lightly browned. Cool on cookie sheet 1 minute. Transfer to a rack; cool. Makes about 56 cookies.

Nutrition Facts per cookie: 66 cal., 3 g total fat (2 g sat. fat), 12 mg chol., 46 mg sodium, 8 g carbo., 0 g fiber, 1 g pro. Daily Values: 3% vit. A, 1% calcium, 2% iron.

Cranberry Sorbet

Canned cranberry sauce gets frosty with this sophisticated sorbet. Place the can of cranberry sauce in the freezer up to three days before making the sorbet. (See the photograph on page 277.)

Prep: 10 minutes   **Freeze:** 6 hours for sauce; 1 hour for sorbet

- 1   **16-oz. can jellied cranberry sauce**
- 1   **Tbsp. lemon juice**
- ½   **to 1 cup Champagne or rosé wine, chilled (optional)**

1 Place the unopened can of cranberry sauce in the freezer for 6 to 8 hours or until frozen. Remove can from freezer and rinse under cold water for a few seconds. Open the can at both ends. Push the frozen sauce into a food processor bowl or blender container. Using a spoon or table knife, break up the sauce into 5 or 6 chunks. Add lemon juice. Cover and process about 10 seconds or blend until smooth and fluffy, but still partially frozen.

2 Transfer mixture to a freezer container or a 2-quart square baking dish. Cover and freeze at least 1 hour until firm or up to 24 hours.

3 To serve, scoop into small glasses or dishes. If desired, spoon chilled Champagne or wine over sorbet. Makes 8 servings.

Nutrition Facts per serving: 90 cal., 0 g total fat, 0 mg chol., 28 mg sodium, 22 g carbo., 1 g fiber, 0 g pro. Daily Values: 1% vit. C.

Very Ginger Pound Cake

See the photograph on page 277.

Prep: 70 minutes   **Bake:** 1 hour

- 1   **cup butter**
- 5   **eggs**
- 1   **cup milk**
- 3   **cups all-purpose flour**
- 1   **tsp. baking powder**
- ¼   **tsp. baking soda**
- ¼   **tsp. salt**
- 2   **cups granulated sugar**
- ¾   **cup packed brown sugar**
- 2   **Tbsp. grated fresh ginger**
- 2   **tsp. vanilla**
- ½   **cup finely chopped candied or crystallized ginger**
- 1   **recipe Blood Orange Topping (see right)**

1 Allow butter, eggs, and milk to stand at room temperature for 30 minutes. Preheat oven to 350°F. Grease and lightly flour a 10-inch tube pan. In a large bowl stir together the flour, baking powder, baking soda, and salt; set aside.

2 In a very large mixing bowl beat the butter with an electric mixer on medium to high speed for 30 seconds. Gradually add the granulated sugar and the brown sugar, beating until well combined. Beat in the fresh ginger and vanilla. Add eggs, one at a time, beating 1 minute after each addition and scraping bowl.

3 Add flour mixture and milk alternately to beaten mixture, beating on low to medium speed after each addition just until combined. Gently stir in half of the candied ginger. Pour batter into prepared pan. Sprinkle top with the remaining candied ginger.

4 Bake for 60 to 70 minutes or until a cake tester or wooden toothpick inserted near the center comes out clean. Cool in pan on a wire rack for 10 minutes. Remove cake from pan. Cool completely on rack.

5 To serve, place cake on a cake stand or serving plate, rounded side up. Spoon Blood Orange Topping over cake. Drizzle with remaining syrup in skillet. Serves 16.

Blood Orange Topping

In a medium saucepan combine 1 cup water and 1½ cups granulated sugar. Bring to boiling. Boil gently for 15 to 20 minutes or until mixture forms a thick syrup, stirring occasionally. Stir more often as syrup begins to thicken (you should have about 1 cup). Meanwhile, thinly slice 3 blood oranges and 12 kumquats; discard ends and any seeds. Add fruit to syrup, stirring to coat. Return to boiling; reduce heat. Simmer, uncovered, about 5 minutes or until fruit is just tender, carefully turning fruit in syrup several times. Using a slotted spoon, gently remove fruit from syrup. Continue to boil syrup, uncovered, for 10 to 15 minutes more or until reduced to ¾ cup. Cool about 15 minutes.

To Make Ahead:

Bake and cool cake as directed, except do not add topping or syrup. Place in airtight container or wrap in foil and store at room temperature for up to 2 days. Or freeze cake for up to 3 months. Thaw. Prepare and add topping just before serving.

Nutrition Facts per serving: 455 cal., 14 g total fat (8 g sat. fat), 100 mg chol., 239 mg sodium, 79 g carbo., 2 g fiber, 5 g pro. **Daily Values:** 14% vit. A, 31% vit. C, 7% calcium, 9% iron.

Top: Cranberry Sorbet (page 276)
Above: Very Ginger Pound Cake (page 276)

Above: Orange-Fennel Autumn Salad (page 258)

Top: Parsnip Potato Mash (page 261), **Above:** Cauliflower Cheese Bake (page 260)

Top: Cranberry-Apple Dressing (page 264), Sage-Sweet Pepper Couscous Dressing (page 264), and
Swiss Chard and Corn Bread Dressing (page 265)
Above: Cumin Butternut Squash Soup (page 263)
Page 281: Green Onion Parker House Biscuits (page 268)

Page 282: Holiday Scalloped Potatoes (page 261)
Top left: Spinach Cheese Puff (page 268)
Top right: Maple-Glazed Sweet Potatoes (page 261)
Left: Cornmeal Skillet Rolls (page 267)

Spiced Pumpkin Cream (page 285)

Spiced Pumpkin Cream

Adorn this fluffy pumpkin dessert with billows of sweetened whipped cream and sugar-glazed pecans. (See the photograph on page 284.)

Prep: 25 minutes **Chill:** 10 minutes

- 2 Tbsp. butter
- ¼ cup packed brown sugar
- 1 Tbsp. dark-colored corn syrup
- 1½ cups pecan halves
- 1 15-oz. can pumpkin
- 1 cup packed brown sugar
- 1½ tsp. finely shredded orange peel
- 1 Tbsp. dark-colored rum or orange juice
- 2 tsp. ground cinnamon
- ½ tsp. ground cloves
- 2 cups whipping cream
   Sweetened whipped cream (optional)

1 For the candied pecans, line a baking sheet with foil. Melt butter in a small saucepan. Stir in the ¼ cup brown sugar and corn syrup. Cook and stir over medium heat about 2 minutes or until sugar dissolves. Cover pan; cook for 1 minute more. Uncover; add pecans. Cook, stirring constantly, about 5 minutes or until nuts are slightly darker. Immediately pour mixture onto the foil-lined baking sheet; spread into a single layer. Cool completely. Break the candied pecans into pieces.

2 In a large mixing bowl combine the pumpkin, the 1 cup brown sugar, the orange peel, rum or orange juice, cinnamon, and cloves. Stir until sugar dissolves. Set aside.

3 In a chilled large mixing bowl beat the whipping cream with the chilled beaters of an electric mixer on medium speed until soft peaks form. Fold whipped cream into pumpkin mixture. Spoon into a serving bowl or into 8 stemmed glasses or dessert dishes. Chill at least 10 minutes or up to 3 hours before serving.

4 To serve, top each serving with sweetened whipped cream, if desired. Sprinkle with candied pecans. Makes 8 one-tablespoon servings.

To Make Ahead:

Prepare candied pecans up to 3 days ahead. Cool as directed. Store in a covered container at room temperature. Sprinkle extra candied pecans on puddings or other desserts.

Nutrition Facts per serving: 535 cal., 40 g total fat (17 g sat. fat), 90 mg chol., 73 mg sodium, 45 g carbo., 4 g fiber, 4 g pro. **Daily Values:** 255% vit. A, 6% vit. C, 11% calcium, 12% iron.

Eggnog Strata with Bourbon Sauce

If you have a craving for this fantastic dessert after the holidays and eggnog has disappeared from the dairy cases, you're still in luck. Canned eggnog works just as well.

Prep: 20 minutes **Chill:** 2 hours
Bake: 50 minutes **Stand:** 20 minutes

- 8 slices cinnamon-raisin bread
- 2 Tbsp. butter or margarine, softened
- 1 3-oz. pkg. cream cheese, cut into ½-inch cubes
- 4 eggs, beaten
- 2 cups dairy or canned eggnog
- ¼ cup butter or margarine
- ⅓ cup packed brown sugar
- 2 Tbsp. water
- 1 Tbsp. pure maple syrup or maple-flavored syrup
- 1 egg yolk, beaten
- 1 to 2 Tbsp. bourbon
   Sifted powdered sugar

1 Evenly spread one side of each slice of bread with the 2 tablespoons butter or margarine. Place half of the slices, buttered side up, in a lightly greased 2-quart square baking dish. Sprinkle evenly with cream cheese. Top with remaining bread, buttered side up.

2 In a medium mixing bowl combine the 4 eggs and eggnog; slowly pour over bread. Press lightly with back of a large spoon to moisten bread. Cover and chill for 2 to 24 hours.

3 Preheat oven to 325°F. Bake, uncovered, about 50 minutes or until a knife inserted near the center comes out clean. Let stand for 20 to 30 minutes before serving.

4 Meanwhile, for sauce, in a small saucepan melt the ¼ cup butter or margarine over medium heat. Stir in brown sugar, water, maple syrup, and egg yolk. Cook and stir the mixture over medium heat until bubbly. Cook and stir for 2 minutes more. Remove from heat; stir in bourbon. Serve warm sauce with strata.

5 To serve, cut strata into squares. Sprinkle each serving with powdered sugar and drizzle with sauce. Makes 6 to 8 servings.

Nutrition Facts per serving: 654 cal., 28 g total fat (12 g sat. fat), 223 mg chol., 292 mg sodium, 87 g carbo., 6 g fiber, 17 g pro. **Daily Values:** 19% vit. A, 2% vit. C, 14% calcium, 24% iron.

Fruit and Brie Dessert Strata

Prep: 30 minutes **Chill:** 8 hours
Bake: 40 minutes **Stand:** 10 minutes

Nonstick cooking spray
½ cup snipped dried apricots
½ cup snipped dried pears
½ cup dried tart red cherries
    or cranberries
¾ cup boiling water
6 cups sourdough bread cubes
8 oz. Brie cheese, cut into
    ¾-inch pieces
2 tsp. finely shredded orange peel
8 eggs, beaten
2½ cups milk
¼ cup packed brown sugar
1 tsp. ground cinnamon
½ tsp. ground ginger
¼ tsp. ground nutmeg
Sweetened Whipped Cream
    (optional)
Orange peel curls (optional)

1 Coat a 3-quart rectangular baking dish with cooking spray; set aside. In a small mixing bowl combine dried apricots, dried pears, and dried cherries or cranberries. Pour boiling water over dried fruit; let stand for 10 minutes to soften fruit. Drain.

2 Meanwhile, layer half of the bread cubes in the prepared baking dish. Top with the Brie pieces. Combine the drained fruit and orange peel. Spoon fruit mixture over brie. Top with remaining bread cubes; set aside.

3 In a large mixing bowl beat together the eggs, milk, brown sugar, cinnamon, ginger, and nutmeg. Pour egg mixture over layers in dish. Press bread lightly with back of a large spoon to moisten bread completely. Cover and chill for 8 hours or overnight.

4 Preheat oven to 350°F. Bake strata, uncovered, for 40 to 45 minutes or until a knife inserted near the center comes out clean. Let stand 10 minutes before serving. Serve with Sweetened Whipped Cream and garnish with orange peel curls, if desired. Makes 12 servings.

Nutrition Facts per serving: 253 cal., 10 g total fat (5 g sat. fat), 164 mg chol., 295 mg sodium, 29 g carbo., 1 g fiber, 11 g pro. **Daily Values:** 17% vit. A, 3% vit. C, 14% calcium, and 9% iron.

Sweetened Whipped Cream

In a chilled mixing bowl combine 1 cup whipping cream, 1 to 2 tablespoons sugar, and ½ teaspoon vanilla. Beat with chilled beaters of an electric mixer on medium speed until soft peaks form.

PRIZE WINNER

Choco Bread Pudding

Douglas Wasdyke
Effort, Pennsylvania
$400—Surefire Potluck Dishes

Prep: 25 minutes **Bake:** 40 minutes
Stand: 30 minutes

12 oz. challah bread, cut into 1-inch
    cubes (about 9 cups)
1½ cups miniature semisweet
    chocolate pieces
4 eggs, beaten
3 cups half-and-half or light cream
1 cup packed brown sugar
¾ tsp. ground cinnamon
Dash salt
1 cup chopped pecans
½ cup packed brown sugar
1 Tbsp. cornstarch
⅓ cup half-and-half or light cream
¼ cup water
2 Tbsp. light-colored corn syrup
1 Tbsp. butter
½ tsp. vanilla

1 Preheat oven to 350°F. In a large mixing bowl combine bread cubes and chocolate pieces. Transfer to a lightly greased 3-quart rectangular baking dish; set aside.

2 In a medium mixing bowl stir together eggs, the 3 cups half-and-half or light cream, the 1 cup brown sugar, the cinnamon, and salt. Slowly pour egg mixture over bread. Press bread lightly with back of a large spoon to moisten bread completely. Sprinkle with pecans.

3 Bake, uncovered, in the preheated oven for 40 to 45 minutes or until egg mixture is set.

4 Meanwhile, for sauce, in a small heavy saucepan combine the ½ cup brown sugar and the cornstarch. Stir in the ⅓ cup half-and-half or light cream, the water, and corn syrup. Cook and stir until thickened and bubbly (mixture may appear curdled at first). Cook and stir for 2 minutes more. Remove saucepan from heat. Stir in butter and vanilla. Pour sauce over hot bread pudding. Let stand 30 minutes before serving. Makes 16 servings.

To Make Ahead:

Prepare bread pudding through Step 2, but do not sprinkle with pecans. Cover and chill up to 24 hours. Sprinkle with pecans and bake as directed.

Nutrition Facts per serving: 400 cal., 20 g total fat (9 g sat. fat), 86 mg chol., 90 mg sodium, 50 g carbo., 1 g fiber, 7 g pro. **Daily Values:** 8% vit. A, 1% vit. C, 9% calcium, 11% iron.

december

IN THIS CHAPTER

30-minute recipes indicated in COLOR.
Low-fat and no-fat recipes indicated with a ♥.
Photographs indicated in italics.
*Bonus recipe

Toasting Made Easy

Lift a glass to life's simple joys: a visit from a favorite uncle, friends invited for dinner, holiday feasts with family. These occasions deserve to be acknowledged with a toast; however, there's no need to be formal about it. Although toasting at banquets has many rules, when you're at home just follow these basics:

● Alcohol isn't necessary—milk or sodas serve just as well.

● Offer the toast either when everyone is seated for the meal or just before dessert, says etiquette expert Hilka Klingerberg.

● To start the toast, the host or hostess lifts his or her glass to eye level and waits until everyone pays attention. (Tapping a glass with a spoon may be required in a large gathering and it may be necessary to stand for groups of more than eight people.)

● Keep it short—two or three sentences are adequate. Thank everyone for attending, say something complimentary about the person being toasted, or add a few thoughts about the season.

● After the toast, everyone except the person being toasted gently clinks glasses with those within easy reach. Avoid awkward reaches, such as across the table, floral arrangements, and burning candles.

Traditionally, toasts are offered with bottles of chilled sparkling wine that yield five or six glasses each. To loosen the cork to open a bottle, hold the cork while twisting the bottle. To remove the cork without letting it pop, twist and wiggle the cork while holding it firmly with a towel. Chill the wine in a bucket filled with ice and water until ready to serve.

Sparkle for the holidays

As an alternative to sparkling white wine, substitute bubbly red Australian wines. These healthful wines complement roasts and turkey, and they also are good served with turkey sandwiches, hard cheeses, chocolate desserts, and as toasting wine. One tasteful example, Sparkling Shiraz (shee-rahz), has a fruity blackberry flavor and brilliant red color.

---

30 MINUTE, NO FAT

Sparkling Cranberry Rosé

Thread a wooden skewer with red cranberries to use as a festive garnish and to stir the drink to dissolve the sugar cube at the bottom of the Champagne flute.

Start to finish: 10 minutes

  8 to 10 sugar cubes
  1 to 1¼ cups cranberry juice
  1 750-ml bottle sparkling extra
     dry rosé wine, Champagne,
     or sparkling white grape
     juice, chilled
     Fresh cranberries (optional)

1 Place one sugar cube in the bottom of 8 to 10 chilled Champagne flutes or other tall, narrow glasses. Pour 2 tablespoons cranberry juice into each glass.

2 Fill each glass with sparkling rosé wine, Champagne, or sparkling white grape juice. Place a wooden skewer of fresh cranberries in each glass, if desired. Makes 8 to 10 servings.

Nutrition Facts per serving: 100 cal., 0 g total fat, 0 mg chol., 1 mg sodium, 11 g carbo., 0 g fiber, 0 g pro. Daily Values: 19% vit. C.

---

30 MINUTE

Pistachios With a Kick

When buying pistachio nuts, select those with partially open shells, which is a sign that the nuts are mature. The partially open shells also make removing the nuts easy.

Prep: 5 minutes **Bake:** 20 minutes

  2 Tbsp. margarine or butter,
     melted
  1 tsp. ground coriander
  ½ tsp. salt
  ¼ tsp. ground cloves
  ¼ tsp. ground red pepper
  1½ cups shelled pistachio nuts

1 Preheat oven to 350°F. In a 9×9×2-inch baking pan combine melted margarine or butter, coriander, salt, cloves, and ground red pepper. Add pistachio nuts, tossing to coat.

2 Bake, uncovered, in the preheated oven for 20 to 25 minutes or until toasted, stirring occasionally. Spread nuts on foil; cool. Store in an airtight container. Makes 1½ cups.

Nutrition Facts per ¼-cup serving: 212 cal., 18 g total fat (2 g sat. fat), 0 mg chol., 239 mg sodium, 9 g carbo., 3 g fiber, 7 g pro. Daily Values: 8% vit. A, 3% vit. C, 4% calcium, 8% iron.

Shrimp and Feta

Marinated in bottled salad dressing and combined with fresh herbs and crumbled feta, this appetizer is as impressive as it is easy. (See the photograph on page 318.)

Prep: 30 minutes **Chill:** 30 minutes

½ cup bottled olive oil and vinegar salad dressing or Italian salad dressing
1 tsp. finely shredded lime peel
3 lb. large shrimp in shells, peeled, deveined, and cooked*
¼ cup snipped fresh herbs, such as dill, cilantro, and/or parsley
¼ cup crumbled feta cheese (1 oz.)
   Salt and pepper
   Lime wedges
1 recipe Garlic Bread Sleds (optional) (see right)

1 In a large bowl stir together salad dressing and lime peel. Add cooked shrimp, tossing to coat. Cover and chill for at least 30 minutes or up to 4 hours.

2 To serve, combine undrained shrimp, snipped fresh herbs, and crumbled feta cheese. Stir gently to combine. Season to taste with salt and pepper. Spoon into a bowl. Serve with lime wedges and, if desired, Garlic Bread Sleds. Makes 18 appetizer servings.

*Note: To cook shrimp, in a Dutch oven bring lightly salted water to boiling. Add shrimp. Simmer, uncovered, for 1 to 3 minutes or until shrimp turn pink, stirring occasionally. Rinse under cold running water; drain.

Nutrition Facts per serving: 95 cal., 5 g total fat (1 g sat. fat), 88 mg chol., 195 mg sodium, 1 g carbo., 0 g fiber, 12 g pro. **Daily Values:** 2% vit. A, 2% vit. C, 4% calcium, 8% iron.

Garlic Bread Sleds

Toasted bread slices are delicious carriers for Shrimp and Feta (see recipe, left), or use them as croutons to serve on a salad.

Prep: 10 minutes **Broil:** 3 minutes

1 8- to 12-oz. loaf baguette-style French bread (about 18 inches long)
½ cup roasted garlic butter with olive oil, softened, or garlic butter

1 Using a serrated knife, cut the bread in half crosswise. Carefully cut each piece horizontally into thirds. Arrange bread slices on a baking sheet. Spread one cut side of each slice with the garlic butter.

2 Broil about 4 inches from the heat for 2 to 4 minutes until toasted. Turn and broil other side about 1 minute or until lightly toasted. Cool on a wire rack. Cut or break into pieces. Makes 18 appetizer servings.

To Make Ahead:

Prepare toasts as directed. Cool completely. Place toasts in an airtight container and store at room temperature for up to 24 hours.

Nutrition Facts per serving: 79 cal., 5 g total fat (2 g sat. fat), 9 mg chol., 119 mg sodium, 7 g carbo., 0 g fiber, 1 g pro. **Daily Values:** 4% vit. A, 1% calcium, 2% iron.

Cheese 'n' Herb Mini Sweet Peppers

To keep these tiny peppers from tipping over, nestle them side by side on the baking sheet. (See the photograph on page 319.)

Prep: 25 minutes **Bake:** 8 minutes

30 red, yellow, and/or orange mini sweet peppers (about 12 oz. total)
18 oz. semisoft goat cheese (chèvre)
¼ cup snipped fresh basil, chives, tarragon, or thyme
   Fresh basil leaves

1 Preheat oven to 350°F. Leaving the stems intact, cut a lengthwise slit down each pepper. Remove the seeds; set aside.

2 In a small bowl stir together the goat cheese and snipped fresh herbs. Spoon cheese mixture into prepared peppers. Arrange filled peppers on a baking sheet.

3 Bake in the preheated oven for 8 to 10 minutes until cheese is heated through and peppers are crisp-tender. Using tongs, arrange warm peppers on a serving dish, stacking peppers into a pyramid. Garnish with fresh basil leaves. Makes 30 appetizer servings.

Nutrition Facts per serving: 65 cal., 5 g total fat (4 g sat. fat), 13 mg chol., 88 mg sodium, 1 g carbo., 0 g fiber, 4 g pro. **Daily Values:** 17% vit. A, 31% vit. C, 5% calcium, 2% iron.

30 MINUTE

Cheese Decked With Fruit

To bring out the fullest flavor of these cheeses, let the wedges stand at room temperature for about 30 minutes before assembling this quick-to-fix appetizer.

Start to finish: 10 minutes

- 1   lb. white cheddar cheese
- 6   to 8 oz. Stilton or blue cheese
- 2   Tbsp. chopped candied apricots
- 2   Tbsp. walnut halves and pieces
     Honey (optional)
     Red currants (optional)

1 On a serving pedestal or plate, place the cheese wedges. Top the cheese with chopped apricots and walnuts. If desired, drizzle with honey and sprinkle with red currants. Makes 22 appetizer servings.

Nutrition Facts per serving: 118 cal., 10 g total fat (6 g sat. fat), 27 mg chol., 236 mg sodium, 1 g carbo., 0 g fiber, 7 g pro. **Daily Values:** 5% vit. A, 19% calcium, 1% iron.

30 MINUTE

Dressed-Up Onion Dip

Begin with a container of sour cream French onion dip, add a couple of crunchy stir-ins, and the result is a fabulous dip that's fancy enough for company. (See the photograph on page 318.)

Start to finish: 15 minutes

- 1   medium fennel bulb
- 1   16-oz. container dairy sour cream French onion dip
- 2   Tbsp. finely chopped red onion
- 2   Tbsp. thinly sliced green onion
     Snipped fresh lemon thyme and/or snipped chives (optional)
     Assorted vegetables for dipping, such as strips of fennel, baby carrots, halved or sliced radishes, sliced cucumbers, and sliced zucchini

1 Wash fennel. Trim off feathery leaves. If desired, chop enough of the leaves to equal 2 tablespoons; set aside. Trim fennel bulb. Chop enough of the bulb to fill 1 cup. Cut remaining bulb into strips to use for dippers.

2 In a medium bowl stir together chopped fennel, onion dip, red onion, and green onion. Spoon the dip into a serving bowl and sprinkle the top with fennel leaves and snipped lemon thyme, and/or snipped chives, if desired. Serve with vegetable dippers. Makes about 2¼ cups dip.

To Make Ahead:
Prepare dip as directed. Cover and chill in the refrigerator for up to 24 hours.

Nutrition Facts per tablespoon dip: 35 cal., 2 g total fat (2 g sat. fat), 0 mg chol., 131 mg sodium, 3 g carbo., 1 g fiber, 1 g pro. **Daily Values:** 1% vit. C.

Spinach and Chicken Cheese Spread

Prep: 25 minutes   **Chill:** 6 hours

- 1   8-oz. pkg. reduced-fat cream cheese (Neufchâtel), softened
- ¼   tsp. lemon-pepper seasoning
- ¼   tsp. dried tarragon or thyme, crushed
- ½   of a 10-oz. pkg. frozen chopped spinach, thawed
- ¼   cup chopped onion
- 2   Tbsp. finely chopped roasted red sweet pepper
- ½   of a 9-oz. pkg. frozen, chopped, cooked chicken, thawed (1 cup)
- 1   5-oz. container semisoft cheese with garlic and herb
     Flowering kale (optional)
     Roasted red sweet pepper strips (optional)
     Assorted bread or crackers

1 Line bottom and sides of a 3-cup mold, bowl, or a 7½×3½×2½-inch loaf pan with clear plastic wrap; set aside. In a medium mixing bowl stir together cream cheese, lemon-pepper seasoning, and tarragon or thyme. Stir in spinach, onion, and sweet pepper. Spread half of the mixture evenly in the bottom of the prepared bowl, mold, or loaf pan.

2 In a food processor bowl combine chicken and semisoft cheese. Cover; process until smooth. Layer over the spinach mixture in the mold. Drop remaining spinach mixture by spoonfuls onto the chicken mixture; spread. Cover; chill at least 6 hours.

3 To serve, invert mold onto a serving platter; remove plastic wrap. Garnish with flowering kale and roasted red pepper strips, if desired. Serve with assorted crackers or bread. Makes 20 appetizer servings.

Nutrition Facts per serving: 134 cal., 6 g total fat (3 g sat. fat), 11 mg chol., 284 mg sodium, 13 g carbo., 1 g fiber, 5 g pro. Daily Values: 23% vit. A, 5% vit. C, 3% calcium, 4% iron.

30 MINUTE

Artichoke-Brie Focaccia

See the photograph on page 318.

Start to finish: 20 minutes

- 1 8-oz. round Brie cheese
- 1 13¾- or 14-oz. can artichoke hearts, drained and chopped
- 4 slices bacon, crisp-cooked, drained, and crumbled
- 1 10-inch square or round Italian flat bread (focaccia), about 2 inches thick, split and toasted
   Fresh rosemary (optional)
   Red grape tomatoes (optional)

1 Preheat oven to 400°F. Trim and discard rind from cheese; cut cheese into large pieces. Place in a medium microwave-safe bowl or 1-quart casserole. Cook in a microwave oven on 100% power (high) for 30 to 45 seconds or until cheese just begins to melt. Stir in artichokes and bacon. Cook on 100% power (high) for 1 to 1½ minutes or until mixture is heated through, stirring once or twice.

2 Spread mixture evenly on bottom half of focaccia. Place focaccia top over mixture. Place on a baking sheet. Bake, uncovered, in the preheated oven for 8 to 10 minutes or until heated through. Cut into 4×1-inch strips or into wedges. Garnish with a sprig of rosemary and a grape tomato, if desired. Makes 12 servings.

Nutrition Facts per serving: 170 cal., 8 g total fat (4 g sat. fat), 20 mg chol., 256 mg sodium, 18 g carbo., 2 g fiber, 8 g pro. Daily Values: 3% vit. A, 1% vit. C, 8% calcium, 6% iron.

EDITOR'S TIP

Open House Strategies

Hosting an open house and serving a variety of appetizers is a great way to entertain during the holidays. Consider these suggestions when planning a holiday gathering to avoid feeling overwhelmed by opening your house to a large group of guests.

● **Time it right.** A two- to three-hour party is long enough for most appetizers to be set out safely.

● **Make it easy for you.** Choose recipes that can primarily be made in advance. On the day of the party, you'll have only last-minute preparations.

● **Focus on variety.** Balance hot-from-the-oven appetizers with cold and room-temperature bites. Present some foods in individual servings and others whole for guests to serve themselves.

● **Pick a place.** At almost every party, the favorite spot for guests to gather is the kitchen. If that's not what you have in mind, make it obvious by positioning the appetizers and beverages in another room.

● **Set the style.** Select a buffet-style table to display the appetizers or keep your guests moving with several food stations located throughout the house.

● **Mix and match.** For serving platters, plates, bowls, and baskets, use a mix-and-match approach, combining transparent and opaque glass plates with pottery and wood serving dishes.

● **Think sturdy.** Use plates that are sturdy and large enough to handle a variety of foods. Be considerate of guests who will carry food while mingling with other guests. Flimsy plates may easily bend, break, or be dropped, causing embarrassment to the guests and a mess for you to clean up.

● **Hire help.** Extra hands make the open house event run smoothly. Whether the helpers are professional or volunteer, assign such tasks as last-minute appetizer assembly, platter replenishing, serving, and cleanup.

● **Appoint a greeter.** Welcome the guests and make them feel comfortable the minute they enter your home. Designate someone to meet and greet the guests if you cannot. Also designate a place for coats so that guests coming and going can find their wraps on their own.

● **Create the mood.** Music provides a pleasant background to a party atmosphere. If you have a musician in the family, recruit him or her to play. When piano or string instrument music provides familiar tunes, guests may use the opportunity to sing along.

● **Focus on fun.** When children are included on the invitation, hire a responsible teenager to take charge. Set aside a room for children with games, the makings for a small take-home craft, and a buffet of simple and nonmessy foods that children especially like.

Smoked Turkey on Wheat Biscuits

Layered with surprises, these tasty little finger sandwiches will quickly disappear. (See the photograph on page 318.)

Prep: 25 minutes **Bake:** 8 minutes

1 cup all-purpose flour
1 cup whole wheat flour
2 tsp. sugar
1 Tbsp. snipped fresh tarragon
1 Tbsp. baking powder
½ tsp. cream of tartar
¼ tsp. salt
½ cup butter
½ cup buttermilk
¼ cup dairy sour cream
2 Tbsp. apple jelly
1 tsp. snipped fresh tarragon
2 to 3 oz. sliced smoked turkey breast, folded into 2-inch pieces
1 to 2 oz. very thinly sliced Emmentaler or white cheddar cheese
   Prepared fig conserve or cranberry relish
   Thin apple slices
   Mizuna leaves (optional)*

1 Preheat oven to 450°F. In a large mixing bowl stir together all-purpose flour, whole wheat flour, sugar, the 1 tablespoon snipped tarragon, baking powder, cream of tartar, and salt. Using a pastry blender, cut in butter until mixture resembles coarse crumbs. Make a well in the center of dry mixture. In a small mixing bowl combine the buttermilk and sour cream; add to dry mixture all at once. Using a fork, stir just until moistened.

2 Turn the dough out onto a lightly floured surface. Quickly knead dough by folding and pressing gently for 10 to 12 strokes or until the dough is nearly smooth. Pat or lightly roll dough to ½-inch thickness. Cut dough with a floured 2-inch oval or round cutter. Place biscuits 2 inches apart on an ungreased baking sheet.

3 In a small saucepan heat apple jelly and the 1 teaspoon snipped tarragon over medium heat until melted. Using a pastry brush, brush tops of biscuits with jelly mixture.

4 Bake for 8 to 10 minutes or until bottoms are lightly browned. Remove biscuits from baking sheet and cool on a wire rack.

5 To assemble, slit biscuits in half. Layer bottom of biscuits with sliced smoked turkey, Emmentaler or white cheddar cheese, fig conserve or cranberry relish, and an apple slice. Replace biscuit tops. Serve on mizuna leaves, if desired. Makes 22 appetizer servings.

***Note:** Mizuna is a feathery, delicate salad green. Select crisp, green leaves that are free of brown spots. When you can't find it, substitute other salad greens.

To Make Ahead:

Prepare and bake biscuits as directed. Cool completely. Place biscuits in a freezer container or bag and freeze for up to 3 months. Thaw before serving. Assemble appetizers as directed.

Nutrition Facts per serving: 103 cal., 6 g total fat (3 g sat. fat), 16 mg chol., 165 mg sodium, 11 g carbo., 1 g fiber, 3 g pro. **Daily Values:** 4% vit. A, 6% calcium, 3% iron.

Have-a-Ball Rolls

Add herbed flavor to frozen bread dough by shaping the dough into tiny balls and topping them with flavorful, crunchy seeds.

Prep: 20 minutes **Rise:** 30 minutes
Bake: 13 minutes

1 16-oz. loaf frozen white or whole wheat bread dough, thawed
1 egg white
1 Tbsp. water
   Fennel seed, mustard seed, and/or dillseed

1 Lightly grease a baking sheet or thirty to thirty-six 1¾-inch muffin cups; set aside.

2 Divide dough into pieces. Shape into small balls. Place rolls on prepared baking sheet or in prepared muffin cups. Cover and let rise in a warm place about 30 minutes or until nearly double in size

3 Preheat oven to 350°F. Beat together the egg white and water. Brush over the rolls. Sprinkle generously with fennel seed, mustard seed, and/or dillseed.

4 Bake in the preheated oven for 13 to 15 minutes or until golden brown. Transfer rolls to wire racks. Serve warm. Makes 30 to 36 mini rolls.

Nutrition Facts per roll: 37 cal., 0 g total fat, 0 mg chol., 2 mg sodium, 7 g carbo., 0 g fiber, 1 g pro. **Daily Values:** 2% calcium, 1% iron.

Grapefruit-Miso Salad

Lori Hall
Erie, Pennsylvania
$200—Citrus Inspirations

Start to finish: 25 minutes

- 2 **cups torn romaine lettuce**
- 2 **cups torn fresh spinach**
- ½ **cup chopped yellow
    sweet pepper**
- 3 **Tbsp. miso paste***
- 2 **Tbsp. rice vinegar**
- 2 **Tbsp. salad oil**
- 2 **tsp. sugar**
- 1 **medium tomato, cut into wedges**
- 2 **to 3 small grapefruit,
    peeled and sectioned**
- ¼ **cup fresh enoki mushrooms**

1 In a large bowl toss together romaine, spinach, and yellow sweet pepper.

2 In a small bowl combine miso paste, rice vinegar, salad oil, and sugar. Whisk mixture until smooth. Pour miso mixture over vegetable mixture, tossing to coat.

3 To serve, transfer salad to a serving bowl. Top with tomato wedges, grapefruit sections, and mushrooms. Makes 4 to 6 servings.

***Note:** Look for miso paste (also called bean paste) in the Asian food section of larger supermarkets or in specialty food stores.

Nutrition Facts per serving: 158 cal., 8 g total fat (1 g sat. fat), 0 mg chol., 488 mg sodium, 20 g carbo., 4 g fiber, 4 g pro. **Daily Values:** 40% vit. A, 152% vit. C, 6% calcium, 9% iron.

TEST KITCHEN TIP

What's Baby Broccoli?

Tender and sweet, baby broccoli is a cross between broccoli and Chinese kale. Completely edible, it has slim stems with a broccoli-like head of flowering buds. Good for you too, it's packed with vitamin C and provides a generous amount of folate, vitamin A, and potassium.

Festive Apple Slaw

All decked out in red and green, this crunchy fruit and vegetable slaw is a glorious side dish to serve with roasted pork or chicken.

Prep: 30 minutes **Chill:** 1 hour

- 1 **recipe Apple Cider Vinaigrette
    (see right)**
- 3 **cups cored and thinly sliced tart
    green apples, such as Newton,
    Pippin, or Granny Smith,
    and/or sweet red apples, such
    as Red Delicious or McIntosh**
- 1 **cup shredded red cabbage**
- ½ **cup seedless green or
    red grapes, halved**
- ⅓ **cup chopped celery**
- ¼ **cup slivered almonds, toasted**

1 Prepare Apple Cider Vinaigrette. Cover and chill until needed.

2 In a large salad bowl place apples, cabbage, grapes, and celery. Toss gently to mix.

3 Shake vinaigrette. Pour dressing over salad, tossing to coat. Cover and chill for 1 hour. Before serving, toss salad with almonds. Serve salad in individual serving bowls. Makes 6 to 8 servings.

Apple Cider Vinaigrette

In a screw-top jar combine ¼ cup cider vinegar, 3 tablespoons salad oil, and 2 tablespoons honey. Cover and shake well. Store in the refrigerator.

Nutrition Facts per serving: 161 cal., 10 g total fat (1 g sat. fat), 0 mg chol., 6 mg sodium, 19 g carbo., 3 g fiber, 2 g pro. **Daily Values:** 1% vit. A, 19% vit. C, 3% calcium, 3% iron.

Lemon-Braised Baby Broccoli

Start to finish: 30 minutes

- 1 **cup reduced-sodium chicken
    broth**
- 1 **Tbsp. snipped fresh dill**
- 2 **slices preserved lemon***
- ⅛ **tsp. crushed red pepper**
- ⅛ **tsp. ground black pepper**
- 2 **Tbsp. butter**
- 1 **lb. baby broccoli or broccoli raab**

1 In a large skillet combine broth, dill, preserved lemon, red pepper, and black pepper. Bring to boiling; reduce heat. Simmer, covered, for 15 minutes.

2 Add butter and baby broccoli to skillet. Cover and cook over medium heat for 6 to 8 minutes or until the broccoli is tender. Drain, if desired; transfer to a serving bowl. Garnish with fresh lemon halves or slices, if desired. Makes 8 servings.

***Note:** Substitute 2 teaspoons finely shredded lemon peel, ½ teaspoon kosher salt, and 1 teaspoon olive oil for the preserved lemon, if desired.

Nutrition Facts per serving: 47 cal., 3 g total fat (2 g sat. fat), 8 mg chol., 489 mg sodium, 4 g carbo., 2 g fiber, 2 g pro. **Daily Values:** 19% vit. A, 84% vit. C, 3% calcium, 3% iron.

Molasses-Tossed Potatoes

A molasses-flavored caramel-like glaze lightly coats these oven-roasted potatoes. For added interest, use more than one variety of small potatoes.

Prep: 15 minutes **Roast:** 35 minutes

	Nonstick cooking spray
2½	lb. tiny new potatoes, small Yukon Gold potatoes, and/or fingerling potatoes
2	Tbsp. cooking oil
2	Tbsp. molasses
2	Tbsp. balsamic vinegar
1	tsp. dried thyme, crushed
½	tsp. salt
½	cup walnut pieces

1 Preheat oven to 450°F. Coat a 13×9×2-inch baking pan with nonstick cooking spray. Scrub and quarter potatoes (halve any large quarters). Arrange potatoes in pan.

2 In a small bowl combine cooking oil, molasses, balsamic vinegar, thyme, and salt. Drizzle mixture over potatoes, tossing gently to coat.

3 Roast potatoes, uncovered, in the preheated oven for 20 minutes. Add walnut pieces, stirring to mix. Roast for 15 to 20 minutes more or until the potatoes are tender, stirring once. Transfer to a serving bowl. Makes 8 side-dish servings.

Nutrition Facts per serving: 219 cal., 9 g total fat (1 g sat. fat), 0 mg chol., 157 mg sodium, 33 g carbo., 3 g fiber, 4 g pro. Daily Values: 1% vit. A, 24% vit. C, 3% calcium, 12% iron.

Christmas Eve Lamb Stew

This spiced blend of lamb, vegetables, and fruits is incredibly delicious served over Mashed Sweet Potatoes (see recipe, right).

Prep: 30 minutes **Cook:** 1½ hours

2	lb. lamb stew meat, cut into 1-inch cubes
¼	tsp. salt
¼	tsp. pepper
2	Tbsp. cooking oil
2	Tbsp. all-purpose flour
2	14½-oz. cans vegetable broth
1	12-oz. can apricot or mango nectar
1	2-inch stick cinnamon or ¼ tsp. ground cinnamon
3	cloves garlic, minced
½	tsp. ground cumin
½	tsp. ground cardamom
⅛	tsp. thread saffron, crushed
3	medium carrots, cut into ½-inch pieces (1½ cups)
1½	cups frozen pearl onions
1	cup dried apricots
1	cup dried pitted plums (prunes)
1	recipe Mashed Sweet Potatoes (optional) (see right)
	Fresh sage leaves (optional)

1 Season lamb with salt and pepper. In a 4-quart Dutch oven brown meat, half at a time, in hot oil over medium-high heat. Drain off excess oil. Return all meat to pan. Sprinkle meat with flour, stirring to coat. Add vegetable broth, apricot or mango nectar, cinnamon, garlic, cumin, cardamom, and saffron; stir to combine. Bring to boiling; reduce heat. Simmer, covered, about 1 hour or until meat is nearly tender.

2 Add carrots, onions, apricots, and dried plums to pan. Return to boiling; reduce heat. Simmer, covered, about 30 minutes more or until vegetables are tender. Remove stick cinnamon, if using. Serve over Mashed Sweet Potatoes or mashed potatoes, if desired. Garnish with fresh sage leaves, if desired. Makes 6 servings.

Nutrition Facts per serving: 418 cal., 12 g total fat (3 g sat. fat), 96 mg chol., 773 mg sodium, 51 g carbo., 6 g fiber, 33 g pro. Daily Values: 209% vit. A, 10% vit. C, 6% calcium, 29% iron.

Mashed Sweet Potatoes

Yogurt gives these mashed sweets a little tang.

Start to finish: 35 minutes

2	lb. sweet potatoes
¼	cup margarine or butter, cut up
¼	cup plain yogurt
	Low-fat or skim milk

1 Peel and quarter the sweet potatoes. In a large saucepan cook potatoes, covered, in a moderate amount of boiling lightly salted water for 20 to 25 minutes or until tender; drain.

2 Mash the sweet potatoes with a potato masher or beat with an electric mixer on low speed. Add the margarine or butter and the yogurt; mash or beat until smooth. If necessary, stir in a little low-fat or skim milk to make of desired consistency. Makes 6 servings.

Nutrition Facts per serving: 195 cal., 8 g total fat (1 g sat. fat), 1 mg chol., 108 mg sodium, 29 g carbo., 4 g fiber, 3 g pro. Daily Values: 522% vit. A, 49% vit. C, 5% calcium, 3% iron.

Citrus-Marinated Lamb Kabobs

For an added burst of orange flavor, squeeze the grilled orange wedges over the couscous.

Prep: 35 minutes **Grill:** 12 minutes
Marinate: 2 hours

- 1 **pink grapefruit**
- ¼ **cup honey**
- 2 **Tbsp. snipped fresh mint**
- ½ **tsp. salt**
- ½ **tsp. freshly ground black pepper**
- ½ **tsp. ground coriander**
- 1 **lb. boneless lamb, cut into
     1-inch pieces**
- 2 **small zucchini and/or yellow
     summer squash, cut into
     ½-inch slices**
- 1 **orange, cut into 8 wedges**
- 1 **medium red sweet pepper, cut
     into 1-inch pieces**
- 1 **to 2 Tbsp. olive oil**
- 2 **cups hot cooked couscous**
- 2 **tsp. snipped fresh mint**

1 Squeeze juice from grapefruit. In a plastic bag set in a medium bowl, combine grapefruit juice, honey, the 2 tablespoons mint, the salt, black pepper, and coriander. Add lamb, turning to coat. Seal bag and chill for 2 to 3 hours, turning bag occasionally.

2 Drain lamb; discard marinade. On four 12-inch skewers alternately thread meat, zucchini or yellow summer squash, orange, and red pepper. Lightly brush vegetables with the olive oil.

3 Grill kabobs on the rack of an uncovered grill directly over medium coals for 12 to 15 minutes or until meat is desired doneness and vegetables are crisp-tender.

4 Meanwhile, stir together hot cooked couscous and 2 teaspoons snipped fresh mint. Serve kabobs with couscous mixture. Makes 4 servings.

Broiler Directions:
Place kabobs on unheated rack of broiler pan. Broil 4 to 5 inches from heat for 12 to 15 minutes or until meat is desired doneness, turning occasionally to brown evenly. Serve as above.

Nutrition Facts per serving: 327 cal., 9 g total fat (2 g sat. fat), 73 mg chol., 168 mg sodium, 33 g carbo., 3 g fiber, 27 g pro. **Daily Values:** 40% vit. A, 130% vit. C, 52% calcium, 18% iron.

PRIZE WINNER

Pork Salad Sandwiches

Tim Bernard
Wirtz, Virginia
$400—Citrus Inspirations

Prep: 25 minutes **Chill:** 2 hours

- 2 **cups cooked pork, cut into thin
     strips or diced**
- 1 **cup diced red, yellow, and/or
     green sweet pepper**
- ½ **cup diced celery**
- ¼ **cup diced red onion**
- ⅓ **cup mayonnaise or
     salad dressing**
- 2 **Tbsp. Dijon-style mustard**
- 1 **Tbsp. finely shredded
     orange peel**
- 1½ **tsp. dried spice blend of lemon,
     basil, and thyme**

WEEKEND LUNCH

- **Pork Salad Sandwiches
  (see left)**

- **Sliced pears and apples**

- **Potato chips**

- **Gingersnap cookies with
  lemon sorbet**

- 1 **tsp. finely shredded lemon or
     lime peel**
- 1 **tsp. sugar**
- 3 **cups packaged shredded cabbage
     with carrot (coleslaw mix)**
- 3 **oranges, peeled and sectioned**
- 1 **lemon or lime, peeled
     and sectioned**
- 6 **to 8 hoagie buns, kaiser rolls,
     or other rolls, split**

1 In a large bowl stir together the cooked pork, sweet pepper, celery, and onion. Set aside.

2 In a small bowl stir together the mayonnaise or salad dressing, Dijon-style mustard, orange peel, spice blend, lemon or lime peel, and sugar. Add mayonnaise mixture to pork mixture, stirring to coat. Cover and chill for 2 to 4 hours.

3 Just before serving, fold coleslaw mix, orange sections, and lemon or lime sections into pork mixture. Spoon filling into buns. Makes 6 to 8 sandwiches.

Nutrition Facts per sandwich: 493 cal., 16 g total fat (3 g sat. fat), 46 mg chol., 743 mg sodium, 64 g carbo., 6 g fiber, 24 g pro. **Daily Values:** 85% vit. A, 167% vit. C, 15% calcium, 18% iron.

- Salad of fresh spinach, apple slices, and crumbled blue cheese drizzled with poppy seed dressing

- Pork Roast with Port Wine Sauce (see below)

- Glazed sweet potatoes

- Buttered steamed broccoli

- Multigrain dinner rolls

LOW FAT

Pork Roast with Port Wine Sauce

A pecan and Parmesan cheese mixture forms a tasty crust to lock in the juices of the roast.

Prep: 20 minutes **Cook:** 10 minutes, sauce
Roast: 1¼ hours **Stand:** 15 minutes

- ⅓ cup finely chopped pecans
- 3 Tbsp. grated Parmesan cheese
- 1 Tbsp. yellow mustard
- 1 tsp. Worcestershire sauce or soy sauce
- 1 2- to 2¼-lb. boneless pork top loin roast (single loin)
- 2 cups port wine or Marsala
- 1 cup snipped dried golden or black figs
- 2 Tbsp. brown sugar
- 1 bay leaf
   Dried golden figs (optional)

1 Preheat oven to 325°F. In a small mixing bowl stir together pecans, Parmesan cheese, mustard, and Worcestershire sauce. Spread pecan mixture on pork roast. Place on a rack in a shallow roasting pan. Insert meat thermometer into center of meat.

2 Roast in the preheated oven for 1¼ to 1½ hours or until thermometer registers 155°F. Cover with foil and let stand for 15 minutes. (Meat temperature will rise 5°F during standing.)

3 Meanwhile, for sauce, in a medium saucepan stir together wine, snipped figs, brown sugar, and bay leaf. Bring to boiling; reduce heat. Simmer, uncovered, for 10 to 15 minutes or until mixture has been reduced to 2¼ cups. Remove bay leaf.

4 Transfer sauce mixture to a blender container or food processor bowl. Cover and blend or process until nearly smooth. Pass mixture through a mesh strainer over a bowl, pressing solids to release juices. Discard solids. (For a seedless sauce, sieve mixture again, using a fine mesh sieve.) Return sauce to saucepan; gently reheat just before serving. Serve sauce with meat. Garnish with additional figs, if desired. Makes 8 servings.

Nutrition Facts per serving: 365 cal., 10 g total fat (3 g sat. fat), 63 mg chol., 110 mg sodium, 28 g carbo., 4 g fiber, 27 g pro. Daily Values: 1% vit. A, 1% vit. C, 10% calcium, 15% iron.

Stout Glazed Ham

Plan to use the ham leftovers in sandwiches or to accompany breakfast or brunch.

Prep: 10 minutes **Cook:** 10 minutes, sauce
Roast: 1 hour, 50 minutes
Stand: 15 minutes

- 1 5- to 6 lb. cooked ham (rump half or shank portion)
   Whole cloves
- ½ cup Irish stout, such as Guinness, or apple cider
- ¼ cup honey
- ¼ cup butter or margarine
- 6 small parsnips, peeled and halved lengthwise
- 1 lb. red boiling onions, peeled and halved, and/or medium red onions, quartered

1 Preheat oven to 325°F. Score ham by making diagonal cuts in a diamond pattern. Stud with cloves. Place ham on a rack in a shallow roasting pan. Insert a meat thermometer. Roast, uncovered, in the preheated oven until thermometer registers 120°F. For rump, roast 1 to 1¼ hours; for shank, roast 1½ to 1¾ hours.

2 Meanwhile, prepare glaze. In a small saucepan combine stout, honey, and butter. Bring to boiling; reduce heat. Simmer, uncovered, for 10 minutes. Set aside.

3 Cook parsnips in a small amount of boiling water for 5 minutes; drain. Arrange onion and partially cooked parsnips around ham. Pour glaze over ham and vegetables. Bake about 50 minutes more or until thermometer registers 135°F and vegetables are tender, spooning pan juices over ham and vegetables once. Remove roasting pan from oven. Cover ham and vegetables with foil and let stand 15 minutes before carving ham. (Meat temperature will rise 5°F during standing.)

4 Remove ham and vegetables to a serving platter, spooning some of the pan juices over vegetables. Makes 14 servings.

Nutrition Facts per serving: 283 cal., 14 g total fat (6 g sat. fat), 76 mg chol., 1,740 mg sodium, 12 g carbo., 1 g fiber, 26 g pro. Daily Values: 3% vit. A, 8% vit. C, 2% calcium, 10% iron.

Tropical Chicken

Add a little sunshine to your winter menu. Bright in color and sweet in flavor, this saucy chicken will transport your thoughts to the tropics.

Start to finish: 35 minutes

- 3 lb. meaty chicken pieces
- 1 Tbsp. olive oil
- ¼ tsp. salt
- ¼ tsp. pepper
- 1 6-oz. container (⅔ cup) frozen orange juice concentrate, thawed
- ½ cup unsweetened coconut milk
- 1 8-oz. can crushed pineapple (juice pack), undrained
- 2 Tbsp. rum
- 1 Tbsp. brown sugar
- 1 Tbsp. grated fresh ginger
- ⅛ tsp. salt

1 Preheat broiler. Arrange the chicken pieces, bone side up, on unheated rack of the broiler pan. Brush lightly with olive oil. Sprinkle with the ¼ teaspoon salt and the pepper. Broil 4 to 5 inches from the heat for 20 to 30 minutes, turning once, until chicken is nearly done.

2 Meanwhile, in a medium saucepan stir together orange juice concentrate, coconut milk, undrained pineapple, rum, brown sugar, ginger, and the ⅛ teaspoon salt. Bring to boiling; reduce heat. Boil gently, uncovered, for 15 to 20 minutes or until reduced to 1¾ cups.

3 Spoon some of the sauce over the chicken. Broil about 5 minutes more until chicken is golden brown and no longer pink inside.

4 To serve, transfer chicken pieces to a serving platter. Pass the remaining sauce to spoon over chicken. Makes 6 servings.

Grill Directions:

Arrange medium-hot coals around a drip pan. Test for medium heat above the pan. Place chicken pieces, bone side down, on grill rack over drip pan. Cover and grill for 50 to 60 minutes or until tender and no longer pink. Cook sauce as directed at left and brush chicken with some of the sauce during the last 15 minutes of grilling. To serve, reheat and pass the remaining sauce with chicken. Serve as directed at left.

Nutrition Facts per serving: 453 cal., 25 g total fat (10 g sat. fat), 130 mg chol., 251 mg sodium, 20 g carbo., 1 g fiber, 34 g pro. **Daily Values:** 5% vit. A, 84% vit. C, 4% calcium, 11% iron.

Cheesy Chorizo Strata

It's the chorizo (chor-EE-zoh), a ground pork sausage that is highly seasoned with garlic, chili powder, and other spices, that gives this egg dish a kick. If the chorizo you purchase has a casing, remove it before cooking.

Prep: 25 minutes **Bake:** 45 minutes
Stand: 15 minutes plus 10 minutes

- 8 oz. chorizo or bulk pork sausage
- ⅓ cup chopped onion
- ⅓ cup chopped red sweet pepper
- 1 clove garlic, minced
- 6 ¾-inch-thick slices Italian bread (8 oz.)
- 1½ cups shredded Monterey Jack cheese with jalapeño peppers (6 oz.)
- 2 eggs, beaten
- 2 cups half-and-half or light cream
- 1 Tbsp. snipped fresh cilantro

1 In a large skillet cook chorizo or pork sausage, onion, sweet pepper, and garlic until sausage is cooked and vegetables are tender. Drain off fat. Set aside.

2 Place four slices of bread in a 2-quart square baking dish. Spread sausage mixture over bread slices. Sprinkle with 1 cup of the Monterey Jack cheese. Place remaining bread slices on top of cheese.

3 In a medium mixing bowl stir together eggs, half-and-half or light cream, and cilantro. Pour evenly over bread in baking dish to moisten. Using the back of a spoon, press the bread down gently. Let stand for 15 minutes. Preheat oven to 325°F.

4 Bake in the preheated oven about 45 minutes or until a knife inserted near the center comes out clean. Sprinkle with remaining ½ cup cheese. Let stand 10 minutes before serving. Makes 6 servings.

Nutrition Facts per serving: 515 cal., 35 g total fat (17 g sat. fat), 159 mg chol., 892 mg sodium, 25 g carbo., 1 g fiber, 24 g pro. **Daily Values:** 24% vit. A, 25% vit. C, 34% calcium, 13% iron.

Santa's Pear Pouches

Bay leaves may be used to decorate the finished pouches, but they are not to be eaten. (See the photograph on page 320.)

Prep: 30 minutes **Bake:** 20 minutes

- 3 medium red or green skinned pears, cored and thinly sliced (about 3½ cups)
- 1 Tbsp. sugar
- 1 Tbsp. all-purpose flour
- ¼ tsp. ground cardamom
- ⅓ cup butter, melted
- 4 sheets frozen phyllo dough (18×14-inch rectangles, thawed)
- ¼ cup caramel ice cream topping
  Sugar or coarse sugar
  Bay leaves (optional)
  Cranberries (optional)

1 For filling, in a medium mixing bowl combine sliced pears, the 1 tablespoon sugar, the flour, and cardamom. Toss gently to coat pears; set aside. Preheat oven to 375°F.

2 Brush four 6-ounce custard cups with some of the melted butter; set aside. Place one sheet of phyllo dough on a cutting board or other flat surface. (Keep remaining phyllo covered with plastic wrap to prevent it from becoming dry and brittle.) Lightly brush the sheet with some of the melted butter. Place another phyllo sheet on top; brush with butter. Repeat with two more phyllo sheets. Cut stack in half lengthwise and then in half crosswise to form four rectangles.

3 Gently ease one stack of phyllo into bottom and up sides of one custard cup (phyllo will extend over edge). Spoon about ¾ cup of the pear filling into the center. Drizzle 1 tablespoon of caramel topping over pears. Bring up phyllo over filling, pinching together to form a ruffled edge. (If desired, arrange a slice or two of pear to poke through the top of the pouch.) Secure pouch with clean kitchen string. Brush again with melted butter. Sprinkle with some of the 1 tablespoon sugar or coarse sugar. Repeat with remaining phyllo, filling, caramel sauce, butter, and sugar. Place the custard cups in a 15×10×1-inch baking pan.

4 Bake in the preheated oven about 20 minutes or until phyllo is golden. Cool 5 minutes in custard cups; remove from cups. Tuck bay leaves under kitchen string and place a few cranberries on serving plate for garnish, if desired. Serve warm or cool. Makes 4 servings.

Nutrition Facts per serving: 364 cal., 18 g total fat (10 g sat. fat), 43 mg chol., 310 mg sodium, 51 g carbo., 4 g fiber, 2 g pro. **Daily Values:** 13% vit. A, 8% vit. C, 3% calcium, 6% iron.

Cake with All the Trimmings

(See the photograph on page 320.)

Prep: 20 minutes

- 2 oz. white chocolate baking squares
- ½ cup dried mango pieces
- ½ cup toasted coconut shards*
- ¼ cup crystallized ginger
- 1 to 2 Tbsp. dried cranberries
- 1 2-layer bakery or homemade frosted cake

1 In a heavy small saucepan melt white chocolate over very low heat, stirring constantly. Remove from heat. Carefully dip one edge of dried mango pieces into melted white chocolate. Set aside to dry on waxed paper.

2 Meanwhile, in a small bowl combine toasted coconut, crystallized ginger, and dried cranberries. Spoon coconut mixture evenly over top of frosted cake. Using your hand, gently press coconut mixture into frosting so it will stick. Sprinkle with mango pieces. Makes 12 servings.

*Note: To make toasted coconut shards, use a vegetable peeler to cut a 2-ounce piece of fresh coconut that is 3 inches long into thin shards. Place shards in a single layer on a baking sheet and bake in a 350°F oven for 5 to 10 minutes or until the coconut shards are lightly toasted.

Nutrition Facts per serving: 487 cal., 20 g total fat (7 g sat. fat), 5 mg chol., 317 mg sodium, 75 g carbo., 2 g fiber, 5 g pro. **Daily Values:** 10% vit. A, 1% vit. C, 12% calcium, 7% iron.

Macadamia Nut Fruit Cakes

Not your average fruit cakes, these golden cakes are chock-full of pears and/or apricots and raisins, and soaked with apricot brandy. They make fancy little gifts when neatly packaged in tins and tied with ribbons.

Prep: 45 minutes **Bake:** 40 minutes
Stand: up to 5 days

½ cup apricot nectar

2 cups chopped dried pears
and/or apricots

½ cup golden raisins or
regular raisins

½ cup butter, softened

1 cup sugar

2 eggs

¼ cup apricot brandy

¼ cup apricot nectar

1 tsp. vanilla

1½ cups all-purpose flour

¼ tsp. baking soda

⅛ tsp. salt

1 cup coarsely chopped macadamia
nuts or almonds

½ cup apricot brandy or
apricot nectar

⅓ cup apricot nectar

1 Preheat oven to 300°F. Grease and lightly flour six 1-cup fluted tube pans, six 1-cup tube pans, or one 9×5×3-inch loaf pan. Set aside pan(s). In a small saucepan bring the ½ cup apricot nectar just to boiling; remove from heat. Stir in pears and/or apricots and raisins. Cover and let stand for 10 minutes.

2 In a large mixing bowl beat butter with an electric mixer on medium speed for 30 seconds. Add sugar; beat until mixture is combined. Add eggs, one at a time, beating on medium speed until combined.

3 In a small bowl combine the ¼ cup apricot brandy, the ¼ apricot nectar, and vanilla; set aside. In a medium bowl stir together the flour, baking soda, and salt. Add the flour mixture and brandy mixture alternately to butter mixture, beating on low speed after each addition just until combined. Fold the soaked fruit

and chopped macadamia nuts into batter. Spread batter into the prepared pan(s).

4 Bake in the preheated oven for 40 to 45 minutes for tube pans or 70 minutes for the loaf pan or until a wooden toothpick inserted into center(s) comes out clean. Cool cake(s) in pans on a wire rack for 10 minutes. Remove from pan(s) and cool completely on a wire rack.

5 Using a wooden toothpick or bamboo skewer, poke holes into cake(s). Soak six 8-inch square pieces (for tube pans) or one 20×8-inch piece (for loaf pan) of double thickness 100% cotton cheesecloth with the ½ cup apricot brandy or nectar. Wrap cakes in soaked cheesecloth. Drizzle any remaining brandy over the cake(s).

6 Wrap cake(s) tightly in foil or seal in plastic storage bags. Store in the refrigerator for 24 hours. Unwrap cakes and drizzle with the ⅓ cup nectar. Rewrap cake(s) and store in the refrigerator for up to 4 more days. Makes 18 servings (6 individual cakes or one loaf).

To Make Ahead:

Prepare cakes as directed, except after drizzling the final ⅓ cup of nectar over the cakes, wrap the cakes securely in freezer wrap and freeze for up to 3 months. To thaw, let stand in the refrigerator overnight.

Nutrition Facts per serving: 297 cal., 12 g total fat (4 g sat. fat), 38 mg chol., 119 mg sodium, 42 g carbo., 3 g fiber, 3 g pro. **Daily Values:** 9% vit. A, 3% vit. C, 2% calcium, 8% iron.

TEST KITCHEN TIP
Cookie Sheets

Before you begin baking for the holidays, take a look at the baking sheets in your cupboard. If they are thin and warped or dark with baked-on grease, or if you have only pans with 1-inch sides, it's time to purchase new pans.

Look for shiny, heavy-gauge sheets with very low or no sides. Avoid dark cookie sheets, which may cause the bottoms of cookies to overbrown.

Use jelly-roll pans (15×10×1-inch baking pans) only for bar cookies. Other types of cookies won't bake evenly in pans with sides. If you must use jelly-roll pans for cookies, turn them over and bake on the bottom.

Nonstick cookie sheets allow you to skip the greasing step; however, the dough may not spread as much and may result in thicker cakelike cookies.

Insulated cookie sheets slow baking and tend to yield pale cookies with soft centers. If you have trouble when using insulated sheets for cookies that contain a large proportion of butter, such as sugar-cookie cutouts, it is probably because the butter melts out before the dough sets. Avoid baking cookies on insulated cookie sheets long enough to brown the bottoms because the cookies will be dry. On the other hand, when an oven heats too hot or browns cookies rapidly, insulated cookie sheets may improve the results.

Greasing cookie sheets makes it easy to remove cookies and to wash cookie sheets after baking. Lightly greasing with shortening or coating with nonstick cooking spray is adequate for most cookie recipes. Using too much fat or greasing when recipes don't call for it causes cookies to spread excessively, to brown too quickly around the edges, or to have very thin edges.

Cookie Heritage

Cookie recipes were included in the first cookbook published in North America in 1796. The book by Amelia Simmons carried the breathtaking title *American Cooking, or the Art of Dressing Viands, Fish, Poultry, and Vegetables, and the Best Modes of Making Pastes, Puffs, Pies, Tarts, Puddings, Custards and Preserves, and all Kinds of Cakes from the Imperial Plumb to the Plain Cake Adapted to this Country, and all Grades of Life.*

The cakes referred to in the title were biscuitlike cookies. One of them, Another Christmas Cookey, called for three pounds of flour, a tea cup of fine powdered coriander seed, one pound of butter, and three tea spoonfuls of pearl ash dissolved in a tea cup of milk. Like most easy cookies, they were shaped by rolling and cutting. Simmons advised that the cookies would be "finer, softer, and better when six months old" after being stored in an earthen pot, dry cellar, or damp room.

The geographical development of the United States was reflected in cookie recipes that became popular. The expansion of the railroad in the early 1800s gave bakers access to coconuts from the South. Later in the century, oranges from the West became an ingredient option.

Around 1900, the Kellogg brothers invested in cornflakes, and cookies made with cereal became the rage. In the 1930s, electric refrigeration made its way into every region of the United States. Icebox cookies, as the chilled slice-and-bake treats were called, were considered an advantage for busy homemakers. The cookies didn't require rolling and were every bit as thin and crisp as rolled cookies.

Hazelnut Bars

Melted white baking bar and milk chocolate offer two-tone design and flavor. Place the bars in a single layer on a tray to serve; otherwise, the coating will stick together.

Prep: 25 minutes **Bake:** 35 minutes

- ½   cup butter, softened
- 2   3-oz. pkg. cream cheese, softened
- ½   cup packed brown sugar
- 1   tsp. vanilla
- 2   cups all-purpose flour
- 3   eggs, slightly beaten
- 1   cup packed brown sugar
- ⅔   cup light-colored corn syrup
- ¼   cup pure maple syrup or maple-flavored syrup
- ¼   cup whipping cream
- ¼   cup butter, melted
- ⅛   tsp. salt
- 2   cups chopped hazelnuts (filberts), toasted
- 4   oz. white baking bar or 2 oz. each white baking bar and milk chocolate bar or pieces

1 Preheat oven to 350°F. Lightly grease a 15×10×1-inch baking pan; set aside. For crust, in a large mixing bowl beat the ½ cup butter, cream cheese, ½ cup brown sugar, and vanilla with an electric mixer on medium to high speed until well combined. Beat in as much flour as you can with the mixer. Using a wooden spoon, stir in any remaining flour. Pat mixture evenly into bottom of the prepared pan. Bake in the preheated oven for 15 minutes.

2 Meanwhile, for filling, in a medium mixing bowl stir together the eggs, the 1 cup brown sugar, corn syrup, maple syrup, whipping cream, the ¼ cup melted butter, and salt. Stir in hazelnuts.

3 Pour filling over partially baked crust in baking pan. Bake an additional 20 minutes or until the mixture is golden and bubbly. Cool in the pan on a wire rack.

4 In a heavy small saucepan melt white baking bar over low heat, stirring constantly. (If using milk chocolate bar or pieces, melt in a second small saucepan.) Drizzle melted white baking bar and melted milk chocolate, if using, over bars in a decorative pattern. Let stand until set. Cut into bars. Store in the refrigerator. Makes 48 bars.

Nutrition Facts per bar: 159 cal., 9 g total fat (4 g sat. fat), 28 mg chol., 63 mg sodium, 18 g carbo., 1 g fiber, 2 g pro. Daily Values: 4% vit. A, 1% vit. C, 2% calcium, 4% iron.

Cranberry Rum Baklava

For long storage, place the pieces in an airtight freezer container and freeze for up to 1 month.

Prep: 1 hour **Bake:** 35 minutes

- 4   cups walnuts, finely chopped (1 lb.)
- ½   cup dried cranberries
- ⅔   cup orange marmalade
- ½   tsp. ground cinnamon
- ¼   tsp. ground nutmeg

1¼ cups butter, melted
1 16-oz. pkg. frozen phyllo
    dough, thawed
1½ cups packed brown sugar
½ cup water
⅓ cup rum
¼ cup honey
½ tsp. finely shredded orange peel
    Dash ground cinnamon
    Dash ground nutmeg

1 For filling, in a large mixing bowl stir together chopped walnuts, dried cranberries, orange marmalade, ½ teaspoon ground cinnamon, and ¼ teaspoon ground nutmeg; set aside.

2 Preheat oven to 325°F. Brush the bottom of a 15×10×1-inch baking pan with some of the melted butter. Unfold phyllo dough. Using scissors or a sharp knife, cut through the whole stack of phyllo dough sheets at one time to make them 15×10-inch rectangles. Discard extra pieces. Keep phyllo covered with plastic wrap, removing sheets as you need them. Layer one-fourth (about 5) of the phyllo sheets in the pan, generously brushing each sheet with melted butter as you layer. Spread about 1⅓ cups of the nut filling onto the phyllo dough. Repeat layering the phyllo sheets, butter, and filling two more times.

3 Layer remaining phyllo sheets on the third layer of filling, brushing each sheet with butter before adding the next phyllo sheet. Drizzle any remaining butter over the top layers. Using a sharp knife, cut through all the layers to make about 60 diamond-, triangle-, or square-shape pieces. (Do not remove pieces from pan.)

4 Bake in the preheated oven for 35 to 45 minutes or until golden. Slightly cool in pan on a wire rack.

5 Meanwhile, for syrup, in a medium saucepan stir together the brown sugar, water, rum, honey, orange peel, a dash of ground cinnamon, and a dash of ground nutmeg. Bring to boiling; reduce heat. Simmer, uncovered, for 20 minutes, stirring occasionally.

6 Pour syrup mixture over slightly cooled baklava in the pan. Cool completely. Can be covered and stored at room temperature for 1 day or in the refrigerator for 1 week. Makes 60 pieces.

Nutrition Facts per piece: 148 cal., 9 g total fat (3 g sat. fat), 11 mg chol., 82 mg sodium, 15 g carbo., 1 g fiber, 2 g pro. **Daily Values:** 3% vit. A, 1% vit. C, 2% calcium, 3% iron.

PRIZE WINNER

Choco-Orange Diamonds

Mary Helms
Anchorage, Alaska
$200—Yuletide Cookies

Prep: 25 minutes **Bake:** 30 minutes

1 cup butter, softened
⅔ cup sugar
¼ tsp. salt
3 eggs
1 egg yolk
3 tsp. finely shredded orange
    peel (set aside)
¼ cup orange juice
1½ cups all-purpose flour
½ cup finely chopped pecans
4 eggs, slightly beaten
1 cup sugar
¼ cup orange juice
3 Tbsp. all-purpose flour
8 oz. bittersweet chocolate,
    finely chopped
1½ cups chopped pecans
3 oz. bittersweet chocolate,
    melted and cooled

1 Preheat oven to 350°F. Grease a 15×10×1-inch baking pan; set aside. For crust, in a large mixing bowl beat butter with an electric mixer on medium to high speed for 30 seconds. Add the ⅔ cup sugar and the salt; beat until combined. Add the 3 eggs and the yolk, one at a time, beating well after each addition. Add ¼ cup orange juice and beat until combined. Add the 1½ cups flour and beat until combined. Using a wooden spoon, stir in 1 teaspoon of the orange peel and the ½ cup finely chopped pecans.

2 Spread crust into the prepared baking pan. Bake in the preheated oven about 15 minutes or until lightly browned (mixture may puff and will fall when removed from the oven).

3 Meanwhile, in a medium mixing bowl use a wire whisk to combine the 4 eggs, the 1 cup sugar, remaining 2 teaspoons peel, ¼ cup orange juice, and the 3 tablespoons flour until smooth. Stir in finely chopped chocolate and the 1½ cups pecans.

4 Spread nut mixture over hot crust. Return to oven. Bake for 15 to 17 minutes more or until set. Cool in pan on a wire rack. Cut into diamond-shape pieces. Place on a plate and drizzle each with melted chocolate. Makes about 60 pieces.

Nutrition Facts per piece: 123 cal., 8 g total fat (4 g sat. fat), 37 mg chol., 51 mg sodium, 12 g carbo., 1 g fiber, 2 g pro. **Daily Values:** 3% vit. A, 2% vit. C, 1% calcium, 3% iron.

Cookie Baking At High Altitudes

Cookie recipes need little adjustment for high altitude. Increase the oven temperature by 25 degrees and decrease the baking time by a minute or two. If further adjustments are necessary, make just one change to the recipe at a time. Reduce the sugar by just a couple of tablespoons. If a recipe calls for baking powder or baking soda, you may need to reduce the amount by ⅛ teaspoon.

White Chocolate Peppermint Drops

Prep: 20 minutes
Bake: 11 minutes per batch

      2   cups all-purpose flour
      1   tsp. baking soda
     ¼   tsp. salt
     ½   cup butter
      1   cup sugar
      2   eggs
      1   tsp. vanilla
   1½   cups white baking pieces
    24   hard striped round peppermint
         candies, crushed (⅔ cup)

1 Preheat oven to 350°F. In a medium bowl stir together flour, baking soda, and salt. Set aside.

2 In a large mixing bowl beat butter with an electric mixer on medium speed for 30 seconds. Add sugar and beat until combined. Beat in eggs and the vanilla until combined. Beat in as much of the flour mixture as you can with the mixer. Using a wooden spoon, stir in any remaining flour mixture. Stir in white baking pieces.

3 Drop dough by rounded teaspoons onto a foil-lined cookie sheet. Bake in preheated oven for 10 to

12 minutes or until edges are lightly browned and cookies are nearly done.

4 Remove cookies from oven and sprinkle with crushed candies (about ½ teaspoon each). Return to oven and bake for 1 minute more or until candy just begins to melt. Cool on the cookie sheet for 1 minute. Transfer cookies to a wire rack and cool completely. Makes about 42 cookies.

Nutrition Facts per cookie: 123 cal., 5 g total fat (4 g sat. fat), 16 mg chol., 83 mg sodium, 18 g carbo., 0 g fiber, 1 g pro. **Daily Values:** 2% vit. A, 2% iron.

Apple Waffle Cookies

Prep: 25 minutes
Bake: 1½ minutes per batch

     ½   cup butter, softened
   1½   cups packed brown sugar
      1   tsp. baking powder
      1   tsp. ground cinnamon
     ½   tsp. salt
     ½   tsp. ground nutmeg
      2   eggs
      1   tsp. vanilla
      2   cups all-purpose flour
     ½   cup coarsely shredded,
         peeled apple
     ½   cup finely chopped toasted
         pecans or walnuts
   1¼   cups apple butter

1 In a large mixing bowl beat butter with an electric mixer on medium speed for 30 seconds. Beat in brown sugar, baking powder, cinnamon, salt, and nutmeg until combined. Beat in eggs and vanilla until combined. Beat in as much of the flour as you can with the mixer. Using a wooden spoon, stir in any remaining flour, the shredded apple, and nuts.

2 Drop dough by a mounded teaspoon onto preheated waffle grids; close lid. Cook for 1½ to 2 minutes or until cookies are set. Using a fork, transfer cookies to a wire rack. Repeat with remaining dough. Cool. Serve with apple butter. Makes 60 cookies.

Nutrition Facts per cookie: 70 cal., 2 g total fat (1 g sat. fat), 11 mg chol., 47 mg sodium, 12 g carbo., 0 g fiber, 1 g pro. **Daily Values:** 1% vit. A, 1% calcium, 2% iron.

PRIZE WINNER

Berry-Sage Thumbprints

Camilla V. Saulsbury
Bloomington, Indiana
$400—Yuletide Cookies

Prep: 25 minutes
Bake: 12 minutes per batch

      2   cups all-purpose flour
     ⅔   cup yellow cornmeal
   1½   tsp. dried sage, crushed
     ¼   tsp. baking powder
      1   cup butter, softened
      1   cup packed brown sugar
      2   egg yolks
      2   tsp. finely shredded lemon peel
   1½   tsp. vanilla
     ¾   cup blackberry preserves

1 Preheat oven to 350°F. In a bowl stir together flour, cornmeal, sage, and baking powder. Set aside.

2 In a large mixing bowl beat butter with an electric mixer on medium speed for 30 seconds. Add brown sugar and beat until combined. Beat in egg yolks, lemon peel, and vanilla until combined. Beat in as much of the flour mixture as you can with the mixer. Using a wooden spoon, stir in any remaining flour mixture.

3 Shape dough into 1-inch balls. Place balls 1 inch apart on an ungreased cookie sheet. Press your thumb into the center of each ball. Fill the centers with about 1 teaspoon blackberry preserves.

4 Bake in the preheated oven about 12 minutes or until bottoms are lightly browned. Cool on cookie sheet 1 minute. Transfer cookies to a wire rack and let cool. Makes about 40.

Nutrition Facts per cookie: 115 cal., 5 g total fat (3 g sat. fat), 24 mg chol., 57 mg sodium, 16 g carbo., 0 g fiber, 1 g pro. Daily Values: 4% vit. A, 1% vit. C, 1% calcium, 3% iron.

Orange Poppy Pockets

Prep: 45 minutes **Chill:** 1 hour
Bake: 8 minutes per batch

- 3   cups all-purpose flour
- 2   tsp. baking powder
- ¾   cup butter, softened
- ½   cup granulated sugar
- ½   cup light-colored corn syrup
- 1   egg
- 1½ tsp. vanilla
- 1   Tbsp. poppy seed
- 4   tsp. finely shredded orange peel
- 1   Tbsp. orange juice
- ¾   cup semisweet chocolate pieces
- ¼   cup whipping cream
- 1   egg white
- 1   Tbsp. water
- 2   Tbsp. coarse sugar or
        granulated sugar

1 Lightly grease a cookie sheet; set aside. In a medium mixing bowl stir together flour, baking powder, and ⅛ teaspoon salt. Set aside.

2 In a large mixing bowl beat butter with an electric mixer on medium speed for 30 seconds. Add the ½ cup granulated sugar and corn syrup. Beat until combined, scraping the sides of the bowl occasionally. Beat in the egg and vanilla until combined. Beat in as much of the flour mixture as you can with the mixer. Using a wooden spoon, stir in remaining flour mixture. Stir in poppy seed, orange peel, and orange juice. Divide dough in half. If necessary, cover and chill dough about 1 hour or until easy to handle.

3 Meanwhile, in a heavy small saucepan cook and stir chocolate pieces and whipping cream over low heat until chocolate is melted. Cover and chill for 15 to 20 minutes or until mixture is firm.

4 Preheat oven to 375°F. On a lightly floured surface, roll half of the dough to about a ⅛-inch thickness. Using a 2-inch round cutter, cut into rounds. Place half of the cookies on the prepared cookie sheet. Spoon about ½ teaspoon of the chocolate mixture in the center of each cookie. Top with remaining cookies. Seal edges with the tines of a fork. Repeat with remaining half of dough and filling, rerolling scraps of dough.

5 In a small mixing bowl beat together egg white and water. Brush the top of each cookie with a little of the egg white mixture. Sprinkle each with some of the coarse sugar. Bake in the preheated oven for 8 to10 minutes or until bottoms are lightly golden. Transfer cookies to a wire rack; let cool. Makes about 54.

Nutrition Facts per cookie: 84 cal., 4 g total fat (2 g sat. fat), 13 mg chol., 54 mg sodium, 11 g carbo., 0 g fiber, 1 g pro. Daily Values: 3% vit. A, 1% vit. C, 2% calcium, 2% iron.

Snowflakes On a Stick

(See the photograph on page 317.)

Prep: 30 minutes
Bake: 15 minutes per batch

- 2½ cups all-purpose flour
- ½   cup granulated sugar
- 2   tsp. finely shredded orange,
        lemon, or lime peel
- 1   cup butter
- 1   Tbsp. milk
- 16 lollipop sticks
       Milk
       White edible glitter, granulated
         sugar, nonpareils, or
         coarse sugar

1 Preheat oven to 325°F. In a bowl combine flour, sugar, and peel. Cut in butter until mixture resembles fine crumbs and starts to cling. Stir in the 1 tablespoon milk. Form mixture into a ball and knead until smooth. Divide dough in half.

2 On a lightly floured surface, roll dough to ½-inch thickness. Using a 3- to 4-inch snowflake cutter, cut out dough. Place cutouts 2 inches apart on an ungreased cookie sheet. Insert a lollipop stick at least 1 inch into each.

3 Brush tops with milk. If using edible glitter, stir together equal proportions of glitter and granulated sugar. Sprinkle glitter mixture, nonpareils, or coarse sugar over cutouts. Bake about 15 minutes or until edges are very light brown. Cool on cookie sheet 1 minute. Transfer cookies to a wire rack to cool. Makes 16.

Nutrition Facts per cookie: 189 cal., 12 g total fat (8 g sat. fat), 33 mg chol., 125 mg sodium, 18 g carbo., 0 g fiber, 2 g pro. Daily Values: 9% vit. A, 1% vit. C, 1% calcium, 4% iron.

CLASSIC CANDIES

Think back. Do you remember your mom or grandmother standing at the stove, stirring and waiting for the bubbly mixture to reach just the right temperature? Do you remember the magic of the syrupy mixture turning into the best candy you've ever tasted—caramels, toffees, and brittles? Now it's your turn to try your hand at making delicious confections for your family and friends. It'll be easy with this collection of treasured recipes and the step-by-step directions.

Exquisite Almond Truffles

As an alternative, dip the truffles in melted white chocolate baking pieces and dust them in cocoa powder instead of dipping them in melted semisweet chocolate.

Prep: 1 hour **Freeze:** 2½ hours

- 16 oz. white chocolate baking pieces
- ¼ cup whipping cream
- ¼ cup cream of coconut
- 1 cup sliced almonds, toasted and chopped
- 2 Tbsp. amaretto
- 18 oz. semisweet chocolate pieces
- 3 Tbsp. shortening
- 4 oz. white chocolate baking pieces
- 2 Tbsp. shortening

1 For filling, in a medium saucepan heat and stir the 16 ounces white chocolate, the whipping cream, and cream of coconut just until white chocolate is melted. Remove from heat. Stir in chopped almonds and amaretto. Cover and freeze 2 hours or until firm. Divide filling into 48 portions; shape each portion into a ball. Freeze 15 minutes.

2 Meanwhile, in a 4-cup glass measure combine the semisweet chocolate pieces and the 3 tablespoons shortening. In a large glass bowl pour very warm tap water (100°F to 110°F) to a depth of 1 inch. Place measure with semisweet chocolate inside large bowl. (Water should cover bottom half of the glass measure.) It is important not to splash any water into the chocolate. Stir semisweet chocolate constantly with a rubber spatula until chocolate is completely melted and smooth. This takes about 20 minutes; don't rush. If water cools, remove glass measure. Discard cool water; add warm water. Return glass measure to bowl with water.

3 Using a fork, dip balls, one at a time, into melted chocolate; place on a waxed-paper-lined baking sheet. Freeze 15 minutes.

4 Meanwhile, in a 1-cup glass measure combine the 4 ounces white chocolate and the 2 tablespoons shortening; melt over hot water. Drizzle over truffles. Chill a few minutes until set. Makes 48.

Nutrition Facts per truffle: 159 cal., 10 g total fat (5 g sat. fat), 6 mg chol., 13 mg sodium, 11 g carbo., 2 g fiber, 2 g pro. **Daily Values:** 1% vit. A, 2% calcium, 1% iron.

Hazelnut Toffee

Similar to candies in the best sweet shops, this buttery toffee is loaded with nuts and topped with chocolate.

Prep: 30 minutes **Cook:** 10 minutes

- 1 cup chopped hazelnuts (filberts), toasted
- ½ cup butter
- 1 cup packed brown sugar
- 1 Tbsp. hazelnut liqueur
- 1 cup semisweet chocolate pieces

1 Line a large baking sheet with foil, extending foil over the edges. Sprinkle ½ cup of the nuts in an 8-inch square on the prepared baking sheet. Set aside.

2 Butter the sides of a heavy 1-quart saucepan. In the saucepan melt the ½ cup butter. Add brown sugar and 1 tablespoon water. Cook and stir over medium-high heat to boiling. Clip a candy thermometer to the side of pan. Cook and stir over medium heat to 280°F, soft-crack stage (about 10 minutes). Remove pan from heat; remove thermometer.

3 Immediately stir in liqueur. Pour over nuts on prepared baking sheet. Sprinkle with chocolate. Let stand for 2 minutes or until chocolate is soft; spread to cover. Sprinkle with remaining nuts. Cool. (If necessary, chill several minutes to harden chocolate.) Holding onto foil, lift candy from baking sheet. Break into pieces. Store in refrigerator up to 2 weeks. Makes about 48 pieces.

Nutrition Facts per piece: 63 cal., 4 g total fat (1 g sat. fat), 5 mg chol., 21 mg sodium, 6 g carbo., 0 g fiber, 0 g pro. Daily Values: 1% vit. A, 1% iron.

Caramels

Once you taste soft and buttery homemade caramels, you'll crave them over the store-bought version.

Prep: 15 minutes Cook: 45 minutes

- 1   cup chopped walnuts (optional)
- 1   cup butter
- 1   16-oz. pkg. (2¼ cups) packed brown sugar
- 2   cups half-and-half or light cream
- 1   cup light-colored corn syrup
- 1   tsp. vanilla

1 Line an 8×8×2- or 9×9×2-inch baking pan with foil, extending foil over edges of pan. Butter foil. If desired, sprinkle nuts onto bottom of pan. Set pan aside.

2 In a heavy 3-quart saucepan melt butter over low heat. Stir in brown sugar, half-and-half, and corn syrup. Cook and stir over medium-

high heat until mixture boils. Clip a candy thermometer to side of pan. Reduce heat to medium; continue boiling at a moderate, steady rate, stirring frequently, until the thermometer registers 248°F, firm-ball stage (45 to 60 minutes).

3 Remove saucepan from heat; remove thermometer. Stir in vanilla. Quickly pour the mixture into the prepared pan. When caramel mixture is firm, use foil to lift it out of pan. Use a buttered knife to cut into 1-inch squares. Wrap each piece in plastic wrap. Makes about 64 pieces.

Nutrition Facts per piece: 76 cal., 4 g total fat (2 g sat. fat), 10 mg chol., 38 mg sodium, 11 g carbo., 0 g fiber, 0 g pro. Daily Values: 3% vit. A, 1% calcium, 2% iron.

Shortcut Caramels
Prepare as directed at left, except substitute one 14-ounce can sweetened condensed milk for the half-and-half or light cream. This mixture takes less time to reach 248°F (about 15 to 20 minutes instead of 45 to 60 minutes).

Nutrition Facts per piece: 68 cal., 3 g total fat (2 g sat. fat), 0 mg chol., 0 mg sodium, 0 g carbo., 0 g fiber, 0 g pro.

Peanut Brittle

Alter this classic candy to feature your favorite nut, such as cashews, hazelnuts, or fancy mixed nuts.

Prep: 15 minutes Cook: 45 minutes

- 2   cups sugar
- 1   cup light-colored corn syrup
- ¼   cup butter
- ½   cup water
- 2½ cups raw peanuts or other coarsely chopped nuts
- 1½ tsp. baking soda, sifted

1 Butter two large baking sheets; set aside. Butter sides of a heavy 3-quart saucepan. In pan combine sugar, corn syrup, butter, and water. Cook and stir over medium-high heat until mixture boils. Clip a candy thermometer to side of pan. Reduce heat to medium-low; continue boiling at a moderate, steady rate, stirring occasionally, until the thermometer registers 275°F, soft-crack stage (about 30 minutes). Stir in nuts; continue cooking over medium-low heat, stirring frequently, until the thermometer registers 295°F, hard-crack stage (15 to 20 minutes more).

2 Remove pan from heat; remove thermometer. Quickly sprinkle baking soda over mixture, stirring constantly. Immediately pour onto prepared baking sheets. Use two forks to lift and pull candy as it cools. Cool completely; break into pieces. Store tightly covered. Makes about 72 pieces.

Nutrition Facts per piece: 69 cal., 3 g total fat (1 g sat. fat), 2 mg chol., 37 mg sodium, 10 g carbo., 0 g fiber, 1 g pro. Daily Values: 2% iron.

COOKING WITH KIDS

Treats for Santa

The word from the North Pole is that even Santa watches what he eats during the holiday season. He needs to keep up his energy level and keep down his weight in preparation for the Big Night. Santa can't tolerate his belly bogging him down in chimneys—throwing off his delivery schedule.

Help Santa stay slim by treating him to a plateful of attractive fruit-and-nut truffles. Packed with delicious, natural, high-energy sugars, this is a great recipe for kids to make—as long as they have adult supervision to use the food processor.

The measuring and shaping are easy, and there's no cooking required. Roll the mixture into balls and dredge them through the coconut coating to make yummy truffles for Santa.

Santa's Snack Truffles

Start to finish: 30 minutes

½	cup flaked coconut
3	Tbsp. powdered sugar
¾	cup coarsely chopped walnuts
8	oz. pitted dates
½	cup raisins
½	cup dried cranberries
⅓	cup flaked coconut
1	Tbsp. unsweetened cocoa powder
¼	tsp. ground cinnamon
¼	cup creamy peanut butter

1 For coating, place the ½ cup coconut and powdered sugar into a food processor bowl. Cover and process until coconut is finely chopped. Transfer mixture to a shallow dish; set aside. (Have an adult operate the blade and transfer the contents to a shallow dish.)

2 For truffles, place walnuts, dates, raisins, cranberries, the ⅓ cup coconut, cocoa powder, and cinnamon in the food processor bowl. Cover and process or blend until finely chopped, stopping to scrape down sides as necessary.

3 Add peanut butter. Cover and process until mixture is moist enough to form a ball. (Have an adult operate food processor.)

4 Using hands, shape the mixture into 1-inch balls. Dredge or roll the balls in coconut mixture, gently patting the mixture onto the balls. Transfer to a storage container. Cover; store at room temperature for up to 1 week. Makes 30 truffles.

Nutrition Facts per truffle: 79 cal., 4 g total fat (1 g sat. fat), 0 mg chol., 11 mg sodium, 11 g carbo., 1 g fiber, 1 g pro. **Daily Values:** 1% calcium, 2% iron.

Ultimate Chocolate Bars

Chocolate for candy-making should be stabilized or tempered during the melting and cooling process. Without tempering, the surface of chocolate develops speckles or gray streaks as it hardens, which affects the appearance and the flavor of the candy.

Prep: 30 minutes **Stand:** 1½ hours

2	6-oz. pkg. bittersweet chocolate squares or 12 oz. semisweet chocolate squares, chopped
1	Tbsp. shortening
¾	tsp. ground ginger
	Whole and/or finely chopped pistachio nuts and/or whole and/or finely crushed pink peppercorns

1 Line a baking sheet with parchment paper or waxed paper. Set aside. Combine the chocolate and shortening in a 4-cup glass measuring cup. Pour very warm water (100°F to 110°F) into a large glass bowl to a depth of 1 inch. Place the measuring cup containing chocolate into the bowl of water. The water should cover the bottom half of the measuring cup. It is important not to splash any water into the chocolate. Using a rubber spatula, stir chocolate mixture constantly until melted and smooth (15 to 20 minutes). If water begins to cool, remove measuring cup and replace water in bowl with additional warm water. Return measuring cup to bowl and continue stirring the chocolate mixture. When chocolate is melted and smooth, stir in ginger.

2 Evenly spread the melted chocolate into a 12×8-inch rectangle onto the prepared baking sheet. Using a knife, score chocolate into 4×1½-inch bars. Working quickly, arrange or sprinkle nuts and/or peppercorns on chocolate. If necessary, press gently into chocolate. Allow chocolate to stand at room temperature 1½ to 2 hours or until set. Use a knife to cut chocolate along the scored lines into bars. Store at room temperature in a sealed container up to 3 days. Makes 16 bars.

Nutrition Facts per bar: 136 cal., 9 g total fat (4 g sat. fat), 0 mg chol., 0 mg sodium, 13 g carbo., 2 g fiber, 2 g pro., **Daily Values:** 1% vit. A, 1% calcium, 7% iron.

Candied Candy Canes

Spread leftover melted chocolate on waxed paper to set. Chop the hardened chocolate to sprinkle on ice cream or stir into cookie dough. (See the photograph on page 320.)

Prep: 25 minutes **Stand:** 1 hour

- 1 cup white baking pieces or semisweet chocolate pieces
- 1 tsp. shortening
- 12 candy canes, about 5½ inches long
  Decorative red sugar, nonpareils, and chocolate-flavored sprinkles

1 In a small saucepan combine baking pieces or chocolate and shortening. Stir over low heat until melted. (Or combine baking pieces and shortening in a microwave-safe bowl. Microwave on 70% [medium] power for 1 to 2 minutes or until baking pieces are melted, stirring every 30 seconds.)

2 Transfer melted baking pieces or chocolate to a 1-cup glass liquid measure. Dip the bottom or top half of each candy cane into the melted chocolate, tilting cup if necessary to coat candy cane. Immediately sprinkle with or roll in decorative sugar, nonpareils, or sprinkles. Place on a baking sheet lined with waxed paper. Let stand for at least 1 hour or until chocolate is firm. Makes 12.

Nutrition Facts per candy cane: 227 cal., 6 g total fat (5 g sat. fat), 0 mg chol., 37 mg sodium, 41 g carbo., 0 g fiber, 0 g pro. **Daily Values:** 1% iron.

30 MINUTE, NO FAT
Vanilla Bean and Brandy Syrup

Start to finish: 25 minutes

- 1 vanilla bean
- 1½ cups sugar
- ¾ cup water
- ¼ cup dark corn syrup
- ¼ cup brandy

1 With a knife, halve vanilla bean lengthwise. In a medium saucepan combine vanilla bean, sugar, water, and corn syrup. Cook and stir over low heat until sugar is dissolved. Bring to boiling over medium-high heat; reduce heat. Simmer, uncovered, about 10 minutes until slightly thickened, stirring occasionally.

2 Strain syrup through a strainer lined with a double thickness of 100% cotton cheesecloth. Discard vanilla bean. Cool. Stir in brandy. Pour syrup into a bottle. Cover and store for up to 2 weeks. Serve over ice cream, gingerbread, or pound cake slices. Makes about 1½ cups.

Nutrition Facts per tablespoon: 62 cal., 0 g total fat, 0 mg chol., 4 mg sodium, 5 g carbo., 0 g fiber, 0 g pro.

Holiday Marmalade

Prep: 30 minutes **Cook:** 36 minutes

- 3 medium oranges
- ⅛ tsp. baking soda
- 2 cups fresh cranberries
- ¼ cup snipped dried pears
- ¼ cup snipped dried pineapple
- 1 cup chopped toasted almonds and/or pecans
- 1 1.75-oz. pkg. powdered pectin
- 4 cups sugar

1 Score each orange into four lengthwise sections; remove peels. Scrape and discard membrane from peels. Cut peels into thin strips (about 1 cup). In a large saucepan bring 1½ cups water, peels, and baking soda to boiling; reduce heat. Simmer, covered, 20 minutes. Do not drain. Remove remaining membrane from oranges. Section oranges over a bowl, reserving juice; discard seeds. Add orange sections, juice, fruits, and nuts to saucepan with peels; return to boiling. Simmer, covered, 10 minutes. Measure 3½ cups fruit mixture.

2 In a 6- to 8- quart kettle combine the 3½ cups fruit mixture and the pectin. Bring mixture to a full rolling boil, stirring constantly. Stir in sugar. Return to a full rolling boil and boil for 1 minute, stirring constantly. Remove from heat; skim off any foam.

3 Ladle into hot, sterilized half-pint jars, leaving ¼-inch headspace. Wipe jar rims; adjust lids. Process in a boiling-water canner for 5 minutes. Remove jars and cool on a rack. Makes 5 half-pints.

Nutrition Facts per tablespoon: 74 cal., 1 g total fat (0 g sat. fat), 0 mg chol., 4 mg sodium, 17 g carbo., 1 g fiber, 1 g pro. **Daily Values:** 11% vit. C, 1% calcium, 1% iron.

30 MINUTE

All-Is-Calm Hot Chocolate Mix

Start to finish: 20 minutes

```
  8  oz. semisweet or bittersweet
       chocolate chunks or pieces
 ⅔  cup sugar
 ½  cup unsweetened cocoa powder
 ½  tsp. anise seed, toasted*
       and crushed
 ½  tsp. ground cinnamon
```

1 For mix, in a large bowl stir together chocolate chunks or pieces, sugar, cocoa powder, anise seed, and cinnamon. Spoon into a container, jar, or self-sealed plastic bag. Cover or seal. Include the following recipe directions.

Recipe Directions:

To make 4 servings of hot chocolate, in a medium saucepan combine ⅔ cup cocoa mix and ¼ cup water. Stir over medium heat until chocolate is melted and mixture is smooth. Whisk in 4 cups milk; heat through, whisking occasionally. Pour into mugs. Top with whipped cream, if desired. Mix makes a total of 12 servings.

*Note: To toast anise seed, place seed in a shallow baking pan. Bake in a 350°F oven about 5 minutes or until toasted and aromatic.

Nutrition Facts per prepared serving: 272 cal., 11 g total fat (6 g sat. fat), 18 mg chol., 122 mg sodium, 30 g carbo., 3 g fiber, 9 g pro. **Daily Values:** 10% vit. A, 4% vit. C, 34% calcium, 4% iron.

30 MINUTE

Holiday Rum Punch

Start to finish: 15 minutes

```
 ½  gallon peppermint ice cream
  4  cups brewed coffee, chilled
  2  cups dairy eggnog
  1  cup light rum
  1  cup whipping cream
 ½  tsp. instant coffee crystals
 ¼  cup crushed hard peppermint
       candies
```

1 In a very large bowl stir ice cream to soften. Gradually stir in chilled coffee, eggnog, and rum.

2 In a chilled mixing bowl combine whipping cream and coffee crystals. Beat with an electric mixer on medium speed until soft peaks form (tips curl). Drop onto punch by tablespoonfuls. Sprinkle with a little crushed candy. Serve at once. Makes 24 servings.

Nutrition Facts per serving: 195 cal., 10 g total fat (7 g sat. fat), 46 mg chol., 64 mg sodium, 17 g carbo., 0 g fiber, 2 g pro. **Daily Values:** 4% vit. A, 1% vit. C, 7% calcium.

Coconut Eggnog

Welcome winter with this smooth and creamy treat. The optional toasted coconut garnish is worth the extra effort. (See the photograph on page 4.)

Prep: 20 minutes **Chill:** 3 hours

```
  3  cups milk
  6  egg yolks, beaten
  1  15- or 16-oz. can cream
       of coconut
 ½  cup rum
  2  tsp. vanilla
 ½  cup whipping cream
  1  Tbsp. sugar
       Toasted coconut* (optional)
```

1 In a medium saucepan combine milk and egg yolks. Cook and stir just until mixture begins to boil; remove from heat. Immediately stir in cream of coconut, rum, and vanilla. Transfer punch to a bowl or pitcher. Cover and chill in the refrigerator about 3 hours or until cold.

2 Just before serving, in a chilled medium mixing bowl beat whipping cream and sugar with an electric mixer on medium speed to soft peaks. Drop tablespoonfuls of the whipped cream on eggnog in a punch bowl or on single servings. Sprinkle with toasted coconut, if desired. Makes 10 servings.

*Note: To toast coconut, place coconut in a shallow baking pan. Bake in a 350°F oven 5 to 10 minutes or until toasted, stirring once or twice.

Nutrition Facts per serving: 287 cal., 24 g total fat (18 g sat. fat), 150 mg chol., 47 mg sodium, 8 g carbo., 1 g fiber, 6 g pro. **Daily Values:** 10% vit. A, 3% vit. C, 12% calcium, 8% iron.

Glossary

adobo sauce [ah-DO-boh]: A dark red Mexican sauce made from ground chiles, herbs, and vinegar. Chipotle peppers are available packed in cans of adobo sauce.

Asiago cheese A cheese made from cow milk with a nutty, rich, and somewhat piquant flavor when young. Originally from Italy, Asiago is made from whole or part-skim milk. Young Asiago has a light yellow interior and small holes. It is delicious for snacking; serve it on an antipasto tray. As the cheese ages, it gets harder and sharper, making it perfect for shredding or grating. Asiago, Parmesan, and Romano may be used interchangeably.

braise To brown food in fat, then cook it, either in the oven or on top of the range, in a tightly covered dish in a small amount of liquid. Food is braised at low heat for a long time. Tougher cuts of meat benefit by being braised, as the process helps break down their fibers.

capers The bud of a spiny shrub that grows from Spain to China. Found next to the olives in the condiment section of the supermarket, capers have an assertive flavor that can best be described as the marriage of citrus and olive, plus an added tang that comes from the salt and vinegar of the packaging brine. Two varieties of capers are available: little buds—which are considered by food experts to be the finest, and the milder, large buds—which also work well in recipes. In a pinch, chopped green olives may be substituted for capers, although they won't bring the hallmark citrus spark of the flavorful buds.

caramelize To heat sugar until it becomes liquefied and brown. The caramelizing process works not only with granulated sugar, but also with such vegetables as onion and garlic because they contain natural sugars. When heated, the natural sugars brown and caramelize, becoming more intense in flavor. To caramelize vegetables, they need to be cooked slowly over low heat in a small amount of fat until browned and sweet.

chipotle peppers (chih-POHT-lay) A smoked, dried jalapeño pepper. Chipotle peppers have wrinkly brown skin and a rich, smoky flavor. They can be found dried or canned in adobo sauce in Hispanic grocery stores or in the specialty foods section of supermarkets. Recipes often call for a small amount of canned chipotle peppers; fortunately, leftovers can be frozen for future use. Pack them, covered with sauce from the can, in a freezer container. Seal, label, and freeze for up to two months; thaw as needed in the refrigerator.

chutney Derived from a Hindi word meaning "strongly spiced," chutney is a condiment used in Indian cuisine. It is made of chopped fruit (mango is a classic), vegetables, and spices enlivened by hot peppers, fresh ginger, or vinegar. Chutney is becoming increasingly popular among American cooks because it is a quick way to spark poultry dishes, salads, and sandwiches. Find chutney alongside such condiments as mustard, ketchup, jellies, and jams or in the specialty food aisles of grocery stores.

cremini mushrooms (kray-MEE-nee) A versatile variety of mushroom that is earthy yet mild in flavor. Use cremini mushrooms whenever you would use white mushrooms. Look for mushrooms that are plump and have no bruises or moistness; avoid spotted or slimy mushrooms. Store fresh cremini mushrooms, unwashed, in the refrigerator for up to two days. Store prepackaged mushrooms in the package. Loose mushrooms, or those in open packages, should be stored in a paper bag or in a damp cloth bag in the refrigerator to allow them to breathe.

crystallized ginger Also known as candied ginger, crystallized ginger is a confection rather than a spice. Bits of fresh ginger are cooked in a sugar syrup then coated with sugar. Look for crystallized ginger in the spice and baking aisle. Store it in a cool, dry, dark place.

cut in To mix a hard, cold fat (butter or shortening) with dry ingredients (flour mixture) until the mixture resembles coarse crumbs or small peas, whichever size is specified by the recipe. This can be done with a pastry blender, two knives worked in criss-cross fashion, a fork, fingers, or a food processor.

deglaze To remove browned bits of food (usually meat) from the bottom of a pan after the food has been sautéed or roasted. Liquid is added to the pan and the bits are loosened by stirring; the resulting mixture is often used as a sauce or a base for a sauce served with the meats.

fennel An aromatic vegetable that has a white bulbous base, light green stalks, and resembles celery. The wispy, green fronds and white bulb impart a gentle, slightly sweet anise (licorice) flavor to foods. To prepare fennel, cut off and discard the stalks (which usually are not eaten). Cut the bulb into wedges or strips, and reserve the fronds for use as a garnish or to add flavor to just about any food.

flax seeds A subtly nutty-flavor seed generally found in health food stores (it is a good source of Omega-3 fatty acids as well as other essential nutrients). When grinding flax seed, a blender works better than a food processor. Store flax seed in the refrigerator or freezer.

ginger The root of a semitropical plant, ginger is used as a spice and prized for its slightly hot flavor and nippy aroma. Ginger should be peeled before using. To peel, cut off one end of the root and peel with a vegetable peeler, moving down the root. To grate ginger for a recipe, use the fine side of the grater. To mince ginger, slice the peeled ginger with the grain (lengthwise) into thin sticks. Bundle the sticks and cut them finely. Ginger stays fresh for two or three weeks in the refrigerator when loosely wrapped in a paper towel. For longer storage, store unpeeled ginger in a freezer bag in the freezer. Ginger will keep indefinitely when frozen and it can be grated or sliced while it is frozen. In a pinch, ground ginger can be used for grated fresh ginger. To substitute 1 teaspoon of grated fresh ginger, use ¼ teaspoon of ground ginger.

Gorgonzola cheese A type of blue cheese made from cow's milk and streaked with greenish veins. Gorgonzola has a softer, creamier, and less pungent flavor than most blue cheeses. In a pinch, substitute another mild blue cheese, such as Saga Bleu, Maytag Blue, or Bleu de Bresse.

hoisin sauce: A tongue-tingling sauce popular in Chinese cooking. American cooks also enjoy this ultimate Asian convenience product. One measure of hoisin sauce brings a multitude of sweet-and-spicy flavors to foods: fermented soybeans, molasses, vinegar, mustard, sesame seed, garlic, and chilies. It is great in Asian stir-fries and can fill in for barbecue sauce. Look for hoisin sauce near the soy sauce in most grocery stores or find it in Asian food markets.

kalamata olive A medium-size greenish-black olive from Greece. It is cured in a wine vinegar brine and has a pungent, fruity flavor. Most kalamata olives are sold unpitted. To remove the pits for cooking, make a small X-shape cut with the tip of a sharp knife on one end of the olive. Pinch the other end between a thumb and forefinger until the pit pops out. Or gently crush the long side of the olive with a knife or the heel of your hand, then pull out the pit.

knead To work dough in a pressing and folding motion until it becomes smooth and elastic. This is an essential step in many yeast breads because it builds a protein structure called gluten, which gives body to the finished bread. To knead, fold the dough over and push down on it with the heels of your hands, curving your fingers over the dough. Give the dough a quarter turn and repeat the process of folding and pushing down until you have an elastic dough with the stiffness called for in the recipe.

Manchego cheese A cheese made from sheep milk and originally made solely from the milk of the Manchego sheep of La Mancha. One of Spain's most famous cheeses, Manchego is prized for its rich, mellow flavor. Unaged Manchego is a white, semifirm cheese that is good for melting and snacking, while aged Manchego is firm, golden, and a top-notch grating cheese (use it as you would Parmesan). Shards of aged Manchego also make a flavorful addition to an appetizer tray.

mascarpone cheese A rich, double- to triple-cream cow's milk cheese that originally hails from the Lombardy region of Italy. The soft, ivory-color cheese, which tastes like a cross between whipped butter and cream cheese, is best known for its role in the classic Italian dessert, tiramisu. It also tastes delicius spooned over fresh fruit, such as strawberries or pear slices. Find Mascarpone in plastic containers in the cheese section of grocery stores or in specialty foods shops. Whipped cream cheese can sometimes be substituted in recipes, although it lacks mascarpone's hallmark buttery richness.

oyster sauce A sauce comprised of oysters, soy sauce, and brine. In Asian cuisine, this concentrated brown sauce is used both in cooking and as a table condiment. It is prized for bringing a distinct rich flavor to foods without overpowering other flavors of the food. Find oyster sauce alongside soy sauce in grocery stores or Asian food markets.

pancetta An Italian-style bacon, which, similar to American bacon, is made from the belly (or *pancia*) of a hog. Also similar to bacon, pancetta has deep pink stripes of flesh streaked with white stripes of fat. Unlike bacon, pancetta is not smoked. Instead it is seasoned with pepper and spices and cured with salt. Look for pancetta, generally available rolled in a sausagelike roll, in some supermarkets, Italian grocery stores, or specialty foods shops. A little of this flavorful ingredient goes a long way to flavor sauces, vegetables, or meat dishes. In a pinch, substitute regular bacon.

phyllo Prominent in Greek, Turkish, and Near Eastern dishes, phyllo consists of tissue-thin sheets of dough that, when layered and baked, results in a delicate, flaky pastry. The word phyllo (sometimes spelled filo), is Greek for "leaf." Although phyllo can be made at home, a frozen commercial product is available that is much handier to use. Allow frozen phyllo dough to thaw while it is wrapped. Once unwrapped, sheets of phyllo quickly dry out and become unusable. To preserve phyllo sheets, keep the stack of dough covered with plastic wrap while preparing recipes. Rewrap remaining sheets of the dough and return them to the freezer.

prosciutto (pro-SHOE-toh) To Italians, prosciutto literally means ham; however, cooks in America use the term to refer to a type of ham that has been seasoned, salt-cured, and air dried (rather than smoked). The process takes at least nine months and results in somewhat sweetly spiced, rose-color meats with a sheen. Parma ham from Italy (prosciutto di Parma) is considered to be the best. Serve prosciutto cold on antipasto platters and in sandwiches, or hot in meat fillings and pasta dishes—it is salty, so be sure to taste the dish before adding salt. Generally, prosciutto is added to hot cooked dishes toward the end of cooking time; otherwise, it may

become brittle. Sliced prosciutto dries out quickly and should be used within a day or frozen for longer storage.

queso fresco (KAY-soh FRES-coh) A soft, white, mild-flavored cow's-milk cheese that often is used in Mexican cooking. Sometimes called queso blanco, it can be sliced, shredded, or crumbled.

rice vinegar A mild-flavor vinegar, popular in Chinese and Japanese cooking, that is made from fermented rice. Rice vinegar is interchangeable with rice wine vinegar, which is made from fermented rice wine. Seasoned rice vinegar, with added sugar and salt, also is available and can be used in recipes that call for rice vinegar, though you may wish to adjust the seasonings accordingly.

roast A specific kind of baking. Roasted food is usually baked uncovered in a shallow pan, which permits browning and crisping. Roasting works best with tender pieces of meat and poultry.

sauté (saw-TAY) From the French word sauter, meaning "to jump." Sautéed food is cooked and stirred in a small mount of fat over fairly high heat in an open, shallow pan. Food cut into a uniform size sautés the best.

shiitake mushrooms An Asian mushroom variety with large floppy caps, tough slender stems, and a smoky and woodsy flavor. Use only the caps—remove and discard the stems before using. Shiitake mushrooms are available dried and fresh. Store unwashed fresh mushrooms in the refrigerator for up to two days; soak dried mushrooms in warm water; rinse well, and remove stems before using.

Swiss chard A mild salad green that is a member of the beet family. Swiss chard is sometimes referred to as chard. One variety has crinkly green leaves attached to an enlarged white stem; another variety, known as rhubarb chard, has dark green leaves and a scarlet stem. The stems of both varieties have a delicate celerylike taste and the leaves have a hearty spinach flavor. Peak seasons for Swiss chard are summer through fall, although in many markets it is available year-round. When you can't find it, substitute fresh spinach.

tomatillos (toh-mah-TEE-yohs) Often called Mexican tomatoes, this small light green fruit is covered with thin, papery husks that are removed before using. Tomatillos offer a hint of lemon, apple, and herb flavors, making it an intriguing addition to fresh salsas and other Mexican food specialties. In most recipes, there is just no substitute for fresh tomatillos—look for them in produce aisles or Hispanic food markets. Choose firm tomatillos with tight-fitting dry husks; cover and refrigerate fresh tomatillos for up to 10 days.

vanilla bean The long, thin pod of an orchid plant. The pod itself, which has been dried and cured, should not be eaten. Instead, the tiny seeds inside the pod are used—they bring an intense vanilla flavor and brown, confetti-like flecks to dishes. Follow recipe directions for extracting the seeds from the pod. Often the pod will be heated in a liquid mixture to make it easier to split open, but even a dry vanilla bean can be cut lengthwise with a paring knife. After it is open, scrape out the tiny seeds.

VALENTINE'S DAY DINNER

Instead of hassling over dinner reservations on a busy eve, put your efforts into this sensational meal for your sweetheart.

- Salad of mixed greens, thinly sliced red onions, thinly sliced red apples, and candied nuts drizzled with a balsamic vinaigrette

- Celebration Shrimp-Stuffed Chicken (page 17)

- Cooked green beans drizzled with butter

- Sesame seed rolls or other dinner rolls

- Hearts and Cherries (page 46)

2 hours before:
- Prepare and bake tortilla hearts

1½ hours before:
- Make chicken rolls and bake

30 minutes before:
- Prepare sauce for chicken
- Assemble salad (except vinaigrette)
- Cook green beans

Just before serving:
- Dress salad
- Drizzle green beans with butter
- Spoon sauce over chicken

Between courses:
- Make cherry sauce
- Assemble desserts

EASTER BRUNCH

With just a little preparation ahead of time, you won't miss a minute of your family gathering.

- Banana Easter Egg Rolls (pages 68-69)

- Camembert Soufflé (page 252)

- Thick ham slice

- Mixed fresh berries including strawberries, blueberries, and red raspberries

- Assorted fruit juices and/or coffee

3 to 4 hours before:
- Prepare and bake rolls; cool and then frost

1¼ hours before:
- Make and bake souffle

30 minutes before:
- Prepare berries
- Heat ham slice; cut into serving size pieces

Just before serving:
- Pour fruit juices and/or coffee

CELEBRATION DINNER

Whatever the celebratory occasion may be, this decadent, mouth-watering meal will be special.

- Icy Shrimp Cocktail (page 138)

- Glorious Greens (page 27)

- Baby Potato Kabobs (page 174)

- Grilled beef tenderloin steaks

- Extreme Chocolate Pie (page 246)

The day before:
- Make pie; cover and chill
- Prepare Hazelnut Vinaigrette; cover and chill

1 hour before (or up to 2 hours before):
- Prepare shrimp; cover and chill

40 minutes before:
- Prepare kabobs
- Compose salads
- Grill steaks until desired doneness

Just before serving:
- Arrange shrimp in cocktail glasses
- Slice steaks, fanning each out on a dinner plate. Add a kabob

Between courses:
- Cut pie and place on dessert plates

DINNER ON THE DECK

Whether it's the deck on your house or the deck on your boat, here's a fresh and fun meal to enjoy on a sunshiny day.

- Onion Burger Melt (page 30)

- Salad of cooked new potatoes, cooked green beans, and Roma tomato wedges drizzled with clear Italian dressing

- Banana Split Trifles (page 165)

- Iced tea or lemonade

The day before:
- Cook new potatoes; cover and chill
- Cook green beans; cover and chill

1 hour before:
- Make trifles; cover and freeze

30 minutes before:
- Prepare and grill burgers
- Arrange potatoes, green beans, and tomato wedges on a platter; drizzle with dressing

Just before serving:
- Assemble open-face sandwiches
- Pour iced tea or lemonade

PICNIC AT THE LAKE

This chilly meal will help beat the heat on a summery hot day. Pack the cooler and head for the lake or your favorite picnic spot.

- **Italian-Style Turkey Hero (page 180)**

- **Salad of halved red grape or cherry tomatoes drizzled with olive oil and white wine vinegar and sprinkled with salt, pepper, and snipped fresh basil and/or thyme**

- **Pasta salad from your favorite deli**

- **Candy Bar Peanut Butter Cookies (page 210)**

- **Assorted cold beverages**

The day before:
- Make and bake cookies; cool and cover

2½ hours before (or up to 8 hours before):
- Prepare sandwich; cover and chill

1 hour before: (or up to 4 hours before):
- Prepare tomato salad; cover and chill

Just before serving:
- Slice sandwich
- Stir salads
- Pour beverages

*Note: Pack the sandwich, salads, and beverages on ice when transporting to a lake/picnic location

AUTUMN AFTERNOON DINNER

When leaves of gold begin to fall, gather family and friends around the table to enjoy some of the season's best flavors.

- **Salad of fresh spinach, thinly sliced sweet onions, halved dried golden figs and golden raisins drizzled with balsamic vinaigrette and a squeeze of fresh orange**

- **Autumn Vegetable and Chicken Stew (page 222)**

- **Have-a-Ball Rolls (page 292)**

- **Sour Cream Harvest Pie (page 233)**

Up to 8 hours before:
- Prepare and bake pie; cool, cover, and chill

4 hours before:
- Thaw dough for rolls

1¼ hours before:
- Make and bake rolls

1 hour before:
- Prepare stew

30 minutes before:
- Prepare salad (except for vinaigrette)

Just before serving:
- Ladle stew into bowls
- Dress salad

Between courses:
- Cut pie and place on dessert plates

BACK TO SCHOOL SUPPER

Treat those tired and hungry students to a hearty, homemade meal. They'll love you for it!

- **Tuna Alfredo Casserole (page 206)**

- **Frozen Italian vegetable blend (zucchini, carrots, cauliflower, lime beans, and Italian beans) cooked and drizzled with butter**

- **Soft breadsticks**

- **Raspberry Fudge Pudding Cake (page 212)**

2¼ hours before:
- Make and bake pudding cake; cool

30 minutes before:
- Prepare and bake casserole
- Cook vegetables; drizzle with butter
- Warm breadsticks, if desired

Between courses:
- Prepare Sweetened Whipped Cream
- Spoon pudding cake into dessert dishes and top with whipped cream

SOUP 'N' SANDWICH LUNCH

When your kids are home on school break, make them this heart-warming lunch. They'll love it because it's so tasty, and you'll love it because it's so easy.

- **Provolone and Ham Melt (page 205)**

- **Tomato soup or other soup**

- **Fresh fruit, including sliced pears or apples, pineapple wedges, and/or grapes**

- **Triple-Dipster Strawberries (page 134)**

1 hour before:
- Wash strawberries; cover and chill
- Prepare sour cream mixture for berries; cover and chill

30 minutes before:
- Prepare soup
- Make and cook sandwiches

Just before serving:
- Ladle soup into bowls
- Arrange sandwiches and additional fruit on plates

Between courses:
- Prepare "dippers" for strawberries

SIMPLE SATURDAY BREAKFAST

Weekend breakfasts are meant to be enjoyed. So, grab the paper or your favorite magazine and sit down to this flash-in-the-pan favorite.

- **Scrambled eggs with diced ham and asparagus pieces sprinkled with crumbled feta cheese**

- **Grilled Muffins (page 65)**

- **Pick-Your-Fruit Smoothie (page 64) or fruit juice**

45 minutes before:
- Dice ham, cut asparagus, and crumble feta cheese for eggs; chill until needed

30 minutes before:
- Grill muffins
- Prepare scrambled eggs
- Make smoothies or pour fruit juice

CHEERS-TO-THE-HOLIDAYS PARTY

As the holiday season is upon you, invite family and friends in to celebrate. This collection of recipes makes a sumptuous appetizer buffet.

- **Cheese 'n' Herb Mini Sweet Peppers (page 289)**

- **Smoked Turkey on Wheat Biscuits (page 292)**

- **Dressed-Up Onion Dip (page 290) with vegetable crudites**

- **Cheese Decked with Fruit (page 290)**

- **Smoked Salmon Appetizers (page 10)**

- **Holiday cookies and candies**

- **Spirited (or Non-Spirited) Cranberry Slush (page 23)**

The day before:
- Prepare slush; cover and freeze
- Prepare dip; cover and chill

Up to 4 hours before:
- Wash mini peppers, cut slits, remove seeds, cover, and chill
- Stir together filling for peppers; cover and chill
- Make and bake wheat biscuits; cool and cover

1 hour before:
- Clean and cut vegetables; arrange on a platter
- Prepare Cheese Decked with Fruit
- Prepare salmon; cover and chill

30 minutes before:
- Fill peppers and bake
- Assemble biscuit sandwiches
- Remove slush from freezer

Just before serving:
- Arrange appetizers, cookies, and candies on platters
- Scrape slush into glasses; add carbonated beverage

CHRISTMAS EVE DINNER

Some of the best traditions of Christmas are those centered around the table. So, gather those who are dear to share old stories, new dreams, and this country-style meal.

- **Christmas Eve Lamb Stew (page 294)**

- **Mashed Sweet Potatoes (page 294)**

- **Festive Apple Slaw (page 293)**

- **Assorted artisan breads**

- **Cake with all the Trimmings (page 298)**

The day before:
- Prepare Apple Cider Vinaigrette; cover and chill

2 hours before:
- Prepare stew
- Decorate cake

1½ hours before:
- Prepare Festive Apple Slaw; cover and chill

40 minutes before:
- Prepare mashed potatoes
- Slice breads

Just before serving:
- Spoon slaw into individual bowls
- Spoon mashed potatoes into shallow bowls or onto plates and ladle stew atop

Between courses:
- Cut cake and place on dessert plates

Snowflakes on a Stick (page 303)

Smoked Turkey on Wheat Biscuits (page 292)

Shrimp and Feta (page 289)

Dressed-Up Onion Dip (page 291)

Artichoke-Brie Foccacia (page 291)

Cheese 'n' Herb Mini Sweet Peppers (page 290)

Santa's Pear Pouches (page 298)

Candied Candy Canes (page 307)

Cake with All the Trimmings (page 298)

INDEX

30-minute recipes indicated in
COLOR.
Low-fat and no-fat recipes
indicated with a ♥.
Bonus recipes indicated with an *.
Photographs indicated in italics.

B

EMERGENCY SUBSTITUTIONS

IF YOU DON'T HAVE:	SUBSTITUTE:
1 teaspoon baking powder	½ teaspoon cream of tartar plus ¼ teaspoon baking soda
1 tablespoon cornstarch (for thickening)	2 tablespoons all-purpose flour
1 package active dry yeast	1 cake compressed yeast
1 cup buttermilk	1 tablespoon lemon juice or vinegar plus enough milk to make 1 cup (let stand 5 minutes before using); or 1 cup plain yogurt
1 cup whole milk	½ cup evaporated milk plus ½ cup water; or 1 cup water plus ⅓ cup nonfat dry milk powder
1 cup light cream	1 tablespoon melted butter or margarine plus enough whole milk to make 1 cup
1 cup dairy sour cream	1 cup plain yogurt
1 whole egg	2 egg whites, 2 egg yolks, or 3 tablespoons frozen egg product, thawed
1 cup margarine	1 cup butter; or 1 cup shortening plus ¼ teaspoon salt, if desired
1 ounce semisweet chocolate	3 tablespoons semisweet chocolate pieces; or 1 ounce unsweetened chocolate plus 1 tablespoon granulated sugar
1 ounce unsweetened chocolate	3 tablespoons unsweetened cocoa powder plus 1 tablespoon cooking oil or shortening, melted
1 cup corn syrup	1 cup granulated sugar plus ¼ cup liquid
1 cup honey	1¼ cups granulated sugar plus ¼ cup liquid
1 cup molasses	1 cup honey
1 cup granulated sugar	1 cup packed brown sugar or 2 cups sifted powdered sugar
1 cup beef broth or chicken broth	1 teaspoon or 1 cube instant beef or chicken bouillon plus 1 cup hot water
2 cups tomato sauce	¾ cup tomato paste plus 1 cup water
1 cup tomato juice	½ cup tomato sauce plus ½ cup water
¼ cup fine dry bread crumbs	¾ cup soft bread crumbs, ¼ cup cracker crumbs, or ¼ cup cornflake crumbs
1 small onion, chopped (⅓ cup)	1 teaspoon onion powder or 1 tablespoon dried minced onion
1 clove garlic	½ teaspoon bottled minced garlic or ⅛ teaspoon garlic powder
1 teaspoon lemon juice	½ teaspoon vinegar
1 teaspoon poultry seasoning	¾ teaspoon dried sage, crushed, plus ¼ teaspoon dried thyme or marjoram, crushed
1 teaspoon dry mustard (in cooked mixtures)	1 tablespoon prepared mustard
1 tablespoon snipped fresh herb	½ to 1 teaspoon dried herb, crushed
1 teaspoon dried herb	½ teaspoon ground herb
1 teaspoon grated fresh ginger	¼ teaspoon ground ginger
1 teaspoon apple pie spice	½ teaspoon ground cinnamon plus ¼ teaspoon ground nutmeg, ⅛ teaspoon ground allspice, and dash ground cloves or ginger
1 teaspoon pumpkin pie spice	½ teaspoon ground cinnamon plus ¼ teaspoon ground ginger, ¼ teaspoon ground allspice, and ⅛ teaspoon ground nutmeg

Better Homes and Gardens.